Cooperative Enterprises

Cooperative Enterprises is the first textbook to examine the evolution of the cooperative enterprise model and the contribution that cooperatives can make to the economy and society.

It provides an accessible overview of the subject, looking at history, cooperative models, theories, legislation, and governance. *Cooperative Enterprises* takes an international approach throughout, drawing on examples from cooperatives from across the globe. The book offers a valuable historical perspective, placing cooperatives within their political, social, cultural, and economic contexts since the Industrial Revolution. It analyses and compares the cooperative law of 26 jurisdictions and showcases key defining moments for cooperative enterprises, cooperative development models, cooperative-specific good practice standards, and compares the cooperative model with the private enterprise model, giving readers a comprehensive view of the subject. The book also demonstrates that cooperatives correct the market, complement the role of the state, support local economic development, reduce income and wealth inequalities, promote social cohesion, and promote economic democracy. Students are supported with a range of pedagogical features, including case studies, tables, figures, chapter summaries, and discussion questions to encourage critical thinking.

This is the ideal textbook for undergraduate and postgraduate courses on cooperative studies, and will also be an illuminating resource for students, researchers, and policymakers interested in social enterprise, business history, economic history, corporate governance, economic democracy, and community development.

Piero Ammirato is an Honorary Fellow at Deakin University. He completed his doctorate on cooperative studies at the University of Adelaide in 1994. Piero taught politics at the University of Adelaide, held positions of director of cooperatives and community organisations, and worked as a manager of research and a principal policy adviser in the Victorian public service. His previous publications include *La Lega: The Making of a Successful Cooperative Network* (1996) and *The Growth of Italian Cooperatives: Innovation, Resilience and Social Responsibility* (2018).

Cooperative Enterprises

Piero Ammirato

LONDON AND NEW YORK

First published 2024
by Routledge
4 Park Square, Milton Park, Abingdon, Oxon OX14 4RN

and by Routledge
605 Third Avenue, New York, NY 10158

Routledge is an imprint of the Taylor & Francis Group, an informa business

British Library Cataloguing-in-Publication Data
A catalogue record for this book is available from the British Library

Library of Congress Cataloging-in-Publication Data
Names: Ammirato, Piero, author.
Title: Cooperative enterprises / Piero Ammirato.
Description: Abingdon, Oxon ; New York, NY : Routledge, 2024. | Includes bibliographical references and index. |
Identifiers: LCCN 2023047759 (print) | LCCN 2023047760 (ebook) | ISBN 9781032216843 (hardback) | ISBN 9781032216829 (paperback) | ISBN 9781003269533 (ebook)
Subjects: LCSH: Cooperative societies. | Cooperation. | Public-private sector cooperation.
Classification: LCC HD2963 .A56 2024 (print) | LCC HD2963 (ebook) | DDC 334—dc23/eng/20231024
LC record available at https://lccn.loc.gov/2023047759
LC ebook record available at https://lccn.loc.gov/2023047760

ISBN: 978-1-032-21684-3 (hbk)
ISBN: 978-1-032-21682-9 (pbk)
ISBN: 978-1-003-26953-3 (ebk)

DOI: 10.4324/9781003269533

Typeset in Sabon
by codeMantra

I dedicate this book to my Mother and Father for their genuine, infinite, and unconditional love and support.

Contents

Illustrations

Figures

Tables

Acknowledgements

My sincerest thanks to Professor Akira Kurimoto for his continuous support and encouragement, for his insightful comments on the manuscript, and for sharing his knowledge on the cooperative sector. I have really enjoyed and greatly benefited from the conversations I have shared with Professor Kurimoto. I would also like to thank Professor Hagen Henrÿ for his encouragement and insightful comments on cooperative law, Professor Vera Zamagni for comments on cooperative economic history, and Professor Seungkwon Jang for sharing documents on the Republic of Korea's cooperative sector.

My very warm thanks also go to Mario Viviani and Antonio Zanotti who are always willing to exchange ideas on the cooperative movement. Mario and Antonio are a rare breed of writers-researchers that combine academic research with practical experience having worked with Legacoop cooperatives, consortia, and the cooperative association. I have found their work on cooperatives to be of the highest quality, and their genuine friendship very rewarding.

This is my third book on cooperatives. Research for my first book on La Lega Nazionale Delle Cooperative e Mutue's network of cooperative enterprises (today's Legacoop) began in 1989, the PhD was completed in 1994, and the book was published in 1996. That experience is still fresh in my mind and the key learnings are still with me today, and for this I am very grateful. To this end, I would like to take the opportunity to thank first of all my then PhD supervisor, Dr John Robbins, for his constant support, intellectual rigour, and genuine friendship; and Alessandro Skuk (then President of Legacoop Bologna) and Giancarlo Pasquini (head of Fincooper at the time, but later President of Legacoop), for their openness, and willingness to transfer their knowledge and understanding on the Italian cooperative sector.

A book such as the one I have written would not have been possible without the body of knowledge available in books and journal papers written by my peers. To this end, I would like to thank all the authors cited in the book for their work and for their insightful knowledge of the cooperative movement. In particular, I am grateful for the work on cooperatives made available by Chris Cornforth, Roger Spear, William Foote Whyte and Kathleen King Whyte, Roy Morrison, Stefano Zan, Renato Zangheri et al., Mark Holmstrom, Mario Viviani, Antonio Zanotti, Vera Zamagni, Carlo Borzaga, Alberto Ianes, Johnston Birchall, Ian MacPherson, Ivano Barberini, and Akira Kurimoto.

I would also like to acknowledge Professor Andrew Scott and Professor Benjamin Isakhan for their continuous support, and Deakin University for providing access to their facilities, to the library, and to their online resources.

Thanks also go to my friend Gaby Jaksa for his continuous support and engaging and challenging thoughts on politics, the economy, and society; and to Martine Hawkes for editing this manuscript and for her professionalism.

Finally, I would like to thank my wife Li-Jun Yao for her constant support, companionship, understanding, compassion, and for sharing her life with me.

Abbreviations

AGA	Annual General Assembly
AGM	Annual General Meeting
BC	benefit corporations
BE	Banca Etica
CG-SCOP	French General Confederation of SCOPs
CLP	Caja Laboral Popular
CEO	chief executive officer
CICOPA	International Organisation of the Industrial and Service Cooperatives
CME	capitalist-led market economy
CQCM	Quebec Council of Cooperatives and Mutuality
CWS	Cooperative Wholesale Society
ESG	environmental, social and governance
GA	General Assembly
GCFF	global cooperative financial framework
GDP	gross domestic product
GFC	global financial crisis
Hew Co-op	Japanese Health and Welfare Cooperative Federation
ICA	International Cooperative Alliance
IOF	investor-owned firms
IDES	Institute for the Development of the Social Economy
ILO	International Labour Organisation
IMF	International Monetary Fund
IPSA	Industrial and Provident Society Act
INACOOP	National Institute of Cooperatives (Uruguay)

JCCU	Japanese Consumers' Cooperative Union
KF	Swedish Co-operative Union & Wholesale Society (Kooperativa Förbundet)
Legacoop	A National Association of Cooperatives – Formerly Lega Nazionale Delle Cooperative e Mutue
LMF	labour-managed firms
LNCM	Lega Nazionale delle Cooperative e Mutue (a National Association of Cooperatives, renamed Legacoop in 1996)
MB	management board
MBA	Masters of Business Administration
MCC	Mondragon Cooperative Corporation
MNC	multinational company
NGC	new generation cooperatives
NFP	not-for-profit
OECD	Organisation for Economic Cooperation and Development
OHADA	Organisation for the Harmonization of Business Law in Africa
RDC	regional development cooperatives
SCE	social cooperative enterprises
TNC	transnational corporations
WBO	worker-buyouts
WTO	World Trade Organization

1 Introduction

This book examines the evolution of cooperative enterprises since the industrial revolution. It adopts a longitudinal, multidisciplinary, and comparative methodology to understand and evaluate the cooperative enterprise model. It discusses the cooperative political and economic history, the cooperative enterprise models, cooperative ideas and theories, cooperative law, and cooperative governance. It analyses cooperatives' interaction with the market economy and compares the cooperative enterprise model with the private enterprise model, especially the modern corporation. It also explores the relationship between cooperatives and the State. This holistic approach will enable the reader to comprehensively assess the role that cooperatives perform in a market economy.

Chapters 2–5 explore the development of cooperative enterprises since the 1750s. Each chapter examines a specific historical period. Each period examines the political, economic, social, and cultural contexts within which cooperatives operated. This includes the political ideas at the time; the nature of the political systems; the relation between the State and the economy and the State and society; and the development of the corporation. Each period identifies the development of key cooperative enterprise models and key cooperative events that have defined the cooperative movement. Chapters 6–9 focus on key areas of cooperative studies. It compares the cooperative law of 26 jurisdictions and considers the impact that cooperative law has on the cooperative enterprise and the cooperative movement. It examines how the relationship between cooperatives and the market has evolved over time. It compares cooperative governance with corporate governance. It compares cooperatives and corporations by examining their purpose, their characteristics and behaviours, their level of entrepreneurship, and their approach to innovation. Chapter 10 concludes the book by summarising key cooperative trends and the contribution made by cooperatives to the market and society, suggesting ways to promote cooperative development on a global scale.

This book contains many key features that enable the readers to develop a comprehensive understanding of the cooperative enterprise model, its potential, and its limitations. The first feature is the focus on key events that have demonstrated how cooperatives met the needs of their members and how they relate to the market and to the State. These events range from the establishment of the early Socialist communities, to the Rochdale consumer cooperative in 1844, to the emerging cooperative enterprise models, to the anti-monopoly strategies of consumer and agricultural cooperatives, and to the more recent development of worker-buyouts (WBO), social cooperatives, and ethical banks. The second feature is the identification of cooperative development models (CDMs) operating in Europe, North America, and Asia that are able to promote new cooperatives,

DOI: 10.4324/9781003269533-1

inter-sectoral cooperation, and are capable of managing change. The third feature is a comparative analysis of cooperative law and the extent to which these cooperative laws align with cooperative principles. The fourth feature is the identification of good practice standards in consumer cooperatives, CDMs, cooperative law, cooperative governance, and in promoting WBOs. The fifth feature is a multidisciplinary analysis that explains why there are fewer cooperatives than private enterprises. The sixth feature compares cooperative governance with corporate governance and discusses various forms of cooperative democratic governance structures. The seventh feature is the discussion on nine key cooperative enterprise risks that need to be identified, measured, and mitigated. The eighth feature is a comprehensive comparison of the cooperative enterprise model with the private enterprise model.

This book discusses a number of key questions regarding cooperative enterprises and the cooperative movement. Key questions include what are the key features of cooperatives, and what benefits do cooperatives provide to members, the community, and the broader economy? Is there one cooperative enterprise model, or are there many cooperative enterprise models that reflect their country's unique political, economic, social, and cultural history? Why are there so few cooperatives compared to conventional enterprises? Are cooperatives and conventional enterprises converging, or are cooperatives developing a new cooperative enterprise model suited to compete in today's global market? How can cooperative governance practices achieve performance in compliance with the law, with cooperative principles, and with community expectations whilst preventing the threat of degeneration and demutualisation? What is the place of cooperatives in the market economy, and how do they compare and contrast to conventional enterprises, state enterprises, and the not-for-profit (NFP) sector? What is the future role of cooperatives in a market economy? What would it take for the cooperative movement to gain a larger share of the global market so that it can significantly influence the market and society?

This book is written in a textbook format. Each chapter is written in a stand-alone format. It identifies key learnings, considers the political and economic contexts, examines key events, describes key cooperative models alongside the evolution of corporations and the State, critically examines concepts and ideas, provides comprehensive summaries for each chapter, and raises a series of questions for readers to consider. The questions aim to encourage further research on cooperative enterprises and the cooperative movement.

The end result of this longitudinal, multidisciplinary, and comparative approach is a comprehensive understanding of the evolution of cooperative enterprises. This allows the reader to make a balanced evaluation of the cooperative movement's achievements, its potential, and its limitations. It should also allow readers to evaluate the role that cooperatives can play in a pluralist market economy and consider how best to promote the cooperative economy globally. The book promotes the view that a larger cooperative sector that can significantly influence the pluralist market economy and society will bring many benefits to the operations of the market, to society, and to the State, and will improve the lives of people and the well-being of their communities.

1.1 Cooperation before Rochdale

The idea of cooperation as a way to solve a problem or to achieve common goals is universal. People across the world have adopted this idea to solve common problems or to share common resources. In Babylon, two centuries before Christ was born, cooperatives were established to co-manage land and co-manage credit for the poor. During Roman times, artisans formed associations for burial societies (Barberini 2009a). In China and Korea,[1] self-governing rural villages established reciprocal social relationships promoting acts of solidarity and mutual help, including common work and the promotion of social welfare for their village (Jung and Rosner 2012). In Japan, there was a rotating credit society that financed new businesses or insured against risks, called Koh, and there were communal groups for crop sowing-harvesting or thatching, called Yui (Kurimoto and Dongre 2020). In Afghanistan, Central America, and the Andes, groups of people managed water in common for irrigation. Since the Middle Ages, credit associations were formed in Europe, across Africa, Mexico, India, and Cambodia to help people access credit and avoid usurers (Muzzarelli 2009, Bruni 2012, Mayo 2017). The Islamic tradition of Takaful provided its members with guarantees and operated on an NFP basis. Caravans trading across the Sahara to the Mediterranean were organised cooperatively. In Finland and Scandinavia, during the sixteenth century, neighbours formed working unions to cultivate land and farm together (Mayo 2017).

After the 1750s, more modern forms of cooperation developed to overcome the insecurities and the poor living conditions created by a capitalist-led market economy (CME),[2] the industrial revolution, and societies governed by a Liberal State. In 1752, Benjamin Franklin founded the Philadelphia Contributionship of the Insurance of Houses from Loss by Fire. In 1755, a building society was formed in Birmingham. In 1780, cotton producers in Greece joined forces to market their produce (Mayo 2017). In 1806, a cooperative dairy of fresh milk and milk products was established at Osoppo, Italy. In 1828, a consumer cooperative was formed in Britain (Barberini 2009a). Shaffer informs that by 1830, 300 cooperatives were registered under the *United Kingdom's Friendly Societies Act* (Shaffer 1999). In 1834, four workers set up the Christian Association of Jewellers inspired by Philippe Buchez (Battilani and Schröter 2012a). Buchez promoted worker cooperatives with a democratic and egalitarian culture that practised the indivisibility of assets (Zanotti 2017). Early Socialists such as Owen, Fourier, and Cabet proposed the formation of communities that would create harmonious societies and could overcome the negative effects of Capitalism and competition (Crick 1987, Zanotti 2017). Unfortunately, bad management, lack of funds, and inappropriate business models meant that these early cooperative and community experiments did not succeed (Bonner 1961, Birchall 2011).

In 1844, the Rochdale Cooperative Society (Rochdale Society) was formed with a business model and a series of cooperative principles that laid the foundations for a successful consumer cooperative enterprise model. The broad objective of the Rochdale Society was the social and intellectual advancement of its members. This was to take place within a CME whilst operating within a unique set of rules (Hilson 2017). According to Holyoake, the Rochdale Society model promoted nine cooperative principles: one-person-one-vote, open membership, fixed and limited return on capital, distribution of the surplus as dividend on purchases, cash trading, sale of only pure and unadulterated goods, education, political and religious neutrality, disposal of assets without profit in the event of the society being wound up (Holyoake 1893, Birchall 2011, 2012). This model paved the way for a successful business model based on cash trading, a broad membership of like-minded people, limited fixed remuneration on members' capital, and the payment of the dividend based on purchases. This model discouraged capitalist investors from becoming members. The success of Rochdale influenced other cooperative societies in the United Kingdom and the British colonies, and through the International Cooperative Alliance (ICA), it also influenced other cooperative movements (Birchall 2011).

1.2 The Cooperative Movement

The cooperative enterprises discussed in this book refer to those inspired by the ICA. The ICA was established in 1895. It developed a set of seven guiding cooperative principles for its members in 1937, of which four were mandatory.[3] These mandatory principles were expanded to six principles in 1966 and then to seven principles in 1995. The ICA defines a cooperative enterprise, its values and principles as follows:

- A cooperative is defined as "an autonomous association of persons united voluntarily to meet their common economic, social, and cultural needs and aspirations through a jointly-owned and democratically controlled enterprise" (ICA 2022).
- Cooperatives are based on the values of self-help, self-responsibility, democracy, equality, equity, and solidarity. In the tradition of their founders, cooperative members believe in the ethical values of honesty, openness, social responsibility, and caring for others.
- Cooperatives operate by seven cooperative principles: open membership; democratic member control; member economic participation; autonomy and independence; education for members; cooperation among cooperatives, and concern for their community (ICA 2022).

The cooperative movement is present worldwide. The International Organisation of the Industrial and Service Cooperatives, CICOPA, a branch of the ICA, estimates that in 2017, there were 2.9 million cooperatives with 1.2 billion members operating globally.[4] These cooperatives employ 279 million people on a full-time and part-time basis. The majority of people employed are producers (252 million), whilst 16 million are employees, and 11 million are worker-members. CICOPA estimates that cooperatives employ close to 9.5 per cent of the world's workforce (CICOPA 2017).

The 2016 World Cooperative Monitor Database revealed that there were 1,420 cooperatives with a turnover of above 100 million USD (Euricse 2016). In 2020, there were 300 cooperatives with a combined turnover of over 2 trillion USD. These operate in insurance (101), agriculture (100), consumer and retail (59), financial services (26), industry and utilities (9), education, health, and social work (3), and other services (2) (Euricse 2022).

A UN commissioner report noted that in 2014 the world cooperative movement's total revenue equated to 4.4 per cent of the world's Gross Domestic Product (DG and Associates 2014). In a number of countries, the cooperative sector's share of the national Gross Domestic Product is more than 10 per cent.[5] In key sectors of a country's economy, however, the cooperative sector holds prominent positions. For instance, cooperative banks hold 40 per cent of the market in France and Holland; mutual insurance companies hold 25 per cent of the world market; agricultural cooperatives hold more than 70 per cent of the market in Japan (Zamagni 2012); consumer cooperatives hold more than 35 per cent of the domestic market in Denmark (International Cooperative Alliance 2016); energy cooperatives in the United States provide electricity service to 42 million people (America's Electric Cooperatives 2016); social cooperatives in Italy provide close to 50 per cent of social services (Zamagni 2017).

1.3 Cooperative Typology

The cooperative enterprise model has served a variety of people with different needs. The most popular cooperatives include consumer cooperatives, cooperative banks, agricultural cooperatives, worker cooperatives, and, most recently, social cooperatives, also known as social enterprises. According to the International Labour Organization's (ILO) definition, cooperatives can be divided into four broad classifications. These include:

- Consumer cooperatives. These cooperatives are formed by members who access goods or services made available by or through a cooperative. These may include consumer co-ops, housing, insurance, banking, electricity, health insurance, and so on. These cooperatives provide fit-for-purpose services and products at reasonable prices to their members.
- Producer cooperatives.[6] These cooperatives are formed by members who own their own private business and form a cooperative to buy inputs or to market and process their produce or services. These may include agricultural cooperatives, artisans, hardware stores, fisheries, taxi drivers, and small businesses.
- Worker cooperatives. These cooperatives are formed by workers or employees who obtain work through their cooperatives. Their goal is to obtain secure employment along with decent working conditions in a democratically managed enterprise. Worker cooperatives operate in many sectors of the economy, including construction, food and catering, maintenance services, manufacturing, transport, and welfare services.
- Multi-stakeholder cooperatives.[7] These cooperatives distinguish themselves by having more than one category of members. These are present in many sectors of the economy, including social services, education, employment for the disadvantaged, child care services, and community services. They are promoted by members with intrinsic values whose goal is to serve the community and promote general interest goals rather than members' interests (ILO 2018).[8]

The above typology refers to primary cooperatives and how they serve their members or stakeholders. These cooperatives, however, are also supported by second-tier cooperatives, which are formed by cooperative enterprises. These second-tier cooperatives include wholesale societies, consortia, manufacturing, marketing, and financial cooperatives. The purpose of these second-tier cooperatives is to provide services or any required input to cooperatives so that they can achieve economies of scale whilst remaining small. Chapters 2–5 will explore these second-tier cooperatives in more detail.

1.4 Cooperatives in a Pluralist Market Economy

Cooperatives' place in a market economy has been debated for quite some time. France coined the term social economy in the 1830s, which included cooperatives and the NFP sector as an alternative sector to the state sector and the private sector (European Commission 2013). Fauquet, in 1935, argued that cooperatives formed the Third Sector of the economy alongside the state sector and the private sector. To Fauquet, cooperatives were democratic enterprises that, through their second-tier structures, helped small producers and artisans compete in the market whilst maintaining their autonomy. He also thought cooperatives could mitigate the conflicts between capital and labour (Fauquet 1941). The United States, however, sees the Third Sector as comprising only non-distributing

NFP associations with a strong volunteer component (Defourny 2001). Recently, South America has promoted the concept of the solidarity economy which includes the social economy, supported by forms of equality (race and gender) and sustainable practices (Borowiak 2015).

In this book, cooperatives are treated as a distinct sector of the economy. They were formed when the State, private enterprises, and the NFP sector already existed. The cooperative principles that have been adopted make them a unique form of enterprise that is democratically managed; focusses on meeting members' needs or general interests rather than focussing on maximising profits; limits the return on capital; and mostly promotes collective ownership and the indivisibility of assets. Cooperatives are also very diverse. Some cooperatives promote general interests and, as such, have more in common with the NFP sector and the State. Other cooperatives support the profit-making operations of producers and artisans and, as such, have more in common with the private sector (Borzaga and Defourny 2001, Sabeti 2011). This discussion will be further developed in Chapter 7. The book, however, views the cooperative sector as a unique sector of the economy with various characteristics from which a variety of benefits flow to their members, to the operations of the market, to the State, and to the communities in which they operate.

1.5 Why Cooperative Studies?

In 2004, MacPherson lamented that cooperative studies comprised those studies that focussed on providing a historical understanding of the cooperative movement and the limited analysis provided by business historians. He lamented that mainstream economics paid little attention to cooperatives by focussing on labour-managed firms and failing to see cooperatives as part of the social economy or as a vital part of a functioning market economy. To MacPherson, this had profound implications that included cooperatives imitating conventional businesses, lawyers, and accountants failing to note cooperative differences, lack of research into cooperative enterprises, and a disjointed public policy debate about cooperatives. To overcome this situation, he proposed a multidisciplinary approach to cooperative studies that would enhance our understanding of cooperatives and provide a deeper analysis of cooperative thought; provide a fuller appreciation of the social, economic, political, and cultural contexts within which cooperatives operate; and establish appropriate frameworks for the development of cooperative enterprises (MacPherson 2007).

Since MacPherson's call to enhance and broaden the focus on cooperative studies, academics and cooperative practitioners have conducted research in a variety of disciplines.[9] There have been studies and publications in the areas of cooperative law covering jurisdictions from all over the world.[10] The field of cooperative economics has been enhanced through studies that note cooperatives' coordinating functions,[11] their behaviours when managing economic crisis,[12] their economic performance,[13] their survival rate,[14] and the financing of cooperatives.[15] Business history academics produced comparative works as well as business histories of individual cooperatives.[16] New forms of cooperative entrepreneurship, such as WBOs[17] and social cooperatives,[18] have been brought to the public's attention. The field of cooperative governance has been explored by highlighting the relationship between members, the general assembly, the board, and management; in encouraging participation in the decision-making process; in achieving performance; in preventing demutualisation; and in managing cooperatives with subsidiaries.[19] Cooperative reporting has been seen as a way to enhance communication with the public, enhance accountability to members and stakeholders, and differentiate from conventional businesses.[20] More reliable cooperative data has been collected in order to highlight the size, importance, global dimension, and possibilities of the cooperative sector.[21] CDMs have been identified in Europe, Asia, and the Americas that demonstrate the global appeal of the cooperative enterprise model.[22] The performance of cooperatives led to publications that promoted cooperatives as a way to transform society, as a key component of a pluralist economy, and as a key component of the economic democracy project.[23]

This book makes a number of key contributions to the field of cooperative studies. First, it provides a comprehensive understanding of the evolution of cooperatives and their key characteristics. The book's multidisciplinary approach includes the study of history, political economy, business history, economics, cooperative law, cooperative governance, and management. It compares cooperative enterprises with private enterprises. This approach provides readers with a holistic understanding of the cooperative enterprise and the cooperative movement, as well as provides a balanced appreciation of their uniqueness, their diversity, their behaviours, their potential, and their limitations. This approach should help co-operators promote cooperative development and develop cooperative-specific strategies and practices in alignment with cooperative principles and values. It should also help public policymakers and governments to promote cooperative-specific policies and public programmes.

Second, this book allows readers to appreciate and value cooperative diversity. The cooperative movement has developed across the world. European countries originally established various types of cooperatives, but all countries have added their own unique features to the original models. Cooperative movements in all countries have developed based on their historical, political, economic, cultural, and social experiences and their international relations with other countries. This has led to a rich, varied, broad cooperative movement that offers solutions to its members and their communities. If cooperative movements could learn from each other's models, cooperate more with each other, and begin to develop global structures to support each other, the cooperative sector could position itself as an alternative economic model to the current CME model.

Third, this study demonstrates that the cooperative enterprise model can contribute to solving many of the problems caused by the CME model. Cooperatives have successfully promoted employment, promoted policies of inclusion, reduced income and wealth inequalities by limiting salary differentials and promoting collectively owned assets, created inter-generational wealth, promoted local economic development, developed fair and just relationships with local communities, and improved the workings of market economies. This book will argue that the cooperative sector could become a key pillar of a more balanced pluralist market economy.

Fourth, this book is important to anyone who wishes to promote economic democracy and strengthen political democracy. Cooperatives operate as 'schools of democracy', giving members the opportunity to learn the art of democratic decision-making and to develop a greater awareness of the relationship between the State, the economy, and society. They also promote a fair distribution of economic resources. Cooperatives overcome the unequal distribution of economic resources, which is a key source of political inequality (Dahl 1998). To this end, cooperatives should be considered a key pillar of market economies and a key contributor to a more sustainable and just economic and social system that serves the needs of every citizen and that strengthens political democracy.

1.6 The Chapter Outline and Content

There are nine other chapters in addition to this introductory chapter. Chapter 2 covers the period from 1750 to 1914. It discusses the passage from the early cooperative communities to the development of the Rochdale enterprise model in 1844. It then introduces the consumer, agricultural, banking, and worker cooperatives enterprise models. It notes how primary cooperatives, second-tier structures, and cooperative federations promoted a unique cooperative enterprise model. The birth and early debates within the ICA are noted. It also analyses the development of the Liberal State, the rise of the modern public company, the rise of the trade union movement and Socialist parties, the democratisation of society, and how these developments affected the development of the cooperative movement.

Chapter 3 covers the period from 1915 to 1945. It discusses the demise of the Liberal State, the rise of Social Democracy, the Russian Revolution, the developments of authoritarian States in Europe, and how these developments changed the relationship between the State and the economy. It discusses how cooperatives fared in authoritarian states. It examines key cooperative-related events such as the role of the Swedish cooperative movements in reducing the power of monopolies, the development of cooperative banking in North America, the role of the State during the New Deal in promoting agricultural and electric cooperatives. It also discusses the role of the ICA during the inter-war period and considers the role that cooperatives could perform in the economy.

Chapter 4 discusses the period from 1945–1990, known for the formation of mixed economies, the Welfare State, and the process of decolonisation. It discusses the development of the Welfare State and the resurgent neo-liberal ideas since the 1980s. It notes that the US corporation becomes the dominant business model. It examines the mixed successes of the consumer cooperative movement and identifies good practice standards for promoting consumer cooperatives. It highlights the CDMs of Mondragon and Italy. These CDMs promoted new cooperatives, developed support services, promoted inter-sectoral cooperation, and proved capable of managing change. It then notes good practices in promoting cooperative development from the Mondragon and Italian experience. The chapter discusses the state-supported cooperative movements in India and Tanzania. The final section discusses the ICA's global development, the updated cooperative principles, and Laidlaw's insightful 1980 report to the ICA.

Chapter 5 discusses how cooperatives have engaged with the global economy since 1990. It analyses the rise of neo-liberalism, the expansion of the global market, and the growth of multinational corporations. It analyses how the State, private enterprises, and cooperatives dealt with market failures. It explores how cooperatives became larger, how they attracted external capital, and how they adopted different legal structures to establish cooperative-led groups of enterprises. It discusses the development of new-generation cooperatives, the demutualisation of financial cooperatives, WBOs, social cooperatives, platform cooperatives, and ethical banking. The CDMs of Trento, Quebec, France, Japan, and Korea are discussed, and good practice standards that promote cooperative development are identified. The chapter concludes by noting that the ICA became a global association, that it updated the cooperative principles to include 'autonomy and independence' and 'concern for the community' as the seventh principle, and that it continued to promote discussions on the relationship between cooperative practice and cooperative principles.

Chapter 6 compares the cooperative law of 26 jurisdictions operating in Europe, North America, South America, Asia, and Africa. It assesses the various phases of cooperative law. It analyses the extent to which cooperative law is aligned with cooperative principles and the extent to which it promotes cooperative development. It identifies a member-owned capital-centred enterprise model and another cooperative enterprise model where cooperatives are members of a cooperative movement that supports community development. It also identifies five types of cooperative enterprises depending on their level of compliance with the cooperative principles. The research suggests good practice standards for cooperative law that can simultaneously promote cooperative principles and cooperative economic development.

Chapter 7 examines the relationship between cooperatives and the market. It summarises how the cooperative sector has engaged with the market, ranging from having an anti-market sentiment, to embracing the market economy, and to establishing cooperatives that promote society's general interests. It then discusses the question: 'Why there are fewer cooperatives compared to capitalist and investor-owned enterprises?' It analyses the views of classical economists, the arguments that identify limits to the cooperative enterprise model, and the roles performed by corporations, the State, and the international cooperative movement. The final section considers the place of the cooperative sector within a pluralist market economy, arguing that the cooperative sector is a distinct and unique sector of the economy.

Chapter 8 focusses on cooperative governance. It explores the historical evolution of corporate governance and the historical evolution of cooperative governance. It discusses six cooperative governance structures used depending on the cooperatives' size and complexity. It analyses nine key cooperative governance risks that need to be identified, measured, and mitigated. A definition of cooperative governance and good practice in cooperative governance concludes this chapter.

Chapter 9 compares cooperatives with private enterprises. The key comparison is between cooperatives and larger private enterprises, especially the corporation. This chapter first considers some of the key features of both enterprises, including purpose, ownership and control, profit distribution, and industrial relations. It then examines the behaviours of both enterprises by comparing their economic performance, entrepreneurship, and innovation. This is followed by considering the impact that cooperatives and corporations have on employment, equality, local economic development, and on economic democracy. The final part considers whether cooperatives and corporations are converging.

Chapter 10 is the concluding chapter. It provides a summary of the CME identifying their virtues and problems. It notes the key cooperative trends and discusses how the cooperative enterprise model contributes to the market economy, to the State, to local economic development, and to economic democracy. It reflects as to why there are few cooperatives compared to conventional enterprises. It proposes a course of action to significantly grow the cooperative sector that includes promoting awareness, education, and good practices; developing a vision of a cooperative-led economy and society; and establishing a global financial and institutional framework that promotes cooperative development.

Notes

1 The text uses the name Korea which is used instead of the Republic of Korea.
2 The term capitalist-led market economies refers to market economies that whilst they include private enterprises, cooperatives, not-for-profits, and state-owned enterprises, the dominant economic actor is the corporation or multinational companies.
3 In 1937, the ICA reduced the nine Rochdale Principles into seven ICA Principles: (1) open membership, (2) democratic control, (3) distribution of surplus in proportion to trade, (4)

payment of limited interest on capital, (5) political and religious neutrality, (6) cash trading, and (7) promotion of education. The ICA declared only the first four principles to be essential and the last three principles less binding (Birchall 2012).

4 This figure may over-represent membership figures because a member can be a member of more than one cooperative. For instance, a person may be a member of a cooperative bank as well as a consumer cooperative and a worker cooperative.
5 These countries include New Zealand, France, the Netherlands, Finland (DG and Associates 2014), and Italy (Borzaga 2015).
6 Coop France refers to some of these producer cooperatives as business cooperatives since the members own a business (Coop France 2023).
7 Another term that may be used instead of multi-stakeholder cooperatives is social and community cooperatives (Zamagni 2012).
8 Please also refer to Zamagni and Birchall for their contribution to developing a cooperative typology (Birchall 2012, Zamagni 2012).
9 I will identify mostly key English language books for readers to consult and peruse, knowing that these do not cover all the books available on these subjects.
10 Key publications include Henrÿ (2012, 2017) and Cracogna, Fici, and Henrÿ (2013).
11 Please refer to Borzaga and Tortia's article on cooperative's coordinating functions (Borzaga and Tortia 2017).
12 Key publications include Birchall and Ketislon (2009), Bajo and Roelants (2011), Ammirato (2018) and Caselli, and Costa and Delbono (2021).
13 Key publications include Craig and Pencavel (1992), Estrin and Jones (1992), Pencavel, Pistaferri and Schivardi (2006), FakhFakh, Perotin and Gago (2012), and Burdin and Andres (2012).
14 Key publications include Government du Quebec (2003), Corcoran and Wilson (2010), Caselli (2014), Bajo and Roelants (2016), and Vieta, Depetri, and Carrano (2017).
15 Key publications on cooperative finance include Zevi (1990), Zevi et al. (2011), Andrews (2015), Chieh and Weber (2015), and Ammirato (2018).
16 Key publications include Battilani and Bertagnoni (2010), Birchall (2011), Battilani and Schroter (2012b), Wilson, Webster, and Vorberg-Rugh (2013), Michie, Blasi, and Borzaga (2017), Hilson, Neunsinger, and Patmore (2017), and Patmore and Belnave (2018).
17 Key publications on WBOs include Soulage (2011), Cecop (2013), Ruggeri (2014), Vieta, Depetri, and Carrano (2017), and Di Stefano (2019).
18 Key publications for social cooperatives include Borzaga and Defourny (2001), Nyssens (2006), Cecop (2009), Borzaga and Galera (2016), Galera (2017), and European Commission (2020).
19 Key publications include Whyte and Whyte (1988), Holmstrom (1989), Spear (2004), Myners (2014), Cornforth (2015), ICA (2015), Fulton and Girard (2015), Sacchetti and Tortia (2016), Birchall (2017), and Basterretxea, Cornforth, and Heras-Saizarbitoria (2020).
20 Key publications include Legacoop (2002), Viviani (2006), Brown et al. (2015), and Novkovic (2021).
21 Key publications include CICOPA (2017) and Euricse (2021, 2022).
22 Key publications that cover the cooperative development models include: for Mondragon, Whyte and Whyte (1988), Morrison (1991), Mondragon Corporation (2012), Barandiaran and Javier (2017); for Italy, Ammirato (1996), Barberini (2009b), Zanotti (2011), OECD (2014), Ianes and Leonardi (2017), Ammirato (2018); for France and Quebec, Corcoran and Wilson (2010), Diamantopoulos (2011), Soulage (2011), Mendell (2015); for Japan, Saito (2010), Kurimoto (2017, 2020); for Korea, Hin and Lee (2013), Lee, Sang-Il and Chung (2014), Kim et al. (2020).
23 Publications that promote cooperatives to transform society include Schweickart (2011), Wolff (2012), Rainis (2016), and Jossa (2020); publications that promote cooperatives as a key component of a pluralist market economy or a key component of economic democracy include Ellerman (1990), Malleson (2014), Ammirato (2018), and Cumbers (2020).

References

America's Electric Cooperatives. 2016. *Powering America*. Accessed June 14, 2017. http://www.electric.coop/our-mission/powering-america/.

Ammirato, Piero. 1996. *La Lega: The Making of a Successful Cooperative Network*. Aldershot: Dartmouth Publishing Company.

———. 2018. *The Growth of Italian Cooperatives: Innovation, Resilience and Social Responsibility*. New York: Routledge.

Andrews, Michael. 2015. *Survey of Co-operative Capital*. ICA Think Piece on Cooperative Capital, Brussels: Filene Research Institute Publication.

Bajo, Claudia Sanchez, and Bruno Roelants. 2011. *Capital and the Debt Trap: Learning from Co-operatives in the Global Crisis*. London: Palgrave Macmillan.

Bajo, Claudia Sanchez, and Bruno Roelants. 2016. "Mainstreaming Co-operatives After the Global Financial Crisis." In *Mainstreaming Cooperatives after the Financial Crisis*, by Linda Shaw, Rachael Vorberg-Rugh Anthony Webster, 14–30. Manchester: Manchester University Press.

Barandiaran, Xabier, and Lezaun Javier. 2017. "The Mondragon Experience." In *The Oxford Handbook of Mutual, Co-Operative, and Co-Owned Business*, by Michie Jonathan, Joseph Blasi and Carlo Borzaga, Chapter 19. Oxford: Oxford University Press.

Barberini, Ivano. 2009a. *Come Vola il Calabrone*. Milano: Baldini Castoldi Dalai.

———.2009b. *How the Bumblebee Flies*. Milan: Baldini Castoldi Dalai Editore.

Basterretxea, Imanol, Chris Cornforth, and Iñaki Heras-Saizarbitoria. 2020. "Corporate Governance as a Key Aspect in the Failure of Worker Cooperatives." *Economic and Industrial Democracy* 1–26.

Battilani, Patrizia, and Giuliana Bertagnoni. 2010. *Cooperation Network Service*. Lancaster: Crucible Books.

Battilani, Patrizia, and Harm G Schröter. 2012a. "Introduction: Principal Problems and General Development of Cooperative Enterprise." In *The Cooperative Business Movement, 1950 to the Present*, by Patrizia Battilani and Harm G Schröter, Introduction. Cambridge: Cambridge University Press.

Battilani, Patrizia, and Harm G Schroter. 2012b. *The Cooperative Business Movement, 1950 to the Present*. Cambridge: Cambridge University Press.

Birchall, Johnston. 2011. *People-Centred Businesses*. London: Palgrave MacMillan.

———. 2012. "A 'Member-Owned Business' Approach to the Classification of Co-operatives and Mutuals." In *The Co-operative Model in Practice: International Perspectives*, by McDonnell Diarmuid and MacKnight Elizabeth, 67–83. Glasgow: CETS Resource.

———. 2017. *The Governance of Large Co-operative Businesses*. Governance Report for Co-operatives UK, Manchester: Co-operatives UK.

Birchall, Johnston, and Lou Hammond Ketislon. 2009. *Resilience of the Cooperative Business Model in Times of Crisis*. Geneva: International Labour Office.

Bonner, Arnold. 1961. *British Cooperation: The History, Principles, and the Organization of the British Cooperative Movement*. Manchester: Cooperative Union Limited.

Borowiak, Craig. 2015. "Mapping Social and Solidarity Economy." In *Social Economy in China and the World*, by Ngai Pun, Ben Hok-bun Ku, Hairong Yan, and Anita Koo, Chapter 2. London: Taylor Francis group.

Borzaga, Carlo. 2015. "Introduzione e Sintesi." In *Economia Cooperativa: Rilevanza, Evoluzione e Nuove Frontiere della Cooperazione Italiana*, by Carlo Borzaga Editor, 5–35. Trento: Euricse.

Borzaga, Carlo, and Jacques Defourny. 2001. *The Emergence of Social Enterprise*. London: Routledge.

Borzaga, Carlo, and Giulia Galera. 2016. "Innovating the Provision of Welfare Services Through Collective Action: the Case of Italian Social Cooperatives." *International Review of Sociology* 31–47.

Borzaga, Carlo, and Ermanno C. Tortia. 2017. "Co-operation as Co-ordination Mechanism: a New Approach to the Economics of Co-operative Enterprises." In *The Oxford Handbook of Mutual, Co-operative, and Co-owned Business*, by Jonathan Michie, Joseph R. Blasi and Carlo Borzaga, 55–75. Oxford: Oxford University Press.

Brown, Leslie, Carla Carini, Jessica Gordon Nembhard, Lou Hammond Ketilson, Elizabeth Hicks, John Mcnamara, Sonja Novkovic, and Daphne, Simmons, Richard Rixon. 2015. *Co-operatives for Sustainable Communities*. Ottawa: Cooperatives and Mutuals Canada and Centre for the Studies of Cooperatives.

Bruni, Luigino. 2012. *Le Prime Radici*. Trento: Il Margine.
Burdin, Gabriel, and Dean Andres. 2012. "Revisiting the Objectives of Worker-managed Firms: An Empirical Assessment." *Economic Systems* 158–171.
Caselli, Guido. 2014. *Osservatorio della Cooperazione in Emilia-Romagna: Partire dai Numeri.* Regional Cooperative Sector Review, Bologna: Unioncamere.
Caselli, Guido, Michele Costa, and Flavio Delbono. 2021. "What Do Cooperative Firms Maximize, If At All? Evidence from Emilia-Romagna in the Pre-Covid Decade." *Annals of Public and Cooperative Economics* 1–27.
Cecop. 2009. *Cooperatives and Social Enterprises*. Brussels: Cecop Publications.
———. 2013. *Business Transfers to Employees Under the Form of a Cooperative in Europe*. Brussels: Cecop-Cicopa Europe.
Chieh, Tan Suee, and Chuin Ting Weber. 2015. *The Capital Conundrum of Cooperatives*. Thematic Report on Cooperative Capital, Brussels: International Cooperative Alliance.
CICOPA. 2017. *Cooperatives and Employment: Second Global Report*. Global Report on Cooperative Employment, Brussels: ICA.
Coop France. 2023. "English." *France Coop*. Accessed May 15, 2023. https://www.entreprises.coop/english.
Corcoran, Hazel, and David Wilson. 2010. *The Worker Co-operative Movements in Italy, Mondragon and France: Context, Success Factors and Lessons*. Calgary: Canadian Worker Cooperative Federation.
Cornforth, Chris. 2015. "The Eternal Triangle: The Crucial Role of the Chair and Chief Executive in Empowering the Board." In *Co-operative Governance Fit to Build Resilience in the Face of Complexity*, by International Cooperative Alliance, 95–103. Brussels: International Cooperative Alliance.
Cracogna, Dante, Antonio Fici, and Hagen Henrÿ. 2013. *International Handbook of Cooperative Law*. Heidelberg: Springer.
Craig, Ben, and John Pencavel. 1992. "The Behavior of Worker Cooperatives: The Plywood Companies." *The American Economic Review* 1083–1105.
Crick, Bernard. 1987. *Socialism*. Milton Keynes: Open University Press.
Cumbers, Andrew. 2020. *Economic Democracy*. Cambridge: Polity Press.
Dahl, Robert. 1998. *On Cooperation*. New Haven: Yale University Press.
Defourny, Jacques. 2001. "Introduction: From Third Sector to Social Enterprise." In *The Emergence of Social Enterprise*, by Carlo Borzaga and Jacques Defourny, 1–29. London: Routledge.
DG and Associates. 2014. *Measuring the Size and Scope of the Cooperative Economy*. Results of the 2014 Global Census of Co-operatives, New York: United Nations Secretariat, Department of Economic and Social Affairs.
Di Stefano, Christina. 2019. "The Business Transfer Through the Cooperative Model. A Comparative Analysis Italy-France." *Journal of Entrepreneurial and Organizational Diversity* 62–86.
Diamantopoulos, Mitch. 2011. "Cooperative Development Gap in Québec and Saskatchewan 1980 to 2010: A Tale of Two Movements." *Canadian Journal of Nonprofit and Social Economy Research* 6–24.
Ellerman, David. 1990. *The Democratic Worker-Owned Firm*. Abingdon: Routledge.
Estrin, Saul, and Derek C. Jones. 1992. "The Viability of Employee-Owned Firms: Evidence from France." *Industrial and Labor Relations Review* 323–338.
Euricse. 2016. *Exploring the Co-operative Economy: Report*. Trento: Euricse.
———. 2021. *Exploring the Cooperative Economy Report 2020*. Cooperative Monitor Report, Trento: International Cooperative Alliance.
———. 2022. *World Cooperative Monitor*. Trento: Euricse and International Cooperative Alliance.
European Commission. 2013. *Social Economy and Social Entrepreneurship*. Social Europe Guide, Volume 4, Brussels: European Commission.
———. 2020. *Social Enterprises and their Ecosystems in Europe*. Comparative Report, Brussels: European Commission.

FakhFakh, Fathi, Virginie Perotin, and Monica Gago. 2012. "Productivity, Capital, and Labor in Labor-Managed and Conventional Firms: An Investigation of French Data." *ILR Review* 847–879.

Fauquet, Georges. 1941. "The Co-operative Sector." *Annals of Public and Cooperative Economy* 342–369.

Fulton, Murray, and Jean-Pierre Girard. 2015. *Demutualization of Co-operatives and Mutuals*. Cooperative Governance Report, Canada: Co-operatives and Mutuals Canada.

Galera, Giulia. 2017. "Social and Solidarity Cooperatives: An International Perspective." In *The Oxford Handbook of Mutual, Co-operative and Co-owned Business*, by Jonathon Michie, Joseph Blasi and Carlo Borzaga, 171–184. Oxford: Oxford University Press.

Government du Quebec. 2003. *Cooperative Development Policy*. Government Policy Document, Quebec: Government du Quebec.

Henrÿ, Hagen. 2012. *Guidelines for Cooperative Legislation*. ILO Guidelines, Geneva: International Labour Organization.

———. 2017. "Co-operative Principles and Co-operative Law Across the Globe." In *The Oxford Handbook of Mutual, Co-operative, and Co-owned Business*, by Jonathan Michie, Joseph Blasi and Carlo Borzaga, 39–54. Oxford: Oxford University Press.

Hilson, Mary. 2017. "Rochdale and Beyond: Consumer Cooperation in Britain before 1945." In *A Global History of Consumer Cooperation Since 1850*, by Mary Hilson, Silker Neusinger and Greg and Patmore, 59–77. Leiden: Brill.

Hilson, Mary, Silke Neunsinger, and Greg Patmore Patmore. 2017. *A Global History of Consumer Co-operation Since 1850*. Leiden: Brill.

Hin, Myung-Ho, and Ah-Reum Lee. 2013. "Factors Affecting the Creation and Sustainability of Cooperatives in the Wonju Region." *Korean Journal of Cooperative Studies* 32–57.

Holmstrom, Mark. 1989. *Industrial Democracy in Italy*. Avebury: Gower Publishing Company.

Holyoake, George Jacob. 1893. *The History of the Rochdale Pioneers 1844–1892*. Brighton: The Socialist Institute.

Ianes, Alberto, and Andrea Leonardi. 2017. *Modelli Cooperativi a Confronto*. Bologna: Il Mulino.

ICA. 2015. *Co-operative Governance Fit to Build Resilience in the face of Complexity*. Brussels: International Cooperative Alliance.

———. 2022. *Cooperative Identity, Values and Principles*. Accessed August 4, 2022. https://www.ica.coop/en/cooperatives/cooperative-identity.

ILO. 2018. *Guidelines Concerning Statistics on Cooperatives*. Guidelines for Collecting Statistics, Geneva: International Labour Office, Department of Statistics.

International Cooperative Alliance. 2016. *Facts and Figures*. 22 December. Accessed December 22, 2016. http://ica.coop/en/facts-and-figures.

Jossa, Bruno. 2020. *The Political Economy of Cooperatives and Socialism*. London: Routledge.

Jung, Hongjoo, and Hans Jürgen Rosner. 2012. "Cooperative Movements in the Republic of Korea." In *The Cooperative Business Movement, 1950 to the Present*, by Patrizia Battilani and Hans Schroter, 83–106. Cambridge: Cambridge University Press (Kindle Edition).

Kim, Sunhwa, Yena Lee, Hyojin Shin, and Seungkwon Jang. 2020. "Korea's Consumer Cooperatives and Civil Society: The Cases of iCOOP and Hansalim." In *Waking the Asian Pacific Co-operative Potential*, by Morris Altman Editor, Chapter 20. London: Academic Press.

Kurimoto, Akira. 2017. "Building Consumer Democracy: The Trajectory of Consumer Co-operation in Japan." In *A Global History of Consumer Co-operation since 1850*, by Mary Hilson, Silke Neunsinger and Greg Patmore, 668–697. Leiden: Brill.

———. 2020. "Consumer Cooperatives' Model in Japan." In *Waking the Asian Pacific Co-operative Potential*, by Morris Altman, Anthony Jensen, Akira Kurimoto, Robby Tulus, Yashavantha Dongre and Seungkwon Jang, Chapter 21. London: Academic Press.

Kurimoto, Akira, and Yashavantha Dongre. 2020. "Emerging Asian Cooperative Models From a Global Perspective." In *Waking The Asian-Pacific Co-operative Potential*, by Morris Altman,

Anthony Jensen, Akira Kurimoto, Robby Tulus, Yashavantha Dongre and Seungkwon Jang, 35–45. London: Academic Press.
Lee, Bokyeong, Yhan Sang-Il, and Soyoon Chung. 2014. "Collective Strategy of Social Economy in Wonju." *Korean Journal of Cooperative Studies* 1–26.
Legacoop. 2002. *Una Forma Complessa di Normazione (tra il Micro e il Meso): il Bilancio Sociale.* Social Reporting Guidelines, Bologna: Legacoop Bologna, Stati Generali della Cooperazione di Lavoro: Soci, Democrazia.
MacPherson, Ian. 2007. *One Path to Cooperative Studies.* Vancouver: British Columbia Institute for Co-operative Studies.
Malleson, Tom. 2014. *Economic Democracy for the 21 Century.* Oxford: Oxford University Press.
Mayo, ED. 2017. *A Short History of Cooperation and Mutuality.* Manchester: Cooperatives UK.
Mendell, Marguerite. 2015. "Democratising Capital: Social and Solidarity Finance in Quebec." In *Social Economy in China and the World*, by Ngai Pun, 94–114. London: Taylor & Francis Group.
Michie, Jonathon, Joseph Blasi, and Carlo Borzaga. 2017. *The Oxford Handbook of Mutual, Co-operative, and Co-owned Business.* Oxford: Oxford University Press.
Mondragon Corporation. 2012. *Corporate Management Model.* Corporate Model, Mondragon: Mondragon Corporation.
Morrison, Roy. 1991. *We Build the Road as We Travel.* Philadelphia: New Society Publishers.
Muzzarelli, Maria Giuseppina. 2009. "Monti di Pieta`." In *Dizionario di Economia Civile*, by Luigino Bruni and Stefano Zamagni, 613–625. Roma: Citta` Nuova Editrice.
Myners, Paul. 2014. *The Cooperative Group: Report of the Independent Governance Review.* Governance Report, Manchester: The UK Cooperative group.
Novkovic, Sonja. 2021. "Cooperative Identity as a Yardstick for Transformative Change." *Annals of Public and Cooperative Economics* 1–24.
Nyssens, Marthe. 2006. *Social Enterprise.* Abington: Routledge.
OECD. 2014. *The Cooperative Model of Trentino.* Local Economic and Employment Development Report, Paris: OECD.
Patmore, Greg, and Nikola Belnave. 2018. *A Global History of Co-operative Business.* London: Routledge.
Pencavel, John, Luigi Pistaferri, and Fabiano Schivardi. 2006. "Wages, Employment, and Capital in Capitalist and Worker-Owned Firms." *Industrial and Labor Relations Review* 23–44.
Rainis, Peter. 2016. *Cooperatives Confront Capitalism: Challenging the Neo-liberal Economy.* London: Zed Books.
Ruggeri, Andres. 2014. "Workers' Cooperative Movement in Argentina." In *Social Economy in China and the World*, by Pun Ngai et al., Chapter 4. London: Taylor Francis Group.
Sabeti, Heerad. 2011. "The For-Benefit Enterprise." *Harvard Business Review* 1–7.
Sacchetti, Silvia, and Ermanno Tortia. 2016. "The Extended Governance of Cooperative Firms: Inter-Firm Coordination and Consistency Values." *Annals of Public and Cooperative Economics* 93–116.
Saito, Yoshiaki. 2010. *A Brief Chronicle of the Modern Japanese Consumer Cooperative Movement.* Tokyo: Japanese Consumers' Co-operative Union.
Schweickart, David. 2011. *After Capitalism.* Plymouth: Rowman&Littlefield Publishers.
Shaffer, J. 1999. *Historical Dictionary of the Cooperative Movement.* Lanham: Scarecrow Press.
Soulage, François. 2011. "France: an Endeavour in Enterprise Transformation." In *Beyond the Crisis: Cooperatives, Work, Finance*, by Alberto Zevi, Antonio Zanotti, François Soulage and Adrian Zelaia, 155–196. Brussels: Cecop Publications.
Spear, Roger. 2004. "Governance in Democratic Member-Based Organisations." *Annals of Public and Cooperative Economics* 33–59.
Vieta, Marcelo, Sara Depetri, and Antonella Carrano. 2017. *The Italian Road to Recuperating Enterprises in Crisis and the Legge Marcora Framework: Italy's Worker-Buyouts in Times of Crisis.* Trento: Euricse.

Viviani, Mario. 2006. *Dire Dare Fare Avere: Percorsi e Pratiche della Responsabilita` Sociale.* Bologna: Il Mulino.

Whyte, William Foote, and Kathleen King Whyte. 1988. *Making Mondragon.* New York: Ithaca Press.

Wilson, John, Anthony Webster, and Rachel Vorberg-Rugh. 2013. *Building Co-operation: A Business History of the Co-operative Group, 1863–2013.* Oxford: Oxford University Press.

Wolff, Richard. 2012. *Democracy at Work: A Cure for Capitalism.* Chicago: Haymarket Books.

Zamagni, Vera. 2012. "A World of Variations: Sectors and Forms." In *The Cooperative Business Movement, 1950 to the Present*, by Patizia Battilani and Harm Schroeder, Chapter 2. Cambridge: Cambridge University Press.

———. 2017. "A Worldwide Historical Perspective on Co-operatives and Their Evolution." In *The Oxford Handbook of Mutual, Co-operatives and Co-owned Business*, by Jonathon Michie and Joseph, Borzaga, Carlo Blasi, 97–114. Oxford: Oxford University Press.

Zanotti, Antonio. 2011. "The Strength of an Inter-Sectoral Network." In *Beyond The Crisis: Cooperatives, Work, Finance*, by Alberto Zevi, Antonio Zanotti, Francois Soulage and Adrian Zelaia, 21–100. Brussels: Cecop Publications.

———. 2017. *Prima di Rochdale: Dal Cooperativismo alla Cooperazione.* Soveria Mannelli: Rubbettino.

Zevi, Alberto. 1990. "The Financing of Cooperatives in Italy." *Annals of Public and Cooperative Economy* 353–365.

Zevi, Alberto, Antonio Zanotti, Francois Soulage, and Adrian Zelaia. 2011. *Beyond the Crisis: Cooperatives, Work and Finance.* Brussels: Cecop Publications.

2 Cooperative Enterprise 1750–1914

2.1 Introduction

This chapter analyses the development of cooperative enterprises from the beginning of the industrial revolution until 1914. It will explain the reasons and motives that led people to form cooperatives to solve their economic and non-economic needs. It will assess how cooperatives developed their early cooperative enterprise models[1] in the consumer, credit, agricultural, and worker cooperative sectors. It will demonstrate that each cooperative enterprise model was established under different economic, social, and political circumstances.

This chapter is divided into 14 parts. Part 2.1 introduces the Chapter. Part 2.2 explains the political and economic context within which cooperatives operated from 1750 to 1860s. Part 2.3 examines the ideas and contributions of the early Socialists before the Rochdale experiment. Part 2.4 introduces the Rochdale consumer society and how the consumer sector evolved in Britain. Part 2.5 discusses the urban and rural cooperative banks that developed in Germany. Part 2.6 analyses the period from 1870 to 1914. This period witnessed the development of businesses as corporations, the early democratisation of the Liberal State, and the rise of working parties and related organisations. During this period, States in industrialised and late industrialising countries became more actively involved in the economy and in society. Part 2.7 explains the development of the Cooperative Wholesale Society (CWS) in Britain, a second-tier cooperative. Part 2.8 examines the second-tier cooperative support structures established by the German rural and urban cooperative banks. Part 2.9 analyses the development of agricultural cooperatives in Denmark. Part 2.10 introduces the Italian worker cooperatives. Part 2.11 discusses the internationalisation of the cooperative movement.[2] This chapter concludes with Part 2.13 providing a Chapter summary and Part 2.14 providing key questions for readers to consider.

Key learnings from this chapter include the following:

- First, readers will be able to understand the reasons that led to the formation of cooperatives and how they set out to meet people's needs.
- Second, readers will be able to understand the differences between the ideas of the early Socialists with those of the Rochdale pioneers.
- Third, readers will become aware of the first-tier (individual cooperatives) and second-tier cooperatives (wholesale, consortia, marketing, service cooperatives) that made up the early cooperative enterprise models.
- Fourth, readers can begin to reflect upon the typology of cooperatives and the commonalities and differences between each cooperative sector.

DOI: 10.4324/9781003269533-2

- Fifth, readers will be able to consider the State's role in supporting or limiting the rise of cooperatives.
- Sixth, readers will appreciate that the cooperative movement was never a homogeneous movement; there were differences in cooperative preferences, in ideas relating to the cooperative's relations with political parties and the State, and the perceived role that cooperatives could perform within a capitalist-led market economy (CME).
- Finally, readers will appreciate how ideas can spread worldwide and the International Cooperative Alliance's (ICA) difficulties uniting a diverse international cooperative movement.

2.2 State, Economy, and Society 1750–1860s

The formation of cooperatives is a response to the precarious social conditions that developed during the industrial revolution. This was a period when private property in the countryside expanded, technological innovations such as the invention of steam power led to the development of the factory system and people migrated from rural to urban areas in search of work, all of which expanded the market system (Chang 2014). It was a period that witnessed the expansion of the CME. In this capitalist market, private property owners hired labour to produce goods and services to be sold at market prices and reserved the privilege to retain the profits from these proceeds. The market, according to Adam Smith, was supposed to be self-regulated. Self-interested individuals and market competition from many players would ensure that business would produce what society wanted at a price people were willing to pay. The factory system would introduce the division of labour and specialisation, increasing production and leading to efficient use of resources. Everyone was supposed to benefit (Heilbroner 1953).

This system operated within a Liberal State whose primary role was confined to protecting private property, maintaining law and order at home, and engaging in external affairs. The State began to regulate the market, enforce contracts, and pass legislation that favoured property owners and capitalists (Poggi 1978). In the *Wealth of Nations*, Adam Smith thought that the State could get involved in infrastructure, education, and health services—all areas where the market did not get involved but that it needed in order to transport its products and to maintain law and order (Heilbroner 1996).

Capitalists thrived in this system. They began to showcase their innovative entrepreneurial spirit and ability to create legal instruments to attract capital. One such venture was the joint-stock company which allowed many individuals to invest in companies that required more capital than what the richest individuals could provide (Chang 2014). In England, 15 joint-stock companies were operating in 1688, and in the United States, there were already 328 corporations operating by 1790 (Bakan 2004). In 1816, the State of New York created the canal fund by selling bonds which were used to build the Eirie Canal. These bonds would be paid for by road tolls. In 1818, a public–private partnership in Baltimore built the railroad (Srinivasan 2017). Businesses could also have access to finance via stock exchanges and universal banks. The London Stock Exchange was established in 1801. The New York Stock Exchange was established in 1817 (Chang 2014). Universal banks provided capital by purchasing equity in companies. They were first established in Belgium in 1822 and later in other parts of Europe. They became very instrumental in Germany's brand of Capitalism (Landes 2003).

Businesses started to increase their average size compared to artisan workshops, but most still employed fewer than 12 employees. Their finance was supplied mainly by their partners. Those who established factories employed up to 200 people in the Manchester cotton mills. The largest smelting firms in Germany's Ruhr region employed up to 450 persons (Amatori and Colli 2011).

Contrary to Adam Smith's prediction, the 'invisible hand' of the market and competition did not benefit everyone. The living conditions were miserable. Working people were required to work 70–80 hours per week, and some worked 100 hours. They lived in crowded conditions—up to 15 people per room, and as many as 100 people shared one toilet. Life expectancy in the United Kingdom was 36 years in 1800 and 41 years in 1860. In the poor areas of Manchester, however, life expectancy was 17 years (Chang 2014).

People excluded from the CME or exploited in the workplaces had few choices to improve their life during the early phase of the industrial revolution. The labour movement was not yet formed. The State left it to the market to provide for the people. The Liberal State was not a Democratic State. In 1860, only one country provided for universal male suffrage, so people could not channel their grievances via the political system (Dahl 1998). One response to this situation was to emigrate. It is estimated that from 1820 to 1850, 2.6 million people emigrated from England, and 800,000 emigrated from Germany (Kenwood and Lougheed 1983). Other members of the community, however, began to look at the principles of cooperation and self-help to solve their problems.

2.3 Early Forms of Cooperation

Cooperation is an activity and an organisational form that allows people to come together to help one another and to solve their immediate economic needs. It has existed throughout the world for over 2,000 years. There is evidence that the act of cooperation to achieve common goals has been embraced by people throughout the world, from every culture, and in response to a variety of economic systems (Barberini 2009, Mayo 2017).

More modern forms of cooperation have responded to the insecurities and poor living conditions that resulted from living within a CME and society governed by a Liberal State. Cooperatives began to be formed all over Europe and America. In 1752, Benjamin Franklin founded America's first mutual, the *Philadelphia Contributionship of the Insurance of Houses from Loss by Fire*. In 1755, the first building society was formed in Birmingham. In 1780, cotton producers in Greece joined forces to market their produce (Mayo 2017). In 1806, the first cooperative dairy of fresh milk and milk products was established at Osoppo, Italy (Barberini 2009). Following unsuccessful strike attempts from 1759 until 1820, workers formed at least 46 flour and bread societies in England and Scotland to retail bread and flour below the prevailing local market price (Patmore and Belnave 2018). Shaffer informs that by 1830, 300 cooperatives were registered under the United Kingdom's *Friendly Societies Act* (Shaffer 1999).

2.3.1 The Idea of Community

A number of Socialist thinkers and activists questioned the capitalist society that was unfolding and declared the living conditions of common people immoral and unacceptable. They identified in competition, individualism, the pursuit of profits, and the excessive powers of landlords and capitalists as the key problems faced by the industrial society. They found unacceptable the powers exercised by landlords and capitalists to exploit working people for the pursuit of profits (Crick 1987, Honneth 2017).

Early Socialists wanted to improve working people's well-being and moral standing by replacing the industrial capitalist system with a cooperative production system. Cooperation would replace competition between people. A cooperative system would create a harmonious society that would benefit and create happiness for all its members. As such, their proposals addressed the whole of society, not one group or class (Zanotti 2017). Key proponents of these early ideas were Robert Owen, Charles Fourier, and Etienne Cabet.

- Following his experience at the New Lanark Mills (1799), where he improved living and working conditions, Robert Owen (1771–1858) proposed establishing self-sufficient communities. These communities would have a population of between 500 and 1,500 people. In these communities, everyone would work to achieve self-sufficiency and be able to exchange goods with other similar villages. He hoped that these self-sufficient communities would spread to the point of replacing the existing capitalist society. The environment created within these communities would eventually create morally superior human beings, leading to human happiness (Owen 1927). Whilst these communities were based on principles of social equality, higher social goals, and provided better living conditions, New Lanark has been described as a benevolent autocracy rather than a cooperative (Thornley 1981).
- Charles Fourier (1772–1837) proposed to form communitarian structures called Grand Hotels. These would include agricultural and handicraft activities. It would consist of 1,600–1,800 people spread over 5,000 acres, guaranteeing food self-sufficiency. Everyone would have a job and be guaranteed a minimum income. Families lived in common buildings but in separate apartments. These communities included shareholders with different sets of remuneration set at 30 per cent for workers and 10 per cent for capitalists. It was hoped that these communities would be replicated and eventually replace the capitalist mode of production. People were to serve their community and not the central State: this was a form of communitarian Socialism (Crick 1987).
- Etienne Cabet (1788–1856) wanted to create communities of at least 1 million people. All production would be held in common, with people taking what they needed. This approach abolished private property. The State was to finance these communities. Cabet, who wrote the book *Voyage en Icarie* in 1840, promoted equality and democracy, ensuring that all positions within the community were elected based on one-person-one-vote (Zanotti 2017).

These communities were tried in Europe and the Americas but did not succeed. Bad management, unsuitable colonists, unsuitable sites, and lack of finance were some of the reasons for their failure (Bonner 1961). These early Socialist theorists, however, have the merit for providing an early critique of the industrial society and for promoting an alternative society to one based on individualism and competition, which placed the unlimited pursuit of profits above the needs and wishes of human beings. Early Socialists also advocated for change from within the system. They hoped that their ideas would spread and that people would accept cooperation, harmonious relations, and a limited role for capital. For these co-operators, cooperation was always a means to an end. The end meant a society that would be able to provide people with the opportunity to develop into better human beings and to find happiness (Crick 1987, Zanotti 2017).

2.3.2 Early Cooperative Principles

Two other key cooperative experiences before Rochdale also developed cooperative guidelines and principles. One experience was that of Doctor King (1786–1865), a Christian Socialist from England who provided some guidelines for consumer cooperatives. The other experience took place in France, where Philippe Buchez (1796–1865) and Louis Blanc (1811–1882) developed a set of guidelines and a strategy for developing worker cooperatives.

Doctor King advocated cooperatives via *The Co-operator* magazine, which was published in 1828. He promoted cooperatives via the Brighton Cooperative Trading Association. The initial goal of these consumer cooperatives was to make profits, which would be invested in workshops to provide jobs for the unemployed. These stores would reduce costs for purchasers and provide an outlet for manufactured goods. Some cooperative articles of association required members to pay a subscription, capital was collectively owned, there was no return on capital, members had to be under 35 years of age and in good health, and a full-time storekeeper was appointed (Patmore and Belnave 2018).

It has been estimated that in 1832, 500 of these cooperatives operated in England. This self-conscious cooperative movement aimed to replace the developing capitalist society with a cooperative economy. By 1834, however, not many had survived. A key reason for not surviving was that people turned to political action in response to the 1832 *Reform Act*, which again denied people the right to vote, and in response to the Poor Laws of 1834, which threatened extremely poor people with the workhouse. Other key reasons were internal weaknesses such as having no legal status and no remedy against fraud; the lack of loyalty; the difficulty in selling their goods through the store; and the abandonment of the cash payment principle as the economic depression hit their members. A fundamental flaw was that people could not withdraw money or have it remunerated. This meant that the only way to get one's investment was to close the cooperative and divide the money (Birchall 2011).

Phillippe Buchez, in 1830–1832, founded an association of cabinet makers and goldsmiths along cooperative lines. He is an important figure because he set the organisational principles that have guided worker cooperatives to this day. These included the democratic election of workers; paying the traditional rates of pay for each craft; the return of surpluses to members proportionate to their work; application of the principle of indivisibility of assets (so that if a society dissolved, its assets would transfer to another society); and providing full membership to all workers after a probationary period of one year. This approach promoted open membership, democratic management, and equality among members (Mellor 1988). Importantly, these principles also prevented cooperatives from degenerating and demutualising. They prevented degeneration by ensuring that everyone could become a member within one year, thus preventing the permanent employment of non-member-workers. In addition, they prevented demutualisation by promoting the collective ownership of assets, thus preventing members from selling the cooperative to capitalists for private gain.

Buchez was also supportive of the State providing financial support to cooperatives. Louis Blanc also advocated State aid in support of cooperatives. In 1839, Blanc published the book *L'Organisation du Travail*, arguing that the government should finance worker-owned enterprises that promoted equal benefits for their members. The idea was for the State to finance cooperatives in their development's early stages and then withdraw support once they became viable. In 1848, the State promoted National Workshops

Laboratories to conduct public works, but these were State-owned companies and did not resemble the type of cooperatives promoted by Buchez and Blanc (Battilani and Schroter 2012). The Work Committee of the Constituent Assembly recorded 175 industrial and artisan associations since 1848, but few remained after an authoritarian government was installed in 1851 (Desroche 1980).

2.4 The Rochdale Model

The Rochdale consumer cooperative was formed in 1844, and it developed a successful cooperative enterprise model that became very influential in England and other countries. The Rochdale cooperative emerged at a time of rapid industrialisation, urbanisation, and economic depression. These circumstances created uncivil living conditions, high unemployment, hunger, lack of proper housing, and public health problems. Life expectancy was 21 years. Unemployment reached 60 per cent. Working people resistance included Owen-influenced communities, forming trade unions to improve working conditions, and supporting parliamentary reforms. None of these actions gave the desired results at the time (Birchall 2011).

Within this context, 28 members formed the Rochdale consumer society. These members were mainly skilled artisans and eight weavers. They had been influenced by Owen's communitarian approach and the Chartists' democratic principles. In developing the cooperative business rules, Rochdale learnt of the potential risks associated with previous consumer cooperatives whilst embracing some principles espoused by other cooperatives. For instance, the Ripponden Cooperative, already practised the democratic principle; Owen had proposed the idea of paying a fixed and limited interest on capital; cooperatives operating in Scotland and Yorkshire in the 1820s already paid dividends on purchases; and the cooperative congress held in 1832 had rejected credit in favour of cash payments (Patmore 2020).

The Rochdale society slowly developed a successful cooperative model that was different from the capitalist enterprise model. The *Industrial and Provident Societies Act* of 1852 (IPSA) facilitated this since it promoted democratic ownership, limited return on capital, and limited shareholding by individuals (Wilson, Webster and Vorberg-Rugh 2013). Unlike previous proponents of cooperative communities or associations, a key feature of the Rochdale model is that it did not question the CME (Hilson 2017). Key features of the Rochdale model included:

- The ability to attract and retain members. Anyone could become a member provided they bought four shares worth one pound each (later increased to five shares). Shares would be remunerated at 5 per cent per annum. Members received a quarterly dividend based on the amount purchased at their store. This approach retained and attracted more members who would become both investors and customers.
- The ability to attract, retain, and grow capital. Capital would be attracted via membership fees which could be paid on a weekly basis. Capital stability would be maintained via the provisions requiring two pounds to remain permanently invested. The rules allowed three pounds to be withdrawn subject to board approval. A portion of the profit would be retained for further investments.
- Democratic governance arrangements. These consisted of the one-member-one-vote principle to elect their representatives on the Rochdale Board. The Board met four times per annum. It comprised a president, a treasurer, and a secretary, plus three

trustees and five directors. Oversight functions included requesting a quarterly report highlighting the level of funds available and the amount of stock sold, the appointment of auditors, and a conflict resolution process that included the right to appeal to the annual general meeting and to access arbitration, if necessary.
- Provisions to prevent demutualisation. These included requiring members to sell their shares to the board; upholding the principle of one-person-one-vote regardless of the number of shares held; limiting the number of shares that each member could hold to 100 shares; limiting the return on capital to 5 per cent, thus preventing speculators from joining the cooperative.
- Unique and prudent cooperative business culture. This includes the goal to sell quality products and no adulteration of goods which was a major problem at the time; the promotion of the democratic principle; the payment of a quarterly dividend on purchases; the principle of limiting the return on capital to 5 per cent; and the devolution of 2 per cent of profits to educational activities which members could enjoy for free. Importantly, it only accepted cash trading and did not provide credit (Birchall 2011, Holyoake 2016).

The Rochdale cooperative formed other businesses to complement the consumer cooperative. It established the Rochdale Cooperative Manufacturing Society in 1854. It invested in private corn mills and other mills, hoping that workers would become shareholders and share the profits. Capitalist investors, however, disagreed, and in 1862 the company was converted into an ordinary profit-making concern. The Rochdale Cooperative Land and Building Company was set up in 1861 with outside investors to build housing for workers. It established a provident, sick, and benefit society (Patmore and Belnave 2018). The Rochdale store was successful. Holyoake notes that 13 years of transactions, from 1844 to 1857, showed receipts amounting to 303,852 pounds. The Store had no debts. It had not incurred losses. It had no law suits (Holyoake 1893).

Further growth for the consumer sector would come from setting up a wholesale society which could guarantee the regular supply of a variety of goods at fair prices. This would overcome the need to deal with unscrupulous suppliers, brokers, and wholesalers. The first attempts to establish a wholesale society, took place at the first cooperative congress held in 1831, but it was unsuccessful. However, the situation improved when the *Industrial and Provident Society Act* of 1862 permitted cooperatives to invest in other cooperatives and to register as limited liability companies. This allowed cooperatives to establish a wholesale society funded and owned by other cooperative societies.[3] These provisions of the IPSA 1862 paved the way for the creation of the CWS in 1863. The CWS would come to dominate the consumer sector and cooperative politics (Wilson, Webster and Vorberg-Rugh 2013).

Before analysing the development of the CWS in the next section of this chapter, we consider the formation of cooperative banking, which began in Germany in 1852.

2.5 Cooperative Banking

The next cooperative sector to develop was the banking sector. Cooperative banks were established in Germany to provide loans to businesses, artisans, and farmers. These groups were excluded from the mainstream banking system because large banks usually intermediated large sums and required collateral from borrowers. Following the large banks' refusal to provide them with loans, businesses, artisans, and farmers found themselves at the mercy of usurers who charged high-interest rates. Some philanthropic-funded credit institutions granted interest fee loans, but these were seen as providing welfare benefits and were not suitable to the needs of businesses. In response, people turned to cooperative banks as a long-term solution to their capital requirements (Goglio and Leonardi 2010). The founders of cooperative banks saw the provision of capital as a prerequisite for small businesses, artisans, and farmers to survive and compete in a CME.

German Capitalism was developing rapidly, and large businesses had formed in the urban areas and the countryside. In the urban areas, small businesses, especially artisans and traders, needed capital to renew their businesses. In the countryside, access to capital was seen as a way to revitalise small farmers and support local communities. In order to satisfy these needs, Hermann Schulze-Delitzsch established the urban banks, called people's banks in 1852, and Friederich Wilhelm Raiffeisen established the cooperative rural banks in 1864 (Birchall 2011).

2.5.1 *People's Banks*

Hermann Schulze-Delitzsch (1808–1893) was the Mayor of Delitzsch and a member of the Prussian National Assembly. He was influenced by Aime Huber, who was aware of Owen and St Simon's views on cooperation. Schulze-Delitzsch had already set up a credit institution supported by wealthy philanthropists in 1850. However, in 1852, he modified it, preferring it to become a self-supporting institution with its members contributing capital (Birchall 2011). The people's banks were founded on the idea of self-help and included the following principles: democratic governance through the one-person-one-vote rule; election of the executive at the general assembly; capital raising requiring individual members to acquire participating shares (which could be paid in instalments); members to acquire more shares if needed; shares to be remunerated via the payment of a regular dividend. The people's banks allowed members access to a loan without needing collateral security apart from the borrower's creditworthiness. The security was provided by all the members, who were all liable for the decisions made by the bank, which operated with unlimited joint liability (Goglio and Leonardi 2010, Blisse and Humme 2017).

Hermann Schulze-Delitzsch considered the people's banks an economic movement. It was a pragmatic way to help traders, artisans, and small businesses to meet the challenges of a CME (Goglio and Kalmi 2017). These banks were not meant to challenge the existing capitalist economic system. Indeed, the payment of interests on capital contributions led to later promoters of people's banks to regard them as pillars against Socialism and supporters of law and order (Goglio and Leonardi 2010).

2.5.2 *Cooperative Rural Banks*

Friedrich Wilhelm Raiffeisen (1818–1888) established rural cooperative banks to supply capital to small farmers from small communities. Raiffeisen was a civil servant in the Prussian State. He was a Conservative and patriotic to the Prussian State. He wanted to address the negative impact that individualism and large-scale industrialisation was having in rural communities such as the spread of poverty, distress, and the indebtedness of small farmers at the hands of usurers. In order to do this, he established rural banks to provide loans to farmers, and to strengthen communities through the cultivation of solidarity and Christian ideals. Whilst he disliked the negative impact that industrialisation was having on rural communities, he too wanted rural banks to operate within the existing social order (Fairbairn 2000, 2017).

The Raiffeisen banks, or cooperative rural banks, initially adopted almost similar statutes as those adopted by the people's banks. In time, however, they developed their own unique cooperative model. First, the democratic governance arrangements were similar to those adopted by the people's banks, except that committee members were not remunerated. Second, the bank's area of operation was the local parish community comprising a few villages. Third, the managers were not remunerated. Fourth, the bank provided long-term loans and allowed farmers to pay their debt at the end of the year when they collected money for their produce. Fifth, profits would not be used to remunerate shares but re-invested in the bank. Sixth, the bank's assets were indivisible, which meant that even if the bank closed down, the assets would be used for the common good. Seventh, the bank practised open membership with shares having a nominal value. Eighth, members would be able to receive a loan based on their reputation and the trust bestowed upon them by other members of the community (Goglio and Leonardi 2010, Birchall 2011).

Compared to the people's banks, there was a big difference in how capital was accumulated. The people's banks hoped to attract more capital from members by paying high interest on capital invested. The rural banks retained all profits in the bank instead and paid no dividends. The people's bank could demutualise because their assets were divisible, whilst the rural banks' assets were indivisible and thus could not demutualise. This ensured that assets were transferred from one generation to the next. The retention of profits improved capitalisation and put rural banks in a position to offer competitive rates to their members (Birchall 2011).

The broad governance structures are similar to those adopted by the people's banks. They include the general assembly, the supervisory board, and the management board. More specific features of the rural banks' governance arrangements include the following:

- The general assembly is the main body where all members exercise their vote to elect the supervisory board and the management board via a democratic voting system based on one-person-one-vote.
- Attendance at meetings was obligatory in order to encourage participation in its affairs (and not only when needing a loan), to learn about cooperative culture, and to be informed.
- The general assembly always retained the right to fix the amount of capital that could be lent, interest rates, the maximum credit limit that could be granted to a member, the terms for repayment of loans, and the level of staff remuneration.
- The management board applied the policies approved by the assembly. It examined loan applications and the ability of members to pay.
- The supervisory board conducted quarterly reviews of the cooperative management and accounts (Goglio and Leonardi 2010).

Both banks became very popular. In 1859, there were 183 people's banks with 18,000 members. As with the British consumer movement, Schulze-Delitzsch had already organised the first congress of the people's banks in 1859, which resulted in the formation of a national federation. In 1867, Prussia enacted the first cooperative law, and subsequently, a national cooperative law was passed in 1871. Cooperative banks, just like the CWS, also established second-tier structures to provide support for independent local cooperatives (Birchall 2011, Kelman 2016).

2.6 State, Economy, and Society 1870–1914

Capitalism development continued at a rapid pace from 1870 to 1914. Compared with the period of the first industrial revolution (the 1760s–1840s), cooperatives would now have to emerge in a different political and economic environment. Private enterprises grew larger, increased their revenue, employed a larger workforce, and were more competitive. The State would become more involved in developing the economy and mediating the excesses of the market. The democratisation of society led to working people joining trade unions and workers' parties. These associations wanted to improve working people's employment conditions and their overall living standards through State welfare services. Workers' parties developed ideas, strategies, and programmes to meet people's immediate needs and their desire to live a life with dignity and hope. For working people, cooperatives would no longer be the only option for a better life. Workers' parties and trade unions now also offered comprehensive policies and programmes that would lead to a better life.

The economic environment of this period benefitted capitalist development. The world population increased from 770 million in 1750, to 1.63 billion by 1900 (Sassoon 2020). New technology, such as steam turbines, refrigeration, and the building of railways, roads, and faster ships, reduced the cost of transport and facilitated trade across the Atlantic. Foreign direct investment from Europe flowed to new European settlements in the Americas, Oceania, and other parts of the world. Colonial powers annexed another 11 million square miles of territory from 1876 to 1910 (Maddison 2007). Forty-six million people emigrated from Europe from 1821 to 1913. People followed capital and opportunities, and in doing so they provided a workforce and a market for investors and businesses (Kenwood and Lougheed 1983). Foreign exchange was based on the gold standard which facilitated trade since businesses and investors could convert foreign currency to gold.

2.6.1 *Corporations*

In this period, businesses grew into very large enterprises, thanks to supportive regulations, access to capital, new production methods, and new organisational structures. Various regulations encouraged entrepreneurship and investment. These included the United States allowing corporations to merge and to operate in more than one State; the legal protection of intellectual property; new bankruptcy laws which allowed businesses to stop paying interest whilst they were re-organising their business; and creditors to write off part of the debt (Amatori and Colli 2011, Srinivasan 2017). Companies could access funds via the stock market, the issuance of bonds, or selling equity to European investment banks or merchant banks. The average size of firms increased. German steel plants employed an average of 1,000 workers, whilst an average of 642 workers were employed in American plants (Frieden 2020). Companies grew larger via mergers and acquisitions, especially railway companies. In the United Kingdom, there were more than 650 mergers from 1898 to 1900 (Cassis 2007). In the United States, 1,800 corporations were absorbed into 157 companies from 1898 to 1904 (Bakan 2004). United Steel employed 100,000 employees and produced the equivalent of 7 per cent of the United States' Gross Domestic Product (Amatori and Colli 2011).

A major innovation which has influenced manufacturing to this day was the Fordism Mode of Production which exploited economies of scale, increased production per unit, and reduced costs. The Ford Motor Company made famous the introduction of the continuous assembly line and the application of Taylor's Principles of Scientific Management which required workers to perform repetitive tasks. The company would be run by professional managers who would coordinate all activities, and it would adopt new management techniques. Companies differentiated between fixed costs and variable costs, and adopted the concept of return on investment to improve decision-making (Cassis 2007). Fordism achieved efficiencies and productivity improvements and reduced the cost of a car from 700 to 350 USD (Frieden 2020). In 1914, Ford doubled workers' wages and introduced the eight-hour day and three daily shifts (Srinivasan 2017).

In the United States, business schools were established to teach these new management techniques governing large complex companies. The Wharton School of Finance and Commerce was the first business school, established in 1881 at the University of Pennsylvania. By 1914, 30 business schools were educating 10,000 graduates yearly (Amatori and Colli 2011). Philanthropists also established or provided seed funding for prestigious universities such as the University of Chicago, John Hopkins University, and Stanford University (Srinivasan 2017).

The State was fully supportive of the CME and mediated its excesses. In addition to regulations that facilitated entrepreneurship, the State began to correct market excesses. A key regulatory change was the United States' *Sherman Anti-Trust Act* of 1890 which prohibited any kind of agreement which resulted in restraint of trade, or that led to a monopoly of trade. As a result, in 1911, Standard Oil was broken up into 34 separate companies (McCraw 1999). Another State function, especially in late developing countries, was that of actively promoting economic development. The State promoted infrastructure by investing in public–private ventures, as was the case in America, or by establishing State-owned enterprises in key areas of the economy, such as railways and steel works, as was the case in some European countries, Japan and China. The State initiated public works (roads, hospitals, and schools) and subsidised and rescued businesses, as in Italy (Millward 2007). A major policy intervention was tariff protection, especially since 1878. Tariffs promoted local industrial sectors by making imports more expensive. Tariffs ranged from 12 to 18 per cent in Europe but were much higher in the manufacturing sector and in the United States (Amatori and Colli 2011, Frieden 2020).

2.6.2 Socialism

The growth of CMEs did not improve working conditions. The relentless pursuit of profit created wealth for the few. Working people began to channel their grievances through the trade union movement and workers' parties. By now, the concept of cooperation espoused by the early Socialists was no longer the only critique of Capitalism nor the only path to improved living standards. Karl Marx wrote *The Communist Manifesto* in 1848. He provided a theory of how capitalists exploited working people (Theory of Surplus Value) and a theory of how history evolved through stages, giving hope to working people that the next stage would be that of a Socialist society (the theory of Historical Materialism). Marx's writings also informed working people that businesses had an insatiable appetite to accumulate capital and grow into large businesses. Socialist parties debating Marx developed strategies to achieve Socialism. One tradition chose revolutionary means. This would entail taking control of the State and nationalising the means of production. Another tradition preferred the parliamentary road to Socialism. This tradition hoped that once it formed government, it could implement State-led reforms that would mediate market failures, reduce the power of businesses, and improve working people's standard of living (Fischer 1973, Wright 1987).

The two key moments of the Socialist strategy before 1914 were the development of the Gotha Program (1875) and the Erfurt Program (1891). Both programs were developed by the German Social Democratic Party (SDP), the most influential in Europe. The Gotha Program proposed policies to promote universal suffrage, freedom of association, conversion of production into common property, State income taxes, better working conditions, and better health conditions at home and at work (Sassoon 1996). The Erfurt Program was more comprehensive and officially declared Marxism the official ideology of Social Democracy. It proposed a parliamentary road to Socialism, the development of the Welfare State, free education, tax on income and property, and better industrial relations and working conditions (SPD 1891). Marx's critique of Capitalism and the SDP programme became the accepted programme of the European Left (Wright 1987). It provided a more comprehensive political and economic theory and a more practical strategy to improve the living standards of working people than that offered by the early Socialists. Most importantly, the policies were to be applied universally, covering everyone, not just cooperative members.

2.6.3 *Rerum Novarum*

In the same year that the SDP released the Erfurt Program, the Catholic Church released the *Encyclical Rerum Novarum*. It became known as the Catholic Social Doctrine. It signalled the Catholic Church's concern for the plight of working people. It was an anti-Socialist document arguing in favour of private property and proposing an inter-classist society where business and government had the responsibility also to help people experiencing poverty. It did not promote cooperatives, but priests that were influenced by the document did. As we have seen, Christians influenced by the Gospel promoted cooperatives before 1891, but the Catholic Church, whilst late in considering the 'Social Question' since 1891, supported activities that helped the poor, their families, and their communities (LEO XIII 1891).

2.6.4 *Democracy and the State*

The rise of the workers' movement was a key factor that led to the democratisation of society. The Liberal States began to democratise and pass legislation that allowed the right to form associations, to form trade unions, to form political parties, and to have the right to vote. By 1914, Socialist parties and trade unions were present throughout Europe. It is estimated that at least 25 per cent of the workforce in Britain and Germany were members of a trade union. Over 15 million members joined a trade union in Europe and 9 million in the United States (Sassoon 1996). France legislated in favour of universal male suffrage in 1845, and slowly other countries initiated electoral reforms extending the right to vote to adult males. Some countries like Finland, and Portugal had implemented full universal suffrage for men and women by 1914 (Sassoon 2020). Dahl notes that by 1920, 15 countries from a total of 66 countries had implemented full male or universal suffrage (Dahl 1998). Socialist parties contested elections and by 1901 got close to 20 per cent of the votes in Germany and Denmark. By 1918, Scandinavian countries, Germany, and Belgium received over 30 per cent of the votes. Socialist parties won municipal elections in Italy and France (Sassoon 1996).

The State responded to working people's grievances and political programmes by implementing reforms. Germany implemented the industrial insurance scheme in 1871. By

1916, all major European countries, but Belgium, had implemented at least one or two of the following schemes: occupational injuries, health, pensions, and unemployment (Sassoon 1996). Uruguay implemented a comprehensive Welfare State from 1903 to 1915 which included free education; comprehensive health system, public pension, and workers compensation (Frieden 2020).

2.6.5 A More Challenging Environment

Cooperatives faced a more challenging competitive environment from 1870 to 1914. Private enterprise was more competitive; companies were larger than before, and they had developed new manufacturing and organisational structures that made them more efficient and productive. The State increased its sphere of influence by adding economic development and welfare to the functions of law and order and external affairs. More importantly, the State relied more and more on the private sector for nation-building activities, employment creation, and, as we shall see later, the preparation of a war-economy. Working people could now rely on trade unions and the Socialist parties to improve working conditions and influence the State. Although, in principle, the Socialist parties and trade unions supported cooperatives but did not think that they could solve people's needs on their own, they questioned the way consumer cooperatives treated workers as simply wage earners and also questioned the economic record of worker cooperatives. They were concerned that cooperatives would take working people away from the fight against Capital. They were also convinced that the State was better suited to develop policies and programmes that would benefit all working people and better suited to build a Socialist society (Bernstein 1889, Lenin 1910, Webb and Webb 1914, Desroche 1980, Jossa 2005, Balnaves and Patmore 2017).

2.7 The Cooperative Wholesale Society

The CWS was formed in 1863 to provide groceries and retail goods at affordable prices to cooperative societies. This would overcome the risk of boycott from private wholesalers who were under pressure to do so from private retailers. Forty-eight cooperative societies joined the CWS, and since there was an investment limit of 200 pounds per member, individuals were also asked to join as members. The CWS grew in line with the growth of the consumer movement, and by 1914 membership increased to 1,345 societies. It developed a unique enterprise model that achieved economies of scale through a federated central organisation (the CWS) which, in turn, was controlled by independent cooperative societies. The CWS was accountable to the societies, and societies were accountable to their members (Wilson, Webster and Vorberg-Rugh 2013).

The CWS displayed a vibrant entrepreneurial spirit. It grew into a large, multi-business, multi-functional organisation that became one of the largest businesses in Britain. The CWS was driven by its desire to meet the immediate needs of its members and the long-term goal of creating a Cooperative Commonwealth. This meant having the CWS as the central hub of a consumer cooperative system which would ultimately replace the CME. To this end, it developed an organisational structure capable of supplying goods nationally, developing its own manufactured and consumer brands, and developing its own international supply chains. Key activities included:

- Manufacturing and agricultural facilities, commencing in the 1870s. These included manufacturing plants producing flour, soap, shoes, biscuits, textiles, pottery, chocolate, printing, and newspapers. From 1890 to 1910, it built or acquired more than 40 factories, workshops, and mills.

- International operations included overseas offices from 1874 in North America, Europe, and Australia. It owned land in various colonies and managed tea plantations in India and Sri Lanka (then called Ceylon). In addition, it owned a creamery and bacon factory in Ireland and a bacon factory in Denmark.
- The CWS banking department (1871) provided financial services to members, such as loans and overdrafts. The cooperative insurance society was incorporated in 1913.
- Management services for members included legal, accounting, and engineering services via its in-house facilities.
- A national distribution service which by 1890 included offices in Manchester, London, and Newcastle, as well as seven subsidiary wholesale branches scattered throughout England (Webster 2012, Wilson, Webster and Vorberg-Rugh 2013, Patmore and Belnave 2018).

The CWS was able to access capital which allowed it to be in a position to invest, to diversify its operations, and to grow. It managed to access capital by retaining profits and tapping into the capital raising ability and the pool of savings held by its 1,345 cooperative society members. Cooperative societies purchased CWS shares, deposited their savings with the CWS bank, and sought loans or overdrafts from the CWS when required. The CWS bank also attracted savings from cooperative members, who numbered 3 million in 1914, and from trade unions. The CWS became a profitable organisation and raised capital by retaining profits. It is estimated that 37 per cent of all goods and groceries purchased by cooperative societies were purchased via the CWS (Webster 2012). In 1905, it became the 16th largest company in England, with a capital of almost 10 million pounds and net sales of almost 35 million pounds (Patmore and Belnave 2018). CWS records indicate that it supplied up to 9 per cent of the retail trade and up to 19 per cent of the grocery and provisions trade (Wilson, Webster and Vorberg-Rugh 2013). It employed 22,000 people (Birchall 2011).

The governance arrangements reflected a complex, democratically managed organisation. Cooperative members elected 12 members to the Board of Directors (The Board). The Board, in turn, used four sub-committees to help with governance. There was a sub-committee for finance, one for drapery, one for grocery and provisions, and another for productive operations. The Board made use of joint-committee meetings to make key decisions. The Board performed a very broad role that included making key appointments and regularly organising conferences for all their buyers. The Board employed a secretary of financial administration, a general manager for operations, and it required all managers to regularly report to the appropriate sub-committee (Wilson, Webster and Vorberg-Rugh 2013).

The CWS governance structure was a complex structure that was quite effective in achieving growth and being aligned to meet the needs of cooperative societies. Its success can be attributed to its enterprise model that achieved horizontal (independent cooperative societies working together) and vertical integration (central provision of goods and services). External factors, such as a doubling of England's population and wage growth of 34 per cent from 1854 to 1914, also contributed. Better transport facilities from railways and steam ships facilitated the importation and delivery of goods (Birchall 2011). The CWS also operated in an advantageous position versus its rivals which were still relatively underdeveloped compared to the CWS (Hilson 2017).

Whilst the CWS success is evident, some issues were emerging which would impact its growth and the cooperative movement in general. First, there was non-alignment between the CWS leadership's mission to build a cooperative consumer-led republic and some of the societies with more limited views about the role of consumer cooperation. In alignment with this view, the CWS expected societies to buy all their produce from the CWS. However, societies would only buy from the CWS if its goods and services were competitively priced and if they satisfied their members. Indeed, some London-based societies purchased less than 30 per cent of their products from the CWS. Second, the CWS could not develop a coherent strategy since local societies operated wholesale societies at a regional level and operated their own manufacturers, bakeries, and mills. Third, there was uneven growth of consumer societies, with lower growth in the South of England. Fourth, the CWS was a very complex organisation that it would become difficult to manage as a result of its geographic expansion and its diversified manufacturing and agricultural holdings (Wilson, Webster and Vorberg-Rugh 2013, Patmore 2020).

Another key issue is the relationship between the CWS and producer cooperatives. At first, the CWS engaged with producer cooperatives by purchasing and selling their products. It also lent them money through the cooperative bank. The producer cooperatives, however, did not do well. They defaulted on loans, and the CWS lost large amounts of money. Following this, the CWS proceeded to form its own companies and took over many producer cooperatives as well. The plight of worker cooperatives was not helped by Beatrice and Sydney Webb's analysis that workers cooperatives failed because of inefficient management, undisciplined workforce, and reluctance towards industrial change. Beatrice and Sydney Webb favoured consumer cooperatives because they benefitted everyone rather than worker cooperatives which benefitted only their members. One of the consequences of this analysis is the long-lasting animosity that has existed between consumer cooperatives and workers cooperatives in England well into the twentieth century (Webb and Webb 1914, Thornley 1981, Webster 2012).

2.8 Cooperative Banks Support Structures

As cooperative banks grew in numbers, there was a need to coordinate the economic growth of the sector and to develop a uniform regulatory regime. To this end, the cooperative banks in Germany developed second-tier cooperative structures, just like the consumer cooperatives in England, in order to achieve economies of scale, promote a cooperative-specific regulatory regime, provide better services to their members, manage capital, and improve accounting standards.

In order to promote a legislative framework and improve the economic performance of banks, the people's banks and the rural banks created second-tier support structures. People's banks created regional federations and central cooperative banks by 1871. The National Federation of Rural Cooperative Societies was established in 1877. It soon established regional federations and a central bank, as well as a number of regional central banks that operated under the guidance of the central bank (Birchall 2011). The rural cooperative banks also established subsidiaries which provided other economic services to agricultural cooperatives in addition to financial services. More specifically:

- The regional federations provided local banks with consultancy services in the training and development of staff, promoted new cooperatives, and represented their members

towards third parties. Their major function, however, was providing annual auditing services, which was compulsory after the passing of the cooperative law in 1889.
- The central bank acted like a clearing house. It distributed funds from local banks with excess liquidity to those local banks that needed credit. This meant that a local bank could access capital outside of its members. These were initially established as a joint-stock company. However, after the cooperative law of 1889 allowed them to establish as second-tier cooperatives with limited liability, they changed their legal status to that of a cooperative.
- The rural banks also provided non-financial services via separate legal entities purchasing fertilisers and marketing agricultural products (Guinnane 2001, Goglio and Leonardi 2010).

The cooperative bank sector became very successful. The people's banks claimed to have over 1,000 banks, with 585,000 members by 1902. The rural banks claimed to have 13,000 cooperative banks with over 1 million members (Birchall 2011). In 1914, there were 19,000 cooperative banks, which held 7 per cent of all German banking liability (Guinnane 2001).

The success of cooperative banks can be attributed to a number of factors. First, the cooperative laws of 1867 and 1889 supported cooperative banks. They upheld the cooperative principles of open membership, and that of members focussed organisations (Blisse and Humme 2017). They required regional associations to conduct annual audits that enhanced accounting practices and the reputation of cooperative banks. The limited liability allowance facilitated the establishment of local banks in poorer areas since banks no longer had to place a higher burden on wealthy members. Finally, the laws did not require cooperatives to meet the minimum capitalisation requirements of corporations. Second, the State provided tax concessions and grants to regional structures that provided auditing services. Third, the tariffs of 1879 helped the agricultural cooperative sector increase their revenue and, as a result, it led to more money being deposited in local banks (Guinnane 2012).

The fourth factor is the cooperative rural banks' enterprise model. The cooperative rural banks' model was successful because (i) it enabled farmers to access credit that they would not have otherwise accessed from other banks; (ii) farmers were able to obtain longer-term loans of between 1 and 10 years, which compared favourably with the 90-day loans offered by commercial banks; (iii) collateral was rarely required except in cases where applicants seeking large loans lived outside the village. In 1901, for instance, only 21 per cent of all outstanding loans from Raiffeisen banks were secured by collateral; (iv) the cooperative banking support structures were very valuable in making better use of the capital available, in providing training, in providing accounting services, and also in reducing costs by providing purchasing and marketing services (Guinnane 2001, Goglio and Leonardi 2010).

Birchall considered which of the two cooperative banking models fared better. He found that the people's bank model were more likely to go bankrupt or to go into liquidation. He found that from 1875 to 1886, 210 people's banks either went bankrupt or into liquidation. One study also found that almost 10 per cent of banks in the Saxony region converted to investor-owned banks in 1892. Key reasons for this turn of events include careless lending, failure to provide enough security, payment of high dividends, and high salaries and commissions. In contrast, the rural banks had only experienced ten cases of fraud up to 1893, and there had been no conversions to investor-owned companies (Birchall 2011). Indeed, the rural banks operated on a model consisting of nominal and minimal shareholding, limited return on capital, and the principle of indivisible assets. These principles would not have attracted investors seeking to receive high-level dividends or investors seeking to capitalise on their investment via demutualisation.

2.9 Agricultural Cooperatives

Agricultural cooperatives established the next major cooperative enterprise model. Agricultural cooperatives were established in a number of European countries, Australia, and the United States by 1870 (Shaffer 1999). A dairy cooperative was established in Italy in 1806 (Barberini 2009). There were 400 cheese factories and creameries operating in the United States in 1867. Denmark, however, is the country most famous for developing agricultural cooperatives. Birchall informs us that a Danish delegation visited the United States in 1876 and, in 1884, established their first creamery at Hjedding. Danish farmers took up the cooperative idea, and by 1900 they established 1,000 cooperative dairies that processed 80 per cent of the country's milk. Other agricultural cooperatives produced 66 per cent of pork, and 800 supply societies imported and manufactured animal feeds (Birchall 2011).

Agricultural cooperatives in Denmark were established in a unique historical and cultural context. The Danish Constitution guaranteed freedom of association and freedom of assembly since 1849, thus facilitating the formation of associations. Denmark boasted a high level of literacy rates, thanks to the Lutheran Church's decision to make it compulsory for candidates of confirmation to read the Bible. Denmark established the Academy for Agriculture in 1769 which encouraged research and the dissemination of ideas and intellectual pursuits. It operated a public school system since 1814; the folk schools since 1844; and the Royal Agricultural College since 1856. There were 16 agricultural schools and 30 public high schools teaching agricultural courses. Education made the Danish people less parochial and more receptive to change. The other key feature to note is that as a result of Denmark's land reforms of 1788–1794, over half of Danish farmers become freeholders by 1814. These farmers had small farms focussing on grain production. Grain prices, however, collapsed in the 1870s due to competition from Russia, America, and Australia. In response, Danish farmers turned to dairy farming and livestock feed production to make a living. However, the small size of their farms made it difficult to compete against the large landlords, leaving farmers open to exploitation from merchants selling agricultural inputs. In response, they turned to cooperatives to access agricultural inputs and to process and market their produce (Stilling-Andersen 1908, Nordstrom 2000).

The agricultural cooperative model offered farmers the opportunity to escape from the control of large capitalist enterprises which paid low rates for milk or from the merchants who charged high prices for corn. To this end, the first modern cooperative creamery was established at Hjedding in 1884. The cooperative model enabled dairy farmers to sell all their milk to their cooperative at a fair price, process the milk into other products such as cream or butter, and sell the produce in the domestic and international markets to increase. In addition, the cooperative would treat members equally by allocating the dividend to each member based on the value of their transaction. The model also included other cooperatives that would lower costs through bulk-buying seeds, fertilisers, machineries, and insurance cover. Overall, the cooperative model allowed small farmers to achieve economies of scale so they could compete against larger businesses whilst maintaining their communal lifestyle (Nordstrom 2000, Birchall 2011).

The cooperative model allowed small milk producers the opportunity to own their own creamery, so they no longer had to take their milk to a privately owned creamery which paid lower prices for their milk and created uncertainty. Creameries were established, thanks to all members accepting liability for the costs of building them. The cooperative capital would come from loans from cooperative members, savings banks, and other banks. Members accepted full liability if the cooperative could not meet repayments. The cooperative hired a manager to run its operations. The contracts stipulated certain standards of cleanliness, feeding practices, and financial arrangements. In addition, they contained clauses that mitigated the risk of members exiting the cooperative early and the risk of members' attempting to adulterate the milk delivered to the creamery. To this end, the contractual arrangements required members to deliver milk for ten years so that the cooperative had a guaranteed milk supply for a long time to generate profits to repay the loan. Leaving before the ten years would jeopardise the repayment of the loan and put more financial pressure on existing members. So exiting early was not welcomed. Adulterating milk by adding water or skim milk was also unacceptable since it would increase costs, reduce profits for all members, and reward guilty farmers (Henriksen, Hviid and Sharp 2012).

A review of 215 creameries found that half the creameries experienced 257 cases where members exited their creameries. Forty-six exits were costless (approved by the cooperative boards as genuine), but the remaining exits had to pay fines. The Danish courts understood the cooperative business and upheld the member requirements stated in the cooperative statutes. The same study also found that 102 creameries had experienced at least one case of milk adulteration. Cooperatives conducted spot checks before the devices to measure milk fat content were introduced in 1905. It also introduced payment based on cream-content. The contracts protected the cooperatives from fraud (adulteration of milk) by having clauses that included damages, penalties, and exclusion. The cases taken to court confirmed that the court generally understood what cooperatives were trying to achieve and the risks they were mitigating (Henriksen, Hviid and Sharp 2012).

In addition to mitigating key risks via the contractual arrangements, dairy cooperatives were able to introduce change and new technologies. The breeding, feeding, and general care improved cow weight and content (milk yield per cow) (Lampe and Sharp 2015). The invention of the continuously spinning milk centrifuge in Denmark (1878) made it worthwhile also to collect milk from small farms, and this enabled the proliferation of cooperatives across Denmark. Another technological invention measured the fat level of milk (1905). This was important because it prevented the dilution of milk with water, and, as a result, the cooperative could pay farmers a fair price for their milk and deal with unfair practices. The development of pasteurisation techniques prevented disease such as bovine tuberculosis and this too improved the quality of milk and productivity (Modhorst 2014).

Cooperatives enjoyed broad community support. Indeed, the Danish narrative on cooperatives is that they are a democratic institution representing the small, free farmers against private capitalist corporations. They are seen as 'Schools for Democracy' that operate in the interest of the nation since they were most responsible for modernising Danish agriculture and successfully transforming its economy. Importantly, cooperative leaders did not see cooperatives just as economic institutions. They viewed cooperatives as a vehicle that modernised the country with the goal to lift the population to a higher moral order, and to make cooperative members better people. For instance, the Danish Encyclopaedia notes that

> An understanding of co-operation [in Denmark] cannot be based on its particular legal, financial, or organizational characteristics alone, but must also include the historical and cultural community, which has its roots in the structure of the rural community in the late nineteenth century. In the minds of the public, the Cooperative Movement is viewed as a unique economic/democratic Danish tradition, which is important to the rise of modern Denmark.
>
> (Mordhorst and Jensen 2019)

Whilst Severin Jørgensen, one of the founding fathers of the Danish cooperative movement in 1903, wrote:

> The movement has a far higher, far more important goal than increasing the population's economic well-being. The most important and most meaningful goal is to lift the population to a higher moral level, to make the members of the cooperative movement more competent and more independent, but most importantly, to make them better people.
>
> (Mordhorst and Jensen 2019)

The cooperative goals of democracy; egalitarianism; sense of fairness; and equitable profit distributions led them to become politically aligned with the SDP. When a Conservative government ruled by decrees in the late nineteenth century and supported landowners, industry, and centralisation, cooperatives supported the Left party because it came to represent farming, nationalism, and decentralisation. In 1913, following debates in the Second International, the Danish SDP and the trade union movement formally supported the formation of cooperatives in urban areas. This was another unique feature of Denmark's cooperative movement (Patmore and Belnave 2018).

The rural areas of Denmark went on to develop a diverse cooperative sector. The cooperative movement was led by a Lutheran Pastor, Sonne, who promoted the first consumer cooperative in Denmark in 1866. It was modelled on the Rochdale experience and quickly grew to 995 societies by 1905. The Dairy cooperatives were formed in 1882; cooperative pork packing houses were formed in 1887; and the Dairy Farmers' Cooperative Egg Export Association was formed in 1895 (Stilling-Andersen 1908). The Federation of Dairy Cooperatives was established in 1899, and it became the vehicle through which cooperatives could influence government policy via the Danish Dairy Board (1912) and the Danish Agricultural Council (1919). It has been estimated that, in all, 4,000 cooperatives were operating in Denmark by 1915 (Modhorst 2014). The overall results from 1874 to 1914 derived from the cooperative-led agricultural economy were remarkable: (i) milk production rose from 1.15 million tons to 3.34 million tons; (ii) butter from 38,000 tons to 110,000 tons; and (iii) pork from 50,000 tons to 210,000 tons. The value of agricultural exports rose by almost five times in the same period (Nordstrom 2000).

The Danish agricultural-led cooperative model offers an interesting contrast to both the urban consumer-led English cooperative model and the cooperative bank-led cooperative model from Germany. Farmers developed a multi-sector cooperative movement formed by agricultural and consumer cooperatives with funding coming from private-sector banks. Politically, they supported Left parties, unlike the rural agricultural and cooperative banks in Germany, which supported Conservative parties. They did, however, have in common with the English and German cooperative models, the establishment of second-tier purchasing and marketing cooperatives and the formation of a federal association to further their interests when dealing with the State.

It is also important to note the role performed by the State in Denmark. Whilst not directly supporting cooperatives with funding or specific legislation, the State provided an advanced education system that taught agricultural studies; it established agricultural research centres that provided knowledge and ideas; it operated an effective legal system that enforced cooperatives contracts; and it established specific State bodies that engaged with cooperative representatives.

2.10 Worker Cooperatives

Worker cooperatives is the next major cooperative enterprise model to develop during this period. It was earlier noted that the organisational principles that have guided worker cooperatives to this day were developed in France. Italy, however, has been the country most receptive to the idea of forming worker cooperatives to provide regular employment and better working conditions to working people. Italy's proximity to France allowed it to become aware of the worker cooperative model. Leaders like Giuseppe Mazzini lived in exile in England where he met cooperative leaders and became aware of the Rochdale consumer cooperative model, as well as Buchez's worker cooperative model (Fabbri 2011a). In addition, leaders from the workers' movement participated at international conferences of the First International (1864 onwards) and the Second International (1889 onwards), where the cooperative model was discussed (Lichtheim 1970).

The cooperative idea began to take hold when the Italian State was formed in 1861. Italy began to industrialise and transform its agrarian economy. Industrialisation and modernisation in the countryside brought similar issues to other European countries: the larger emerging industrial businesses made it difficult for artisan firms to compete in the market, and farmers could not get access to credit and suffered at the hands of usurers. In 1861, agriculture accounted for 63 per cent of the labour force. Large corporations and tenant farmers, who held long leases, employed a large pool of landless labourers as casual labourers. Working people's living standards were poor: the average living age was 30, and close to 40 per cent of the population lived close to the absolute poverty line, defined as sufficient income to buy the essentials in life (Toniolo 2013). In Bologna, more than 30 per cent lived off charities (D'Attorre 1986).

The cooperative idea was promoted as a way to organise artisans, small businesses, farmers, workers, and landless peasants so that they could improve their economic and social positions within the emerging CME. To this end, in 1854, the first consumer cooperative was established in Turin by the Turin Workers Association. Conservative leaders such as Luzzatti established the first popular banks in 1864, and Wollenberg established the first rural bank in 1883. Catholic priests became strong promoters of cooperative rural banks and agricultural cooperatives to support small farmers. The Liberals promoted cooperatives to ensure working people had minimum health care and sufficient food (Zan 1982, Ianes 2013). Italy's unique contribution to the international cooperative movement of this period, however, has been the promotion of a large and sustainable worker cooperative sector (Zangheri 1987).

The first worker cooperative was formed in 1854 by the glass blowers of Altare, a town in the region of Liguria. This industrialised region was the birthplace of Mazzini, who actively promoted cooperatives. He had an inter-classist view of society and viewed cooperatives as the vehicle through which the middle classes and artisans achieved social mobility. The Mazzinians' favourite saying was that cooperatives ensured that capital and labour were in the same hands. After Altare, many other artisans, such as printers, stone masons, carpenters, local carvers, tailors, coffee makers, hairdressers, shoemakers, and boatbuilders, soon formed cooperatives (Fabbri 2011b). These early worker cooperatives did not follow Buchez's cooperative principles. The Altare Glass Blowers cooperative was dominated by a few families who did not allow people from other municipalities to be admitted as members. The Cooperative Society of Crockery and Majolica of Imola, near Bologna, had an open membership and distributed profits also to casual workers. The Construction Cooperative of Cesena (in the region of Emilia Romagna) distributed its profits as follows: 50 per cent to shareholders, 35 per cent reserve fund, 10 per cent to a pension fund for retired workers, their widows and children, and 5 per cent for health cover. In many other cooperatives, the number of shareholders exceeded the member-workers by 10:1. As a result, the distribution of profits mostly went to remunerate capital. For instance, a study of 15 cooperatives conducted in 1887 found that 54 per cent of profits were assigned to capital, whilst worker-members only received 14 per cent on average. There is no doubt that some of these early cooperatives resembled joint-stock companies rather than Buchez-type cooperatives (Zangheri 1987). As was the case in England and France, not many artisan cooperatives survived (Degl'Innocenti 1990).

Working people, however, persevered and identified the worker cooperative model as one that could provide them with a job and dignified life at a time when the State and the market were unable or unwilling to meet their needs. To this end, from the 1880s to 1915, the number of workers' cooperatives increased from 109 in 1888; to 607 in 1902; to 3,936 in 1915. Considering that in 1915 the total number of cooperatives was 8,251 (excluding cooperative banks), worker cooperatives represented close to 48 per cent of all cooperatives (Zangheri 1987, Battilani 2005, Fabbri 2011). There are a number of factors that explain the growth in worker cooperatives. First, the specific link between the economy and the labour market in specific regions. Second, the democratisation of society and the rise of the Socialist party and workers' movement. Third, the political strategy of the cooperative movement. Fourth, the Liberal State's nation-building policies and its response to the demands of the cooperative sector. Fifth, the performance of a cooperative model based on intersectoral unity, and second-tier support structures led by a national federation.

Like other European countries, the economy faced an economic crisis in the 1880s. Competition from agricultural products from low-cost-producing countries like America, Russia, and India, created an economic crisis. For example, the price of wheat was 30 per cent lower from 1880 to 1887, whilst imports increased by 8.5 millions of tonnes at the expense of local production (Castronovo 2013). This led to strikes from landless labourers across the Po Valley. They no longer could work as sharecroppers or rent small plots of land but worked for tenant farmers who hired them as needed. Landless peasants, who numbered 55 per cent to 65 per cent of the rural populations in some areas, began to form cooperatives to provide them with long-term employment. Landless labourers were joined by other workers who had completed land reclamation projects and could not find work, and others still who had been thrown off long held land (Clarke 1996). The cooperatives formed were quite unique in that some focussed on renting land leased from the local government. In contrast, others focussed on construction work like road building, land reclamation projects, or other public works.

Some cooperatives were active in both types of activity. The most famous of these was the Federation of Landless Workers of Ravenna, formed in 1883, which went on to drain the marshes in Ostia, near Rome (Earle 1986).

The Socialist party and the workers' movement were becoming well-organised and, along with other democratic forces, were demanding democratic reforms. Basic rights like freedom of association and the right to vote began to be implemented in line with other European countries (Sassoon 2020). In a 20-year period from 1886 to 1906, working people established the National Cooperative Federation (Lega Nazionale delle Cooperative e Mutue—'LNCM' hereafter) (1886); the workers' associations known as Camere del Lavoro, which housed the Socialist party, the trade union, and the cooperative movement (1891); the Socialist Party (1892); the Federation of Landless Labourers (1901); and the Trade Union Federation (1906). In 1907, the trade union federation, LNCM, and the mutual aid societies formed the Triple Alliance with a political programme seeking welfare measures, better working conditions, and access to public works (Zangheri 1987). In the 1882 elections, in which 6.9 per cent of the population voted, Andrea Costa, a key promoter of municipal Socialism and cooperatives, became the first Socialist to be elected to parliament. In the elections of 1904 and 1909, the Socialists won close to 20 per cent of the votes (Clarke 1996). In 1909, 60 members of parliament, including Socialists, Catholics, Republicans, and Liberal members, formed the Friends of Cooperation Group (FCG). Luzzatti, who also served as the treasurer in the Italian government, led the FCG. LNCM also became a member of a number of parliamentary bodies (Galasso 1987).

LNCM lobbied the national government and local governments. At the local level, it supported the Socialist strategy to win local elections so that they could create employment opportunities for working people. This was possible because local governments had authority over many areas, including education, public works, hygiene, demesne land, welfare services and hospitals, and local policing (Clarke 1996). The Socialists promoted public works, allocation of land to agricultural cooperatives, allocation of land for public housing, as well as lower local taxes (Galasso 1987).

The national government, especially under the Giolitti leadership 1903–1914, enacted a series of cooperative-specific laws which enhanced cooperative principles and enabled cooperatives to access public works. Giolitti used these projects as part of a nation-building activity and as a way to contain the demands of the Socialist party. The 1882 law granted small cooperatives exemption from stamp duty, limited the number of member shares, promoted the principle of one-person-one-vote, and required the manager to be a cooperative member. The 1889 law allowed cooperatives to bid for public contracts, and it permitted local authorities to outsource work to cooperatives for a sum of 100,000 lire without recourse to competitive tender. The law also required the majority of members to be workers, the maximum return on members' shares not to exceed 5 per cent, and the surplus to be distributed according to amount of work performed by both members and non-members. The 1909 law allowed cooperative consortia to bid for public contracts outside their local council. There were laws which allowed cooperatives to bid for railway projects, to access cheap loans for housing, and to buy land at public auctions. In 1913, the National Institute for Cooperative Credit was formed with an initial capital of over 7 billion lire (Ammirato 1996).

LNCM was very supportive of its cooperative members. In addition to political representation, it promoted an intersectoral unified cooperative sector and cooperative support structures, which would become a feature of its cooperative model. This cooperative model included local consortia to help small cooperatives bid for public works, achieve economies of scale, and develop technical expertise; provincial consortia, which operated across cities; and national consortia, which operated on large national projects. LNCM also established 33 local offices across Italy with technical staff who could help with cooperative formation. Its membership included cooperatives from all economic sectors (D'Attorre 1986, Galasso 1987, Degl'Innocenti 1990, Ammirato 1996).

The cooperative strategy was successful. It was estimated that from 1889 to 1909, a total of 4,426 public works were assigned to cooperatives. Of these, 86.2 per cent of the total were assigned to cooperatives from Northern Italy, of which 50.1 per cent went to Emilia Romagna (Degl'Innocenti 1977). In the period 1910–1912, Emilia-Romagna received a further 58 per cent of all public works assigned to cooperatives. In the Socialist strongholds of Bologna, Ravenna, and Ferrara, more than 75 per cent of all public works were assigned to cooperatives (Degl'Innocenti 1990).[4] Some cooperatives grew into large businesses. The Association of Landless Workers of Ravenna, which rented and managed land collectively or worked on land reclamation projects, employed 330 labourers in 1883, but more than 2,500 workers three years later (Menzani 2015). The Ravenna-based construction cooperative, Cooperativa Muratori e Cementisti, formed by bricklayers and cement makers, boasted 700 members in 1909 (Zamagni 2011).

Degl'Innocenti has noted that all the cooperatives of landless labourers established in the 1880s–1890s in Emilia-Romagna were still operating in 1915 (Degl'Innocenti 1990). These cooperatives, however, were different from the early cooperatives. The cooperative laws enacted since 1882 now required cooperatives to be registered, apply the principle of one-person-one-vote; place a limit on their members' shares; limit capital remuneration to less than 5 per cent; ensure the majority of members were workers; and distribute the surplus to both members and non-members according to work performed. In addition, cooperatives could not subcontract work. The Socialist egalitarian ideals ensured that workers were paid a fair wage, salary differentials were limited, and that cooperatives focussed on providing long-term job security (Ammirato 1996).

This period of cooperative development laid the foundations of what would become a feature of the Italian cooperative model. First, broad support from political parties. Second, the national cooperative federation's intersectoral membership and the consortia system would benefit cooperative formation, competitiveness, and growth in years to come. Third, the large construction cooperatives and consortia would become a key component of the Italian cooperative movement alongside the consumer, agricultural, and banking sectors.

2.11 Key Features of Cooperative Models

This first period of cooperative development led to the rise of the consumer, banking, agricultural, and worker cooperative sector. These are still core cooperative sectors today. They all helped their members meet a need that was not being met by the private sector and by the State. They all formed democratic organisations and various support structures to help them compete in the market. Their ideas, external influences, and their broader goals, however, differed. Some cooperative models promoted private property, some promoted cohesive communities, whilst some, influenced by Socialism, promoted collective goals. Table 2.1 provides a summary of the five cooperative enterprise models discussed thus far.

Table 2.1 Cooperative Enterprise Models

Model	*Ideas and Influences*	*Immediate Goal*	*Broader Goals*	*Enterprise Model—Structure*
Consumer (UK)	Owenism, Christianity, Chartism, Consumer-led Socialism Food prices, food quality, and boycotts from private wholesalers	Lower prices, safe food and quality products	Consumer-led Cooperative Republic developing from within a market economy Collectively-owned structure promoting collective goals	Local cooperative societies National wholesaler supporting local units National wholesaler operating as a group of enterprises
Cooperative Rural Bank (Germany)	Christian values Rural conditions and farmers' lack of access to credit	Loans to farmers and other services	Cohesive sustainable community operating within a market economy Collectively-owned structure promoting private property	Local Cooperative Banks Regional Support Structures Federal Structure
Cooperative People's Banks (Germany)	Self-help and economic utility Precarious conditions for small businesses and a lack of access to finance	Loans to artisans and small businesses	Viable small businesses operating within a market economy Private ownership model with divisible assets	Local cooperative banks Regional Support Structures Federal Structure
Agriculture (Denmark)	Christianity and community spirit Farmers wanted direct access to the market without intermediaries	Access to market and support for farmers' produce	Cohesive farming community promoting democratic practices whilst operating within a market economy Collectively-owned structure promoting private property	Local Cooperatives Marketing cooperatives National Cooperative Association
Worker Cooperatives (Italy)	Municipal Socialism High unemployment and poverty	Provision of secure, long-term employment	Socialist-egalitarian society developing from within a market economy with support from the State and local municipalities Collectively-owned structure promoting secure jobs.	Local cooperatives Consortia to bid for public works National Cooperative Association

2.12 The International Cooperative Movement

The cooperative movement developed into a world movement. The rise of Capitalism and industrialisation created similar problems worldwide, and people responded by setting up cooperatives to solve their needs. Shaffer informs us that by 1900, cooperatives had been formed in 40 countries, of which 20 had passed legislation covering cooperatives. Cooperatives laws were enacted all over the world, for instance: in the United Kingdom in 1852, the United States in 1865, Germany and Turkey in 1867, Australia in 1881, Algiers in 1893, Japan in 1900, Brazil in 1903, India in 1904, Argentina in 1905, and Botswana in 1910. Cooperatives were formed in the consumer, credit, agriculture, and worker cooperative sectors (Shaffer 1999).

The spread of the cooperative idea throughout the world took place in multiple ways. First, the idea was spread by early Socialists from France and England. Their utopian ideas reached the United States, where several communities were established. Second, the Rochdale idea spread throughout Europe via people from various countries who learned about it and then spread the idea in their country of origin. For instance, Victor Aime Huber in Germany, Mazzini in Italy, and Lutheran Pastor Sonne in Denmark. Third, international trade also helped spread the cooperative model, especially from the CWS since it had offices in many parts of the world or from Danish dairy cooperatives exhibiting at the Paris World's Fair in 1900. Fourth, the International Labour Movement since 1864 discussed the role of cooperatives and the social question, thus informing delegates from all over the world about the role of cooperatives. Fifth, colonial governments spread the ideas of cooperation in their colonies. This was the case of Britain, which introduced credit cooperatives along the lines of the German model in India in 1904; the French promoted cooperative organisations under French law of provident societies and association in Algeria, Marocco and Tunisia; and Japan promoted cooperatives in Korea. Sixth, proximity to a country with cooperative activity helped absorb new ideas: so Germany influenced nearby areas to the uptake of credit cooperatives; Italians became aware of French worker cooperatives; Sri Lanka adopted the Indian law on cooperatives. Seventh, English, Scandinavian, Ukrainian, Russian, and Jewish immigrants established agricultural and other cooperatives in the United States; English immigrants established consumer cooperatives in Australia and Canada; German, Italian, French and Japanese immigrants established cooperatives in South America. Eighth, writers and researchers spread cooperative ideas, as the Utopian Socialists and Holyoake had done, by writing books on cooperatives or by teaching overseas, as was the case of Germany's Ugo Eggert, who taught in Japan in 1890. Finally, as already noted, religious leaders were active in establishing or supporting mainly credit and agricultural cooperatives in Germany, Italy, Denmark, Canada, and other parts of the world (Stilling-Andersen 1908, Develtere 1992, Paulin 2000, Merrett and Walzer 2004, Birchall 2011, Fabbri 2011a, Münkner 2013, Hilson 2018, Patmore and Belnave 2018).

2.12.1 The International Cooperative Alliance

The formation of the ICA in 1895 also contributed to the spread of cooperative ideas around the world. The Idea of forming an international movement had been discussed earlier than 1895. Robert Owen established the Association of all Classes of all Nations in 1835 with the goal of creating a central cooperative association with branches across the world. However, it was not successful, and it ceased operations in 1839. The idea was then revived by the French, who wanted to hold an international conference in Paris in 1867, but the French government opposed it (Shaffer 1999).

The ICA was established on 19 August 1895 in London. In attendance were delegates from cooperatives from Argentina, Australia, Belgium, England, Denmark, France, Germany, Holland, India, Italy, Switzerland, Serbia, and the United States. The four primary forms of cooperation were represented—consumer, credit, agricultural and worker. At this meeting, the representatives agreed on three main objectives: (i) sharing of information among its members; (ii) defining and defending the cooperative principles; and (iii) developing international trade among cooperatives (Brouder 2010). A 15-member central committee and executive officers were elected. Britain provided most of its funding, and as a result, held six committee positions and all the executive positions (Patmore and Belnave 2018).

The ICA had the difficult task of keeping under one organisation many different cooperative movements from different countries and different sectors. It held seven conferences until 1915. They were held in European cities, where members debated key issues such as definition of producer cooperatives and profit sharing cooperatives; political and religious neutrality; international trade cooperation among cooperatives; role of the State supporting cooperative development; production versus consumer cooperatives; relationship with the trade union movement and international organisations (Desroche 1980, Shaffer 1999).

The ICA could claim a few achievements during this period. It did manage to establish a self-funded organisation with an organisational structure and an executive. It upheld the principles of political and religious neutrality, and in 1913 it passed a resolution promoting world peace (Shaffer 1999). On other key matters, however, it could not reach a consensus. The ICA could not agree on a definition of co-partnership. Subsequently, the issue of worker participation in profit sharing was not a key priority after the Paris Congress of 1896 (Rosati 2017). The ICA initially refuted any State support for cooperatives at the Delft Congress held in 1897. This position was altered slightly at the Budapest Congress held in 1904, where the majority of representatives supported the French motion that limited the support from the State to promoting cooperative law and tax concessions as long as the State did not replace private initiative, and cooperatives retained their autonomy (Vagnini 2017). The ICA wanted to promote inter-cooperative trade between producers and consumers and inter-cooperative trade between consumer wholesalers but this too did not eventuate. The reality was that the British CWS was much bigger than the rest, and it could satisfy its needs without forming an international cooperative wholesale society (Hilson 2018).

The ICA congresses revealed some of the divisions within the movements. The Austrian and German movements withdrew from the ICA following its support for consumer cooperatives to expand in rural areas in 1904. Similarly, the Hungarian agricultural cooperatives withdrew because the ICA had not fully supported their arguments for State aid (Patmore and Belnave 2018). This also revealed differences between cooperatives operating in countries that favoured free trade (such as England) and late industrialising countries which required State intervention to catch up with more economically advanced countries (Vagnini 2017).

The key differences, however, were between a dominant, well-established, competitive consumer movement and other cooperative sectors. The consumer cooperatives could access capital via their vast membership and a ready market, whilst the agriculture and worker cooperatives had fewer members, limited capital, and faced stronger competition. Consumer cooperatives had also developed a fairly strong argument favouring the consumer-led cooperative commonwealth. They argued that consumer cooperatives would benefit everyone since everyone is a consumer, whilst independent worker cooperatives or agricultural cooperatives only served their members and would end up speculating and becoming monopolies just like private enterprises (Vergnanini 1907, Webb and Webb 1914, Hoyt 2004). Charles Gide had a clear strategy on how to achieve the Cooperative Commonwealth:

> In a first triumphant stage we shall conquer the distribution and sales sector; in the second, the manufacturing sector; and in the third and last, the agricultural sector. This should be the program of the cooperative movement in every country.
>
> (Hirschfield 1976)

The strength of the consumer movement within the ICA and the strong relations it generally had with working-class organisations, influenced relations with the more Conservative credit and agricultural-based movements. For instance, at its 1904 congress, the ICA noted the anti-capitalist nature of cooperation, and at its 1910 congress held in Hamburg, it welcomed the Second International's position that regarded cooperatives as the third pillar of the International Labour Movement whilst affirming the autonomy of the cooperative movement (Hilson 2018). This should not have been a surprise since it is well documented that the consumer and worker cooperative movement had a close relation with the labour movements in the United Kingdom, Scandinavia, Austria, Belgium, Italy, Germany, and so on. These cooperative and labour movements shared anti-capitalist ideas, an egalitarian culture, leaders and supporters, and, as in the case of Italy, a common strategy to win local government elections.

2.13 Summary

- The capitalist economy and society that developed during the industrial revolution created insecure and inhumane working conditions for working people. The Liberal State focussed on maintaining internal order and managing foreign affairs and did not intervene to overcome market failures. The State was not a Democratic State. The Trade Union and Socialist parties were not well established. Marx wrote *The Communist Manifesto* in 1848. The Catholic Church formally considered the Social Question in 1891. Thus, in the initial stages of the industrial revolution working people, farmers, and their communities turned to cooperatives to meet their economic and social needs.
- The Early Socialists proposed cooperatives as communities or as associations as a means to overcome the negative capitalist culture based on individualism, competition, and profit seeking. They proposed to establish communities and societies based on cooperation and harmony where everyone would share the fruits of their labour, would become better human beings, and would achieve happiness. These experiments were not successful, but early Socialists did provide the first critique of the capitalist system and the idea that, through cooperation, everyone could lead a better life.
- Buchez provided governance principles for worker cooperatives. These included the democratic election of workers, paying the traditional rates of pay for each craft, returning surpluses to members proportionate to their work, applying the principle of indivisibility of assets (so that if a society dissolved, its assets would transfer to another society), and providing full membership to all workers after a probationary

period of one year. These principles promote internal financing, equality among members, the open door principle, and prevent degeneration and demutualisation through the creation of inter-generational wealth.

- The Rochdale Pioneers established a consumer cooperative in 1844 with an enterprise model that could successfully compete in a CME. The Rochdale model established a democratic structure based on one-person-one-vote. It was able to attract and retain members, and it did not provide credit to consumers. It paid a limited return on capital, paid a dividend based on the amount purchased during the year, and was able to pay out capital invested by members without negatively impacting the cooperative.
- The cooperative model expanded in different countries and in different sectors such as consumer, credit, agriculture, and worker cooperatives. Each of these cooperatives was established to solve a problem or meet a need that individuals could not meet on their own. To this end, consumer cooperatives provided quality goods at affordable prices, cooperative banks provided access to credit to farmers and artisans, agricultural cooperatives provided access to markets and lower input and marketing costs, and worker cooperatives provided long-term employment to its members. These four cooperative models soon developed second-tier economic structures to provide economic support to their cooperative members. They also promoted a national association to promote the interests of cooperatives versus the State.
- The second-tier cooperative structure is an innovative business model. Second-tier structures—cooperative wholesale society; central banks; marketing agricultural cooperatives; or consortia bidding for public works—allowed cooperatives to remain small and democratic whilst achieving economies of scale. They helped cooperatives to reduce costs, to access markets, to share risks, to provide better services, and to facilitate entrepreneurship. This model was in stark contrast to the model proposed by corporations in which large businesses grew by buying out other businesses, by merging with other businesses, or by driving other businesses out of the market.
- Cooperatives accessed finance internally via their members or via the second-tier cooperative structures. They also accessed finance externally through different means. The UK cooperatives opened their own bank and accessed savings from cooperatives, co-operators, and trade union members. The German farmers accessed credit via their cooperative banks. The Danish farmers accessed credit via private-sector banks. The Italian worker cooperatives accessed finance via local banks and, later, the State.
- The State's behaviour towards cooperatives was not consistent, but it did provide a level of support to cooperative movements. The State passed legislation in England, Germany, and Italy that acknowledged the unique features of cooperative enterprises and allowed them to operate as a proprietary limited company. The German cooperative law required the cooperative association to audit cooperative members. The Danish State did not have a cooperative law but it provided a supportive educational environment and a legal system that understood and enforced cooperative contractual arrangements. The Italian State provided cooperatives with access to public works and with financial assistance. The State did not prevent the CWS from issuing bonds, owning its insurance company, having its own bank, and owning various subsidiaries.
- The relationship between cooperatives and politics is not unanimous. The English consumer movement was stronger in working-class cities and supported labour politics. The Italian worker cooperatives, particularly in Emilia Romagna, supported the Socialist party in winning local elections, and the national association had a close alliance with the trade union and mutual aid societies. The Danish farmers entered into

an alliance with the workers' parties against the Liberals who supported large corporations. The German farmers and credit union were Conservative and anti-Socialists.

- The cooperative models noted so far have different origins and characteristics. The English consumer movement promoted a Cooperative Commonwealth where the consumer wholesaler owned financial, service-related, manufacturing, and agricultural subsidiaries. Consumer cooperatives were to lead and dominate the whole movement. In Germany, a bank-led cooperative model developed. The banks provided agricultural cooperatives and farmers with loans and with technical support. They owned subsidiaries which provided fertilisers and machinery. The Danish cooperative model was led by dairy cooperatives and it expanded to form consumer cooperatives and agricultural cooperatives, including marketing cooperatives. They later formed one association with the urban consumer cooperatives supported by working people. The Italian cooperative movement is multi-faceted and multi-political. However, the area covered so far suggested a model that had a strategy of alliances with the Socialist party to win local elections and to influence the national government in order to access public works and create employment for the landless labourers.
- All cooperative models had good leaders and aspirations that went beyond the needs of the enterprise and of their members. The English consumer movement promoted anti-capitalist, Socialist views of society with limited State intervention. The German leaders of the rural cooperatives wanted to preserve local communities and a way of life by creating cooperatives. The Danish cooperative movement promoted a successful national economy and democratic values. As a result, the Danish cooperative movement is seen as having served the country, having protected small farmers, and having strengthened democracy. Italian worker cooperatives promoted Socialism so that everyone could benefit from the land and the fruits of their labour. To these early co-operators, cooperation meant more than just serving their members and more than managing an enterprise. They also promoted higher goals, such as building stable, cohesive, democratic, and egalitarian communities. Some accepted working within the capitalist system, but others wanted to build a more egalitarian Socialist society.
- The establishment of the ICA in 1895 provided an opportunity for cooperative movements to exchange ideas, promote trade, discuss common cooperative principles, and to establish a lasting organisational structure. The early years, however, demonstrated the differences between consumer and worker cooperatives, between the various views on the role of the State, and the differences between late and early industrialised countries. All of these made it difficult to find common ground. The ICA agreed on the principle of political neutrality but it did not deter cooperative movements from being involved in national politics.
- The political, economic, and social context of 1914 was different to that encountered by the early co-operators. Cooperatives faced more competition from Corporations who had greater access to credit via the stock market, investment banks, and an international financial framework; to a more educated managerial class; and modern organisational method of production (Fordism). They were also much larger than cooperative enterprises. Cooperatives would also face a more difficult environment to convince people to join cooperatives since the trade union and Left political parties offered a credible alternative view on how working people could improve their living conditions. They offered hope that through the democratic process and the use of State powers and resources, they could improve workplace conditions and offer everyone a social safety net. It would become known as the 'cradle to grave' policy, and it was available to everyone.

2.14 Key Questions

Some of the key important questions relating to this chapter include:

- Consider and comment on the early Socialists' communitarian views of the economy and society. Do you agree with their critique of a capitalist society? What are your views on the idea that cooperation and the development of a harmonious society can lead to happiness?
- Why was there a transition from the early Socialist community model of cooperation to the Rochdale-based business model? What are the main differences between the two cooperative models? What is the Rochdale Pioneers' major contribution to cooperatives?
- What are the key features and benefits of the four cooperative enterprise models discussed? What are the innovative features of their business models? How do they differ from capitalist firms?
- The second-tier cooperative structures are regarded as an important innovation in the cooperative enterprise model. What are the economic and social benefits of these innovative structures? How important are they to cooperatives and their communities?
- In what way does the political, economic, social, and cultural environment influence cooperative development? Consider and contrast the cooperative developments in the rural areas of Germany, Denmark, and Italy, for instance.
- What role did the State perform in cooperative development from 1750 to 1914? Was the State's involvement supportive or hostile to cooperative development? In your opinion, what roles should the State perform in promoting cooperatives?
- Cooperative leaders promoted cooperatives as a means to a broader end that involved the community, the nation, democracy, Socialism, and the building of a cooperative commonwealth. To what extent did this approach benefit cooperative development? Should cooperatives have higher, broader goals or should they simply focus on developing a successful enterprise on behalf of their members?
- What are the key features of cooperatives until 1914? How do these features make cooperatives different to conventional corporations? Do you agree with all these features?
- The governance principles of Buchez's worker cooperatives, and Germany's cooperative rural banks, supported the indivisibility of cooperative reserves and cooperative assets. This approach supported the creation of inter-generational cooperative assets. What, in your view, are the short-term and long-term benefits of this principle? What are the risks if reserves and assets can be distributed to members during the life of a cooperative?
- What are the early achievements and limits of the International Cooperative Alliance?

Notes

1 A cooperative enterprise model refers to the way a cooperative is organised to produce and sell goods and services in the market in order to meet the needs of its members. Cooperatives meet the economic, social, cultural, and aspirational needs of their members by competing in the market on their own, or as a member of a second-tier cooperative. Whilst the term enterprise model is synonymous with the term business model, this book will opt to use the term cooperative model interchangeably with the term cooperative enterprise model.

2 Cooperative movement is a term that refers to cooperatives from various economic sectors that are members of a national sectoral or intersectoral association or federation, through which they promote common ideas, beliefs, policies, and common cooperative principles.

3 The *Industrial and Provident Society Act* of 1852 had made provisions for the applications of cooperative principles such as member democratic control and restrictions on share ownership, but did not yet allow cooperatives to invest in other cooperatives and form second-tier structures (Hilson 2017).

4 To put this in perspective, the public works assigned to cooperatives represented 5.6 per cent of all public works assigned nationally (Galasso 1987).

References

Amatori, Franco, and Andrea Colli. 2011. *Business History*. Routledge: New York.

Ammirato, Piero. 1996. *La Lega: The Making of a Successful Cooperative Network*. Aldershot: Dartmouth Publishing Company.

Bakan, Joel. 2004. *The Corporation*. London: Constable and Robinson.

Balnaves, Nikola, and Greg Patmore. 2017. "The Labour Movement and Cooperatives." *Labour History* 7–24.

Barberini, Ivano. 2009. *Come Vola il Calabrone*. Milano: Baldini Castoldi Dalai.

Battilani, Patrizia. 2005. "I Mille Volti della Cooperazione Italiana: Obiettivi e Risultati di una Nuova Forma di Impresa dalle Origini alla Seconda Guerra Mondiale." In *Verso Una Nuova Teoria della Cooperazione Italiana*, by Enea Mazzoli, Stefano Zamagni and Editors, 97–140. Bologna: Il Mulino.

Battilani, Patrizia, and Harm G Schroter. 2012. *The Cooperative Business Movement, 1950 to the Present*. Cambridge: Cambridge University Press.

Bernstein, Edward. 1889. "Evolutionary Socialism." *Marxists Internet Archive*. Accessed January 13, 2022. https://www.marxists.org/reference/archive/bernstein/works/1899/evsoc/index.htm.

Birchall, Johnston. 2011. *People-Centred Businesses*. London: Palgrave MacMillan.

Blisse, Holger, and Detlev Humme. 2017. "Raiffesenbanks and Volksbanks for Europe: The Case for Co-operative Banking In Germany." In *The Oxford Handbook of Mutual, Cooperative and Co-owned Business*, by Jonathon Mitchie, Blasi. Joseph and Carlo Borzaga, 398–411. Oxford: Oxford University Press.

Bonner, Arnold. 1961. *British Cooperation: The History, Principles, and the Organization of the British Cooperative Movement*. Manchester: Cooperative Union Limited.

Brouder, Alan. 2010. "International Cooperative Alliance." In *Handbook of Transnational Economic Governance Regimes*, by Christian Tietje and Alan Brouder, 155–167. Leiden: Brill/Nijhoff.

Cassis, Youssef. 2007. "Big Business." In *The Oxford Handbook of Business History*, by Jones Geoffrey and Jonathon Zeitlin, 171–193. Oxford: Oxford University Press.

Castronovo, Valerio. 2013. *Storia Economica D'Italia*. Turin: Piccola Biblioteca Einaudi.

Chang, Ha-Joon. 2014. *Economics: The User's Guide*. London: Penguin Books.

Clarke, Martin. 1996. *Modern Italy: 1871–1995*. London: Longman.

Crick, Bernard. 1987. *Socialism*. Milton Keynes: Open University Press.

Dahl, Robert. 1998. *On Cooperation*. New Haven: Yale University Press.

D'Attorre, Pier Paolo. 1986. "La Politica." In *Bologna*, by Renato Zangheri, 63–191. Bari: Editori Laterza.

Degl'Innocenti, Maurizio. 1990. "Le Origini della Cooperazione in Emilia Romagna." In *Emilia-Romagna Terra di Cooperazione*, by Angelo Varni, 21–36. Bologna: Eta / Analisi.

———. 1977. *Storia della Cooperazione in Italia*. Rome: Editori Riuniti.

Desroche, Henri. 1980. *Il Progetto Cooperativo*. Milano: Jaca Books.

Develtere, Patrick. 1992. *Co-operatives and Development: Toward a Social Movement Perspective*. Occasional Paper Series, Saskatoon: University of Saskatchewan.

Earle, John. 1986. *The Italian Cooperative Movement: A Portrait of the Lega Nazionale Delle Cooperative e Mutue*. New York: Harper Collins Publishers.

Fabbri, Fabio. 2011a. "Le Origini della Cooperazione Italiana: Tra Mazzini e il Socialismo di Cattedra (1854–1886)." In *L'Italia Cooperativa*, by Fabio Fabbri, 25–66. Roma: Odiesse.

———. 2011b. *L'Italia Cooperativa*. Rome: Odiesse.

Fairbairn, Brett. 2000. "Raiffesen and Desjardins: Co-operative Leadership, Identity and Memory." In *Canadians Cooperatives in the Year 2000*, by Brett Fairbairn, Ian MacPherson and Nora Russell, 13–27. Saskatoon: University of saskatchewan.

———. 2017. "Raiffesan as a Social Innovator." *Annals of Public and Cooperative Economics* 425–448.

Fischer, Ernst. 1973. *Marx in his Own Words*. New York: Penguin Books Limited.

Frieden, Jeffry A. 2020. *Global Capitalism*. New York: WW Norton and Company.

Galasso, Giuseppe. 1987. "Gli Anni Della Grande Espansione e la Crisi del Sistema." In *Storia del Movimento Cooperativo in Italia: 1886–1986*, by renato Zangheri, Giuseppe Galasso and Valerio Castronovo, 219–486. Turin: Giulio Einaudi Editore.

Goglio, Silvio, and Andrea Leonardi. 2010. "The Roots of Cooperative Credit from a Theoretical and Historical Perspective." *Euricse Working Papers* 26.

Goglio, Silvio, and Panu Kalmi. 2017. "Credit Unions and Co-operative Banks Across the World." In *The Oxford Handbook of Mutual, Co-operative, and Co-owned Businesses*, by Jonathon Michie, Joseph Blasi and Carlo Borzaga, 145–158. Oxford: Oxford University Press.

Guinnane, Timothy W. 2001. "Cooperatives as Information Machines: German Rural Credit Cooperatives, 1883–1914." *The Journal of Economic History* 366–389.

———. 2012. "State Support for the German Cooperative Movement." *Central European History* 208–232.

Heilbroner, Robert. 1953. *The Worldly Philosophers*. New York: Penguin Books.

———. 1996. *Teachings from the Worldly Pholisophers*. New York: Norton Paperback.

Henriksen, Ingrid, Morten Hviid, and Paul Sharp. 2012. "Law and Peace: Contracts and the Success of the Danish Dairy Cooperatives." *The Journal of Economic History* 197–224.

Hilson, Mary. 2017. "Rochdale and Beyond: Consumer Cooperation in Britain Before 1945." In *A Global History of Consumer Cooperation Since 1850*, by Mary Hilson, Silker Neusinger and Greg and Patmore, 59–77. Leiden: Brill.

———. 2018. *The International Co-operative Alliance and the Consumer Co-operative Movement in Northern Europe, 1860–1939*. Manchester: Manchester University Press.

Hirschfield, Andre. 1976. "Some Thoughts on 'Co-operative Socialism'." *Annals of Public and Cooperative Economy* 87–101.

Holyoake, George Jacob. 1893. *The History of the Rochdale Pioneers 1844–1892*. Brighton: The Socialist Institute.

———. 2016. *The History of the Rochdale Pioneers: 1844–1892*. London: Kindle Edition, Routledge.

Honneth, Axel. 2017. *The Idea of Socialism*. Cambridge: Polity.

Hoyt, Ann. 2004. "Consumer Ownership in Capitalist Economies: Applications of Theory to Consumer Cooperation." In *Cooperatives and Local Development*, by Christopher Merrett and Norman Walzer, 265–290. New York: Routledge.

Ianes, Alberto. 2013. *Introduzione Alla Storia della Cooperazione in Italia (1854–2011)*. Soveria Mannelli: Rubbettino Editore.

Jossa, Bruno. 2005. "Marxism and the Cooperative Movement." *Cambridge Journal of Economics* 3–29.

Kelman, James. 2016. *The History of Banking*. Scotts Valley: CreateSpace Independent Publishing Platform.

Kenwood, Albert George, and Alan Leslie Lougheed. 1983. *The Growth of the International Economy*. London: Allen and Unwin.

Lampe, Markus, and Paul Sharp. 2015. "Just Add Milk: A Productivity Analysis of the Revolutionary Changes in Nineteenth-Century Danish Dairying." *Economic History Review* 1132–1153.

Landes, David S. 2003. *The Unbound Prometheus*. Cambridge: Cambridge University Press.

LEO XIII. 1891. *Rerum Novarum*. Encyclical, Rome: Libreria Editrice Vaticana.

Lenin, V.I. 1910. "The Question of Co-operative Societies at the International Socialist Congress in Copenhagen." *Marxist Internet Archive*. 25 September. Accessed January 13, 2022. https://www.marxists.org/archive/lenin/works/1910/sep/25.htm.

Lichtheim, George. 1970. *A Short History of Socialism*. Glasgow: William Collins and Sons.

Maddison, Angus. 2007. *Contours of the World Economy, 1-2030 AD*. Oxford: Oxford University Press.

Mayo, ED. 2017. *A Short History of Cooperation and Mutuality*. Manchester: Cooperatives UK.

McCraw, Thomas K. 1999. "American Capitalism." In *Creating Modern Capitalism*, by Thomas K McCraw, 301–348. Cambridge: Harvard University Press.

Mellor, Mary, et al. 1988. *Worker Cooperatives in Theory and Practice*. Milton Keynes: Open University Press.

Menzani, Tito. 2015. *Cooperative: Persone Oltre che Imprese*. Soveria Mannelli: Rubbettino Editore.

Merrett, Christopher, and Norman Walzer. 2004. *Cooperatives and Local Development*. New York: Routledge.

Millward, Robert. 2007. "Business and the State." In *The Oxford Handbook of Business History*, by Geoffrey Jones and Jonathon Zeitlin, 529–557. Oxford: Oxford University Press.

Modhorst, Mads. 2014. "Arla and Danish National Identity." *Business History* 116–133.

Mordhorst, Mads, and Kristoffer Jensen. 2019. "Co-operatives." In *The Routledge Companion to the Makers of Global Business*, by Teresa Silva Lopes, Christina Lubinski, Heidi Tworek and Editors, 217–233. Milton: Taylor Francis Group.

Münkner, Hans-Hermann. 2013. *Worldwide Regulation of Co-operative Societies: An Overview*. Working Paper 53/13, Trento: Euricse.

Nordstrom, Byron J. 2000. *Scandinavia Since 1500*. Minneapolis: University of Minnesota.

Owen, Robert. 1927. *A View of Society and Other Writings*. London: JM Dent and Sons.

Patmore, Greg. 2020. *Innovative Consumer Cooperatives: The Rise and Fall of Berkeley*. London: Routledge.

Patmore, Greg, and Nikola Belnave. 2018. *A Global History of Co-operative Business*. London: Routledge.

Paulin, Pierre. 2000. "The Origins of Savings and Credit Co-operatives in North America." In *Canadian Cooperatives in the Year 2000*, by Brett Fairbern, Ian MacPherson and Nora Russell, 28–39. Saskatoon: University of Saskatchewan.

Poggi, Gianfranco. 1978. *The Developmental of the Modern State*. Stanford: Stanford University Press.

Rosati, Generoso. 2017. "I Congressi ICA di Delft e di Amburgo." In *Alle Origini dell'International Cooperative Alliance (1895–1913)*, by Andrea Ciampani and Paolo Acanfora, 69–82. Soveria Mannelli: Rubbettino Editore.

Sassoon, Donald. 1996. *One Hundred Years of Socialism*. London: Fontana Press.

———. 2020. *The Anxious Triumph: A Global History of Capitalism, 1860–1914*. London: Penguin Books.

Shaffer, J. 1999. *Historical Dictionary of the Cooperative Movement*. Lanham: Scarecrow Press.

SPD, Social Democratic Party of Germany. 1891. *German History in Documents and Images*. 14 October. Accessed November 12, 2021. https://www.marxists.org/history/international/social-democracy/1891/erfurt-program.htm.

Srinivasan, Bhu. 2017. *Americana: A 400 Year History of American Capitalism*. New York: Penguin Books.

Stilling-Andersen, B. 1908. "The Co-operative Movement in Denmark." *Transvaal Agricultural Journal* 234–237.

Thornley, Jenny. 1981. *Workers' Co-operatives: Jobs and Dreams*. London: Heinemann Educational Books.

Toniolo, Gianni. 2013. "An Overview of Italy's Economic Growth." In *The Oxford Handbook of the Italian Economy Since Unification*, by Gianni Toniolo, 1–38. Oxford: Oxford University Press.

Vagnini, Alessandro. 2017. "Il Congresso di Budapest." In *Alle origini dell'International Cooperative Alliance*, by Andrea Ciampani and Paolo Acanfora, 83–98. Soveria Mannelli: Rubbettino Editore.

Vergnanini, Antonio. 1907. "Cooperazione Integrale." *International Cooperative Alliance*, 1–43. Cremona: Edizione Tipografia Giulio Mandelli.
Webb, Sydney, and Beatrice Webb. 1914. "Special Supplement on the Co-operative Production and Profit Sharing." *The New Statesman*, 30 May: 1–34.
Webster, Anthony. 2012. "Building the Wholesale: The development of the English CWS and British Cooperative Business 1863–1890." *Business History* 883–904.
Wilson, John, Anthony Webster, and Rachael Vorberg-Rugh. 2013. *Building Co-operation: A Business history of the Co-operative Group, 1863–2013*. Oxford: Oxford University Press.
Wright, Anthony. 1987. *Socialisms*. Oxford: Oxford University Press.
Zamagni, Vera. 2011. *Da Ravenna al Mondo*. Bologna: Il Mulino.
Zan, Stefano. 1982. *La Cooperazione in Italia*. Bari: De Donato.
Zangheri, Renato. 1987. "Nascita e Primi Sviluppi." In *Storia del Movimento Cooperativo in Italia*, by Renato Zangheri, Giuseppe Galasso and Valerio Castronovo, 1–218. Turin: Giulio Einaudi Editore.
Zanotti, Antonio. 2017. *Prima di Rochdale: Dal Cooperativismo alla Cooperazione*. Soveria Mannelli: Rubbettino.

3 Cooperatives, Monopolies, and the State

1915–1945

This chapter will discuss how cooperatives evolved from 1915 to 1945. Part 3.1 examines how the economy, business, labour, and the State evolved from 1915 to 1945. Part 3.2 will analyse the relationship between cooperatives and the State in Russia following the 1917 revolution and the totalitarian regimes present in Italy and Germany. Part 3.3 will discuss how the Swedish consumer movement competed against monopolies and how it created an international consumer wholesaler. Part 3.4 focussed on "Cooperative Banks in North America". It will discuss the Desjardins cooperative banks in Quebec and credit union movements in the United States. Part 3.5 will analyse the 'New Deal' public policies that promoted agricultural and electricity cooperatives in the United States. Part 3.6 will discuss the evolution and the politics of the international cooperative movement. This will include a discussion on cooperative development, the role of cooperatives in the economy, and the 1935 cooperative principles. Part 3.7 provides a summary of the chapter and Part 3.8 provides key questions for readers to consider.

Key learnings from this chapter include the following:

- Readers will gain an appreciation of the context within which cooperatives operated from 1915 to 1945 and the opportunities and risks associated with operating in different political and economic contexts.
- Readers will gain an appreciation of the role that cooperatives can perform in the economy, including promoting economic development, reducing the power of monopolies, operating as a countervailing power to big business in the interest of producers and consumers, and promoting the community's interests in response to market failures.
- Readers will appreciate the development of the agricultural and credit union experience in the United States and will benefit from comparing them with the European experiences.
- Readers will be able to examine the debates about the role of cooperatives in the economy alongside a more interventionist State and the dominant role of corporations.
- Readers will appreciate the varied relationships that can develop between the State and cooperatives by comparing the events of Sweden, Russia, Italy, Germany, and the United States.
- Readers will be able to understand the difficulties faced by the International Cooperative Alliance (ICA) when developing policies or strategies for a diverse cooperative movement.

DOI: 10.4324/9781003269533-3

3.1 State, Economy, and Society: 1915–1945

The period from 1915 to 1945 witnessed two world wars, the first world economic depression, and the end of the Liberal State. The Liberal State promoted free markets, prudent financial management, including minimal taxation and balanced budgets, and minimal involvement in the economy. Capitalist-led market economies (CMEs) demonstrated that they could not guarantee continued growth, they could not provide full employment, and they could not guarantee a fair distribution of wealth. Businesses continued to grow, to innovate, to expand, and to become multinational companies, but were not able to provide solutions to the unfolding economic crisis of 1929. The Liberal State was not able to develop appropriate public policies to deal with emerging economic and social issues. The policies of balanced budgets and a minimalist State could not deal with the problems unfolding in the 1920s and 1930s.

3.1.1 End of Liberalism

The world economy during this period suffered inflationary pressures but the major shock came with the stock market crash of 1929, which led to the first world economic depression. The depression had devastating consequences. In Europe, 670 banks failed from 1929 to 1937, of which 276 were joint stock banks (Landes 2003). In the United States, 2,294 small banks failed by 1931 (Srinivasan 2017). The price of corn and the price of wheat fell to a third of the pre-depression prices. The Gross Domestic Product (GDP) of most countries in Europe and South America shrank 15–30 per cent. The US economy also shrank by 30 per cent from 1929 to 1933 (Frieden 2020). Businesses were failing, farms were foreclosed, and unemployment reached unforeseen levels. During the worst period (1932–1933), unemployment in the United States and in European countries reached 22 per cent in Britain, 27 per cent in the United States, 32 per cent in Denmark, and 44 per cent in Germany (Hobsbawm 1994).

The Liberal States' inability to deal with the crisis resulted in the rise of different political economic systems that re-arranged the role of the State in the economy and in society. The Russian Revolution installed a one-party-State where the State slowly took control of the economy, nationalising every business employing more than 50 employees (Neusinger 2017). The State would provide 'cradle to grave' support via a State-led economic plan. It proved to be economically successful, growing income per capita by 5 per cent per year from 1928 to 1938. This compared favourably with the rest of the world, where income grew at less than 2 per cent per year (Chang 2014). In Italy and Germany, totalitarian dictatorships replaced the Liberal State. These were reactionary regimes that used violence to defeat their opponents and eliminate their opposition. Everyone now had to be part of a Totalitarian State and be incorporated into its State agencies. In Germany, the State led a CME which comprised over 2,000 cartels which benefitted from the State's re-armament policies. A closer State-business relation, however, unfolded in Italy, where State had been rescuing businesses since the early 1920s. After 1933, the Institute of Industrial Reconstruction (IRI), a State-owned holding company, was established to rescue a number of investment banks and, in the process, became a major shareholder of both banks and businesses. IRI's holdings included 80 per cent of shipbuilding, 50 per cent of the steel industry, and 25 per cent of the mechanical industry as well as holdings in the telecommunication and aviation industry (Amatori and Colli 2011). In 1934, IRI controlled 1,500 companies and 44 per cent of the capital of all public companies (Castronovo 2013).

3.1.2 Social Democracy

During the same period, the State in Sweden and the United States developed a different approach known as 'the third way', or Social Democratic way, to manage the economy. It basically involved a greater level of State involvement in a market economy without stifling private initiative. Whilst the approaches in Sweden and the United States were not identical, generally, the Social Democratic State dealt with the crisis by regulating the financial system, promoting welfare measures, and initiating public works programmes to create jobs. More specifically, State action included guaranteeing people's savings, regulating the banking sector by separating the commercial from the investment arm of banks, promoting collective bargaining between capital and labour, regulating the economy by limiting the powers of business, increasing consumer protection, promoting public works to create employment, providing welfare services (pension, unemployment, and health benefits), guaranteeing farm prices, and establishing credit facilities to promote business activity. This new relationship between the State, the economy, and society required the State to increase taxes and increase public spending. These policies were now deemed acceptable because the State was rescuing the CMEs and solving the unemployment crisis. The Social Democratic State coordinated and reconciled the interest of business and labour, the interests of urban and rural people, and the interests of businesses and consumers (Chang 2014, Srinivasan 2017, Frieden 2020).

3.1.3 Corporations and the State

During this period, businesses continued to grow, innovate, and expand. They also showed different approaches to entrepreneurship. The US corporations, by the 1920s, became multinational businesses, having established thousands of subsidiaries worldwide, including 400 in Britain and 200 each in France and Germany (Amatori and Colli 2011). The power of the US corporations came from size, money, ideas, and management expertise. It was estimated that in 1938, for instance, there were 5 million executives, of whom 100,000 occupied major executive positions (McCraw 1999). In Europe, thousands of cartels were operating at this time, and almost all leading European businesses were members of a cartel. Some European firms, especially family-owned firms, used the holding company legal structure to access capital. This structure allowed them to develop horizontal and vertical business integration whilst retaining control. Ford's management production methods were adopted by the European automobile industry (Amatori and Colli 2011). In Japan, the key business groups were the Zaibatsu. These were family-owned, financially integrated groups that controlled subsidiaries through cross-shareholding and inter-locking directorships. Mitsui, for instance, controlled over 100 subsidiaries. Five Zaibatsu accounted for one-third of the total manufacturing output in Japan. These Zaibatsu controlled over 25 per cent of Japan's GDP before the 1930s (Bernstein 1999).

What stands out during this period is the relationship between the State and capital. The Italian model already introduced a State-owned holding company rescuing and controlling public companies via holding shares. But the State-Business relationships varied. In Japan, the State helped the Zaibatsu through military spending, which reached 55 per cent of public expenditure in 1935. Public procurement also helped to propel industry. For instance, in 1918, out of the 14,000 aircraft built in the United States, 13,991 were purchased by the military. It was these same businesses which later built a further 48,000 aircraft within 12 months of the 1941 attack on Pearl Harbour (Srinivasan 2017). The US Federal Government also increased research expenditure from 80 million in 1940 to 1.3 billion USD in 1945. This research helped make technological advances in chemicals, pharmaceuticals, air transport, electronics, and new materials (synthetic fibres) commercialised by businesses (Amatori and Colli 2011). The State and business needed each other. Sassoon concluded that Capitalism had become the unavoidable backbone of State power and that "the triumph of Capitalism, in the decades before the First World War, meant that no government, regardless of its inclination, could ignore industrialisation" (Sassoon 2020).

What does this mean for cooperatives? We have already noted how, since the 1870s, the democratisation of society, the rise of the labour movement and Socialist parties, and the beginning of State involvement in the economy and society meant that cooperatives were no longer the only alternative available to working people who were excluded or dissatisfied with their position in society. Working people could now rely on trade unions to improve their working conditions in the workplace and, in a Left government, to provide more rights and better social security provisions.

During 1915–1945, the role of the State expanded further to the point that it was now managing CMEs and controlling the Russian economy through State ownership and economic planning. In the latter case, the State positioned itself to be able to look after its citizens from 'cradle to grave'. Corporations and large businesses were more sophisticated and dominated the industrial and manufacturing sector globally. As a result, cooperatives established in the industrial and manufacturing sector would find it difficult to compete. In some countries, however, the consumer, banking, and agricultural cooperatives managed to grow and to satisfy the needs of their members.

3.2 Authoritarian States and Cooperatives

3.2.1 Cooperatives in Russia

The government of the Soviet Union was ambivalent towards cooperatives. Initially, the State passed a law in 1917 which facilitated the establishment of cooperatives. Soon, however, the State quickly exerted its authority and took control of the cooperative sector. The State promoted communal-led or State-led collective farms. It required consumer cooperatives to include a State representative on their board of directors. It absorbed credit cooperatives into the Soviet State Bank in 1918. It transformed consumer cooperatives into State-owned organisations for distributing food in 1919. The State also transformed Tsentrosouiz, the consumer association, into a central organisation that absorbed the functions of agricultural and credit cooperatives. Membership in these State-owned based cooperatives was compulsory. Following the New Economic Policy in 1923, there was a brief period when cooperatives again became voluntary and self-governing. During this period, cooperative membership grew to 43 million, and Tsentrosouiz began running many facilities, including grain elevators, canneries, and soap works, plus educational and welfare activities (De Luca 2013, Neusinger 2017, Patmore and Belnave 2018). This phase, however, was short-lived and in 1935, urban consumer cooperatives were transformed into State enterprises (Birchall 2011).

State control culminated in the passage of the 1936 Constitution, which required cooperatives to be members of a government-supervised local union of cooperatives. Cooperatives were classified as a form of Socialist ownership and were required to promote collective work and to meet set production targets. To this end, agricultural land was placed under State control (De Luca 2013). By 1941, the State brought 98 per cent of agricultural land under the control of State or collective farms (the State controlled only 2 per cent in 1928). It is estimated that several million farmers were forcefully removed from the land. Collective farms operated as cooperatives or under communal ownership: they comprised 50–100 households; they operated democratically using the general assembly as the decision-making body, although, according to reports, democracy was constantly challenged. Peasants did not receive wages, but once the government targets were met, cooperatives could distribute the remaining income to members based on work performed. Peasants also managed their own land, usually one acre, and could sell their produce in the local market (Westwood 1981, Neusinger 2017). In any case, by 1941, the State had brought consumer, credit, agricultural, and worker cooperatives under its control.

3.2.2 *Cooperatives under Fascist Italy*

The Fascist period in Italy from 1922 to 1943 was a disaster for the Italian cooperative movement. The totalitarian regime did not tolerate democratic organisations. It adopted legal and non-legal methods, including the use of violence, to incorporate the cooperative sector within the corporatist institutions of the Fascist State.

The Fascist Party was formed in Milan in 1919. It was the party of the middle classes, retailers, landlords, and public servants. In 1922, the Catholic Church began to support the regime. The Fascist used violence to intimidate its opponents. Procacci notes that in the first four months of 1921, acts of violence on labour organisations, including cooperatives and also other anti-Fascist Republican and Liberal leaders, were almost a daily occurrence (Procacci 1991). During the first half of 1921, before the Fascists formed government in 1922, hundreds of cooperatives were attacked by Fascist squads (Earle 1986, Galasso 1987).

After forming government in 1922, the Fascists began to take control of the cooperative movement. In 1921, the Fascist Union of Cooperatives (FUC) was formed to attract cooperatives via violence and intimidation. In 1923, the Cooperative Association of ex-servicemen joined the FUC. In 1923, the Fascists began to use the Cooperative Institute of Credit to force cooperatives into liquidation by asking for quicker loan repayments. The final blow to the independent cooperative sector came in 1926 when a government decree dissolved all cooperative associations and their newspapers. The same decree also established the National Agency for Cooperation (ENC) as the sole representative body of the cooperative movement. This agency had the power to dissolve any cooperative or expel any person who was deemed to be subversive. The ENC also changed the status of consortia (second-tier cooperatives) into government institutions removing any direct link with cooperatives (Bonfante 1981, Galasso 1987). The Fascists proceeded to purge left-wing members from cooperatives, replacing them with loyal Fascists by placing Fascist members on the cooperative boards; and using the powers of the government Prefects to either dissolve cooperatives or force them to join the ENC (Garotti 1990).

The Fascist impact on the cooperative movement was devastating. From March 1921 to 1927, the number of cooperatives (excluding credit cooperatives) declined from 17,976 to 4,830. More specifically, for the same period, worker cooperatives declined from 7,643 to 1,777; consumer cooperatives from 6,481 to 3,333; and agricultural cooperatives from 2,239 to 1,777 (Battilani 2005). Those agricultural cooperatives destroyed by Fascism included close to 600 collectively managed agricultural cooperatives linked to La Lega Nazionale Delle Cooperative E Mutue (La Lega) and the Catholic-led Confederation (Menzani 2009). It is clear that Fascism targeted those collectively owned cooperatives that were close to the labour movement, such as consumer cooperatives, worker cooperatives, and collectively managed agricultural cooperatives. This is further confirmed by La Lega's own data, which show that its cooperative members declined from 8,000 in 1920 to only 600 cooperatives just before it was dissolved in 1926 (Galasso 1987).

Once cooperatives close to the Socialist Party and Catholic-led cooperatives with anti-Fascist views and their leaders were removed, the Fascist State used cooperatives for its own ends, including using consumer cooperatives to reduce prices; allocating some public works to worker cooperatives to create jobs after the Great Depression; supporting agricultural production to meet the State's goal of food self-sufficiency. Cooperatives under Fascism were legally classified as cooperatives, but they did not comply with the cooperative principles of democracy, open membership, and autonomy from the State. In any case, State records indicate that by 1937, there were 9,766 cooperatives in Italy (excluding cooperative banks), fewer than the 17,976 cooperatives that were operating in 1921. The cooperative rural banks numbered 2,545 in 1925 but only 861 in 1943. The government established the national wholesaler for the consumer movement in 1938 (EICA), which could be regarded as a positive contribution to the cooperative sector, but considering that the English Cooperative Wholesale Society was formed in 1863, it re-inforces the view that the Fascist Government held the cooperative movement back economically and culturally since it was prevented from developing new business models (Menzani 2009, Ianes 2013, Neusinger 2017).

3.2.3 *Cooperatives under Nazi Germany*

The Nazi Regime came to power in 1933 and focussed on destroying the consumer movement. It did not act upon the agricultural cooperatives nor credit cooperatives since they were deemed neutral or supporters of the regime (Patmore and Belnave 2018). The consumer movement had established a central association in 1903 and reached 3.29 million members by 1929. It was regarded as the third pillar of the labour movement alongside the trade union movement and the Social Democratic Party (Prinz 2017).

As was the case in Italy, the Nazis used violence, intimidation, and the media to undermine consumer cooperatives before forming government in 1933. Their threat to destroy consumer cooperatives led many members to withdraw their cash and investments which led to bankruptcy. Once in power, the Nazis used legal measures to weaken and ultimately liquidate the consumer cooperative sector. Key activities included: (i) in 1933, it dissolved the Socialist and Catholic-leaning consumer associations to form the Reich Union of Consumer Cooperatives (Prinz 2017); (ii) in 1933, it limited dividend payments to 3 per cent of the turnover (Menzani 2009); (iii) in 1934, it enacted the *Discount Act* which capped the interest paid on the dividend to a maximum of 4 per cent (Prinz 2017); (iv) the State did not allow banks to provide credit to consumer cooperatives (Neusinger 2017); (v) in 1935, the *Law on Consumer Cooperatives* led to 100 consumer cooperatives in financial difficulty to be privatised or liquidated; (vi) it promoted mergers; (vii) it replaced cooperative personnel with Nazi supporters (Menzani 2009).

The consumer movement was liquidated in 1941 when a government decree transferred consumer cooperatives to the Labour Front, the Nazi-controlled trade union organisation. The consumer movement was no longer owned and managed by members for the benefit of members but it was there to serve the nation (Menzani 2009). The consumer movement slowly re-emerged after the war, but by 1948 it only attracted 756,000 members (Prinz 2017).

3.3 Cooperatives and Monopolies: The Case of Sweden

The Swedish consumer movement offers another type of cooperative experience compared to the experience of cooperatives in Russia, Italy, and Germany. The experience of the Swedish consumer cooperative movement demonstrates the effectiveness of the consumer sector in countervailing the powers of monopolies and cartels. In doing so, the consumer sector improved the workings of the market, it lowered prices for consumers, it lowered costs for industry, it created employment, and it generally improved the spending power of the whole community.

Consumer cooperatives in Sweden were established in the 1860s, and after a few difficult decades, 200 cooperative societies were operating in the 1890s. Kooperativa Forbunded (KF), the Swedish Central Association of the whole cooperative sector, was founded in 1899. Since 1904, it has been responsible for the wholesale operations of the consumer sector (Friberg et al. 2012). The consumer movement grew steadily and by 1930, there were 837 cooperatives which managed 4,849 stores supported by 635,000 members (Johnson 2017). It controlled 20 per cent of the retail market (Patmore and Belnave 2018).

The consumer cooperative sector was successful because consumer cooperatives' turnover was nine times larger than the average turnover of private retailers (Bonow 1938); cooperative governance and the cooperative enterprise model[1] improved competitiveness; of their ability to get support from society; and because of their strategic and objective clarity in defining their role in the economy, in politics, and in society.

The governance arrangements are based on democratic principles. Cooperative members have one vote, they are required to buy a certain amount of shares (ten shares at ten Kronor each, later increased to 15 shares), and they elect cooperative members to the board. Cooperative surpluses were distributed as follows: a limited amount to remunerate shares, 15 per cent to the reserve fund for future investment, and the remaining amount distributed as a dividend to members and non-members in proportion to their purchasers. Members received cash returns, but non-members could use the refund to purchase shares and become members if they wished. The governance arrangements of KF are typical of a second-tier cooperative. KF divided the whole country into 18 cooperative districts, each governed by elected bodies. The KF congress is the supreme body elected by local cooperative societies. The KF congress meets annually in Stockholm to elect the KF board and to approve key policy resolutions (Bonow 1938, Gillespie 1950).

The economic arrangements are in part as expected of second-tier structures, and in part, they are quite innovative. The KF was a highly centralised organisation providing a variety of services to its members. It comprised 12 regional wholesalers to serve their local cooperative members. Wholesale societies made use of the 30 industrial establishments which KF owned on behalf of their members. These establishments produced flour, meat products, rubber goods, tyres, shoes, electric bulbs, pottery, cash registers, fertilisers, and pulp. KF supplied close to 35 per cent of cooperatives' total purchases.

Interestingly, 35 per cent of KF's total revenue was made up by goods sold to the public and private sector (Gillespie 1950).

KF supplied a variety of services to its members. In 1909, KF established a solidity department which supported cooperatives on economic matters and kept an oversight over potential insolvency situations. In 1916, following the German model, it established an audit department to improve cooperative financial management and, in the process, provided consultancy services to cooperative members. Since cooperative failures continued—up to 300 cooperative societies ceased operations by 1918—in the same year, KF required the cooperative's funds to be placed with KF in order to expedite payments. In 1923, it established a company to conduct rescue operations and to establish new cooperatives in areas with low populations (Gillespie 1950, Kyleb 1986). KF was also active in educating its members about cooperative principles. It owned a correspondence school and a residential college, as well as a publishing house. It organised study groups and study circles. KF had the capacity to provide cooperative business and other courses to more than 30,000 members each year (Bonow 1938).

KF and the Swedish consumer sector had a very clear view of how it related to society and its role in the economy. KF was aware of the British consumer model, which was mostly anchored in working-class areas and which had its own political party since 1917; of the French Nîmes School, which promoted an inter-classist cooperative culture; and of the Danish approach to cooperation which managed to harmonise the interests of consumers and producers and the interests of urban and rural areas. KF's approach was to create a movement open to all classes and to maintain political neutrality even though its members were close to the Social Democratic Party (Hilson 2017).

KF promoted a pluralist market economy. It would cooperate with the private sector, but would intervene in the market against monopolies and trusts whenever these would make unjustified profits at the expense of the consumers and the community. Its anti-monopoly policy was clear: KF would intervene only when there was a risk to the supply of goods, and only when KF could control at least 15 per cent of the market so that it could succeed in reducing the prices of goods. Its anti-monopoly policy was not intended to replace the private sector (Hilson 2017, 2018).

In summary, KF was a key component of the Social Democratic consensus that would be established in the 1930s culminating with the State-Business-Union Agreement of 1938. This tri-partite consensus agreed that business would control the market, the unions would represent workers via collective bargaining, and the State would take care of market failures and economic crises by managing the economy and by providing social and welfare services (Frieden 2020). Within this consensus, the cooperative sector would provide food and other products at lower prices via consumer cooperatives, and cheaper affordable housing via housing cooperatives. These cooperative services would reduce costs which would benefit workers by increasing their spending powers, and would benefit business by putting less pressure on wages. The CME and private property were not challenged but simply questioned when capitalists abused their powers. When monopolies and cartels did exploit the community, cooperatives successfully intervened to curb their powers and protect consumers.

KF's first anti-monopoly action was against the Pellerin margarine cartel. In 1908, following pressure from Swedish retailers, the Pellerin cartel stopped supplying margarine to the cooperative sector. In response, KF mobilised its members and trade union members to boycott Pellerin products. At the same time, it took the strategic step of buying its own margarine factory. In response, Pellerin resumed supplies immediately and also reduced the price of margarine. KF sold the initial factory, but it built a bigger factory in 1921. It soon controlled 25 per cent of the market, and the price of margarine was reduced by close to 60 per cent (Gillespie 1950).

KF took another anti-monopoly action against the producers of rubber shoes (galoshes). In 1922, the monopoly sold rubber shoes at 7.5 Kronor a pair even though the cost was only 1.2 Kronor a pair. The price was further increased to 8.5 Kronor a pair in 1927. Investors were making excessive profits receiving 50 million Kronor in profits over 15 years after having made an initial investment of only 4 million Kronor. This equates to an average return of 80 per cent dividend payment per annum. KF bought a factory and produced its own rubber shoes. As a result, the price of shoes fell from 8.5 Kronor to 3.5 Kronor; overall production increased by 50 per cent; and the total employment in the rubber industry increased from 4,090 in 1926 to 5,672 in 1929. KF's own production facilities held a market share not exceeding 30 per cent (Bonow 1938).

KF conducted many other anti-monopoly activities against tyres, fertilisers, and building materials monopolies and cartels. Still, the most famous anti-monopoly stand was its fight against the international light bulb cartel based in Geneva. The Phoebus cartel controlled light bulb production in inter-war Europe. When KF announced that it would be building a light bulb factory, prices immediately fell from 1.35 Kronor to 1.10 Kronor. KF eventually built a factory (called Luma) in 1931, producing 8,000 bulbs per day (Hilson 2018). Luma successfully performed countervailing powers by breaking the monopoly of light bulbs and reducing the cost of light bulbs by 37 per cent (Kyleb 1986). Luma's other milestone is that it became an international cooperative venture. First, in cooperation with the other Norden cooperative associations, it established the Kooperativa Lumaforbundet in Copenhagen in May 1931. Second, in 1934, Luma helped the Norwegian Norges Kooperative Landsforening to build its own lamp factory. Third, in 1939, it opened a Luma factory in partnership with the Scottish Cooperative Wholesale Society. This was the first international factory established by the cooperative movement. The Nordic movement achieved something that the ICA was not able to do so (Hilson 2018).

The ability of the Scandinavian cooperative associations to promote international collaboration in the light bulb industry should not have been a surprise since years earlier, the Nordic consumer associations had also established an international consumer wholesale society. In response to the disrupted international trade experienced during the First World War, the consumer societies of Sweden, Norway, and Denmark initially arranged to purchase supplies via the Danish consumer wholesaler, Fællesforeningen for Danmarks Brugsforeninger (FDB), in 1918. Two years later, in 1920, they formed a new international wholesale organisation, Nordisk Andelsforbund (NAF), registered in Copenhagen. One year later, NAF opened an office in London. By 1927, the two Finnish consumer societies also joined. The operating formulae were simple: NAF raised capital from each cooperative association based on their annual turnover; NAF negotiated prices with suppliers on behalf of members for a variety of products, especially coffee, but members were not under any obligations to purchase the products; and NAF would pay a dividend based on the amount purchased. It became a significant importer of Brazilian coffee and dried fruits from California (Hilson 2018).

3.4 Cooperative Banks in North America

North America encountered the same economic and social changes that took place in Europe. The processes of industrialisation, international trade, urbanisation, the power of corporations, and market failures led to lower agricultural prices in times of crisis; a lack of access to credit by farmers, artisans, small businesses, and working people; poverty and inequalities; emigration from Quebec to the United States; and high unemployment, especially during the Great Depression of 1929. In response to this situation, leaders, community and religious organisations, farmers' associations, and enlightened bureaucrats promoted financial, agricultural, and electricity cooperatives to satisfy the needs of farmers, small businesses, and consumers. The following two sections will explore financial cooperatives in Quebec and the United States. Part 5 will explore the agricultutal cooperatives and the electric cooperatives promoted in the United States during the New Deal.

3.4.1 Desjardins Community Cooperatives

The first cooperative bank in North America was established in 1900 in the town of Levis, Quebec. The leader of this movement was Alphonse Desjardins, a French-speaking stenographer working at the House of Commons, who was concerned with the impact that Capitalism, industrialisation, and urbanisation were having on the French-Canadian community. He was concerned with the financial insecurity of the working classes, the growing social inequality, the economic difficulties encountered by farmers, and the high level of emigration to the United States (MacPherson 2007). Indeed, by 1900, nearly 500,000 people emigrated from Quebec to the United States, posing a demographic problem for a province of 1.65 million people (Richard 2015).

Desjardins embarked on a fact-finding journey and found that the causes of Quebec's problems were an economy dominated by British and North American capital and big corporations. English-speaking people were 20 per cent of the population but held a lot of economic power (Levasseur and Rousseau 2001). The large banks did not lend money to workers or farmers, who were then exploited by usurers. To find answers, he turned to the Catholic Social Doctrine. His Christian beliefs led him to help working people and farming communities. He was aware of the Rochdale cooperative movement but became more drawn to the community-based cooperative systems established in Germany, Italy, and France. He became aware of the urban and rural banks in Germany, read the works of Wolff, was influenced by the principles of social economy defined by Frederick le Play, and appreciated the Luzzatti-inspired Italian banking model (Poulin 2000, MacPherson 2007).

By the 1900s, Desjardins developed clear ideas about how to solve issues faced in Quebec. He wanted to improve the economic well-being of French-Canadian working people and farmers living in Quebec by promoting local economic development. His guiding principles included Quebec economic independence, Christian values of 'love thy neighbour', and 'self-help'. Ultimately, Desjardins thought that the local cooperative community bank was the economic institution most likely to achieve his goals.

Desjardins established the cooperative banks by enlisting the help and support of the Catholic Church. Each Catholic parish promoted a community bank. They encouraged parishioners to become members and to provide voluntary services. Each bank served the parish's catchment area. The role of the Church cannot be overestimated since parish priests comprised over 66 per cent of the presidents of the 30 banks that operated in 1909 (Fairbairn 2000, Levasseur and Rousseau 2001). The government rewarded Desjardins for his efforts and in 1906 passed the *Quebec Cooperative Association Act* that reflected Desjardins' views as well as the major features of the European cooperative banks. Key features of the Desjardins community banks include the following:

- The cooperative bank was defined as a savings and credit bank, but it was represented as a community institution that was open to all members of the community, and that had the dual identity of a cooperative and a social project.
- Membership would be available to members of all classes. They would need to buy a share to the value of 5 CAD which could be withdrawn at any time.
- The cooperative bank was democratically managed, with each person holding one vote regardless of capital invested.
- Credit would be available to persons from all classes—from those of humble origins to the bourgeoisie—and their character would be considered when applying for a loan.
- The cooperative bank was collectively owned, and its reserves and assets were indivisible. In addition, the value of shares remained constant.
- The cooperative bank would be based on the principle of limited liability and could not be sold to another cooperative (Poulin 2000, MacPherson 2007).

The Desjardins banks had a reputation for good governance. The governance arrangements consisted of three governing bodies, all democratically elected. The Board of Directors oversaw the organisation's day-to-day affairs. The Credit Committee reviewed loan applications. The Supervisory Committee had oversight over the banks' recordkeeping. Volunteer leadership was encouraged, and, except for managers, all office holders did not get paid (Richard 2015). The Desjardins banks further improved their governance arrangements by establishing regional and provincial federations from 1920 to 1932 and a rigorous auditing system. The federations conducted State-funded audit inspections (Levasseur and Rousseau 2001). The community banks had a good reputation. In the first seven years, they made 2,900 loans without a single loss. The movement grew to 175 cooperative banks by 1920, the year Desjardins passed away. By 1940, cooperative banks numbered 562 and held assets worth 25 million CAD (Birchall 2011).

3.4.2 Credit Unions

Desjardins was instrumental in promoting community banking in the United States. In 1908, Reverend Pierre Hevey, and the Massachusetts State Commissioner for Banking, Pierre Jay, invited Desjardins to promote community banking in New Hampshire and Massachusetts. Jay was concerned with money lenders, and led an investigation to find out how money lenders were victimising factory workers in Boston. Invitees included 150 businessmen, who were urged to create credit unions for their employees (Nadeau 2012). Desjardins also spoke to the Parliamentary Committee on Banks and Banking, where he mentioned that cooperative banks in Quebec had not lost any money (Richard 2015).

French-Canadian immigrants living in New Hampshire formed the first credit union in 1909. Credit unions became more popular after the state of Massachusetts passed the law on credit unions in 1909. The law required credit unions: to manage savings and deposits from members; uphold the principle of one-person-one-vote; to operate within a prescribed geographic boundary, such as a parish or a workplace; to form a board of directors, a credit committee, and a supervisory committee; to have a credit committee to approve loans; to encourage savings, and to provide loans to working people at moderate rates (MacPherson 2007, Richard 2015).

Credit Unions became popular throughout the United States, thanks to the work of a Boston philanthropist Edward Filene, and a lawyer named Roy Bergengren. Filene, who had supported the Massachusetts law on credit unions of 1909, and had met Desjardins, funded the Credit Union National Extension Bureau (Bureau hereafter) in 1921, and hired Bergengren to manage it. They developed a four-point strategy to promote credit unions. It included promoting adequate legislation across the country; promoting credit unions across the country; establishing State leagues of credit unions to promote local credit union development; and finally, organising credit union national associations to provide direction and leadership (Nadeau 2012).

The Bureau's plan was successful. Workplace credit unions became popular because of low administrative costs, easy deductions from salaries, and low-risk loans. They were also supported by professionals, teachers, enlightened employers, the Federal Government, the trade unions, the churches, and established consumer and agricultural cooperatives. The number of credit unions increased steadily from 190 in 1921, to 1,300 in 1930. In 1934, 33 State credit union leagues formed the Credit Union National Association (Nadeau 2012). The North American movement via State leagues offered education and training courses for elected officials and treasurers and encouraged the formation of local chapters facilitating access to training courses (MacPherson 2007).

The *Federal Credit Union Act* of 1934 (*Credit Union Act*) provided further impetus to the development of credit unions. The *Credit Union Act* is important to analyse because of the reasons for its implementation and also because it supported credit union principles and objectives. Emmons and Schmid inform us that the reasons why the *Credit Union Act* was implemented were because credit unions had not failed during the Great Depression,[2] they served the general public, which had been ignored by conventional banks, and they represented a common bond uniting members. The latter was a key factor for their success since members knew each other, and they would be reluctant to default. Credit unions were not taxed due to the fact that they could not access equity, so tax concessions allowed them to build up capital (Emmons and Schmid 1999). Tax concessions would be challenged on numerous occasions, but the Credit Union National Association always managed to defend this policy (Jerving 2006).

The key features of the *Credit Union Act* of 1934 were influenced by the *Massachusetts Act* of 1909. The *Credit Union Act* supported democratic governance, supported the principle of having a common bond, supported the principle of mutuality and self-help, and promoted credit union growth. First, credit unions were organised for the purpose of promoting thrift among its members and for creating a source of credit for provident or productive purposes. Second, membership was limited to groups having a common bond of occupation or association or to groups within a well-defined neighbourhood, community, or rural district. Members were required to purchase a share worth 5 USD. Third, lending practices allowed credit unions to borrow 50 per cent of their capital and surplus; to issue loans to members with loan maturities not exceeding two years, and charge interest not exceeding 1 per cent per month. Fourth, democratic governance arrangements included members having one vote, and each credit union having a board of directors, a credit committee, and a supervisory committee. Office holders were not compensated for their work. Fifth, surplus distribution required the board to deposit 20 per cent of surpluses in the reserve fund, and to be able to pay dividends. Sixth, credit unions, being mutual, did not pay taxes. Seventh, the Federal Government provided supervision and examination (Croteau 1956, Richard 2015).

In 1937 and 1949, minor modifications were made, which did not change the direction of the Act. These included credit unions making loans to other credit unions within limits. It exempted credit unions from all taxation except on real and personal property. It required federal employee credit unions to be provided free office space in federal buildings (Croteau 1956). By 1934, 10,000 credit unions with 3.3 million members were established (Patmore and Belnave 2018).

We can identify a number of key differences between the US and Desjardins models. The United States was a lay movement, whilst Desjardins was religious, nationalist, community focussed. The United States promoted mostly workplace credit unions and not parish or community-based cooperative banks. The United States focussed on consumer credit to help employees and workers buy consumer goods such as radios and household products at moderate interest rates. Desjardins provided credit for productive purposes to farmers and local businesses (Fairbairn 2004). The two models have in common the principles of self-help, and democratic governance. Desjardins, however, promoted community-based banks to support farmers and small businesses to compete against corporations; credit unions performed a complementary role to the CME. There are also differences and similarities with the other two cooperative bank models developed in Germany. Table 3.1 compares the four cooperative banking models, comparing their vision, objectives, membership, governance, profit distribution, asset management, and remuneration policies.

3.5 The New Deal and Cooperatives

3.5.1 Agricultural Cooperatives

Agricultural cooperatives in the United States provide a good case study that explores the close relationship that evolved between farmers via cooperatives and political activity and the federal and state governments. Governments supported cooperatives via legislation, regulations, provision of credit, provision of technical and managerial skills, access to education, and promotional activities. Government support grew gradually since the 1880s, especially during the New Deal, a period when the State promoted a new relationship between the State, the market, and society. The State became the manager of the economy. The State intervened in the economy when the CME was unable to resolve the problems that it caused or was unable to meet the basic needs and aspirations of working people. The State also intervened to limit the market power of corporations where it was deemed to be excessive.[3]

Farmers operated in precarious positions. They were too reliant on others for agricultural inputs when purchasing their crops or livestock and when transporting their produce to market. In the dairy industry, the introduction of new technologies and the costs involved in processing milk were beyond the capabilities of small farmers (Nadeau 2012). Small farmers were especially at a disadvantage when negotiating prices and when entering into contractual arrangements with profit-maximising business intermediaries and monopolists. This was especially the case with railway owners and grain elevators, who charged excessive prices and operated with unethical business practices (Torgerson, Reynolds and Fray 1998). Farmers also had to be resilient to market fluctuations as a result of over-production in world markets or as a result of lower prices following the First World War (Fairbairn 2004).

Farmers responded by forming farmers' associations to represent their interests. They recruited members, promoted cooperatives, influenced public opinion, and influenced the State. Considering farmers and ranchers accounted for about 40 per cent of the US workforce in the late 1880s and early 1900s, farmers were in a strong position to influence political decisions (Nadeau 2012). One of the earliest organisations to represent

Table 3.1 Cooperative Banking Models

	Schulze- Delitzsch	*Raiffeisen*	*Desjardins*	*Credit Unions*
Vision	Immediate economic utility Provide credit to urban small businesses and artisans	Harmonious rural community based on Christian values via the provision of credit to farmers	Promote the well-being of Quebec's local economy and community based on Christian values	Provide credit to employees and working people to buy consumer goods
Membership	One town but with a large catchment area. Otherwise unlimited growth	Parish-based rural community—an average of 400 people	Parish community catchment area—open to all classes	Common bond of occupation or association or defined rural, community or district area
Entry conditions	Share(s) paid in instalments	Nominal share	Nominal share	Nominal share
Voting rights	One-person-one-vote	One-person-one-vote	One-person-one-vote	One-person-one-vote
Governance Structure	General Assembly, Supervisory Board, Management Board	General Assembly, Supervisory Board, Management Board	General Assembly, board, supervisory and credit committees	General Assembly, Unitary Board, supervisory and credit committees
Cooperative structures	Federation—second-tier cooperatives	Federation—second-tier cooperatives	Federation—second-tier cooperatives	Federation—second-tier cooperatives
Type of lending	Short, three months as the norm (to meet the needs of traders and artisans)	Long-term, up to ten years (to meet the needs of farmers)	Loans to all classes for providential purposes only	Short-term consumer loans to members—less than two years
Guarantee	Pledges, land mortgages, collateral, reputation	Reputation, solidarity, mutual knowledge	Reputation, mutual knowledge, character	Reputational—common bond
Profits	Dividend payment allowed—sometimes a high percentage	Non-distribution of profits. All profits to indivisible reserves	Non-distribution of profits. All profits to indivisible reserves	Dividend payment allowed—20 per cent of the surplus to reserves
Assets	Divisible	Indivisible assets	Indivisible assets	Indivisible assets
Remuneration	Remuneration to committee members and managers	Only the cashier received remuneration	Remuneration only for the Manager	No remunerations for committee and board members

Sources: Croteau (1956); Poulin (2000); Levasseur and Rousseau (2001); Birchall (2011); Richard (2015).

farmers was the Grange Society. The Grange was established by public servants in 1869, and by 1875, it counted on 25,000 branches, with 858,000 members, and a presence in 32 States. The Grange organised cooperatives such as grain elevator, flour milling, central wholesale, and also fire insurance (Fairbairn 2004).

The Farmers' Alliance was another major farmers' association formed in Texas in 1877. This organisation was more ambitious than the Grange and wanted to form marketing cooperatives that would operate nationally and internationally. It organised cooperatives across Kansas, Missouri, Nebraska, and Dakotas. In 1887, it established the Texas Cotton Exchange, a cooperative marketing association. In Dakota, farmers responded to monopoly powers of railroads and grain elevators by establishing a state-wide farmers' exchange and 30 cooperative warehouses. At the 1890 Kansas State election, Farmers' Alliance-affiliated candidates won 96 of the 125 seats in the legislature (Fairbairn 2004). In 1921, a number of farmers' organisations met with Republican and Democratic Party representatives to voice their concerns about the severity of the agricultural economy. They wanted Congress to address issues like farm credit, transportation, and legislation. These elected representatives pledged their support to farmers and exerted political influence in Washington on their behalf (Nadeau 2012).

The State began to respond to farmers' needs after the 1880s. It has already been noted that it was public servants who established the Grange in 1877. The *War Revenue Act* of 1888 and the *Income Tax Act* of 1913 exempted agricultural cooperatives from taxation (Zeuli and Cropp 2004). The Federal Government's *Country Life Commission* produced a report in 1909 which identified a number of issues faced by farmers. Key findings included a lack of knowledge of the exact agricultural conditions, a lack of training in country schools, disadvantages faced against established business systems and interests preventing farmers from receiving adequate returns for their produce, a lack of highways, widespread depletion of soils, a lack of adequate agricultural credit, and a need of new and active leadership (Country Life Commission 1909). The Commission also initiated fact-funding surveys at home and sent a study group to Europe in 1912 and 1913 to study cooperative land-mortgage banks, rural credit unions, and other institutions that promoted agriculture and rural development (Farm Credit Administration 2021).

The Federal and State governments, through their own commissioned reports, active public servants, and farmers' associations and their parliamentary representatives, were aware of the needs of farmers and acted accordingly. The government's activity can be divided into three areas: legal legitimacy; promotional activity, including educational, management, and technical assistance; and credit assistance through government-funded agencies.

The two key legal documents that defined cooperatives, especially agricultural cooperatives, are the *Wisconsin Cooperative Law* of 1911 and the *Capper-Volstead Act* of 1922. The *Wisconsin Law* defined cooperatives as distinct businesses that practised democratic governance and placed limits on the remuneration of capital. The law noted that a cooperative could start with a minimum of five people and is a democratic institution based on one-person-one-vote. The members elected and removed the board directors. The composition of the cooperative board included at least five directors. Board directors elect officers of the board from existing board members. The law required cooperatives to allocate 5 per cent of surpluses to the education fund; to limit payments to capital stock to a maximum rate of 8 per cent; to place an amount to the reserve fund; and to fund the patronage refund from the surplus made from members' transactions only. The surpluses with non-member transactions, however, could be used to remunerate stock. The Articles of Association amendments and mergers had to be approved by a two-thirds majority.

The cooperative second-tier associations could have weighted voting based on the total amount of business transactions (Zeuli and Cropp 2004).

The *Capper-Volstead Act* of 1922 complemented the *Wisconsin Act*. It granted farmers the right to unite and market their products without being in violation of the anti-trust laws.[4] This allowed cooperatives to form marketing cooperatives and federations. It granted limited exemption from anti-trust laws to agricultural producers who act together in association to market or process their goods. The Act granted limited exemption provided cooperatives: (i) operate to benefit members; (ii) members must have one vote; may not pay dividend stock or membership capital more than 8 per cent per annum; and (iii) member business must always exceed 50 per cent of total business (Volkin 1985).

The governance structure of agricultural cooperatives is that of a Unitary Board Model. Cooperative members choose the board members. The board members choose the Chair, and appoint committee members from existing board members. The board appoints a Chief Executive Officer (CEO) and holds the CEO and management to account. The CEO implements the board's strategic directions, appoints and manages staff, and reports regularly to the board. In accordance with the law, the cooperative model developed either as a central structure or as a second-tier structure. In a central structure, farmers are members of one cooperative that is either located in one location or via branches located in multiple locations. Alternatively, as had been the case in Europe, a number of cooperatives form a second-tier structure to achieve economies of scale or to provide services that cooperatives cannot access individually. These second-tier structures provide purchasing, marketing, or processing services to other cooperatives (Zeuli and Cropp 2004).

The second area includes the government's broad suite of promotional activity towards the agricultural sector and cooperatives. It began with the *Morrill Land-Grant College Act* of 1862, which set about educating rural North Americans about advances in agricultural technology and practices. The *Smith-Lever Act* of 1914 formalised the cooperative extension programmes. The *Cooperative Marketing Act* of 1926, for the first time, pledged the United States Department of Agriculture (USDA) to support and encourage the formation of agricultural cooperatives. The USDA conducted research, disseminated information, and provided technical assistance to cooperatives. The *Agricultural Marketing Act* of 1929 established the Federal Farm Board, which was assigned the task of expanding the agricultural cooperative sector. It also provided a 500 million USD fund to assist cooperatives and to stabilise farm prices (Zeuli and Cropp 2004).

The Federal Government's third key contribution was the provision of credit. In response to the Wilson Commission's recommendations, the Federal Government enacted the *Farm Loan Act* of 1916. It created a system of agricultural banks to provide long-term (land-mortgage credit) and Federal Land Banks. The latter were present in 12 districts and could count on hundreds of National Farm Loan Associations, which served as agents. In response to the Great Depression of 1929, and the numerous farm foreclosures, the government intervened through the *Emergency Farm Mortgage* Act of 1933 and The *Farm Credit Act* of 1933. The *Emergency Farm Mortgage Act* extended loan repayment schedules and offered emergency financing. The *Farm Credit Act* extended the provisions of the *Farm Loan Act* of 1916 by making available short-term and other loans. The *Farm Credit Act* system established various layers of financial institutions. These included

- Twelve Federal Land Banks that provided long-term agricultural real estate loans.
- Twelve Federal Intermediate Credit Banks that made available short and intermediate-term credit to local production credit associations, and other lending institutions serving agricultural producers.

- Twelve Banks for Cooperatives to provide credit for farmers' cooperatives, and a central bank for cooperatives to participate in loans that exceeded their lending capacities.
- The Farm Credit Administration, an independent supervisory body for all agricultural credit organisations (Farm Credit Administration 2021).

In 1935, the government also established the Farm Security Administration to combat rural poverty. It encouraged forms of mutual aid among farmers. The Farm Security Administration provided start-up loans to approximately 25,000 cooperatives covering about 4 million farmers. This scheme backed cooperatives for the supply of purchasing raw materials, product marketing, farm machinery, breeding stock, veterinary services, insurance, water, and medical care. The Farm Security Administration supported 'land leasing' cooperatives, where farmers collectively leased large plantations and managed them under the supervision of agricultural experts. The Farm Bureau opposed this type of cooperative, eventually leading the Farm Security Administration to discontinue this practice and revert to providing loans for farmers to buy land and for cooperatives (Curl 2009).

3.5.2 Electricity Cooperatives

The US Federal Government's New Deal policies included the passage of the *Rural Electrification Administration Act* of 1936 (REA). The purpose of the REA was to provide electricity to rural areas. Electrification in rural areas varied from 27.5 per cent of rural areas having access to electricity in the state of Oregon, to less than 2 per cent in the states of Arkansas, Louisiana, and Mississippi (Schneiberg 2011). The unit cost of electricity in rural areas was four times higher than the cost charged in urban areas (Curl 2009).

The government initially wanted to provide electricity in rural areas by subsidising the incumbent investor-owned companies. These investor-owned companies, however, were not interested in providing electricity to rural communities. They claimed that the costs would run over 2,000 USD per mile, which was well above the feasibility target of 1,000 USD per mile. Further, they claimed that they could only receive a return on investment of 1–4 per cent, compared to the 8–12 per cent return they received from their investment in urban areas (Taylor 2021).

The government was aware that an alternative to incumbent companies already existed. Indeed, since the late 1800s, municipal governments, mutual societies, and cooperatives had already formed electric utilities that served economically under-developed areas. The *Commission for Country Life Report* of 1908 had already noted the existence of electricity cooperatives. In addition, the Tennessee Valley Authority, established in 1933, was already promoting electricity cooperatives. By 1935, there were 49 electricity cooperatives operating in the rural areas of the United States. In accordance with the purpose of the REA, the REA administration invited rural communities to form cooperatives and to own and manage electric utilities. The REA provided long-term affordable loans for building transmission and distribution networks, as well as business planning skills and personnel with technical expertise to work with cooperatives to help drive down costs. This partnership was very successful. The REA engineers successfully developed new poles and new assembly line systems, which eventually drove down the overhead costs to 548 USD per mile. This cost was lower than the 2,000 USD per mile estimates provided by investor-owned companies (Schneiberg 2011, Taylor 2021).

The REA programme was very successful. REA provided finance, planning, and technical expertise, whilst cooperatives managed to organise popular support and demand as well as manage the electric utilities. By 1941, 800 electric cooperatives were formed, and 350 miles of line were built out. These cooperatives helped to achieve 100 per cent electrification by the late 1940s. Importantly, cooperatives paid back all the loans at a profit to US taxpayers (Taylor 2021).

REA-funded Cooperative involvement produced many positive outcomes for rural communities. Cooperatives helped to create a national electricity network providing electricity access to millions of people. They helped rural US communities modernise their farms and, in the process, promoted economic development in rural areas. They pressured investor-owned private utilities to reduce rates or sell their utilities to cooperatives. They reduced the need for local government to intervene by managing to produce a public good without State-ownership (Curl 2009, Schneiberg 2011, Nadeau 2012). These cooperatives promoted democratic practices and a business culture that focussed on managing a business with the purpose of serving the community and not maximising returns for shareholders.

3.5.3 The State: Responding to Need and Promoting Countervailing Powers

The State has been very responsive and supportive of agricultural cooperatives. We have noted a favourable cooperative law; various forms of promotional and management support; and the provision of credit via a very well-planned and comprehensive framework of banks and offices spread throughout the country. The question is, why did the State behave like this?

The first reason is that the State acknowledged that there was a public need to solve a number of problems faced by farmers. These needs included access to credit, access to knowledge, or monopoly powers. These needs were well known and articulated by farmers' associations and promoted via their friendly politicians. Subsequently, the State became more informed; it developed appropriate laws, appropriate programmes, and effective plans implemented by fit-for-purpose administrative structures.

The second reason is a classic case of government intervention to correct a market failure.[5] This was the case with the Federal Government making available loans to rural cooperatives via the REA to promote electric cooperatives. This action was taken only after the private sector declared that it was not interested in providing a public good, such as electricity access to rural communities, because it preferred to focus on the more profitable urban markets (Taylor 2021).

The third reason is that the severity of the Great Depression required a different approach from government. The situation was so severe that President Roosevelt suggested a broader role for government in the economy in order "to prevent the return to conditions which came very close to destroying what we call modern civilization" (Roosevelt 2014). The prevailing economic orthodoxy at the time—limited government intervention, balanced budgets, and faith in the market mechanism—was not working. Roosevelt's policies led the State to effectively manage the economy. This new role assigned to government was quite different to the previous limited role that governments performed. Roosevelt saw this new approach as a partnership between the State, farming, industry, and transportation, in the implementation of plans to solve the crisis. Within this context, the government got involved in promoting public works; providing funding for farmers; enhancing the power of unions; protecting retailers and consumers; helping home-owners and businesses to repay loans (Roosevelt 2014).

Finally, the political culture of the United States has always supported curbing the powers of trusts and large corporations. This political culture, which has become known as the 'concept of countervailing powers', has placed restraints of the power of private interests. Galbraith notes that in the economic sphere, Theodore Roosevelt's government first intervened through the *Sherman Antitrust Act* of 1890 which prescribe the rules of free competition and made it illegal any form of restraint of trade or price fixing. It also passed regulations barring impure food and drugs. It banned corporate political donations in order to curb corruption and their influence on politics. The New Deal continued this tradition in promoting countervailing powers. It promoted legislations reforms giving labour the right to bargain collectively, giving small investors protection from financial fraud, and giving small businesses protection from large retail chains (Galbraith 2001, Reich 2016). The broad promotion and support of agricultural cooperatives is also part of a countervailing culture because small farmers, through cooperatives, were able to break free from the grain elevator monopolies and intermediaries who wielded excessive powers to the detriment of farmers' economic well-being. This approach was aligned with the influential cooperative thinking of Professor E.G. Nourse, who argued that cooperatives could be organised to represent a limited share of marketing activity which would provide a checkpoint on other businesses that would eventually be forced to become more competitive (Torgerson, Reynolds and Fray 1998).

3.6 The International Cooperative Movement

The International cooperative movement continued to grow during the inter-war period. Shaffer informs us that cooperatives were operating in 119 countries by 1945, compared to 72 countries in 1915. Similarly, 86 countries enacted cooperative laws by 1945, compared to 52 countries in 1918. Some of the new countries that embraced cooperatives included Argentina, Brazil, Ecuador, Egypt, Ghana, Malaysia, Mexico, Morocco, Nigeria, the Philippines, and Tanzania. The cooperative movement continued to promote schools and colleges that taught cooperative studies. Educational facilities were established all over the world, including Australia, France, Germany, Iceland, Iran, Japan, Peru, Sweden, the United States, and Western Nigeria (Shaffer 1999).

The ICA organisation held four congresses during the inter-war years. It established three committees covering international cooperative banking, international cooperative insurance, and another focussing on encouraging women in the cooperative movement (Patmore and Belnave 2018). It established good relations with the International Labour Organization (ILO). The ILO operated a cooperative unit headed by George Fauquet, a French cooperative theorist, who supported Buchez's idea of worker cooperatives and their inter-generational approach. He also valued the cooperative's focus on pursuing general interests, on avoiding cyclical crises, and on contributing towards social justice and peace (Bayo 2019). The ICA, with limited success, continued to promote international trade by establishing the International Cooperative Wholesale Society, and the International Cooperative Trading Agency in 1937 (Shaffer 1999).

The key issue faced by the ICA during this period was to define its identity and its values in a world that was much different than the one in which the early Socialists established their communities and cooperatives, and the Rochdale Pioneers established their consumer society. MacPherson notes that by the 1920s, the early generation of co-operators was being replaced by a new generation and that the cooperative model of growth via forming federations (second-tier structures) was coming under pressure (MacPherson 2008). The major issue, however, was how to respond to Socialists who wanted cooperatives to be the third pillar of the labour movement or to the Russians who wanted cooperatives to be supportive of class struggles and revolutions? In addition, how should the ICA respond to what was happening in the totalitarian regimes of Italy and Germany, knowing that some parts of the cooperative movement were being targeted (consumer cooperatives and worker cooperatives) whilst others were supported (agricultural and credit cooperatives)?

The ICA did not accept membership of Nazi Germany or Fascist Italy's cooperative federations and made it clear that it stood for peace, free trade, and anti-Fascism. In relation to the Soviet Union, the ICA sent a delegation to Russia to understand how cooperatives were operating, and it concluded that they were operating within cooperative principles. The ICA would have also considered the fact that the Russian Federation was a major financial contributor to the ICA, second only to Britain, and that it boasted a membership of 33 million people. This equalled 70 per cent of the ICA's total membership. Most importantly, there was a general feeling that perhaps a new society was emerging that could lead to the promotion of a consumer commonwealth (Hilson 2018).

To the question of whether the cooperative movement was to be the third pillar of Socialism or support class struggle, the ICA responded by maintaining its political neutrality and by allowing each cooperative movement to decide for themselves. The ICA also developed a set of cooperative principles that would define cooperatives and would differentiate them from private and State-owned enterprises (Hilson 2018).

The political neutrality argument was informed by Vaino Tanner's paper presented at the 1937 ICA Congress held in Paris. Tanner was the ICA President. He described how cooperatives were operating in various countries under different political systems. He argued that cooperatives could coexist in any system, and were not incompatible with economic planning, provided cooperatives were autonomous, could set their own prices, were allowed to grow, and were not discriminated against. He also argued that cooperatives do not dominate any system but they supplement other existing economic systems and mitigate their defects. The ICA Congress approved a resolution that reflected Tanner's argument that cooperatives needed to operate free from political interference, have freedom of activity, and reject any type of interference. The resolution also rejected policies that would concentrate everything in the hands of the State (Tanner 1937).

In 1935, George Fauquet, head of the ILO Cooperative Unit, wrote the essay *The Cooperative Sector* in which he stated that the cooperative sector was the third sector of the economy, alongside the private sector and the State sector. He argued that since each of these three sectors could not control the whole economy, they should coexist. Fauquet was aware that mixed economies led by a more interventionist State would eventually replace the CME governed by a Liberal State. Within a mixed economy, cooperatives could perform an important role as the third sector of a country's economy. He noted that cooperatives have a dual structure: that of a democratic association of people and that of a business providing a service to their members. He identified in cooperatives' federalist structures the ability of cooperatives to organise small basic units (artisans, farmers, consumers, small businesses, workers, small shopkeepers, fishermen) whilst maintaining their individual autonomy. Fauquet's contribution is quite important because it identified limits within the cooperative ideas of building a cooperative commonwealth, as well as identifying opportunities within the emerging mixed market economy (Fauquet 1941).

The cooperative movement could have explored Fauquet's ideas, but it was not united, it was not cohesive, and the best it could achieve was the development of cooperative principles.

The ICA agreed to review cooperative principles in 1930. In 1932, it established a special committee to review the Rochdale principles. The Committee presented the seven principles at the ICA London Congress of 1934, which were later approved in Paris in 1937. The first four principles were obligatory: (i) open membership, (ii) democratic control, (iii) dividends to be paid on purchases, and (iv) limited interest to be paid on capital invested. The other three principles of (v) political neutrality, (vi) cash trading, and (vii) education were not obligatory. The principles promoted cooperatives as a uniquely democratic enterprise that placed a limited return on capital. These aligned with some of the key principles espoused by the Rochdale Pioneers. They seemed to reflect how cooperatives operated but did not yet promote inter-cooperative trade or community development. Inter-cooperative trade was actively promoted by the ICA (without success), whilst community development was the goal of early Socialists and the Rochdale Consumer Society. There was no mention of building a cooperative commonwealth. Within the ICA, there were too many differences between consumer and other cooperatives; Socialists and Conservatives; free traders and protectionists from developing countries; political activists and politically neutral Nordic cooperative sectors. Within this context, it was impossible for the ICA to approve more ambitious principles whilst wanting to maintain unity (Hilson 2017, Patmore and Belnave 2018).

3.7 Summary

- The State and businesses expanded their sphere of influence from 1915 to 1945. The development of the Welfare State in Sweden, and the rise of the Welfare-developmental State in the United States during the New Deal, increased State involvement in the economy and society. Businesses became more central to national economies because they increased their size, internationalised their operations, developed sophisticated management techniques, operated within a diverse set of legal structures, and found new ways to access credit. Business became a very indispensable part of any State strategy to encourage economic growth, to create employment, to modernise the economy, or to lead war economies. Business became a formidable opponent to cooperatives.
- Cooperatives survived under different political and economic systems. Right-wing regimes used violence and have discriminated against consumer and worker cooperatives with Socialist sympathies. In Russia, the concept of State ownership and management of the economy brought the cooperative sector under State control. The Welfare State began to occupy spaces that cooperatives could have managed, such as housing, welfare, and health insurance. All of these developments halted the growth of the cooperative sector, especially the growth of those cooperative movements that operated in Totalitarian States.
- The Swedish consumer cooperative model demonstrated its anti-monopoly credentials and suitability to overcome market failures. They performed a countervailing role against monopolies and cartels. They developed clear investment policies and, through their own manufacturing plants, produced goods at lower prices than those offered by private monopolies. This led to lower market prices for a variety of goods.
- The Credit Unions of the United States were established to provide consumers with short-term credit at competitive rates to enable members to buy consumer goods.

These credit unions differed from the urban and rural cooperative banks operating in Germany and the Desjardins banks promoted in Quebec. The latter banks provided loans to local businesses in support of productive activity and in support of local economic development.

- The agricultural sector in the United States provides an ideal approach to how public-cooperative partnerships could work. The State provided appropriate laws, credit, education facilities, an exemption from anti-trust laws, and tax concessions to revitalise the agricultural sector during a crisis. The cooperative movement was well organised, it was able to articulate its needs, it was able to influence public policy, and, most importantly, it provided a successful enterprise model (through cooperatives and second-tier cooperative structures) that proved capable of increasing productivity and improving the living standards of farmers and rural areas.
- Electricity cooperatives in the United States demonstrated that cooperatives are a good partner in overcoming market failure. Electricity cooperatives were established in response to private investors declining the offer to provide electricity to rural areas because not deemed profitable for their shareholders. Farmers and citizens, with the State providing financial and technical support, successfully used the cooperative model to provide electricity to rural areas demonstrating the cooperative organisational model's appropriateness and effectiveness in overcoming market failures.
- The cooperative sector broadened its areas of operation with the establishment of credit unions and electric cooperatives. The cooperative enterprise model, however, remained mostly the same. It still comprised the first-tier cooperative, where members or farmers form a cooperative to provide a service; the second-tier cooperative, where cooperatives get together to form a wholesaler, a marketing cooperative, a purchasing cooperative, or a processing cooperative; and the third-tier structure, namely a state or federal unitary association to represent their interests versus the State. The Scandinavian cooperative movement established an international consumer wholesale society and a number of joint ventures that led to light bulb factories being established in Denmark, Norway and Scotland. This was an important event but did not constitute a worldwide approach to cooperative development.
- Fauquet defined the cooperative sector as the third sector of the economy alongside the State sector and the private sector. He argued that since neither of the three sectors could control the whole of the economy, they should coexist. He argued that cooperatives in cooperatives' federalist structures could help small units of artisans, small businesses, farmers, and cooperatives to achieve economies of scale whilst retaining their autonomy. He identified limits within the cooperative ideas of building a cooperative commonwealth, as well as identifying opportunities within the emerging CMEs.
- Cooperatives were operating in various countries under different political systems. Tanner, the ICA President argued that cooperatives could coexist in any system, and were not incompatible with economic planning, provided cooperatives were autonomous, could set their own prices, were allowed to grow, and were not discriminated against.
- The ICA successfully maintained a degree of unity and developed the ICA cooperative principles in 1937. The ICA developed into a broad movement with members from different sectors, members from diverse countries with different levels of economic development, and cooperative movements with different cooperative histories and political views. This diverse group of cooperative movements made it difficult for the ICA to develop a clear strategy delineating the role of cooperatives in the economy.

3.8 Key Questions

- Compare and contrast the Swedish and British consumer movements. In doing so, consider their similarities and differences in their approach to the market; in their relations with the private sector; in the way the wholesaler engages with individual cooperative societies; and in their approach to international trading. What are the factors that have led these two successful consumer movements to adopt different strategies? Which of the two is more effective? Which of the two strategies is more appropriate today?
- Consider the information in Table 3.1, which compares the various cooperative banking models. If you were being asked to promote a cooperative bank for your area, which of the four models would you promote and why? What are your key objectives for choosing a model? Which model best supports local community development?
- The United States was very supportive of agricultural and electricity cooperatives. How would you define the relationship between the State and cooperatives in the United States? In what way was this relationship different from the cooperative-State relationships being established in Germany, Italy, or Sweden? Would you regard the State-cooperative relationship that developed in the United States in the 1930s as an ideal type of public-cooperative partnership model?
- Why did the United States Federal State behave the way it did during the 1930s? Are there some nation-specific features of US political culture that explain their unique approach to public policy during the 1930s? In your view, what would it take for the US government to promote pro-cooperative public policies today?
- Consider the cooperative experiences discussed in this chapter and identify the key benefits that flow to cooperative members and to the local communities in which they operate. Please consider the strategies and activities of the Swedish consumer cooperative sector, the Desjardins cooperative banks, the North American credit unions, the agricultural cooperatives, and the electric cooperatives developed in the United States.
- Compare, contrast, and evaluate the cooperative enterprise models with the business models of private enterprises and corporations. What are the reasons that led the private sector to innovate their legal frameworks, organisational structures, and financial systems faster than cooperative enterprises?
- Cooperatives have survived under various political and economic systems. Consider the views of Tanner and Fauquet, and compare and contrast the position of cooperatives within each political and economic system. According to you, which political and economic system offers cooperatives the best chance to grow into a diverse and large sector of the economy?
- The ICA has promoted political neutrality and a set of cooperative principles that identify cooperatives as democratically managed businesses. In your opinion, what factors prevented the ICA from promoting a cooperative movement that also focussed on social change, as was advocated by the early Socialists, by the Rochdale Pioneers, by supporters of a Cooperative Commonwealth Republic, and by those that advocated Municipal Socialism?

Notes

1 A cooperative enterprise model refers to the way a cooperative is organised to produce and sell goods and services in the market in order to meet the needs of its members. Cooperatives meet the economic, social, cultural, and aspirational needs of their members by competing in the market on their own, or as a member of a second-tier cooperative. Whilst the term enterprise model

is synonymous with the term business model, this book will opt to use the term cooperative model interchangeably with the term cooperative enterprise model.

2 In fact, during the Great Depression, credit unions lost less than 7 per cent of their deposits compared to banks and Savings and Loans societies which lost more than 30 per cent of their deposits (Birchall 2011).

3 For more information on the New Deal, please refer to these books from Frieden and Gerstle (Frieden 2020, Gerstle 2022).

4 The government had enacted the *Sherman Anti-Trust Act* in 1890. This act was an anti-monopoly act that made it illegal to restrain trade or commerce. Until 1910, many cooperatives were indicted under state anti-trust laws in six states. The *Clayton Act* of 1914 exempted those cooperatives that practised mutual help from anti-trust laws but did not exempt those that had capital stock or conducted for a profit. Finally, the *Capper-Volstead Act* of 1922 clarified cooperatives' relation with anti-trust laws (Zeuli and Cropp 2004).

5 There are many different types of market failures, including imperfect competition, public goods, externalities, incomplete markets, information failures, unemployment-inflation, and disequilibrium. Please refer to Chapter 4 of Joseph Stiglitz's book *The Economics of the Public Sector* (Stiglitz 2000).

References

Amatori, Franco, and Andrea Colli. 2011. *Business History*. New York: Routledge.

Battilani, Patrizia. 2005. "I Mille Volti della Cooperazione Italiana: Obiettivi e Risultati di una Nuova Forma di Impresa dalle Origini alla Seconda Guerra Mondiale." In *Verso Una Nuova Teoria della Cooperazione Italiana*, by Enea Mazzoli, Stefano Zamagni and Editors, 97–140. Bologna: Il Mulino.

Bayo, Claudia Sanchez. 2019. "Work and Cooperatives." In *Cooperatives and the World of Work*, by Bruno Roelants et al., 1–21. London: Taylor Francis Group.

Bernstein, Jeffrey R. 1999. "Japanese Capitalism." In *Creating Modern Capitalism*, by Thomas K McCraw, 439–489. Boston: Harvard University Press.

Birchall, Johnston. 2011. *People-Centred Businesses*. London: Palgrave MacMillan.

Bonfante, Guido. 1981. "La Legislazione Cooperativistica." In *Il Movimento Cooperativo in Italian: Storia e Problemi*, by Giulio Sapelli, Torino: Einaudi Editore.

Bonow, Mauritz. 1938. "The Consumer Movement in Sweden." *The Annals of the American Academy of Political and Social Science* 171–184.

Castronovo, Valerio. 2013. *Storia Economica D'Italia*. Turin: Piccola Biblioteca Einaudi.

Chang, Ha-Joon. 2014. *Economics: The User's Guide*. London: Penguin Books.

Country Life Commission. 1909. *Report of the Country Life Commission*. Governmenet Report, Washington: United States Senate.

Croteau, John T. 1956. "The Federal Credit Union System: A Legislative History." *Social Security Bulletin* 10–17.

Curl, John. 2009. *For All the PeopleUncovering the Hidden History of Cooperation, Cooperative Movements, and Communalism in America*. Oakland: PM Press.

De Luca, Nicola. 2013. "Russia." In *International Handbook of Cooperative Law*, by Dante Cracogna, Antonio Fici and Hagen Henry, 667–686. Heidelberg: Springer.

Earle, John. 1986. *The Italian Cooperative Movement: A Portrait of the Lega Nazionale Delle Cooperative e Mutue*. New York: Harper Collins Publishers.

Emmons, William R, and Frank R Schmid. 1999. "Credit Unions and the Common Bond." *Federal Reserve Bank of St. Louis* 41–64.

Fairbairn, Brett. 2000. "Raiffesen and Desjardins: Co-operative Leadership, Identity and Memory." In *Canadians Cooperatives in the Year 2000*, by Brett Fairbairn, Ian MacPherson and Nora Russell, 13–27. Saskatoon: University of saskatchewan.

———. 2004. "History of Cooperatives." In *Cooperatives and Local Development Theory and Applications for the 21st Century*, by Christopher D Merrett and Norman Walzer, Chapter 2. New York: Taylor and Francis.

Farm Credit Administration. 2021. *About Us*. 12 October. Accessed February 22, 2022. https://www.fca.gov/about/history-of-fca.

Fauquet, Georges. 1941. "The Co-operative Sector." *Annals of Public and Cooperative Economy* 342–369.

Friberg, Katarina, Rachael Vorbergh-Rugh, Anthony Webster, and John Wilson. 2012. "The Politics of Commercial Dynamics: Cooperative Adaptations to Postwar Consumerism in the United Kingdom and Sweden, 1950–2010." In *The Cooperatrive Business Mopvement, 1950 to the Present*, by Harm. G Schroter and Patrizia Battilani, 243–262. Cambridge: Cambridge University Press.

Frieden, Jeffry A. 2020. *Global Capitalism*. New York: WW Norton and Company.

Galasso, Giuseppe. 1987. "Gli Anni della Grande Espansione e la Crisi del Sistema." In *Storia del Movimento Cooperativo in Italia*, by Renato Zangheri, Giuseppe Galasso and Valerio Castronovo, 219–496. Torino: Giulio Einaudi Editore.

Galbraith, John Kenneth. 2001. *The Essential Galbraith*. Boston: Houghton Mifflin Company.

Garotti, Luciana Ricci. 1990. "La Cooperazione In Emilia Romagna nel Periodo Fascista." In *Emilia-Romagna Terra di Cooperazione*, by Angelo Varni, 37–45. Bologna: Eta / Analisi.

Gerstle, Gary. 2022. *The Rise and Fall of the Neoliberal Order*. New York: Oxford University Press.

Gillespie, James Edward. 1950. "Swedish Cooperatives." *Current History* 331–336.

Hilson, Mary. 2017. "Consumer Cooperatives in the Nordic Countries, c.1860–1939." In *A Global History of Consumer Co-Operation Since the 1850s*, by Mary Hilson, Silke Neunsinger and Greg Patmore, 121–144. Leiden: Brill.

———. 2018. *The International Co-operative Alliance and the Consumer Co-operative Movement in Northern Europe, 1860–1939*. Manchester: Manchester University Press.

Hobsbawm, Eric. 1994. *Age of Extremes: The Short History of the Twentieth Century 1914–1991*. London: Penguin.

Ianes, Alberto. 2013. *Introduzione Alla Storia della Cooperazione in Italia (1854–2011)*. Soveria Mannelli: Rubbettino Editore.

Jerving, Jim. 2006. "The Long and Winding (Credit Union) Road." *The Credit Union Journal* 34–36.

Johnson, Pernilla. 2017. "From Commercial Trickery to Social Responsibility: Marketing in the Swedish Co-operative Movement in the Early Twentieth Century." In *A Global History of Consumer Co-Operation Since 1850*, by Mary Hilson, Silke Neunsinger and Greg Patmore, 642–667. Leiden: Brill.

Kyleb, Hugo. 1986. *Co-operatives Today - Selected Essays from Various Fields of Co-operatives Activities - A Tribute to Prof. V. Laakkonen (ICA, 1986, 542 p.)*. Accessed January 18, 2022. http://www.nzdl.org/cgi-bin/library?e=d-00000-00---off-0cdl--00-0----0-10-0---0---0direct-10---4-------0-0l--11-en-50---20-about---00-0-1-00-0-0-11----0-0-&a=d&c=cdl&cl=CL2.3&d=HASH01e58d563aadbe4e1f5faafb.21.

Landes, David S. 2003. *The Unbound Prometheus*. Cambridge: Cambridge University Press.

Levasseur, Roger, and Yyan Rousseau. 2001. "Social Movements and Developments in Quebec." *Annals of Public and Cooperative Economy* 549–579.

MacPherson, Ian. 2007. *One Path to Cooperative Studies*. Vancouver: British Columbia Institute for Co-operative Studies.

———. 2008. "The Co-operative Movement and the Social Economy Traditions: Reflections of the Mingling of Broad Visions." *Annals of Public and Cooperative Economics* 625–642.

McCraw, Thomas K. 1999. "American Capitalism." In *Creating Modern Capitalism*, by Thomas K McCraw, 301–348. Cambridge: Harvard University Press.

Menzani, Tito. 2009. *Il Movimento Cooperativo fra le due Guerre*. Rome: Carocci.

Nadeau, E.G. 2012. *The Cooperative Solution: How the United States Can Tame Recessions, Reduce-Inequality, and Protect the Environment*. Create Space Independent Publishing Platform.

Neusinger, Silke. 2017. "Challenges to Democracy - State Intervention: Introduction to Section Two." In *A Global History od Consumer Co-operation since 1850*, by Mary Hilson, Silke Neusinger and Greg Patmore, 229–242. Leiden: Brill.

Patmore, Greg, and Nikola Belnave. 2018. *A Global History of Co-operative Business*. London: Routledge.

Poulin, Pierre. 2000. "The Origins of the Savings and Credit Cooperatives in North America." In *Canadian Cooperatives in the Year 2000*, by Brett Fairbairn, Ian MacPherson and Nora Russell, 28–39. Saskatoon: University of Saskatchewan.

Prinz, Michael. 2017. "German Co-operatives: Rise and Fall 1850–1970." In *A Global History of Consumer Co-Operation Since 1850*, by Mary Hilson, Silke Neusinger and Greg Patmore, 243–267. Leiden: The Netherlands.

Procacci, Giuliano. 1991. *History of the Italian People*. London: Penguin Books.

Reich, Robert. 2016. *Saving Capitalism*. London: Icon Books.

Richard, Mark Paul. 2015. "'The Humble Parish Bank': The Cultural Origin of the US Credit Union Movement." *The New England Quaterly* 449–482.

Roosevelt, Franklyn Delano. 2014. "Second Fireside Chat (1933)." In *American Capitalism: A Reader*, by Louis Hyman and Edward E Baptist, Chapter 16. New York: Simon and Schuster.

Sassoon, Donald. 2020. *The Anxious Triumph: A Global History of Capitalism, 1860–1914*. London: Penguin Books.

Schneiberg. 2011. "Toward an Organisationally Diverse American Capitalism? Cooperative, Mutual and Local State-Owned Enterprise." *Seattle University Law Review, 34*, 1409–1434.

Shaffer, J. 1999. *Historical Dictionary of the Cooperative Movement*. Lanham: Scarecrow Press.

Srinivasan, Bhu. 2017. *Americana: a 400 Year History of American Capitalism*. New York: Penguin Books.

Stiglitz, Joseph. 2000. *Economics of the Public Sector*. New York: W.W. Norton and Company.

Tanner, Vaino. 1937. "The Place of Cooperatives in Different Economic Systems." *Annals of Collective Economy* 240–265.

Taylor, Keith. 2021. "An Analysis of the Entrepreneurial Institutional Ecosystems Supporting the Development of Hybrid Organizations: the Development of Cooperatives in the U.S." *Journal of Environmental Management* 112244.

Torgerson, Randall E, Bruce J Reynolds, and Thomas W Fray. 1998. "Evolution of Cooperative Thought, Theory and Purpose." *Journal of Cooperatives* 1–20.

Volkin, David. 1985. *Understanding Capper-Volstead*. Cooperative Information Report 35, Washington: US Department of Agriculture.

Westwood, J N. 1981. *Endurance and Endeavour: Russian History 1812–1980*. Oxford: Oxford University Press.

Zeuli, Kimberley A, and Robert Cropp. 2004. *Cooperatives: Principles and Practices in the 21st Century*. Wisconsin: University of Wisconsin Centre for Cooperatives.

4 Cooperatives, Mixed Economy, and Decolonisation

1945–1990

This chapter will discuss how cooperatives evolved from 1945 to 1990. Part 4.1 will examine the relationship between the State and the economy and the evolution of private enterprises. It will discuss the 1945–1975 period, characterised by the primacy of the State and the development of mixed economies and the Welfare State, and the period from 1975 to 1990, characterised by neo-Liberal policies and the primacy of the capitalist-led market economy (CME). Part 4.2 analyses how cooperatives in traditional sectors met the challenges posed by corporations. Part 4.3 discusses how consumer cooperatives in various countries managed change. Part4.4 discusses the Mondragon Cooperative Corporation. Part 4.5 discusses the Lega Nazionale delle Cooperative e Mutue's (LNCM) cooperative network of enterprises. Part 4.6 considers the process of decolonisation with reference to India and Tanzania. Part 4.7 focusses on the International Cooperative Alliance's (ICA) organisational growth, organisational structure, and the question of cooperative identity. Part 4.8 will summarise the key points made in this chapter. Part 4.9 will identify key questions for readers to consider.

The key learnings from this chapter include the following:

- Understand the evolving relation between the State, the economy, and society, the continued growth and influence of corporations, the integration of world markets, and the challenges that these changes posed for the cooperative sector.
- Appreciate how the cooperative sector responded to the challenges faced in world markets and the challenges of large corporations.
- Examine how consumer movements across the world managed to compete against supermarket chains, and be able to identify and contrast those strategic, operational, and cultural factors that have led to their success or decline.
- Appreciate the Mondragon cooperative corporate model and evaluate the advantages that this diverse network of cooperative businesses and support structures provide to their members.
- Appreciate the LCNM's cooperative network model, identify its key success factors, and consider the significance of its inter-sectoral approach to cooperative development.
- Understand and critically examine the relationship between the State and cooperatives in the newly independent countries of India and Tanzania.
- Consider how the ICA's organisational structure changed to become more inclusive to new types of cooperatives and to cooperative movements from developing countries.
- Understand the reasons why the ICA considered the question of cooperative identity very important and crucial for cooperative development.

DOI: 10.4324/9781003269533-4

4.1 State, Economy, and Society: 1945–1990

The world that emerged after World-War-Two was divided between developed Western countries, communist countries, and developing countries. The United States emerged after 1945 with the largest economy producing 60 per cent of total world output and capital stock (Hobsbawm 1994). In response to the failures of the post-1914 international order, the United States and delegates from allied countries met at Bretton Woods, New Hampshire, in 1944 to establish a new international trade and development system that would promote world trade. Fearing a depression, The United States also funded post-war reconstruction in Europe through the Marshall Aid Plan and by opening its markets to European products (Chang 2014).

The Bretton Woods system consisted of a number of institutions designed to promote world trade. These included the International Monetary Fund to provide short-term lending; the World Bank to fund specific infrastructure projects; and The General Agreements on Trade and Tariffs, later re-named World Trade Organization, to reduce tariffs and other trade barriers. In 1961, the Organisation for Economic Cooperation and Development (OECD) was established to provide a platform for countries to promote a CME. The Bretton Woods system also promoted fixed exchange rates which were only allowed to deviate 1 per cent from the fixed rate (Chang 2014, Steger 2020). These institutions removed 90 per cent of trade quotas by 1955 (Landes 2003).

4.1.1 The Mixed Economy and the Welfare State

Post-war OECD countries featured the development of capitalist mixed economies where governments were given the responsibility to manage the economy and achieve full employment. This approach was a continuation of the practical policies implemented by the United States and Sweden during the Great Depression. Governments could now manage economies by making use of these experiences and by adopting Keynesian economic management tools, which included adjusting disposable income, making credit available, and increasing public investments (Stretton 2000). This approach led states to intervene in the economy in a variety of ways, including providing subsidies and tax concessions, pro-business procurement policies, business access to public works, and funding research and development. Research and development spending in the United States, for instance, increased from 30 billion USD in 1955 to 90 billion USD in 1969 (Chang 2014). National political and economic approaches supporting a capitalist mixed economy differed across countries. For instance, France, Japan and Korea promoted indicative planning; France, Italy and Britain promoted the nationalisation of key industries; Germany and Sweden promoted co-determination with trade union representation on company boards; and Japan promoted a state-led industrial policy. Each of these capitalist models reflected their country's history, business culture, economic development, and the nature of engagement with the world economy (Armstrong, Glyn and Harrison 1984, McGraw 1995, Yergin and Janislaw 1998, Hall and Soskice 2001).

All OECD countries developed comprehensive welfare policies. As noted in earlier chapters, welfare provisions commenced in the late nineteenth century. After 1945, however, welfare policies became a key aspect of capitalist societies and could count on broad social and political support. The growth of Left parties, plus working people demanding a better life after having lived through two world wars and the Great Depression, led to broad support for the Welfare State. Whilst approaches to welfare differed, by 1970, most countries had implemented universal public health service or insurance; much-improved income support; services for the aged; regular public incomes for most of the sick, handicapped, and unemployed; family allowances and day care, maternity leave and other services for people with children; and personal social services for a variety of human needs (Birch 1974, Hicks 1999, Stretton 2000).

Businesses continued to grow and expand in new markets and in new activities. Businesses grew via mergers and acquisitions. In 1969 alone, 6,000 mergers and acquisitions took place in the United States. A year earlier, 4,000 corporations disappeared. There was greater access to investments from institutional investors, which in the United Kingdom already controlled 33 per cent of capital by 1963. Investor-owned firms dominated new industries of telecommunications, aviation, biotechnology, the internet, and personal computers. Many of these new industries were spin-offs from state-funded research. Foreign direct investment grew from 13 billion USD in 1970 to 207 billion USD by 1990, turning corporations into global firms. The US corporations' multi-divisional organisational structure became the world's preferred business model (Amatori and Colli 2011, Chang 2014).

Corporations improved their organisational culture and performance. The Japanese manufacturers achieved success by focussing on quality improvements, on quality circles, and by operating lean production systems to improve relations with suppliers and reduce inventory costs. In response to the Japanese challenge, corporations began to place more emphasis on quality management and developed broad-based quality management systems to improve overall performance and competitiveness. By the 1990s, lean production systems, quality management, international organisational standards, and tools such as Six Sigma or Baldridge's Quality Performance Standards were widely used to improve business performance (Evans and Lindsay 2008).

After 1945, the United States promoted Masters of Business Administration (MBA) and Executive Training worldwide. This internationalisation of management education promoted US Capitalism. The United States, via the Marshall Aid Plan and the European Productive Agency, arranged for Europeans to visit the US universities and for US professors to teach in Europe. The Ford Foundation funded business schools in France, Manchester, Brussels, and Finland. By 1980 there were 100,000 MBA degrees awarded annually in the United States. In 1998, there were at least 1,600 MBA programmes worldwide, including in China (Amdam 2009). In 1945, Harvard established executive focussed 13-week education courses, and by 1968 there were 50 such programmes in the United States. Faculty members of Harvard were actively involved in establishing top executive schools in France, Spain, Switzerland, Italy, and India, as well as the London Business School in 1965. In all, the US business schools and the Ford Foundation established 22 executive educational programmes across the world from 1949 to 1968 (Amdam 2019).

The capitalist mixed market economies with welfare measures and businesses operating in a more open global market were quite successful. Industrialised countries achieved gross domestic product growth averaging 4.9 per cent from 1950 to 1970[1] (Kenwood and Lougheed 1983). From 1945 to 1973 unemployment was virtually eliminated. There was general support for this new type of social democratic Capitalism which generated wealth, full employment, and redistributed wealth to those most in need via the Welfare State. European Socialists and Eurocommunist parties had chosen the parliamentary road to Socialism and acknowledged the achievements of mixed economies. Socialist parties dropped nationalisation from their political programme (Berlinguer 1982, Sassoon 1997).

Anthony Crosland, the English Labour Member of Parliament, went further, arguing that Capitalism had resolved the problem of accumulation and that the role of the State plus strong unions would be able to redistribute wealth and achieve an equitable redistribution of the fruits of one's labour. He was adamant that there was a broad consensus in support of the mixed economy and the Welfare State and that economic growth and full employment would continue. As a result, he believed that state ownership of the means of production was no longer needed (Crosland 1956).

4.1.2 Neo-Liberalism

Crosland's views turned out to be overly optimistic. The Golden Age did not last. Competition among firms from Europe, the United States, and Japan reduced profit margins. Full employment increased the bargaining power of working people, and this led to wage rises and falls in profit rates. In 1974, Industrial production fell by 10 per cent. When the Organisation of Petroleum Exporting Countries increased the price of oil by 10 per cent, and later by 25 per cent, it led to inflationary pressures. The culmination of these events was stagflation: inflation and unemployment occurring at the same time. Unemployment in industrialised countries increased to 8.4 per cent in 1983. The United States devalued its currency in 1971 by more than 9 per cent, signalling the end of fixed exchange rates. Keynesian policies did not seem to work because whilst attempting to create employment, increasing public spending or increasing the money supply would increase inflation. In response to this, Britain and the United States resorted to neo-Liberal policies to solve the economic crisis (Armstrong, Glyn and Harrison 1984).

Neo-Liberal policies set out to dismantle the post-war consensus. Neo-Liberals were concerned about the growth of the State since, in OECD countries, government spending had grown from 27 per cent of GDP in 1965 to 39 per cent of GDP by 1995. Neo-Liberal policies included privatisation, deregulation, outsourcing public services to businesses, and tax cuts. They promoted the rights of individuals over collective action. They believed that the market was better suited to deliver jobs, goods and services than the government. They fought inflation by increasing interest rates and by re-stating the policy of balanced budgets to contain public spending (Armstrong, Glyn and Harrison 1984, Chang 2014). These policies did not lead to greater economic growth than the previous period,[2] whilst tax cuts and deregulation created wider inequalities.[3]

4.1.3 Implications for Cooperatives

The predominant world view from 1945 to 1989 favoured CMEs, individualism, and the Welfare State over cooperatives. The Left parties and working people turned to the State to solve their problems in the workplace and to help them meet their expectations of having a job, a home, a good education, and a pension after retirement. Neo-Liberals turned to individualism and the market to create economic growth, employment, and opportunities. Corporations were larger, had access to credit via institutional investors, and operated with fewer trade barriers in world markets. Cooperatives faced more competition from business and were viewed as marginal players in the economy. Yet cooperatives managed to survive and grow. This period also witnessed the growth of worker cooperatives, the dynamism of some consumer movements, and the growth of retail cooperatives. New independent countries identified the cooperative sector as a key feature of their economy. Further, the State and the market had not met all of people's needs or expectations. The various political and economic systems could not create stable economies and stable societies. Within this context, cooperatives continued to provide solutions to people's needs and expectations.

4.2 Responses to Post-War Capitalism

The cooperative response to this new world order has been threefold: (i) to grow the cooperative enterprises via mergers and, where possible, via acquisitions; (ii) to find ways to access capital needed to grow the cooperative enterprises; (iii) to compete in the market with new legal structures.

4.2.1 Larger Cooperatives

Cooperatives from the traditional sectors, consumer, credit and agriculture, focussed on creating larger enterprises to achieve economies of scale and improve their competitiveness. The United Kingdom's Cooperative Wholesale Society (CWS) and the Cooperative Retail Society absorbed close to 200 societies. By 1976, this strategy created 20 large societies that provided 62 per cent of the total turnover (Wilson, Webster and Vorberg-Rugh 2013). In 1950, the Swedish consumer sector comprised 681 cooperatives and 8,000 retail outlets. In 1990, however, it comprised 120 societies and 1687 retail outlets, whilst cooperative members doubled to over 2 million (Pestoff 2012). The Swiss consumer sector reduced its cooperatives from 491 in 1965 to 28 in 1990 (Degen 2017). The Italian consumer sector reduced its cooperatives from 3,300 in 1956 to 431 by 1990. Twenty-one cooperatives controlled over 75 per cent of the total retail area (Ammirato 1996).

The agricultural cooperatives provide a similar story. The Danish dairy cooperatives numbered 1,300 in 1960, but concentrated their operations so much that by 1993 Arla controlled 90 per cent of the dairy market (Modhorst 2014). The Japanese agricultural sector reduced its cooperatives from 8,800 in 1970 to 3,200 in 1993, whilst their turnover remained unchanged (Hoyt and Menzani 2012). In the United States, agricultural cooperatives were reduced from over 10,000 in 1950 to 5,625 cooperatives by 1985. Their turnover, however, increased from 8 billion USD to 65 billion USD (Zeuli and Cropp 2004). Canadian agricultural cooperatives were reduced from 186 to 162, but their turnover increased from 3.3 billion CAD to 11 billion CAD (Hoyt and Menzani 2012).

Credit cooperatives also concentrated resources in fewer cooperatives. The Indian credit unions, which numbered 83,000 in 1970, were reduced to 41,500 in 1995 whilst servicing an almost identical membership of 43 million members. Credit unions in the United States were reduced from 23,000 in 1970 to 11,880 by 1995, whilst their membership increased from 24 million members to 71 million members. Canadian credit unions increased their average membership per cooperative from 1,542 to over 4,500 members (Hoyt and Menzani 2012). In 1972, The German and the Dutch cooperative bank movements merged their associations to form one central-national body in each country (Patmore and Belnave 2018).

4.2.2 Legal Structures

In order to access capital and markets, the cooperative sector began to adopt conventional legal structures to better serve its members. These structures allowed cooperatives to attract external capital so they could grow their business. They allowed cooperatives to buy conventional companies to achieve scale or to enter new market segments. They allowed cooperatives to form joint ventures with private companies so that cooperatives could access know-how and have a better chance of winning public works. Key examples of this strategy include Crédit Agricole and Rabobank adopting the joint stock company format whilst ownership remained with cooperative members (Zamagni 2012); the Visentini Law of 1983, allowing Italian cooperatives to form holding companies subject to profits made being retained as profit reserves (Bonfante 2011); and cooperatives forming joint ventures with private enterprises to co-invest in shared projects (Ammirato 1996, Zamagni, Battilani and Casali 2004).

4.2.3 Access to Capital

Cooperatives also began to explore new ways to access capital. The traditional cooperative way to access capital, such as members' capital, members' loans, retained surplus, and external loans (from cooperative banks, private banks, and the State), no longer met the financial needs of large cooperatives. As a result, the cooperative laws of some European countries encouraged cooperatives to find new ways to access capital. Since 1973, the German law removed any restriction on the amount of dividend paid or interest paid on members' share capital. Germany also allowed the cooperative to allocate a portion of the reserve funds to departing members (Munkner 2013). Cooperative movements began to develop their own financial companies to coordinate investments and provide cooperatives with short- and long-term loans and with equity investments. Cooperative financial institutions include the Mondragon Cooperative Bank (Whyte and Whyte 1991), the Fincooper financial consortium in Italy (Ammirato 1996), and the Socoden finance company in France (Soulage 2011).

Financial joint ventures between the State and cooperatives also began to emerge to promote the social economy and worker-buyouts. Cooperazione Finanza Impresa was established in Italy in 1987 by the State, the cooperative movement, and the labour movement. It provided short- to medium-term loans to cooperatives that promoted innovation and focussed on productivity improvements. They also provide loans to cooperatives formed from enterprises in crisis. The Institute for the Development of the Social Economy (IDES) was established in France in 1983 by the State, local authorities, and the cooperative sector. Its role is to invest in cooperative bonds (participatory shares), which pay interest but do not provide voting rights (Corcoran and Wilson 2010, Zevi, Zanotti, et al. 2011). In Quebec, the labour movement established the Solidarity Bank (Caisse D'économie Solidaire Desjardins) in 1971 and the Workers Solidarity Fund (Fonds de Solidarité des Travailleurs) in 1983 to provide loans to cooperatives and other social economy enterprises (Mendell 2015).

4.3 The Consumer Sector

This period was one of major changes for the retail sector. After the 1950s, the large supermarket chains that managed ten or more supermarkets began to dominate the market. The factors of their success consisted in operating large supermarkets that offered a diverse range of goods for their customers, a centralised, cost-effective purchasing and marketing structure, the use of standardised procedures throughout the stores, an integrated distribution function, and a readiness to meet the needs and wants of all consumers. Indeed, by 1971, the chain stores held up to 50 per cent of the retail market in the

United Kingdom and more than 20 per cent in most other European countries (Zamagni, Battilani and Casali 2004).

The Cooperative sector, until the 1950s, had been broadly characterised by small cooperatives. These cooperatives used a second-tier structure, a local wholesaler, to bulk purchase their produce at lower prices. Their federal consumer association provided common administrative services and political representation. The English CWS and the Swedish Co-operative Union & Wholesale Society (Kooperativa Förbundet, KF) had already embarked on establishing self-service shops, but generally, the above picture reflected the state of the other cooperative sectors. The consumer movements provided a mixed response to the challenges posed by the supermarket chains. The cooperative sectors of the Netherlands, Belgium, France, Austria and Germany had either collapsed or reduced to holding a limited share of the retail market. Britain and Sweden experienced decline, whilst the cooperative sectors of Denmark, Finland, Italy, Japan, and Norway, maintained or increased their market share (Birchall 2011, Patmore and Belnave 2018).

4.3.1 Consumer Cooperative Models

Eckberg analysed the major consumer cooperative enterprise models[4] to explain the different fortunes experienced by the national consumer cooperative movements. He considered the federal model, the centralised model, and a hybrid model. More specifically

- The federal structure consists of a clear division of roles and responsibilities between the cooperatives and the wholesaler. In this model, cooperatives manage the retail outlets, whilst the wholesaler purchases goods and provides services to cooperatives members. This model led cooperatives to merge into larger units and to use contractual arrangements to govern their commercial relations. This took place in Italy, Norway, France and Belgium.
- The second model is the national centralised structure, where a central organisation manages all retail outlets. In this model, all consumers are members of one national organisation. There are no independent cooperative societies. This model operates in Germany, Austria, Switzerland and Spain.
- The third model is a hybrid model where the roles of the wholesaler and the cooperative societies are not clear. In this model, the consumer sector did not develop a clear alignment between its strategy, structure, and its stated goals. In these cases, a federal structure worked alongside a national wholesaler that wanted to develop a fully centralised movement. The hybrid model was operating in the United Kingdom, Sweden, Denmark, and the Netherlands.

Eckberg concluded that the cooperative model chosen did not provide an answer as to why some cooperative movements did well and others had difficulty managing change. He found some consumer cooperative movements operating under each model did well, whilst others operating under each model had difficulty managing change (Ekberg 2012).

The reason why some consumer movements have succeeded, and some failed or had difficulties in meeting the challenges posed by the supermarket chain stores lay elsewhere. A good starting point is to consider all the components that make an enterprise successful. These would include leadership and innovation; strategy and planning processes; data, information and knowledge; quality of people; customer/member focussed culture; the quality of processes, products and services; and finally, the capacity to achieve sustainable economic performance (Australian Quality Council 2000, SAI 2007). More specifically to a cooperative, it is important to examine the extent to which cooperatives have access to capital; employ managers that understand cooperative governance; practice democratic governance; engage with members; practice inter-cooperative co-operation; engage with the local community; and have the capacity to manage change (Cornforth et al. 1988, Ammirato 1996). A second consideration is to examine the extent to which cooperatives matched the chain stores' capacity to establish supermarkets supported by centralised wholesale/distribution systems. This is important because these methods were cost-effective, they facilitated a unified marketing strategy, and they provided consumers with an inviting store that was convenient and fully assorted with a diverse range of food and brand-name products. A third consideration is the cooperative's ability to understand and meet affluent consumers' changing needs and expectations. A fourth consideration is to analyse the interaction between the consumer movement and the external political, legal and competitive environment (Ekberg 2012).

The following case studies will inform us of some of the nation-specific factors that have led to consumer movements experiencing different fortunes and help us identify cooperative good practice standards.

4.3.2 France and Germany

France and Germany are two countries that have not managed change well. France adopted a federated model whilst Germany operated a centralised structure by 1981. Germany's consumer movement was re-established after 1945, and it grew until 1954. However, a series of bad decisions led it to declare bankruptcy in 1989. First, Germany's consumer movement was slow to adapt to the supermarket challenge. By 1960, cooperatives owned only 9 per cent of the total supermarkets. The private sector grew much faster. Cooperatives promoted an alternative called Rapid Service, but it did not work. Second, consumer cooperatives were also too focussed on catering for working people and did not meet the needs of the emerging middle class, who had more money to spend. This led to fewer members from the 1960s, which also meant fewer members' capital available to finance growth. Third, the consumer sector started to accumulate losses throughout the 1970s. It borrowed money to keep operating, but this led to more debt repayments. Borrowing was unavoidable since the cooperative law prevented consumer cooperatives from attracting members' savings. Fourth, the sector stopped paying the dividend, which led to further members leaving and more financial difficulties. Fifth, a strategy was developed in the early 1970s to create a central structure supported by 20 regional associations. This took place in 1981, with the Central Association becoming a holding company controlling three regional associations. This approach did not seem to work because some regional associations had their own wholesale network, so it did not lead to a centralised buying system. Sixth, in 1985, the Central Association borrowed more money to fund growth strategies. This strategy failed, and it led to higher debt repayments. Seventh, in 1986, it was discovered that management became the majority shareholder in the central public company and engaged in fraudulent activity, yet members could not replace them. Finally, in 1989 the Central Association went bankrupt, and members were not aware of financial difficulties because the Board had withheld information. Those cooperatives which did not join the Central Association survived. In 1990 there were 20 cooperatives left with 600,000 members (Zamagni, Battilani and Casali 2004, Ekberg 2012, Prinz 2017).

The French consumer sector comprised over 3,000 cooperatives with 876,000 members in 1914. In 1960, membership had grown to 3.5 million, and five cooperative societies produced 50 per cent of the total turnover. Concentration was promoted to counter the high level of competition from Carrefour and Leclerk (the cooperative for private retailers). By 1980, the consumer sector managed 2,200 stores compared to the 7,700 retail outlets it operated in 1965 (Lambersens, Artis and Demoustier 2017).

A number of factors led to the consumer sector's decline. First, it faced a lot of opposition from Carrefour hypermarkets and Leclerk. These two supermarket chains established supermarkets in the best locations, had mass sales and low costs, provided food and goods at competitive prices, provided a diversified product range, and designed appealing and convenient stores. Second, there were too many cooperative stores concentrated in towns with less than 50,000 people. Third, over 80 per cent of new members were practical and focussed on the dividend. The dividend, however, was constantly reduced: from 2.6 per cent in 1970 to 0.5 per cent in 1990. Fourth, management came from business schools and did not engage with cooperative members. They also made bad decisions, such as purchasing equipment at high costs, and they were slow to computerise or improve their marketing strategies. It was found that the retail stores were not managed efficiently, the running costs were high, and this led to a low rate of return. Fifth, the governance arrangements were not effective since members were not able to replace management. Finally, the relations between the cooperative associations and the central wholesaler were inadequate. This led to a decline in trade between consumer associations and the wholesaler. These factors led to a steady decline in the consumer movement, which by 1986 was reduced to 1.4 million members mainly operating in the Northeast (Lambersens, Artis and Demoustier 2017).

4.3.3 United Kingdom

The United Kingdom operated a hybrid model within which the CWS wanted to unify the movement under one central organisation. It operated in a very competitive market, having to compete with the likes of Sainsbury and Tesco. The consumer movement in Britain did innovate early, and by 1953 it already managed 1,700 self-service outlets. It promoted mergers that created larger cooperative societies. This policy reduced the number of cooperative societies from 859 in 1960 to 77 in 1990 (Ekberg 2012). In spite of this activity, its market share declined from 10 per cent in 1950 to 4.4 per cent in 1990. During the same period, its membership declined from 11.2 million members to 8 million members (Secchi 2017).

A number of factors explain the diminished importance of the consumer sector in the United Kingdom. First, there was a misalignment between the centre and the periphery. The consumer sector developed with three main players: the CWS wholesaler, which also became a retailer controlling a quarter of cooperative trade; the Cooperative Retail Society established in 1934 to promote cooperatives, which by 1985 managed 172 retail societies; and 20 regional associations which controlled 62 per cent of the total cooperative trade. The latter had its own wholesaler and distribution network and organised its own marketing and store setting. So there was neither a centralised approach nor a federalist approach via contractual agreements. The second factor is that only 25 per cent of cooperative societies were operating supermarkets, and these were not as modern as their competitors. The third issue is that changed economic conditions, unemployment and the rise of individualism weakened cooperative's membership base. Lower membership meant lower share capital to the tune of 95 per cent in real terms as at 1985. When cooperatives decided to cancel the dividend, membership declined further. Third, inept management was a key factor in 56 per cent of all retail stores failing, leading to a loss of 97,000 jobs. Management did not encourage member participation resulting in weak governance arrangements and oversight. A number of societies also suffered from management's corrupt behaviour. Fourth, the retail market was very competitive, with the multiples winning more and more of the grocery market: from 20 per cent in 1950 to 81 per cent in 1998. Fifth, the consumer sector's leadership failed to reconcile the views of the centre, which wanted a centralised movement, and the views of the regionals and local societies, which jealously guarded their independence. The movement did not go bankrupt and was able to recover during the 1990s through the creation of a centralised structure and a greater focus on the needs of the modern consumer (Ekberg 2012, Wilson, Webster and Vorberg-Rugh 2013, Secchi 2017).

4.3.4 *Norway*

The consumer movement in Norway successfully operates under a federalist model. It held 24 per cent of the food market by 1970. It operated in a market where in 1990, the independent stores still held 50 per cent of the retail food market. When supermarkets arrived, the cooperative sector was well prepared because it had modernised its stores, its distribution system, and its policies aligned with the needs of consumers.

A number of factors have helped the Norwegian cooperative sector manage change. First, Norway was an early adapter of the self-service model and the supermarket model. Its first self-service was established in 1947, and its first supermarket in 1968. Since the 1950s, the consumer sector had started to create larger cooperative societies and larger stores. It succeeded in halving its stores from just over 1,000 stores operating in 1950 to less than 450 stores operating in 1990. Second, it successfully raised capital by attracting a larger portion of members' savings. It is estimated that this campaign increased savings eightfold, and it set the scene for future capital raisings. Third, since the 1950s, the Central Association had been promoting standardisation and a more centralised distribution system. This strategy was accomplished in 1990 when a centralised purchasing wholesaler, standardised procedures, and a cohesive distribution centre were established. This was established within an enterprise model where the retail stores continued to be independently owned, and the division of responsibilities between the retail stores and the wholesaler was clear and without any overlapping functions. Fourth, the consumer movement's strategies were aligned with consumer expectations. Consumers in Norway were deemed to be very practical after the war. Generally, they were not ideologically minded. Indeed, the cooperative movement considered a member as an active member when a member conducted at least 60 per cent of their daily household consumption in the consumer cooperative. To this end, the Norwegian movement provided a variety of store formats ranging from the local store; soft discount stores; large supermarkets, and very large hypermarkets to attract consumers. These stores contained a wide variety of food and goods to meet their tastes and preferences. In addition, the cooperatives treated members with bonuses, special discounts, and the dividend, which further encouraged loyalty and differentiation from their competitors. This approach enabled Norway to maintain its share of the market whilst competing with large private retailers (Ekberg 2012, 2017).

4.3.5 *Italy*

Italy also developed a federalist consumer model. Consumer cooperatives operated in a highly regulated post-war market dominated by small retailers. The first supermarket was established in 1968, Carrefour established the first hypermarket in 1973, and by 1980 chain stores held 26 per cent of the retail market (it had been 17 per cent in 1970) (Tassinari 2015). Consumer cooperatives declined from 3,320 cooperatives operating in 1948 to 341 in 1990, whilst their membership increased from 1.5 million to 2.26 million members. So larger cooperatives were created (Battilani 2017).

There are many factors that led the consumer sector associated with the Central Association, LNCM, to manage change and lay the foundations for future growth.[5] First, it modernised its stores in response to competition from the chain stores. In doing so, it benefitted from the earlier experiences of other European cooperative sectors, and also considered the business models of the conventional retail sectors operating in Europe and the United States (Tassinari 2015, Battilani 2017). Second, cooperatives operated in a supportive political environment that broadly accepted a mixed pluralist economy and promoted inter-classist alliances. Within this environment, consumer cooperatives benefited from tax concessions[6] and developed a strategy that catered for the needs of all consumers. Third, in the 1960s, the Central Association encouraged cooperatives to merge and compete against large businesses. It was an anti-monopoly strategy implemented across the organisation. Cooperative societies merged into larger ones, at first within a city, then within a province, and then within a region. The strategy was successful, and by 1990, 22 cooperatives controlled 43 per cent of retail outlets, 75 per cent of the total retailing area, and 85 per cent of total sales (Ammirato 1996). Fourth, the Coop Italia national wholesaler was formed in 1968. It was made possible through the amalgamation of 32 provincial wholesalers. Its role was to negotiate agreements with suppliers, modernise warehouses, cut costs, improve services, and lower food prices. It did not manage retail outlets (Casali 2000). Fifth, cooperatives raised 2.26 billion euros by 1990 to modernise their retail outlets and to build large supermarkets and hypermarkets. Funds were raised from new members' one-off joining fees and mostly via members' loans, which also benefitted from a tax incentive (Zamagni, Battilani and Casali 2004).[7]

A Sixth reason was the ability of the Central Association to manage a crisis that could have derailed the consumer sector in 1975. In that year, three large cooperative associations from three Northern Italian regions encountered financial difficulties. The problem lay in the enterprise model that had Coop Italia acting as a guarantor to their suppliers. When the three consumer associations were in financial difficulties, the whole system was at risk. The Central Association resolved this with the help of the Unipol insurance company, which bought these cooperatives' properties at market rates, and with the help of major consumer cooperatives from Tuscany and Emilia Romagna, which provided financial and managerial support. Coop Italia no longer guaranteed payments but kept the role of purchasing, contractual arrangements, managing coop brand products, and national marketing. From then on, each cooperative would be solely responsible for managing its own warehousing. The changes were well implemented to the point that cooperatives now purchase 90 per cent of their products from Coop Italia (Tassinari 1991, Barberini 2009). Seventh, consumer cooperatives catered for all consumers. To this end, cooperatives developed a broad typology of retail outlets ranging from the local outlet, to the small supermarket, to large stores, and to hypermarkets. They promoted consumer protection and product quality assurance. They provided other services such as insurance products and travel agencies. Coop Italia sought consumers' views on coop-label products and on their favourite products. Finally, the Central Association managed to eliminate competition among its major consumer societies by encouraging mergers and by promoting expansion without direct competition. For instance, Tuscan-based cooperatives expanded along the Tyrrhenian coast, whilst Emilian-based cooperatives expanded along the Adriatic coast (Ammirato 1996, Zamagni, Battilani and Casali 2004, Battilani 2017).

A unique feature of the Italian consumer sector is that it did not aim to produce goods and services through its own manufacturing or agricultural businesses. Other than one manufacturing plant,[8] it purchases its products from other cooperatives and from private sector firms. Secondly, the consumer sector actively promotes inter-sectoral cooperation. For instance, agricultural and manufacturing cooperatives supplied 12.5 per cent of total purchases, 45 per cent of Coop Italia's own coop brand products, and 28 of the 37 organic products sold under its own label (ANCC 1990, Tassinari 1991). Inter-sectoral cooperation also flowed to co-investing in the Unipol insurance company and outsourcing transport services, cleaning, maintenance, security, food and catering to other cooperatives.

4.3.6 Japan[9]

Johnstone Birchall regarded the Japanese consumer cooperative movement as the best example of a successful consumer cooperative movement after 1945. It managed to succeed within a hostile political and retail environment whilst cultivating a friendly civil society. Private retailers numbered 1.7 million in 1982 and were hostile to consumer cooperatives, as was the case in Europe. The national cooperative law restricted consumer cooperatives to trade only with members, to operate within one prefecture and prohibited them from operating wholesale societies until 1954. The Law also prohibited consumer cooperatives from providing any credit facilities or from having their own bank. The broad regulatory framework for the retailing industry allowed consumers to operate only small stores until 1998. In spite of this, the movement got support from various groups in civil society, especially consumer associations and universities, and it grew from 2 million members in 1970 to 14 million members in 1990 (Birchall 2011). How did they do it?

Japan's consumer movement expanded in the 1960s in response to consumer and health-related issues. Consumers were most concerned with food adulteration caused by arsenic-laced powder milk, which killed over 100 babies in 1955. Consumers were further concerned with misleading labelling and environmental pollution caused by industrialisation and chemical industries. In response, Japanese housewives started the '10 yen milk movement'. It led to groups of housewives buying milk from reputable local producers instead of commercial producers. These groups of housewives came to be known as 'Han Groups', and they began buying safe and unadulterated products from the local cooperatives who would deliver them to their homes since it was difficult to open department stores. This unique cooperative model overcame at once the imposed legal restrictions. The cooperative model was cost-effective. The Han Groups operated with local cooperatives that managed warehouses, used computers to process orders and owned delivery vans that delivered the orders once a week. There was no need for a building, a store and furniture. There was no need for sophisticated management techniques. Transactions were facilitated by introducing simple administrative innovations such as computer-related orders, withdrawals from members' bank accounts, and semi-automatic sorting at warehouses. All of these innovations reduced costs and improved service delivery.

The consumer movement promoted broad membership to enhance their market share and attract capital. Members were invited to join because the Han Group-based cooperatives offered good unadulterated quality food at good prices and offered home delivery. Most importantly, the cooperative movement supported their members' broader concerns as consumers, such as food quality, the environment, anti-war (anti-nuclear) movement, misleading product labelling, and so on. Membership swelled from 2 million to 14 million. Considering that by 1990 each member had invested, on average, 300 USD, the large membership raised sufficient capital to finance their operations.

The university-based consumer cooperatives provided further growth. University members supported the cooperative movement and were instrumental in promoting cooperatives outside the campus. They promoted the ideas of establishing regional consortia and cooperative's own brand products. Many also became cooperative managers of new cooperatives.

This consumer cooperative model became an avenue for active democratic management. Han Group members, mostly housewives, participated in district committees and consumer panels, took part in developing coop-label products, as well as participating in the annual general meeting. Many became Board members. It is noted that the close contact between delivery staff and Han Groups provided the cooperative with real-time feedback on products and service which was quickly relayed to the cooperative administration.

The consumer movement in Japan has had a real impact on Japan's consumer legislation. It promoted an ethical consumer culture and enabled 100,000 female members to become active members of civil society by becoming members of various organisations and entering politics. In 1990, with a membership of 14 million, it had more members than the United Kingdom, Italy, France, Germany, and Norway combined.

4.3.7 *Summary: Good Practice*

The Consumer movement did not perform consistently from 1945 to 1990. The evidence suggests that cooperative movements that have managed change well have displayed a number of good practice features that improved their competitiveness. These include the following:

- Clear alignment between the consumer sector's strategy, organisational structure, and consumer culture. This entailed having clear roles and responsibilities between the retailing and wholesaling functions and the avoidance of duplication of responsibilities and activities.
- Capacity to represent all consumers, not just one class of consumers. This should be the focus regardless of whether consumers are practical and focussed on material benefits or whether they are part of social movements. Those who focussed on a variety of typologies for their stores, sold socially responsible products, and made available a diversity of products to please all subsets of consumers did well.
- Strong engagement with members by promoting dialogue and democratic participation. Member involvement leads to more members joining, more access to capital, more ideas, and continuous feedback. Ultimately, member engagement promotes a culture of continuous improvement, less apathy, and monitoring of management. All of these factors reduce the risk of mismanagement or fraudulent activity.

- Leadership and good management. Leadership is important in giving the overall direction, identifying and dealing with risks, managing crises, and being resilient when faced with difficulties. Cooperatives should appoint ethical managers, monitor management, and remove managers that promote forms of demutualisation or disregard democratic practices.
- Leadership, management and all members should promote a culture that equally values economic performance and democratic governance. Practising sound financial management is as important as practising cooperative principles. Everyone involved with cooperatives should understand and support the principle that capital is a means to serve cooperative members and their community.
- The State can be a partner for cooperative development. The State has such influence as a lawmaker, an industry regulator, a tax regulator, and a mediator of conflicts. Overall, it influences the nature of the political and economic system and the place and role of cooperatives within it. Cooperatives should reflect on how to approach the State so that it recognises cooperative uniqueness and cooperative autonomy at the same time.

The brief analysis of the consumer movement has once again shown how diverse and rich the cooperative experience is. This period has identified the unique consumer movements of Italy and Japan, which have developed different cooperative enterprise models to those practised in the United Kingdom and Sweden. There is no right or wrong model as long as they enable sound financial performance, promote the principles of cooperation, develop the capacity and capability to manage change, and are able to serve their members and their community.

4.4 The Mondragon Experience

During the post-war period, cooperative movements in Spain and Italy developed cooperative development models (CDMs). The term CDM refers to how an association or federation and their support structures promote and support an ever-changing inter-sectoral cooperative movement. A successful CDM is capable of promoting new cooperatives in all sectors of the economy, support existing cooperatives, facilitate inter-sectoral cooperation, and manage change. The CDMs operating in Spain and Italy demonstrated that worker cooperatives successfully competed in CMEs, just like the consumer, agriculture and credit cooperatives had previously demonstrated. Research findings indicate that worker cooperatives developed as members of a cooperative network of enterprises. These Networks provided financial, research, marketing, and management support to their cooperative members. This support improved their competitiveness, their survival rate, and their capacity to manage change. To explore the development of these CDMs, we will discuss the Mondragon cooperative network from the Basque region in Spain and the LNCM's cooperative network model which is mostly based in the region of Emilia Romagna in Italy.

4.4.1 Introduction

The Mondragon cooperative network commenced in 1956 when students from the local technical college formed Ulgor, Mondragon's first cooperative. By the 1980s, Mondragon comprised 172 cooperatives, mostly operating in the manufacturing sector. Mondragon cooperatives successfully increased employment from 11,417 in 1974 to 18,795 in 1984 at a time when the rest of Spain was losing jobs (Quarter 1989). How did Mondragon achieve this? What original contribution has Mondragon made to the study of cooperative development?

There are many factors that have contributed to Mondragon's success. In answering this question, this section will consider the external environment, the far-sighted leadership of Father Jose Maria Arizmendiarrieta, the effective cooperative governance arrangements, the high-level support structures that promoted cooperative start-ups and cooperative growth, the capability and the capacity to manage change, and the ability to compete whilst complying with their own set of cooperative values.

4.4.2 *External Environment*

Mondragon developed within an environment that supported the cooperative idea. Fishing, farming, and forests had been managed in common in the Basque region (Whyte and Whyte 1991). The Basque community placed a lot of emphasis on trust and solidarity (Oakshott 1978). The Basque trade union movement supported all types of cooperatives during the 1930s (Thomas and Logan 1982). Basque nationalism and its unique language are a source of unity among the Mondragon community. The community financially supported the Mondragon technical school in 1943, the first cooperative Ulgor in 1956, and the cooperative bank, Caja Laboral Popular (CLP), in 1959 (Oakshott 1978). Finally, Spain's late entry into the European Union allowed Mondragon manufacturing cooperatives to sell household manufacturing products to the emerging Spanish middle class under tariff protection until 1993 (Whyte 1995).

4.4.3 *The State*

The State was the other external institution that supported Mondragon. It implemented a number of policies that supported cooperative development. These include favourable tax concessions in lieu of the State not providing social security provisions and in lieu of the cooperative's requirement to place 10 per cent of the surplus into the social fund (Clayre 1980). State policies did not require cooperatives to pay tax for the first ten years and to pay 50 per cent of the ongoing rate thereafter. The State also provided short- to medium-term loans to cooperatives and 20 per cent of start-up capital for each new cooperative (Oakshott 1978). The central government accredited and funded the Mondragon technical school (Meek and Woodworth 1990). The Basque regional government provided Ikerlan, the research and development cooperative, with 50 per cent of its costs; cooperatives with 2,000 USD for every new job created[10]; grants and credit guarantees totalling 28.6 million USD from 1985 to 1987 to 31 cooperatives engaged in new and competitive technologies (Morrison 1991). Overall, the State's tax concessions and favourable environment had a positive impact on Mondragon's development.

4.4.4 *Jose Maria Arizmendiarrieta*

The Catholic priest Jose Maria Arizmendiarrieta is the visionary of the Mondragon experiment. He was a strategic thinker and a leader of educational dialogues. He was aware of Robert Owen's cooperative experiments and of the Rochdale model. He was influenced by the Catholic Social Doctrine. He was an anti-capitalist and anti-collectivist and disliked Taylorist organisational methods. He was pragmatic and promoted a culture equilibrium, a balance between pragmatism and idealism, the needs of workers, the enterprise, the community, and economic growth. Molina and Miguez note that his principles derived from Catholicism, Marxism, and Liberalism tempered by the Catholic Social Doctrine (Molina and Miguez 2008). He was the inspiration behind the formation of the vocational-technical school, the CLP, Lagun Aro insurance cooperative, and the cooperative statute, which included innovative governance arrangements and profit distribution mechanisms. These institutions became the foundation for the Mondragon model (Whyte and Whyte 1991, Whyte 1995).

4.4.5 Cooperative Governance

The Mondragon cooperatives' governance arrangements included unique membership policies and decision-making structures. Membership policies were quite strict. Mondragon practised the principle of open membership and required at least 80 per cent of workers to be members. Each member invested the equivalent of their annual salary. Salaries could fluctuate between 80 per cent and 110 per cent of the set rate, depending on the cooperative's economic performance. Salary differentials were initially set at 4.5:1 but were later increased to 6:1. Profit distribution was divided between the enterprise reserves (at least 20 per cent), member's capital accounts (maximum of 70 per cent), and the social fund (10 per cent). The profit split between capital accounts and the reserves varied according to prevailing economic conditions. For instance, during the 1980s economic recession, 50 per cent of surpluses were allocated in the reserve fund. The reserve fund is indivisible, and the members' capital accounts are not transferable. This profit distribution policy retains capital and prevents demutualisation (Whyte and Whyte 1991).

Democratic governance arrangements were experimented with at Ulgor and later became accepted throughout the Mondragon network. Each member has one vote, which is exercised each year at the General Assembly (AGA). The AGA is the supreme governing body of the cooperative, where key decisions are taken, and other representative bodies are elected. More specifically, the key governing bodies include:

- The Annual General Assembly. The AGA approves the budget; key strategic decisions such as mergers or joining other cooperative structures; membership entry fees and distribution of earnings and losses; and the appointment of the Governing Council (Board of Directors) and the Monitoring Commission (audit committee).
- The Governing Council performs the classic role of providing direction and control. It is responsible for implementing the overall strategy approved by the AGA. It appoints, supervises and removes the CEO and manager. It determines job classifications, and it proposes management plans and profit distributions to the AGA. In large cooperatives, it also appoints a formal senior management committee.
- The three-member Monitoring Commission performs an arbitration and auditing role (although in large cooperatives, external auditors are used).
- The Social Council is a unique Mondragon-specific governance body. It may comprise up to 50 members appointed by workers at the departmental or work unit level. The process allows one elected member for every ten workers. The Social Council is a consultative body representing the interest of members as employees. It counterbalances the managerial focus of the Board and the management committee. It engages in matters relating to pay and conditions, health and safety, and work activities.

The Governing Council appoints the Chair of the Social Council, thus re-enforcing the Social Council's status as an advisory body (Morrison 1991, Barandarian and Lezaun 2017).

4.4.6 *Support Structures*

Mondragon's cooperative support structures are major contributors to Mondragon's success. They have helped cooperatives achieve economies of scale, access knowledge on technology and markets, lower administrative costs, provide health and social security benefits to their members, and access to capital. Lagun Aro, Mondragon's insurance company, was the first support organisation. It provides social security and health insurance to Mondragon workers since they are not covered by the national scheme. Lagun Aro is financed via payroll tax. It provides unemployment benefits of up to 80 per cent of workers' wages and a pension payment equivalent to 60 per cent of workers' wages. Other support structures include Ikerlan, which conducts Mondragon's research and development activities, and Lankide Exports, which supports cooperatives' exporting activities. The Ularco consortium, established in 1965, grouped cooperatives from a particular area. It required cooperatives to pool resources, and in return, Ularco provided their members with legal and administrative services, financed new activities, and coordinated employee transfers between cooperatives (Whyte and Whyte 1991). The CLP bank, however, became the pillar of the Mondragon system.

4.4.7 *Mondragon Bank*

The CLP cooperative bank was formed in 1959 as a savings bank but soon developed into a unique cooperative development bank, providing loans, services, entrepreneurial, and coordinating and unifying roles. The CLP provided loans to cooperatives with interest rates lower than the ongoing market rate. Sometimes it charged no interest. The CLP provided cooperative start-ups with a moratorium on payment for the first two years, thus improving their chances of survival. The CLP wrote off loans amounting to 1 million USD and declared an interest moratorium on 40 per cent of the remaining loans during the recession of the 1980s (Morrison 1991).

The CLP established an Entrepreneurial Division to promote new cooperatives, as well as provide consultancy and auditing services. It employed 116 persons in 1982 (Whyte and Whyte 1991). It provided feasibility studies, training, and funding to managers who wished to start new cooperatives. CLP's feasibility studies could take two years to develop original ideas. This approach led to the formation of four to five cooperatives each year (Corcoran and Wilson 2010). The CLP provided advance payments totalling 60 per cent of total funding to establish new cooperatives and a moratorium on payments for the first couple of years. The CLP supports cooperatives throughout their lifecycle (Whyte and Whyte 1991).

CLP also performs a coordinating and unifying role for the Mondragon cooperative network. It required every Mondragon cooperative to sign a 'Contract of Association' as a condition for accessing CLP loans and services. It included five key requirements. First, members had to agree on key principles of democracy, wage solidarity, open admission, and fixed interest on capital contributions. Second, the cooperative had to become a member of CLP with voting rights and obligations to invest its capital, its surpluses, and its liquid assets with the CLP. Third, cooperatives were required to distribute surpluses to its indivisible reserves (at least 20 per cent), to the social fund (10 per cent), and the remainder to member accounts. These accounts are deposited with CLP until members exit the cooperative. Fourth, cooperatives are required to provide the CLP with their monthly accounts and their financial statements. Fifth, CLP audits the cooperative accounts at least every four years (Morrison 1991).

4.4.8 *Managing Change*

The Mondragon network has successfully managed a number of issues and economic crises. First, at Ulgor, in 1974, workers went on strike protesting against pay, working conditions, and Tayloristic organisational methods. The cooperative responded by introducing group activities, limiting the size of the cooperative to 500 employees, and establishing the Social Council to represent workers versus management (Thomas and Logan 1982).

Second, Mondragon overcame the recession of the late 1970s–1980s and the temporary loss of competitiveness. To improve their competitiveness, cooperatives decided to temporarily reduce workers' pay by 14 per cent from 1978 to 1984 (Zabaleta 1986) and introduce more flexible working hours, replacing the eight-hour day. Where there was an oversupply of labour, the Ularco consortium or Lagun Aro managed to either re-train or transfer workers to another cooperative. Those employees eligible for unemployment benefits received 70 per cent of their salary from Lagun Aro and 30 per cent from their cooperative. Some employees were given the opportunity to retire early with an indemnity and a pension.

Third, the CLP has been instrumental in helping cooperatives manage change and deal with crises. It has provided financial support and consultancy services to one-third of all cooperatives. These cooperatives faced financial difficulties or had to restructure to recapture market share. Where cooperatives faced financial difficulties, the CLP introduced a moratorium on payments, reduced interest rates, or wrote off payments. Joe Maria Ormachea, CLP's general manager, noted that between 1973 and 1986, CLP provided subsidies totalling 100 million USD. He affirmed that more than 50 per cent of Mondragon's cooperatives would not exist if CLP had not rescued them (Whyte and Whyte 1991).

The Mondragon approach seemed to work. At the start of 1988, 166 cooperatives employed 21,000 people, compared to almost 19,000 in 1984 (Morrison 1991). Unemployment at Mondragon was non-existent, whilst in the Basque region, the unemployment rate rose to 20 per cent (Axworthy 1985). Smith informs us from inception until 1992, Mondragon witnessed eight cooperative failures out of 120 cooperative start-ups (Smith 2001). Major changes took place after 1987. Mondragon developed a more centralised structure which took over many of the functions previously performed by the CLP.

4.4.9 *Cooperative Principles*

In 1987, Mondragon developed a set of formal principles which differed from the ICA principles. These formalised the Mondragon practices and the teachings of Father Arizmendiarrieta. The ten Mondragon principles are:

1 Free membership: there are no barriers to membership for those who want to be part of the Mondragón experience, provided they respect its basic principles.
2 Democratic organisation: equality of worker-members expressed in the election of the cooperative's representative bodies (one-member-one-vote).

3 Sovereignty of labour: labour is the transformative factor in society and in human beings and is, therefore, the basis for the distribution of wealth.
4 The instrumental and subordinated character of capital: capital is an instrument and should be subordinated to labour.
5 Self-management: worker-members should be provided with opportunities (and mechanisms to participate in the management of the firm).
6 Pay solidarity: a fair and equitable return for labour.
7 Inter-cooperation: a commitment to cooperation among different cooperative firms.
8 Social transformation: a commitment to transform society by pursuing a future of liberty, justice, and solidarity.
9 Universalism: the Mondragón experience is part of the broader search for peace, justice, and development of the international cooperative movement.
10 Education: a commitment to dedicate the necessary human and economic resources to cooperative education (Mondragon Corporation 2012, Barandarian and Lezaun 2017).

The Mondragon principles are quite unique. The key focus is the sovereignty of labour over capital. The rights of workers to a fair distribution of wealth and participation in the cooperative decision-making process. Inter-firm collaboration is a requirement for being part of Mondragon. They see the cooperative as an instrument of social transformation that is universally applicable (Corcoran and Wilson 2010). It is a holistic approach, with very explicit operational boundaries within which cooperatives members are required to operate.

4.4.10 Summary: Key Features

Mondragon has developed a CDM with a number of features that facilitate cooperative development.

- The first feature is access to capital. This has been achieved via members' investment (equivalent to their annual salary); depositing a portion of profits into the members' capital account; depositing profits into the indivisible reserves; access to CLP loans; CLP's advance payments to promote new cooperatives; and, finally, Ularco Group's policy to pool profits.
- The second feature is education and training. The technical school and Mondragon research centres have provided technical and managerial skills, research and development research, and knowledge of export markets and practices.
- The third feature is entrepreneurship. The CLP entrepreneurial division established new cooperatives every year by conducting feasibility studies, providing patient capital, and advance payments to cooperative start-ups (Whyte and Whyte 1991).
- The fourth feature is effective democratic governance arrangements. Key institutions include the General Assembly, the Governing Council, the Monitoring Commission, and the Social Council. The Social Council is an important innovation because it is elected by workers and because it balances the interests of workers and management when managing conflicts.
- The fifth feature is Mondragon's membership policy. It allows all workers and employees to become members and elect representatives to the Governing Councils of all cooperatives, including the CLP bank; agriculture cooperatives; and the retail

cooperative, Eroski. This is quite an innovative feature that is aligned with the principles of sovereignty of labour, self-management, and social transformation.

- The sixth feature are the cooperative principles. The focus on worker sovereignty provides guidance to Mondragon's governance arrangements, pay differentials, profit distribution, employment policies, crisis management practices, and, ultimately, workers controlling capital and not vice versa.
- The final feature is the ability to manage change as a united network of enterprises. Mondragon managed change via the CLP. The CLP united the movement via providing funds, management support, and a set of rules and principles set out in the 'Contract of Association'. The CLP Board is able to coordinate Mondragon responses because it is led by leaders of other cooperatives. Indeed, Ularco's president was also the CLP Chair of the Board until 1983. This centralised governance approach, based on an interlocking directorship model that formally links cooperatives with the CLP, could make binding decisions for the Mondragon network of cooperative enterprises.

4.5 Lega Nazionale delle Cooperative e Mutue

The Central Cooperative Association, LNCM, was formed in 1886. In 1920 it numbered 8,000 cooperatives. By 1926, Fascist aggression and intimidation reduced its members to only 600. LCNM ceased to operate in 1926 after the Fascist Government declared the National Agency for Cooperation as the sole agency representing cooperatives. After 1945, with the Fascists defeated, it re-established itself as the leading cooperative association in Italy. In 1947, it associated 4,722 cooperatives with 1.5 million members. In 1989, it associated 12,889 cooperatives, with a membership of 4.1 million that employed 230,000 people. Its members included 1,410 worker cooperatives from the construction and manufacturing sector and 2,060 worker cooperatives from the services sector employing a combined 150,000 persons (Ammirato 1996).

As was the case with Mondragon, there are a number of factors that have led to the development of LNCM since 1945. These factors include a supportive external environment; the role of the State; an egalitarian, cooperative culture and value system; the leadership role performed by the Central Association and its associated network of territorial, sectoral, and consortia; the level of inter-sectoral cooperation; entrepreneurship; and the capacity to manage change.

4.5.1 External Environment

The cooperative movement in Italy has always received a level of support from Catholics, Conservatives, Liberals, Socialists and Communists. They all supported cooperatives as a legitimate form of enterprise. The Left cooperative sector favoured consumer, housing and worker cooperatives. The Catholic-led cooperative sector favoured cooperative banks and agricultural cooperatives. The Liberal-Conservatives favoured cooperative banks (in urban areas), consumer cooperatives, as well as mutual societies providing health insurance. The Left wanted cooperatives to promote social change, whilst the others thought cooperatives could promote social cohesion within the existing capitalist system. After 1945, cooperatives were seen as democratic, anti-fascist organisations and received broad support from political parties, the trade union, and the general public (Zangheri, Galasso and Castronovo 1987).

4.5.2 The State

This broad political support influenced the State's attitude towards the cooperative sector. Indeed, in 1946, the cooperative movement could count on 108 friendly members of parliament. The State recognised the cooperative sector via article 45 of the Constitution, which acknowledged the social role performed by cooperatives and the State's responsibility in promoting cooperatives. Over the years, the State would provide enabling legislation, tax concessions, loans, and access to public works. In 1947, the State passed the cooperative law, which was generally aligned with the ICA principles, provided some tax concessions, and enshrined the principle of indivisibility of reserves. The State provided loans via the cooperative branch of the Banca Nazionale Del Lavoro, which in 1971 made available approximately 75 million USD. The State provided tax concessions between 25 per cent and 100 per cent depending on the type of cooperative. In 1973, the State enabled cooperatives to access funds via members' loans. In 1977, profits deposited in the indivisible reserves were tax-free. Changes to the cooperative law in 1983 allowed an increase in remuneration of members' capital accounts from a fixed 5 per cent to 2.5 per cent above the postal bond rate, allowed cooperatives to own subsidiaries, and it increased the maximum amount members could invest in their capital accounts and in loans to 30,000 USD. The State also continued to provide cooperatives with access to public works, including public buildings, roads, and railways. It also promoted a number of job-creation schemes which will be discussed in the Entrepreneurship Section below (Bonfante 1981, Ammirato 1996, Bonfante 2011, Fici 2013).

4.5.3 Cooperative Culture

The LNCM's cooperative culture is a pluralist socialist culture. It has been influenced by the egalitarian traditions of landless labourers and workers. This tradition favoured secure employment and lower salary differentials. It has been influenced by Prampolini's view of creating a cooperative republic formed by consumer, agricultural, and worker cooperatives. It has been influenced by Andrea Costa's Municipal Socialism, where local governments would support cooperative formation and provide access to public works and public resources. It has also been influenced by the Communist vision of the cooperative movement being part of a broad coalition of Left forces, working people and the middle class, cooperatives and small businesses, with the intention to promote Socialism. To this end, LNCM promoted cooperatives as the Third sector of the economy supported by programmes to tackle key issues faced by society, such as unemployment, housing, jobs for young people, and economic development in Southern Italy. Through the influence of Socialist and Communist parties, LCNM has also viewed the State as a partner and as an institution with which it could work (Zangheri, Galasso and Castronovo 1987). Professional managers joining LCNM cooperatives from the 1970s onwards introduced conventional management practices and a desire to promote long-term enterprise growth (Battilani and Zamagni 2010).

4.5.4 Network of Cooperative Enterprises

The LCNM network of cooperative enterprises is governed by a Central Association. It comprises territorial structures representing cooperatives in a given area (for example, Emilia Romagna), sectoral divisions representing cooperatives from a given sector of the economy (for example, manufacturing or consumer), and the consortia network, which group cooperatives from a given sector of the economy (construction or agricultural or service consortia). These structures are funded by their cooperative members. In return, they provide their members with political representation, leadership, professional services, improved economic competitiveness, access to inter-cooperative trade, and a greater capacity to manage change and manage crises.

4.5.5 Cooperative Governance

Cooperatives are democratic organisations where each member has one vote. At least 50 per cent of working people are required to be members. The initial investment requirement was set at a legal maximum of 250 USD in 1947. Members' capital account receives an annual remuneration not exceeding 5 per cent, later increased to 2.5 per cent above the bond rate. Workers are paid market rates as per collective agreements. Pay differentials were limited to 1.5:1 until the 1970s but increased to 4.5:1 by the 1980s. Worker cooperatives can pay members a 20 per cent bonus on top of their wages. The focus has been to promote re-investments of profits in the indivisible reserve fund in return for secure employment (Zangheri, Galasso and Castronovo 1987, Ammirato 1996).

The Cooperative governance structures include the Annual General Assembly (AGA), where members exercise their rights and elect a Management Council (the Board of Directors) and a supervisory committee. In addition to electing the governing bodies and holding them to account, the AGA approves the budget and cooperative strategy, approves policies and procedures, decides on profit distribution, and has the final say on membership issues. The Board implements the strategy, appoints the senior management committee (in large cooperatives), and reports annually to the AGA. The Supervisory Committee appoints external auditors. It supervises the operations of the Board to ensure it is complying with performance targets, the law, and the principles of mutuality. It also deals with workers' complaints towards management. It, too, reports annually to the AGA (Bonfante 2011, Genco 2011).

4.5.6 Support Structures

The Central Association's structures are all democratically elected by their cooperatives. Cooperatives elect the boards and supervisory body of the consortium, the sectoral associations, and the territorial structures. More specifically:

- The LCNM national assembly comprised 805 delegates in 1991. Cooperatives elect at least 50 per cent of delegates. The consortia elected 85 delegates, and the territorial regional councils elected the rest (Zotti 1983, LNCM 1991). This broad representation ensures that once strategic decisions are taken, the network and large cooperatives will implement them because they were all part of the decision-making process.
- The Central Association develops the overall strategy, engages with the State, engages with the trade union movement, promotes cooperatives nationally, and monitors the implementation of the strategic plan.
- The 20 regional territorial structures provide market-related information and updates on relevant public policies and legislation; promote cooperative awareness; negotiate collective bargaining agreements with the trade union movement; promote new cooperatives in existing economic sectors and in new sectors of the economy; mediate conflicts between cooperatives; and provide advice on how to manage change. The

region of Emilia-Romagna also had eight local offices covering its major cities, providing administrative, legal, accounting, and financial services.

- The ten sectoral associations provide cooperatives that represent members' interests with government departments, review monthly performance, promote inter-firm collaboration, promote large cooperatives via mergers, mediate conflicts among cooperatives, and coordinate cooperative strategies and practices.
- Consortia's main function is to improve cooperative competitiveness by achieving economies of scale. There were 87 consortia operating by the late 1980s. Through the consortia, cooperatives have achieved economies of scale, have reduced the costs of raw materials through bulk buying or other contractual arrangements, have won public contracts, have marketed their products, have accessed new technology, and have had access to technical and managerial expertise. They maintain a cohesive network by managing conflicts and by distributing work among members. They have also promoted inter-sectoral trade (Zan 1982, Ammirato 1996, Zamagni and Felice 2006).

4.5.7 *System of Authority*

The Central Association has developed a system of authority that enabled it to promote an overall strategy, new economic sectors, and manage a number of crises. First, the Central Association managed to direct and coordinate activities because it provided a range of support services through its network, which helped to create a cohesive network. Second, interlocking directorships of cooperatives, consortia, sectoral, and territorial structures enabled collective decisions to be made and implemented across the network. Third, many leaders had worked in cooperatives and in various parts of the network, developing a comprehensive knowledge of how the organisation worked and forging good working relations with other leaders across the organisation. This made it easier to make and implement collective decisions and deal with conflicts. Fourth, LNCM's formalised political factions imposed discipline and power-sharing arrangements. This provided unity, cohesiveness, and an open and predictable decision-making process. Finally, the LNCM executive included well-respected leaders, who were politically connected, possessed good leadership skills, had high moral standing, and were respected by cooperative members (Zan 1982, Viviani 2013, Ammirato 2018).

The following are some of the decisions made by the Central Association that led to cooperative growth and successfully managing change and dealing with crises:

- The Central Association developed an anti-monopoly strategy in the 1960s that led to the development of large cooperatives via mergers and acquisitions. The strategy was successful, and by 1989, the largest 394 cooperatives produced 54 per cent of LNCM's total turnover (Petralia 1988).
- The Central Association proposed to create national consortia across the movement so that they could achieve economies of scale, reduce costs, and provide better services to cooperative members. To this end, local and provincial consortia were merged and eventually, national consortia were established: Coop Italia became a national consortium servicing all consumer cooperatives; the Consortium, CCC (Consorzio Cooperative Costruzioni), became the national consortium for the construction and building cooperatives focussing on winning public and private contracts throughout Italy; CNS (Consorzio Nazionale Servizi) became the national consortia for the service sector (Ammirato 1996, Felice 2010).

- In 1962, the Central Association promoted Conad, the national consortium servicing private retailers so they could compete against large supermarkets. LNCM leaders convinced the consumer sector to provide Conad access to its wholesale consortium and to release some of its top managers to help start up Conad (Gombi 1990, Viviani and Dessi 2005). This strategy was implemented well, and by 1990, Conad held 5 per cent of the national food sales market (Putzolu 1991).
- In the 1970s, the Central Association managed to rescue four large regional consumer cooperatives from Northern Italy. These consumer cooperatives faced financial difficulties resulting from bad management, slow modernisation, overspending in new supermarkets, and accumulated financial losses. The LNCM leadership persuaded Unipol (the insurance company) and other consumer cooperatives to purchase their assets to reduce their debt; they developed a new strategic plan; persuaded the consumer sector to allocate top managers to each of these cooperatives. All of these cooperatives survived, and the consumer sector remained a viable national sector (Zamagni, Battilani and Casali 2004, Barberini 2009).

4.5.8 *Inter-sectoral Cooperation*

A unique characteristic is LNCM's capacity to promote inter-sectoral cooperation and inter-sectoral trade. In 1969, LNCM organised 200 cooperatives from the consumer, construction, manufacturing and services sectors to join forces and establish Fincooper, its financial consortium. In 1990, over 2,000 cooperative members had joined. Fincooper managed members' excess liquidity, paid interests on deposits, provided loans, and acted as a guarantor for cooperatives that borrowed from private banks. Most importantly, Fincooper established LNCM's initial financial framework, which consisted of the cooperative bank (BANEC), a merchant bank (FINEC), and Unipol, the movement's own insurance company founded by 195 cooperatives in 1962. Fincooper also invested in 41 companies offering leasing, factoring, real estate and consultancy services to the whole cooperative movement (Lega Nazionale Delle Cooperative e Mutue 1990, Ammirato 1996, Zamagni and Felice 2006, Viviani 2013).

Inter-sectoral cooperation operates in different economic settings. Coop Italia purchases from industrial and agricultural cooperatives up to 45 per cent of the products sold under its own coop label. In addition, consumer cooperatives outsource transport, maintenance, cleaning, security, and catering services to other cooperatives. The National Construction Consortium conducted 49 per cent of its total work on behalf of housing cooperatives in 1976. ACAM, the National Consortium for Purchasers and Supplies, servicing 390 construction and manufacturing cooperative members, bought 14.5 per cent of the total purchasers from other cooperatives (Ammirato 1996). Other linkages took place in the tourism industry between consumers, travel agents, cooperative owned hotels, and Unipol insurance.

4.5.9 *Entrepreneurship*

The formation of new cooperatives associated with LNCM took place via a variety of channels. In post-war Italy, a diverse group of people, organisations, and institutions established close to 9,000 cooperatives from August 1944 to September 1946. Many were set up spontaneously by people in search of jobs or a home. The Resistance Brigades formed cooperatives because they were democratic organisations. The National

Committees of Liberation established cooperatives to build roads, build houses, and distribute food because they created jobs and did not speculate. Co-operators returning from exile formed cooperatives. Local authorities actively supported the consumer cooperatives because they could keep food prices low during the difficult post-war period (Zangheri, Galasso and Castronovo 1987).

Following this initial euphoria, people that formed new cooperatives received support from other cooperatives or from the local LNCM offices. Up to the late 1960s, LNCM policy was to promote one cooperative per sector in each town. These cooperatives operated in their local economies. Usually, the leader or an experienced person from an established cooperative would help establish a new cooperative operating in another town. In other cases, the local LNCM offices provided cooperative start-ups with legal, administrative, accounting, and financial advice and helped them engage with other cooperatives or to join a consortium. Some local offices established cooperatives in new sectors of the economy. The Bologna office established the first cultural cooperative that managed a local theatre and the first insurance company. These two initiatives led to the formation of more cooperatives in the cultural sector and the formation of the Unipol insurance company. Local offices, following solicitation from workers, the trade union, or the local mayor, helped workers buy out private enterprises in crisis. In these cases, they would conduct feasibility studies, prepare a cooperative statute, and provide advice on how to manage a cooperative. LNCM reported that 94 worker-buyouts took place from 1981 to 1987 (Oakshott 1978, Ammirato 1996, Bulgarelli 2006).

The Italian government promoted job-creation programmes that led to the formation of new cooperatives. These were developed in response to lower economic growth, unemployment, and de-industrialisation. In 1977, the state provided all enterprises access to finance and public works if they employed young people. Through this programme, 1,248 cooperatives were established from 1977 to 1979. In 1986, a job-creation scheme targeting unemployed youth in Southern Italy provided start-up capital, funds to conduct a feasibility study, loans, and grants. Through this programme, 110 cooperatives were established. Finally, in 1985 the Parliament approved the Marcora Law. This law provided 150 million USD for cooperatives to restructure or innovate their operations and for cooperatives formed from worker-buyouts of private enterprises. The Marcora programme supported 273 cooperatives and established 86 cooperatives from worker-buyouts of private enterprises (Ammirato 1996).

4.5.10 Summary: Key Features

LNCM has built a successful network of cooperative enterprises. The key features of this successful CDM can be summarised as follows:

- The first feature is that LNCM has operated in a non-hostile political environment where all major political traditions support the principle of cooperation.
- The second feature consists in leading and developing a comprehensive, cohesive cooperative network. It includes a central-national association, local and regional territorial structures, and the consortia network. It provides leadership, a cohesive decision-making process based on interlocking directorships and common cooperative culture, a capacity to develop a common strategy, a variety of business services, a capacity to grow cooperative enterprises, a capacity to develop new cooperative sectors, and a capacity to manage crises.

- The third feature is the role of large cooperative enterprises. These large cooperatives provide leadership to each sector, provide most funds to the network, and support the financial sector. They provide LNCM with the economic capacity and the technical and financial capabilities to promote cooperatives.
- The fourth feature is inter-cooperative and inter-sectoral collaboration. Inter-sectoral collaboration led to the creation of strategic cooperatives like Unipol and the private retail sector, and promoted inter-cooperative trading. Inter-sectoral trading has promoted cooperative growth and cooperative diversity.
- The fifth feature is LNCM's respectful relationship with the State. It views the State as a partner rather than a hostile institution. The State has promoted a cooperative law that reflects cooperative values and cooperatives' economic and financial needs. The State has provided cooperatives access to finance (albeit limited),[11] access to public works, and access to housing and job-creation programmes that have benefited the cooperative sector.
- The Sixth feature is the ability to promote new cooperatives. LNCM has promoted entrepreneurship via its own cooperatives, via its local offices, and via supporting state-led employment and business programmes. In the post-war years, local authorities and civil society organisations also promoted cooperatives.

4.6 New Independent States

The cooperative movement was given a boost from the newly independent states of Africa and Asia that emerged after 1945. At the time of independence, their economies were already integrated with the world economy by selling cash crops to developed countries in return for manufactured goods. Colonial governments did not modernise the colonies' economic systems. They promoted only one of the four standard modernisation policies that had been used by the United States and other European countries to modernise their economies so they could catch up with Britain. The four modernisation policies are railways, schools, money, and tariff protection. The colonial governments built railways and roads to take goods to the ports so they could then be transported and sold overseas, but they did not build an effective education system, nor an effective financial system, nor did they use tariffs to promote local industries. This ensured that independent states occupied a weak and precarious place in the world economy and would face difficulties catching up with developed economies (Allen 2011).

The newly independent states turned to the modernisation model that had been successfully applied by the Soviet Union and by Japan to catch up with the developed countries. This model consisted in promoting state-led economic development. This entailed the State establishing economic plans, providing direction to business and the economy, providing adequate laws and regulations, and providing financial and other technical support. Cooperatives figured prominently within this state-led development model (Allen 2011). Cooperatives were viewed favourably because they were accepted as being part of a socialist economy, as being capable of modernising agriculture, as being able to promote a cohesive society, and as being capable of distributing wealth more equitably.

The State and cooperatives had a close, continuous, and evolving relationship. Develtere provides a succinct analysis of the relationship between the State and cooperatives as it evolved until the early 1990s. Deltevere highlights that a pattern emerged where states led, controlled, coerced, and included cooperatives within their industrial plans. This led to the speedy growth of the cooperative sector to the point that it could not be matched with adequate management expertise and with an appropriately skilled and educated membership. In addition, members' apathy, the practice of political appointees, and inadequate governance processes led to corrupt activity. As cooperatives did not achieve the desired results, governments would conduct an inquiry. The inquiry's recommendations normally led to more state controls and state intervention as cooperatives were not deemed capable of meeting the Government's economic targets. Within this context, cooperatives became quasi-state agencies that coordinated agricultural production on behalf of the state-run marketing boards (Develtere 2008). We will draw on the experiences of India and Tanzania to explore this thesis further.

4.6.1 *India*

The cooperative movement in India was promoted by the colonial government to help farmers by pass money lenders and to access credit through their own cooperative banks. The cooperative banks were based on the German Raiffeisen banks. The Government passed the *Cooperative Credit Act* in 1904 and the *Cooperative Societies Act* in 1912. The latter covered all cooperative societies. From inception, the colonial government created a unitary system with one law covering the whole country and with one registrar registering all cooperatives. The system included district and provincial unions as well as a national federation[12] (Birchall 2011). The registrar had broad powers which severely limited cooperative autonomy. The registrar could refuse registration, appoint a person to take over management, call general meetings, compulsory amend by-laws, and could dissolve a cooperative (ALC India 2019).

After gaining independence in 1947, the government promoted a state-led mixed economy. Indian leaders were influenced by Fabian-style democratic Socialism and by the Soviet Union's centrally planned economic model based on five-year economic plans. The key pillars of India's political economy included state ownership, no foreign direct investment, self-sufficiency, and a system of control based on a highly regulated licencing system. In the latter case, the State had to approve a company's willingness to change production from one product to another. The State also reviewed the decisions, and the board composition, of any company worth more than 20 million USD (Yergin and Janislaw 1998).

The Government assigned cooperatives the role to modernise the agricultural sector. Cooperatives were seen as a people's movement organised at a village level. The State hoped that cooperatives would alleviate poverty, improve productivity, and improve the overall quality of life. In accordance with the recommendations from the All India Credit Rural Survey Committee of 1954, the government performed a very active role in promoting cooperatives. It provided capital, technical and managerial support, and financial assistance to different types of cooperatives. Financial assistance included loans, subsidies and financial guarantees (Vaswani 2012, Dash 2021).

In 1965, the Mirdha Committee reviewed the cooperative sector and concluded that it had been politicised. Indeed many chairpersons and managers of the sugar cooperatives had links with political parties (Vaswani 2012). The Committee's recommendations led to further controls of cooperatives via the cooperative registrar. The registrar now had the powers to appoint a cooperative's management committee; to compulsorily divide, merge, and amalgamate cooperatives; to appoint supervisory staff; and to set wages and conditions. The Government also required compulsory membership of cooperatives, required cooperatives to bank with cooperative rural banks, and also required cooperatives to market products via government-run marketing boards (ALC India 2019). People soon viewed cooperatives as government agencies and not as autonomous member-owned organisations (Dash 2021).

The cooperative sector in India managed to grow and also expand in other sectors of the economy, including agri-business, fishing, textile, irrigation, electricity, and transport. By 1995, there were 446,000 cooperatives registered in India with close to 183 million members (Shaffer 1999). The cooperative sector, however, was deemed to be too dependent on state aid; it was not autonomous and was regarded as a state agency. The high level of government control and poor cooperative management has developed poorly functioning cooperatives. According to Vaswani, a huge gap has been created between the expectations and the actual performance.[13] This has given cooperatives a poor image and has also created a lack of trust (Vaswani 2012).

4.6.2 *Tanzania*

Cooperatives first emerged in Tanzania in 1925 when local coffee growers formed their own marketing association. In the late 1940s, the British colonial government granted marketing cooperatives a monopoly to market cotton and by-pass middlemen who paid low prices. It is estimated that by 1958, 273 societies sold 83 per cent of all cotton (Birchall and Simmons 2010). When Tanzania won independence in 1961, the Nationalist government embraced Socialism as the political and economic model to make Tanzania truly independent. Socialism allowed Tanzania to control and distribute wealth. Cooperatives were seen as part of a Socialist economy and society and became part of the Government's economic plan to modernise the country. It is estimated that one-third of the national assembly supported cooperatives. Aid organisations and international organisations also supported cooperatives hoping they would help with modernisation and the fair distribution of wealth (Birchall 2011).

The Tanzanian Government gave cooperatives the responsibility to market all crops produced. This policy helped the cooperative sector to grow. In 1961, there were 275 cotton societies and 182 coffee societies operating in Tanzania. By 1965, 1287 primary cooperatives marketed over 20 types of crops and controlled over 80 per cent of agricultural production and marketing (Birchall and Simmons 2010). Cooperatives found it difficult to manage this rapid growth and to meet government expectations. As was the case in India, this led to the special Presidential Commission of Enquiry in 1966. The inquiry concluded that without government control, cooperatives could not guarantee their democratic nature (especially at the secondary and apex levels) and could not guarantee their contribution to the national economy. To this end, the State took over sixteen cooperative unions and hundreds of societies (Develtere 2003).

In 1967, the government introduced a policy to nationalise the commanding heights of the economy and simultaneously made local villages (instead of traditional cooperatives) responsible for agricultural production, marketing, and distribution. This new policy dissolved cooperatives and their unions. The concept of the traditional Ujamaa villages was based on four principles: people live together in villages; the means of production are communally owned; people work together; and they share the fruits of their work. These villages were to link traditional culture with socialist-led modernisation, the principles of equality, and the distribution of wealth (Develtere 2003).

In 1984, the government realised that the new policies of village-based production and marketing had not worked and re-established traditional cooperatives. However, these cooperatives and their unions were required to follow the directions of the ruling party. These cooperative unions had accumulated debt, which the ruling party admitted was accumulated as a result of government policies (Birchall 2011).

International organisations had supported cooperative development in Tanzania and Africa and showed concern that the professed goals were not being achieved. The International Labour Organisation (ILO) passed the ILO Recommendation No. 127, titled *Concerning the Role of Co-operatives in the Economic and Social Development of Developing Countries*. It called on governments to form one central organisation to support independently managed cooperatives, to promote a national cooperative law, and to include cooperatives in the economic and planning processes. The ILO saw cooperatives as organisations, not as enterprises (Bayo 2019). A report from the United Nations Research Institute for Social Development declared that cooperatives had not achieved their performance target. It found that they were government-led, were small, and had little impact on society. An ICA report found that politics restricted the flourishing of cooperatives in Africa because they prevented voluntary membership and prevented cooperatives from operating as independent organisations (Birchall 2011). A 1991 World Bank discussion paper found that the problems with cooperative development in Africa were due to internal and external factors. These included excessive government interference; unrealistic expectations; problems with undercapitalisation; lack of member involvement in decision-making; and lack of management expertise. The report concluded that governments and international donors used cooperatives as quasi-government agencies or donor-led agencies to carry out their programmes (Braverman et al. 1991).

The ICA conducted a review in the early 1990s, identifying a new set of issues faced by cooperatives in developing countries that were implementing the International Monetary Fund (IMF) structural adjustments policies. Developing countries were forced to apply structural adjustment policies in order to receive IMF loans to repay public debt. The ICA report noted that cooperatives have difficulties competing in more liberalised markets because of low business efficiency, weak capital base, heavy indebtedness and limited creditworthiness, the limited entrepreneurial capability of managers and board members, and the unbalanced organisational structures of the movement (Develtere 2008). Yet some positive developments did take place during this period. Tanzania's number of cooperatives did increase to over 8,000, with more than 1.3 million members by 1993 (Shaffer 1999). The Credit Union movement made progress in Cameroon, Rwanda and Benin and close to 5,000 operated throughout Africa (Braverman et al. 1991). Cooperative education and training were extended to members and managers, and international donors began to engage directly with cooperative federations rather than government departments (Develtere 2008).

4.6.3 Summary

Promoting economic development in a developing country after independence was difficult. Newly independent countries occupied a precarious position in the world economy, had poor infrastructure, inadequate financial frameworks, and faced political instability.[14] The State became the preferred institution to drive change, as had been the case in late industrialising countries. Cooperatives were part of this change and were given an enormous responsibility to help modernise the countryside and agricultural production. The State's overall control of the economy and of cooperatives led to a growth in cooperatives as legal entities and as organisations capable of coordinating production for their members. These cooperatives, however, lacked autonomy and democratic structures and came to be seen as state agencies.

Would cooperatives have fared better had they been free from government control? Considering the position of newly independent countries in the world economy, the modernisation issues faced by new modern states, the general lack of understanding of cooperative principles and governance, the lack of education among the masses of people, and the cooperative limits of undercapitalisation and lack of managerial expertise, it is difficult to affirm that autonomous cooperatives would have performed better. At the same time, however, it is not correct for institutions to judge cooperatives negatively because cooperatives were not given the opportunity to operate autonomously and demonstrate what they could have achieved.

4.7 The International Cooperative Movement

The ICA extended its global presence during this period. For the first time, the majority of ICA members resided in developing countries. The ICA became a more diverse organisation, with cooperatives operating in many sectors of the economy. The growth of cooperatives through mergers and their need to compete with larger capitalist enterprises led them to adopt conventional legal structures which tested their democratic governance arrangements. The evolution of cooperatives and the passing of old leaders created an identity crisis for the ICA (MacPherson 2008).

The ICA became a truly global organisation by the 1990s. It is estimated that the ICA-affiliated cooperatives boasted over 670 million members worldwide, of which over 56 per cent resided in developing countries. Over 82 per cent were members of agricultural and credit cooperatives, but consumer, fisheries, housing and industrial cooperatives were also represented, making it a diverse cooperative sector (Develtere 2003). The ICA took note of this development and established various sectoral departments[15] as well as ICA international offices in India in 1960, Tanzania in 1968, and Costa Rica in 1984 (Shaffer 1999).

The ICA's global reach translated into further international recognition. The United Nations awarded the ICA with representative function status and, in 1968, it sought ICA's assistance in promoting cooperative development in developing countries. The ICA helped to establish the Committee for the Advancement of Cooperatives, which included the ILO, three United Nations agencies, three non-government organisations, and three cooperative development agencies. In 1982, the ICA moved its offices from London to Geneva (Brouder 2010).

The 1954 ICA Congress affirmed the ICA's role in promoting cooperatives across the world. In addition to international cooperation with the United Nations and other international bodies, the ICA promoted education and training. Cooperative schools were established in France, Nigeria, Germany, Tanzania, Kenya and Benin. Japan established its International Cooperative Training Centre in 1963 (Granata 2019). Cooperative centres were established in Nova Scotia, Wisconsin, Quebec, Saskatchewan, Montreal, and the University of California at Davis (Fairbairn 2004). The ILO International Directory of Cooperative Organisations identified 86 countries that had cooperative education institutes (Shaffer 1999). These cooperative institutes performed an important role in educating cooperative members at a time when the study of cooperatives was disappearing from mainstream economic textbooks (Kalmi 2007). Whilst the number of institutes worldwide may sound impressive, Laidlaw's report to the ICA Conference held in Moscow in

1980 concluded that cooperatives and the cooperative movements had neglected cooperative education (Laidlaw 1980).

The biggest issue faced by the ICA was a crisis of identity. As we have seen so far, there are major differences between consumer, worker cooperatives, agricultural cooperatives, and cooperative banks. We have noted that the 1937 ICA principles emphasised the economic over the communitarian aspects of cooperation. Since 1945, the growth of large cooperatives of national dimensions has weakened democratic participation. The promotion of legal structures that allowed ownership of subsidiaries made cooperatives look like conventional businesses with management exerting too much power. In 1966, the ICA reviewed its cooperative principles and added the fifth principle, 'education, training, and information', and the sixth principle: 'cooperation among cooperatives'. But more needed to be done, so the ICA commissioned Laidlaw to prepare a report to be discussed at the 1980 ICA conference to be held in Moscow.

Laidlaw presented the *Cooperatives in the Year 2000* report at the ICA Moscow conference in 1980. He noted that the international cooperative movement faced a credibility crisis and a managerial crisis and that cooperatives were behaving like other businesses. More specifically, there were different types of cooperatives with different forms of ownership and different types of members (workers, farmers, middle class, retail owners); cooperatives were becoming more like conventional enterprises with similar industrial relations practices; and management began to exert control in the larger, more complex cooperatives. In large cooperatives, member apathy and weak democratic management practices were key concerns. Laidlaw also made four key suggestions to promote cooperatives: focus on providing food to the world; encourage worker cooperatives which had been neglected in the past; continue to promote consumer cooperatives; and promote cooperative communities where a variety of cooperatives provide many goods and services for urban communities (Laidlaw 1980).

The ICA continued to explore the issues raised by the Laidlaw report. At the 1984 Congress, the Russian Federation encouraged the ICA to address global issues such as poverty, hunger, war, and pollution. At the 1988 Congress held in Sweden, the ICA president, Lars Marcus, emphasised that cooperatives were being influenced by Capitalism, especially its shareholding companies. He found that weak national cooperative movements, the decline in democratic practices, the lack of cooperative international institutions, and a decline in member commitment were issues that needed to be addressed. The debate led the ICA to assign Sven Ake Book with the task of conducting a worldwide consultation. This consultation eventually led to the updated 1995 ICA principles. The consultation process would be conducted post-Soviet Union, and there was hope that a Post-Cold-War world would welcome a more open debate and lead to improved cooperative principles (MacPherson 2012).

4.8 Summary

- After 1945, the development of capitalist mixed economies and the Welfare State promoted economic growth, provided employment, and made available a variety of goods and services that society needed and wanted. States, universities, foundations, and philanthropists actively promoted the CME and the modern corporation. Corporations continued to grow, invest, innovate, improve their operations, and start new sectors of the economy. They dominated the CMEs. The Welfare State provided people with the added security of universal health cover, improved income support, services for the aged, regular public incomes for most of the sick, handicapped and unemployed, family allowances and daycare, maternity leave, and personal social services for a variety of human needs.

- Corporations and states created an international liberal economic order that supported Capitalism and trade without (or with limited) tariffs and other barriers to trade. International organisations such as the IMF, the World Bank, the World Trade Organisation, and the OECD promoted the CME, individualism, and free trade. Philanthropic organisations and US Universities developed and taught MBAs. Managers with MBAs, in turn, promoted the multi-divisional Corporation and the concept of profit maximisation.
- The cooperative movement responded to the new competitive environment by growing its size, accessing finance and operating under new legal structures. Cooperatives grew via mergers and/or acquisitions. Cooperatives accessed finance through their own banks or financial companies and by legislating financial incentives to attract finance from members. Cooperative movements promoted legal structures such as joint stock companies and holding companies to grow faster and to access capital from external sources.
- Nation-specific consumer cooperative movements developed across many countries. Consumer cooperatives can be successful by adopting a variety of models and strategies. The research demonstrated that a successful consumer movement requires good business practices alongside the application of cooperative principles. First, there should be a clear alignment between the consumer sector's strategy, its organisational structure, and its consumer-focussed culture. Second, consumer sectors need to represent and satisfy the needs of all consumers, not just one class of consumers. Third, the consumer cooperatives need to raise sufficient funds from their members and/or retained profits to fund their operations. Fourth, consumer cooperatives need to elect competent leaders and employ competent managers. Fifth, consumer cooperatives should engage with their members by promoting dialogue and forms of democratic participation. Sixth, the cooperative leadership, management, and members need to promote a cooperative culture that equally values economic performance and adherence to cooperative principles, especially adherence to the principle of democratic governance.
- The Mondragon network demonstrated that worker cooperatives can be successful and can be very innovative. Mondragon cooperatives compete in the market by being part of a network of cooperatives and support organisations that provide education, finance, business, insurance and marketing services. The network facilitates the formation of new cooperatives, provides support to cooperatives experiencing economic difficulties, and provides support to cooperatives that want to grow. The network operates cohesively as a result of having a shared common history and workplace culture, adhering to the CLP bank's contract of association and financial policies, being able to access services from support structures, sharing cooperative principles, being part of continuous acts of solidarity and support, especially in difficult times.
- LNCM is a successful network of cooperatives. The network is led and coordinated by a Central Association, and it comprises consortia, territorial, and sectoral associations. These bodies provide administrative services, finance, managerial expertise, and economic direction that enable cooperatives to compete in the market. LNCM has engaged with and influenced the State, which created an enabling environment that includes cooperative legislation, tax laws, providing access to public works, job-creation

programmes, and financial support. LNCM has promoted new cooperatives, promoted the development of large cooperatives, promoted new cooperative sectors, promoted inter-sectoral trade, and provided support in times of crisis. LNCM network is a successful inter-sectoral cooperative network that is embedded in the region of Emilia-Romagna and that operates at a national level.

- India and Tanzania promoted a state-led Socialist economic development that included cooperatives as a key component of the new economy. The ICA and other international organisations considered it appropriate for the State to lead cooperative development because the local cooperative movements lacked the knowledge, experience, and money to promote a viable cooperative sector. This led to the State exercising too much control, and cooperatives came to be seen as state agencies rather than independent organisations.
- The ICA developed into a global and more diversified organisation. It was no longer dominated by consumer cooperatives. It facilitated changes to its organisational structure to accommodate new cooperatives. It opened new international offices to accommodate the growth of cooperatives in developing countries. It established good relations with the United Nations and the ILO. It promoted formal reviews on cooperative identity conducted by Laidlaw and Book. These eventually led the ICA to update the ICA Principles in 1995.
- The international cooperative movement faced a crisis of identity. The findings from Laidlaw's 1980 report, the evidence from cooperative practice in developing countries, member apathy and lack of democratic governance in large and complex cooperatives, the conventional legal structures adopted by large cooperatives, and the different types of cooperatives with diverse goals, all contributed to cooperative members and the cooperative movement questioning the cooperative identity.

4.9 Questions

- Identify the various strategies, institutions, policies, and programmes developed by states, corporations, universities, and philanthropic organisations in promoting the capitalist-led international economic system. Why was this strategy successful? Why was the cooperative movement not able to counter this pro-capitalist strategy? What could the cooperative movement have done, or could do in the future, to promote an international economic system that better reflects the ideals of the cooperative movement?
- Examine the evolution of the State, the market, and corporations from 1945 to 1990. What were the threats and opportunities faced by cooperatives during the post-war boom and during the early period of neo-Liberalism?
- Consider the consumer cooperative movements of the United Kingdom, Sweden, Italy, and Japan and develop an 'ideal type' consumer cooperative model. What policies or laws would you propose to raise finance; establish a united movement with clear goals; engage with members; promote democratic management; to engage with the local community?
- Consider the consumer movements explored in this chapter. What are the key risks faced by consumer cooperatives? How would you go about identifying, mitigating, and monitoring the key risks faced by consumer cooperatives?
- Consider, evaluate and compare Mondragon's cooperative principles with the ICA cooperative principles and/or with the Wisconsin cooperative principles. According to

your values and experience, which of these three sets of cooperative principles could best represent the ideals, expectations, and values of the cooperative movement?

- Consider the role of the Mondragon Cooperative Bank (CLP) and compare it with the Cooperative Rural Banks (Raiffeisen Model) or the Credit Unions established in the United States. Which bank model best promotes cooperative principles and cooperative development? Which cooperative bank model makes the biggest impact on people, on cooperative development, and on local communities?
- Consider the key features of LNCM network of cooperatives. What are the advantages of this cooperative model compared to having individual cooperatives competing on their own? What are the most striking features of the LNCM cooperative model? What aspects of this model are transferable to the cooperative model operating in your country?
- Review the cooperative development approach in India and Tanzania. What were the key issues faced by the cooperative sector? If cooperatives had been more autonomous from the State, would they have been more successful?
- Compare and contrast the role that the State has performed in the United States during the New Deal period, in post-war Italy, In Mondragon, in Japan, and in India. What is the most appropriate role of the State in supporting cooperative development? Which state actions or policies have supported cooperative development, and which state actions or policies have been detrimental to cooperative development?
- Examine Laidlaw's report to the ICA Moscow Conference of 1980. Why are Laidlaw's findings important? Which finding would you prioritise in order to promote a viable cooperative movement? Which finding is most detrimental to the credibility of the cooperative movement? What measures would you put in place to prevent these practices from occurring?
- Consider the ICA's strategy, its organisational structure, and its key activities. Critically identify and discuss the areas where the ICA is adequately promoting cooperative development and the areas where the ICA could do more to promote cooperative development across the globe?
- Consider the cooperative enterprise models discussed in this chapter, and identify areas where cooperatives have been very innovative in developing their enterprise models. Innovation may include cooperative strategy, organisational structure, business culture, access to capital, managing change, governance arrangements, democratic structures and processes, relations between cooperatives, and so on.

Notes

1 This compares favourably to the 2.6 per cent achieved from 1870 to 1913; and the 1.9 per cent achieved from 1913 to 1950 (Kenwood and Lougheed 1983).

2 The World Bank data indicates that from 1974 to 1989 world economic growth ranged from 0.4 per cent to a high of 5.3 per cent whilst from 1961 to 1973 world economic growth ranged from 3.8 per cent to 6.6 per cent (The World Bank 2020).

3 In the United States from 1977 to 1989, the top 1 per cent of families received 70 per cent of the rise in average family income (Stretton 2000).

4 A cooperative enterprise model refers to the way a cooperative is organised to produce and sell goods and services in the market in order to meet the needs of its members. Cooperatives meet the economic, social, cultural and aspirational needs of their members by competing in the market on their own, or as a member of a second-tier cooperative. Whilst the term enterprise model is synonymous with the term business model, this book will opt to use the term cooperative model interchangeably with the term cooperative enterprise model.

5 The Central Association, Lega Nazionale delle Cooperative e Mutue (LNCM) is also known by its abbreviated title 'La Lega' (Ammirato 1996). In 1996, it changed its name to Legacoop. This book will use the abbreviated LNCM for events until 1996, and then use the new name Legacoop thereafter.

6 The 1947 cooperative law provided 25 per cent tax concession on consumer cooperative profits. The law of 1977 exempted 100 per cent of profits deposited into the indivisible reserve account until 2004. Since 2004, at least 65 per cent of consumer cooperative profits are taxed (Balboni 1991, Fici 2013).

7 In 1971, a government law allowed cooperative members to lend money to consumer cooperatives with the incentive of having to pay a flat tax on returns equivalent to 12.5 per cent, rather than the flat tax of 25 per cent charged on bank deposits (Zevi 1990).

8 Co.Ind is the cooperative owned manufacturing company. In 1990, it employed 86 people. It produced coffee, tea, and cocoa, and is a shareholder in other companies. In later years, it diversified its production (Battilani 2001).

9 The information on the Japan Consumer Cooperative movement reflects the work of Professor Akira Kurimoto unless otherwise stated. Please refer to the following two articles: Kurimoto (2017, 2020).

10 It is important to note that the technical School is open to all students, and Ikerlan's research and development activity serves all Basque businesses.

11 For instance, FIAT received over 1.5 billion dollars to build a factory in Southern Italy. This is much more than the amount spent on the job-creation programmes mentioned in this Section. Further, the Department of Treasury noted that cooperatives received 1.75 per cent of the total grants and tax exemptions that the State makes available to business and non-business entities (Ammirato 1996). The State never approved LNCM to open its own banks or insurance company. LCNM was able to start Unipol because it bought the insurance licence from a private company but the government never granted it a new licence (Mazzoli 2005, Zamagni and Felice 2006).

12 The British colonial government applied the Indian model of cooperation with a unitary law and a powerful register throughout the British colonies of Africa and South East Asia (Birchall 2011).

13 In the mid-1980s, 40 per cent of the rural population still lived in poverty and 55 per cent of villagers earned less than 300 USD per annum (Wang 1994).

14 Dane Kennedy informs us that new nation states often exacerbated regional, occupational, linguistic, ethnic, and other differences among distinct communities within colonies. He notes that from 1945 to 1999, there have been 127 civil wars and 25 interstate wars in the same period. Those civil wars produced 16.2 million casualties, vastly outnumbering the 3.3 million who died in interstate wars (Kennedy 2016).

15 The ICA established the International Organisation of Industrial and Service Co-operatives in 1947; the International Co-operative Agricultural Organisation in 1951; the International Cooperative Housing committee in 1952; the International Co-operative Fisheries Organisations in 1966; The International Association of Tourism Co-operative in 1976 (International Cooperative Alliance 2022).

References

ALC India. 2019. *Autonomy and Independence of Cooperatives in India*. New Delhi: International Cooperative Alliance.

Allen, Robert C. 2011. *Global Economic History*. Oxford: Oxford University Press.

Amatori, Franco, and Andrea Colli. 2011. *Business History*. Routledge: New York.

Amdam, Rolv Petter. 2009. "Business Education." In *The Oxford Handbook of Business History*, by Geoffrey G Jones and Jonathon Zetlin, 581–602. Oxford: Oxford University Press.

———. 2019. "The Internationalization of Executive Education." In *The Routledge Companion to the Makers of Global Business*, by Teresa da Silva Lopes, Christina Lubinski and Heidi JS Tworek, 125–137. London: Taylor Francis Group.

Ammirato, Piero. 1996. *La Lega: The Making of a Successful Cooperative Network*. Aldershot: Dartmouth Publishing Company.

———. 2018. *The Growth of Italian Cooperatives: Innovation, Resilience and Social Responsibility*. New York: Routledge.

ANCC. 1990. *La Cooperazione dei Consumatori*. Rome: Associazione Nazionale Cooperative dei Consumatori (ANCC).

Armstrong, Philip, Andrew Glyn, and John Harrison. 1984. *Capitalism Since World War II*. London: Fontana Paperbacks.

Australian Quality Council. 2000. *Business Excellence: An Overview*. Australia: Australian Quality Council.

Axworthy, Chris. 1985. *Worker Cooperatives in Mondragon, the UK and France: Some Reflections*. Working Paper, Saskatchewan: Centre for the Studies of Cooperatives, University of Sasketchewan.

Balboni, Michele. 1991. "L'impresa Cooperativa: Aspetti Legislativi e Fiscali." In *Il Movimento, Il Sistema, La rete: Un Decennio di Cambiamenti nelle Imprese Cooperative*, by Carella Francesco, 56–58. Bologna: Editrice Emilia Romagna.

Barandarian, Xabier, and Javier Lezaun. 2017. "The Mondragon Experience." In *The Oxford Handbook of Mutual, Cooperative and Co-Owned Business*, by Jonathon Michie, Joseph R Blasi and Carlo Borzaga, Chapter 19. Oxford: Oxford University Press.

Barberini, Ivano. 2009. *Come Vola il Calabrone*. Milano: Baldini, Castoldi Calai editore.

Battilani, Patrizia. 2001. *CoInd: Un Successo Costruito sulla Diversita`*. Bologna: Il Mulino.

———. 2017. "Consumer Co-operation in Italy: A Network of Co-operatives with a Multi-class Constituency." In *A Global History of Consumer Co-operation since 1850*, by Mary Hilson, Silke Neunsinger and Greg Patmore, 584–613. Leiden: Brill.

Battilani, Patrizia, and Vera Zamagni. 2010. *The Managerial Transformation of Italian Co-operative Enterprises: 1946–2010*. Working Paper DSE N° 789, Bologna: University of Bologna.

Bayo, Claudia Sanchez. 2019. "A Century of ILO Interaction with the Cooperative Movement." In *Cooperatives and the World of Work*, by Bruno Roelants, 13–33. London: Taylor and Francis Group.

Berlinguer, Enrico. 1982. "Le Ragioni della Terza Via." In *La Terza Via: Una Nuova Fase di Lotta per il Socialismo in Italia e in Europa*, by Partito Comunista Italiano, 4–14. Rome: Partito Comunista Italiano.

Birch, RC. 1974. *The Shaping of the Welfare State*. Harlow: Longman Group Limited.

Birchall, Johnston. 2011. *People-Centred Businesses*. London: Palgrave MacMillan.

Birchall, Johnstone, and Richard Simmons. 2010. "The Cooperative Reform Process in Tanzania and Sri Lanka." *Annals of Public and Cooperative Economics* 467–500.

Bonfante, Guido. 1981. "La Legislazione Cooperativistica." In *Il Movimento Cooperativo in Italian: Storia e Problemi*, by Giulio Sapelli, Torino: Einaudi Editore.

———. 2011. *Manuale di Diritto Cooperativo*. Bologna: Zanichelli.

Braverman, Avishay, J. Luis Guasch, Monika Huppi, and Lorenz Pohlmeier. 1991. *Promoting Rural Cooperatives in Developing Countries: The Case of Sub-Saharan Africa*. Discussion Paper, Washington: The World Bank.

Brouder, Alan. 2010. "International Cooperative Alliance." In *Handbook of Transnational Economic Governance Regimes*, by Christian Tietje and Alan Brouder, 155–167. Leiden: Brill-Nijhoff.

Bulgarelli, Marco. 2006. "Coopfond e la Nuova Promozione Cooperativa." In *La Promozione Cooperativa: Coopfoond tra Mercato e Solidarieta`*, by Marco Bulgarelli and Mario Viviani, 39–80. Bologna : Il Mulino.

Casali, Antonio. 2000. *Per Una Storia di Coop Italia: Mauro Cesari (1926–1968)*. Bologna: Il Mulino.

Chang, Ha-Joon. 2014. *Economics: The User's Guide*. London: Penguin Books.

Clayre, Alasdair. 1980. "Some Aspects of the Mondragon Federation." In *The Political Economy of Co-operation and Participation*, by Alasdair Clayre, 171–173. Oxford: Oxford University Press.

Corcoran, Hazel, and David Wilson. 2010. *The Worker Co-operative Movements in Italy, Mondragon and France: Context, Success Factors and Lessons*. Calgary: Canadian Worker Cooperative Federation.

Cornforth, Chris, Alan Thomas, Jenny Lewis, and Roger Spear. 1988. *Developing Successful Worker Cooperatives*. London: Sage Publications.

Crosland, Anthony. 1956. *The Future of Socialism*. London: Constable.

Dash, Tapas R. 2021. "Emerging Issues in the Management of Cooperatives in India." In *Cooperatives in the Global Economy*, by Tapas R Dash, 249–260. London: Lexington Books.

Degen, Bernard. 2017. "Consumer Societies in Switzerland: From Local Self-Help Organizations to a Single National Co-operative." In *A Global History of Consumer Co-operation since 1850*, by Mary Hilson, Silke Neunsinger and Greg Patmore, Chapter 24. Leiden: Brill.

Develtere, Patrick. 2008. "Cooperative Development in Africa up to the 1990s." In *Cooperating Out of Poverty: The Renaissance of the African Cooperative Movement*, by Patrick Develtere, Ignace Pollet and Fredrick Wanyama, 1–37. Geneva: International Labour Organization.

———. 2003. *Co-operatives and Development: Towards a Social Movement Perspective*. Occasional Paper for the Centre for the Studies of Cooperatives, Saskatchewan: University of Saskatoon.

Ekberg, Espen. 2012. "Organization: Top Down or Bottom up? The Organizational Development of Consumer Cooperatives, 1950–2000." In *The Cooperative Business Movement, 1950 to the Present*, by Harm Schroter and Patrizia Battilani, 222–242. Cambridge: Cambridge University Press.

———. 2017. "Against the Tide: Understanding the Commercial." In *A Global History of Consumer Co-operation since 1850*, by Mary Hilson, Silke Neunsinger and Greg Patmore, 698–726. Leiden: Brill.

Evans, James R, and WIlliam M Lindsay. 2008. *Managing for Quality and Performance Excellence*. Mason: Thomson South-Western.

Fairbairn, Brett. 2004. "History of Cooperatives." In *Cooperatives and Local Development Theory and Applications for the 21st Century*, by Christopher D Merrett and Norman Walzer, Chapter 2. London: Taylor and Francis.

Felice, Emanuele. 2010. "The Strategies and Development of the CNS." In *Cooperation Network Service*, by Patrizia Battilani and Giuliana Bertagnoni, 65–117. Lancaster: Crucible Books.

Fici, Antonio. 2013. "Italy." In *International Handbook of Cooperative Law*, by Dante Cracogna, Antonio Fici and Hagen Henry, 479–502. Heidelberg: Springer.

Genco, Roberto. 2011. *Il Diritto delle Societa' Cooperative*. Bologna: Il Mulino.

Gombi, Mario. 1990. "Cooperazione tra Dettaglianti:Storia di un Successo." In *Emilia-Romagna Terra di Cooperazione*, by Angelo Varni, 252–254. Bologna: Edizioni Tecniche Associate.

Granata, Mattia. 2019. "Breve Storia dell'International Cooperative Alliance." In *Identita` e Valori dell'Impresa Cooperativa: Scritti e Discorsi di Ivano Barberini*, by Michele Dorigatti and Tito Menzani, 25–42. Soveria Mannelli: Rubbettino Editore.

Hall, Peter, and David Soskice. 2001. *Varieties of Capitalism*. Oxford: Oxford University Press.

Hicks, Alexander. 1999. *Social Democracy and Welfare Capitalism*. Ithaca: Cornell University.

Hobsbawm, Eric. 1994. *Age of Extremes: The Short History of the Twentieth Century 1914–1991*. London: Penguin.

Hoyt, Ann, and Tito Menzani. 2012. "The International Cooperative Movement: a Quite Giant." In *The Cooperative Movement, 1950 to the Present*, by Harm G Svchroter and Patrizia Battilani, Chapter 1. Cambridge: Cambridge University Press.

International Cooperative Alliance. 2022. *History of the Alliance*. Accessed May 7, 2022. https://www.ica.coop/en/history-alliance.

Kalmi, Panu. 2007. "The Disappearance of Cooperatives from Economics Textbooks." *Cambridge Journal of Economics* 625–647.

Kennedy, Dane. 2016. *Decolonization: A Very Short Introduction*. Oxford: Oxford University Press.

Kenwood, AG, and AL Lougheed. 1983. *The Growth of the International Economy*. London: Allen and Unwin.

Kurimoto, Akira. 2017. "Building Consumer Democracy: The Trajectory of Consumer Co-operation in Japan." In *A Global History of Consumer Co-operation since 1850*, by Mary Hilson, Silke Neunsinger and Greg Patmore, 668–697. Leiden: Brill.

———. 2020. "Consumer Cooperatives' Model in Japan." In *Waking the Asian Pacific Co-operative Potential*, by Morris Altman, Anthony Jensen, Akira Kurimoto, Robby Tulus, Yashavantha Dongre and Seungkwon Jang, Chapter 21. London: Academic Press.

Laidlaw, AF. 1980. *Cooperatives in the Year 2000*. A paper prepared for the 27th Congress of the International Cooperative Alliance, Moscow: International Cooperative Alliance.

Lambersens, Simon, Amélie Artis, and Danièle Demoustier. 2017. "History of Consumer Co-operatives in France: From the Conquest of Consumption by the Masses to the Challenge of Mass Consumption." In *A Global History of Consumer Co-operation Since 1850*, by Mary Hilson, Silke Neunsinger and Greg Patmore, 99–120. Leiden: Brill.

Landes, David S. 2003. *The Unbound Prometheus*. Cambridge: Cambridge University Press.

Lega Nazionale Delle Cooperative e Mutue. 1990. *Il Sistema Finanziario delle Cooperative*. Bologna: Lega Nazionale Delle Cooperative e Mutue.

LNCM. 1991. *Documento Politico: 33mo Congresso Nazionale Roma 1991*. Congress Report, Roma: Lega Nazionale Delle Cooperative e Mutue.

MacPherson, Ian. 2008. "The Cooperative Movement and the Social Economy Traditions: Reflections on the Mingling of Broad Visions." *Annals of Public and Cooperative Economics* 625–642.

———. 2012. "What Is the End Purpose of It All?": The Centrality of Values for Cooperative Success in the Marketplace"." In *The Cooperative Business Movement, 1950 to the Present*, by Harm G Schroter and Patrizia Battilani, 107–140. Cambridge: Cambridge University Press.

Mazzoli, Enea. 2005. "Gli Sviluppi della Cooperazione Italiana dal Dopoguerra ad Oggi. Ripercorsi di un Protagonista." In *Verso unaNuova teoria sulla Cooperazione*, by Enea Mazzoli and Stefano Zamagni, 57–95. Bologna: Il Mulino.

McGraw, Thoma K. 1995. *Creating Modern Capitalism*. Boston: Harvard University Press.

Meek, Christopher, and Warner Woodworth. 1990. "Technical Training and Enterprise: Mondragon's Educational System and Implications for Other Cooperatives." *Economic and Industrial Democracy* 505–528.

Mendell, Marguerite. 2015. "Democratising Capital: Social and Solidarity Finance in Quebec." In *Social Economy in China and the World*, by Ngai Pun, 94–114. London: Taylor & Francis Group.

Modhorst, Mads. 2014. "Arla and Danish National Identity." *Business History* 116–133.

Molina, Fernando, and Antonio Miguez. 2008. "The Origins of Mondragon: Catholic Co-Operativism and Social Movement in a Basque." *Social History* 284–298.

Mondragon Corporation. 2012. *Corporate Management Model*. Mondragon: Mondragon Corporation.

Morrison, Roy. 1991. *We Build the Road as we Travel*. Santa Cruz: New Society Publishers.

Munkner, Hans-H. 2013. "Germany." In *International Handbook of Cooperative Law*, by Dante Cracogna, Antonio Fici and Hagen Henry, 413–429. Heidelberg: Springer.

Oakshott, Robert. 1978. *The Case for Workers' Cooperatives*. London: Routledge and Keegan Paul.

Patmore, Greg, and Nikola Belnave. 2018. *A Global History of Co-Operative Business*. London: Routledge.

Pestoff, Victor. 2012. "Hybrid Tendencies in Consumer Co-operatives: The Case of Sweden." In *The Co-operative Model in Practice*, by Diarmuid McDonnell and Elizabeth Macknight, Chapter 7. Aberdeen: CETS.

Petralia, Rino. 1988. *Movimento Cooperativo: Prospettive e Problemi*. Rome: Lega Nazionale delle Cooperative e Mutue.

Prinz, Michael. 2017. "German Co-operatives: Rise and Fall 1850–1970." In *A Global History of Consumer Co-operation since 1850*, by Mary Hilson, Silke Neunsinger and Greg Patmore, 243–266. Leiden: Brill.

Putzolu, Placido. 1991. "Offerta Diversificata e Unione delle Forze." *La Cooperazione Italiana* 31.

Quarter, Jack. 1989. "Starting Worker-Owned Enterprises: Problems and Prospects." In *Partners in Enterprises: The Worker Ownership Phenomenon*, by Jack Quarter and George Melnyk, 33–58. Montreal: Black Rose Books.

SAI. 2007. *The Business Excellence Framework*. Sydney: SAI Global Limited.

Sassoon, Donald. 1997. *One Hundred Years of Socialism*. London: Harper Collins.

Secchi, Corrado. 2017. "Affluence and Decline: Consumer Co-operatives." In *A Global History of Consumer Co-operation since 1850*, by Mary Hilson, Silke Neunsinger and Greg Patmore, 527–547. Leiden: Brill.

Shaffer, Jack. 1999. *Historical Dictionary of the Cooperative Movement*. London: The Scarecrow Press.

Smith, Stephen. 2001. *Blooming Alone or Wilting Alone? Network Externalities and the Mondragon and Lega Cooperative Networks*. UN-WIDER Working Paper 2001-27, New York: United Nations University.

Soulage, François. 2011. "France: an Endeavour in Enterprise Transformation." In *Beyond the Crisis: Cooperatives, Work, Finance*, by Alberto Zevi, Antonio Zanotti, François Soulage and Adrian Zelaia, 155–196. Brussels: Cecop Publications.

Steger, Manfred. 2020. *Globalization*. Oxford: Oxford University Press.

Stretton, Hugh. 2000. *Economics: a New Introduction*. Sydney: University of New South Wales.

Tassinari, Vincenzo. 2015. *Noi, Le Coop Rosse: Tra Supermercati e Riforme Mancate*. Soveria Mannelli: Rubbettino.

———. 1991. *Relazione del Presidente del Consiglio di Amministrazione*. Presentation at Coop Italia Annual General Assembly, Bologna: Coop Italia.

The World Bank. 2020. *World Bank Data*. Accessed March 17, 2022. https://data.worldbank.org/indicator/NY.GDP.MKTP.KD.ZG?end=2020&start=1961&view=chart.

Thomas, Henk, and Chris Logan. 1982. *Mondragon: An Economic Analysis*. London: George Allen and Unwin.

Vaswani, L K. 2012. "Government to Governance: The Challenge of Co-operative Revival in India." In *Hidden Alternative: Co-Operative Values, Past, Present and Future*, by Anthony Webster and David Stewart, John K. Walton, Linda Shaw Alyson Brown, 266–287. New York: United Nations University Press.

Viviani, Mario. 2013. *Piccola Guida Alla Cooperazione*. Soveria Mannelli: Rubbettino.

Viviani, Mario, and Roberto Dessi. 2005. *Conad: Prudenti capitani e Bravi Commercianti*. Bologna: Il Mulino.

Wang, James. 1994. *Comparative Asian Politics:Power, Politics and Change*. New Jersey: Prentice Hall International Editions.

Whyte, William Foote. 1995. "Learning from the Mondragon Experience." *Studies in Comparative International Development*, 58–67.

Whyte, William Foote, and Kathleen King Whyte. 1991. *Making Mondragon*. Ithaca: ILR Press.

Wilson, John, Anthony Webster, and Rachael Vorberg-Rugh. 2013. *Building Co-operation: A Business History of the Co-operative Group, 1863–2013*. Oxford: Oxford University Press.

Yergin, Daniel, and Joseph Janislaw. 1998. *The Commanding Heights: The Battle for the World Economy*. New York: Simon Schuster.

Zabaleta, Ma Jesus. 1986. "Mondragon: Un'Esperienza Integrata." In *Cooperare e Competere*, by Avitabile Anna, 18–30. Milano: Feltrinelli Editore.

Zamagni, Vera. 2012. "A World of Variations: Sectors and Forms." In *The Cooperative Business Movement: 1950 to the Present*, by Harm Schroter and Patrizia Battilani, Chapter 2. Cambridge: Cambridge University Press.

Zamagni, Vera, and Emanuele Felice. 2006. *Oltre il Secolo: La Transformazione del Sistema Cooperativo Legacoop Alla Fine del Secondo Millennio*. Bologna: Il Mulino.

Zamagni, Vera, Patrizia Battilani, and Antonio Casali. 2004. *La Cooperazione di Consumo in Italia*. Bologna: Il Mulino.

Zan, Stefano. 1982. *La Cooperazione In Italia: Strutture, Strategie e Sviluppo della Lega Nazionale delle Cooperative e Mutue*. Bari: De Donato.

Zangheri, Renato, Giuseppe Galasso, and Valerio Castronovo. 1987. *Storia del Movimento Cooperativo in Italia*. Turin: Giulio Einaudi Editore.

Zeuli, Kimberley A., and Robert Cropp. 2004. *Cooperatives: Principles and Practices in the 21st Century*. Wisconsin: University of Wisconsin Centre for Cooperatives.

Zevi, Alberto. 1990. "The Financing of Cooperatives in Italy." *Annals of Public and Cooperative Economies* 353–365.

Zevi, Alberto, Antonio Zanotti, Francois Soulage, and Adrian Zelaia. 2011. *Beyond the Crisis: Cooperatives, Work and Finance*. Brussels: Cecop Publications.

Zotti, Nicola. 1983. *Lega Nazionale delle Cooperative: la sua Storia, la sua Immaggine, la sua Politica*. Rome: Editrice Cooperativa.

5 Cooperatives and the Global Economy since 1990

This chapter examines how cooperatives have evolved since 1990. The term globalisation refers to a higher level of global trade, faster movement of capital and foreign direct investment between many more countries, standardised products sold globally that lead to economies of scale, and a greater number of multinational corporations that operate in more than one country (Levitt 1983, Steger 2020). The global market expanded when countries that were previously part of the Soviet Union, China, and developing countries, opened their economies to those of developed countries. This development provided threats and opportunities for cooperatives but, above all, it required cooperatives to manage change and innovate their cooperative enterprise model.[1]

There are six parts to this chapter. Part 5.1 analyses the political and economic context within which cooperatives have operated since 1990. It will assess the neo-Liberal political and economic policies and their institutions; the impact of neo-Liberalism on the economy and society; and how states and corporations have responded to the challenges posed by neo-Liberalism, globalisation, and economic crisis. Part 5.2 explores how cooperatives have responded to globalisation. It will assess how cooperatives have achieved economies of scale and improved access to capital. It will explore the cooperative enterprise models. It will assess the new types of cooperative enterprises that emerged in the 1990s, such as worker-buyouts (WBOs), social welfare cooperatives, platform cooperatives, and ethical banking. Part 5.3 explores the cooperative development models (CDMs)[2] of Trento, Quebec, Japan, the General Confederation of Société Coopérative et Participative (CG-SCOP) in France, and the emerging Wonju Cooperative Network. Part 5.4 will explore the role of the International Cooperative Alliance (ICA) in promoting cooperative development and cooperative principles and in dealing with emerging cooperative issues. Part 5.5 will provide a summary of the chapter, and Part 5.6 will provide a set of questions for readers to consider.

Readers will gain an appreciation of how the world political economy has evolved during this period and how cooperatives have responded to meet economic and social challenges. This chapter will enable readers to:

- Appreciate the evolution of capitalist-led market economies (CMEs), the evolving role of the State and corporations at different stages of economic development, the impact that markets have on societies, and the opportunities and threats to cooperative development.
- Understand how some cooperatives have adopted traditional cooperative approaches to compete in the market, such as second-tier structures and by limiting the power of capital.

DOI: 10.4324/9781003269533-5

- Explore how some cooperatives have used dual structures combining traditional cooperative approaches alongside conventional legal structures. In these instances, external capital has been given a legitimate role, including access to limited voting rights.
- Appreciate how new types of cooperatives have developed to meet the emerging needs of society. These new experiences include social cooperatives providing welfare services; community cooperatives providing services to the whole community and not just members; WBOs of private enterprises; and the emerging ethical banking movement.
- Analyse the reasons that have led cooperatives to demutualise, the impact this has on the cooperative movement, and consider ways to prevent demutualisation from re-occurring.
- Consider, compare and contrast the CDMs operating in France, Japan, Korea, Quebec, and Trento.
- Examine the role of the ICA in coordinating the cooperative movement and in promoting cooperative development and cooperative principles across the globe.

5.1 Globalisation

The neo-Liberal model proceeded triumphantly after 1989. The Soviet Union disintegrated and accepted a CMEs. China promoted a mixed economy but maintained a large state sector; it attracted foreign direct investment, accepted private property, and legitimised private enterprises. There was broad consensus in favour of international trade and the neo-Liberal economic framework. The International Monetary Fund (IMF), the World Bank, and the World Trade Organization (WTO) promoted neo-Liberal policies. These organisations imposed 'Washington Consensus' policies worldwide that included austerity measures, the privatisation of state-owned enterprises, and the liberalisation of markets. More specifically, they included balanced budgets; privatisation; deregulation; free movement of financial resources; market-determined exchange rates and interest rates; reduction in public spending; trade liberalisation and reduction of licencing regimes and tariffs; attracting foreign direct investment; and the protection of private property (Steger and Roy 2015).

5.1.1 Neo-Liberalism

Elected governments, new trading blocs, and international organisations all promoted neo-Liberal policies. The United States deregulated the financial sector and repealed the *Glass-Steagall Act* of 1933, allowing banks to operate as commercial and investment banks. Europe and North America developed major trading blocs to advance trade between member states. To this end, the European Union signed the Maastricht Treaty,[3] and the United States, Canada, and Mexico signed the North America Free Trade Agreement. Other trading blocs emerged in the Asia Pacific Region (Asia-Pacific Economic Cooperation) and South America (Southern Common Market). The IMF and the World Bank forced debtor countries to implement neo-Liberal policies as a condition for its financial support. They also imposed neo-Liberal policies on Russia, Brazil, Mexico, Malaysia, Indonesia, and Thailand following their currency crisis of 1995. The IMF forced Korea to open up its capital markets and reduce trade barriers in 1997. From the 1990s, market-based solutions were imposed on many Socialist-led developing countries. The programme was renamed the *Structural Adjustment Program*, but it contained the same neo-Liberal policies (Chang 2014, Stiglitz 2018).

The neo-Liberal approach to governing national economies and world trade transferred more power to business. Corporations could transfer capital to low-wage, low-taxing countries[4] and pressure governments to lower taxes and deregulate the economy. The flow of Foreign Direct Investment increased from 75 billion USD per annum in the 1980s to 1.5 trillion USD from 2008 to 2012 (Chang 2014). Institutional investors had invested 35 trillion USD by 2000 and controlled more than half of all equity issued in the United States (Amatori and Colli 2011). Multinational companies[5] (MNCs) grew from 7,000 in 1970 to over 100,000 in 2015. They controlled world trade and output. MNCs increased their share of world trade from 40 per cent in 2000 (Jones 2008) to 70 per cent in 2019, and the top 200 MNCs produced 50 per cent of the world's industrial output (Steger 2020).[6]

The neo-Liberal strategy expanded the world economy and increased world trade. The world Gross Domestic Product (GDP) continued to grow, but not as high as during the golden age. The World Bank indicates that from 1990 to 2020 the world economy grew by more than 4 per cent on six occasions, and achieved negative growth on two occasions (World Bank 2022).[7] World trade increased from 12 per cent of the world GDP in the 1960s to 29 per cent by 2011 (Chang 2014), whilst the value of world trade increased from 57 billion USD in 1947 to 19.5 trillion USD by 2018 (Steger 2020).

5.1.2 *Issues with Neo-Liberalism*

The Washington Consensus strategies revealed weaknesses and caused instability. The neo-Liberal policies led to constant financial crises around the world, a greater level of inequalities, and the weakening of democracy. Financial crises took place all over the world, commencing in Sweden, Finland and Norway in the early 1990s, then Mexico from 1994 to 1995, then the Asian economies in 1997, then Russia in 1998, then Brazil in 1999, and then Argentina in 2002 (Chang 2014). In 2007, the world experienced the Global Financial Crisis (GFC) caused by the collapse of the housing market in the United States. It affected banks, insurance companies, and investment banks, and when banks stopped lending, the crisis worsened. In 2009–2010 the Greek government faced financial difficulties. The GFC caused some 80 million people around the world to lose their jobs, and the unemployment rate five years after the crisis was still 7–8 per cent in Sweden, the United States, and Britain. In Southern Europe, it was much higher, especially among the young (Chang 2014, Frieden 2020).

Neo-Liberal policies had a negative impact on wealth distribution. Its focus on individualism, the market, and on profit maximisation, along with the limited influence of Social Democracy and the trade union movement, led to higher levels of inequalities. Social Democracy focussed on distributing wealth when it could, and it was no longer an alternative to Capitalism. As a result, their appeal waned across the world. Trade Union membership declined from 21 per cent of the workforce across Organisation for Economic Cooperation and Development (OECD) countries in 1999 to 17 per cent in 2014 (Sassoon 2019). Without effective countervailing powers, business and the wealthy kept more of the profits (Reich 2016). In 2017, Oxfam revealed that 1 per cent of the world's population owned more wealth than the remaining 99 per cent (Oxfam 2017). Robert Reich noted that the richest 400 US citizens have more wealth than 50 per cent of US citizens (Reich 2016). In 2015, the pay of US CEOs was 204 times more than the pay of workers (Picketty 2014). Further confirmation of this bleak reality is the fact that in 2019, 40 per cent of US families did not have sufficient cash to pay for a 400 USD emergency (Bakan 2020).

Wealth inequalities have also had an impact on politics and democracy. The very wealthy and corporations have a greater capacity to influence elected officials and government decisions. Henderson notes that in the United States, proposals supported by 90 per cent of the general population are no more likely to pass than proposals supported by 10 per cent of the population, but when the rich wanted something done, they managed to get it done (Henderson 2020). The negative effects of globalisation have led to the rise of Populist movements that questioned free trade and the free movement of business, capital, and people. Populists want to protect local economies and local identity and have reverted to tariff protection as a way to protect jobs (Steger and Roy 2015, Mudde and Kaltwasser 2017).

5.1.3 Dealing with Market Failures

The State, corporations, and cooperatives all responded to the GFC in their own distinct way. The deregulated market could not solve the problems arising out of the GFC, so the State had to intervene. States had privatised state-owned enterprises and outsourced government services, but were still managing the economy through regulations, the provision of services, and the transfer of payments to those in need. In 2020, the majority of OECD governments collected revenue that exceeded 40 per cent of the GDP and spent more than 40 per cent of the GDP.[8] In Western Europe, the State employs 15–20 per cent of the workforce (Picketty 2014). The State's response to the GFC was to rescue the market and install confidence into the system. The United States, Europe, and Britain alone injected 12 trillion USD into the economy. The money was used to buy–up companies, buy corporate bonds, offer guarantees to bank depositors, initiate public works programmes, and transfer payments to families in need (Steger and Roy 2015).[9] The State intervened to save Capitalism, but the neo-Liberal capitalist-led system remained in place.

The corporations adopted five broad approaches. First, corporations continued to promote the same neo-Liberal policies through intellectuals, business associations, academic think tanks, major newspapers, and television stations across the world. Second, businesses continued to grow their market share and grow their dimension. In 2011, for instance, just over 1,300 MNCs controlled the majority of the world's blue-chip companies; and in 2018, MNCs spent a further 4.6 trillion USD on mergers and acquisitions (Steger 2020). Third, business sought direct and indirect help from the State during the GFC, and during the COVID-19-led crisis of 2020. Fourth, corporations attempted to redefine the image of Capitalism and the corporation from one focussed on profit maximisation to one focussed on stakeholders. Business promoted this strategy via business associations, business leaders, and intellectuals. The Business Roundtable in 2019 promoted 'Stakeholder Capitalism', where the interests of workers, the community, and the environment are also considered. The 'Inclusive Capitalism' group promoted a capitalist system that is equitable, inclusive, and sustainable.[10] The Davos conference suggested that corporations are to fill the void left by governments. Gates promoted 'Creative Capitalism', arguing that Capitalism rather than philanthropy can solve the world's biggest problems. In his vision, the role of government is to create incentives for business activity to solve the problems of the poor (Bakan 2020). Porter promoted the concept of 'Shared Value'. Within this concept, businesses embed social considerations into the decision-making process, enabling them to achieve profit maximisation whilst promoting social and community benefits at the same time (Porter 2011). The fifth approach came from institutional investors who promoted investment in companies that met environmental, social, and governance (ESG) criteria. In 2018, ESG-related investment totalled 19 trillion USD, 20 per cent of the total funds invested in the US stock market (Henderson 2020). Bakan, Reich, and Stiglitz, however, make a very strong argument that the bottom line of all these concepts is to expand the power of business, to continue to maximise profits, and to reduce the power of governments (Reich 2016, Stiglitz 2019, Bakan 2020).

5.1.4 Implications for Cooperatives

Globalisation and neo-Liberalism posed great challenges for the cooperative movement. The size, competitiveness, and multinational reach of corporations made it more difficult for cooperatives to compete in world markets. The language used by corporations about inclusiveness, shared value, and social responsibility was closer to the language used by cooperatives. Social Democracy no longer posed a threat to Capitalism, nor did they propose alternative societies where cooperatives could perform a major role. Society's overall support for individualism, profit maximisation, and Capitalism marginalised cooperatives. As Sassoon correctly noted, the strength of Capitalism was clearly on display since, during the GFC, everyone rushed to save the same system that caused it (Sassoon 2019).

This period, however, also offered opportunities for a cooperative movement whose inherent values and behaviours mitigate the negative consequences of globalisation and corporate behaviour. The cooperative sector went on to portray itself as anti-cyclic because during the GFC: it continued to grow; cooperative banks continued to lend money; worker cooperatives shared work instead of sacking people; consumer cooperatives continued to keep prices low; worker cooperatives took over private enterprises in crisis; and social cooperatives were relieving Welfare State failures. Cooperatives were considered enterprises that could mitigate wealth inequalities via policies that kept a portion of profits in indivisible reserves, policies that limited the remuneration of capital, and policies that limited salary differentials between management and employees.

5.2 Cooperatives and Globalisation

The cooperative sector actively responded to the challenges of globalisation, neo-Liberal policies, and competition from corporations. First, cooperatives continued to grow via organic growth, mergers, and acquisitions to achieve economies of scale. Second, cooperatives developed new ways to access capital. Third, cooperatives managed change via a variety of enterprise models. This included strengthening the traditional cooperative model, forming cooperative corporations, forming New Generation Cooperatives (NGCs), and forming a cooperative group of companies. Fourth, some cooperatives demutualised. Fifth, new types of cooperatives were formed to meet emerging needs. These included WBOs of private enterprises, social cooperatives operating in the welfare sector, platform cooperatives, and ethical banking.

5.2.1 Economies of Scale

Cooperatives focussed on becoming larger and to achieve economies of scale. This strategy lowered costs, and led to a diversification of products, services, and markets, and made cooperatives more competitive.

The consumer sector improved competitiveness by forming central wholesale associations and by creating larger cooperative societies. In 2001, the United Kingdom's

Cooperative Wholesale Society (CWS) and the Cooperative Retail Service Society merged to form the Cooperative Group. The CWS Group merged with other cooperative societies, and by 2010, it conducted 85 per cent of all cooperative trade. Policies focussing on food, better retail typology, ethical products, and the reinstatement of the dividend increased its market share from 5.5 per cent in 1990 to 8 per cent by 2010 (Ekberg 2012, Wilson, Webster and Vorberg-Rugh 2013). The Swedish cooperative sector concentrated its operations: in 1990, it associated 120 societies with 2.1 million members, but by 2010, it counted 28 societies with 3.7 million members (Pestoff 2012, Kooperativa Förbundet 2022). In Switzerland, consumer societies formed one central cooperative in 2001, with 2.5 million members by 2020 (Degen 2017, Coop Group 2021). In 1993, The Japanese consumer movement comprised 663 cooperatives with more than 16 million members. In 2020, it numbered 428 cooperatives with over 25 million members. The top ten cooperatives contributed over 50 per cent of its total turnover (Hoyt and Menzani 2012, JCCU 2022). In 2018, Coop Italia, the national consumer wholesaler in Italy, serviced just 83 cooperatives, compared to the 431 it serviced in 1990. The top seven cooperatives produced 95 per cent of the total turnover (ANCC 2018).

The cooperative banks in Europe and North America pursued policies of mergers leading to fewer cooperatives with a larger asset base. These policies reduced costs, created larger banks, and improved competitiveness. The idea of creating larger units came from farsighted leadership groups; it came from cooperative banks in economic difficulties seeking to survive via a merger with a larger cooperative bank; and it also came from government regulations seeking to create larger cooperative banks (Goglio and Palmi 2017, McKillop et al. 2020). In Germany, cooperative banks accelerated mergers which reduced the number of banks from 2,514 in 1996 to 772 in 2021. Each bank increased its assets from 140 million euros in 1993 to 790 million euros in 2016. In 2016, the Raiffeisen banks and the Volksbanks merged to create one Central Bank (Blisse and Hummel 2017, BRV 2022). In the Netherlands, Rabobank and the 100 autonomous local cooperative banks merged in January 2016. The 100 cooperative banks became operating units of the new central organisation (Poli 2019). The three French cooperative associations maintained their regional banks steady from 83 in 2003 to 86 in 2020 but increased their combined membership from 14 million to over 27 million members (Marchetti and Sabetta 2010, EACB 2019). In Italy, there were 788 cooperative banks in 1988 but only 289 in 2017 (Carretta and Boscia 2009, Poli 2019). From 1995 to 2020, the United States witnessed a reduction in credit unions from 11,880 to 5,206, an increase in membership from 71 million to 125 million, and an increase in assets from 336 billion USD to 1.8 trillion USD (Hoyt and Menzani 2012, WOCCU 2020). Australia witnessed a reduction in credit unions from 293 in 1995 to 64 in 2020, but with an increase in membership from 3.2 to 5.2 million (Jain, Keneley and Thomson 2015, WOCCU 2020). Canada's credit unions embarked on a similar trajectory: from 905 credit unions in 1995 to 449 in 2020, whilst members increased from 4.1 million to 10.6 million (Hoyt and Menzani 2012, WOCCU 2020).

Agricultural cooperatives also increased the size of each cooperative to achieve economies of scale. Denmark has achieved a high level of concentration following decades of mergers. In 1960, there were more than 1300 cooperative dairies in Denmark. Almost forty years later, there were 16 cooperatives left. The largest of these cooperatives, Arla, controlled 90 per cent of the market (Modhorst 2014). In New Zealand, a special law enacted in 2001 allowed two large dairy cooperatives and the New Zealand Dairy Board to merge. The merger established Fonterra, New Zealand's largest company, employing over 17,000 people and controlling 90 per cent of the New Zealand raw milk market (Shadbolt and Duncan 2015). In the United States, agricultural cooperatives declined from 4,783 in 1995 to over 2,100 today. Their membership also declined from 4.7 million members to over 2 million members (Hoyt and Menzani 2012, NCBA-Clusa 2022).

Worker cooperatives operating in the manufacturing, construction, and services industries created larger units to compete with multinational organisations and publicly listed companies. In Italy, the process of mergers and concentration commenced in the 1960s. The second-tier consortia network, which numbered 1734 in 2011, consolidated their activities so much that the largest 64 consortia produced 75 per cent of their total consortia revenue (Linguiti 2014). A study conducted in 2016 also revealed that the largest 250 cooperatives with a turnover above 50 million euros produced close to 62 per cent of the cooperative sector's total turnover and employed 21 per cent of the sector's total employment (Ammirato 2018). A study focussing on Emilia-Romagna found that five cooperatives generated 65 per cent of the cooperative sector's total exports from that region (Caselli 2016).

Over 100 cooperatives from the industrial, finance, distribution and knowledge sector formed the Mondragon Corporation to promote growth, manage crises, and facilitate change. It had the same structures as a cooperative with a Congress (Annual General Meeting), a Standing Committee (the Board) and the General Council (the Executive). It incorporated Lagun Aro, the insurance company, the research and development bodies, and the inter-cooperative solidarity fund. It still boasted the Caja Laboral Cooperative Bank as a member (Baraijoa, Errasti and Begiristain 2004, Barandiaran and Javier 2017). In addition to forming a Corporation, Mondragon cooperatives also grew their size and international reach. The flagship cooperative Fagor, employed 11,000 (including those working in subsidiaries) in 2005, and by 2013, 27 cooperatives controlled 122 foreign subsidiaries (Errasti, Bretos and Etxezarreta 2016).

5.2.2 Access to Capital

Cooperatives adopted various strategies to access an adequate amount of capital that would complement the strategies of growth. The larger cooperatives that operated in a very competitive environment and with international aspirations found ways to access external capital. This section explores how cooperatives access finance at the enterprise level; via the cooperative movement's own financial structures, via the State, and via attracting capital from external investors.

Cooperatives have traditionally raised funds from members and from retaining a portion of their surpluses for future investment. First, members usually invest a nominal amount as a condition of membership which is held in members' accounts. The amount varies depending on the cooperative, and it can increase over time. Member accounts attract a fixed interest if the cooperative can afford it. Second, members can also provide loans to the cooperative for which they receive a fixed return. Third, surplus not returned to members is deposited in the reserve fund, which in some countries it is indivisible. Fourth, in the United States, NGCs have linked member shares to cooperative usage, hoping to raise more funds in capital-intensive ventures. This means that the more shares you own, the more produce you can sell to the cooperative. These shares reflect the value of the cooperative assets and can be sold to achieve capital gain (Andrews 2015, Roelants 2015).

Cooperatives are also accessing capital via financial instruments owned and operated by the cooperative movement. Cooperative banks can support the cooperative sector, although they are mostly focussed on supporting agricultural cooperatives. Credit guarantee companies or financial consortia operate in many countries, helping cooperatives access loans from private banks at favourable rates. Mondragon established its own bank, Caja Laboral Popular, to provide loans and many other financial services to cooperative members. Since 1993, Italy and France have established cooperative development funds. These are funded from a percentage of cooperative surplus or their turnover. They are used to establish new cooperatives, fund cooperative growth, help cooperatives manage a crisis, and help cooperatives restructure their operations. The Cooperative movement has also established financial companies, with cooperative and private capital, that invest in cooperatives (Whyte and Whyte 1991, Corcoran and Wilson 2010, Zevi et al. 2011, Roelants 2015, Ammirato 2018).

The State has also been a source of funding for the cooperative sector. We have already noted how the State has supported agricultural development in the United States by establishing farm credit banks for the farming sector. The state-owned banks have provided loans to cooperatives in Italy, Spain, France and Quebec. The State also provides tax concessions to cooperatives. Tax concessions were granted to support the retention of profits as indivisible reserves, to avoid double taxation, and to help a sector that did not have access to the share market. The State has also become an investor in those cooperatives that allow external or institutional investors, such as those operating in Italy, France and Spain (Corcoran and Wilson 2010, Zevi et al. 2011).

Cooperatives can now also access external capital from investors and institutions. A study promoted by the ICA has noted that 58 per cent of the largest cooperatives are using some form of external equity (Andrews 2015). External equity consists of many financial instruments. First, cooperatives can issue cooperative bonds or preferred shares that have economic rights but do not have voting rights and are non-transferable. Second, cooperatives can also issue a small portion of cooperative shares, or cooperative bonds, that have economic rights (right to a dividend), are transferable, and are tradeable on a country's stock market. These tradeable financial instruments also do not have voting rights. Third, in some countries, cooperative laws allow external investors to invest in a cooperative, granting them economic and voting rights. These cooperative shares are not tradeable and do not reflect the value of the cooperative. Voting rights are limited (ranging from a maximum of 33 per cent in Italy to 49 per cent in France), thus ensuring that cooperative members retain control of their cooperative. Fourth, some cooperatives have chosen to access capital by listing a controlled subsidiary on the stock market. This approach allows cooperatives to list less than 50 per cent of the total shares, thus maintaining control of the enterprise. Fifth, cooperatives can be a majority-shareholder of subsidiaries, thus accessing the remaining capital from the private sector. Sixth, cooperatives can establish a holding company which is co-owned with private investors and/or the State (Kuijpers and Groeneveld 2015, Shadbolt and Duncan 2015, Ammirato 2018).

5.2.3 *Traditional Cooperatives*

The traditional cooperative structure operates in compliance with the ICA principles of one-person-one-vote; limited return on members' accounts; democratic decision-making processes; no external capital; and conducts the majority of transactions with members. One cooperative that has managed to grow whilst maintaining its traditional cooperative structure is the Japanese consumer cooperative. The Japanese consumer movement managed to grow and consolidate in a restrictive regulatory environment whilst maintaining a traditional structure. The regulatory environment prevented consumer cooperatives from trading beyond their prefecture, from trading with non-members, and from operating their own credit facilities. To this day, consumer cooperatives are democratically managed, with members having only one vote, with the right to elect their representatives to the Board and to elect the audit committee. The Board could also include three independent directors approved at the annual general meeting. All the capital required comes from members' shares and retained earnings. The return on capital is limited to less than 10 per cent per annum (Kurimoto 2020).

The consumer movement in Japan managed to compete post-1990 through a very clever and country-specific strategy. First, it introduced regional consortia to achieve economies of scale and lower costs without having to merge cooperatives. This enabled the consortia to operate across prefectures and keep cooperatives autonomous. Second, it introduced individual home delivery services to complement the group buying segment and the local stores segments, which were losing market share. Third, it continued to focus on increasing its membership, which grew from 9 million in 1990 to 22.2 million in 2020. Fourth, it raised capital from members by asking them to top up their members' account. Members responded by depositing on average 221 USD per member, amounting to a total of 5.1 billion USD in 2021. Fifth, the consumer movement continued to promote social causes, pro-environment policies, and organic foods, so it continues to build a high reputation with the public and with consumers. Finally, The Japanese Consumers' Cooperative Union (JCCU), through its own companies, provided 5,400 cooperative brand products as well as providing business support services such as online marketing, quality systems, and distribution centres (Kurimoto 2020, Kurimoto and Akeda 2021, JCCU 2022).

The Japanese consumer cooperatives have managed to grow whilst maintaining their traditional structure. They are democratically managed, they trade only with members, and capital needs are met via retained earnings and from members' accounts. They do not access external capital, and their legal structure has maintained its traditional cooperative governance arrangements.[11]

5.2.4 *Cooperative Corporations*[12]

The cooperative corporation refers to a cooperative that is a large enterprise with a centralised organisational structure. Key features are governance arrangements with a clear division between the Board and management; management has a high degree of autonomy; the organisation has many divisions; and it provides many services whilst operating in a complex, competitive environment. Rabobank is an example of a corporation-type model. The Dutch credit cooperatives established Rabobank in 1972 following the merger of its two central cooperative banking associations. In 1972, Rabobank was a cooperative central association providing financial services to its cooperative members. Its fundamental tasks included ensuring liquidity within the group; providing cash clearing; providing commercial, leasing, insurance, and merchant banking; and providing credit guarantee facilities.

The competitive environment, and the bank's strategy to expand to the international market, led to a concentration of activities to lower costs, improved competitiveness, and access external capital. This process accelerated after the GFC. The concentration of activities included cooperative banks merging (889 local banks in 1989 were reduced to 100 in 2016), reducing bank branches from 1643 in 2004 to 446 in 2017, and reducing staff from 53,900 in 2014 to 43,800 in 2017. Rabobank also conducted most of its business with non-members.[13] By 2013, it operated 769 branches in 42 countries. To expand overseas, Rabobank needed finance beyond the amount provided by members' equity and retained earnings. To this end, Rabobank issued member certificates from 2000 to 2005. These corporate bonds were not listed on the stock exchange and had no voting rights but were transferable within an internal Rabobank-managed market. In 2014, Rabobank Certificates were open to external investors. These new tradeable certificates were listed on the stock market, and were paid up to 2 per cent above the Dutch government bond rate. In 2021, Rabobank issued certificates worth 7.8 billion euros (Cotugno 2010, Kuijpers and Groeneveld 2015, Poli 2019, Rabobank 2021).

In 2016, Rabobank amalgamated all its remaining 108 cooperative banks under one central organisation that operated under one banking licence. The cooperative banks became Rabobank branches. Each branch's assets were translated into Rabobank equity. Each branch's members elected a Local Members Council (LMC) that, in turn, elects a local board. The Board appoints a bank manager to manage each local branch. The LMC has the right to monitor and advise management, but Rabobank can remove these rights. Each branch also has voting power at the Rabobank annual general meeting based on the amount of equity they hold. It is not based on the principle of one-member-one-vote. Rabobank has centralised all functions, including information technology, product development, marketing, external funding, internal policies and procedures, risk management, and reporting requirements (Poli 2019).

Rabobank is regarded as a socially responsible cooperative bank that has developed a corporate-style culture. It has centralised its powers so that management has more control compared to local units and members. It makes profits, and it remunerates external capital as well as member capital. It operates with equity-based voting rights rather than the democratic principle of one-person-one-vote. It conducts most of its business with non-members. Rabobank has over 1.9 million members, and in 2021 made 3.7 billion euros in profits (Rabobank 2021).

5.2.5 New Generation Cooperatives

NGCs were established in the United States. NGCs are distinct from traditional cooperatives because they operate under a closed membership; require substantial up-front investment; enforce delivery rights and obligations; and issue tradable shares. The delivery rights or obligations are in direct proportion to the investment made into the cooperative. These changes allow cooperatives to access more capital, achieve economies of scale, and become more competitive (Zeuli and Cropp 2004).

Fonterra was established in 2001 from the merger of two dairy cooperatives and the New Zealand Dairy Board. The deal was enabled by special legislation, the *Dairy Industry Restructuring Act 2001 (NZ)*. It produces dairy consumer products and sells them in over 100 countries. It purchased 90 per cent of milk locally. It is New Zealand's largest company and, in 2014, became the world's largest dairy company for processing milk (Shadbolt and Duncan 2015).

In order to exploit global opportunities and meet the costs of processing capacity, Fonterra embarked on radical changes. First, farmers can become members if they buy one share for every one kilogram of milk solids they wish to deliver to Fonterra. Under this scheme, if farmers produce less milk, then they have to relinquish their shares. This scheme caused financial instability because Fonterra was obliged to buy the shares.

Second, in 2009, to overcome this financial risk, Fonterra allowed farmers to purchase non-voting shares with economic rights. They could purchase two non-voting shares for each full share they already had. With this system, farmers would be eligible for an annually set milk price plus a dividend on their non-voting shares. Third, in 2012, Fonterra went further and allowed the equivalent of 525 million NZD worth of non-voting shares to list on the New Zealand stock market. These shares are classified as permanent shares that can be traded on the stock market. Fonterra has no obligation to buy these shares back (Shadbolt and Duncan 2015). Fourth, from 2021, members could purchase four shares for each voting share with a minimum purchase of 1,000 shares. These shares were open to all farmer stakeholders, not just members. In addition, shareholders that no longer supply milk to Fonterra were given at least ten years to dispose of their non-voting shares (it was previously three years) (Fonterra 2021c).

In addition to capital raising from members and external shareholders, Fonterra also altered its governance arrangements. The closed membership structure has also introduced a plural voting system. When voting to elect the board and constitutional matters, plural voting applies and it is proportionate to shareholding. The Board comprises up to 11 directors. Seven directors are elected by members, whilst the Board appoints four competency-based directors. Fonterra also has a 25-member Shareholders Advisory Council that is democratically appointed by members (Fonterra 2022).

The decision to become a global player has led to changes in Fonterra's capital structure and governance arrangements that have led it to move away from the traditional agricultural model. It now operates a closed membership model rather than an open membership model. It has introduced a plural voting system rather than a democratic system, giving more power to those who hold more shares. Farmer-members now earn their income partly from milk production and partly from a return on capital invested. Fonterra shares are tradeable, and their value is linked to the value of the cooperative assets rather than having a nominal value as is the case in traditional cooperatives. Fonterra is more prone to profit-maximising operations since non-members supply a portion of the milk, since it is obliged to return a dividend to external investors, and since the value of its shares reflects the value of the cooperative assets. It has been noted that the complexity of global operations enables management to escape democratic control and that these changes threaten cooperative identity (Apps 2020). Fonterra's public documents for instance, emphasise revenue, profits, dividends, and shareholders' return, more than cooperative principles (Fonterra 2021a, 2021b).

5.2.6 *Cooperative Group of Companies*

The formation of business groups is one of four major organisational models that businesses adopt to compete in the market. These models include the multi-divisional firms represented by large US companies; business groups led by a holding company that fully or partly owns subsidiaries (Coplan and Takashi 2010); industrial districts where firms co-operate and compete whilst accessing common services provided by local business associations and local governments (Zeitlin 2007); and inter-firm networks like the Keireitsu System practices by Toyota which relies on thousands of suppliers to provide parts to manufacture its cars (Fruin 2007). A cooperative group of companies is another type of cooperative model which operates under a dual legal structure. This structure consists of a cooperative parent company that, via full ownership or via a controlling share of a holding company, owns and controls many subsidiaries. In this situation, the parent company is registered and managed as a cooperative, but the subsidiaries operate as conventional companies.

Cooperative groups of companies operate in all sectors of the economy. For instance, the agricultural cooperative Granlatte is the major shareholder of Granarolo Holding Company which owns or controls many subsidiaries (Granarolo Group 2022). The Crédit Agricole cooperative bank is a third-tier central association servicing the cooperative banks that is listed on the stock exchange. Crédit Agricole is majority owned by cooperative banks and regional cooperative associations, but it has floated a third of its shares on the stock exchange (Poli 2019). This section discusses the Sacmi cooperative group, a manufacturing cooperative from Imola, near Bologna.

Sacmi is a cooperative founded in 1909. In 1949 it employed 84 workers. In 2020, Sacmi operated in 28 countries with 80 production facilities, distribution and sales departments. It employs 4,720 employees worldwide. Initially, it produced presses for ceramic tiles, but later, through acquisitions, it diversified into other areas such as packaging plants for agricultural products, ceramic sanitary and homeware products, manufacturing machinery for food packaging, machinery to produce ice cream, brick handling solutions, filtering and purification systems, and wine cellar technology. Italian cooperatives usually develop via local consortia, a second-tier cooperative that enables small cooperatives to compete in the market by working together with similar or complementary cooperatives. Sacmi, however, could not be part of a consortium because it was the sole cooperative operating in this market segment (Ammirato 2018).

Sacmi decided to grow and diversify its products and geographic markets to become more competitive, create employment, maximise its engineering capabilities, and exploit market opportunities. The acquisition and control of subsidiaries allowed Sacmi to access know-how, increase market share, have quicker access to new product and geographic markets, access local knowledge, and have a more flexible operational structure. This structure allows the parent cooperative to mitigate financial risks via its subsidiaries. It is important to note that, unlike Rabobank and Fonterra, Sacmi did not go to the stock market to access capital. It accessed capital via very traditional means: member shares (currently at 5.75 million euro), members' loans (currently at 22 million euro), loans from local banks, and retained surplus held in the indivisible reserves. Sacmi fully owns the holding company and its subsidiaries. Joint venture investments are not significant when compared with its assets. Indeed, Sacmi's net equity stood at 682 million euros in 2020 (Sacmi 2020a).[14]

The Governance arrangements reflect the cooperative's dual structure. The headquarters employs 1,097 of the 4,720 employees, of whom only 385 are members. An employee can become a member after five years of service. The pay and conditions of all employees that work at the Imola headquarters are based on collective agreements negotiated with the unions that include enterprise-based pension schemes, canteen, welfare, and childcare support. However, patronage payments and remuneration of member loans go to members only. Sacmi employees who work in overseas subsidiaries are employed under local collective agreements (Ammirato 2018). Sacmi supports the cooperative movement and the community with annual support amounting to close to 1.8 million euros (Sacmi 2020a).

Sacmi has adopted the Unitary Governance Model. Its members elect a Board at the Annual General Assembly (AGA), and the Board appoints a general manager. The general manager is responsible for operational matters, the appointment and recruitment of staff, and meeting the AGA approved strategic goals. Members participate in the budget process and specialised committees. A number of AGA meetings are held each year where key decisions are made. It is expected that the Board will delay making a decision on any issue that lacks broad consensus. The AGA decides on any issue affecting membership, key strategic directions, any decision that overrides the strategic plan, and matters relating to the cooperative movement. The attendance rate at Annual General Meetings is over 80 per cent. Imola-based cooperatives agree that they work better with fewer active, dedicated members who invest in the cooperative (Hancock 2007, Benati and Mazzoli 2009, Sacmi 2015). In 2020, members invested 72,000 euros on average (Sacmi 2020).

This dual structure has enabled Sacmi to diversify its products and markets, to grow, and to create employment. It has maintained democratic governance processes for members. It is a socially responsible enterprise. It is not under pressure from external investors to make profits. It operates under Italian industrial law that promotes equal pay for equal work for all workers. It operates under cooperative law that includes limited return on member accounts and member loans, limited bonus payments not exceeding 20 per cent of one's pay, and that requires the remaining profits to be held as indivisible reserves (Fici 2013).

Sacmi's dual structure, however, weakens cooperative values because the majority of employees are not members and do not have access to bonus payments and do not participate in the democratic governance process. Sacmi faces similar problems faced by Mondragon cooperatives, and that is: how to expand the cooperative business internationally in countries that have different cooperative laws and where the workforce is not aware of cooperative principles and practices? How can the parent cooperative keep control of the group when the majority of its workforce, and potential members, are based overseas? This discussion continues in the chapter on cooperative governance.

*5.2.7 **Demutualisation***

During the neo-Liberal era, some financial and agricultural cooperatives converted to investor-owned companies. Cases of demutualisation occurred prior to 1990, but in the 1990s, they were more frequent, at least until the GFC. In post-Socialist countries, farmers preferred privatisation because they equated cooperatives with the old collectivist system. In the United States, 72 cooperative mutual societies converted to capitalist firms from 1981 to 1999 (Battilani and Schröter 2012). In Australia, 75 cooperatives demutualised from 1990 to 2019 (Patmore, Balnave and Marjanovic 2021). This is quite detrimental to the reputation of the cooperative movement because it implies a weakness of the cooperative model to compete in deregulated global markets or signals that the cooperative model may be transitory and no longer valid. Whilst demutualisation is restricted to a couple of cooperative sectors and mainly took hold in English-speaking countries with a strong neo-Liberal culture, it is still important to analyse why demutualisation happened so that the causes can be identified and preventive measures can be implemented.

Cooperative studies conducted in Australia, Britain, Canada and the United States have provided valuable insights into the reasons that have led to demutualisation. First, cooperatives were forced to operate in a new regulatory environment that encouraged deregulation, privatisation of public assets, higher regulatory costs, and generally promoted a more competitive environment. In this environment, Isomorphism was encouraged. Second, cooperatives were usually in financial difficulties or needed more capital to grow their business and could not, or did not know how to, increase capital within a mutually owned or cooperative structure. Third, cooperative managers with private sector experience promoted demutualisation and conversion to an investor-owned firm to improve competitiveness and access more capital. In this endeavour, managers were supported by hired consultants and received hefty pay rises following demutualisation (Fulton and Girard 2015). Fourth, board members either supported the change or did not have the capabilities to challenge management and consultants' advice. The fifth reason is member apathy. Members of mutual or agricultural cooperatives were disengaged from cooperative governance, they were not fully informed on the state of the challenging environment, and they did not know how to challenge management. They also thought that there was not much difference between a cooperative and its competitors because they offered similar products and services. Finally, the cooperative law allowed demutualisation and the distribution of inter-generational assets to current members[15] (Chaddad and Cook 2004, Battilani and Schröter 2012, Fulton and Girard 2015, Patmore, Balnave and Marjanovic 2021).

The discussion on demutualisation also identified ways to prevent it. Barberini, the late president of the ICA, stated that to avoid demutualisation: boards must ensure that cooperative practice is always aligned with cooperative ideals; managers must be able to understand, interpret, and implement cooperative goals and mission and not just have technical skills; cooperative members must actively participate in the decision-making process (Barberini 2009). Cooperatives must also demonstrate good financial management so that cooperatives are not in financial distress when managing change (Fulton and Girard 2015). The recruitment of managers and staff should attract, retain and train people that believe in and support cooperative values. Boards should consult the cooperative movement's various cooperative-based approaches to manage change before entertaining demutualisation.[16] The regulatory regime can help by making cooperative rules that reflect cooperative culture, such as making collective reserves indivisible. The reserves and assets should remain collectively owned and be made available to future generations to use and hold in trust for other generations (Barberini 2009).

Demutualisation took place as a result of external factors, internal factors, and cultural factors. External factors include government decisions, neo-Liberal ideas, and ready-made organisational structures available to convert to. Internal factors relate to governance arrangements that allocate appropriate powers, roles and responsibilities to the Board, management and members. Cultural factors related to having everyone appreciating and supporting cooperative values; understanding the political and economic environment; promoting economic democracy; appreciating the concept of inter-generational wealth; and understanding that capital is a means to an end, not an end in itself (Battilani and Schröter 2012, Fulton and Girard 2015, Patmore, Balnave and Marjanovic 2021). The cooperative movement needs to work at all levels to prevent demutualisation.

5.2.8 Worker-Buyouts

Whilst some cooperatives demutualised, many small to medium size businesses converted into cooperatives. These have become known as WBOs because workers (and employees) buy out the firm they worked for. WBOs took place before the 1990s, but they accelerated after the 1990s as a result the economic crisis and the de-industrialisation caused by globalisation and the neo-Liberal policies. WBOs have been occurring in Europe, North America, and South America (Zevi et al. 2011, Vieta, Depedri and Carrano 2017, Bernardi et al. 2022). WBOs have mostly taken place when workers buy out a business that is facing economic difficulty or bankruptcy. On some occasions, WBOs have occurred when business owners have willingly transferred their business to their employees. What follows are examples from France, Italy and Argentina that reflect three different approaches to WBOs.

France has the highest concentration of WBOs in the world. It is estimated that WBOs account for 23 per cent (793 cooperatives) of all the 3,451 cooperatives associated with the CG-SCOP that were formed from 1989 to 2010 (Soulage 2011). WBOs accounted for 31 per cent of all new cooperatives from 2016 to 2021 and accounted for 49 per cent of the 71,000 jobs provided by CG-SCOP cooperatives (CG-SCOP 2022c).

The unique aspect of the French experience is that most of the WBOs have been created from non-ailing enterprises. These are enterprises where the owner willingly transferred to existing employees because their family members were not willing to take over the business, because they did not wish to sell the business to a competitor, or because they could get a better price selling the company to employees (Soulage 2011).

French WBOs are established within a very supportive external environment comprising the cooperative network, the legal framework, and financial support. More specifically, The CG-SCOP network consists of a central association, 13 regional structures, and three sectoral associations. The regional structures provide workers with support such as feasibility studies; developing a business plan; legal advice; and trade links to financial support structures and to the cooperative movement (CG-SCOP 2022b). Cooperatives themselves have noted that they would not have been established without this support (Di Stefano 2019).

The legislation allows for external funding in the form of non-voting cooperative bonds and cooperative equity of up to 49 per cent of total equity. Cooperative equity holders may hold up to 35 per cent of the votes (Soulage 2011). Since 2014, the law also allows workers to manage WBOs even though they are not majority equity holders. In these cases, workers are required to purchase more than 50 per cent of shares within seven years, and equity holders are required to sell their shares until workers reach this target. In the meantime, workers control the cooperative (Di Stefano 2019).

A few specialised companies supply finance. CG-SCOP's own Socoden provides credit guarantees and subsidised personal loans to members so they can purchase equity. Socoden also co-invests with the finance company SPOT,[17] a venture capitalist company, which purchases equity in cooperatives. The Institute for the Development of the Social Economy (IDES), funded by the State, cooperative banks, and mutual societies, purchases non-voting cooperative bonds. From 1983 to 2010, IDES invested 60 million euros in 403 enterprises, of which 280 were cooperatives (Corcoran and Wilson 2010, Soulage 2011).

Soulage found that from 1989 to 2010, WBOs had a better survival rate than other cooperatives. Whereas new cooperatives had a survival rate of 42 per cent; owner-transferred WBOs had a survival rate of 62 per cent; and WBOs from ailing enterprises had a survival rate of 49 per cent. The findings also indicate that the success factors for WBOs from owner-transferred companies include the company being in good shape, senior executives remaining but not recruiting managers from outside, good results and the distribution of profits, and access to the cooperative network's administrative, professional, and financial services. Some of the risks to consider include high debt level, loss of customers, lack of leadership, and profit risk (Soulage 2011).

The Italian WBO experience commenced in the 1970s, and it has since become an integral part of the cooperative movement since the passing of the Marcora law in 1985. The Marcora Law provided funding for WBOs, allowed workers to access their unemployment benefits, and it established a specialised company, Cooperazione Finanza Impresa (CFI), to manage the programme. CFI included the three cooperative associations, the three trade union confederations, and state representatives. The Marcora Law was a response to de-industrialisation at a time when Italy was experiencing high public debt, high unemployment, and high inflation, and firms were either ceasing to operate or relocating overseas. In promoting WBOs, the Marcora programme set out to save local businesses and local jobs (De Micheli, Imbruglia and Misiani 2017).

The first phase of the programme (1986–2001) involved CFI providing three times the equity capital invested by workers. Workers could invest their severance pay and unemployment insurance on condition that they could not access unemployment benefits for three years. CFI provided funding as a non-returnable grant. Cooperative-owned financial companies could also provide up to 25 per cent of workers' capital. CFI, with support from the cooperative associations, would conduct feasibility studies and develop business plans for approved projects. In this first phase, from 1986 to 2001, CFI supported 157 WBOs which employed 6,000 people (Zanotti 2011, Zevi and De Bernardinis 2016, Vieta, Depedri and Carrano 2017).

The Marcora programme introduced key changes in 2001 that became operational in 2003. CFI became a consortium allowing it to attract cooperatives as members. CFI no longer offered grants. Instead, it now offered loans and equity investments to be repaid within ten years. This made the fund a revolving fund, and it enabled CFI to invest in cooperatives throughout their lifecycle. CFI also developed a broader financial network that included the national consortium Cooperfidi, which provided credit guarantees; the three cooperative development funds, which provided equity and loans; and a number of cooperative banks or local banks; in particular Banca Etica (BE), which provided initial funding to get WBOs started whilst they waited for their severance pay. The cooperative law of 1992 further supported the formation of WBOs by allowing external investors (with less than one-third of votes) to invest in cooperatives. In 2014, employees were given the right of first refusal should they seek to buy out companies in crisis or companies that are undergoing liquidation or bankruptcy procedures (Zanotti 2011, Vieta, Depedri and Carrano 2017, Ammirato 2018).

A rigorous process is used to assess the viability of a potential WBO. First, employees enquire about forming a WBO following advice they receive from the union, local government, a local business consultant, or the cooperative associations. Second CFI, the cooperative developing funds, and the cooperative associations conduct a feasibility study and determine whether the project is feasible. Third, financial commitment is sought from CFI and its partners. Finally, once a WBO is established, CFI and the Central associations monitor it to ensure that it remains viable and that any risk is identified and managed on time. The WBO can access finance and managerial support throughout their lifecycle. The review process is important because it mitigates key risks. It ensures group cohesiveness; no carryover of debt; that the previous owner is not involved; that key skilled staff are retained; and that workers are willing to become collective entrepreneurs (Laurini 2016, Viola 2016).

CFI established 323 WBOs from 1985 to 2020. These 323 WBOs have provided 10,408 jobs, of which 80 per cent are in the manufacturing sector. Of these, 113 cooperatives or 35 per cent are active today. The average lifespan for each WBO is 18 years which compares favourably with the average lifespan of two–five years experienced by private sector firms. Data also confirms that those WBOs that are members of a cooperative association have an average lifespan of 21 years, compared to other WBOs' lifespan of 15 years.[18] The WBOs that are members of a cooperative association produce 97 per cent of turnover and almost all the profits (Legacoop 2020, Bernardi et al. 2022). Bernardi et al. have calculated that for every 203,000 euros that CFI spent to establish a WBO, the return to the State on tax revenue, based on a cooperative's lifespan, amounts to 7.9 million euros (Bernardi et al. 2022). The CFI consortium today has 177 member cooperatives (not all WBOs), 98 million euros in equity capital, and a further 9 million euros in indivisible reserves. Approximately, 37 per cent of its investments are directed to WBOs (CFI 2022).

Argentina's WBO movement developed in direct response to the economic crisis of the 1990s, which led to business closures and unemployment. Facing a loss of wages and witnessing asset stripping by company owners, workers occupied their factories, hoping that the government and the courts would allow them to manage their factories in lieu of lost wages and severance pay. Mobilisation at first was linked to political activity directed against neo-Liberal policies, but after 2001 workers wanted to save jobs and their factories (Ruggeri and Vieta 2015).

The Argentine workforce was supported by the union and three associations that promoted self-management. They established WBOs the hard way. It is estimated that 140 WBOs were established from 1990 to 2002. In 2013, there were 311 WBOs operating across most sectors of the economy. These WBOs employed over 13,462 persons averaging over 43 persons per WBO. These WBOs were established without having access to the management and financial support afforded to workers in France and Italy. In addition, the legal system was initially focussed on paying creditors by selling assets. In 2011, the law required judges to consider WBOs to continue production subject to two-thirds of the workforce agreeing to form a WBO. Whilst this legal requirement was an improvement, Ruggeri and Vieta found that only 16 per cent of applications had been approved (Ruggeri and Vieta 2015).

Argentinian WBOs encountered difficulties that are common with WBOs. According to Rainis, key issues included administrative staff leaving once owners and managers left; suppliers demanding cash payment; difficulty in establishing credit lines; lack of investment capital; difficulty accessing the market; and workers having to work long hours in the early stages of the new cooperative's life. Other difficulties included educating the workforce on cooperative values and democratic management and linking the WBOs with the traditional cooperative movement. The early signs of economic democracy indicate that these WBOs favour forms of direct democracy, with the general assembly meeting regularly to make binding decisions (Ruggeri 2015, Ruggeri and Vieta 2015, Ranis 2016).

The success of WBOs is clearly based on the tenacity and resilience of employees wanting to save their jobs. The three examples have highlighted cooperative good practice in establishing WBOs. Key good practice standards include:

- An enabling legislative framework. The legislative framework should facilitate the establishment of WBOs as well as enable access to external capital.
- A supporting cooperative environment. The cooperative movement should provide legal, managerial, and financial support throughout a WBOs lifecycle so they can survive, grow, and manage change.
- A supportive external environment. The external environment—the State, social economy institutions, trade unions, and professionals—should provide financial and management support.

- A formal assessment process for each WBO. This process should conduct feasibility studies, develop business plans, understand and mitigate WBOs' specific risks, be able to retain skilled staff and assess the level of commitment to collective ownership and democratic management.

It is important to note the uniqueness of each experience: France established WBOs from non-ailing enterprises; Argentina succeeded without the supportive legal and cooperative environment afforded to cooperatives in Italy and France; and Italy developed a formal approach to establishing WBOs which is supported by the State, the trade unions, and the cooperative associations.

5.2.9 Social Cooperatives

The economic and social changes that took place since the 1970s left sections of the population marginalised and excluded. Key events that led to marginalisation and exclusion include the emergence of long-term unemployment following the economic crisis of the 1970s; neo-Liberal policies of privatisation and outsourcing of government services; the inability of families to cater for their elderly parents at a time when people were living longer whilst both husband and wife had to work; lack of childcare centres and lack of policies to meet the needs of disadvantaged people; the structure of labour markets that left many people in precarious employment, especially the young, the uneducated, and the disabled. This context provided cooperatives with an opportunity to provide goods and services to people experiencing difficulties. The level of opportunities for cooperatives differed between countries, and they depended on the maturity of the Welfare State, the extent of the State's capacity or willingness to meet people's needs, and the culture, capacity, and capability of a country's cooperative sector (Roelants 2009, Galera 2017).

The traditional cooperative movement comprising worker cooperatives and consumer cooperatives had already been active in the provision of health services, aged care, youth unemployment, and childcare. Birchall informs us that Serbia established the first health cooperative in 1920, and others followed in the United States and Japan (Birchall 2011). The Japanese consumer movement established medical cooperatives in the 1950s (JCCU 2022). The Italian cooperative sector began to cater for the disadvantaged, the elderly, and young people suffering from drug addiction and unemployment from the late 1970s (Marzocchi 2012). The Swedish cooperative sector established childcare centres in the 1980s (Galera 2017). Korean activists did likewise (ILO 2017). The Cooperative Home Care Associates, a worker cooperative from New York, was established in 1985 to provide immigrant workers with better working conditions in the home care services sector (Berry 2017).

In the 1990s, however, a new type of cooperative, the social cooperative enterprise (SCE) was established. This model was formalised in Italy with the passing of a specific cooperative law in 1991. It established a new type of cooperative whose key objective was to satisfy general interests or the community interests rather than the interests of members. It also promoted a stakeholder governance model where everyone with interest in the cooperative activity could become a member with voting rights. This contrasted with traditional cooperatives, where only workers or consumers or users could become members. What follows is a discussion of the Italian law, differences between jurisdictions, and key areas of SCE activities.

The Italian Parliament formally recognised SCEs by passing the Social Cooperative Law 381/1991. It is estimated that by 1991, associations of volunteers and worker cooperatives had already established 2,000 cooperatives providing services to drug addicts, shelters for homeless people, and home-based services for the elderly (Borzaga and Galera 2016). The Cooperative Law 381/1991 is important because it gave a formal recognition and a unique definition of SCEs. The law acknowledged that a social cooperative's mission is to operate in the best interest of the community, that volunteers and disadvantaged workers had to become actively involved, and that SCEs could adopt a stakeholder governance model. The Law defined social cooperatives as having:

> the purpose of pursuing the general interests of the community, promoting human development, and the social integration of citizens through
>
> - Type A cooperatives, which engage in the management of social, health and educational services; and
> - Type B cooperatives, which carry out different activities, including agricultural, industrial, commercial, or services, with the aim of integrating disadvantaged persons into the labour market.[19]
> - Other key features include the following: volunteers cannot exceed 50 percent of total members; at least 30 percent of the workforce in Type B cooperatives must be comprised of disadvantaged workers[20]; the stakeholder governance structure may include voluntary personnel, external investor-members, legal entities, as well as worker-members; and social cooperatives can form consortia with private enterprises provided 70 percent of its members are social cooperatives.
>
> (Fici 2013)

The success of the social cooperative law in Italy encouraged other countries across Europe and other parts of the world to enact legislation supporting SCEs. A recent study by the European Commission has revealed that all European countries have enacted a law on social enterprises or have a public policy promoting them. Nine countries have passed specific legislation supporting the formation of social cooperatives. Finland has passed a law on social enterprises that includes cooperatives. Germany updated its cooperative regulations to include social cooperatives. Whilst the United Kingdom made an adjustment to its company law to accommodate SCEs. The names given to SCEs differ. Italy uses the term social cooperatives. France calls them Collective Interest Cooperative Societies. The United Kingdom calls them Community Interest Companies. Social Solidarity Cooperatives is used in Portugal, and Social Initiative Cooperatives is used in Spain (European Commission 2020). In Korea, they are called social cooperatives (ICA Asia and Pacific 2019). In Quebec, they are known as Solidarity Cooperatives. In Ontario, they are known as Community Ownership Cooperatives, whose purpose is to meet a geographic need (Petrou 2013, Publications Quebec 2022).

The legislations broadly support similar general interest goals and stakeholder governance, but there are some differences in membership rights; voting rights, distribution of profits; and asset management.[21] More specifically:

- Membership. For work integration cooperatives, a percentage of members must be disadvantaged workers (30 per cent in Italy, 40 per cent in Greece, and 50 per cent in Poland). France requires three stakeholder groups to be represented, whilst Quebec requires two stakeholder groups to be members. In the United Kingdom, anyone can be a member.

- Voting Rights. In principle, all support one-person-one-vote. Spain, however, does not allow voluntary personnel to vote. France requires each of the three stakeholder groups to hold between 10 per cent and 50 per cent of the votes. The UK voting rights are the same as shareholders' rights as defined by the *Companies Act 1985*.
- Distribution of profits.[22] Countries usually place a limit on the distribution of profits, but Portugal, Spain, Poland and Korea forbid any distribution of profits.
- Destination of assets in case of liquidation. In most countries, assets cannot be distributed, but Poland allows 20 per cent distribution to members.
- External Investors are permitted in most countries except Korea (Girard and Langlois 2009, Roelants 2009, ICA Asia and Pacific 2019, Kurimoto and Akeda 2021).

Three types of SCEs have been established. The first provides welfare services. These SCEs provide services for the aged, disabled, disadvantaged, and childcare services. The second type is work integration SCEs. These cooperatives operate in all sectors of the economy and support the long-term unemployed and people with disabilities in finding work. The third segment, possibly less studied, are community or proximity SCEs. These cooperatives are formed mainly in local rural or isolated de-populated communities which have limited access to services. These community cooperatives may provide an essential service like a supermarket, a service station, a café, the postal service, a pub, a sporting facility, a supermarket, tourism activity, hospitality services, and so on. It may also organise an electricity cooperative involving the whole town or revitalise tourism activities alongside the hospitality services (Borzaga and Defourny 2001, Nyssens 2006, Mori 2017, Legacoop 2019a).[23]

These SCEs are being established in many parts of the world. In Italy, the number of SCEs increased from 2,000 in 1991 to 19,800 in 2019. They employed 437,000 people in 2019 (Carini and Borzaga 2015, Legacoop 2019b). In France, there were 1,084 SCEs employing over 10,000 people in 2021 (Coop France 2022). There were 1,351 SCEs operating in Korea (ICA Asia and Pacific 2019). Quebec recorded 453 active solidarity cooperatives in 2019 (Canadian Government 2019).

The emergence of SCEs is important because they clearly espouse the economic and social dimensions of cooperatives. To this end, their goal of promoting the community and general interests is aligned with the ideas of the early Socialists. They also introduce a new stakeholder governance model that encourages inclusion policies towards the disadvantaged. SCEs also demonstrate the flexibility of the cooperative model in meeting people's needs. In this case, cooperatives filled the void left by the Welfare State by supporting people in need and by contributing towards a more inclusive, just, and humane society. As in other sectors of the economy, SECs face strong competition from corporations operating with social ends, not-for-profit organisations, foundations, mutual societies, and public-benefit-companies.[24]

5.2.10 Platform Cooperatives

Platform cooperatives refers to cooperative-owned digital platforms (that include a website or an App) that act as an intermediary between a producer and consumer, or between working people providing services and consumers, or working people and businesses who purchase their services. The term came to prominence at a conference hosted by the New School University of New York in 2015 titled: *Platform Cooperativism: The Internet, Ownership, and Democracy*. The promoters' goal was to replace the digital platform capitalist ownership model that focussed on the pursuit of profits on behalf of shareholders with a digital platform cooperative ownership model that distributed profits among its members (Scholz et al. 2021).

As with all existing cooperatives, the cooperative model is often used when there is a need or a problem to solve that neither the market nor the State can solve. In this case, there has been strong criticism of companies like Uber and TaskRabbit, which use digital platforms to act as intermediaries between customers and working people and make high profits without accepting any responsibilities as an employer. In fact, because workers are classified as contractors or independent workers, the digital platform owner is not deemed responsible for providing a regular salary, social security contributions, or welfare payments. In the case of Uber drivers, working people are paid on piecemeal rates but are responsible for owning their own car and paying for car insurance, maintenance, and petrol. These companies keep 70–75 per cent of earnings. Uber keeps up to 30 per cent of earnings in lieu of managing the platform (Poole 2016). Along with low pay, precarious work, and loss of benefits, criticisms have also centred on excessive surveillance, transparency, and privacy issues. There are also negative externalities associated with their impact on traditional jobs and inequalities (Calvo, Kenney and Zysman 2021).

Platform Cooperatives plan to replace capitalist-led platform models by blending existing technologies with the existing cooperative models that are aligned with the ICA principles. The cooperative model is deemed appropriate because of its long-standing principles of democratic management, profit sharing, and improving the pay and working conditions of working people. The cooperative models suited to Platform Cooperatives are the worker cooperative model or the multi-stakeholder model, where employees, investors, suppliers, and local authorities, can become members. Scholz has proposed ten Platform Cooperatives Principles that promote democratic management, worker involvement, and good working conditions, supported by a legal framework (Scholz 2016).[25] To further the growth of Platform Cooperatives, a group of collaborators from the Berggruen Institute have proposed a set of public policies that encourage governments to provide access to early finance, provide access to procurement, develop an appropriate legal framework, direct state investment in platform cooperatives, and to promote hubs for Platform Cooperatives (Scholz et al. 2021).

The information supplied by the 'Internet of Ownership–Platform Cooperative Directory' suggests that in 2022 there were over 300 Platform cooperatives or supporting organisations currently registered. There are Platform Cooperatives for taxis, professional and tradespersons, entertainment artists, photographers, online retailers, agriculture, as well as Fairbnb instead of Airbnb (Internet of Ownership 2022). According to Zhu and Marjanovic, there are over 40 key research papers on this subject, but there is a dearth of in-depth studies focussing on the governance and impact of Platform Cooperatives (Zhu and Marjanovic 2021). Data available on early experiences, however, demonstrates the value of the cooperative model:

- Fairbnb, an Airbnb equivalent, shares the commission it charges landlords with local communities who decide whether to allocate that money to support local associations or local economic development. Unlike Airbnb, it allows hosts to rent only one house (Fairbnb 2022).

- Smart, from Belgium, provides administrative, legal, and management services to freelancers. Smart also manages their invoicing and recoups money from their clients. In doing so, Smart becomes the freelancer's employer for the duration of the contract and pays the freelancer a proper income, as well as providing social security benefits and a pension scheme. This allows freelancers to keep their freedom whilst protecting their work rights and facilitating their business (Martinelli et al. 2019).
- Green Taxi in Colorado is a member-owned cooperative of taxi drivers. It charges members 80 USD per week for administrative support compared to 800 USD charged by competitors. Green Taxi also returns 90 per cent of taxi fares to drivers compared to the approximately 75 per cent returned by competitors, including Uber's return to drivers. In 2019, Green Taxi controlled 37 per cent of the taxi market in Denver, Colorado (Wiener 2019).

Online platforms are a growing cooperative model. It is estimated that they are present in 70 per cent of service sectors in the United States, representing 5.2 million establishments. Researchers have found over 500 active platforms in Europe as well as over 750 labour platforms worldwide. Their overall impact is difficult to ascertain, considering that whilst 30 per cent of the working population in Europe have been involved in platform work, only 1.1 per cent earn more than 50 per cent of their income from this type of work (Calvo, Kenney and Zysman 2021). Nevertheless, on the basis of what we know about the disruption caused by the case studies like Uber, Airbnb and TaskRabbit, cooperatives can perform a key humanising role by providing an alternative workplace to the exploitative conditions offered by Investor-owned Digital Platforms.

5.2.11 Banca Etica—Ethical Banking

This research has so far noted a number of cooperative bank models. These included the rural banks, which focussed on providing credit and support services to farmers and their community; the urban cooperative banks, which provided access to credit to artisans and small businesses; the credit unions, which focussed on providing credit to consumers so they could purchase consumer goods and access home loans; and the Mondragon Bank, Caja Laboral Popular, a development bank which focussed on providing credit, business services, and monitoring services to Mondragon cooperatives. BE adds another dimension to cooperative banking because it provides finance solely for the third sector of the economy and because it has developed unique operational features that align its mission with its practices (Biggeri 2014). It also operates under the 2016 Italian banking law, which sets licencing requirements for Ethical Banks. This section explains the Italian banking law on ethical banking and analyses the alignment between BE's stated mission, its democratic governance, and credit policies and practices.

The Italian law makes a few prescriptive requirements for any Ethical bank covering credit allocation, governance, profit distribution, pay scales, and tax provisions. The Law requires ethical banks to demonstrate that they evaluate loans in accordance with international ethical rating standards, including their social and environmental impact; publish on the website all loan recipients; allocate at least 20 per cent of the loan portfolio to non-profit organisations or social enterprises; re-invest all profits; practice a democratic governance model that encourages participation and a broad-based shareholding structure; ensure salary differentials do not exceed the scale of 5:1.[26] If they meet these requirements, ethical banks will be eligible to tax concessions equivalent to 75 per cent of the profits destined to increase the profit reserves (Ardu 2016, Banca Etica 2016).

BE has a clear vision of how a bank can contribute to a better society. This vision guides its governance, policy development, and policy implementation. BE's Manifesto supports a society based on justice and fraternity, which values the distribution of wealth and promotes economic activity to serve people and their communities. It supports the primacy of people over the market. Its economic development model integrates economic development, social cohesion, and environmental protection. It counteracts social exclusion and economic inequalities through its banking products, socio-cultural activities, and economic-financial education. It is committed to removing obstacles of an economic, social, and cultural nature that limit the freedom and equality of citizens and that prevent people from achieving their potential (Banca Etica 2022b).

BE's credit policies are clear and are aligned with its vision and the law. Its credit policies prioritise areas such as welfare, renewable energy, environment, organic food, international cooperation with developing countries, social-cultural activities, SCEs, and support for people and their families. The Bank does not support activities that are harmful to people and the environment. These include arms production and trade, intensive farming, the tobacco industry, gambling and activities related to the extraction of fossils. It provides loans that address primary needs (such as a first home) but does not support the purchase of luxury items and expensive real estate. It follows that in 2021 almost 66 per cent of its total loans were provided to cooperatives and not-for-profit associations, and cooperatives and associations received 42 per cent of all funds dedicated to start-ups, with the remaining funds loaned to other social and private businesses.

All approved loans must meet economic and social responsibility indicators covering governance, industrial relations, environment, community engagement, corporate social responsibility measures, and product quality. The criteria include 40 specific indicators measuring social impact. The social-environmental impact statement or review is conducted by members who are trained as social evaluators. There are 87 evaluator branches scattered throughout Italy. In 2021 over 94 per cent of loan applications were evaluated by members. In addition, all loan approvals are publicly listed on its website (Banca Etica 2022c).

The Bank's governance arrangements comply with law requirements and principles of democratic management. The General Assembly appoints the Board of Directors, which, in turn, appoints management. Management's role is to implement the strategy and policies approved by the Board and the Assembly. The Assembly appoints an Oversight Committee, which monitors compliance, risks and mutuality. The Assembly appoints the auditors upon recommendation from the Oversight committee. There is also an Ethics Committee and a Membership Committee. Three thousand people participated in the Board election of 2022. Each member has one vote and cannot own more than 1 per cent of shares. The shares are not remunerated but are revalued each year by the Bank of Italy. Salary differentials are less than 5:1, and all profits are placed in the statutory reserve (Banca Etica 2022d).

BE was formed in 1999, and it has been very successful. In 2021, it had 45,000 members who invested 82 million euros. It services 100,000 clients who have deposited 2.2 billion euros. In the same year, it made a profit of 16.7 million euros. It has branches throughout Italy and Spain. It owns a fund management company, Etica SGR,[27] which is totally dedicated to ethical investments. It manages five platforms to raise funds for a variety of projects. It produces a publicly available annual impact report which informs how bank lending impacts the economy, the environment and society (Banca Etica 2022a, 2022c).

BE is worth studying because it is a successful bank specifically dedicated to the social economy and ethical banking and that operates under specific Ethical banking regulations since 2016. It has a clear vision of society and the role that a bank can play in building a better, more egalitarian society. Its focus on providing finance that does not harm humans and the environment, its policy to conduct member-led social evaluations of loans, its transparent approach in publishing all loan recipients, and its production of a social impact report to demonstrate alignment with its mission is to be commended.

BE is part of a global banking movement that declares to be a socially responsible bank. The Federation of Alternative and Ethical Banks was formed in 2001 and has 15 members. It supports building a fairer, more inclusive, and sustainable society (FEBEA 2021). The Global Alliance for Banking and Values was formed in 2009, and it has attracted 61 banks from 44 countries. It supports banks that put people and communities first and adopt a triple-bottom-line approach to promoting a long-term sustainable business (GABV 2021, 2022).

5.3 Cooperative Development Models

In the previous chapters, we identified three cooperative models and two CDMs. The first cooperative model was the consumer cooperatives-centred model. This model was pioneered by the CWS in the United Kingdom. It owned and controlled a number of companies operating in different sectors of the economy that provided a variety of goods and services to cooperatives and consumers. The second cooperative model was the German cooperative rural banks model. It provided credit to local farmers and local families as well as marketing and business services to agricultural cooperatives. The third cooperative model is the US agricultural model. In this model, the State established agricultural banks, promoted higher education facilities, and supplied management expertise to agricultural and electric cooperatives, which successfully modernised rural United States. The fourth model was the Mondragon CDM model. It was initially led by the Caja Laboral Popular Bank. It later developed into the Mondragon Corporation, which included multi-sector cooperatives, a university, multiple support structures, internationally focussed manufacturing cooperatives, a set of Mondragon-specific ten work-life principles, and a capacity to manage change and support cooperatives in crisis. The fifth model we identified is the Lega Nazionale delle Cooperative e Mutue's (Legacoop) CDM.[28] This inter-sectoral networking model is centred on the cooperative Central's capacity to lead and coordinate change via its territorial, consortia, and financial framework; the formation of large cooperative groups; the capacity to promote new cooperatives; a culture of inter-sectoral cooperation and trade; and a capacity to manage change and support cooperatives in crisis.

This section discusses the CDMs of Trento, Quebec, the urban-consumer movement in Japan, GS-SCOP in France, and Wonju in Korea. These experiences have been chosen because of their uniqueness and because they also display features typical of CDMs such as having a national association, having an inter-sectoral membership, provision of support services, promotion of new cooperatives, and the capacity to manage change and economic crises.[29]

5.3.1 *Trento*

The Italian province of Trento has developed a successful CDM. Trento established its first consumer cooperative in 1890, its first rural 'Raiffeisen' cooperative bank in 1892, and the first agricultural wine cooperative in 1893. These three sectors form the core of the Trento cooperative movement. The movement later expanded in the 1980s to include cooperatives from the housing, construction, services, and social welfare sectors (Ianes 2014). Today, the Trento province, with a population of close to 550,000 people, boasts 436 cooperatives that are supported by 290,000 members. They produce 7.6 per cent of the province's GDP and provide direct employment to 24,000 employees. Cooperatives account for only 1 per cent of the province's total businesses, but they employ 21 per cent of all private sector employees (ISTAT 2019). Cooperatives control over 80 per cent of agricultural production, over 50 per cent of banking activities, and over 38 per cent of the retail market (OECD 2014). Trento has succeeded in forming a successful cooperative district for the following reasons: solid leadership and foundations embedded into the local community; a cooperative, friendly state; the formation of a solid cooperative network; and the ability to manage change at the enterprise level and at the network level.

Trento cooperatives were formed in response to high unemployment, poverty, and emigration. Trento is a mountainous area and did not experience the industrialisation of other Northern regions. Peasant holdings were small as a result of the Napoleonic Code that divided land equally among the family's children. In response, local Catholic priests influenced by the Catholic Social Doctrine, led by Lorenzo Guetti, promoted cooperatives to help families and their communities. To this end, consumer cooperatives were established to provide food on credit and to sell local produce; local banks were established to provide farmers with credit so they could buy equipment and seeds; and agricultural cooperatives were established to help farmers process and market their products. In support of these cooperatives, second-grade cooperatives were formed, including the Federation of Rural Banks and Cooperatives in 1893, representing the whole cooperative sector; the Trentino Catholic Bank in 1899 to provide financial coordination and inter-banking loan functions; and the consumer wholesale society (SAIT) in 1899. By 1914, there were already 265 consumer cooperatives operating alongside 177 rural banks. Solid foundations for future growth had been laid: sound selfless leadership from Catholic priests who put the needs of families and communities above profits; cooperatives meeting the needs of the local community; local embeddedness through small-scale cooperatives present in every small village; an inter-sectoral, united, cooperative movement; one central cooperative federation; and a consortium for every economic sector (Ianes 2014).

The State has always supported cooperative development in Trento. The Austrian government established the Provincial Agricultural Department in 1881, which promoted agricultural cooperatives throughout the Province.[30] In 1948, the Autonomous Provincial Government of Trento was granted powers to promote cooperatives and to ensure compliance with the national cooperative law. To this end, the provincial government provided cooperatives with business services and funding. In the 1980s, it promoted job creation programmes for cooperatives providing employment to long-term unemployed and for people reaching retirement age (Ianes 2014, OECD 2014). Since 1992, the local government has been a joint shareholder with the Trentino Federation of Cooperatives (the Federation) in Promosviluppo, a finance company that manages the cooperative development fund and invests in local cooperatives as an equity partner (Promosviluppo 2018).

In 2004, the Trento Provincial Government delegated the Federation the powers to keep oversight, including regular auditing, of the Trentino cooperatives (Ianes 2014).

The Italian Constitution, as per Article 45, requires the Italian state to promote cooperatives. To this end, the Italian state's laws on cooperatives have facilitated their formation, growth and access to finance. The State facilitated the formation of cooperatives by allowing only three persons to start a cooperative; it facilitated access to credit via provisions on members' shares, member loans, access to external investors, and various tax concessions for profits re-invested in the cooperative; it enabled cooperative growth by allowing the formation of cooperative groups and joint ventures; it promoted cooperatives in perpetuity by enforcing the indivisibility of cooperative reserves. The law promotes democratic management based on the principle of one-person-one-vote. In 1991, it passed the law on social cooperatives, and in 1992 it promoted cooperative development funds. The law requires cooperatives to deposit 3 per cent of profits into the Federation's fund, Promocoop (Fici 2013, Ammirato 2018).

The Trento model, like the Legacoop model, can be described as a successful intersectoral cooperative network. The model consists of individual cooperative members, a major consortium for each economic activity, the Federation as a coordinating body, and a series of public companies providing financial and related services to cooperative members. The network has also evolved to include external partners from Italy and overseas that have improved its competitiveness. There are four key features of this network. First, the Trentino Federation, unlike other parts of Italy, represents all the cooperatives in the Trento area, including those formerly associated with Legacoop. The Federation performs a coordinating role, an auditing function, and provides technical expertise. It also manages the cooperative development fund and other financial companies. The second feature is the consortia. These have been established for over 100 years, but since the 1980s, the strategy has been to have one consortium per economic sector in order to achieve economies of scale. These consortia perform the processing and marketing functions on behalf of producers. These provincial consortia reduce costs, achieve economies of scale, market all products, process raw materials, conduct research, provide training, and have even formed holding companies to form groups of companies. These Consortia perform for Trento the same leadership role that large cooperatives perform for Legacoop.[31] In doing so, they keep cooperatives small and embedded in local economies, just like Father Guetti suggested over one century ago.

The third feature is the Trentino Federation's support network. The Federation, in partnership with the cooperative banks, cooperative consortia, and the local government, have established companies that provide financial, training, and health services. These include Promocoop (equity and loans); Cooperfidi (credit guarantees); Fincoop Spa (equity finance); Formazione Lavoro (education and training); Assicura Brokers (insurance); Cooperazione Salute (health cover); Coopersviluppo (consumer cooperative development).

The fourth feature is the formation of alliances. The Trento model has extended its alliances and partnerships beyond its province. Its consumer sector buys products from Legacoop's Coop Italia, and its agricultural sector sells products via Coop Italia. The consumer consortium SAIT also services the nearby region of Friuli. The Central Bank for Trento, formed in 1974, broadened its market by becoming the central bank for North East Italy in 2004. It is now one of the two cooperative banking groups in Italy, and it has welcomed equity investment from the DZ Cooperative Bank from Germany (Dorigatti 2014, Ianes 2014, OECD 2014). Finally, in 2008, the Federation established Euricse, the European Research Institute on Cooperatives and Social Enterprises. This centre has become a world-renowned research centre. It publishes the annual data on the top 300 cooperatives from around the world (Euricse 2021).

The Trentino movement is over 130 years old. During this time, it has demonstrated its capacity to manage change. Salvadori notes that the Trentino movement successfully managed to navigate change when it joined Italy after 1919; in surviving under Fascism and growing after 1948; and finally in overcoming the crisis of the 1980s when the Trento province faced competition from large businesses, and Italy was experiencing high unemployment and high public debt (Salvadori 2011). The difficulties of the 1980s were overcome by making changes at all levels of the network. The consumer and cooperative banks merged but still maintained retail outlets and bank branches throughout the territory.[32] All sectors formed one provincial consortium per sector, thus achieving economies of scale and promoting agricultural exports. The Federation coordinated the formation of a number of financial services companies that provided credit guarantees, equity finance, and loans. For instance, in 2016 alone, Promocoop invested 23.5 million euros in 40 cooperatives and consortia (Cooperazione Trentina 2017). The Federation promoted a more pluralist association by merging with Legacoop cooperatives and by promoting new cooperative sectors such as worker cooperatives, service cooperatives, social cooperatives, and housing cooperatives. These new cooperatives numbered 290 by 2014. They had 24,000 members and employed more than 10,000 people (Dorigatti 2014). The consumer movement formed an alliance with Coop Italia, accessing more products at a lower price, and the Central Cooperative Bank extended its reach throughout Italy, providing services to 69 affiliated banks, including 17 from Southern Italy (Cassa Centrale Banca 2022).

The Trentino Model can be classified as unified, multisector cooperative network. Its cooperative culture promotes cooperatives to solve community problems that are embedded in the local economy. It promotes a learning culture that, whilst it absorbs ideas from other cooperative movements (the Consumer and the Raiffeisen movements, for instance), promotes its own unique version of cooperation, such as promoting a unitary system, adopting a consortia-led economic model and, in pioneering the laws on social cooperatives. It has built a respectful partnership with the local government that has led to the Federation conducting audits on its behalf, becoming partners in job creation schemes, and becoming co-financiers of the cooperative sector. It has managed change, and it has diversified into new areas of the economy to meet the needs of the local community.

5.3.2 *Quebec*

The first cooperative in Quebec was established in 1865. Desjardins formed the first popular bank in 1900. Along with cooperative banks, agricultural cooperatives were soon established. In the 1930s, forestry cooperatives were formed. The cooperative movement diversified further from the 1980s with the formation of worker cooperatives, housing cooperatives, solidarity cooperatives, school cooperatives, and funeral cooperatives. The Quebec Council of Cooperatives and Mutuality (CQCM), the sector's peak body, notes that in 2021 there were 3,000 cooperatives (2,800 are non-financial cooperatives) operating in Quebec with 11 million members and 122,000 employees. The non-financial cooperatives associate 1.3 million members and employ 46,000 people (Ministry of Economy and Innovation 2022). The Quebec cooperative sector produces 52 billion CAD of revenue, which equals 14.5 per cent of the region's GDP (CQCM 2022, Ministry of Economy and Innovation 2022).

The factors for Quebec's cooperative success include the cooperative's embeddedness with the local economy and local society; the cooperative movement's capacity to create networks to promote new cooperatives and business services; the State's enabling and supporting role; the supporting financial structures; and the cooperative movement's success in managing change.

Cooperatives have always been a key part of Quebec society. The Desjardins popular banks movement was established to give the French-speaking population their own financial institution so they could access credit and not rely on British or US finance. From the beginning, the Catholic Church, its parish system, and the local communities supported Desjardins. In the 1980s, when Quebec faced high unemployment, civil society organisations, including universities, the trade union movement, social economy coalitions, and the State, supported the cooperative movement to create employment, provide affordable housing, and provide welfare services. This coalition linked the old and new cooperatives and provided new ideas about cooperative networks, cooperative finance, and cooperative legislation (Diamantopoulos 2011). The Desjardins movement also provided confidence in how to manage change, considering it managed to overcome difficulties during the great depression, during economic downturns following the end of the great boom, and during the GFC (Bajo and Roelants 2011).

The second key factor is Quebec's cooperative network's ability to represent the movement, promote new cooperatives in new sectors, and provide business services throughout Quebec. The network consists of the CQCM, which is the peak body; 12 sectoral organisations, which support cooperative development, coordinate economic activity, and provide business services; 11 Regional Development Cooperatives (RDCs), which represent and support over 1,100 cooperatives throughout their lifecycle[33]; the Desjardins cooperative banking group; and mutual societies (Ministry of Economy and Innovation 2022). The CQCM manages the RDCs, which group cooperatives from all sectors and provide start-up, legal, financial, and management support. It has been estimated that in the first 25 years of operation, RDCs helped create 16,000 jobs (Reliess 2013). They also helped establish 243 new cooperatives from 2016 to 2021 (CDRQ 2021). The cooperative network is supported by external organisations, including the ministries for housing, agriculture and the social solidarity economy; the universities of Montreal, Quebec, and Sherbrooke, which all teach cooperative studies; the unions; community organisations; and the peak organisation for the social economy, the Chantier de l'Economie Sociale (Government du Quebec 2003).

The Quebec state has been very supportive, especially since the economic recession of the 1980s. The State has promoted an enabling cooperative legislation, funded cooperative programmes, and provided tax concessions. First, the cooperative legislation facilitates cooperative growth, capitalisation, and cooperation among cooperatives and promotes cooperative values. The law requires five people to form cooperatives. Each member has one vote. It promotes capitalisation via retention of surplus, via members' rebates that can be used to increase members' capital accounts, and by allowing the issuing of preferential shares with non-voting rights. Governance arrangements have been improved by allowing members representing the CQCM or a financial cooperative to sit on cooperative boards. The law promotes cooperation among cooperatives by specifically noting the role that the CQCM performs in coordinating the activity of the cooperative movement (Petrou 2013). Second, the State supports cooperative capitalisation via tax concessions. In 1985, the State promoted the Cooperative Re-investment Plan, which allows the cooperative to issue preference shares to members and employees whilst receiving a 125 per cent tax deduction. This programme facilitated close to 500 million CAD in investment from 1985 to 2009 (Forsey 1989). Third, the State provides financial support. The State provided 20 million CAD in support of promotional activities to RDCs from 2003 to 2006 (Government du Quebec 2003). The finance company, Investissement Quebec, founded in 1997, raised 15 million CAD in 2001 to provide loans and credit guarantees to cooperatives. Quebec also established 57 Community Future Development Corporations, which provided loans of up to 416 million to members of the social economy, including cooperatives (Mendell 2015).

The cooperative sector has access to a number of social instruments created by cooperatives and social economy stakeholders. In 1971, the Labour movement created the Bank for the Solidarity Economy.[34] It has more than 21,000 members, including 4,000 cooperatives, social economy associations, and 16,000 individuals. Its 2021 loan portfolio amounts to 1.2 billion, of which 323 million are lent to over 1,000 cooperatives (Caisse Déconomie Solidaire Desjardins 2021). In 1997, a public–private partnership created the Réseau d'Investissement Social du Québec (Quebec Social Investment Network Fund), which by 2011 provided 14 million CAD in loans and credit guarantees to 354 cooperatives (Mendell 2015). Two public-private funds are providing long-term patient capital. The Social Economy Trust Fund (Fiducie) was formed with a capitalisation of 22.6 million CAD in 2007, and by 2021 provided 116 million CAD to 315 cooperative projects (Fiducie 2022). The Co-Investissement Coop Fund, with 30 million CAD in capitalisation, provides cooperatives with access to patient capital from 50,000 to 1 million CAD (Mendell 2015).

The Quebec cooperative network has been very resilient. The economic recession of the 1980s led to the failure of many cooperatives and to the CQCM's loss of credibility. Yet, the movement regrouped, supported by new civil society stakeholders, and it was able to create unity between the old cooperative leadership and new cooperatives. They improved the cooperative law, created a broad cooperative network that included public-social economy-cooperative partnerships, and provided cooperatives with access to finance and managerial support structures. This enabled the movement to overcome the crisis and to demonstrate to the government that it could contribute to solving economic and social problems. From 1995 to 2000, the number of new cooperatives established each year grew from 85 to 169. Cooperative jobs increased by 46 per cent compared to an increase of 9 per cent by the whole economy. The cooperative survival rate for five years was 64 per cent, much higher than the 36 per cent survival rate of the rest of the economy (Government du Quebec 2003, Diamantopoulos 2011). There were 479 solidarity cooperatives established from 1997 to 2007, amounting to 28 per cent of all new cooperatives formed in that period (Girard and Langlois 2009). Total employment for the cooperative sector increased from almost 74,000 jobs in 2007 to 122,000 direct jobs in 2021. The cooperative sector produces 14.5 per cent of Quebec's GDP (CQCM 2022). The cooperative sector in Quebec has been operating for over 100 years and has developed into a key economic sector that can work in partnership with the State and civil society to meet people's needs and solve community problems.

5.3.3 Japan

The Japanese cooperative movement has developed into two broad multi-purpose and multi-sectoral movements: one led by the agricultural cooperatives in rural areas and the other by the consumer movement in urban areas. *The Agricultural Cooperatives Act* of

1947 allowed agricultural cooperatives to carry out economic, banking, insurance, and health services activities to serve their rural members. *The Consumer Cooperatives Act* of 1948 also allowed consumer cooperatives to operate in retail and welfare but did not allow them to own their own bank and imposed restrictive trade practices (Kurimoto and Akeda 2021). This did not prevent the Japanese consumer movement from growing into a multi-sector group. The movement is led by JCCU, which coordinates the affiliated retail sector, the insurance sector, the health and welfare sector, and the housing sector. In 2020 the consumer movement associated close to 30 million members, generating a turnover of 3.8 trillion yen, and providing employment to 74,000 employees (JCCU 2022). This section will focus on the consumer sector. It explains the reasons for its success by examining: the Consumer Cooperative Act; the consumer retail sector's innovative community-based culture; the leadership role of the JCCU; the capacity to deal with adversity and manage change.

The Consumer Cooperatives Act of 1948 promoted democratic cooperative principles based on one-person-one-vote, limited return on capital, allowed members to hold more than one share, and prevented demutualisation. The Act does not allow external shareholders. The law acknowledged cooperatives' role in elevating the cultural and economic standards of the daily life of their members, and it allowed multi-sector activity. Cooperatives are taxed at a lower rate than corporations, but the difference has been reduced from 12.3 per cent in 1984 to only 4.4 per cent in 2016. The Law prevented consumer cooperatives from developing a 'European type' growth model based on national wholesale associations and large supermarkets. The Law restricted consumer cooperatives to trade only with members (health cooperatives could trade with non-members), prevented them from operating a wholesale society until 1954, allowed them to operate only small stores until 1998, and required them to trade within one prefecture until 2007. Consumer cooperatives are still excluded from banking activity. They could operate an insurance company subject to it being separate from the retailing business (Kurimoto and Akeda 2021). In conclusion, the law prevented the consumer sector from growing to its full potential, but it did allow the development of a multi-purpose consumer-led cooperative and allowed cooperatives to attract members who were willing to purchase more shares to finance its growth.

The Japanese consumer movement's unique community-based culture is a major reason for its success. Unlike the European consumer sector's working-class roots, the Japanese movement was focussed on broader societal issues, as well as providing quality grocery and food items at fair prices. The consumer sector in Japan came to prominence in the 1960s out of its concerns for consumer and health-related issues. It was concerned with food adulteration, especially in powdered milk, misleading labelling, and environmental pollution caused by industrialisation and the chemical industry. It was a pacifist movement and campaigned against war and against nuclear weapons. This broad consumer culture focussed on protecting consumers and engaging with citizens on broader political issues. This activism led to consumer cooperatives attracting millions of members and promoting welfare services for Japanese citizens. Indeed, the Nada-Kobe cooperative formed the 'Co-op Mutual Associations', providing home services to handicapped persons and 'group lunches' for elderly persons from 1991. Other cooperatives soon followed in providing welfare services (Saito 2010).

The Japanese consumer movement developed an innovative, unique cooperative model. Their response to legal restrictions to establish supermarkets was to promote housewife-led group buying activity (Han Groups) and, from 1990, individual home delivery activities. This strategy was supported by flexible, cost-effective organisations that used information technology software, warehouses to store food, and vans for home deliveries (Kurimoto 2020). Their popularity as a democratic organisation promoting consumer rights, engaging in political issues, and supplying healthy products, attracted close to 25 million members. They purchased more than one share, and by 2020, the value of members' accounts amounted to 736 billion yen (5.4 billion USD) (JCCU 2022). Having a large membership that purchased multiple shares provided capital to finance their operations without requiring access to their own banking facilities or external shareholders.

A major factor in the success and development of a multi-sector consumer movement is the role performed by JCCU, the consumer movement's central association. The JCCU was established as the national consumer cooperative federation in 1951. It has performed a leading role for the retail consumer sector by consolidating buying power and supplying goods from local suppliers, developing its own Coop-brand products (including from overseas partners), providing legal and consulting services, and by providing strategic directions such as promoting joint-buying groups, and a larger membership. JCCU also provides political representation on behalf of the consumer movement (Saito 2010, JCCU 2022).

JCCU was instrumental in promoting the health and welfare sector and the insurance sector. The JCCU founded the Japanese Health and Welfare Cooperative Federation in 1957 (HEW CO-OP). Initially a branch of the JCCU, it began to attract established welfare cooperatives formed by consumer cooperatives or by retirees. The welfare branch grew to 77 medical cooperatives in 1970 and to 105 in 1980. HEW CO-OP became an independent association in 2010 but is still affiliated to JCCU (Saito 2010). Today there are 104 cooperative societies with close to 3 million members. They own 75 hospitals, 333 primary health care centres, 75 dental facilities, and over 350 nursing care facilities. HEW CO-OP provides employment to over 39,000 employees, including over 2,000 doctors and 235 dentists (HEW CO-OP 2020).

The JCCU commenced selling insurance in 1975. Initially, it was an agent of the union-led cooperative insurance company Zenrosai. In 1987, JCCU developed its own life and health insurance products and sold them via consumer cooperatives. In 2020, 151 consumer cooperatives sold over 8 million JCCU insurance policies worth 1.5 billion USD. JCCU also affiliates the larger Kokumin Kyosai Co-Op, which offers insurance mainly to trade union members. The latter has the support of 58 cooperative societies, and it sells 29 million insurance policies worth over 4 billion USD (Saito 2010; JCCU 2022).

The consumer movement has shown resilience and the ability to manage change and innovate. First, in 1990, when more Japanese women joined the workforce, and the 'Han Group' delivery strategy was no longer viable, the consumer movement introduced individual home delivery. Today, this new segment accounts for over 70 per cent of all home delivery sales (JCCU 2022). Second, in the 1990s, the consumer movement faced a reputational crisis as a result of mismanagement, some fraudulent activity, and mislabelling. Some cooperatives went bankrupt, and others faced bankruptcy. To this end, the JCCU and other consumer cooperatives established a solidarity fund which lent money to consumer cooperatives in need. They also provided financial and management support, made improvements to governance practices, and improved access to reliable food suppliers. All these actions helped the consumer movement to overcome the crisis. Third, when the government passed the *Long-Term Care Insurance Act* in 1997, the consumer movement quickly established daycare facilities, nursing homes, and other services in support of their members, in alignment with the government law. It has also managed to organise some 30,000 Han Groups that promote preventive medicine and conduct health check-ups for their members (Restakis 2010, HEW CO-OP 2015, 2020).

The Japanese model can be described as a consumer-led multisector urban-based cooperative network. Each consumer activity is autonomous, yet it is linked via JCCU's coordinating role; via inter-sectoral linkages between consumer cooperatives and the insurance, health and welfare sectors; and via promoting common cooperative-community goals. There is also some level of inter-sectoral cooperation between consumer and agricultural cooperatives and health and welfare sector and worker cooperatives. It is important to stress the uniqueness of the Japanese consumer retail movement, which consists of (i) an enterprise model based on a home delivery service led by Han Groups, and (ii) multi-sector services performed by autonomous national associations. This approach differed from the European models, which are based on promoting supermarket chains supported by the provision of services owned and controlled by the consumer cooperatives.

5.3.4 CG-SCOP

The CG-SCOP network of cooperatives represents worker cooperatives, social cooperatives, and participatory companies. It represents cooperatives operating in the industries and services sectors of the French economy. The CG-SCOP cooperative network is part of France Coop, which associates cooperatives from all sectors of the economy. France Coop is a large movement comprising 22,589 cooperatives, with over 28 million members, and employing close to 1.3 million employees. The largest sectors are the banking, agriculture, and retail sectors. The CG-SCOP network is smaller, but it has grown continuously over the years. The CG-SCOP was formed in 1978. It associated 736 cooperatives in 1980. In 2009 it associated 1927 cooperatives which employed 40,000 persons. Today CG-SCOP associates 3,801 cooperatives that employ over 71,000 persons, of whom 13,000 are employed by social cooperatives (Corcoran and Wilson 2010, Soulage 2011, Cooperatives Europe 2021, CG-SCOP 2022).

The ideology of French worker cooperatives can be summarised as anti-capitalist with a desire of members to have control over their working lives and to distribute fairly the fruits of their labour. This culture is a result of a long cooperative tradition beginning in the eighteenth century with the Utopian Socialists, Fourier and Cabet, and continuing in the nineteenth century with Buchez and Louis Blanc. Buchez developed the accepted worker cooperative governance principles that are still adhered to today.[35] Fauquet's concept of cooperatives as the third sector of the economy proposed in 1935,[36] and the concept of workers' self-management of the 1970s also influenced the worker cooperative movement in France. These ideas promoting cooperation were always tempered by the Left political parties and the trade union, which always focussed on the State and workplace struggles to improve working people's living standards (Espagne 2001, Espagne 2009).

CG-SCOP operates within a supportive legislative framework that is in compliance with ICA principles. The Law allows external shareholders (with limited return on capital and voting rights limited to 35 per cent of total votes), allows the formation of cooperative groups, and prevents assets and reserves from being distributed. The law allows cooperatives associated with CG-SCOP to distribute up to 40 per cent of profits to all employees (including non-members). Cooperatives are required to finance the CG-SCOP association via a fee equivalent to 0.42 per cent of their annual revenue. The State provides tax concessions if profits are placed in the indivisible reserve fund and if bonus payments are re-invested in the cooperative for five years (Soulage 2011, Hiez 2013, Douvitsa 2021).

The CG-SCOP confederation comprises one central association, four sectoral associations, 12 regional unions, and a financial network. The network supports cooperatives throughout their lifecycle. First, the CG-SCOP central association promotes cooperatives, coordinates and represents the network in public fora, and performs oversight functions to ensure compliance with the law and with cooperative principles. Second, the 13 regional unions support the formation of cooperatives at a local and regional level. Third, the sectoral associations (building, communication, manufacturing, and social cooperatives) provide economic, technical and legal support and promote inter-cooperative support. Fourth, CG-SCOP cooperatives can access equity and long-term loans from a financial network consisting of (i) CG-SCOP's own financial company, Socoden, which provides equity and loans; (ii) Socoden and another financial society, SPOT, provide finance for WBOs; (iii) two regional financial societies provide credit guarantee (with support from Credit Cooperatif); and (iv) IDES, formed in 1983, and funded by the State and social economy stakeholders, provides finance via purchasing cooperative bonds or equity as an external investor. Socoden funds up to 150 cooperatives each year with loans ranging from 5,000 to 600,000 Euros, whilst IDES financed 280 cooperatives from 1983 to 2010 (Corcoran and Wilson 2010, CG-SCOP 2022a).

The CG-SCOP cooperative network has developed sectoral, territorial and financial support structures. It has formed partnerships with the social economy and the State. The network has grown steadily by offering its members support throughout their lifecycle. It is a unique model that requires cooperatives to fund the operation of the CG-SCOP network; requires 40–45 per cent of profits to be distributed to all workers, thus acknowledging every worker's contribution to wealth creation (CG-Scop 2023).

5.3.5 Wonju

The Wonju Network of the Social Economy is a small multi-sector network of 29 cooperatives formed in the City of Wonju, Republic of Korea. It comprises the Balgeum Credit Union, Hansalim consumer-producer cooperative, the Wonju medical cooperative, and other cooperatives operating in the education, childcare, culture, and environment sectors. The network develops common goals, and they jointly invest to create new cooperatives. The Wanju cooperative movement focusses on community goals that consider the needs of stakeholders and not just members. The key features to note are the leaders' original ideas and their influence on cooperative development; how the network supports new cooperatives; the Hansalim consumer cooperative's goals and broad membership; the cooperative law; and how the Network has managed change.

Hak-soon Ji, a Catholic Bishop, and Il-soon Chang, a human rights activist, promoted the Wonju cooperative movement. Ji was influenced by the Second Vatican Council teachings and promoted democracy, solidarity, social justice, and civil society associations. Chang was a local civil movement activist who promoted environmentally responsible living, expressed via 'thoughts of life' a concept. In 1972, with support from Germany, they established the Balgeum (Bright) credit union. Balgeum supported small businesses, farmers, and cooperatives. In 1985, it sponsored Hansalim producer-consumer cooperative. In 2002, the Wonju Medical Cooperative was established. In 2009, 29 Wonju cooperatives formed the Wonju Network of the Social Economy (The Network). This Network coordinates the work of its members and promotes new cooperatives. The Network upholds the cooperative principles of common ownership, democratic decision-making, humanistic social service, contribution to the local community, and cooperation among the cooperatives. Their goal is to emulate the cooperative models operating in Trento and Mondragon (Han, Chung and Park 2013).

The Wonju model's core group of cooperatives, Balgeum, Hansalim, and the Wonju consumer cooperative, over time, promoted a multi-sector cooperative network. These cooperatives have encouraged the formation of new cooperatives to meet the emerging needs of the people of Wonju. They promoted eco-friendly farming household cooperatives in 1989, various welfare services cooperatives in the 1990s, a medical cooperative in 2002, a cooperative providing jobs for the elderly in 2005, organic rice cooperative in 2008 and so on. The process used to establish a new cooperative included forming an organising committee; coordinating the support from existing cooperatives to support new cooperatives; encouraging cooperatives and individual members to invest capital; providing management expertise; and promoting inter-cooperative trade, especially via Hansalim. The Network was strengthened through the promotion of interlocking directorships (the chair of one cooperative would also be chair of a new cooperative, or members would join more than one cooperative). New cooperatives were also able to access a socially active workforce that had been formally educated in cooperative principles (Hin and Lee 2013).

The Wonju model is enhanced through the Hansalim consumer-producer cooperative. Consumers and producers are both members of Hansalim and have developed common goals that go beyond the interests of consumers. The name Hansalim means 'to save all living things on earth'. Hansalim's key goal is to build a society where the urban areas and the rural areas, as well as humans and the environment, can coexist. One of its slogans says that "producers have to be responsible for consumers' life, and consumers take responsibility for producers' livelihood" (Stories.coop 2011). This way, urban consumers help farmers improve their standard of living through receiving a stable income. Likewise, farmers provide consumers with organic, authentic food to ensure that consumers avoid food safety problems. To this end, Hansalim gets consumers and producers to trade directly and to jointly set prices, thus bypassing the market. This creates a harmonious and respectful relationship between urban and rural areas. The Hansalim cooperative is headquartered in Seoul. It comprises 23 cooperatives nationwide, 114 producer associations, 640,000 members, and 215 stores (Stories.coop 2011, Kim et al. 2020).

The *Framework on Cooperatives Act* of 2012 (FCA) promotes cooperatives' development of local economies. The FCA states its legislative purpose is to facilitate independent self-supportive cooperatives so they can contribute to social integration, contribute to local communities by engaging in purchasing, production, sales, and provision of goods or services, and contribute to a balanced development of the national economy. The FCA requires consumer cooperatives to trade with members only and requires welfare cooperatives to demonstrate that at least 50 per cent of their transactions are with members. Three members are needed to form a social cooperative, and 300 are needed to form a consumer cooperative. Members can hold up to 30 per cent of the total capital raised (20 per cent in consumer cooperatives), but still hold one vote. The FCA does not allow external investors, but member accounts can be remunerated up to 10 per cent per annum after depositing a portion of profits in the reserve fund. Social cooperatives can distribute up to 40 per cent of profits as a patronage refund. Social cooperative shares are indivisible, but other cooperatives can distribute assets if they dissolve. It seems that the focus is to promote members' only trade and members' only capitalisation, supported by generous remuneration of shares and patronage (Jang 2013, ICA Asia and Pacific 2019).

The Wonju Network has continually evolved in order to respond to people's needs following the economic and social changes experienced in Korea as a result of industrialisation, the financial crisis of the 1990s, and the GFC. The Wonju experience commenced with two leaders, and it evolved through the formation of key cooperatives in the banking and consumer sector. These, in turn, formed medical cooperatives and welfare cooperatives that catered for the elderly. Once a key group of cooperatives had been formed, they established the Wonju Social Cooperative Network, along with key principles to further unite and promote the cooperative sector in Wonju (Lee, Sang-Il and Chung 2014).

The Wonju cooperative network is a unique network because its ultimate goals are to solve community problems via a strong, cohesive, humane community of cooperatives. It differs from the traditional cooperative principles because their goals are broader than just serving their members' interests. The blending of the Korean philosophy on life principles with those of Catholic solidarity and social justice enables them to promote cooperatives like Hansalim within which the interests of consumers and producers and urban and rural needs can coexist. This culture contrasts with traditional consumer cooperatives, which have seen their role as predominantly protecting and advancing the interests of consumers.

5.3.6 Summary: Good Practice

As was the case with other cooperative models considered in previous chapters, the cooperative models of Trento, Quebec, Japan, CG-SCOP, and Wonju all have displayed unique country-specific features and also common features that are present in all cooperative models that operate CMEs.

The common good practice features of these cooperative models include those features that allow cooperatives to develop, to grow, to manage change, and to pass on their assets and acquired know-how to the next generation. They also propose forms of interaction between cooperatives, the cooperative movement, civil society, and the State. These key features are:

- Having a vision for society or goals that are higher than enterprise-specific goals. These visions or goals influence cooperatives or make cooperatives complementary to their goals. These may include the Catholic Social Doctrine, community and French identity in Quebec, Catholicism and community identity in Trento; the anti-war and holistic consumer movement in Japan; Korea's philosophy of life principles; or the egalitarian culture of CG-SCOP cooperatives.
- A coordinating cooperative association that can provide leadership and direction, promote entrepreneurship, provide administrative and business services, and provide access to finance.
- A multi-sectoral network of cooperatives that support one another, and that support cooperative structures, the formation of new cooperatives, and new cooperative sectors.
- An enabling legislation that supports cooperative principles, access to capital, and cooperative formation.
- A supportive State which in addition to an enabling cooperative law, supports cooperatives through the provision of finance (equity or loans), cooperative-specific tax policies, access to public resources and job creation schemes.

- A supportive civil society that supports the cooperative movement with its ideas, social movements, financial structures, and new needs for cooperatives to solve.
- A cooperative movement with the capacity, capability, and will to manage change and to support cooperatives in crisis.
- A cooperative movement that appreciates the need to be competitive in alignment with cooperative principles.

5.4 International Cooperative Movement

Since the 1990s, the ICA has coordinated a larger, more diverse international cooperative movement. In 1991 the ICA claimed to represent 79 countries and 670 million cooperative members (Develtere 1992). In 2022, the ICA represented 112 countries, 2.9 million cooperatives, and more than 1.2 billion cooperative members. The Cicopa-led cooperative census of 2017 noted that 2.9 million cooperatives employed 27 million employees and 252 million primary producers. This means that cooperative employment equals 9.46 per cent of total world employment (CICOPA 2017, International Cooperative Alliance 2022). The Asian region organised the majority of cooperatives (73 per cent), the majority of employees (62 per cent), as well as 45 per cent of all members (CICOPA 2017).[37]

The cooperative movement became more diverse. These changes reflected cooperatives' responses to globalisation, de-industrialisation, the weakening of the Welfare State, demographic changes, and to information technology. Cooperatives now operated as corporations, as holding groups, they owned subsidiaries, they promoted worker buy-outs, promoted stakeholder cooperatives, and promoted the use of platform technology to counter emerging businesses. This provided the cooperative movement with opportunities but also with risks. Sven Ake Book noted these risks in his report to the ICA congress held in Tokyo in 1992. Just like Laidlaw's report to the ICA's Moscow Congress in 1980, Book's report highlighted concerns about cooperatives' democratic practices and member participation, the tendency to deviate from the principle of limited return on capital, and the practice of forming joint-stock companies. He also noted that the ICA needed to have better data on the cooperative movement, needed to understand better the transformation of planned economies, and needed to support cooperatives in their dealings with the State. Book went on to highlight three core recommendations for updating the ICA principles: strengthen the concept of limited interest on capital (and capital formation); include the participation of employees in cooperative administration; and emphasise the autonomy and independence of cooperatives (Book 1992).

The ICA responded to these challenges in a number of ways. First, in 1992 it modified its organisational structure to accommodate the various cooperative geographic areas, and to this end, it established the four regional offices of Europe, the Americas, Africa, and Asia-Pacific. It also established eight sectoral associations and five committees dealing with gender equality, cooperative research, cooperative law, youth network, and international cooperative development network (ICA 2022a).

The second response was to update the Cooperative principles of 1966 at the 1995 ICA Congress held in Manchester. The Congress agreed on a definition of a cooperative, added cooperative values to the cooperative principles, and added a seventh principle: 'concern for the community'. A cooperative was now defined as: "an autonomous association of persons united voluntarily to meet their common economic, social and cultural needs and aspirations through a jointly-owned and democratically-controlled

Table 5.1 Cooperatives, Employment, and Membership

Regions and Number of Countries	*Number of Cooperatives*	*Employment*			*Total Employment (A+B+C)*	*User members (D)*	*Total members (B+C+D)*
		Employees (A)	*Worker members (B)*	*Producer Members (C)*			
Europe (37)	221,960	4,710.595	1,554,687	9,157,350	15,422,632	152,064,608	162,776,645
Africa (35)	375,375	1,939.836	37,836	20,410,298	22,387,970	33,638,298	54,086,432
Asia (33)	2,156,219	7,426,760	8,573,775	219,247,186	235,247,721	320,130,233	547,951,194
America (39)	181,378	1,896,257	983,285	3,237,493	6,116,035	417,580,396	421,800,174
Oceania (12)	2,391	75,438	0	147,071	222,509	30,696,144	30,843,215
Total 156	**2,937,323**	**16,048,886**	**11,148,583**	**252,199,398**	**279,396,867**	**954,109,676**	**1,217,457,660**

Source: Cicopa (2017).

enterprise" (ICA 2022). The emphasis is on autonomy, democracy, and social and economic needs. Cooperative values included self-help, self-responsibility, democracy, equality, equity, and solidarity. The seven principles consisted of voluntary and open membership, democratic member control, member economic participation, autonomy and independence, education, training and information, cooperation among cooperatives, and concern for the community (ICA 2022). Since 1966, there has been more emphasis on cooperation among cooperatives, which is one way of creating a cooperative movement; and concern for the community, which emphasises that cooperatives are not just concerned with members' welfare but have concerns for all stakeholders and for their community. In 2016, the ICA produced guidance notes to help cooperators understand and apply these principles (ICA 2017). In 2022, the ICA is again conducting a review of the cooperative principles to make sure they reflect the needs and aspirations of today's cooperators and society.[38]

The third response was to promote cooperative development and cooperative principles internationally. To this end it received strong support from the United Nations and the International Labour Organisation (ILO). The United Nations approved the *United Nations Guidelines Aimed at Creating a Supporting Environment for the Development of Cooperatives* in 2001. The ILO approved *Recommendation 193 on the Promotion of Cooperatives* in 2002. These two documents explicitly endorsed the ICA principles, the definition of a cooperative, and the cooperative sector. They recommend that states support cooperatives whilst preserving their autonomy and their cooperative identity. They also encourage States to promote cooperatives through appropriate legislation, access to credit, and education and training. They also suggested that states promote cooperative research and data gathering, as well as collaborative partnerships (United Nations 2001, ILO 2002). The ICA encouraged governments in some developing countries to perform an enabling role rather than a controlling role on cooperatives. International recognition culminated with the United Nations declaring the Year of Cooperatives in 2012. The ICA responded by developing a strategy for the next decade that focussed on five themes: participation, sustainability, identity, legal framework, and capital (ICA 2013).

The fourth ICA response was to develop more reliable data on the cooperative sector worldwide so that it could have a clearer picture of the contribution cooperatives were making to the economy and to society. To this end, it engaged Cicopa Europe to prepare a report on the world cooperative sector. Cicopa produced a report in 2014 and another in 2017. In addition, Euricse was commissioned to prepare a report of the largest 300 cooperatives in the world. Euricse has published its tenth report demonstrating that cooperatives can grow large businesses in all sectors of the economy (Euricse 2021).

Finally, the ICA, through its various regional areas and specific committees, has been informing the public on cooperative finance, cooperative governance, and cooperative legislation. These are important topics for promoting cooperative identity and for promoting cooperative development. A key promotional tool is the Coop4Development website developed by the ICA in partnership with the European Union. This project provides key data on cooperative movements around the world, as well as an analysis of each country's legislative framework. It successfully informs cooperators, governments, and scholars about good practice in cooperative law (ICA 2016).[39] The ICA also engaged cooperative scholars to prepare reports on cooperative governance and cooperative access to capital.[40]

The ICA is currently reviewing the cooperative principles and has developed another ten-year plan. It will be interesting to see how the new cooperative values and principles will reflect some of the current themes, such as global poverty; inequality; gender balance; sustainability, and climate change. It will also be interesting to see how it will accommodate all the organisational and cultural differences, from cooperative groups to stakeholder cooperatives. The ICA has been able to promote cooperative principles, and establish good relations with international bodies like the United Nations and the ILO (Granata 2019). The biggest challenge will be to get cooperatives and cooperative movements to work closer together internationally in the same way that some cooperative movements are working together nationally. If the best national practices highlighted so far can be replicated internationally, then the cooperative-led market economy can begin to challenge the CME as the preferred way to meet people's economic, social and cultural needs.

5.5 Summary

- Nation states and international bodies like the IMF, the World Bank, and the WTO promoted a neo-liberal world economic order. They promoted the 'Washington Consensus' policies of privatisation, deregulation, lower taxes, and the liberalisation of global markets. Within this context, Corporations increased overseas investments, and MNCs grew from 7,000 to 100,000. The top 200 MNCs produced 50 per cent of the world's industrial output and dominated the world economy. Corporations promoted their own ideas about the economy and society, influenced government policies, and succeeded in promoting a world economy suited to their needs. The power and influence of corporations prevented cooperatives' ideas from becoming mainstream and to influence the public debate.
- The State, whilst weakened as a result of neo-Liberal policies and ideology, still collected revenue that exceeded 40 per cent of the GDP and spent more than 40 per cent of the GDP in most OECD countries. The State, however, privatised most or all of their government enterprises, faced difficulties in funding the welfare services, and faced higher debt levels following their rescue operations during the GFC. The retreat of the State from directly providing welfare services, along with the problems of inequalities, wealth distribution, the exclusion of disadvantaged people from the economy, and precarious working conditions provided cooperatives with an opportunity to expand into new economic areas and to promote their cooperative model as an alternative to the neo-Liberal CME.
- Cooperatives responded to globalisation by creating larger enterprises via mergers and acquisitions, increasing their members, and increasing their assets. Larger cooperatives found more avenues to access capital. Originally cooperatives had access to capital via members' investments, member loans, and retained profits. Today cooperatives access capital by attracting external capital from individuals or institutional investors; controlling a holding company that attracts external investors; co-owning subsidiaries; holding shares in listed companies; via cooperative-owned financial companies; via cooperative development funds; and via state-cooperative-civil society partnerships.
- Cooperatives responded to globalisation by developing various cooperative enterprise models. Some cooperatives continued to adopt the traditional cooperative model, whilst others adopted the corporate model, the NGC model, and the cooperative group model. The non-traditional models successfully attracted finance and achieved growth but also introduced practices that deviated from the traditional cooperative approach. These included plural voting, accepting external capital with voting powers,

linking the value of member capital to cooperative assets, and practising closed or quasi-closed membership practices.

- Some cooperatives chose to demutualise into capitalist businesses. Demutualisation took place mainly in English-speaking countries where the neo-Liberal ideology was strongest. Demutualisation took place in cooperatives from the financial and agricultural sectors that faced financial difficulties, that were led by management who promoted demutualisation, and that were governed by an ineffective board supported by a passive membership. These members and their leaders no longer believed that the cooperative model was appropriate to serve their needs.
- New types of cooperatives successfully responded to new opportunities and met new public demands. These included cooperatives formed from WBOs of private enterprises; social cooperatives providing social services or employment to disadvantaged citizens; cooperatives that used technology platforms to provide goods and services; and ethical banking offered an alternative to traditional banking.
- Social cooperatives introduced a stakeholder membership model and promoted the general interests. This is a major innovation to the cooperative enterprise model in that it meets the needs of the community and the general interests of society rather than the needs of a limited membership. SCEs also promoted a stakeholder governance model where a different class of voters had the right to elect the Board.
- The cooperative enterprise model has demonstrated that it is an acceptable model to solve the needs of people from every part of the world. Each country has developed a cooperative model that is suited to its needs, reflects its national culture, and is aligned with its political-economic framework. Previous chapters noted the cooperative models developed by the consumer sector in the United Kingdom; the rural cooperative bank model in Germany; the State-agricultural societies partnership model developed in the United States, especially during the New Deal; and the Mondragon and Legacoop CDMs with a strong emphasis on worker cooperatives and inter-cooperative collaboration, trade, and support. In the twenty-first century, other unique CDMs have emerged: in Trento, a network model with a strong role performed by the provincial consortia for each sector; in Quebec, a multi-sector cooperative association with territorial structures, operating in partnership with the State and civil society; in Japan, the consumer movement providing retail, financial, and health and welfare services to all urban consumers; and in Korea, where the Wonju Social Network is an inter-sectoral network that unites urban consumers and agricultural producers in a win-win partnership.
- The ICA has been able to act as the representative body of the global cooperative movement. It has developed inclusive territorial structures. It has highlighted issues that needed to be addressed. It has promoted cooperative principles. It has established good working relations with international bodies. It has promoted debates on cooperative principles, cooperative law, cooperative finance, and cooperative governance, and is beginning to gather reliable data on the cooperative movement. The ICA has not been able to get cooperative movements to work closer together internationally as they do at the local or national level. The ICA continues to have issues with the cooperative identity considering that there are major differences: between national cooperative laws; in how countries view the role of cooperation in society and the economy; between cooperative sectors; and between traditional cooperatives and cooperatives that operate with dual structures.

5.6 Key Questions

- Corporations actively influence governments, universities, the media, and international institutions, to promote their worldview and pro-capitalist policies that enable them to grow, control markets, and maximise profits. What should the cooperative movement do to promote a cooperative-led market economy or a more pluralist view of the economy and society that would benefit every person and every community?
- The State is still the most influential institution in our society. The State performs legislative, regulatory, social, and economic management functions. It spends, on average, 40 per cent of the GDP across OECD countries. Consider the role of the State during the New Deal and the way it supported cooperatives in Italy, Mondragon, France and Quebec. What is an ideal state-cooperative sector relation in your view? What should the State do to support cooperatives, and what should the State not do? Which cooperative-specific policies can be regarded as fair and reasonable?
- Cooperatives have grown into large enterprises, and in order to compete with corporations, they have attracted external capital and adopted legal forms similar to conventional firms. Imagine that you are the Chair of a cooperative board or the chief executive officer of a cooperative, and you have been asked to prepare a document with various options designed to achieve cooperative growth. You have three strategic options: (1) use the traditional strategy of growing organically and by being part of second-tier cooperative structures? (2) Remain small, locally based, and compete via being part of a consortia or second-tier cooperative structure? (3) Adopt a corporate structure (Fonterra, for instance) or dual structure (Italian or Mondragon cooperatives) and grow via mergers, acquisitions, and conventionally managed subsidiaries? What advice would you give to the Board? What are the risks and rewards for each option? How would you engage with members to discuss these options and arrive at a decision?
- Consider the non-traditional cooperative models: the corporate model, the 'New Generation Cooperative' model, and the cooperative group model. To what extent have they deviated from traditional cooperative principles, and to what extent have they met the needs and aspirations of their members? Do you consider their strategies to be a form of degeneration or do you think that their strategies are a legitimate way for members to promote cooperatives in the twenty-first century?
- Compare and evaluate the three WBO experiences of France, Italy, and Argentina and develop a public policy programme designed to promote WBOs in your country. In answering this question, consider the legal framework, the role of the State, the role of support organisations, workers' culture and their commitment, the leadership qualities needed, and the potential organisational and business risks encountered by newly established worker-cooperatives?
- Compare social cooperatives' mission and membership and governance model with those of traditional cooperative enterprises. What are the major differences between the two cooperative models? Which is your preferred model and why?
- Compare BE's vision for the role of banking in society and its banking practices to the banking practices of credit unions or mutual banks. What are the main differences between these two cooperative banking models? Which of the two banking models has more impact on the economy and society? Which of the two banking models performs a transformative role in society? Should banks perform a transformative role in society?

- Do you agree that in order to develop a united, successful CDM, cooperatives and cooperators need to have, and need to support, a vision of society where cooperatives are a means to a higher goal, and are not considered an end to themselves? In other words, the above statement asserts that people or areas that promote cooperatives as pure enterprises will have less chance of developing a cooperative movement or a successful CDM. Please consider the CDMs of Mondragon, Legacoop, Trento, Quebec, Japan, Korea, and France and any other model of your choice.
- Compare the CDMs from Europe and Quebec with the CDMs developed in Japan and Korea. What are the similarities and differences between the two cooperative traditions? What are the key reasons that led to the development of diverse CDMs?
- Consider the various types of cooperative enterprises and evaluate the extent to which their practices are aligned with the ICA cooperative principles of 1995.
- Examine the history, structure, policies, and practices of the ICA and analyse its strengths and weaknesses. What are the ICA's key achievements, according to you, and where do you think the ICA can improve further so that it can successfully promote the cooperative movement worldwide as an alternative to the CME model?

Notes

1 A cooperative enterprise model refers to the way a cooperative is organised to produce and sell goods and services in the market in order to meet the needs of its members. Cooperatives meet the economic, social, cultural and aspirational needs of their members by competing in the market on their own, or as a member of a second-tier cooperative. Whilst the term enterprise model is synonymous with the term business model, this book will opt to use the term cooperative model interchangeably with the term cooperative enterprise model.

2 Cooperative development model refers to cooperative movements that are able to promote the whole cooperative sector. These are usually led by a cooperative association or federation providing political, strategic, cultural, and economic leadership to an inter-sectoral cooperative movement. Cooperative development models have the capability and capacity to promote new cooperatives, new cooperative sectors, support existing cooperatives, and manage economic or organisational crises that beset the cooperative movement.

3 Key compliance requirements from the Maastricht Treaty included the following: annual budget deficit below 3 per cent of GDP; public debt less than 60 per cent of GDP; inflation rate within 1.5 per cent of the three European Union countries with the lowest rate; long-term interest rates and exchange rates to be contained within certain limits (Steger and Roy 2015).

4 The Panama papers revealed that the wealthy have deposited 7.6 trillion USD in offshore tax havens (Picketty 2014).

5 A Multinational company is one where a parent company owns one or more subsidiaries in other countries which have a coherent system of decision-making and a common strategy (Steger 2020).

6 Apple's capitalisation for instance equals to France's Gross National Product. According to the NASDAC index, on 15 May 2022, Apple's had a capitalisation of 2.38 trillion, which equals the GDP of France, the world's fifth largest economy of 2.32 trillion Euro in 2022. The exchange rate in May was almost identical: 1:1.04 in favour of the Euro (OECD 2022).

7 This performance was weaker than the performance achieved during the period 1961–1973 when it grew 11 years above 4 per cent, and it never experienced negative economic growth (World Bank 2022). The US economy also grew less after 1980. From 1947 to 1980, the United States grew at an annual rate of 3.7 per cent, whilst for the last third of a century, from 1980 to 2017, the average growth rate has been only 2.7 per cent, a full percentage point lower (Stiglitz 2019).

8 Government revenue among OECD countries consisted of 25 per cent of GDP in 1965; 34 per cent in 2011 (Sassoon 2019), and 40 per cent in 2020 (OECD 2022). Government spending among OECD countries was 27 per cent of GDP in 1965, 36 per cent in 2000 (Yergin and Janislaw 1998), and 40 per cent in 2020 (OECD 2022).

9 More specifically states involvement included: States took the following action during the 2020 COVID-19 crisis: kept interest rates low, helped business keep people employed and pay rent, provided one-off payments to low-income families to encourage spending, bought corporate bonds, and made available the COVID-19 vaccine (Steger and Roy 2015).
10 Please refer to the following document for information on Inclusive Capitalism (Coalition for Inclusive Capitalism 2022).
11 The Danish agricultural cooperative ARLA has also maintained a traditional cooperative structure whilst operating internationally (Arla Foods 2021).
12 The term 'corporatisation' refers to cooperatives that adopt the legal, organisational structures, governance arrangements, the language, and reporting formats that is similar to those of corporations.
13 The member-client ratio fluctuated from 16 per cent to 22 per cent from 2004 to 2017. The majority of clients are non-members (Poli 2019).
14 Equity represents the amount of money that would be returned to a company's shareholders if all the assets were liquidated and all of the company's debt was paid off in the case of liquidation. In Sacmi's case, all the net assets are indivisible, so in case of liquidation they would be deposited into the Cooperative Development Fund. Otherwise, the next generation will have the right to use the net assets in accordance with their member's wishes.
15 For instance, five demutualised British building societies transferred 35 billion pounds to their current members in 1995 (Reserve Bank of Australia 1999).
16 In the agricultural and financial sectors many models have been developed in order to access finance and improve competitiveness. Please refer to the following Chaddad and Cook (2004), EACB (2019), and McKillop et al. (2020).
17 SPOT is an equity company owned by the General Confederation of Worker Cooperatives and the ESFIN Group to provide equity to small business and cooperatives formed from private enterprises (Soulage 2011).
18 Legacoop is the more active Central Association considering that WBOs associated with Legacoop generate 87 per cent of the total turnover and 91 per cent of the total profits generated by WBOs (Legacoop 2020).
19 Please refer to the Italian Law on Social Cooperatives: Law of 8 November 1991/381, Article 1.
20 Disadvantaged workers could include: people with mental and physical disabilities, alcoholics, drug addicts, prisoners on probation, and minors with family problems.
21 Here I have considered the legislation on social cooperatives or social enterprises from Belgium, France, Greece, Korea, Italy, Quebec, Portugal, Poland, Spain, and the United Kingdom.
22 By 'profit' is meant revenue minus costs. At times cooperatives also use the term surplus, which refers to revenue minus costs, taking into account only those transactions with members. Throughout the book, I will use the term profit because it will be easier for the general public to understand and easier to compare with private enterprises.
23 Many examples are provided by two books produces by the EMES group titled *The Emergence of Social Enterprise* published in 2001 (Borzaga and Defourny 2001) and *Social Enterprise* published in 2006 (Nyssens 2006).
24 For an overview of the Social Enterprises please refer to Ridley-Duff's book titled: *Understanding the Social Economy: Theory and Practice* (Ridley-Duff 2015). For an introduction to Public-Benefit Companies refer to Heerad Sabeti's article *The For-Benefit-Enterprise* (Sabeti 2011).
25 The ten principles are (1) collective member-based ownership; (2) decent pay and income security; (3) transparency and data portability; (4) appreciation and acknowledgement; (5) co-determined work involving workers; (6) a protective legal framework; (7) portable worker protections and benefits; (8) protection against arbitrary behaviour; (9) rejection of excessive workplace surveillance; (10) the right to log off (Scholz 2016).
26 The Italian cooperative movement and the Mondragon cooperatives have always supported low salary differentials, but this is the first time that this practice is enshrined in law.
27 SGR stands for Societa di Gestione di Risparmio or Asset Management Company.
28 The Central Association, La Lega Nazionale delle Cooperative e Mutue is also known by its abbreviated title 'La Lega' (Ammirato 1996). In 1996, it was renamed Legacoop. This book uses the abbreviation LNCM for events until 1996, and uses the new name Legacoop thereafter.
29 There are other cooperative development models emerging. An OECD study notes how cooperative development has become very popular in Andalusia in Spain, Costa Rica, Uruguay,

and Västra Götaland in Sweden (OECD 2014). Argentina with its multi-sector cooperative economy, a developing worker cooperative sector, well developed cooperative legislation, the National Institute of the Social Economy providing oversight, and a self-funded cooperative education development fund, is also developing a distinct cooperative model (Cracogna 2013, Gonzales 2020).

30 Austria governed this region from 1815 until 1919.

31 Please refer to Ammirato which contains a case study on Cavit, the Trentino Winegrowers Consortium, and Chapters on consortia and cooperative groups (Ammirato 2018).

32 The consumer sector comprises 68 cooperatives in 2022 (there were 178 in 1990) but still has retail outlets in some 200 villages where it is the only retail outlet where locals can buy goods at reasonable prices. The cooperative banks number 15 (there were 113 in 1990) but still are the only local bank branches in some 600 villages or small towns (OECD 2014, Cooperazione Trentina 2022).

33 Regional Development Cooperatives were first formed in 1985 but have been managed by the Counsel since 2005.

34 This bank was initially called Caisse D'économie des Travailleuses et Travails de Québec or Labor Savings Bank of Quebec.

35 Please refer to Chapter 2, Part 2.3.2.

36 Please refer to Chapter 3, Part 3.6.

37 The information provided by the International Organisation on Industrial and Service Cooperatives (CICOPA) may include double counting and also counting of employees employed in cooperative-owned subsidiaries that are managed as conventional enterprises (CICOPA 2017). The ILO is concerned that cooperative statistics are not reliable and thus cannot measure its influence. In 2018, the ILO released the document tilted: "Guidelines Concerning Statistics of Cooperatives" hoping that it will lead to coherent and consistent cooperative reporting across the globe (ILO 2018). Until reporting is conducted according to ILO guidelines, we will use the CICOPA Report as a point of reference.

38 A good reference to understand the role of the ICA principles is the work of the late Ian MacPherson. Please refer to the following contributions (MacPherson 2007, 2012).

39 The cooperative for development website can be found here: https://coops4dev.coop/en/coops4dev (ICA 2016).

40 Key ICA reports include *The Capital Conundrum of Cooperatives* (Chieh and Weber 2015), *Survey of Cooperative Capital* (Andrews 2015), and *Co-operative Governance Fit to Build Resilience in the Face of Complexity* (ICA 2015).

References

Amatori, Franco, and Andrea Colli. 2011. *Business History: Complexities and Comparisons*. New York: Routledge.

Ammirato, Piero. 2018. *The Growth of Italian Cooperatives: Innovation, Resilience and Social Responsibility*. New York: Routledge.

ANCC. 2018. *Le Cooperative Coop*. 31 December. Accessed June 6, 2022. https://www.e-coop.it/noi/cooperative.

Andrews, Michael. 2015. *Survey of Co-operative Capital*. ICA Think Piece on Cooperative Capital, Brussels: Filene Research Institute Publication.

Apps, Ann. 2020. *National Report of New Zealand. Legal Framework Analysis*. Country Law Report, Brussels: International Cooperative Alliance.

Ardu, Barbara. 2016. "Via libera alla prima legge sulla finanza etica." *Economia*. 7 December. Accessed March 29, 2017. http://www.repubblica.it/economia/2016/12/07/news/etica-153593375/.

Arla Foods. 2021. *Arla Foods Consolidated Annual Report 2021*. Annual Report, Copenhagen: Arla Foods.

Bajo, Claudia Sanchez, and Bruno Roelants. 2011. *Capital and the Debt Trap: Learning from Cooperatives in the Global Crisis*. London: Palgrave Macmillan.

Bakan, Joel. 2020. *The New Corporation: How "Good" Corporations Are Bad for Democracy*. New York: Vintage Books.

Banca Etica. 2016. "Per La Prima Volta La Legge Riconosce la Finanza Etica." *Banca Etica Blog*. 16 December. Accessed March 29, 2017. http://www.bancaetica.it/blog/per-prima-volta-europa-legge-riconosce-finanza-etica.

———. 2022a. *Company profile*. Company Profile - Press kit, Padova: Banca Popolare Etica.

———. 2022b. *IL Manifesto di Banca Etica*. Accessed July 13, 2022. https://www.bancaetica.it/la-nostra-missione/il-manifesto-di-banca-etica/.

———. 2022c. *Report di Impatto*. Annual Impact Report, Padova: Banca Etica.

———. 2022d. *Statuto di Banca Popolare Etica*. Company Statute, Padova: Banca Etica.

Baraijoa, Baleren, Anjel Errasti, and Agurtzane Begiristain. 2004. "Governance of the Mondragon Corporacion Cooperativa." *Annals of Public and Cooperative Economics* 61–87.

Barandiaran, Xabier, and Lezaun Javier. 2017. "The Mondragon Experience." In *The Oxford Handbook of Mutual, Co-operative, and Co-owned Business*, by Michie Jonathan, Joseph Blasi and Carlo Borzaga, Chapter 19. Oxford: Oxford University Press.

Barberini, Ivano. 2009. *Come Vola il Calabrone*. Milano: Baldini, Castoldi, Calai Editore.

Battilani, Patrizia, and Harm Schröter. 2012. "Demutualisation and its Problems." In *The Co-operative Business Movement, 1950 to the Present*, by Patrizia Battilani and Harm Schröter, 150–171. Cambridge: Cambridge University Press.

Benati, Benito, and Marco Mazzoli. 2009. *Partecipazione, Ricerca, Innovazione*. Imola: La Mandrangora.

Bernardi, Andrea, Andrea Cori Cori, Mattia Granata, Lelo, Keti, and Salvatore Monni. 2022. "Mapping Worker Buyouts in Italy." *33 International Ciriec Congress Held in Valencia*. Brussels: Ciriec, 1–25.

Berry, Daphne. 2017. "The Worker Co-operative Form in the Home Care Industry in the USA." In *The Oxford Handbook of Mutual, Co-operative and Co-owned Business*, by Jonathon Michie, Joseph Blasi and Carlo Borzaga, 15 Pages. Oxford: Oxford University Press.

Biggeri, Ugo. 2014. *Il Valore dei Soldi*. Milan: Edizioni San Paolo.

Birchall, Johnston. 2011. *People-Centred Businesses*. London: Palgrave MacMillan.

Blisse, Holger, and Detlev Hummel. 2017. "Raiffeisenbanks and Volksbanks for Europe: The Case for Co-operative Banking." In *The Oxford Handbook of Mutual, Co-operative, and Co-owned Business*, by Jonathan MIchie, Joseph Blasi and Carlo Borzaga, Chapter 28. Oxford: Oxford University Press.

Book, Sven Ake. 1992. *Cooperatives in a Changing World*. Report to the ICA Congress Tokyo, October, 1992, Geneva: International Cooperative Alliance.

Borzaga, Carlo, and Giulia Galera. 2016. "Innovating the Provision of Welfare Services Through Collective Action: the Case of Italian Social Cooperatives." *International Review of Sociology* 31–47.

Borzaga, Carlo, and Jacques Defourny. 2001. *The Emergence of Social Enterprise*. London: Routledge.

BRV. 2022. *Cooperative Financial Framework*. Accessed May 27, 2022. https://www.bvr.de/About_us/Cooperative_Financial_Network.

Caisse Déconomie Solidaire Desjardins. 2021. *Portrait of the Caisse Déconomie Solidaire Desjardins*. Annual Report, Quebec: Caisse Déconomie Solidaire Desjardins.

Calvo, Angela Garcia, Martin Kenney, and John Zysman. 2021. *Understanding Work in the Online Platform Economy: A Critical Review*. Working Paper, Berkeley: Berkeley Roundtable on the International Economy (BRIE).

Canadian Government. 2019. *Canadian Cooperatives 2019*. Annual Report, Ottawa: Canadian Government.

Carini, Chiara, and Carlo Borzaga. 2015. "La Cooperazione Sociale: Dinamica Economica ed Occupazionale tra il 2008 ed il 2013." In *Terzo Rapporto Euricse sull'Economia Cooperativa*, by Carlo Borzaga, 172–192. Trento: Euricse.

Carretta, Alessandro, and Vittorio Boscia. 2009. *Il RuoloEconomico delle Banche d Credito Cooperativo nel Sistema Finanziario*. Rome: Ecra.

Caselli, Guido. 2016. *Osservatorio della Cooperazione dell'Emilia Romagna*. Bologna: Unioncamere Emilia-Romagna.

Cassa Centrale Banca. 2022. *Company Profile*. Company Profile, Trento: Cassa Centrale Banca.

CDRQ. 2021. *Rapport Annuel 2020–2021*. Annual Report, Quebec: Cooperative de Developpement Regional du Quebec.

CFI. 2022. *CFI in Cifre*. Accessed June 23, 2022. https://www.cfi.it/cfi-in-cifre.php.

CG-SCOP. 2022. *Welcome to the Website of the General Confederation of Scop*. Accessed May 8, 2022. https://www.les-scop.coop/chiffres-cles.

———. 2022a. *Outils Financiers*. Brochure on CG-SCOP Financial Programs, Paris: CG-SCOP.

———. 2022b. *The CG-SCOP Movement*. Accessed August 8, 2022. https://www.les-scop.coop/le-mouvement-scop.

———. 2022c. *Welcome to the Website of the General Confederation of CG-SCOP - Key Figures*. Accessed May 8, 2022. https://www.les-scop.coop/chiffres-cles.

———. 2023. "The Scops." *Les Scops Cooperative Sociaties*. Accessed May 3, 2023. file:///C:/Users/ammir/Documents/Downloads/Tableau%20comparatif%20cr%C3%A9ation%20en%20Scop_0.pdf.

Chaddad, Fabio, and Michael Cook. 2004. "The Economics of Organization Structure Changes: A US Perspective on Demutualization." *Annals of Public and Cooperative Economics* (Annals of Public and Cooperative Economics) 575–594.

Chang, Ha-Joon. 2014. *Economics: a User's Guide*. London: Penguin Books.

Chieh, Tan Suee, and Chuin Ting Weber. 2015. *The Capital Conundrum of Cooperatives*. Thematic Report on Cooperative Capital, Brussels: International Cooperative Alliance.

Chomsky, Noam, and Mary Waterstone. 2021. *Consequences of Capitalism: Manufacturing Discontent and Resistance*. United Kingdom: Penguin Random House.

CICOPA. 2017. *Cooperatives and Employment: Second Global Report*. Global Report on Cooperative Employment, Brussels: ICA.

Coalition for Inclusive Capitalism. 2022. *What Is Inclusive Capitalism*. Accessed May 16, 2022. https://www.coalitionforinclusivecapitalism.com/what-is-inclusive-capitalism/.

Coop France. 2022. *Survey of Cooperatives: Summary*. Annual Report, Paris: Coop France.

Coop Group. 2021. *2020 Annual Report*. Annual Report, Basel: Coop Cooperative.

Cooperatives Europe. 2021. *National Report France*. Mapping Report, Brussels: International Cooperative Alliance.

Cooperazione Trentina. 2017. "Promocoop: Crescono Le Partecipazioni." *Cooperazione Trentina*, June: 33–34.

———. 2022. *Our Cooperatives*. Accessed July 25, 2022. https://www.cooperazionetrentina.it/it/cooperative.

Coplan, Asli M., and Hikino Takashi. 2010. "Foundations of Business Groups." In *The Oxford Handbook of Business Groups*, by Asli Coplan, Hikino Takashi and James Lincoln, 15–66. Oxford: Oxford University Press.

Corcoran, Hazel, and David Wilson. 2010. *The Worker Co-operative Movements in Italy, France and Mondragon*. Kentville: Canadian Worker Cooperative Federation.

Cotugno, Matteo. 2010. "Cooperative Banking in the Netherlands: Rabobank Network." In *Cooperative Banking in Europe*, by Vittorio Boscia Boscia, Carretta, Alessandro and Schwizer Paola, 107–128. London: Palgrave MacMillan.

CQCM. 2022. *Rapport D'Activite 2021*. Annual Report, Montreal: Conseil Québécois de la Coopération et de la Mutualité.

Cracogna, Dante. 2013. "Argentina." In *International Handbook of Cooperative Law*, by Dante Cracogna, Antonio Fici and Hagen Henry, 189–206. Heidelberg: Springer.

De Micheli, Paola, Stefano Imbruglia, and Antonio Misiani. 2017. *Se Chiudi Ti Compro: Le Imprese Rigenerate dai Lavoratori*. Milano: Guerrini e Associati.

Degen, Bernard. 2017. "Consumer Societies in Switzerland: From Local Self-Help Organizations to a Single National Co-operative." In *A Global History of Consumer Co-operation since 1850*, by Mary Hilson, Silke Neunsinger and Greg Patmore, Chapter 24. Leiden: Brill.

Develtere, Patrick. 1992. *Co-operatives and Development: Toward a Social Movement Perspective.* Occasional Paper Series, Saskatoon: University of Saskatchewan.

Di Stefano, Christina. 2019. "The Business Transfer Through the Cooperative Model. A Comparative Analysis Italy-France." *Journal of Entrepreneurial and Organizational Diversity* 62–86.

Diamantopoulos, Mitch. 2011. "Cooperative Development Gap in Québec and Saskatchewan 1980 to 2010: A Tale of Two Movements." *Canadian Journal of Nonprofit and Social Economy Research* 6–24.

Dorigatti, Michele. 2014. "Le Peculiarita del Modello Trentino." In *Guida alla Cooperazione Trentina*, by Cooperazione Trentina, 55–86. Trento: Federazione Trentina della Cooperazione.

Douvitsa, Ifigeneia. 2021. *National Report: France.* Legal Framework Analysis, Brussels: International Cooperative Alliance.

EACB. 2019. *Models of Groups and Networks of Cooperative Banks.* Key Statistics, Brussels: European Association of Co-operative Banks.

Ekberg, Espen. 2012. "Organization: Top Down or Bottom Up? The Organizational Development of Consumer Cooperatives, 1950–2000." In *The Cooperative Business Movement, 1950 to the Present*, by Harm Schroter and Patrizia Battilani, 222–242. Cambridge: Cambridge University Press.

Errasti, Anjel, Ignacio Bretos, and Enekoitz Etxezarreta. 2016. "What Do Mondragon Coopitalist Multinationals Look Like: The Rise and Fall of Fagor Electrodomesticos S Coop and Its European Subsidiaries." *Annals of Public and Cooperative Economics* 433–456.

Espagne, François. 2001. "111 Year History of the GSSCOP." *CG-SCOP - Doctrines.* Accessed August 26, 2022. https://www.les-scop.coop/system/files/inline-files/111-ans-histoire-scop.pdf.

———. 2009. "Crises and Mutations." *CG-SCOP - Ideology.* Accessed August 26, 2022. https://www.les-scop.coop/system/files/inline-files/crises-mutations.pdf.

Euricse. 2021. *Exploring the Cooperative Economy Report 2020.* Cooperative Monitor Report, Trento: International Cooperative Alliance.

European Commission. 2020. *Social Enterprises and their Ecosystems in Europe.* Comparative Synthesis Report, Brussels: European Union.

Fairbnb. 2022. *Fairbnb Coop- Community Powered Tourism.* Accessed July 8, 2022. https://fairbnb.coop/how-it-works/.

FEBEA. 2021. *Annual Report.* Annual Report, Brussels: European Federation of Ethical and Alternative Banks.

Fici, Antonio. 2013. "Italy." In *International Handbook of Cooperative Law*, by David Cracogna, Antonio Fici and Hagen Henrÿ, 479–502. Heidelberg: Springer.

Fiducie. 2022. *It's Party: 15 Years of Trust.* Accessed July 19, 2022. https://fiducieduchantier.qc.ca/cest-la-fete-15-ans-deja-15ansfiducie/.

Fonterra. 2021a. *Our Path to 2030.* Corporate Document, Aukland: Fonterra.

———. 2021b. *2022 Quarter One Update.* Auckland: Fonterra.

———. 2021c. *Fonterra Capital Structure.* Accessed December 8, 2021. https://www.fonterra.com/nz/en/capital-structure/our-choice.html.

———. 2022. "Governance and Management." *Fonterra.* June. Accessed June 12, 2022. https://www.fonterra.com/content/dam/fonterra-public-website/fonterra-new-zealand/documents/pdf/governance-and-management/fonterra-co-operative-group-limited-constitution.pdf.

Forsey, Helen. 1989. *The Cooperative investment Plan.* Program Review, Ottawa: Canadian Co-operative Association and Conseil Canadien de la Coopération et de la mutualité.

Frieden, Jeffry A. 2020. *Global Capitalism.* New York: W.W.Norton and Company.

Fruin, Mark. 2007. "Business Groups and Inter-firm Networks." In *The Oxford Handbook of Business History*, by Geoffrey Jones and Jonathon Zeitlin, 244–267. Oxford: Oxford University Press.

Fulton, Murray, and Jean-Pierre Girard. 2015. *Demutualization of Cooperatives and Mutuals*. Saskatoon: University of Saskatchewan.

GABV. 2021. *Annual Report*. Annual Report, Amsterdam: Global Alliance for Banking Values.

———. 2022. "Principles of Value-Based Banking." *Global Alliance for Banking on Values - About Us*. Accessed July 14, 2022. https://www.gabv.org/wp-content/uploads/2022/02/Principles_def.pdf.

Galera, Giulia. 2017. "Social and Solidarity Cooperatives: an International Perspective." In *The Oxford Handbook of Mutual, Co-operative, and Co-owned Business*, by Jonathon Mitchie, Jonathon R Blasi and Carlo Borzaga, 15 pages. Oxford: Oxford University Press.

Girard, Jean-Pierre, and Genevieve Langlois. 2009. "How Social Enterprises Can Combine Social and Economic Goals." In *The Changing Boundaries of Social Enterprises*, by OECD, Chapter 5. Paris: OECD.

Goglio, Silvio, and Kanu Palmi. 2017. "Credit Unions and Co-operative Banks Across the World." In *The Oxford Handbook of Mutual, Co-operative, and Co-owned Business*, by Jonathan Michie, Joseph Blasi and Carlo Borzaga, Chapter 10. Oxford: Oxford University Press.

Gonzales, Carlos. 2020. *National Report: Argentina*. Mapping: Key Figures Country Report, Brussels: International Cooperative Alliance - Cooperatives of the Americas Division.

Government du Quebec. 2003. *Cooperative Development Policy*. Government Policy Document, Quebec: Government du Quebec.

Granarolo Group. 2022. "About Us." *The Granarolo Group*. May. Accessed June 15, 2022. https://www.granarologroup.com/about-us/the-granarolo-group.

Granata, Mattia. 2019. "Breve Storia dell'International Cooperative Alliance." In *Identita` e Valori dell'Impresa Cooperativa: Scritti e Discorsi di Ivano Barberini*, by Michele Dorigatti and Tito Menzani, 25–42. Soveria Mannelli: Rubbettino Editore.

Han, Sang-Il, Moo-Kwon Chung, and Mun-su Park. 2013. "Local Stakeholder Involvement and Social Innovation in Korean Co-operatives: The Cases of Wonju and Ansung Cities." *Oxford University Press and Community Development Journal*.

Hancock, Matt. 2007. *Compete to Cooperate: The Cooperative District of Imola*. Imola: Bacchilega Editore.

Henderson, Rebecca. 2020. *Reimagining Capitalism*. London: Penguin Business.

HEW CO-OP. 2015. *Promoting Health and Inclusion in Aging Population*. 9 January. Accessed June 28, 2022. https://stories.coop/stories/promoting-health-and-inclusion-in-an-aging-population.

———. 2020. *The Basic Philosophy of Health and Welfare Co-ops*. Accessed June 30, 2022. http://www.hew.coop/english/.

Hiez, David. 2013. "France." In *International Handbook of Cooperative Law*, by Dante Cracogna, Antonio Fici, Hagen Henry and editors, 393–412. Heidelberg: Springer.

Hin, Myung-Ho, and Ah-Reum Lee. 2013. "Factors Affecting the Creation and Sustainability of cooperatives in the Wonju Region." *Korean Journal of Cooperative studies* 31–57.

Hoyt, Ann, and Tito Menzani. 2012. "The International Cooperative Movement: A Quite Giant." In *The Cooperative Movement, 1950 to the Present*, by Harm G Svchroter and Patrizia Battilani, Chapter 1. Cambridge: Cambridge University Press.

Ianes, Alberto. 2014. "La Storia. La Cooperazione Trentina e Italiana Un Modo Diverso di Leggere e Interpretare l'Economia e la Società." In *Guida alla Cooperazione Trentina*, by Cooperazione Trentina, 55–86. Trento: Federazione Trentina della Cooperazione.

ICA. 2013. *Blueprint for a Cooperative Decade*. Strategic Plan, Brussels: International Cooperative Alliance.

———. 2015. *Co-operative Governance Fit to Build Resilience in the face of Complexity*. Brussels: International Cooperative Alliance.

———. ICA. 2016. *Coops4Dev*. March. Accessed 2022. https://coops4dev.coop/en/coops4dev#coops4dev

———. 2017. *Guidance Notes to the Co-operative Principles*. Guidance Notes, Geneva: International Cooperative Alliance.

———. 2022a. *Cooperative Identity, Values and Principles*. Accessed August 4, 2022. https://www.ica.coop/en/cooperatives/cooperative-identity.

———. 2022b. *Organigram*. Accessed August 5, 2022. https://www.ica.coop/en/about-us/our-structure/alliance-organigram.

ICA Asia and Pacific. 2019. *National Report of Republic of Korea: Legal Framework Analysis*. Country Legal Framework Report, Brussels: International Cooperative Alliance.

ILO. 2002. *Recommendation 193 - Promotion of Cooperatives*. Recommendation on Cooperatives, Geneva: International Labour Organization.

———. 2017. *The Case of the Republic of Korea*. Geneva: International Labour Organization.

International Cooperative Alliance. 2022. *Facts and Figures*. Accessed August 3, 2022. https://www.ica.coop/en/cooperatives/facts-and-figures.

Internet of Ownership. 2022. "Internet of Ownership." *PlatformCoopDirectory*. Accessed July 9, 2022. https://docs.google.com/spreadsheets/d/1RQTMhPJVVdmE7Yeop1iwYhvj46kgvVJQnn11EPGwzeY/edit#gid=674927682.

ISTAT. 2019. *Strutture e Performance delle cooperative Italiane, anno 2015*. Research Report, Rome: Italian National Institute of Statistics.

Jain, Ameeta, Monica Keneley, and Dianne Thomson. 2015. "Customer-Owned Banking in Australia: From Credit Unions to Mutual Banks." *Annals of Public and Cooperative Economics* 465–478.

Jang, Jongick. 2013. "Republic of Korea." In *International Handbook of International Law*, by Dante Cracogna, Antonio Fici and Hagen Henry, 653–666. Heidelberg: Springer.

JCCU. 2022. *Profile of the Japanese Consumer Cooperative Union: 2021–2022*. Annual Report, Tokyo: Japanese Consumers' Co-operative Union.

Jones, Geoffrey. 2008. "Globalisation." In *The Oxford Handbook of Business History*, by Geoffrey Jones and Jonathon Zeitlin, 92–101. Oxford: Oxford University Press.

Kim, Sunhwa, Yena Lee, Hyojin Shin, and Seungkwon Jang. 2020. "Korea's Consumer Cooperatives and Civil Society: The Cases of iCOOP and Hansalim." In *Waking the Asian Pacific Co-operative Potential*, by Morris Altman Editor, Chapter 20. London: Academic Press.

Kooperativa Förbundet. 2022. "About KF." *Kooperativa Förbundet*. Accessed May 25, 2022. https://kf.se/om-kf/.

Kuijpers, Arnold, and Hans Groeneveld. 2015. "Co-operative Capital of a Large Financial Co-operative: The Capitalization Evolution of Rabobank." In *The Capital Conundrum for Co-operatives*, by Tan Suee Chieh and Chuin Ting Weber, 45–87. Brussels: International Cooperative Alliance.

Kurimoto, Akira. 2020. "Consumer Cooperatives' Model in Japan." In *Waking the Asian Pacific Co-operative Potential*, by Morris Altman, Anthony Jensen, Akira Kurimoto, Robby Tulus, Yashavantha Dongre and Seungkwon Jang, Chapter 21. London: Academic Press.

Kurimoto, Akira, and Tsukuru Akeda. 2021. *Legal Framework Analysis - National Report of Japan*. April. Accessed August 10, 2021. https://coops4dev.coop/sites/default/files/2021-06/Japan%20Legal%20Framework%20Analysis%20National%20Report.pdf.

Laurini, Gianluca, interview by Piero Ammirato. 2016. *Coopfond and Employee Buyouts* (20 May).

Lee, Bokyeong, Yhan Sang-Il, and Soyoon Chung. 2014. "Collective Strategy of Social Economy in Wonju." *Korean Journal of Cooperative Studies* 1–26.

Legacoop. 2020. *Italy's Worker Buyout Mapping. A Historical Review*. WBO Program Review, Rome: Legacoop Area Studi.

———. 2019a. *Le Cooperative di Comunità Legacoop: Una realtà in Crescita*. Sectoral Briefing, Rome: Area Studi Legacoop.

———. 2019b. *Le Cooperative Sociali Italiane*. Research Briefings, Rome: Legacoop Area Studi.

Levitt, Theodore. 1983. "The Globalization of Markets." *Harvard Business Review* 92–101.

Linguiti, Francesco. 2014. "I Consorzi tra Societa` Cooperative." In *La Cooperazione Italiana Negli Anni della Crisi: Secondo Rapporto Euricse*, by Carlo Borzaga, 53–72. Trento: Euricse.

MacPherson, Ian. 2007. *One Path to Cooperative Studies.* Vancouver: British Columbia Institute for Co-operative Studies.

———. 2012. "What Is the Purpose of It All." In *The Cooperative Business Movement, 1950 to the Present*, by Harm G Schroter and Patrizia Battilani, Chapter 4. Cambridge: Cambridge University Press.

Marchetti, Pietro Marchetti, and Arianna Sabetta. 2010. "The Cooperative Banking System in France." In *Cooperative Banking in Europe*, by Vittorio Boscia, Alessandro Carretta and Paola Schwizer, 51–94. London: Palgrave Macmillan.

Martinelli, Francesca, Samuele Bozzoni, Simone Caroli, Francesca Tamascelli, and Giuseppe Guerini. 2019. *Platform Cooperativism in Italy and in Europe.* Working paper - No. 2019/27, Brussels: CIRIEC.

Marzocchi, Franco. 2012. *A Brief History of Social Cooperation in Italy.* Forli: Aiccon.

McKillop, Donal, Declan French, Barry Quinn, Anna L. Sobiech, and John O.S Wilson. 2020. "Cooperative Financial Institutions: A Review of the Literature." *International Review of Financial Analysis* 1–11.

Mendell, Marguerite. 2015. "Democratising Capital: Social and Solidarity Finance in Quebec." In *Social Economy in China and the World*, by Ngai Pun, 94–114. London: Taylor & Francis Group.

Ministry of Economy and Innovation. 2022. *Overview / Cooperative Movement in Quebec.* Accessed July 16, 2022. https://www.economie.gouv.qc.ca/bibliotheques/bref/mouvement-cooperatif-au-quebec/.

Modhorst, Mads. 2014. "Arla and Danish National Identity." *Business History* 116–133.

Mori, Pierangelo. 2017. "Community Co-operatives and Co-operatives Providing Public Services: Facts and Prospects." In *The Oxford Handbook of Mutual, Co-Operative, and Co-Owned Business*, by Joseph R. Blasi, and Carlo Borzaga Edited by Jonathan Michie, 13. Oxford: Oxford University Press.

Mudde, Cas, and Cristobal Rovira Kaltwasser. 2017. *Populism, A Very Short Introduction.* New York: Oxford University Press.

NCBA-Clusa. 2022. *Agriculture Co-ops.* 28 May. Accessed May 28, 2022. https://ncbaclusa.coop/resources/co-op-sectors/agriculture-co-ops/.

Nyssens, Marthe. 2006. *Social Enterprise.* London: Routledge.

OECD. 2014. *The Cooperative Model of Trentino: A Case Study.* Local Economic and Employment Development Report, Paris: OECD.

———. 2022a. "Central Government Spending (2020)." *OECD Data.* May. Accessed May 16, 2022. https://data.oecd.org/gga/general-government-spending.htm#indicator-chart.

———. 2022b. "General Government Revenue (2020)." *OECD Data.* May. Accessed May 16, 2022. https://data.oecd.org/gga/general-government-revenue.htm#indicator-chart.

———. 2022c. *National Accounts of OECD Countries: France.* Accessed May 15, 2022. https://read.oecd-ilibrary.org/economics/national-accounts-of-oecd-countries-volume-2022-issue-1_675610e6-en#page1.Oxfam. 2017. *An Economy for the 99 Per cent.* Oxford: Oxfam.

Patmore, Greg, Nicola Balnave, and Olivera Marjanovic. 2021. "Resistance Is Not Futile: Co-operatives, Demutualization, Agriculture and neo-Liberalism in Australia." *Business and Politics* 1–19.

Pestoff, Victor. 2012. "Hybrid Tendencies in Consumer Co-operatives: The Case of Sweden." In *The Co-operative Model in Practice*, by Diarmuid McDonnell and Elizabeth Macknight, Chapter 7. Aberdeen: CETS.

Petrou, Timothy. 2013. "Canada." In *International Handbook of Cooperative Law*, by Antonio Fici and Hagen Henry Dante Cracogna, 289–316. Heidelberg: Springer.

Picketty, Thomas. 2014. *Capital in the Twenty-First Century.* Cambridge: Harvard University Press.

Poli, Federica. 2019. *Co-operative Banking Networks in Europe: Models and Performance.* Berlin: Springer International Publishing AG.

Poole, Steven. 2016. "Book of the Day." *The Guardian.* 2 April. Accessed July 8, 2022. https://www.theguardian.com/books/2016/apr/02/whats-yours-is-mine-against-the-sharing-economy-tom-slee-review.

Porter, Michael. 2011. "Creating Shared Value." *Harvard Business Review* 17.

Promosviluppo. 2018. "Fondo Mutualistico." *Promosviluppo.* Accessed September 17, 2018. http://www.promocoop.it/fondo-mutualistico/.

Publications Quebec. 2022. "Cooperatives Act." *Legis Quebec - Official Source.* April. Accessed October 6, 2021. http://legisquebec.gouv.qc.ca/en/showdoc/cs/c-67.2.

Rabobank. 2021. *Annual Report 2021.* Annual Report, Amsterdam: Rabobank.

Ranis, Peter. 2016. *Cooperatives Confront Capitalism.* London: ZED Books.

Reich, Robert. 2016. *Saving Capitalism: For the Many, Not the Few.* London: Icon Books.

Reliess. 2013. *To Support the Development of Cooperatives in the Territories of Quebec; The Regional Development Cooperatives CDR.* Brief Number 8, Centre Reliess.

Restakis, John. 2010. *Humanizing the Economy: Co-operatives in the Age of Capital.* Canada: New Society Publishers.

Ridley-Duff, Rory. 2015. *Understanding Social Enterprise: Theory and Practice.* Newbury Park (California): Sage Publications.

Roelants, Bruno. 2015. "Capital Building in Industrial and Service Co-operatives." In *The Capital Conundrum for Co-operatives*, by Tan Suee Chieh and Chuin Ting Weber, 22–31. Brussels: International Cooperative Alliance.

———. 2009a. "Conclusion." In *Cooperatives and Social Enterprises: GOvernance and Normative Frameworks*, by Bruno Roelants, 109–130. Brussels: CECOP.

———. 2009b. *Cooperatives and Social Enterprises: Governance and Normative Frameworks.* Brussels: CECOP Publications.

Ruggeri, Andres. 2015. "Workers' Cooperative Movement in Argentina." In *Social Economy in China and the World*, by Pun Ngai, Hok Bun, KU, Yan Hairong and Anita Koo, 60–76. London: Taylor and Francis Group.

Ruggeri, Andres, and Marcelo Vieta. 2015. "Argentina's Worker-Recuperated Enterprises, 2010–2013: A Synthesis of Recent Empirical Findings." *Journal of Entrepreneurial and Organizational Diversity* 75–103.

Sabeti, Heerad. 2011. *The For-Benefit Enterprise.* Cambridge: Harvard Business Review.

Sacmi. 2015. *Bilancio di Sostenibilita.* Annual Sustainability Report, Imola: Sacmi.

———. 2020a. *Annual Report.* Annual Report, Imola: Sacmi.

———. 2020b. *Sacmi in Figures.* Corporate Information, Imola: Sacmi.

Saito, Yoshiaki. 2010. *A Brief Chronicle of the Modern Japanese Consumer Cooperative Movement.* Tokyo: Japanese Consumers' Co-operative Union.

Salvadori, Gianluca. 2011. *LA COOPERAZIONE IN TRENTINO ATTRAVERSO 120 ANNI DI TRASFORMAZIONI.* Working Paper, Trento: Fondazione Euricse.

Sassoon, Donald. 2019. *The Anxious Triumph.* London: Allen Lane.

Scholz, Trebor. 2016. *Platform Cooperativism: Challenging the Corporate Sharing Economy.* New York: Rosa Luxemburg Stiftung.

Scholz, Trebor, Morshed Mannan, Jonas Pentzien, and Hal Plotkin. 2021. *Policies for Cooperative Ownership in the Digital Economy.* Los Angeles: Berggruen Institute.

Shadbolt, Nicola, and Alex Duncan. 2015. "Perspectives from the Ground: Fonterra Co-operative Case Study." In *The Capital Conundrum for Cooperatives*, by Tan Suee Chiech and Chuin Ting Weber, 94–103. Brussels: International Cooperative Alliance.

Soulage, François. 2011. "France: an Endeavour in Enterprise Transformation." In *Beyond the Crisis: Cooperatives, Work, Finance*, by Alberto Zevi, Antonio Zanotti, François Soulage and Adrian Zelaia, 155–196. Brussels: Cecop Publications.

Steger, Manfred B., and Ravi K Roy. 2015. *Neoliberalism: A Very Short Introduction.* Oxford: Oxford University Press.

Steger, Manfred. 2020. *Globalization: A Very Short Introduction.* Oxford: Oxford University Press.

Stiglitz, Joseph. 2018. *Globalization and Its Discontents: Anti-globalization in the Era of Trump*. New York: W W Norton and Company.

———. 2019. *People, Power and Profits*. London: Allen Lane.

Stories.coop. 2011. *Hansalim*. 19 December. Accessed July 31, 2022. https://stories.coop/hansalim/.

United Nations. 2001. "Guidelines Aimed at Creating a Supportive Environment for the Development of Cooperatives." New York: United Nations.

Vieta, Marcelo, Sara Depedri, and Antonella Carrano. 2017. *The Italian Road to Recuperating Enterprises and the Legge Marcora Framework*. Research Report, Trento: Euricse.

Viola, Alessandro. 2016. WBO. WBO Program Review, Rome: 2016. *WBO Program Review*. WBO Program Review, Rome: Cooperazione Finanza Impresa (internal report)).

Whyte, William Foote, and Kathleen King Whyte. 1991. *Making Mondragon*. Ithaca: ILR Press.

Wiener, Jason. 2019. *Platform Coop Showcase 3*. Accessed July 8, 2022. https://www.youtube.com/watch?v=vNPYxLI3GEM.

Wilson, John, Anthony Webster, and Rachel Vorberg-Rugh. 2013. *Building Co-operation: A Business History of the Co-operative Group, 1863–2013*. Oxford: Oxford University Press.

WOCCU. 2020. *Statistical Report*. Statistical Report, Washington: World Council of Credit Unions.

World Bank. 2022. *GDP Annual Growth Rate*. Accessed March 17, 2022. https://data.worldbank.org/indicator/NY.GDP.MKTP.KD.ZG?end=2020&start=1961&view=chart.

Yergin, Daniel, and Joseph Janislaw. 1998. *The Commanding Heights: The Battle for the World Economy*. New York: Simon Schuster.

Zanotti, Antonio. 2011. "Beyond the Crisis: Cooperatives, Work, Finance." In *Beyond the Crisis: Cooperatives, Work, Finance*, by Zevi, Alberto, Antonio Zanotti, François Soulage and Adrian Zelaia, 21–100. Brussels: Cecop Publication.

Zeitlin, Jonathon. 2007. ""Industrial Districts and Regional Clusters." In *The Oxford Handbook of Business History*, by Geoffrey Jones and Jonathon Zeitlin, 219–243. Oxford: Oxford University Press.

Zeuli, Kimberley A, and Robert Cropp. 2004. *Cooperatives: Principles and Practices in the 21st Century*. Wisconsin: University of Wisconsin Centre for Cooperatives.

Zevi, Alberto, and Camillo De Bernardinis. 2016. *L'Italia che ce la fa: 1986–2016*. Rome: Cooperazione Finanza Impresa.

Zevi, Alberto, Antonio Zanotti, François Soulage, and Adrian Zelaia. 2011. *Beyond the Crisis: Cooperatives, Work, Finance*. Brussels: Cecop Publication.

Zhu, Jiang, and Olivera Marjanovic. 2021. "A Different Kind of Sharing Economy: A Literature Review of Platform Cooperatives." *Proceedings of the 54th Hawaii International Conference on System Sciences | 2021*. Hawaii: International Conference on System Sciences. 4128–4137.

6 Legislation

The study of cooperative law is fundamental to understanding the history, principles, values, and economic and social development of the cooperative movement. Cooperative law defines cooperatives, specifies what they can and cannot do, and distinguishes them from other type of enterprises. These laws provide cooperatives with a variety of organisational and legal structures to choose from. Cooperative laws regulate the relationship between cooperatives and their members, between cooperatives and their consortia, between cooperatives and their national or regional associations or federations, between cooperatives and the community, between current members and future members, and between the cooperatives and the State. Cooperative law does this by attributing each stakeholder powers, rights and obligations, and duties and responsibilities.

The study of cooperative law will help the reader develop a deeper understanding of cooperative development across the world. A longitudinal analysis of cooperative law will inform the readers of the many phases it has encountered at various times, in different regions, and under various political systems. The study of cooperative law is a good tool of analysis to compare how countries have promoted cooperative development. It can offer insights into examining the extent to which cooperative law has upheld cooperative principles, whether cooperative law has promoted economic and social development, or whether cooperative law has facilitated or discouraged the conversion of cooperatives into capitalist firms, also known as demutualisation.

This chapter will enable the reader to have an appreciation of

- The fundamental features of cooperative law.
- The evolution of cooperative law.
- The extent to which cooperative law aligns with the International Cooperative Alliance's (ICA) seven cooperative principles.
- The national approaches to asset management and demutualisation.
- How cooperative law has facilitated cooperative economic development.
- How cooperative law has influenced cooperative enterprise models across the world.
- The various cooperative enterprise models[1] that are emerging.

This chapter comprises ten parts. Part 6.1 will discuss the key features of cooperative law and how to approach the study of cooperative law. Part 6.2 will discuss the various phases of cooperative law. Part 6.3 will focus on assessing the extent to which the current cooperative law, as practised across all continents, aligns with the ICA's cooperative principles. Part 6.4 will summarise the findings. Part 6.5 will examine how cooperative laws promote cooperative economic development. Part 6.6 will examine two different

DOI: 10.4324/9781003269533-6

broad cooperative enterprise models that can develop within cooperative law. Part 6.7 will describe and provide a definition for five different types of cooperative enterprises that can operate within cooperative law. Part 6.8 identifies good practice standards. Part 6.9 provides a summary, and Part 6.10 suggests key questions to consider.

6.1 Cooperative Law

Henrÿ defined cooperative law as

> all those legal rules—laws, administrative acts, court decisions, jurisprudence, co-operative by-laws/statutes, or any other source of law—which regulate the structure and/or the operations of cooperatives as enterprises in the economic sense and as institutions in the legal sense.
>
> (Henrÿ 2012)

It reflects specific laws on cooperatives (cooperative law) but also other laws that regulate cooperative governance and its operations. This would include industrial relations law, taxation law, competition laws, accounting and audit rules, bankruptcy rules, and so on (Henrÿ 2012).

Cooperative law can be specified in a single legal document dedicated to cooperatives Germany or the Republic of Korea,[2] or in a general instrument, such as the civil code or commercial code, that cover commercial enterprises and including cooperative laws (Italy and France). In some countries, there are national laws and also state or regional laws that govern cooperatives, as is the case in Canada, India, Spain, Tanzania, and the United States. Japanese cooperatives, however, operate under specific sector-based cooperative laws covering agriculture, consumer and credit cooperatives (Kurimoto 2020). Countries such as Denmark and the United Kingdom do not have a specific cooperative law (Münkner 2013a).

Cooperative law performs a number of functions. Its key function is to distinguish cooperatives from other forms of enterprises, promote cooperative principles, encourage entrepreneurship, and promote cooperative economic development. It consists of a set of rules regarding the definition and purpose; cooperative formation; membership rights and obligations; financial instruments; governance arrangements; allocation of profits;[3] relations among cooperatives; relations between cooperative associations and the State; procedures dealing with cooperative dissolution, mergers, demerger, and conversions. The Law also emphasises reporting requirements to authorities to verify compliance with the law and to verify bonafide cooperative practices (Fici 2013a).

A key task is to assess the appropriateness and effectiveness of cooperative law. In other words, is the law fit-for-purpose? Does the law promote cooperative principles and development? Henrÿ makes a distinction between cooperative law that aligns with cooperative principles and those laws that deviate from those principles (Henrÿ 2017). Fici and Münkner share Henrÿ's approach. Fici suggests that only where the cooperative laws enforce the social function of cooperatives can cooperatives be seen as different to private enterprises. Key requirements supporting the social function include (i) the function to meet members' needs and not to remunerate capital or promote capital appreciation; (ii) member participation in managing the enterprise and the open door principle; (iii) support for third-party 'external persons' via the open door principle; support for other cooperatives, the associations, and the community (Fici 2013a). Münkner is more specific, noting that the law should discourage or limit the bad practices of unlimited business with non-members; admission of rent-seeking investors as members; the focus of management on making a profit for distribution among capital owners; undemocratic distribution of voting rights; and external control replacing member control (Münkner 2013a). In summary, the cooperative law should require cooperatives to serve their members; that members democratically govern the cooperative; that members control capital; and that cooperatives are open to others.

Another way of approaching the study of cooperative law is to consider cooperative law as a living, flexible, adaptable instrument that seeks to meet cooperative needs across different industries and across different political and social cultures. This is a legitimate way to approach cooperative law since the core principles date back to the Rochdale principles of 1844 and may not be suited to other cooperatives, especially worker cooperatives (Birchall 2012). This approach would enable us to understand how cooperative law has evolved and how it has met the needs of cooperatives that operate in global markets. This approach would consider whether the changes in cooperative law have facilitated the development, adaptation, or enhancement of cooperative principles. This method adopts a critical approach to cooperative law but does not view changes to the original principles necessarily as a form of degeneration.

Another approach is to consider the effectiveness of cooperative law. We would expect that an effective cooperative law would simultaneously promote the seven cooperative principles, cooperative economic development, and cooperative oversight. This approach considers whether cooperative law is fit-for-purpose to support the current needs of cooperatives. In examining the effectiveness of cooperative law, we would consider the extent that cooperative law promotes the principle of open membership and economic participation; promotes appropriate democratic practices; facilitates cooperative economic development so that cooperative enterprises can compete in global markets; provides adequate oversight of all cooperatives to ensure the public that cooperative enterprises operate in compliance with the cooperative law and cooperative principles (Ammirato 2018).

6.2 Phases of Cooperative Law

Cooperative law has evolved since the United Kingdom's *Industrial and Provident Societies Act* of 1852 (IAPSA 1852) recognised the legal status of cooperatives. The cooperative model has spread throughout the world, and in each country, it reflects unique political and economic and social circumstances. What follows is an explanation of how cooperative law has evolved from a phase which focussed on distinguishing cooperatives form from investor-owned companies to the internationalisation of cooperative law that reflects the ICA cooperative principles.

6.2.1 *Legal Recognition*

In the first phase, cooperatives sought recognition that they were an organisation engaged in a business activity with their members that was different from that of an investor-owned company.[4] In this phase, cooperatives also sought a level playing field (Henrÿ 2012). The *IAPSA Act* of 1852 gave cooperatives in the UK recognition, and they no longer had to register as an investor-owned company. The updated *IAPSA Act* of 1862 provided cooperatives with limited liability status and exemption from income tax from profits arising from trade with members. It also allowed members to make loans to cooperatives (Patmore and Belnave 2018). Canada modelled its first cooperative law on IAPSA in 1865. Prussia enacted the *Cooperative Act* in 1867. It included voting based on one-person-one-vote and executive and board positions reserved for members (Blisse and Humme 2017). France developed its first cooperative law in 1867. In Italy, the Commercial Code of 1882 included cooperatives with provisions of equal voting rights and non-transferability of shares. The Law of 1911 allowed cooperatives to bid for public contracts and required them to allocate a portion of profits to a reserve fund, limit the remuneration on members' capital accounts,[5] and require directors to be members (Fici 2013b). In the United States, the *Capper-Volstead Act* of 1922 allowed agricultural cooperatives that collectively processed and marketed commodities to unite without violating anti-trust laws. This provision was subject to cooperatives operating for the mutual benefit of agricultural producers, applying equal voting rights, applying a maximum of 8 per cent return on their capital accounts, and ensuring that non-member business did not exceed 50 per cent of total business (Zeuli and Cropp 2004).

6.2.2 *Autonomy*

In the second phase, cooperatives at first lost and then recovered their autonomy from the State in a number of countries. Key experiences in the state-led cooperative formations include India, The Republic of Korea, the Soviet Union, Italy, and Germany.[6]

In India, the State promoted credit cooperatives in 1904 and later other cooperatives. As late as 1995, the State gave the cooperative registrar powers to replace management, appoint board directors, compulsory amend by-laws, reject by-laws, re-instate expelled members, and decide whether to dissolve a cooperative. The State of Andhra Pradesh passed an Act in 1995 rejecting colonial law and declared cooperatives free to establish, manage, control and dissolve cooperatives. In 2002, the national government passed the *Multi-State Societies Act*. It is aligned with the ICA cooperative principles and covers cooperatives operating in more than one State. In 2011, a constitutional amendment declared cooperatives to be autonomous bodies. As of today, seven Indian States followed the lead of Andhra Pradesh and the Constitutional Amendment of 2011, but other states still conserve those State laws that limit cooperative autonomy (Veerakumuran 2013, ALC India 2019).

In Korea, the Japanese imperialist government introduced financial and industrial cooperative acts in 1907 and in 1926. The State appointed cooperative officials and denied voting rights and the right to hold a general assembly. After gaining independence in 1945, Korea endured a military government from 1962 to 1992. The military government controlled the national cooperative body, appointed cooperative leaders, and approved the cooperative budgets. This changed in 1988 when the new cooperative act gave cooperatives more autonomy. The recent *Framework Act on Cooperatives* of 2012 is aligned with the ICA Principles (Jung and Rosner 2012, Jang 2013).

In Italy, The Fascist government (1922–1943) established The National Agency for Cooperation in 1926 as the sole representative body for all cooperatives, thus abolishing existing cooperative associations associated with the Socialists and the Catholics. This body had the power to dissolve any cooperative deemed subversive, dismiss independent cooperative executives, and replace them with Fascist members or sympathisers. The National Agency for Cooperation later changed the status of consortia to government institutions. Following the defeat of Fascism at the end of the Second World War, the Republican Constitution, via Article 45 of the Constitution, and the Basevi Law of 1947, fully restored cooperative autonomy (Galasso 1986, Menzani 2009, Ianes 2013).

The German Nazi government exercised State control over cooperatives. First, it tried to weaken consumer cooperatives by reducing its dividend payout to 4 per cent. Later, it forced the election of Nazi leaders, limited democratic decision-making, forbade the creation of new cooperatives, forced mergers, and privatised some cooperatives. In 1941 a government decree liquidated consumer cooperatives. The State incorporated agricultural marketing and housing cooperatives. Agricultural Cooperatives and Cooperative banks were left untouched as these sectors were either neutral or supportive of the regime (Menzani 2009). Following the defeat of Nazism at the end of the Second World War, cooperative autonomy was restored.

In the Soviet Union following the Revolution of 1917, the State promoted collective farms, which were communal-led or state-led. State representatives sat on the board of consumer cooperatives from 1918. In 1919, they were transformed into consumer communes which also absorbed the functions of agricultural and credit cooperatives. Membership in these commune-based cooperatives was compulsory. There was a brief period following the New Economic Policy in 1923, when cooperatives became voluntary and self-governing again, but it was short-lived. Urban consumer cooperatives became state enterprises in 1935. State control culminated in the passage of the 1936 Constitution, which required cooperatives to be members of a government-supervised local union of cooperatives. The State classified cooperatives as a form of Socialist ownership and were required to promote collective work and to meet government-set production targets. Subject to achieving government targets, cooperatives could distribute the remaining income to members based on work performed. The Gorbachev-led Perestroika reforms led to a re-appraisal of cooperatives. The cooperative law of 1988 gave cooperatives their autonomy from the State (De Luca 2013, Patmore and Belnave 2018).

6.2.3 *Corporatisation*

The third phase witnessed the corporatisation of cooperative law. Henrÿ notes that this was a major change to cooperative law: "the key change has been the alignment of cooperative law to the law of joint stock companies. This especially concerns the nature and structure of capital, as well as management and control mechanisms" (Henrÿ 2017).[7] This phase commenced in the 1970s and became more prominent in the early 1990s. It reflects the large cooperative's need to access finance and to find alternative legal structures in order to compete in global markets. It is important to note that the changes towards corporatisation are not uniform across countries or sectors, but the trend towards corporatisation is real. Key changes towards corporatisation include cooperative boards having more autonomy from the general assembly and having the power to appoint and dismiss management; cooperative law placing no limit on the remuneration of shares; non-member business or transactions more than 50 percent; cooperatives allowing members to access the cooperative reserve fund as they leave the cooperative or cooperative assets in case of dissolution or demutualisation, cooperatives having access to external capital from non-members and granting them limited voting rights; cooperatives issuing tradeable corporate bonds; cooperatives forming holding companies to attract external capital and own conventional enterprises; cooperatives being major shareholders of listed companies.[8]

6.2.4 General Interests

The fourth phase of cooperative law equates to the rise of social cooperatives (also known as social enterprises). This is a type of cooperative that operates in the general interest of the community. Their general interest purpose and multi-stakeholder membership model are significantly different than the traditional member-based cooperative model.

Social cooperatives emerged in the 1980s in response to demands for aged care, social services, and for employing people left-out of the job-market. They also emerged in response to neo-liberal policies of privatisation and outsourcing of government services and in response to the State's fiscal crisis following the end of the long post-war economic boom in the 1970s. The Italian Cooperative Law 381/1991 gave formal recognition to social cooperatives, defining them as having: "the purpose of pursuing the general interests of the community, promoting human development and the social integration of citizens through cooperatives".[9] Korea's *Framework Act on Cooperatives* of 2012 defines a social cooperative as "[carrying] out a business activity related to the enhancement of rights, interests, and welfare of local residents or the provision of social services or jobs to disadvantaged people" (Jang 2013).

Social cooperatives have been formed worldwide. Some countries have passed specific legislation in support of cooperatives Italy, France, Spain, Portugal, Hungary, Poland, and Korea. Other countries have passed a law on social enterprises that includes cooperatives (Finland), have adjusted their cooperative regulations to include social cooperatives (Germany), or have made adjustments to their company law (United Kingdom). Social cooperatives are known under different names,[10] but they have a common purpose, and that is to provide goods or services that are in the public or general interest. This can be the interest of the community, a specific group of people, or an activity with a social outcome (provision of employment to long-term unemployed or healthcare services). Their uniqueness also lies in having a multi-stakeholder-based membership that includes workers, users, voluntary staff, supporting institutions, and representatives of local communities (Roelants 2009, Jang 2013, European Commission 2013).

6.2.5 Internationalisation

The fifth phase of cooperative law development is the internationalisation of the ICA cooperative principles. The ICA approved the cooperative principles in 1937, then updated them in 1966, and again in 1995. The ICA principles have influenced cooperative law. For instance, the United States Supreme Court decision of 1966 relating to the Puget Sound Plywood case considered the original Rochdale principles (Beckett 2020), and Argentina's 1973 cooperative law explicitly aligned its rules with the ICA principles (Cracogna 2013a). Since 1995, the UN and the International Labour Organization (ILO) have formally promoted ICA principles. The UN General Assembly approved the *United Nations Draft Guidelines Aimed at Creating a Supporting Environment for the Development of Cooperatives* in 2001 (United Nations 2001). The ILO adopted *Recommendation 193 on the Promotion of Cooperatives* in 2002 (ILO 2002). These two documents explicitly endorse the ICA principles and the cooperative sector. They also recommend that States support cooperatives whilst preserving cooperative autonomy and cooperative identity. This added influence has led cooperative principles to influence cooperative law-making in all countries. The ICA principles are explicitly acknowledged by Portugal, Norway, Argentina, Uruguay, India's Multi-State Cooperative Law of 2002, and Zanzibar in Tanzania (Cracogna, Fici and Henrÿ 2013). The ICA, the ILO, and the UN have also influenced the harmonisation of cooperative law among neighbouring countries. Attempts to harmonise cooperative law include the Organisation for the Harmonization of Business Law in Africa (OHADA), which now covers seventeen States in Western and Central Africa (Diez and Tadjudje 2013); the European Cooperative Society Regulation (Fici 2013); the Statute of Mercusor Cooperatives (Cracogna 2013b); and the Framework Law for Cooperatives in South America (Cracogna 2013c).

6.3 Current State of Cooperative Law[11]

The previous section analysed the key phases in the development of cooperative law. This section examines the extent to which cooperative law as practised in twenty-six jurisdictions from Africa, Asia, Europe, North America, Oceania and South America align with the ICA cooperative principles.[12] This section is divided into seven parts, each of which discusses one of the seven ICA cooperative principles: Voluntary and Open Membership; Democratic Member Control; Member Economic Participation; Autonomy and Independence; Education, Training and Information; Cooperation among Cooperatives; and Concern for the Community.[13]

6.3.1 Principle 1: Open and Voluntary Membership

The first ICA Principle is open and voluntary membership. This requires cooperatives not to discriminate against anyone and to be open to all who are prepared to accept the responsibilities of membership.

Every jurisdiction reviewed complied with the principle of open and voluntary membership without any form of discrimination. The cooperative laws also have affordable membership entry requirements that do not pose a barrier to entry. The only notable exceptions are the New Generation (Agricultural) Cooperatives. This type of cooperative practices a closed membership, and it ties membership shares to delivery rights. The more shares a member owns, the higher the quantity that can be delivered to the cooperative. These delivery rights are also transferable (Czachorska-Jones, Finkelstein and Sansami 2013).

One way of measuring the effectiveness of compliance with the principle of open and voluntary membership is the extent of cooperative transactions with members versus non-members. Cooperatives are expected to transact mostly with members as this demonstrates their compliance with the mutuality principle and their willingness to accept others as cooperative members. To this end, the results are mixed. Cooperative laws in 15 countries encouraged cooperatives to have a high membership rate by limiting transactions with non-members to less than 50 per cent of total transactions or by providing tax incentives to those cooperatives that conduct the majority of transactions with members.[14] The research, however, also found that the remaining 11 jurisdictions pose no limit or are silent on non-member transactions.[15]

The cooperative laws operating today have changed the composition of cooperative membership. Cooperatives have had homogenous memberships until the 1970s. This comprised members with similar interests who engaged with the cooperative as a consumer, as a worker, or as a producer. Since then, the rise of social cooperatives and the need to access capital has led cooperatives to attract a diverse set of members. These members include workers, consumers, volunteers, state agencies, businesses, external investors, and other cooperatives. All social cooperatives adopt a multi-stakeholder member approach regardless of their jurisdiction. Investor members are welcomed in 17 jurisdictions, with nine jurisdictions not admitting external investors in the affairs of their cooperative.[16]

We could summarise the results relating to the principle of open and voluntary membership as follows:

- All jurisdictions promote the principle of open and voluntary membership.
- From a homogenous to a diverse membership, which also includes external investors.
- The majority of jurisdictions reviewed require at least 50 per cent of employees/users/producers to be members.
- Social cooperatives' stakeholder-based membership approach enhances the concept of open and voluntary membership.

6.3.2 Principle 2.1: Democratic Member Control

The second ICA principle is Democratic Member Control. It defines who is in control and how cooperatives are governed. It requires members to control the organisation by participating in setting policies, making decisions, and serving as elected members. In primary cooperatives, the principle of one-person-one-vote applies. In stakeholder cooperatives and secondary cooperatives other democratic systems (proportional voting or a set number of positions for each category of stakeholders) may apply (International Cooperative Alliance 2017).

Democratic governance is the decision-making framework through which members elect the board, keep the board and management accountable, and participate in key decisions to ensure the cooperative achieves economic performance in compliance with the cooperative law and national laws and in alignment with cooperative principles. Cooperative law upholds this principle by providing members with voting rights and with governance structures and procedures that enable them to democratically control the cooperative enterprise. The research found that the following key features generally apply across jurisdictions:

- Members hold the majority of votes giving them the power to make all key decisions.
- Members, via the Annual General Assembly (AGA),[17] approve and review the articles of associations or by-laws which govern the cooperative.
- Members, via the AGA, elect, review and hold to account the Board of Directors and related operational structures via reviewing the annual report on economic performance and compliance with the law and cooperative principles and the annual financial statements.
- Members, via the AGA, except where a Unitary Board model is used, select or approve the external auditors who report to the AGA.
- Members hold the majority of votes in all cooperatives in spite of changes which have allowed multiple voting and the inclusion of external investors with limited voting powers.

The Review found that 16 jurisdictions allow for multiple voting rights.[18] Three countries provide multiple voting based on share ownership. Canada provides one extra vote to members who also purchase an investor share (Petrou 2013). Belgium has legislated that voting rights are based on one-share-one-vote and that members can hold up to 10 per cent of total votes (Coates 2013). New Zealand allows the one-share-one-vote principle, provided transacting members hold 60 per cent of total votes (Apps 2020). Two countries allow multiple-member voting. Germany allows up to three votes, but can only be allowed to 'persons who further the cooperative society in a special manner' (Münkner 2013), whilst Finland allows members to have up to ten votes (Henrÿ 2013). The remaining 11 countries that allow multiple voting usually provide multiple-weighted voting to other cooperatives or institutional investors or external investors that are members of the cooperative, or to agricultural cooperatives. In agricultural cooperatives, multiple voting is based on the level of business transaction with the cooperative. In all these countries, the law ensures that active members always have the majority of votes at the AGA. Limiting those who hold multiple votes allows cooperatives to affirm that members still have control of the cooperative, but the democratic principle of one-member-one-vote has been undermined, especially in those jurisdictions where voting rights are tied to shareholding.

Cooperative members have kept control of cooperatives that allow external investors with voting rights. The Review found that most jurisdictions accept external investors, but only seven jurisdictions, Belgium, China, France, Italy, New Zealand, Russia, and Spain provide investors with voting rights.[19] Total voting rights allocated to investors range from a low of 20 per cent in China (Ren and Yuan 2013) to a high of 40 per cent in New Zealand (Apps 2020).[20] Providing investors with limited voting powers enables cooperatives to comply with the democratic control principle because active members still control the majority of votes in the general assembly.

A key source of member democratic control is member control of the AGA, which is the cooperative's principal decision-making body. The AGA's key functions, albeit with some differences across jurisdictions, generally include the approval of the articles of association or by-laws, which provide cooperatives with a set of rules and procedures that guide their governance and the decision-making process; electing the Board of Directors; approving the cooperative strategic plan and annual budget; appointing or approving the external auditors; reviewing the annual report; and reviewing the annual audited financial statements. The AGA is also the body where members, subject to legal constraints, decide the distribution of profits, the level of share remuneration, the level of patronage refund, and the admission of new members. The AGA is also the body where important decisions such as mergers, dissolution, demutualisation, and key investments are made (Cracogna, Fici and Henrÿ 2013).

Cooperative members are required to hold the majority of seats on cooperative boards. The Review found that most jurisdictions allow stakeholders to sit on cooperative boards. These stakeholders may include investors who are members, independent persons with technical expertise, directors nominated by other cooperatives, cooperative federations, businesses, government-owned businesses, or government agencies. Other than Belgium, whose cooperative act has few articles concerning governance (Coates 2013), all other jurisdictions considered here provide for members to hold always the majority of board seats. For instance, board places reserved for investor-members range from 25 per cent to 33 per cent of total board places.[21] Quebec allows 33 per cent of cooperative board seats to be allocated to financial cooperatives or nominees from the cooperative federation (Petrou 2013). India's multi-state act allows two independent members to be co-opted (Veerakumuran 2013). Japan, Korea, and Spain allow up to 33 per cent of independent directors (Kurimoto 2020, Jang 2013, Fayardo Garcia 2013). Italy limits the combined board places reserved for investor-members and independent board members to less than 50 per cent (Fici 2013). All jurisdictions, other than Belgium, explicitly require the majority of board members to be active members.

6.3.3 Principle 2.2: Governance Structures

Cooperative members retain control of the cooperative by being able to hold cooperative boards and management to account. Considering cooperatives vary in size and operate under different cultural contexts, three core governance models are being used. These are (1) the monistic model, a one-tier governance model consisting of the General Assembly (GA); (2) a dualistic model, a two-tiered governance model, consisting of the AGA appointing the cooperative Board of Directors or a supervisory board which, in turn, appoints the management board (MB)); and (3) a tri-partite body consisting of the AGA appointing both the cooperative Board of Directors and a supervisory committee.

The one-tier governance model comprises the GA. It is suitable for small cooperatives, usually employing up to 20 members. Cooperatives that adopt this model make decisions collegially. The AGA may appoint a cooperative representative and may appoint an auditor to audit its financial statements. These are cooperatives that adopt direct democracy. In these cases, every member is generally well-informed of the cooperative model and is accustomed to participating in the decision-making process. All jurisdictions may adopt this model.

The second governance model is the two-tier model which is popular in France. In this model, the AGA elects a Board of Directors. The Board performs the role of executive management and usually appoints a President. The President represents the cooperative externally and is responsible for preparing the strategic plan, the annual business plan, the Board agenda, and the annual report to be tabled at the AGA. The Board develops and implements the cooperative strategy. The Board needs to comply with the requirements of the cooperative by-laws, and it needs to report to the AGA. In this model, the AGA appoints an independent auditor to prepare annual financial statements (Hiez 2013, Jang 2013).

The third governance model is the two-tier model known as the German model. In this model, the AGA elects a Supervisory Board to which it delegates the power to appoint the MB[22] and to perform an internal oversight function. The MB includes executives and non-executive members; it may appoint management sub-committees; and is responsible for preparing the strategic plan, business plan and implementation plan. The Supervisory Board does not take part in making decisions but keeps the MB accountable via performing an internal auditing and compliance function. In addition to appointing the Supervisory Board, cooperative members keep the MB accountable via the by-laws, making decisions on annual returns and allocation of surplus, reserving major decisions such as mergers or conversions to the AGA. Ten per cent of members can also call a general meeting (Münkner 2013). Importantly, the German Cooperative Auditing Federation audits large cooperatives before registration and annually thereafter and audits small cooperatives every two years. These audits consider financial and cooperative principles matters (Münkner 2013).

Another two-tier governance model is the Unitary Board Model which is used in the United States. This fourth model also operates in Australia, Finland, India, Japan, Korea, New Zealand, Norway, Tanzania, and the United Kingdom. The key features of this model, as is practised in the United States, include having the AGA elect the Board of Directors. The Board, in turn, elect a CEO. The CEO is responsible for selecting a management team and implementing the cooperative strategic plan. In this model, the Board provides direction and exercises control of the cooperative. It provides direction by approving the strategic plan, business plans, and risk management plans, and by appointing the CEO. It keeps control by appointing external auditors, regularly monitoring management performance, and regularly reviewing risk and compliance reports at Board meetings. The Board may appoint sub-committees such as audit and risk committee or governance committee to monitor the performance and the compliance requirements (Zeuli and Cropp 2004, New South Wales Government 2012, Czachorska-Jones, Finkelstein and Sansami 2013, Jang 2013, Veerakumuran 2013, Kurimoto 2020, Rutabanzibwa 2020)

New Zealand and Norway have applied two notable innovations in cooperative governance worthy of note. In New Zealand, directors are required to pass an annual resolution to confirm that their cooperative has been operating as a cooperative company during the financial year (Apps 2020). In Norway, since 2007, cooperatives that employ more than 30 employees must have employee representation on their Board (Fjortoft and Gjems-Onstad 2013).[23]

The fifth and final cooperative governance model is the tri-partite model. This is a three-tiered model where the AGA elects both the Supervisory Committee and the Board of Directors. This model is common in Argentina, Finland, Italy, OHADA members, Portugal, Russia, Spain, and Uruguay. In the Italian model, the three key bodies are allocated the following roles:

- The AGA approves the by-laws, elects the Board of Directors, elects the Supervisory Committee, approves the annual budget, approves policies and procedures, approves the annual dividend payment, and approves patronage refunds. It also approves new members.
- The Board of Directors, of whom at least 50 per cent must be members, implements the AGA-approved strategy. It appoints the senior management team, some of whom may be Board members. It reports to the AGA on economic performance and compliance matters.
- The Supervisory Committee is an AGA-appointed stand-alone committee. It comprises at least one registered accountant. It supervises the operations of the Board and examines whether Board decisions are aligned with cooperative principles. It appoints an external auditor, reviews member complaints against management, and reports directly to the AGA on performance and compliance matters and on the application of cooperative principles.
- Further, the major cooperative federations review cooperative financial statements annually (every two years for small cooperatives) to confirm compliance with the cooperative law (Bonfante 2011, Fici 2013, Ammirato 2018).

The other Jurisdictions that adopt the tri-partite governance model have unique features that differ slightly from the Italian model. For instance, in Uruguay, the Board appoints an audit commission as well as an education committee, and an electoral committee. The composition of the Board of Directors differs among countries: Italy requires 50 per cent of the Board directors to be members; Spain requires at least 66 per cent to be members; Portugal requires 75 per cent to be members; Argentina and Uruguay do not admit non-members as directors. The external auditors are appointed by the supervisory committee in Italy, by the cooperative federation in Uruguay, and by the AGA in other jurisdictions. The Italian supervisory committee and the cooperative directors of Valencia, Spain, report to the AGA whether the cooperative activity is aligned with cooperative principles. Spain allows one board member to represent employees in cooperatives employing more than 50 employees (Cracogna 2013a, Fayardo Garcia 2013, Fici 2013b, Namorado 2013, Lavega 2020, Kutko 2021).

In summary, the dualistic, tri-partite, and Unitary Board governance models distribute power between the AGA, the Board of Directors, and management. The more power is devolved to the Board and to management, the less control for the AGA and cooperative members. Out of the five governance models explored in this section, it seems that the one-tier model is suitable for small cooperatives, and the tri-partite model reserve more power to the AGA. In fact, the AGA appoints the Board, it appoints the Supervisory Committee to perform an oversight function and it also appoints external auditors. The Unitary Board Model, gives more power to the Board of Directors, which has delegated powers to appoint the CEO and the auditors, and to the CEO, who has the right to appoint and dismiss senior management. This unitary model is similar to the governance models adopted by large corporations. Cooperative by-laws and approved internal policies articulate further these divisions of powers. Cooperative governance will be explored further in Chapter 8, which compares cooperative governance with corporate governance.

6.3.4 *Principle 3: Member Economic Participation*

The third ICA Principle is Member Economic Participation. This principle is fulfilled if cooperatives (i) make a distinction between profit and surplus; (ii) set up an indivisible reserve fund; (iii) pay limited return on members' capital accounts; and (iv) pay a patronage refund based on member transactions with the cooperative.

The distinction between profit and surplus is one which promotes the distinctiveness of the cooperative model by encouraging cooperatives to attract more members and preventing members from taking advantage of non-members. In a nutshell, a cooperative profit is the annual positive result of business trading (revenue minus cost), and it includes transactions incurred with everyone, members and non-members. Surplus is that portion of the profit that is generated with transactions with members only. Usually, the surplus has been open to allocation to members as a patronage refund (as was the case at Rochdale), and profit is allocated to remunerate members' capital accounts and to increase the reserve fund. The Review has found that 16 of the countries surveyed do not appear to explicitly make a distinction between profits and surplus.[24] Only ten jurisdictions explicitly declare that only surplus funds can be used to provide members with a patronage refund.

The approach to remunerating patronage refunds differs among jurisdictions. In 15 jurisdictions,[25] cooperative by-laws determine how much of the profits and surplus can be returned to members as patronage refunds. The remaining 11 countries have prescribed legal requirements for paying patronage refunds. These 11 countries either allow for rebates to be paid after other distribution requirements have been met (such as payment to reserves, educational fund, remuneration of investor capital); or state a percentage of profits that can be distributed as patronage rebate as is done in Korea (50 per cent), China (60 per cent), or Spain (75 per cent) (Fayardo Garcia 2013, Jang 2013, Ren and Yuan 2013).

The establishment of an indivisible (collectively owned) reserve has always been a key feature of cooperative culture and cooperative law. These reserves strengthen the financial viability of the cooperative business, represent the contributions made by generations of co-operators, promote inter-generational solidarity, and prevent demutualisation (International Cooperative Alliance 2017). The Review found that 16 jurisdictions require a percentage of profits to be deposited into the reserve fund ranging from 5 per cent to 35 per cent.[26] More specifically, it ranges from 5 per cent in Argentina and Finland; 10 per cent in the Republic of Korea and Japan; 15 per cent in France; 20 per cent in Quebec, Spain, OHADA Member States and Tanzania; 25 per cent in Uruguay; 30 per cent in Italy; and 35 per cent in India. The other 11 jurisdictions left it to the cooperative statutes to decide whether to have or not have a reserve fund, other than Belgium, which had a requirement to establish a reserve fund but did not prescribe an amount to be deposited (Cracogna, Fici and Henrÿ 2013).

This Review found that whilst social cooperatives are prevented from distributing the reserve fund during the life of the cooperative or after dissolution, a different picture emerges when considering traditional cooperatives. The Review revealed that in 18 jurisdictions, the reserve fund can be distributed upon dissolution. Of these, Germany, Denmark and China make provisions for departing members to receive a portion of the reserve fund, based on their contribution as members, upon exiting the cooperative (Fjortoft and Gjems-Onstad 2013, Münkner 2013a, Ren and Yuan 2013). The remaining eight jurisdictions prohibit the distribution of the reserve fund whilst the cooperative is active, and in case of dissolution, the net assets remaining are to be deposited either in a cooperative fund or with a cooperative agency with the responsibility to promote the cooperative sector[27] (Cracogna, Fici and Henrÿ 2013).

Limited remuneration of members' capital accounts is a long-standing principle that defines the cooperative movement. Capital invested by members is not primarily an investment to generate a capital return. Instead, its function is to provide the necessary initial capital to establish the cooperative. The ICA's Third Principle acknowledges that a limited rate of return should be allowed (International Cooperative Alliance 2017). All jurisdictions reviewed pay a dividend on members' capital accounts. In 14 jurisdictions, the remuneration of members' capital is determined via by-laws. In these 14 jurisdictions, the cooperative law is either silent or, as is the case in Canada, Denmark, Finland, Germany, and Sweden, it places no upper limit on member capital remuneration.[28] The remaining 12 jurisdictions provide for capital remuneration via a variable rate. In some countries, it is a percentage above the government bond rate (in Italy, it is set at 2 per cent above the bond rate; and in Argentina, at 1 per cent). In other countries, the law places a maximum rate of remuneration on member capital of 8 per cent in the United States and 10 per cent in Korea. China has a more distinct approach in allowing for 40 per cent of its profits to remunerate capital invested (Cracogna, Fici and Henrÿ 2013).

A major change to cooperative membership or capitalisation has been the acceptance of the external investors as members—a non-active person or business—that receive a return on their investment. The Review found that 17 jurisdictions accept external investors.[29] Of these, 12 jurisdictions[30] remunerate external investors as per cooperative by-laws or via decisions taken at their AGAs. Subject to making a profit, these 12 jurisdictions do not place any regulatory limits on how external investors can be remunerated. Indeed, Belgium and Sweden explicitly note that there is no upper limit on distributions (Coates 2013, Fjortoft and Gjems-Onstad 2013). The remaining five jurisdictions, China, France, Italy, Quebec, and Spain, remunerate external investors as prescribed in their cooperative law. For instance, in Italy, the maximum remuneration is set at 4 per cent above the government bond rate (Fici 2013); and in Spain, cooperatives can pay 8 per cent above the set government rate (Fayardo Garcia 2013). Quebec has set a maximum rate of return of 25 per cent for preferred shares (Petrou 2013). In China, 40 per cent of the distributable profit can be used to remunerate capital invested by members and external investors (Ren and Yuan 2013).

Key findings for Principle Three: Member Economic Participation are:

- Most cooperatives do not adhere to the principle of paying patronage refunds based on surplus rather than profits.
- Half the jurisdictions allow cooperative by-laws rather than legislation to set the return on investments, which may not comply with the principle of limited return on capital.
- Most countries distribute the cooperative residual assets to members upon dissolution, and three countries distribute cooperative residual assets before dissolution.
- The majority of jurisdictions allow cooperatives to admit external shareholders. Their remuneration is either set via the cooperative law (at a higher rate than member capital remuneration) or is set in the cooperative by-laws.

6.3.5 Principle 4: Autonomy and Independence

Principle four: Autonomy and Independence. This principle affirms that cooperatives are to be controlled by their members and should be autonomous from other organisations, governments, or financial institutions. The principle of Autonomy and Independence is further enhanced when cooperatives promote educational activities to enhance member awareness of cooperative principles and increase member capabilities in managing their own cooperative (International Cooperative Alliance 2017).

Almost all of the jurisdictions reviewed do promote autonomous cooperatives enterprises. Cooperative law requires governments to perform a regulatory role in setting cooperative's rules and conduct and to perform an administrative role by facilitating registration and data collection. A high degree of State control is still exercised in those Indian States where cooperatives operate under the local state laws (ALC India 2019) and in the Tanzanian mainland where the registrar may appoint up to one-third of board members if deemed to be in the public interest, and exercises controls on loans, and cooperative investments from reserve funds (Rutabanzibwa 2020).

6.3.6 Principle 5: Education, Training, and Information

The fifth ICA principle is Education, Training, and Information. Cooperatives are required to train their members so that they can contribute to the development of their cooperatives and participate in the decision-making process. This means training in technical skills and all the skills necessary to govern the cooperative. They should also educate the public on the history of cooperatives, their ideals and practice (International Cooperative Alliance 2017).

The Review found that nine jurisdictions require cooperatives to set aside part of their profits towards educational activities.[31] Seven jurisdictions, Spain, Portugal, Argentina, Uruguay, Wisconsin, Tanzania (Zanzibar), and OHADA members, require cooperatives to set aside a percentage of profits towards their educational fund. It ranges from an unspecified amount in Portugal to 20 per cent for OHADA members. Most set aside 5 per cent. Italy, India and Uruguay deposit money into funds externally managed by cooperative movement. The Italian cooperatives pay 3 per cent of profits into a cooperative development fund managed by cooperative federations. India deposits 1 per cent of profits into the education fund managed by the National Cooperative Union of India. Cooperatives from Uruguay pay 0.15 per cent of their revenue into a provisional fund for cooperative promotion development and education that is managed by the National Institute of Cooperatives (INACOOP), a public-cooperative body (Cracogna, Fici and Henrÿ 2013).

The cooperative law in the other 17 jurisdictions does not explicitly promote educational activities. This does not mean that cooperatives in those countries do not engage in cooperative education and training, but it does imply that their legislators did not view education and training as a core component of cooperative law.

6.3.7 *Principle 6: Cooperation among Cooperatives*

In 1966, the ICA included the sixth ICA cooperative principle: 'Cooperation among Cooperatives'. Cooperatives have been practising this principle for over a century. It was practised by every traditional cooperative sector through the formation of second-tier cooperatives: wholesalers, consortia, central banking associations, and agricultural marketing or supply cooperatives. The ICA Guidance Notes indicate that this principle has an inherent inspiration to transform society by getting cooperatives to work together. It is an indication that cooperatives are part of a movement and that they do not operate on their own (International Cooperative Alliance 2017).

All the jurisdictions reviewed do not prevent cooperatives from forming cooperative federations and second-tier cooperatives, but only eight jurisdictions actively promote cooperation among cooperatives. The eight jurisdictions include the following:

- The Argentinian law requires cooperatives to pay a 2 per cent tax to the Cooperative Education Promotion Fund to support cooperative development (Cracogna 2013a).
- The French Law explicitly promotes second-tier cooperatives and the formation of cooperative groupings (Hiez 2013, Douvitsa 2021).
- The Indian law requires cooperatives to pay 1 per cent of their profits to the National Cooperative Union of India for the purpose of education, training and for promoting the cooperative movement (Veerakumuran 2013).
- Italian law requires cooperatives to deposit 3 per cent of their profits into a cooperative development fund. The cooperative federations use these funds to support cooperative development, including promoting cooperative education (Ammirato 2018).
- The Japanese law promotes second-tier cooperatives to conduct economic activities, and promotes cooperative federations or unions to represent their cooperative members when engaging with administrative authorities and to provide business services (Kurimoto 2013, 2020).
- The Quebec Law on cooperatives outlines the role of the Quebec Council for Cooperatives and Mutual. A key role includes the coordination of the State-funded Regional Development Cooperatives Centres, which promote cooperative economic development in Quebec (Petrou 2013).
- In Spain, the State and the autonomous regions partly fund the administrative costs of cooperative federations. They also require cooperatives to fund the cooperative federation-managed Educational and Promotion Fund (Fayardo Garcia 2013).
- In Uruguay, INACOOP is a public-cooperative-funded body which promotes the economic, social, and cultural development of cooperatives. In 2015, it created Fondes-Inacoop, a cooperative development fund to support sustainable cooperative projects (Gonzales 2020, Lavega 2020).

The current state of cooperative law does not prevent cooperatives from cooperating with each other, but generally, the law does not promote cooperation among cooperatives.

6.3.8 *Principle 7: Concern for the Community*

The seventh ICA cooperative principle, 'Concern for the Community', was added to the ICA Principles of 1995. It encourages cooperatives to work for sustainable development,[32] the promotion of social justice, and the need to combat inequalities and poverty (International Cooperative Alliance 2017). Cooperatives would demonstrate compliance with this principle if they

- Promote collective ownership of assets and prevent demutualisation. This enables cooperatives to be embedded in local communities and to ensure that their collective assets, capabilities, and know-how are passed on to the next generation in perpetuity.
- Establish cooperative support structures to promote local economic development.
- Promote the well-being and the general interests of the community. In this model, cooperatives would serve the community and not just their members. This is demonstrated by tackling issues such as unemployment, exclusion, welfare services such as aged care, and community services.

The Review found that only eight jurisdictions require assets to be indivisible (asset lock) at all times.[33] The Review found that the remaining 18 cooperative jurisdictions reviewed in this study allow the distribution of assets upon dissolution, thus promoting cooperatives as private businesses and not as inter-generational cooperatives whose assets are passed on to future generations. The jurisdictions of China, Denmark, and Germany allow members to access a proportion of the reserve fund when departing the cooperative (Fjortoft and Gjems-Onstad 2013, Münkner 2013, Ren and Yuan 2013).

The cooperative law of 16 jurisdictions allows cooperatives to demutualise and convert cooperatives into private enterprises.[34] This usually involves the majority of members voting in favour of demutualisation. Four countries, Argentina, India, Japan, and Uruguay do not allow demutualisation. Six other jurisdictions make it difficult for cooperatives to demutualise. Italy, the OHADA members, Quebec, and Portugal allow demutualisation subject to the net assets being returned to the cooperative movement. Spain requires the obligatory reserve fund and the education and promotion fund to be assigned to the cooperative federation or to the Treasury or to another cooperative. France requires the net assets to be locked for ten years from the date of demutualisation before they can be distributed to members (Cracogna, Fici and Henrÿ 2013).

Almost all Cooperative laws do not explicitly promote local economic cooperative development agencies or instruments. Only the law in Italy, Quebec, Spain, and Uruguay explicitly promote local economic development agencies. The Italian law requires cooperatives to deposit 3 per cent of their profits into a cooperative development fund that invests in new and existing cooperatives throughout their lifecycle (Ammirato 2018). The Quebec cooperative law promotes the Quebec Council of Cooperation and Mutuality as the coordinator of the Regional Development Corporations (RDCs). RDCs support local economic development by creating new cooperatives, supporting existing cooperatives, and organising a cooperative network in each region. These RDCs are primarily funded by the government based on the number of jobs created (Petrou 2013).

The Spanish law requires a percentage of profits to be deposited into the Education and Promotion Fund, whose function is to promote cooperatives and cooperation among cooperatives (Fayardo Garcia 2013). The Uruguayan cooperative law enabled the formation of the Fondes-Inacoop, a cooperative development fund that provides financial and non-financial support to cooperative projects (Inacoop 2015).

The arrival of social cooperatives has greatly strengthened the cooperative movement's community focus and credentials throughout the world. The purpose of social cooperatives is to pursue the general interest of the community in terms of human development and the social integration of the citizens. This research found that jurisdictions promote social enterprises via a variety of laws, including a specific social cooperative law (Italy, Portugal, and Spain); social cooperative requirements included in the main cooperative law (Canada, Germany, Japan, Korea, Quebec, and Uruguay); or social cooperatives formed via social enterprise laws or generic laws (Cecop 2009, Cracogna, Fici and Henrÿ 2013).

Japan also offers a unique experience in community development. The Japanese cooperative law for the agricultural and consumer sectors promotes community development. These laws enable agricultural and consumer cooperatives to engage in multi-activities that include welfare and health care. To this end, the Welfare Federation of Agricultural Cooperatives has been managing medical centres since 1951. Consumer cooperatives also provide educational and health care services as well as welfare activities for the elderly and handicapped (Kurimoto 2020).

In summary, the majority of jurisdictions do not implicitly support community development, just like they did not actively support education and training activities and cooperation among cooperatives. The majority of jurisdictions allow members to access cooperative assets when cooperatives cease to operate. Most jurisdictions also allow the demutualisation of cooperatives without major barriers. The formation of social cooperatives throughout the world, the multi-purpose form of cooperation practised in Japan, and the cooperative development and regional funds operating in Italy, Quebec, Spain, and Uruguay, indicate support for a cooperative model that supports community development. This model has a broader vision and broader goals than those models that focus on the enterprise and its members only.

6.4 Summary of Results

The results demonstrate the diversity of the cooperative laws that operate across the world. The results based on this sample of 26 jurisdictions indicate that non-compliance with the cooperative principles exceeds compliance. Only ICA principle two, Democratic Member Control, is fully complied with because members hold the majority of votes in the AGA and are able to elect, dismiss, and hold the Board to account. The principle of Autonomy and Independence is almost fully complied with, as only two countries still interfere in cooperative governance. Most jurisdictions, however, do not fully comply with the other cooperative principles. Table 6.1 provides a summary of results and a brief concluding comment for each ICA principle.

6.5 The Law and Cooperative Development

One way to assess the effectiveness of cooperative law is to consider the extent to which the law facilitates or prevents cooperative development. Since cooperatives produce goods and services to be sold in the market in competition with other firms, this is very

Table 6.1 Summary of Compliance with the ICA Cooperative Principles

Principle	Definition	Results
Principle 1	Voluntary and Open Membership	• All jurisdictions practice open membership without discrimination. • The majority of jurisdictions require at least 50 per cent of employees/users/producers to be members.
Principle 2	Democratic Member Control	• Members control the cooperative decision-making process in-spite of the introduction of plural voting and investor members in some countries. • Members hold the majority of votes and control the AGA, by-laws, and the election and dismissal of board representatives.
Principle 3	Member Economic Participation	• In the majority of jurisdictions, cooperative by-laws determine the level of remuneration for patronage refunds, member shares, and other financial instruments. • Most jurisdictions allow the distribution of residual assets (reserves) upon dissolution. This facilitates cooperative degeneration into capitalist enterprises.
Principle 4	Autonomy and Independence	• Principle applied in all but two countries.
Principle 5	Education, Training and Information	• Ten jurisdictions prescribe an active contribution towards education.[a]
Principle 6	Cooperation among Cooperatives	• Eight jurisdictions actively promote cooperation among cooperatives. • Most jurisdictions neither prevent nor encourage cooperation among cooperatives.
Principle 7	Concern for the Community	• Eight jurisdictions actively support the principle: Concern for the Community. • Most jurisdictions allow members to access net assets and allow cooperatives to demutualise. • Only four jurisdictions promote cooperative economic development funds. • Most jurisdictions do not have a cooperative-specific law on social cooperatives.

Note: [a] This includes the Wisconsin Law representing the United States.

important. To answer this question, we consider how cooperative law promotes the formation of cooperatives, access to economic activities, access to finance, access to appropriate legal business structures, and taxation policies.

Overall, the cooperative laws reviewed in this study provide cooperatives with the opportunity to start a business without obstacles, to operate in almost all sectors of the economy, to access capital through a variety of capital instruments, to choose a variety of legal structures, and to operate within non-hostile tax laws. Cooperative sectors from all over the world have a lot of choice when promoting their ideal cooperative economic environment. More specifically:

- The formation of cooperatives has been facilitated by requiring few members in order to form a cooperative. Most jurisdictions require from three to ten members to form a cooperative. Finland allows one member to start a cooperative. Agricultural, consumer, and banking cooperatives require more members but still quite a reachable number.

- The requirement to trade with members only to maintain their mutuality credentials of open membership and democratic management has been modified. The great majority of jurisdictions allow trading with non-members: most allow trading up to 50 per cent of total trade with non-members, with some allowing unlimited trading with non-members.
- Cooperatives can operate in almost all sectors of the economy. At times there are restrictions in the financial sector, such as the management of pension funds, insurance, and finance companies. This, however, has not prevented cooperatives from owning insurance companies registered as stock companies or listed on the stock market.
- Accessing finance has been improved over the years. Initially, finance was raised internally from member shares, member loans, and retained profits. Today, most jurisdictions allow external investors to invest in cooperatives either by purchasing shares with or without voting rights, by buying cooperative bonds, or by purchasing other capital instruments. Cooperative federations have established credit guarantee companies, manage their own finance companies, and some manage their own cooperative development funds or cooperative regional funds. Some cooperatives have listed a portion of their shares or bonds in stock markets.
- There are a variety of legal structures available to grow cooperatives. All jurisdictions allow cooperatives to cooperate with other cooperatives by forming second-tier structures or by forming federations. Cooperatives are allowed to form joint-ventures with private companies or with other cooperatives. Most of the jurisdictions reviewed allow cooperatives or second-tier organisations to buy stocks and purchase private companies. This has led to the rise of corporations and cooperative groups of companies. These legal structures allow the formation of holding companies to attract capital and to buy other companies to pursue growth policies whilst minimising business risks.
- Finally, cooperative-specific government tax policies do not pose a barrier to cooperative growth. The jurisdictions normally allow cooperatives to claim tax deductions for patronage refunds and/or for dividends paid to members subject to these amounts being included in members' taxable income. Governments provide tax exemptions to cooperatives with a legal requirement to deposit a portion of profits to the indivisible reserve fund. In addition, some tax incentives are more nation-specific. For instance, Spain provides a 90 per cent tax concession for five years to worker cooperatives (Fayardo Garcia 2013); India provides tax concessions for ten years on new industrial projects and also on exports (Veerakumuran 2013); whilst Quebec provides a 125 per cent tax rebate to investors that invest in Investment Income Preference Shares (Petrou 2013).

6.6 One Cooperative Enterprise Model?

The findings from this Review verified Hagen Henrÿ's insights when he warned that:

This approximation of the features of cooperatives with those of stock companies is indicative of the difficulties in practice and in law of finding an appropriate balance between the economic and the social objectives of cooperatives. The reaction to these difficulties might lead to a new divide between cooperative laws: those which support the idea of cooperatives doing business as capital-centred enterprises, albeit in a different way (Australia, Northern European countries, and North America), and those which reflect the re-emerging social and solidarity economy idea (Central and South American countries and Southern European countries) (Henrÿ 2017).

6.6.1 *Cooperative Enterprise Model 1: Cooperatives as a Member-owned Capital-Centred Enterprise*

The first cooperative model is that of cooperatives as member-owned businesses with a unique organisational model. These jurisdictions are mostly concerned with the first four ICA principles, which focus on membership, democratic control, economic participation, and autonomy.

The jurisdictions favouring this approach mostly allow for plural voting and allow cooperative by-laws to determine the extent of non-member trading, the level of remuneration on members' capital accounts, the level of patronage refunds, and the level of remuneration of external investments. These jurisdictions allow net cooperative assets to be distributed at dissolution or at times when members depart the cooperative. These jurisdictions also allow cooperatives to demutualise and convert into capitalist enterprises and allow member access to cooperative assets.

Cooperatives that operate under this model may still choose to approve by-laws that adhere to cooperative principles and, therefore, operate as democratically managed cooperatives that operate on behalf of their members. Should cooperative by-laws not comply with traditional cooperative principles, they would then operate as profit-maximising, profit-sharing cooperatives. This model would allow members to pay high dividends, introduce profit-sharing schemes, access cooperative assets, and demutualise for financial gain. This cooperative model would resemble investor-owned firms. The cooperative law opens the possibility for this type of cooperative enterprise model to develop in Northern Europe, North America, and Oceania and also in some of the countries where the State had played a more prominent role in managing the cooperative sector, such as Russia, China, Tanzania, and South Africa.[35]

6.6.2 *Cooperative Enterprise Model 2: Cooperatives as Members of a Cooperative Movement Supporting Community Development*

The second trend comprises jurisdictions that encourage cooperatives to be part of a cooperative movement that also promotes community development. In this cooperative model, cooperatives are still seen as enterprises competing in the market with unique characteristics, but they do so as part of a cooperative movement and with responsibilities towards their community, not just their members. In these jurisdictions, the cooperative law prescribes the limited return on members' investment, the limited return on patronage refunds, and the limited return on external investment. The law requires cooperatives to support educational activities, to actively support cooperation among cooperatives, and to actively support their community. Concern for the community is demonstrated via promoting active cooperative development or promotional funds managed by the cooperative federations; preventing the distribution of assets at all times; preventing demutualisation, or making it very difficult to demutualise (for instance, requiring net assets to be returned to the cooperative sector). These jurisdictions support social cooperatives' goals of promoting community interests or general interests. Control of the cooperative governance arrangements is always vested with members whilst allowing external investors and independents to sit on their Boards.

These jurisdictions have more prescribed legal arrangements that define cooperative practices in alignment with the seven ICA principles. These jurisdictions are mainly found in Argentina, France, Italy, Japan, Quebec, Portugal, Spain, and Uruguay. Table 6.2 compares how key aspects of cooperative law are applied across the 26 jurisdictions.

Table 6.2 Comparative Analysis of Cooperative Jurisdictions

Country	One Vote / Plural Vote	Trading with Non-members	Patronage Refund	Return Member-Accounts	Demutual-isation	Indivisible Reserves—Assets[a]	Education Support	Cooperation Among Cooperatives	Community Development[b]
1 **Argentina**	One Vote	CL-Limited[d]	CL-Limited	Limited	Not Allowed	Indivisible	Yes	Yes	High
2 **Australia**	One Vote	CL-Limited	By-laws	By-Laws	Allowed	Divisible	Silent	Silent	Low
3 **Belgium**	Plural	By-laws	By-laws	Limited	Allowed	Divisible	Silent	Silent	Low
4 **Canada**	Plural-LA[c]	By-laws	By-laws	By-Laws	Allowed	Divisible	Silent	Silent	Low
5 **China**	Plural-LA	CL-Limited	CL-Limited	Limited	Silent	Divisible	Silent	Silent	Low
6 **Denmark**	Plural	By-laws	By-laws	By-laws	Allowed	Divisible	Silent	Silent	Low
7 **Finland**	Plural	By-laws	By-laws	By-laws	Allowed	Divisible	Silent	Silent	Low
8 **France**	Plural-LA	CL-Limited	CL-Limited	Limited	Allowed-Difficult[e]	Indivisible	Silent	Yes	high
9 **Germany**	Plural-LA	By-laws	By-laws	By-laws	Allowed	Divisible	Silent	Silent	Low
10 **India**	Plural-LA	By-laws	CL-Limited	By-laws	Not Allowed	Mixed[f]	Yes	Yes	Moderate
11 **Italy**	Plural-LA	CL-Limited	CL-Limited	Limited	Allowed-Difficult	Indivisible	Yes	Yes	High
12 **Japan**	One Vote	CL-Limited	CL-Limited	Limited	Not Allowed	Divisible	Yes	Yes	High
13 **Korea**	Plural-LA	CL-Limited	CL-Limited	Limited	Allowed	Divisible	Silent	Silent	Low
14 **NZ**	Plural-LA	CL-Limited	By-laws	By-Laws	Allowed	Divisible	Silent	Silent	Low
15 **Norway**	Plural-LA	By-laws	By-laws	Limited	Allowed	Divisible-difficult[g]	Silent	Silent	Low
16 **OHADA**	One Vote	By-laws	By-laws	By-laws	Allowed-Difficult	Indivisible	Yes	Silent	Moderate
17 **Portugal.**	Plural-LA	CL-Limited	CL-Limited	limited	Allowed-Difficult	Indivisible	Yes	Silent	High
18 **Quebec**	One Vote	CL-Limited	By-laws	By-laws	Allowed-Difficult	Indivisible	Silent	Yes	High
19 **Russia**	One Vote	CL-Limited	By-laws	By-laws	Allowed[h]	Divisible	Silent	Silent	Low
20 **South Africa**	One Vote	CL-Limited	By-laws	By-Laws	Allowed	Divisible	Silent	Silent	Low
21 **Spain**	Plural-LA	CL-Limited	CL-Limited	Limited	Allowed-Difficult	Indivisible	Yes	Yes	High

Country	One Vote / Plural Vote	Trading with Non-members	Patronage Refund	Return Member-Accounts	Demutual-isation	Indivisible Reserves—Assets[a]	Education Support	Cooperation Among Cooperatives	Community Development[b]
22 **Sweden**	Plural	By-laws	By-laws	By-laws	Allowed	Divisible	Silent	Silent	Low
23 **Tanzania**	One Vote	By-laws	By-laws	By-Laws	Allowed	Divisible	Yes	Silent	Low
24 **UK**	One Vote	By-laws	By-laws	By-Laws	Allowed	Divisible	Silent	Silent	Low
25 **Uruguay**	One Vote	CL-Limited	CL-Limited	limited	Not Allowed	Indivisible	Yes	Yes	High
26 **USA**	Plural-LA	CL-Limited	CL-Limited	Limited	Allowed	Divisible	Silent	Silent	Low

Notes:

[a] Indivisible reserves of assets relates to all cooperatives other than social cooperatives. Social Cooperatives, in almost all cases, are not allowed to divide their assets among members. Please refer to Part 5.2.9 in Chapter 5.

[b] The community development column combines data on collective asset ownership, prevention of demutualisation, social cooperatives law or equivalent, and cooperative local development support structures. Please refer to Part 6.3.8.

[c] Plural-LA (Plural Voting with Limited Application), means that a number of stakeholders may hold plural voting rights, but the majority of votes is always reserved for members. Please refer to Part 6.3.2.

[d] CL-Limited (Cooperative Law-Limited), means that the Cooperative Law limits trading with non-members. Please refer to Part 6.3.1.

[e] Allowed-difficult, means that: demutualisation is allowed but the cooperative law requires the assets to be deposited with a cooperative development fund, or government fund, or makes it difficult to distribute to members. Please refer to Part 6.3.8.

[f] Cooperatives that operate in multi-states may distribute assets. Those cooperatives that operate under state laws are required to transfer the residual capital and assets to the government (Veerakumuran 2013).

[g] In Norway, 80 per cent majority must vote in favour of distributing the collective equity fund (reserve fund) and must have a good reason. The decision needs to be approved by the Foundation Authority (Fjortoft and Gjems-Onstad, 2013).

[h] Russia does not allow consumer cooperatives to demutualise (De Luca 2013).

6.7 One Cooperative Enterprise Definition?

Within these two broad cooperative enterprise models, the variety of cooperative laws across the globe allows for the development of various types of cooperative enterprises. One cooperative enterprise type fits the existing ICA definition of a cooperative, but at least four other cooperative enterprise types do not. Based on the previous historical analysis conducted in Chapters 2–5, and the analysis and data collected in this chapter, we can identify five different types of cooperative enterprises with unique definitions.

6.7.1 *Traditional Cooperative Enterprise*

The first type of cooperative enterprise is the traditional model of a cooperative that complies with the first four ICA principles. This cooperative is democratically managed, does not distribute net assets at any time, limits the return on capital accounts, and limits the number of profits distributed as patronage refunds. This cooperative suits the current cooperative ICA definition: "A cooperative is an autonomous association of persons united to meet their economic, social, and cultural needs and aspirations through a jointly-managed and democratically controlled enterprise" (International Cooperative Alliance 2017).

6.7.2 *Member-Owned, Capital-Centred Cooperative Enterprise*

The second type of cooperative enterprise is a cooperative that does not fully comply with the ICA's first four principles. As we have seen, many jurisdictions allow the distribution of net assets and allow cooperatives to demutualise. They allow by-laws to determine the level of remuneration to capital owned by members and investors and to determine the amounts paid as patronage refunds. These could be democratically owned enterprises. I emphasise 'member-owned enterprises' because members are able to access the assets and distribute profits without limits. An appropriate definition for this type of cooperative is: *A cooperative is a member owned, democratically controlled, profit maximising business that shares profits and cooperative assets with its members.*[36]

6.7.3 *Cooperatives as Active Members of a Cooperative Movement*

The third type of cooperative enterprise is one which is part of a cooperative movement. These cooperatives would add to the practices of the traditional cooperative model by being more active with the cooperative federations, the consortia and second-tier structures, and other cooperative support structures. This cooperative would comply with the first six ICA principles. This research has noted how some jurisdictions require cooperatives to pay a portion of their profits to an educational fund or to the cooperative federation to access business services, funding, auditing, oversight functions and so on. The definition of this cooperative would add the phrase 'active member of the cooperative movement' to the current ICA definition. The definition of this cooperative would read: *A cooperative is an autonomous association of persons united to meet their economic, social, and cultural needs and aspirations through a democratically controlled enterprise that is an active member of the cooperative movement.*

6.7.4 *Cooperatives as Members of a Community Focussed Cooperative Movement*

The fourth cooperative enterprise type describes those cooperatives that apply all seven cooperative principles, including 'Concern for the Community'. The archetypal cooperative that fits this model is the social cooperative. Their concern for the community, however, can be better expressed if they are part of a cooperative movement which can provide a variety of support services. In this case, an appropriate definition would note that the focus is not to meet the needs of their members or profit sharing but to meet the needs of the community. The definition of this cooperative could read: *A cooperative is an autonomous association of persons united to provide goods and services that meet the general interests of the community through a member-led, or stakeholder-led, democratically controlled enterprise that is an active member of the cooperative movement.*

6.7.5 *Cooperative-owned Group of Companies*

The fifth cooperative enterprise model is that of the cooperative-owned group of companies. These are cooperatives that own business subsidiaries managed as conventional businesses. Some cooperatives usually form groups by acquiring subsidiaries via a separate holding company or directly via the cooperative structure. The cooperative legislation is silent on how these cooperative groups should apply ICA principles throughout the group. These cooperatives operate with dual structures, which require the cooperative to comply with the ICA cooperative principles, yet it allows the same cooperative to control subsidiaries that are managed as profit-maximising conventional companies. This may be an effective way to enable cooperatives to grow their business, but it is a form of degeneration because cooperatives manage another enterprise as a capitalist enterprise violating the principles of open membership, democratic principles, limited return on capital, and so on. A cooperative definition that would reflect the dual functions of cooperative groups where the lead cooperatives may comply with all seven ICA principles, yet their holding companies own capitalist-managed subsidiaries, would be: *A cooperative is an autonomous association of persons united to meet their economic, social and cultural needs and aspirations via managing a cooperative-owned group of companies which engages in profit maximising activity to further the interests of their members, the cooperative movement, and the community in which they operate.*

If the leading cooperative of the cooperative group does not fully comply with the first four ICA principles, then the cooperative group would operate solely to maximise profits for the benefit of their members. To this end, it would be re-classified as a 'Member-owned, Capital-centred Cooperative Corporation'.

6.8 Good Practice Standards

This study has noted that most of the scrutinised jurisdictions do not align cooperative law requirements with ICA principles and guidelines. At the same time, many jurisdictions have in place regulations that fully comply with the ICA principles. It is possible to collate the best that cooperative law has to offer to develop a good practice guide that is able to promote economic performance in compliance with ICA principles. Below is an attempt at developing a good practice guide to cooperative law, taking into consideration the findings from this Review, the suggestions made by Henrÿ, Fici, and Münkner, and the ICA Guidance Notes.

What follows are suggestions for each ICA principle and the potential outcome if these suggestions are implemented:

- **Principle 1: Voluntary and Open Membership.** At least 50 per cent of potential members are members at all times. Persons access membership after one-to-two years, subject to meeting economic and social requirements. These requirements will promote bonafide cooperatives and promote inclusion.
- **Principle 2: Democratic Member Control.** One person-one vote in all primary cooperatives. Majority of members on the Board of Directors or Supervisory Boards at all times. AGA appoints the Board, managers, auditors, supervisory boards, and independent directors. AGA makes key decisions, including budget approval, profit distribution, membership approval, mergers, and acquisitions. Forms of participatory democracy in place for members and non-members. Employees are to elect their Board representatives in all cooperatives with over 30 employees, as is the case in Norway. These requirements will encourage member control and a greater level of participation from members and non-member employees.
- **Principle 3: Member Economic Participation.** Limited fixed return on member accounts, member patronage refunds, and other financial instruments. At least 50 per cent of profits to be deposited into the indivisible reserve fund. Up to 20 per cent of profits are to be used for patronage refunds. Remuneration for capital accounts or members' loans up to 10 per cent per annum, as is the case in Korea, or a percentage above the government bond rate. The patronage refunds should be available to members and non-members because it is a recognition of the transactions between individuals and the cooperative, as is practised in France. Salary differentials should not exceed 5:1, as legislated for ethical banks in Italy. This approach will encourage investment from members, it will encourage inclusion and equal treatment of workers/users/producers, will promote financial prudence, will promote inter-generational wealth, and will reduce salary differentials and promote a more egalitarian culture.
- **Principle 4: Autonomy and Independence.** Government performs a variety of roles without interfering with cooperative governance. The government could be involved in legislation; registration; regulatory oversight; non-discriminatory access to public works or outsourcing of government services; provision of long-term patient capital; promoting public-cooperative partnerships; promoting cooperative-specific job creation schemes; developing cooperative-specific tax policies; integrating the subject of cooperatives into the research and education curricula,[37] and so on. These requirements enhance cooperative autonomy, promote bona-fide cooperatives, and pave the way for respectful relations with their government.
- **Principle 5: Education, Training, and Information.** Cooperatives to deposit at least 10 per cent of profits to their own fund or to the cooperative federation education fund. Cooperatives to develop an education programme that enhances the knowledge and capabilities of members in understanding cooperative principles and the cooperative model, so they can actively and confidently engage in the decision-making process and governance. These requirements will encourage active members, discourage passive members, and will promote cooperative development and cooperative values.
- **Principle 6: Cooperation among Cooperatives.** Cooperatives to deposit at least 10 per cent of profits deposited into the cooperative federation economic fund to promote

cooperatives throughout their lifecycle. The law should actively promote federations, cooperative support structures, and regional structures that promote broad-based, inter-sectoral cooperative networks. These requirements would unite, strengthen, and promote an inter-sectoral cooperative movement that is able to promote new cooperatives, support existing ones at various stages of their lifecycle, and manage economic crises.
- **Principle 7: Concern for the Community**. Cooperative specialist law on social cooperatives or cooperative law with a clear definition of social cooperatives. Cooperative reserves and assets are collectively owned and indivisible. The law should prevent demutualisation. Cooperative development funds to promote economic development in all communities. These requirements will strengthen cooperatives economically, enhance the reputation of cooperatives as collectively owned enterprises that promote inter-generational wealth; promote trust in cooperatives since they will be collectively owned in perpetuity; and will enhance community development via asset lock and the community development fund.

The above good practice cooperative law standards can be modified to suit national circumstances. They can also be enhanced further. For instance, a percentage of profits could be placed in an international cooperative development fund to promote cooperatives in developing countries; to promote inter-cooperative trade; to promote strategic cooperatives in new innovative areas; or to invest 'patient capital' in cooperatives around the world.

6.9 Summary

- Cooperative principles have been modified to reflect the character of the cooperative movement. They have influenced cooperative law, and they have been recognised by the UN, the ILO, and national governments.
- Cooperative law has changed over time to reflect cooperative principles and the needs of cooperatives operating in changing political and economic contexts. Cooperative law is quite diverse across jurisdictions and has been flexible in accommodating the needs of cooperatives that operate in different economic sectors.
- Cooperative governance makes use of various governance models: a one-tier model, a dualistic model, a unitary board model, a tri-partite model. These models are suited to cooperatives of different dimensions and complexity. They distribute power between the GA, the Board of Directors, management, and supervisory bodies. The level of control that members hold depends on the distribution of powers between these bodies. Members will have less control when authority and decision-making powers are transferred to the Board of Directors and management.
- The development of social cooperatives serving the general interests demonstrates that the communitarian and social traditions of the cooperative movement are still appropriate to solve people's needs. The development of capital-centred cooperative enterprises and cooperative groups of companies demonstrates the extent to which the neo-liberal ideology and the capitalist-led market economy influence cooperative development.
- The cooperative laws and taxation laws generally do not pose a barrier to cooperative formation or cooperative economic development.
- Cooperative law in the majority of the jurisdictions reviewed in this book does not comply with most ICA principles. This has led to the development of two different broad

cooperative enterprise models. One broad cooperative enterprise model promotes cooperatives as a business. The other cooperative enterprise model sees cooperatives as part of a cooperative movement supporting their members and their local community.

- The diversity in cooperative law has also led to the emergence of at least five types of cooperative enterprises. These cooperatives are managed democratically, with members ultimately exercising their powers over the decision-making process and control via controlling the general council and cooperative by-laws. They are different, however, in the way they align with cooperative principles, distribute profits, manage and dispose of assets, relate to the cooperative movement, and relate to their communities.
- The 'Member-Owned Centred Cooperatives' and the 'Cooperative-owned group of enterprises' display some of the characteristics of private enterprises. These include the possibility to operate as profit-maximising cooperatives, unlimited remuneration of capital accounts, and access to cooperative assets and reserves. The 'Cooperative-owned group of enterprises' manage subsidiaries as conventional firms.
- The traditional cooperative enterprise model, the cooperatives as active members of a cooperative movement model, and the cooperatives as active members of a community focussed cooperative movement, offer enterprise models that are an alternative to capitalist enterprises. The 'traditional cooperatives' uphold the principles of limited capital remuneration, the indivisibility of assets, and inter-generational wealth. The other two cooperative enterprise models have closer relations with their cooperative movement and their communities and offer a greater chance to positively influence the economy and society.
- The best cooperative law practices from around the globe offers the opportunity to develop a cooperative enterprise that balances the needs of members, the enterprise, the cooperative movement, and the community. Key features could include democratic practices with at least 50 per cent of members and with employees accessing membership after two years, member control via the general assembly, forms of active participation, and co-determination policies. Salary differentials to be limited to 5:1. Profit distribution to be apportioned to indivisible reserves, education; cooperative movement (federation, cooperative development fund), capital accounts remuneration; and cooperative patronage refunds based on work or transactions. Patronage refunds are available to all employees (members and non-members). Cooperative federations and cooperative economic integration are explicitly supported. Cooperative assets are inter-generational and cannot be distributed. Cooperative conversions are not allowed.

6.10 Key Questions

- How would you go about analysing whether a cooperative law is appropriate (fit-for-purpose for a cooperative enterprise) or effective (allows cooperatives to achieve their economic and social objectives)?
- Cooperative law has undergone many phases. Examine the various phases in the evolution of cooperative law and discuss which phase do you think is the most significant for the development of the cooperative sector? In what way has this phase of cooperative law development strengthened or weakened the cooperative movement?
- Cooperative practices towards non-members, the distribution of profits, the retention of net assets, and demutualisation define cooperative culture and cooperative identity. Explain the policies you would propose relating to membership, profit distribution, net assets, and demutualisation that would enable the cooperative to successfully

achieve its economic and social goals. In other words, what would your ideal cooperative law and cooperative practices look like?

- Cooperatives are present in all sectors of the economy and come in all shapes and sizes. It seems difficult to develop a law that suits all types of cooperatives. To this end, what is the best approach to developing cooperative law: (a) one size fits all? (b) A general law with specific sections addressing unique features of each type of cooperative, such as social cooperatives or cooperative groups? (c) A specific law for each cooperative sector?
- Cooperatives need to simultaneously achieve economic and social goals. Critically examine the profit distribution allocation below, and determine whether it facilitates cooperative development in compliance with the ICA principles. Suggested profit distribution: indivisible reserve fund (at least 50 per cent of total profit); patronage refund (up to 20 per cent of profits); remuneration of member accounts (up to 10 per cent of profits); cooperative development funds (up to 10 per cent of profits); educational fund (up to 10 per cent of profits).
- Cooperatives have formed groups of companies to grow nationally and to expand in foreign markets. What would cooperative groups need to demonstrate to convince you that they are bonafide cooperatives?
- Some jurisdictions tax cooperatives the same way as other businesses. Please examine the cooperative-specific tax policies of the United States, Spain, Uruguay, Finland, and India and discuss whether there are compelling reasons why States should develop cooperative-specific tax laws? Why should cooperatives be treated differently from private enterprises?
- The author has identified five cooperative enterprises and has given each one a unique cooperative definition. Do you agree with this classification? Consider various cooperatives in your location and analyse their enterprise model? Are these cooperative enterprises similar, or do they differ from the ones identified in this chapter?

Notes

1 A cooperative enterprise model refers to the way a cooperative is organised to produce and sell goods and services in the market in order to meet the needs of its members. Cooperatives meet the economic, social, cultural and aspirational needs of their members by competing in the market on their own, or as a member of a second-tier cooperative. Whilst the term enterprise model is synonymous with the term business model, this book will opt to use the term cooperative model interchangeably with the term cooperative enterprise model.

2 I will refer to the Republic of Korea as Korea hereafter.

3 By 'profit' is meant revenue minus costs. At times cooperatives also use the term surplus, which refers to revenue minus costs, taking into account only those transactions with members. Throughout the book, I will use the term profit because it will be easier for the general public to understand and easier to compare with private enterprises.

4 Investor-owned companies are also known as joint-stock companies.

5 Members' capital accounts include members' initial investment to join a cooperative as a member, further investments by members, bonus payments as practised in worker cooperatives, and dividend payments as per legal requirements or as per by-laws.

6 Cooperative autonomy was also limited in Western-controlled colonies where the laws provided registrars with wide powers to intervene. Key countries here would include Sri Lanka, Tanzania and Zimbabwe (Birchall and Simmons 2010). It was also limited in other European countries which either came under the control of Germany during the inter-war years, such as Austria and Czechoslovakia or countries which were governed by authoritarian regimes such as Latvia, Estonia or Spain (Patmore and Belnave 2018).

7 Henrÿ uses the word 'companisation' and not 'corporation' to describe these changes. Companisation is described as the splitting of a functional unit from a company and incorporating it as a separate company. I use the term 'corporatisation' implying that cooperatives adopt the legal, organisational, governance structures, the language, and reporting formats that is similar to those of corporations.

8 For further information, in addition to the information available later in this chapter, please refer to Parts 4.2, 5.2, and 8.2.

9 Please refer to the Italian Law of 8 November 1991/381, Article 1. The full definition is as follows:

> the purpose of pursuing the general interests of the community, promoting human development and the social integration of citizens through: a) the management of social, health and educational services (via Type A cooperatives); b) the carrying out of different activities including agricultural, industrial, commercial or services with the aim of integrating disadvantaged persons into the labour market (via Type B cooperatives).

10 Social cooperatives is used in Italy, Collective Interest Cooperative Societies in France; Community Interest Companies in the United Kingdom; Social Solidarity Cooperatives in Portugal; and Social Initiative Cooperatives in Spain; Solidarity Cooperatives in Quebec; Community Investment Cooperatives in Ontario (Guy, Fici and Roelants 2009, European Commission 2013, Petrou 2013).

11 The data on cooperative law, unless otherwise stated, is derived from the country case studies contained in the International Handbook on Cooperative Law (Cracogna, Fici and Henrÿ 2013), and from the more recent country case studies contained in the International Cooperative Alliance website titled Coops4Development (International Cooperative Alliance 2023).

12 This research has reviewed the cooperative law practised in 26 jurisdictions, including 24 countries plus the Province of Quebec and the Organisation for the Harmonization of Business Law in Africa, which covers 17 States in Western and Central Africa. The 24 countries are Argentina, Australia, Belgium, Canada, China, Denmark, Finland, France, Germany, India, Italy, Japan, Korea, New Zealand, Norway, Portugal, Russia, Spain, Sweden, South Africa; Tanzania, the United Kingdom, the United States, and Uruguay. In the text, I will use the term jurisdictions to cover all 26 cooperative laws.

13 Please note that this section compares the relationship between a jurisdiction's cooperative law and the ICA cooperative principles. There may be times when the jurisdiction may not reflect the cooperative's practical experiences. For instances, if a country does not have a specific cooperative law on social cooperatives, it does not mean that social cooperatives are not promoted in that country.

14 The 15 jurisdictions which limited the amount of member trading usually below 50 per cent include Argentina, Australia, China, France, Italy, Japan, Korea, New Zealand, Portugal, Quebec, Russia, South Africa, Spain, Uruguay, and the United States. Japan allows only health and welfare cooperatives unlimited trade with non-members (Kurimoto 2020).

15 The jurisdictions whose cooperative law is either silent or poses no limits to non-member trading include Belgium, Canada, Denmark, Finland, Germany, India, Norway, Sweden, Tanzania, the United Kingdom, and OHADA.

16 Jurisdictions not allowing external investors include Argentina, Canada, Denmark, India, Japan, Korea, Norway, South Africa, and OHADA members.

17 Members can choose to hold a number of general assemblies during the year.

18 The jurisdictions that allow multiple voting are Belgium, Canada, China, Denmark, Finland, France, Germany, India, Italy, Korea, New Zealand, Norway, Portugal, Spain, Sweden, and the United States.

19 Tanzania, the United Kingdom, and the United States defer this decision to cooperative by-laws.

20 Jurisdictions adopt different voting arrangements for investors. In addition to China and New Zealand's approach, Russia allows a maximum of 25 per cent of total votes; Spain 30 per cent; Italy and France one third of all votes. The Belgium Cooperative law leaves it to cooperative by-laws to decide the maximum votes allocated to investors (Tilquin and Bernaertz 2020).

21 For instance, France and Italy allow up to one third of investor-members to sit on boards; Germany and Russia and Portugal allocate 25 per cent of board places.

22 The German Cooperative Law actually refers to the management board as the Board of Directors but it really performs the function of management. The Supervisory Board is also called Supervisory Council (Münkner 2013, 2013a). I have used the terms used in the German Corporate Governance Code because the functions are the same and it helps to distinguish this governance model with the other cooperative governance models (Regierungskommission 2022).
23 In a number of European countries, namely: Germany, Austria, Slovenia, Denmark, Sweden, and Norway, workers can elect their representatives to company Boards (Pendleton and Gospel 2013, Thomsen, Rese and Kronborg 2016). This form of industrial democracy is referred to as 'co-determination' and it also applies to cooperatives Münkner 2020.
24 These Jurisdictions include Australia, Belgium, China, Denmark, Finland, India, Italy, Japan, Korea, New Zealand, Norway, OHADA, Russia, South Africa, Sweden, and Tanzania.
25 These Jurisdictions are Australia, Belgium, Canada, Denmark, Finland, Germany, New Zealand, Norway, OHADA, Quebec, Russia, South Africa, Sweden, Tanzania, and the United Kingdom.
26 The 16 jurisdictions include Argentina, Finland, France, India, Italy, Japan, Korea, OHADA, Portugal, Quebec, South Africa, Spain, Sweden, Tanzania, the United Kingdom, and Uruguay.
27 The eight jurisdictions are Argentina, France, Italy, OHADA, Portugal, Quebec, Spain, and Uruguay.
28 The 14 jurisdictions are Australia, Canada, Denmark, Finland, Germany, India, New Zealand, OHADA, Quebec, Russia, South Africa, Sweden, Tanzania, and the United Kingdom.
29 The 17 jurisdictions that accept external investors are: Australia, Belgium, China, Finland, France, Germany, Italy, New Zealand, Portugal, Quebec, Russia, Spain, Sweden, Tanzania, the United Kingdom, the United States, and Uruguay.
30 The 12 Jurisdictions are Australia, Belgium, Finland, Germany, New Zealand, Portugal, Russia, Sweden, Tanzania, the United Kingdom, the United States, and Uruguay.
31 The nine Jurisdictions are Argentina, India, Italy, Japan, OHADA, Portugal, Spain, Tanzania, and Uruguay.
32 The Brundtland Report of 1987, *Our Common Future*, defines sustainability as: "development that meets the needs of the present without compromising the ability of future generations to meet their own needs" (United Nations 2023).
33 The eight jurisdictions are Argentina, France, Italy, OHADA, Portugal, Quebec, Spain, and Uruguay.
34 The 16 Jurisdictions are Australia, Belgium, Canada, China, Denmark, Finland, Germany, Korea, New Zealand, Norway, Russia, South Africa, Sweden, Tanzania, the United Kingdom, and the United States. Note that, whilst included in these 16 jurisdictions, Russia prohibits consumer cooperatives to demutualise (Kutko 2021).
35 It is important to note that the Italian law and the Belgian law allow a type of cooperative to also operate without having to comply with those aspects of the cooperative law that adhere to the ICA principles. In Italy, these cooperatives do not receive tax concessions as a result (Coates 2013, Fici 2013b).
36 This definition differs slightly from the one given by Johnstone Birchall in that I emphasise profit maximisation and the distribution of profits rather than benefits. I also regard this definition to represent one type of cooperative not the whole cooperative movement. Birchall's definition is as follows: "business organization that is owned and controlled by members who are drawn from one (or more) of three types of stakeholder—consumers, producers and employees—and whose benefits go mainly to these members" (Birchall 2012).
37 This is a requirement of the ILO Recommendation 193, Paragraph 8.

References

ALC India. 2019. *Autonomy and Independence of Cooperatives in India.* New Delhi: International Cooperative Alliance.

Ammirato, Piero. 2018. *The Growth of Italian Cooperatives: Innovation, Resilience and Social Responsibility.* New York: Routledge.

Apps, Ann. 2020. *National Report of New Zealand.* Legal Framework Analysis, Brussels: International Cooperative Alliance.

Beckett, Thomas. 2020. *National Report for the United States of America.* Legal Cooperative Framework Analysis, Brussels: International Cooperative Alliance.

Birchall, Johnston. 2012. "A 'Member-Owned Business' Approach to the Classification of Co-operatives and Mutuals." In *The Co-Operative Model in Practice: International Perspectives*, by McDonnell Diarmuid and MacKnight Elizabeth, 67–83. CETS Resource.

Birchall, Johnston, and Richard Simmons. 2010. "The Co-operative Reform Process in Tanzania and Sri Lanka." *Annals of Public and Cooperative Economics* 467–500.

Blisse, Holger, and Detlev Humme. 2017. "Raiffeisenbanks and Volksbanks for Europe: The Case for Co-operative Banking In Germany." In *The Oxford Handbook of Mutual, Cooperative and Co-Owned Business*, by Jonathon Michie, Joseph Blasi and Carlo Borzaga, 398–411. Oxford: Oxford University Press.

Bonfante, Guido. 2011. *Manuale di Diritto Cooperativo.* Bologna: Zanichelli.

Cecop. 2009. *Cooperatives and Social Enterprises.* Brussels: Cecop Publications.

Coates, Astrid. 2013. "Belgium." In *International Handbook of Cooperative Law*, by Dante Cracogna, Antonio Fici and Hagen Henrÿ, 251–270. Heidelberg: Springer.

Cracogna, Dante. 2013a. "Argentina." In *International Handbook of Cooperative Law*, by Dante Cracogna, Antonio Fici and Hagen Henrÿ, 189–206. Heidelberg: Springer.

Cracogna, Dante. 2013c. "The Framework Law for the Cooperatives in Latin America." In *International Handbook of Cooperative Law*, by David Cracogna, Antonio Fici and Hagen Henrÿ, 165–188. Heidelberg: Spring.

Cracogna, Dante, Antonio Fici, and Hagen Henrÿ. 2013. *International Handbook of Cooperative Law.* Heidelberg: Springer.

Czachorska-Jones, Barbara, Jay Gary Finkelstein, and Bahareh Sansami. 2013. "United States." In *International Handbook of Cooperative Law*, by Dante Cracogna, Antonio Fici and Hagen Henrÿ, 760–778. Heidelberg: Springer.

De Luca, Nicola. 2013. "Russia." In *International Handbook of Cooperative Law*, by Dante Cracogna, Antonio Fici and Hagen Henrÿ, 667–686. Heidelberg: Springer.

Diez, David, and Willy Tadjudje. 2013. "The OHADA Cooperative Regulation." In *The International Handbook of Cooperative Law*, by David Cracogna, Antonio Fici and Hagen Henrÿ, 89–114. Heidelberg: Springer.

Douvitsa, Ifigeneia. 2021. *National Report: France.* Legal Framework Analysis, Brussels: International Cooperative Alliance.

European Commission. 2013. *Social Economy and Social Entrepreneurship.* Social Europe Guide, Volume 4, Brussels: European Commission.

Fayardo Garcia, Isabel-Gemma. 2013. "Spain." In *International Handbook of Cooperative Law*, by Dante Cracogna, Antonio Fici and Hagen Henrÿ, 701–718. Heidelberg: Springer.

Fici, Antonio. 2013a. "Introduction to Cooperative Law." In *International Handbook of Cooperative Law*, by Dante Cracogna, Antonio Fici and Hagen Henrÿ, 3–62. Heidelberg: Springer.

———. 2013b. "Italy." In *International Handbook of Cooperative Law*, by David Cracogna, Antonio Fici and Hagen Henrÿ, 479–502. Heidelber: Springer.

———. 2013c. "The European Cooperative Society Regulation." In *International Handbook of Cooperative Law*, by David Cracogna, Antonio Fici and Hagen Henrÿ, 115–152. Heidelberg: Springer.

Fjortoft, Tore, and Ole Gjems-Onstad. 2013. "Norway and Scandinavian Countries." In *International Handbook of Cooperative law*, by Dante Cracogna, Antonio Fici and Hagen Henrÿ, 563–584. Heidelberg: Springer.

Galasso, Giuseppe. 1986. "Gli Anni della Grande Espansione e la Crisi del Sistema." In *Storia del Movimento Cooperativo in Italia*, by Renato Zangheri, Giuseppe Galasso and Valerio Castronovo, 219–496. Torino: Giulio Einaudi Editore.

Gonzales, Carlos. 2020. *Uruguay.* National Report: Uruguay, Brussels: International Cooperative Alliance.

Guy, Boucquiaux, Antonio Fici, and Bruno Roelants. 2009. "Annex: Comparative Table of Existing Legislation in Europe." In *Cooperatives and Social Enterprises*, by Bruno Roelants, 10. Brussels: Cecop.

Henrÿ, Hagen. 2012. *Guidelines for Cooperative Legislation.* ILO Guidelines, Geneva: International Labour Organization.

———. 2013. "Finland." In *International Handbook of Cooperative Law*, by Dante Cracogna, Antonio Fici and Hagen Henrÿ, 373–392. Heidelberg: Springer.

———. 2017. "Co-operative Principles and Co-operative Law Across the Globe." In *The Oxford Handbook of Mutual, Co-Operative, and Co-Owned Business*, by Jonathan Michie, Joseph Blasi and Carlo Borzaga, 39–54. Oxford: Oxford University Press.

Hiez, David. 2013. "France." In *International Handbook of Cooperative Law*, by Dante Cracogna, Antonio Fici and Hagen Henrÿ, 393–412. Heidelberg: Springer.

Ianes, Alberto. 2013. *Introduzione alla Storia della Cooperazione in Italia (1854-2011).* Soveria Monnelli: Rubbettino.

ILO. 2002. *Recommendation 193 - Promotion of Cooperatives.* Recommendation on Cooperatives, Geneva: International Labour Organization.

Inacoop. 2015. *Development Fund.* August. Accessed August 15, 2023. https://www.inacoop.org.uy/fondes-inacoop.

International Cooperative Alliance. 2017. *Guidance Notes to the Co-operative Principles.* Guidelines, Brussels: International Cooperative Alliance.

———. 2023. *Coops4Dev: Legal Framework.* Accessed 2022-2023. https://coops4dev.coop/en/world.

Jang, Jongick. 2013. "Republic of Korea." In *International Handbook of International Law*, by Dante Cracogna, Antonio Fici and Hagen Henrÿ, 653–666. Heidelberg: Springer.

Jung, Hongjoo, and Hans Jürgen Rosner. 2012. "Cooperative Movements in the Republic of Korea." In *The Cooperative Business Movement, 1950 to the Present*, by Patrizia Battilani and Hans Schroter, 83–106. Cambridge: Cambridge University Press (Kindle Edition).

Kurimoto, Akira. 2013. "Japan." In *International Handbook of Cooperative Law*, by Dante Cracogna, Antonio Fici and Hagen Henry, 503–524. Heidelberg: Springer.

———. 2020. "Legal Framework Analysis - National Report of Japan." *Coops4Dev.* April. Accessed August 10, 2021. https://coops4dev.coop/sites/default/files/2021-06/Japan%20Legal%20Framework%20Analysis%20National%20Report.pdf.

Kutko, Victoria. 2021. *National Report: Russia.* Legal Framework Analysis, Brussels: International Cooperative Alliance.

Lavega, Sergio Reyes. 2020. *National Report of Uruguay.* Legal Cooperative Framework Analysis, Brussels: International Cooperative Alliance.

Menzani, Tito. 2009. *Il Movimento Cooperativo fra le due Guerre.* Rome: Carocci.

Münkner, Hans. 2020. *National Report Germany.* Legal Framework Analysis, Brussels: International Cooperative Alliance.

Münkner, Hans-Hermann. 2013a. "Germany." In *International Handbook of Cooperative Law*, by Dante Cracogna, Antonio Fici and Hagen Henrÿ, 413–429. Heidelberg: Springer.

———. 2013b. "Worldwide Regulation of Co-operative Societies - an Overview." *Euricse Working Paper Series* 1–30.

Namorado, Rui. 2013. "Portugal." In *International Handbook of Cooperative Law*, by Dante Cracogna, Antonio Fici and Hagen Henrÿ, 635–652. Heidelberg: Springer.

New South Wales Government. 2012. "Co-operatives (Adoption of National Law) Act 2012 No 29." New South Wales Government.

Patmore, Greg, and Nikola Belnave. 2018. *A Global History of Co-Operative Business.* London: Routledge.

Pendleton, Andrew, and Howard Gospel. 2013. "Corporate Governance and Labor." In *The Oxford Handbook of Corporate Governance*, by Mike Wright, Donald S Siegel, Kevin Keasey and Igor Filatochev, 634–657. Oxford: Oxford University Press.

Petrou, Timothy. 2013. "Canada." In *International Handbook of Cooperative Law*, by Dante Cracogna, Antonio Fici and Hagen Henrÿ, 289–316. Heidelberg: Springer.

Regierungskommission. 2022. *German Corporate Governance Code.* Corporate Governance Code, Berlin: Regierungskommission.

Ren, Dapeng, and Peng Yuan. 2013. "China." In *International Handbook of Cooperative Law*, by Dante Cracogna, Antonio Fici and Hagen Henrÿ, 339–354. Heidelberg: Springer.

Roelants, Bruno. 2009. "Conclusion." In *Cooperatives and Social Enterprises*, by Bruno Roelants, 109–130. Brussels: Cecop Publications.

Rutabanzibwa, Audax Peter. 2020. *Tanzania - National Report*. Legal Framework Analysis, Brussels: International Cooperative Alliance.

Thomsen, Steen, Caspar Rese, and Dorte Kronborg. 2016. "Employee Representation and Board Size in the Nordic Countries." *Eur J Law Econ* 471–490.

Tilquin, Thierry, and Maika Bernaertz. 2020. *National Report: Belgium*. Legal Framework Analysis, Brussels: International Cooperative Alliance.

United Nations. 2001. "Guidelines Aimed at Creating a Supportive Environment for the Development of Cooperatives." New York: United Nations.

———. 2023. "Report of the World Commission on Environment and Development: Our Common Future." *United Nations Digital Library*. Accessed May 4, 2023. file:///C:/Users/ammir/Documents/Downloads/A_42_427-EN.pdf.

Veerakumuran, Govindaraj. 2013. "India." In *International Handbook of Cooperative Law*, by Dante Cracogna, Antonio Fici and Hagen Henrÿ, 449–466. Heidelberg: Springer.

Zeuli, Kimberley A, and Robert Cropp. 2004. *Cooperatives: Principles and Practices in the 21st Century*. Wisconsin: University of Wisconsin Centre for Cooperatives.

7 Cooperatives and the Market

This chapter examines the relationship between cooperatives and the market. Part 7.1 summarises how the cooperative sector has engaged with the market, ranging from having an anti-market sentiment to eventually embracing the market economy. Part 7.2 discusses the question: 'Why are there fewer cooperatives compared to capitalist and investor-owned enterprises?'. In this section, we consider the views of classical economists, the arguments that identify limits to the cooperative enterprise model,[1] and the roles performed by corporations, the State, and the cooperative movement. Part 7.3 will analyse the debate surrounding the place of the cooperative sector within a pluralist market economy. Part 7.4 provides a summary of the chapter's key findings, and Part 7.5 provides key questions for readers to consider.

Key learnings for this section include the following:

- Greater awareness of the changing relationship between cooperatives and the market.
- Greater appreciation of how cooperatives have improved the working of the market through the following practices: market inclusion, ethical conduct, anti-monopoly practices, anti-crisis behaviour, and cooperative responses to market failure, state failures, and business failures.
- Appreciate the value and limits of classical economists' theories about the cooperative firm.
- Consideration of a broad range of internal and external factors that explain why there are fewer cooperatives than private firms.
- An understanding of the cooperative sector's position and its unique role in a pluralist market economy that comprises the State, the private sector, the cooperative sector, and the not-for-profit (NFP) sector.
- Ability to differentiate the location of cooperatives in a continuum of organisational forms that display commercial objectives and social objectives.

7.1 Cooperatives and the Market

The role of cooperatives in the market, as has been explored in Chapters 2–5, spans from being in opposition to the market to embracing the market economy. Key cooperative behaviours since the industrial revolution can be summarised as being against the market; wanting to dominate the market; encouraging market inclusion; correcting the market; actively dealing with market, State, and business failures; embracing the market; and, in promoting the general interests within a market economy.

DOI: 10.4324/9781003269533-7

7.1.1 *Against the Market*

The communitarian Socialists like Owen, Fourier, and Cabet saw private property, competition, and the excessive power of capitalists and landlords, as the main reason why people were living under extremely poor conditions. They proposed self-sufficient communities that would provide everyone with a job, housing, and all their needs without having to engage with the market. They hoped that this approach would spread to other communities to the point that this form of Socialism would overthrow the capitalist system. Through this approach, they also hoped that people would become more civil and more educated and would also find happiness. These early Socialists did not succeed, but they were the first to develop a critique of Capitalism. To them, the key to a better society was to replace market competition with a harmonious society based on cooperative communities that would benefit everyone (Crick 1987, Honneth 2017, Zanotti 2017).

7.1.2 *Dominating the Market*

The consumer movement across Europe, but predominantly via leaders such as the British Co-operative Wholesale Society (CWS) and Charles Gide, developed a fairly strong argument in favour of creating a consumer-led cooperative commonwealth. They argued that consumer cooperatives would benefit everyone and would offer working people a way to win the struggle against Capitalism (Vergnanini 1907, Webb and Webb 1914). Charles Gide developed a three-stage strategy to achieve the Cooperative Commonwealth:

> In a first triumphant stage we shall conquer the distribution and sales sector; in the second, the manufacturing sector; and in the third and last, the agricultural sector. This should be the program of the cooperative movement in every country.
> (Hirschfield 1976)

The most advanced consumer movement in the nineteenth century was established in Britain, where the CWS managed 40 manufacturing and agricultural facilities; a national distribution service; various international agricultural facilities and trade operations; and banking and insurance services (Webster 2012, Wilson, Webster and Vorberg-Rugh 2013, Patmore and Belnave 2018).

This idea of the consumer commonwealth went on to influence consumer movements worldwide. These consumer movements still provide a wide variety of goods and services ranging from food, insurance, telecommunication, tourism, legal, health and wellbeing, and cultural activities, but they no longer aim to replace capitalist-led market economies (CMEs) (Hilson, Neunsinger and Patmore 2017).

7.1.3 *Market Inclusion and Coordination*

Cooperatives have always been a vehicle that consumers, workers, artisans, farmers, and retailers have used to join the market in a more competitive position. Cooperatives allow consumers to access goods at lower prices; workers to democratically manage their own enterprise and improve their working conditions; farmers to access credit via rural banks and by-pass usurers; farmers to reduce input costs and sell all their produce; artisans to obtain loans from urban banks at lower interest rates; retailers to achieve economies of scale via establishing their own wholesalers.

In these instances, cooperatives act as a voluntary coordination mechanism for market activity on behalf of their members that improves their market position, reduces their costs, increases their benefits, and provides them with a more stable existence. Cooperatives allow members to reduce the risks of having to engage directly with the market or having to engage in subordinate hierarchical relations with large companies. As a result, cooperatives improve the competitiveness and the living conditions of their members beyond what independent action could have delivered (Borzaga and Tortia 2017).

7.1.4 *Correcting the Market*

Cooperatives have demonstrated to correct or mediate market excesses for the benefit of their members, their communities, and the market itself. Cooperatives can correct the operations of the market by adopting anti-monopoly strategies and promoting anti-crisis behaviour at the enterprise and cooperative network levels.

One way that cooperatives corrected the market is via anti-monopoly behaviour. The Swedish consumer movement demonstrated this during the inter-war years intervening in areas where monopolies and trusts were making excessive profits. The Swedish consumer movement intervened in selected areas such as margarine, rubber shoes, tires, fertilisers, and building materials and in disrupting the international light bulb cartel. In these cases, the cooperative would intervene to the point of controlling at least 15 per cent of the market so that it could influence prices. It was very successful as light bulbs prices fell by 37 per cent; rubber shoe prices by more than 50 per cent; and margarine prices by close to 60 per cent (Bonow 1938, Gillespie 1950, Hilson 2018).

The second way that cooperatives correct the market is via anti-crisis behaviour. The Global Financial Crisis (GFC) in the twenty-first century provided a good example of how cooperatives mitigated the negative impact that such a crisis could have had on workers, consumers, and communities. It has been well documented that during the GFC, whilst banks were reducing their lending and companies were laying off staff, cooperative banks and worker cooperatives were doing the opposite. Cooperative banks continued to lend money to their members because their purpose is to serve their members and not to maximise profits for their shareholders. The Mondragon cooperative network dealt with the crisis by reducing working hours or transferring workers between cooperatives as much as possible. Research conducted on the Italian cooperative movement indicates that during the crisis, cooperatives increased investment and increased employment. Research also showed that where cooperatives had to reduce working hours, it was implemented fairly between members and non-members whilst avoiding job losses. The Mondragon Corporation, and the Legacoop Cooperative Development Fund (Coopfond), also supported cooperative members in restructuring their operations in order to survive the crisis. Whilst there are limits to what cooperatives can do, there have demonstrated an inclination to save employment and to support other cooperative members in times of crisis (Birchall and Ketislon 2009, Bajo and Roelants 2011, Zevi et al. 2011, Roelants et al. 2012, Birchall 2013, Ammirato 2018).

7.1.5 *Market, State, and Business Failures*

Market and State failures occur when they cannot provide goods or services in a fair and transparent manner that meets the needs and expectations of people, business, and the community. Six areas of market failure include imperfect competition, public goods, externalities, incomplete markets, imperfect information, high unemployment, and other macroeconomic disturbances. State failure occurs when there is limited information, limited control over private markets, limited control over the bureaucracy, and limitations imposed by the political process (Stiglitz 2000). Business failure refers to businesses that close their operations, leading to their employees losing their jobs.

Cooperatives have been formed to deal with all three types of failures. The electricity cooperatives formed during the New Deal period are key examples of cooperatives overcoming a case of market failure.[2] In this situation, the US Government failed to convince the private sector to provide electricity to rural areas where electricity coverage ranged from 2 to 27.5 per cent of the total households. The private sector provided this service in urban areas but deemed it unprofitable to invest in rural areas. Farmer-organised co-operatives, with the State's support, managed to provide electricity to rural areas at a lower cost than that offered by the private sector. By 1941, 800 electric cooperatives were formed, and they helped achieve 100 per cent electrification in the United States by the late 1940s (Schneiberg 2011, Taylor 2021).

The classic case of State failure that we discussed in Chapter 5 is the inability or unwillingness to provide adequate social services to the elderly or people with disabilities. This may be due to a high level of public debt, political ideologies, or limitations imposed by the political process. Cooperatives throughout the world have demonstrated a willingness and a capacity to provide these services through worker cooperatives, social cooperatives, and consumer-owned or rural cooperatives-owned welfare service providers, as is the case in Japan.

Cooperatives are also providing an alternative to overcome business failure via the promotion of worker-buyouts of privately owned companies. In Chapter 5, we examined the experiences of France, Italy and Argentina, where hundreds of private enterprises were converted into cooperatives. This includes cooperatives formed by ailing businesses, as well as the French experience where business owners transferred their business to existing employees.

It could be argued that the Wonju cooperative model in Korea, especially the Hansalim consumer cooperative model, which has been discussed in Chapter 5, is a response to simultaneous market failure and State failure. The State's industrialisation policies led to the formation of large corporations, large cities attracting people from rural areas, and food supplies being controlled by large corporations. This type of development did not suit the urban consumers who were not being able to buy organic and safe produce, nor the rural areas who were losing residents. The strategy of creating an alliance between urban and rural people via the Hansalim consumer cooperative ensured that people remained in the countryside, farmers received a good price for their produce, and urban people could buy organic, local produce at fair prices from their own consumer cooperative. Co-op Sanchoku, from Japan, has developed a similar approach since the 1970s. Sanchoku links consumer cooperatives with local producers and local food businesses. Their approach promotes local communities, eco-friendly agriculture, and sustainable development. Sanchoku buys rice, husbandry, fish, and forestry products. It also actively promotes better agricultural practices in cooperation with local farmers (Asiedu and Hayashi 2012).

7.1.6 Embracing the Market

Cooperatives today have embraced the market to sell their goods and services, access capital, and engage in trade relations with corporations or other private companies. Banks like Credit Agricole and Rabobank access capital from financial markets and have subsidiaries overseas offering services to clients just like a private bank would. Consumer cooperatives in Europe have grown their market share, made acquisitions, and owned listed real estate and insurance companies. Large agricultural cooperatives, like Fonterra and others, access capital from financial markets, own subsidiaries, and focus on profit-making operations. Worker cooperatives in Italy since the 1970s have formed joint ventures with private sector firms in order to win public works contracts. Mondragon subsidiaries have located overseas to be closer to supply chains and their customers. Manufacturing cooperatives in Italy subcontract work to private enterprises from the local economy.[3]

7.1.7 *Promoting the General Interests*

Since the 1990s, cooperatives have been formed throughout the world to provide services that benefit the general interests or community interests. These types of cooperatives are known as social cooperatives or collective interest cooperative societies or community interest companies, or solidarity cooperatives. The key point is that a variety of stakeholders have voluntarily formed a cooperative to meet a need of society or their community and not only the need of their members. There are three types of social cooperatives. The first type provides welfare services for the aged, disabled, and disadvantaged, childcare services, education, and healthcare services. The second type provides work integration services for the long-term unemployed and people with disabilities. The third type provides community or proximity services to local rural or isolated communities that have suffered from de-population. Key services may include the provision of electricity, a supermarket, a service station, the postal service, a local pub, a sporting facility, tourism activity, hospitality services, and so on.[4]

7.1.8 *Summary*

The evolution of how cooperatives have engaged with the market reflects how cooperatives have responded to different market situations in support of their members. The flexibility of cooperative law in applying cooperative principles allows for the formation of different types of cooperatives that meet their members' needs whilst reflecting their country's political, economic and cultural traditions. As noted in Chapter 6, this has led to the development of a plurality of cooperative enterprises that engage with the market to meet the needs of their members and, in some cases, the needs of the cooperative movement and of the community in which they operate.

7.2 Why Are There Fewer Cooperatives Than Private Enterprises?

In 1989, Jon Elster asked the question: "if cooperatives are so desirable why don't workers desire them?". His research was inconclusive, but he supported worker cooperatives because they promoted economic justice (Elster 1989). The reality is that there are fewer cooperatives than conventional enterprises, and cooperatives employ fewer people than the State and the private sector. Cicopa reported in 2017 that there were 2.9 million cooperatives employing 27 million employees and 252 million primary producers. This means that cooperatives employ 9.46 per cent of total world employment (CICOPA 2017). Considering that cooperatives have been formed for over 200 years, it seems fair to ask the question: why are there fewer cooperatives?

Part 7.2 is divided into eight parts. Part 7.2.1 discusses the views of neo-classical economists, which were very influential until the early 1990s. Part 7.2.2 discusses the views of neo-institutionalists, which focus on transaction costs. Part 7.2.3 will discuss the view that various barriers prevent the cooperative sector from growing. Part 7.2.4 will examine the cooperative formation rate. Part 7.2.5 will focus on the cooperative's capacity to grow. Part 7.2.6 explores the role of corporations and the private sector. Part 7.2.7 explores the role of the State. Part 7.2.8 explores the limits of the cooperative movement in promoting cooperative development: Part 7.2.9 provides a summary.

7.2.1 Classical Economists

Classical economists such as Ward and Vanek attempted to develop a theory of the labour-managed firm (LMF) after conducting research on the Yugoslavian model.[5] They concluded that the LMF would maximise income per worker and, as a result, would have a tendency to under-employ. These authors based their findings on theoretical assumptions that viewed individuals as selfish, who focussed on maximising their income; that cooperatives were financed only from retained earnings; that workers receive wages plus a limited return on capital; that all profits would be reinvested and would be collectively owned; and in the short-term, they displayed a static decision-making process. The argument concluded that whilst private enterprises maximised profits to be distributed to shareholders, in an LMF, the interests of workers would be to maximise income per worker. This would lead to under-employment because, in times of high demand, they would increase prices instead of increasing production and employment. Increasing prices without employment would maximise income per worker by allowing the existing workforce to share higher profits (Ward 1958, Vanek 1971).

Furubotn and Pejovich, also using Yugoslavia as a model, enhanced the Ward-Vanek model by suggesting that the LMF model also leads to under-investment and under-capitalisation. They argued that members could deposit profits either in the LMF's Investment Fund, which is not owned by workers, or the workers' own Wages Fund. They concluded that this LMF model would lead workers to prefer depositing more money into the Wages Fund because it belongs to them, leading to under-capitalisation. These authors also noted that older workers would rather not place profits into the LMF Investment Fund because they would retire soon and would not benefit from any long-term investment. As a result, LMFs would also under-invest because of their short-term investment horizon (Furubotn and Pejovich 1970).

Alchian and Demsetz claimed that shirking was an issue with LMFs. They claimed that teamwork made it difficult to observe the productivity of individual workers and that unless individuals are paid according to their productivity, it will lead to shirking. This can be avoided in a capitalist firm where the owner, or appointed manager, is able to monitor productivity and pay employees accordingly. The owner would make use of contractual arrangements to renegotiate pay and conditions. The owner has an interest in monitoring productivity because higher productivity will lead to lower monitoring costs and higher profits (Alchian and Demsetz 1972).

Classical economists wrote about LMFs from the 1950s to 1970s, a period when corporations and market economies were growing strongly. It was also a time when the successful models of Mondragon and Italy were not known to the outside world. The International Cooperative Alliance (ICA) was also not in a position to provide up-to-date statistics on the cooperative sector. These authors have the merit to attempt to develop a theory of the LMF, and to stimulate a debate among academics about cooperative economics and the cooperative firm. The weakness of the classical economist model is that their findings were not based on empirical evidence based on a cooperative enterprises that were operating in a non-socialist country. Empirical research on cooperative enterprises, as noted in Chapters 2–5, has demonstrated that cooperative enterprises do have a long-term horizon; the cooperative law and tax incentive promote internal investments; workers may favour long-term job security rather than short-term gains; cooperative enterprises have grown in order to achieve economies of scale and to diversify their products, markets, and services. Research on cooperatives has also not found evidence of shirking.

7.2.2 *Neo-Institutionalism*

Neo-Institutional economists have a view that investor-owned-firms (IOF) or cooperatives form in response to transaction costs incurred from market-based contracting or from ownership. Market-based costs are incurred when there are monopolies (power over prices) or a monopsony (power over suppliers), post-power lock-in, or there is asymmetric information. Costs of ownership include the costs of governance, monitoring, and decision-making. Patrons, investors, consumers, farmers, retailers, and so on decide to form a cooperative or an IOF, depending on which form can best reduce market or ownership costs (Hansmann 1999).

Hansmann applied the transaction costs approach to understanding when cooperatives are most likely to form and why there are so few cooperatives. He concluded that cooperatives are formed when there are market failures citing agricultural cooperatives or energy cooperatives forming against monopolies in the United States. Hansmann, however, regarded cooperative formation as transitional and that they would no longer be required once governments improved the market through regulations (anti-trust laws; pro-competitive laws; consumer protection laws, information laws, and so on) and/or when the market became more competitive. So as the market becomes more efficient, the costs of market contracting no longer warrant the formation of cooperatives because IOFs would have re-established their market dominance (Hansmann 2013).

Hansmann also concluded that another reason why there are few cooperatives is that their ownership costs are higher than those incurred by IOF. This is because cooperatives have a heterogeneous membership that has multiple goals, such as income, job security, working conditions, quality of services, and democratic management. Hansmann argues that having multiple goals leads to high governance costs when making decisions and when trying to discipline staff. This makes cooperatives uncompetitive compared to IOF because IOFs have a homogeneous membership formed by shareholders that want a return on their investment. This clear focus facilitates the decision-making process and the disciplining of staff (Hansmann 1999, 2013, Dow 2018a).

Hansmann's sound theoretical discussion, as was the case with classical economists, has made a contribution to the cooperative debate by encouraging academics to reconsider the economics of the cooperative firm. The evidence provided in Chapters 2–5, however, clearly demonstrates that cooperatives are continuing to operate in very competitive markets. Cooperatives from all economic sectors are formed for a variety of economic and non-economic reasons. Whilst democratic governance in a cooperative may be more costly than governance in a hierarchical IOF, there are also advantages with democratic governance that lead to productivity improvements and workplace flexibility, both of which benefit cooperative economic performance and cooperative resilience (Spear 2000, Zamagni and Zamagni 2010, McDonnel and Macknight 2012). The reasons why there are fewer cooperatives are more complex than those outlined by classical and institutional economists.

7.2.3 Cooperative Barriers

Promoters, activists, and authors have identified a number of factors that prevent cooperative formation, consolidation, and growth. The early Socialists realised that access to finance was an issue, so they sought the help of philanthropists or the State to finance cooperatives.[6] Sydney and Beatrice Webb thought that worker cooperatives would eventually degenerate because some workers would exploit others and retain more profits for the few (Webb and Webb 1914). Vanek argued that cooperatives could not get finance because they had no collateral, because workers had no assets, and because banks would not be inclined to fund cooperatives (Vanek 2000, Jossa 2015). The Open University Cooperative Group studied British cooperatives in the 1980s and identified a number of cooperative barriers that limited the development of British worker cooperatives, namely entrepreneurship, lack of finance, attracting and retaining management skills, internal limits to growth (democratic management and limited return on capital), weak place of cooperative in the economy, constraints on takeovers of private enterprises, and forms of discrimination from the State and the private sectors (Cornforth, Thomas and Lewis et al. 1988, Cornforth and Thomas 1990).

These findings were nation-specific and time-specific. They were mostly related to small worker cooperatives operating in the United Kingdom and the United States. These worker cooperatives were also competing on their own against large corporations that were operating in deregulated liberal market economies. These studies are important to understand nation-specific cooperative development. They also formed a good tool of analysis for comparing cooperative development in different countries.

Chapters 4 and 5 have noted that cooperative development has been very dynamic and very diverse. The research thus far has demonstrated that from the 1970s, cooperatives began to overcome many of the previously highlighted cooperative barriers. They have achieved this via promoting legislative changes that provided better access to credit and facilitated the formation of larger enterprises; via forming second-tier cooperatives that allowed small- and medium-sized cooperatives to achieve economies of scale, reduce costs, and access knowledge; via introducing legal structures that allowed cooperatives to grow into large enterprises that own overseas subsidiaries, and to form joint ventures with other firms; via promoting competitive strategies within cooperative networks that provide finance and management support; and via establishing support mechanisms that have helped cooperatives buy out private enterprises.[7]

In addition, research on LMFs confirmed that in industries where both cooperatives and capitalist firms exist, cooperative productivity appears to be at least as high as capitalist firm productivity and sometimes higher. And in industries where both cooperatives and capitalist firms exist, cooperatives' survival rates appear to be at least as high as capitalist firm survival rates and sometimes higher (Dow 2018b). Indeed, there are many studies that show that worker cooperatives' survival rate is higher than private enterprises (Government du Quebec 2003, Roelants et al. 2012, Caselli 2014, Smith and Rothbaum 2014, Vieta, Depetri and Carrano 2017).

In spite of the fact that cooperatives have demonstrated that they are well equipped to compete in markets, the question as to why there are fewer cooperatives still remains valid, considering that there are many more private enterprises than cooperatives. The challenges may be different than those confronted by small cooperatives up to the 1980s. Today cooperatives face a different set of challenges because they have grown in size and aspirations, people's needs and expectations have changed, and the global economy has increased competition and opportunities. Considering the knowledge we have today, cooperative challenges can be divided into two categories that had been previously identified by the Open University Cooperative Group: entrepreneurship or low rate of cooperative formation, and limits to cooperative growth potential (Cornforth, Thomas and Lewis et al. 1988).

7.2.4 Cooperative Formation

A key challenge for the cooperative sector is the low cooperative rate of formation. If more cooperatives could be established, considering they have a better longevity record and, at least, an equal productivity record than private enterprises, a larger cooperative sector could be established. The first reason for having a low rate of cooperative formation is the lack of cooperative awareness in society. Cooperative studies are not taught at many universities, and the popular media regularly extols the virtues of private enterprises. This makes it difficult for people to get to know the benefits of cooperatives and to consider starting a cooperative rather than a small business (Kalmi 2007). A second reason is that whilst one person can start a private enterprise, more are needed to start a cooperative (Jossa 2015). In many countries, however, three people can start a cooperative, yet the formation rate is still low compared to the private sector (Cracogna, Fici and Henrÿ 2013).[8] A third reason is that because of a lack of awareness, cooperatives can still suffer from being considered transient enterprises (Hansmann 2013).

There is no doubt that many more people prefer to become wage earners, public sector employees, embark on a professional career, become self-employed tradespersons, franchisors, or start a private enterprise instead of starting a cooperative. There may be country-specific reasons for this. In Scandinavia, Lindkvist and Westenholz noted that the reason for an absence of a collective entrepreneurial culture was that working people managed to create successful economies through the trade union movement and political parties. As a result, they did not need cooperatives, considering the low unemployment rates supported by an elaborate unemployment relief and social security system (Lindkvist and Westenholz 1987). In countries which were formerly members of the Soviet Union, cooperatives have not been popular because they have been associated with Soviet collectives. These preferences, however, are generally present worldwide regardless of political, social, cultural, and religious preferences. The higher unemployment rates after the GFC may have revived the cooperative sector, but it did not change people's overall work preferences.

The extent to which these work preferences can change if cooperatives were better known is a question that still needs to be answered. Further research to answer this question is required, but an answer will not be known until people are fully informed about cooperatives, they are able to compare the full benefits and inherent limits of both cooperatives and private enterprises without fear or favour, and they are able to start either a cooperative or private enterprise in an entrepreneurial environment that equally supports both types of enterprises.

7.2.5 *Cooperative Growth*

Another key challenge for the cooperative sector wanting to increase its share of the economy is to deal with challenges relating to the internal democratic structure; access to adequate finance; access to cooperative managers; and nation-specific cooperative law. It is important to note here that we are referring to challenges that prevent cooperatives from achieving their full potential because cooperatives have already demonstrated that they can grow into large successful businesses (Euricse 2021).

The cooperative, democratic structure may pose a challenge to cooperative growth. For those cooperatives that want to retain a democratic structure that values direct democracy, then there will be limits to how much they can grow (Cornforth, Thomas and Lewis et al. 1988). In a sense, this would be similar to family owned businesses that stopped growing once a size that meets their aspirations is reached. Those worker cooperatives that accept a form of representative and participatory democracy, however, have managed to grow. For instance, the catering cooperative Camst employs over 15,000 people, Arla has a democratic structure with an international membership, and Japan's consumer movement has grown and yet has a very democratic and participatory structure in place. This study, however, has also shown that cooperatives from the banking, agricultural, consumer and industrial and manufacturing sectors have resorted to a corporate model (Fonterra, Rabobank) or dual structures (Samci, Credit Agricole, Mondragon) in order to grow via overseas subsidiaries.

The second challenge for promoting cooperative growth is access to finance. The initial discussions on finance noted that worker cooperatives could not get loans as a result of discrimination, for having low collateral, and for having to raise capital internally (member shares, member loans, or retained profits). This argument may still hold in some less developed cooperative economies, but in places like France, Italy, Spain, and Quebec, this is not the case. In these countries and jurisdictions, local banks, cooperative development funds, local development agencies, and financial consortia provide loans to start-ups or existing cooperatives. There are credit guarantee companies that act as guarantors making it easier to get loans. Small cooperatives that operate in labour-intensive sectors, such as social cooperatives where human resources rather than capital is most important, also do not have a problem accessing the required capital to start and grow cooperatives.

Access to capital seems to be a challenge for large cooperatives that operate in capital-intensive industries, that want to internationalise their operations, or that want to grow quicker than organic growth would allow. In many countries, these cooperatives have access to external capital via issuing voting, non-voting, or preference shares; issuing cooperative bonds; attracting investors to co-invest in a cooperative majority-owned holding company; establishing joint ventures with other cooperatives or private companies; accessing capital via cooperative owned financial companies; accessing capital via issuing a limited amount of tradeable shares on the conventional stock market. As noted in Chapter 5, some of these large cooperatives have used dual structures to access capital and compete in global markets. Sacmi and Mondragon cooperatives, however, whilst they use dual structures (where a cooperative owns conventional subsidiaries), they do not need external capital.[9] Arla uses a traditional structure to compete internationally, but it has accessed external capital via issuing bonds without voting rights (Arla 2022).

In relation to finance, we could tentatively say that in areas where the cooperative economy is well positioned, small cooperatives can have access to credit. We can also say that there are many financial instruments that cooperatives can use to access credit that enables them to maintain the traditional cooperative form. We have noted that some co-operatives have adopted dual organisational structures and more corporatist approaches to access finance. The latter may pose a reputational risk for cooperatives if their firm behaviour is found to be similar to that of capitalist corporations.

The third challenge is attracting managers that understand cooperative principles and cooperative values (Borzaga and Galera 2012). Managers in agricultural, credit, consumer, and worker cooperatives in various sectors are well-paid. Salary differentials in manufacturing cooperatives that used to be as low as 3:1 in the 1970s have grown to 10:1 in some cases. Salaries of managers leading large cooperative banks, agricultural cooperatives, consumer cooperatives, or insurance companies earn more than 1 million USD per annum.[10] Large cooperatives, therefore, are able to attract external managers when needed. Large cooperative movements are also able to attract young graduates who could have a career within the cooperative sector and are thus able to bridge conventional management values and cooperative values (Battilani and Zamagni 2011). Whilst the cooperative sector welcomes their strategic, technical, and administrative skills and their ability to implement the strategic plans approved by the cooperative board, the key risk for cooperatives is that managers are trained in conventional business thinking that is more suited to capitalist corporations than cooperatives. This may lead managers to mirror IOF practices by focussing on profit maximisation, promoting hierarchical work culture, promoting company legal structures such as holding companies and cooperative groups, promoting higher salary differentials, treating cooperative members as clients, promoting cooperative demutualisation with support from opportunistic members, and suggesting cost-cutting at the expense of member values and expectations (Battilani and Zamagni 2011, Battilani and Schroter 2012, Borzaga and Galera 2012, Fulton and Girard 2015, Patmore, Balnave and Marjanovic 2021). There is no doubt that this is an area where the cooperative movement needs to improve. Cooperatives cannot grow without the support of competent, cooperative managers, yet they cannot allow conventional managers to dominate decision-making nor overly influence cooperative culture. Cooperative movements would benefit by promoting cooperative education for managers at the highest level, just like capitalist philanthropists and businesses have done.

The fourth issue that may prevent cooperative expansion overseas is the lack of consistency with cooperative law (Borzaga and Galera 2012). As we have explored in Chapter 6, the nation-specific cooperative legislation is very diverse. There are differences relating to almost every aspect of cooperative law, including cooperative formation, profit distribution, capital remuneration, cooperative governance, accessing external capital, asset management, and demutualisation. The cooperative sector is beginning to harmonise cooperative law in regions such as West Africa, South America and Europe. Hopefully, this may lead to a worldwide approach to cooperative law that can facilitate cooperative growth internationally (Cracogna, Fici and Henrÿ 2013).

The extent to which these four barriers prevent cooperatives from growing into a large and possibly more dominant sector of the economy requires further research and further analysis. Research on the four challenges discussed will undoubtedly provide different results depending on the historical period being studied, the size and aspirations of co-operatives, the cooperative typology being examined, whether cooperatives operate in a friendly or hostile cooperative environment, whether cooperatives are engaging or hostile to the State, whether cooperatives compete alone or as part of a cooperative network, whether cooperatives want to grow slow or want to grow fast, whether cooperatives are new or well established, and whether the legislative framework facilitates entrepreneurship and enables cooperative growth.

7.2.6 *The Corporation*

A key reason why there are few cooperatives is that private enterprises, especially corporations, have been very successful. Gregory Dow has identified four key advantages of capitalist firms. These are ease of establishing firms as one person can hire many other people and also can employ people in more than one location; access to capital; ease of changing ownership without changing the structure of the firm; and the fact that capitalist firms are better suited for capital intensive industries (Dow 2018). These advantages allow capitalist firms to access vast amounts of capital via global stock markets and to quickly grow into global firms much faster than cooperative firms that adopt traditional organisational principles.

In Chapters 2–5, we examined the evolution of private enterprises, especially corporations, and have identified many other factors that have led to the growth of private firms and corporations. Some key factors include:

- Corporations operating in the manufacturing sector were established before cooperatives. They controlled the industrial and manufacturing sector and became the chosen partner by the nation States for nation-building projects and for conducting wars. This allowed private businesses and corporations to grow and broaden their impact on the economy and on society.
- Businesses developed the public company in the eighteenth century, which allowed them to access external capital and separate ownership (shareholders) from governance (company board). This structure allowed public companies to access capital from international shareholders and attract competent leaders and managers. This made corporations more competitive.
- Businesses have been very innovative. Businesses have regularly innovated products and services, ownership models, governance arrangements, organisational structures, management models, communication techniques, and inter-firm arrangements. This innovative spirit has allowed businesses to grow, achieve economies of scale, improve their competitiveness, and occupy newly emerging markets.
- Capitalism has developed a legal, financial, and media architecture worldwide that promotes the capitalist enterprise. Key features of the capitalist architecture include worldwide acceptance of private property and the right of capital to keep profits; the law of contracts; bankruptcy laws; international financial markets that allows the buying and trading of company shares;[11] fund managers and institutional funds that link shareholders with companies across the world; a sophisticated media that informs the public about financial markets and investment opportunities.
- Capitalist firms, philanthropists, foundations, and the State have founded and funded universities to teach Masters of Business Administration that train managers across the world. These universities provided a pool of ready managers and executives for capitalist corporations across the world.
- Capitalist businesses have been very flexible in being able to coexist within all types of regimes (other than the State-led economic systems operating in the Soviet Union and China up to the 1980s). They have been flexible in accommodating improved industrial relations laws and taxation policies to support the Welfare State

and, more recently, have promoted the idea of corporations operating as socially responsible companies.

- Capitalists, via their business associations, think tanks, and political representatives, have been very successful in promoting their views of the economy and society to political parties, to the State, and to international organisations. States, the World Bank, The International Monetary Fund, and the World Trade Organization have promoted free, deregulated markets with limited state intervention that favours the development of corporations (Bakan 2004, Jones and Zeitlin 2007, Amatori and Colli 2011, Chang 2014, Srinivasan 2017).

The power of private enterprise is such that even when they cause a world crisis like the GFC of 2008, States worldwide rescued corporations because they were deemed too big to fail and too important for the world economy. The power of private businesses is also reflected in the way cooperatives throughout the world have been adopting governance, legal, and management approaches first adopted by private enterprises. These include joint ventures, holding companies with subsidiaries, listed investment companies, financial companies, wide salary scales, quality management frameworks, independent cooperative board members, cooperative CEOs having more operational powers, appointing competency-based board directors, and applying formal risk management practices.

7.2.7 The State

The State's attitude towards cooperatives has been inconsistent. Since the 1750s, we could summarise its attitude as indifferent, supportive, hostile, and at times very violent towards parts of the cooperative movement. The State's responses to cooperatives have been highlighted in Chapters 2–5. The purpose of this section is to highlight those key aspects of the State's role in the economy and in society that have influenced cooperative formation and growth.

The research thus far has shown that the State has evolved from dispensing the limited functions of law and order and foreign affairs that are typical of the Liberal State, to the more comprehensive functions of managing the economy and welfare provisions that are typical of the Liberal/Social Democratic State (Poggi 1978). Managing the economy includes functions such as promoting economic development, dealing with market failures and externalities, dealing with economic crises, and managing conflicts. The States' wider functions, and its subsequent economic and social achievements, have reduced people's immediate need to experiment with alternative firms. More specifically:

- The State's nation-building activities included establishing a financial and banking system, infrastructure, education system, energy sources, and public-works programme. The State also supported industrial development via tariff protection, and it facilitated business transactions through the enforcement of contracts. The State's nation-building activity supported the growth of private enterprises. This generated economic activity, more jobs for more people, contributed to rising living standards, and promoted more competitive businesses.
- The State has intervened to deal with market failure and to improve the operations of the market by encouraging competition and preventing monopoly powers. This has included passing anti-trust laws, appropriate industry standards, reducing barriers to market entry, promoting consumer protection laws, preventing business

non-discriminatory behaviours, and so on. These measures improved the operations of markets, making them more efficient and better suited to meet the needs of consumers and businesses.

- The State manages market excesses and mediates the power of capital by improving people's living standards in the workplace and in society. The democratisation of society allowed people to elect political representatives who could best articulate their needs. To this end, since the end of the nineteenth century, States have been passing laws and implementing public policies designed to improve living standards and living conditions. Key measures have included shorter working weeks, usually less than 40 hours today, unemployment benefits, health benefits, public housing, and a pension on retirement.
- The State manages the economy and mediates the negative impacts caused by economic crises. Especially since the time of the New Deal, the State has managed the economy and economic crisis. Key governance tools include the following: Keynesian fiscal and monetary management policies to stimulate or slow the economy; public works programmes; business buy-outs; buying corporate bonds; cash handouts to stimulate spending; a guarantor of bank deposits; and direct involvement in the economy. The State also intervenes to manage the negative consequences of market externalities such as unemployment, inequalities, homelessness, and business bankruptcies (Poggi 1978, Stiglitz 2000, Stretton 2000, Chang 2014, Frieden 2020, Sassoon 2020).
- The role of the State in promoting economic development, dealing with market failures, and managing the economy has reduced most people's need to form cooperatives because the negative aspects of living in a CME and society have been mitigated. In addition, the State has demonstrated to have a clear advantage over cooperatives and the private sector in that only the State can guarantee universal health cover, universal education, and universal social security coverage, and only the State has sufficient resources to manage an economic crisis. This is very appealing to working people because they could rely on their elected government to mediate the negative aspects of CMEs, without having to risk forming cooperatives to solve their immediate issues.

The State is continually evolving. We have noted in Chapter 5 how the neo-liberal State has created opportunities for social cooperatives providing social and wellbeing services to young people and the aged. It is also important to note that regardless of the State's success in dealing with market failures, and its capability to provide universal social services, cooperatives will always be formed because of people's desire to own their enterprise collectively, to promote economic democracy, and to promote stable communities, can only be met by forming their own cooperatives. What has been highlighted here is that the State's broader role in the economic and social sphere has reduced the need to form cooperatives. This is a key reason why there are fewer cooperatives.

7.2.8 The Cooperative Movement

The cooperative movement, at national and international levels, has not provided the cooperative sector with the support it needs to achieve its full potential. There are four key areas where the cooperative movement needs to perform better. These include creating a more united movement; safeguarding cooperative identity by discouraging organisational practices similar to conventional companies; promoting international institutions or structures (especially education and finance); and articulating a vision of a cooperative-led society with broad public support to influence the State.

The cooperative sector has often been divided. The first division took place between consumer cooperatives and worker cooperatives, as articulated by Sydney and Beatrice Webb, which influenced the debate in the United Kingdom and later influenced the ICA. The ICA principles of 1937 were more aligned with the needs of consumer cooperatives rather than worker cooperatives (Birchall 2012). The ICA membership also included differences of opinion between free traders and protectionists and between political activists and those that preferred political neutrality. There have also been divisions between Socialist-led and Catholic-led cooperatives splitting the cooperative movement (Desroche 1980, Hilson, Neunsinger and Patmore 2017, Patmore and Belnave 2018). Laidlaw's 1980 report to the ICA noted how worker cooperatives had been neglected (Laidlaw 1980). These divisions have limited the level of inter-sectoral cooperation between different cooperative sectors. All of these factors have negatively impacted the growth of the whole cooperative movement.

The second major area that has weakened the overall development of cooperatives is their loss of identity. This issue first surfaced in the 1920s when the early generation co-operators were replaced by a new generation, and the federation-led growth model was coming under pressure (MacPherson 2008). Laidlaw also noted that cooperatives suffered a credibility crisis as a result of large cooperatives: operating with poor democratic practices, having members with low levels of involvement, and operating subsidiaries managed as private companies (Laidlaw 1980). Lars Marcus, in 1988, and Sven Ake Book, in 1992, made similar findings, noting a deviation from the limited return on capital principle and the practice of forming joint ventures. These reports affirmed that cooperatives were being influenced by Capitalism and that they resembled conventional firms (Book 1992, MacPherson 2008, MacPherson 2012). The ICA has updated its principles, developed guides on how to apply cooperative principles, and it promoted discussions on finance and governance. However, more needs to be done to develop a more cohesive movement that operates in alignment with cooperative principles.

Third, whilst the cooperative movement has made efforts to promote educational facilities, especially in developing countries, and has developed national financial structures (banks, insurance companies, and financial companies), they do not meet the overall needs of the cooperative movement. Managers are still trained in conventional Master of Business Administration courses, and cooperatives have had to resort to conventional financial markets to access capital via issuing bonds, tradeable shares, or listing cooperative-owned companies. The cooperative movement has not managed to convince universities in every country to provide comprehensive cooperative studies courses, including cooperative management courses, to meet the demand of cooperatives. The cooperative movement has not established an international cooperative financial framework, as the capitalist sector has done for more than two centuries. It does not have an international cooperative bank that invests in cooperatives, nor has it established a financial network of banks, managed funds, pension funds, or cooperative capital funds that attract investments from individuals and invest in cooperative enterprises in accordance with cooperative principles of limited return on capital and indivisibility of assets. As a result, cooperatives have used conventional markets and financial instruments to access capital and possibly have missed out on attracting savings from people who support the cooperative movement and an alternative society.

Four, the international cooperative movement has not developed a coherent vision articulating what a cooperative economy and society would look like. It has not articulated what an appropriate, cooperative-friendly political framework would look like. The ICA has recently been gathering accurate data on the cooperative sector, and this should assist in promoting the cooperative sector to governments and international bodies (CICOPA 2017, Euricse 2021). Ultimately, the ICA and national movements need to promote a cooperative vision of the economy and society that rivals the vision promoted by capitalists and investor-owned firms, which is based on individual freedoms; freedom of enterprise; private property; maximisation of profits; and a CME linked to the rule of law supported by a liberal/social democratic state. This is a vision which is repeated every day in newspapers, specialised journals, television, universities, in the workplace and so on. The cooperative movement needs to develop its own vision that best suits a cooperative economy operating to meet the needs of everyone. This would allow it to influence governments worldwide to promote a legislative and policy framework that promotes cooperative development in accordance with cooperative principles and values.

7.2.9 Summary

There are many reasons why there are fewer cooperatives than conventional firms. The reasons put forward by classical economists and institutionalists do not provide adequate explanations. The legitimate evolution of the State and the constant capacity of the private sector to grow and innovate provide a sound explanation as to why there are fewer cooperatives. Together, the State and the private sector have created a political, economic, educational, and industrial relation system supportive of the capitalist economic system and the welfare state. Whilst imperfect, this combination has constantly improved living standards and contributed to developing a more humane society. In order to challenge this state of affairs, the cooperative movement needs to promote cooperative awareness, provide cooperative study courses in all universities, educate cooperative-friendly managers, develop a global cooperative-focussed financial framework, engage with the media and seek more space in media outlets. Most importantly, the cooperative movement needs to develop a vision of what a cooperative-led economy would look like, identify public policies that would advance its cause, and spell out clearly the advantages of a cooperative-led market economy compared to a CME.

7.3 Cooperatives in a Pluralist Economy

The cooperative sector has always displayed unique characteristics which distinguished it from other economic sectors. When cooperatives were first formally defined by Buchez in the 1830s and later by Rochdale in 1844, the economy already included the State, the private sector, and the charity sector. The State was a Liberal State which spent almost all its revenue on law and order, the army, and public administration. It had little direct involvement in the economy and welfare services. Private enterprises operated as privately owned, profit-making enterprises for the pursuit of personal gains or in the interest of their shareholders. Charity organisations, which had been active since the Middle Ages, provided educational, welfare, and banking services on an NFP basis. Cooperatives became a part of the market economy as an enterprise with social and economic objectives. In particular, it was an association of people that practised democratic management based on the principle of one-person-one-vote; practised limited return on capital; and distributed part of its surplus to members based on their transactions with the cooperative. Buchez also promoted the indivisibility of reserves (Mellor 1988, Birchall 2011, Holyoake 2016).

These four types of economic and social actors promoted different ownership models with different purposes:

- The State, provided public services, was responsible for law and order, promoted infrastructure and industry development, and promoted welfare measures since the 1870s.
- The private sector provided goods and services via privately owned businesses for the pursuit of private gain. Private enterprises varied from family businesses to investor-owned firms. The latter were externally funded and managed by a board of directors.
- The charity sector, religious and non-religious, were usually community-owned and provided general interest services to the community on an NFP basis. They were managed via a trust, funded by donors, and predominantly made use of voluntary labour.
- The cooperative sector included member-owned and democratically managed cooperatives that satisfied their members' needs through the provision of work or the provision of goods and services. This also included making a surplus to meet the enterprise's needs, paying a dividend to members based on their transactions with the cooperative, and paying members a limited return on capital (Jones and Zeitlin 2007, Webster 2016, Zamagni 2020).

7.3.1 The Third Sector

In 1935, George Fauquet, Head of the International Labour Organisation cooperative unit, wrote the essay *The Cooperative Sector*, where he argued that cooperatives were the third sector of the economy. By 1935, the boundaries within the economy occupied by the four sectors had changed since the previous century. In Russia, the State had abolished private property and limited cooperative autonomy. The 1929 Great Depression revealed that the CME was not able to provide full employment and stability. As a result, the State began to take a greater interest and involvement in managing the economy, regulating labour markets, and providing welfare services at the expense of the charity sector and mutual aid societies. The cooperative sector was growing in the consumer, agricultural, and credit sectors but felt under threat from the events in Russia and the Fascist regimes of Italy, Germany and other European countries. Within this context, Fauquet argued that the State, the private sector, or cooperatives should coexist, considering that neither of these sectors would be able to control the whole of the economy on their own. He suggested that cooperatives had a dual structure of being a democratic association of people and a business providing services to members. He promoted cooperatives' federalist structures as being able to support the workers, consumers, self-employed, farmers, and small businesses to compete in the market whilst respecting their autonomy. Fauquet also promoted cooperatives as being able to solve the conflicts between capital and labour, and, in citing the example of Denmark, he noted how cooperatives improve the material and moral standards of people (Fauquet 1941).

The ICA President, Vaino Tanner, in a paper presented to the ICA Congress of 1937, argued that cooperatives could complement any existing system and mitigate their defects by overcoming middlemen and the capitalist struggle for profits (Tanner 1937). In 1937, the ICA published the first cooperative principles, which reinforced cooperatives as democratic enterprises with an open membership that practised limited return on members' capital (Patmore and Belnave 2018).

7.3.2 Economic Boundaries

The four key economic actors, whilst keeping their core defining characteristics, all have adapted to changing political and economic conditions by broadening their functions or roles in the economy. All four sectors have encroached into the space that had formally been the domain of the other sectors. The State has slowly expanded its role. Especially since 1945, it has performed a more active role in managing the economy, it has been a key provider of welfare services and infrastructure, and in some countries, it has nationalised businesses that actively compete in the market. The private sector has promoted forms of corporate social responsibility to improve its image by promoting the concept of 'inclusive Capitalism' and the concept of 'shared value'. The latter suggests that social considerations should be embedded into a corporation's decision-making processes. This would simultaneously improve the competitiveness of the company and the social conditions of the communities in which it operates (Porter and Kramer 2011). The private sector also promoted Benefit Corporations (BCs). BCs focus on achieving goals that are broader than the profit maximisation objective. BCs are allowed to make decisions on behalf of stakeholders, are required to demonstrate a reliance on earned income, and are required to report annually how they have met their social purpose goals (Sabeti 2011).

Cooperatives, as we have seen in Chapters 2–5, have developed a variety of different approaches. Some have adopted the form of a corporation, and some that of a holding company that owns conventional businesses. Some cooperatives can demutualise and share the proceeds from cooperative assets, similar to private firms. Cooperatives have also formed social cooperative and community enterprises that promote general or community interests rather than member-only interests. As a result, their objective is similar to the general interest purpose promoted by the NFP sector.

Charity or NFP organisations have also been promoting the social enterprise model. This model differs from the traditional NFP organisation in that social enterprises derive a portion of their income from trading (a benchmark is 50 per cent of turnover). They generally practice asset lock and do not distribute profits like charity organisations. Social enterprises can take the form of private companies, charities, or cooperatives.[12]

What these approaches demonstrate is that each sector is adaptable and can change in response to the nature of the State, the problems faced by society, the prevailing ideas at the time, and the capacity, capability, and willingness of each sector to solve society's problems. However, whilst each sector has borrowed ideas from other sectors, their core features have remained the same. In relation to cooperatives, they have remained a unique sector because they are owned by members who are also users, their purpose is to provide a service to members, they are democratically governed, they generally limit the return on investments, and in most cases, assets are collectively owned. Until cooperatives demutualise, they can be regarded as being part of the cooperative sector of the economy. This should not, however, underestimate the changes that have taken place that have seen cooperatives operating like corporations or controlling holding companies. These changes are a matter of concern for the cooperative movement.

7.3.3 A Diversity of Views

The four sectors have been described based on their core characteristics of their ownership model, their governance model, and their purpose. Other views define these economic sectors differently depending on their cultural and historical background. The prevailing view in the United States is that only NFP organisations are part of the third sector. These must be private formal organisations with a legal personality, be self-governing, cannot distribute profits, and must have a contribution from volunteers (Defourny 2001). The United Kingdom is one of many countries that sees the third sector comprising cooperatives, community interest companies, and NFPs (Lyons 2001, Webster 2016, Pestoff 2021). The French concept of the Social Economy, first mentioned in the 1830s, divides the economic sectors into three distinct parts: State, private, and the social economy. This concept came to prominence again in the 1980s, proposing an alternative economic system to the State sector and the private sector (European Commission 2013).[13] According to the European Commission, social economy organisations pursue social aims, are democratically governed, and emphasise people instead of capital. Social economy organisations would include cooperatives, mutuals, for-profit and NFP associations, and social enterprises. South America has developed the concept of the Solidarity Economy. It includes all the players that are present in a social economy, but it adds the need to promote equity in all dimensions (including race and gender) and sustainable practices (Borowiak 2015).

7.3.4 *Continuum of Cooperative Forms*

This discussion has identified cooperatives as one of the four sectors that comprise the market economy. These four sectors have evolved, and each sector has crossed over the sphere of influence occupied by other sectors. The core characteristics of each sector relating to ownership, governance, and overall purpose, have largely remained the same. The cooperative form, as discussed in this chapter, but also in Chapters 2–5, has evolved to include different legal forms, including the social enterprise form, and has found different routes and legal forms to access external capital. Chapter 6 identified five different types of cooperative enterprises with unique definitions and characteristics. A good way to visualise the different types of cooperatives is to place them in a continuum of organisational forms ranging from purely commercial objectives to social objectives.

As Figure 7.1 shows, cooperatives that have adopted a corporate model that does not fully comply with the ICA cooperative principles one to four are closest to the commercial axis. The Member-owned, capital-centred cooperative enterprises that apply ICA cooperative principles one to four but allow assets to be distributed and allow unlimited profit distribution are also close to the commercial axis. The Cooperative-owned group

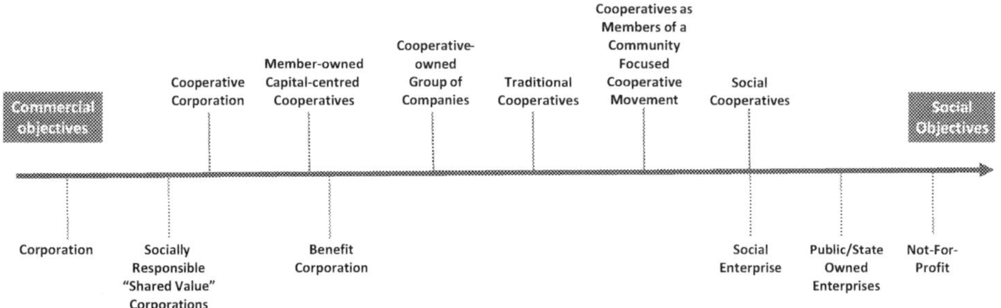

Figure 7.1 Continuum of Organisational Forms

Source: Adaptation from the figure produced by Sacchetti and Tortia (2020).

of enterprises that adopt dual structures sit closer to the middle of the axis. Those traditional cooperatives that apply ICA cooperative principles one to four and do not distribute net assets at any time, limit the return on capital accounts, and limit the amount of profits distributed as patronage refunds sit between the commercial and the social axis. Those cooperatives that see themselves as members of a community focussed cooperative movement that apply ICA cooperative principles one to seven and encourage cooperation among cooperatives, promote community development, do not distribute assets, and practice a limited return on capital, are closer to the social axis. The social cooperatives that promote general interests and rarely distribute profits are located on the social objectives axis, are very close to NFP associations.[14]

Figure 7.1 also shows the position of private companies and NFP associations facilitating a comparison with cooperatives along the commercial and social objective axis. For instance, corporations are profit-maximising companies so they sit closest to the commercial objective axis; BCs which consider stakeholder interests rather than maximising value for shareholders, sit closer to the middle of the axis; social enterprises sit opposite social cooperatives because both sets of enterprises promote the general interests, do not distribute assets, and practice limited return on capital; and, finally, NFPs sit closest to the social objective axis because they solely focus on providing a service to the community and because they do not distribute any surplus.

7.4 Summary

- Cooperatives have engaged with the market in a variety of ways ranging from being hostile to the market, to wanting to dominate the market, and to embracing the market. This embracement of the market does not mean that cooperatives have an uncritical view of the CME. Indeed, within the market, cooperatives still promote an alternative business culture to that promoted by private enterprises. This is demonstrated through adherence to the principles of democratic management, limited return on capital, inter-cooperative cooperation, and community development.
- Cooperatives coordinate consumers, farmers, workers, and businesses' entry and engagement with the market. Cooperatives operate as a coordinating mechanism on behalf of their members, thus facilitating their inclusion in the market whilst improving their market position vis-à-vis their competitors. Cooperative's enterprise model and level of competitiveness allowed them to perform a complementary role to the State and private sector. They have performed this role by intervening where there have been State failures or market failures. They have corrected market power by challenging monopolies. Cooperatives have also mediated market excesses during the economic crisis by continuing to focus on meeting members' needs in difficult circumstances.
- Classical economists and institutionalists have the merit of stimulating the debate on cooperative economics. This led the cooperative sector and cooperative-friendly academics to come to the defence of cooperative enterprises. This led to progress being made in developing a theory of cooperative economics and in identifying some of the strengths and weaknesses of cooperatives as well as their unique characteristics when competing in the market. This debate has also firmed the belief that a multidisciplinary approach is best suited to understand the cooperative model.
- Cooperatives have a greater chance of starting, growing, consolidating, restructuring, and managing a crisis, if they are part of a cooperative movement or network of cooperatives that operate in a non-hostile environment. The cooperative network provides

support services throughout the cooperative lifecycle, whilst the State can provide an enabling legal environment and access to public resources. When cooperatives compete alone, without being a member of a mature cooperative sector, they will find it more difficult to grow and navigate difficulties encountered along their cooperative lifecycle.

- Cooperatives still face obstacles that limit their formation and limit their growth. Obstacles such as lack of awareness preventing cooperative formation, the lack of capital-intensive funding via the stock market, and the lack of cooperative educated managers are real. However, understanding the extent of the problem worldwide requires further research that considers a multitude of global and nation-specific factors such as the maturity of the cooperative sector; its relation with the State; the size of cooperatives, the maturity of cooperatives, type of economic sector, and the cooperative's own aspirations; the preferred democratic governance model; cooperative's position in the economy; and whether cooperatives want to grow organically or grow faster through conventional means.
- Explanations as to why there are a few cooperatives have focussed mostly on explaining internal cooperative limits and the negative impact that an external, hostile environment has had on cooperatives. This study has also emphasised that a more in-depth understanding of the role of the nation-state, the evolution of the corporation, and the history of cooperative movements and the ICA, adds value to our understanding as to why there are fewer cooperatives than private firms. Having a broader understanding may lead the cooperative movement to develop a more comprehensive approach to promoting and growing cooperatives.
- The international cooperative movement has not yet managed to match the CME in articulating a vision for a cooperative economy and how it would interact with the State, society and other economic actors. It has also shown its limitation in promoting a worldwide educational system that includes cooperative studies. Most importantly, it has not yet developed an international cooperative financial framework that is able to attract and direct funds to the cooperative sector whose remuneration and expectation would align with cooperative principles.
- Cooperatives are a key sector of a pluralist market economy. The major four sectors of the economy: the State, the private sector, the cooperative sector, and the NFP sector, have existed since cooperatives were formed in the eighteenth century. All four sectors have evolved and have encroached on the economic space of other sectors. Cooperatives have evolved and have adopted legal structures that allow them to incorporate elements of the private sector and, at times, elements of the NFP sector. In Figure 7.1, we have allocated cooperatives along a continuum of organisational forms to illustrate how cooperatives relate to other sectors of the economy.

7.5 Questions

- Consider how the relation between cooperatives and the market has evolved since the industrial revolution, and identify (i) the type of cooperatives that most likely would fully embrace a CME; and (ii) the type of cooperatives that whilst operating in a market economy, challenge the key aspects of a CME and a capitalist-led society.
- Review the cooperative sector in your city, region or country and examine the cooperative rate of formation. What is driving people to form or reject cooperatives? Are there any barriers faced by people wanting to form cooperatives? What should

the cooperative sector and local and national authorities do to encourage the rate of cooperative formation?

- Review the cooperative sector in your city, region or country and examine the cooperatives' rate of growth. Have cooperatives managed to grow since their inception? How did they manage to grow? Did they finance their operations internally or externally? Did cooperatives grow through organic growth, or did they grow faster through mergers and acquisitions? Did cooperatives manage to grow whilst complying with cooperative principles?
- This research has claimed that the role of the State, the growth of corporations, and the limits faced by the cooperative movement have limited the growth potential of the cooperative sector. According to you, are the reasons why there are fewer cooperatives than private enterprises to be found in the cooperative model or in external factors such as the power of corporations, the role of the State, and the limits of the cooperative movement?
- Do you think that cooperatives should simply be seen as part of the third sector or part of the social economy or be seen as one of the four sectors that comprise the cooperative sector alongside the State sector, the private sector, and the NFP sector? What distinguishes the cooperative sector from the other sectors? You may consider ownership, governance, and overall purpose.
- Georges Fauquet noted that since the State sector, the private sector, or the cooperative sector, cannot dominate the economy on their own, they should find ways to coexist. Do you agree with this statement? If you do, what is the most appropriate role for each sector? Should they have a clearly defined role in the economy, or should they compete as they do today? Should the market determine their role, or should politics determine their role according to economic and non-economic criteria?
- Please review Figure 7.1 which describes the positioning of cooperatives along the two axes of commercial objectives and social objectives. How would you allocate the various types of cooperatives within these two axes?

Notes

1 A cooperative enterprise model refers to the way a cooperative is organised to produce and sell goods and services in the market in order to meet the needs of its members. Cooperatives meet the economic, social, cultural and aspirational needs of their members by competing in the market on their own, or as a member of a second-tier cooperative. Whilst the term enterprise model is synonymous with the term business model, this book will opt to use the term cooperative model interchangeably with the term cooperative enterprise model.
2 Please refer to Chapter 3, Part 3.5.2.
3 Please refer to Chapter 5.
4 Please refer to Chapter 5, Part 5.2.9.
5 Gregory Dow provides a good overview of the debates on the Labour Managed Firm in an article published in the *Annals of Public and Cooperative Economics* in 2018 (Dow 2018).
6 Please refer to Chapter 2.
7 Please refer to Chapter 5.
8 In Finland, one person can start a cooperative and in Norway, two people can start a cooperative.
9 For further information on Sacmi see (Ammirato 2018).
10 For instance, the CEOs of Arla, Cooperative Group Limited, Fonterra, Rabobank, Vancity, and Unipol, all earn salaries above 1 million USD.
11 The London Stock Exchange was established in 1801, and the New York Stock Exchange in 1817 (Chang 2014).

12 Ridley-Duff and Mike Bull, in their informative book *Understanding Social Enterprise*, include cooperatives, mutual enterprises, socially responsible businesses, and charitable trading companies under the term 'social enterprise' (Ridley-Duff and Bull 2019).
13 Please also refer to Jack Quarter's *Canada's Social Economy* for a good discussion on the concept of social economy (Quarter 1992).
14 For further information on the five cooperative enterprises noted in Figure 7.1, please refer to Chapter 6, Part 6.7.

References

Alchian, Armen A., and Harold Demsetz. 1972. "Production, Information Costs, and Economic Organization." *American Economics Review* 777–795.

Amatori, Franco, and Andrea Colli. 2011. *Business History*. Routledge: New York.

Ammirato, Piero. 2018. *The Growth of Italian Cooperatives: Innovation, Resilience and Social Responsibility*. New York: Routledge.

Arla. 2022. *Investing in Arla: Bond Programme*. Accessed September 30, 2022. https://www.arla.com/company/investor/bond-programme/.

Asiedu, Isaac Yaw, and Kumpei Hayashi. 2012. "Japanese Consumers' Co-operative Union." *Publications*. Accessed May 4, 2023. https://jccu.coop/eng/public/pdf/coop_sanchoku.pdf.

Bajo, Claudia Sanchez, and Bruno Roelants. 2011. *Capital and the Debt Trap: Learning from Cooperatives in the Global Crisis*. London: Palgrave Macmillan.

Bakan, Joel. 2004. *The Corporation*. London: Constable and Robinson.

Battilani, Patrizia, and Harm G Schroter. 2012. "Demutualization and Its Problems." In *The Cooperative Business Movement, 195 to the Present*, by Patrizia Battilani and Harm G. Schroter, Chapter 6. Cambridge: Cambridge University Press.

Battilani, Patrizia, and Vera Zamagni. 2011. "The Managerial Transformation of Italian Cooperative Enterprises 1946–2010." *Department of Economics of the University of Bologna Working Papers Number 789* 39.

Birchall, Johnston. 2011. *People-Centred Businesses*. London: Palgrave MacMillan.

———. 2012. "A 'Member-Owned Business' Approach to the Classification of Co-operatives and Mutuals." In *The Co-Operative Model In Practice: International Perspectives*, by McDonnell Diarmuid and MacKnight Elizabeth, 67–83. CETS Resource.

———. 2013. *Resilience in Downturn: The Power of Financial Cooperatives*. Financial Report, Geneva: International Labour Organization.

Birchall, Johnston, and Lou Hammond Ketislon. 2009. *Resilience of the Cooperative Business Model in Times of Crisis*. Geneva: International Labour Office.

Bonow, Mauritz. 1938. "The Consumer Movement in Sweden." *The Annals of the American Academy of Political and Social Science* 171–184.

Book, Sven Ake. 1992. *Cooperatives in a Changing World*. Report to the ICA Congress Tokyo, October, 1992, Geneva: International Cooperative Alliance.

Borowiak, Craig. 2015. "Mapping Social and Solidarity Economy." In *Social Economy in China and the World*, by N. Pun, BH Ku, H. Yan and A. (Editors) and Koo, Chapter 2. London: Taylor Francis Group.

Borzaga, Carlo, and Ermanno C. Tortia. 2017. "Co-operation as Co-ordination Mechanism: A New Approach to the Economics of Co-operative Enterprises." In *The Oxford Handbook of Mutual, Co-Operative, and Co-Owned Business*, by Jonathan Michie, Joseph R. Blasi and Carlo Borzaga, 55–75. Oxford: Oxford University Press.

Borzaga, Carlo, and Giulia Galera. 2012. *Promoting the Understanding of Cooperatives for a Better World*. Trento: Euricse.

Caselli, Guido. 2014. *Osservatorio della Cooperazione in Emilia-Romagna: Partire dai Numeri*. Regional Cooperative Sector Review, Bologna: Unioncamere.

Chang, Ha-Joon. 2014. *Economics: The User's Guide*. London: Penguin Books.

CICOPA. 2017. *Cooperatives and Employment: Second Global Report.* Global Report on Cooperative Employment, Brussels: ICA.

Cornforth, Chris, and Alan Thomas. 1990. "Cooperative Development: Barriers, Support Structures and Cultural Factors." *Economic and Industrial Democracy* 451–461.

Cornforth, Chris, Alan Thomas, Jenny Lewis, and Roger Spear. 1988. *Developing Successful Worker Cooperatives.* London: Sage Publications.

Cracogna, Dante, Antonio Fici, and Hagen Henrÿ. 2013. *International Handbook of Cooperative Law.* Heidelberg: Springer.

Crick, Bernard. 1987. *Socialism.* Milton Keynes: Open University Press.

Defourny, Jacques. 2001. "Introduction: from Third Sector to Social Enterprise." In *the Emergence of Social Enterprise*, by Carlo Borzaga and Jacques Defourny, 1–29. London: Routledge.

Desroche, Henri. 1980. *Il Progetto Cooperativo.* Milano: Jaca Books.

Dow, Gregory. 2018a. *The Labour-Managed Firm: Theoretical Foundations.* Cambridge: Cambridge University Press.

———. 2018b. "The Theory of the Labor-Managed Firm: Past, Present and Future." *Annals of Public and Cooperative Economics* 65–86.

Elster, John. 1989. "From Here to There, or, If Cooperatives Ownership is so Desirable, Why are There so Few Cooperatives." *Social Philosophy and Policy* 93–111.

Euricse. 2021. *Exploring the Cooperative Economy Report 2020.* Cooperative Monitor Report, Trento: International Cooperative Alliance.

European Commission. 2013. *Social Economy and Social Entrepreneurship.* Social Europe Guide, Volume 4, Brussels: European Commission.

Fauquet, Georges. 1941. "The Co-operative Sector." *Annals of Public and Cooperative Economy* 342–369.

Frieden, Jeffry A. 2020. *Global Capitalism.* New York: WW Norton and Company.

Fulton, Murray, and Jean-Pierre Girard. 2015. *Demutualization of Co-operatives and Mutuals.* Cooperative Governance Report, Canada: Co-operatives and Mutuals Canada.

Furubotn, Eirik, and Svetozar Pejovich. 1970. "Property Rights and the Behaviour of the Firm in a Socialist State: The Example of Yugoslavia." *Zeitschrift ffir NationalSkonomie* 431–454.

Gillespie, James Edward. 1950. "Swedish Cooperatives." *Current History* 331–336.

Government du Quebec. 2003. *Cooperative Development Policy.* Government Policy Document, Quebec: Government du Quebec.

Hansmann, Henry. 1999. "Cooperative Firms in Theory and Practice." *LTA* 387–403.

———. 2013. "All Firms are Cooperatives and So Are Governments." *Journal of Entrepreneurial and Organisational Diversity* 1–10.

Hilson, Mary. 2018. *The International Co-operative Alliance and the Consumer Co-operative Movement in Northern Europe, 1860-1939.* Manchester: Manchester University Press.

Hilson, Mary, Silke Neunsinger, and Greg Patmore Patmore. 2017. *A Global History of Consumer Co-operation since 1850.* Leiden: Brill.

Hirschfield, Andre. 1976. "Some Thoughts on "Co-operative Socialism"." *Annals of Public and Cooperative Economy* 87–101.

Holyoake, George Jacob. 2016. *The History of the Rochdale Pioneers: 1844-1892.* London: Kindle Edition, Routledge.

Honneth, Axel. 2017. *The Idea of Socialism.* Cambridge: Polity.

Jones, Geoffrey, and Jonathon Zeitlin. 2007. *The Oxford Handbook of Business History.* Oxford: Oxford University Press.

Jossa, Bruno. 2015. "A Few Reflections on the Reasons Why Cooperative Firms Have Failed to Gain a Foothold." *Open Journal of Business and Management* 265–280.

Kalmi, Panu. 2007. "The Disappearance of Cooperatives from Textbooks." *Cambridge Journal of Economics* 625–647.

Laidlaw, AF. 1980. *Cooperatives in the Year 2000.* A Paper Prepared for the 27 Congress of the International Cooperative Alliance, Moscow: International Cooperative Alliance.

Lindkvist, Lars, and Ann Westenholz. 1987. *Employee Owned Companies in the Nordic Countries: A Historical Parenthesis or a Future Possibility*. Copenhagen: Nordic Council of Ministers.

Lyons, Mark. 2001. *Third Sector.* Sydney: Allan and Unwin.

MacPherson, Ian. 2008. "The Co-operative Movement and the Social Economy Traditions: Reflections of the Mingling of Broad Visions." *Annals of Public and Cooperative Economics* 625–642.

———. 2012. "What Is the Purpose of It All." In *The Cooperative Business Movement, 1950 to the Present*, by Harm G Schroter and Patrizia Battilani, Chapter 4. Cambridge: Cambridge University Press.

McDonnel, Diarmuid, and Elizabeth Macknight. 2012. *The Co-operative Model in Practice: International Perspectives.* Aberdeen: CETS.

Mellor, Mary, et.al. 1988. *Worker Cooperatives in Theory and Practice.* Milton Keynes: Open University Press.

Patmore, Greg, and Nikola Belnave. 2018. *A Global History of Co-Operative Business.* London: Routledge.

Patmore, Greg, Nikola Balnave, and Oliveira Marjanovic. 2021. "Resistance Is Not Futile: Co-operatives, Demutualization, Agriculture and Neoliberalism in Australia." *Cambridge University Press* 1–19.

Pestoff, Victor. 2021. *Co-Production and Japanese Healthcare.* London: Taylor and Francis Group.

Poggi, Gianfranco. 1978. *The Developmental of the Modern State.* Stanford: Stanford University Press.

Porter, Michael E, and Mark R Kramer. 2011. "Creating Shared Value." *Harvard Business Review* 1–17.

Quarter, Jack. 1992. *Canada's Social Economy.* Toronto: James Lorimer and Company.

Ridley-Duff, Rory, and Mike Bull. 2019. *Understanding Social Enterprise.* London: Sage Publications.

Roelants, Bruno, Diana Dovgan, Hyungsik Eum, Terrasi, and Elisa. 2012. *The Resilience of the Cooperative Model.* Economic Report, Brussels: Cecop.

Sabeti, Heerad. 2011. "The For-Benefit Enterprise." *Harvard Business Review* 1–7.

Sacchetti, Silvia, and Ermanno Tortia. 2020. "Social Responsibility in Non-Investor-Owned Organisations." *Corporate Governance* 343–363.

Sassoon, Donald. 2020. *The Anxious Triumph: A Global History of Capitalism, 1860-1914.* London: Penguin Books.

Schneiberg, Marc. 2011. "Toward an Organisationally Diverse American Capitalism? Cooperative, Mutual and Local State-Owned Enterprise." *Seattle University Law Review 34* 1409–1434.

Smith, Stephen C., and Jonathon Rothbaum. 2014. "Cooperatives in a Global Economy: Key Issues, Recent Trends and Potential Development." In *Co-operatives in Post-Growth Era: Creating Co-operative Economics*, by Sonja NOvkovic and Tom Webb, 221–242. London: Zed Books.

Spear, Roger. 2000. "The Co-operative Advantage." *Annals of Public and Cooperative Economics* 507–523.

Srinivasan, Bhu. 2017. *Americana: A 400 Year History of American Capitalism.* New York: Penguin Books.

Stiglitz, Joseph. 2000. *Economics of the Public Sector.* New York: W.W. Norton and Company.

Stretton, Hugh. 2000. *Economics: a New Introduction.* Sydney: University of New South Wales.

Tanner, Vaino. 1937. "The Place of Cooperatives in Different Economic Systems." *Annals of Collective Economy* 240–265.

Taylor, Keith. 2021. "An Analysis of the Entrepreneurial Institutional Ecosystems Supporting the Development of Hybrid Organizations: The Development of Cooperatives in the U.S." *Journal of Environmental Management* 112244.

Vanek, Jaroslav. 1971. "The Basic Theory of Financial Participatory Firms." In *Self Management: Economic Liberation of Man*, by Jaroslav Vanek, 445–455. Harmondsworth: Penguin Books.

———. 2000. "Cooperative Economics." *New Renaissance Magazine* Volume 5, Number 1.

Vergnanini, Antonio. 1907. "Cooperazione Integrale." *International Cooperative Alliance.* Cremona: Edizione Tipografia Giulio Mandelli. 1–43.

Vieta, Marcelo, Sara Depetri, and Antonella Carrano. 2017. *The Italian Road to Recuperating Enterprises in Crisis and the Legge Marcora Framework: Italy's Worker-Buyouts in Times of Crisis.* Trento: Euricse.

Ward, Benjamin. 1958. "The Firm in Illyria: Market Syndicalism." *The American Economic Review* 566–589.

Webb, Sydney, and Beatrice Webb. 1914. "Special Supplement on the Co-operative Production and Profit Sharing." *The New Statesman*, 30 May: 1–34.

Webster, Anthony. 2012. "Building the Wholesale: The Development of the English CWS and British Cooperative Business 1863-1890." *Business History* 883–904.

———. 2016. "The Third Sector: Cooperatives, Mutuals, Charities and Social Enterprises." In *The Routledge Companion to Business History*, by John Wilson, Chapter 9. London: Taylor Francis Group.

Wilson, John, Anthony Webster, and Rachael Vorberg-Rugh. 2013. *Building Co-operation: A Business History of the Co-operative Group, 1863-2013.* Oxford: Oxford University Press.

Zamagni, Stefano, and Vera Zamagni. 2010. *Cooperative Enterprise.* Cheltenham: Edward Elgar Publishing.

Zamagni, Vera. 2020. *Forme D'Impresa: Una Prospettiva Storico-Economica.* Bologna: Il Mulino.

Zanotti, Antonio. 2017. *Prima di Rochdale: Dal Cooperativismo alla Cooperazione.* Soveria Mannelli: Rubbettino.

Zevi, Alberto, Antonio Zanotti, Francois Soulage, and Adrian Zelaia. 2011. *Beyond the Crisis: Cooperatives, Work and Finance.* Brussels: Cecop Publications.

8 Governance

Corporate or cooperative governance[1] is a term that refers to how companies, cooperative enterprises,[2] and organisations make decisions, how they comply with the law, and how they are held to account for their decisions, their performance, and their compliance with the law. Good governance helps organisations achieve performance in compliance with the law, with industry standards and principles, and in meeting community expectations. Good governance practices have been promoted to help countries maintain their competitiveness and protect and promote their prevailing economic system. Many high-profile corporate governance reviews conducted since the 1990s have led to legislative and regulatory changes and industry good practice guides. These reviews have made recommendations to strengthen the role of the Board of Directors, to provide more protection to shareholders, to strengthen the integrity of financial markets, and to provide more regulatory oversight (Du Plessis et al. 2015, OECD 2015).

This chapter explores the evolution, structures, and risks associated with corporate and cooperative governance. Part 8.1 will explore the concept, structures, and evolution of corporate governance. Part 8.2 will explore the evolution of cooperative governance. Part 8.3 will discuss cooperative governance structures. Part 8.4 will analyse key cooperative governance risks that cooperatives need to mitigate. Part 8.5 will provide a definition of cooperative governance. Part 8.6 provides a summary. Part 8.7 suggests key questions for further consideration.

This chapter will enable the reader to

- Understand the concept, evolution, structures and good practice in corporate governance.
- Understand the development of cooperative governance structures and practices.
- Analyse the key risks associated with cooperative governance and consider how best to mitigate these risks.
- Appreciate how good reporting can help improve cooperative awareness, enhance the reputation of the cooperative sector, and keep cooperatives accountable.
- Identify and analyse the similarities and differences between corporate governance and cooperative governance.
- Discuss how best to define cooperative governance.
- Consider reforms that would enhance cooperative governance.

DOI: 10.4324/9781003269533-8

8.1 Corporate Governance

In the private sector, corporate governance is synonymous with the rise of the modern corporation and joint stock companies.[3] These companies were formed because the new industrial companies (railways especially) needed more money than could be raised through partnerships. Legislative changes in Britain and the United States facilitated the formation of joint stock companies. In Britain, the 1844 *Joint Stock Companies Act* allowed joint stock companies to form without a Royal Charter or an Act of Parliament. In the United States, the New Jersey and Delaware States removed many restrictions for corporations in 1899. The new laws allowed corporations to operate for broader purposes (rather than a single purpose), to operate in perpetuity (rather than for a limited period), to operate in many locations (rather than only in one State), and to merge and buy stock in another company (which was previously not allowed). Within this new legislative environment, the State no longer oversaw the activities of the company to ensure that it acted in the public interest. This role would now be performed by the company's Board of Directors (Bakan 2004, Bevir 2012).

In the twentieth century, corporations continued to grow in size and complexity and began to attract investments from a broader set of investors via the stock markets of London and New York. General Motors, for instance, developed the multi-divisional organisational structure, which allowed key divisions a degree of autonomy whilst still linked to a centralised executive and financial team. Railways and oil companies were already large enterprises. Berle and Means's *Modern Corporation and Private Property*, published in 1932, was the first major study on corporate governance. Their research found that ownership was separated from those who controlled the corporation. It found that whilst many shareholders owned the corporation, control rested with the Board and management—with the latter having more effective control than the Board. This new development eliminated the checks and balances that owners previously exercised over management. As a result, management could pursue its own interests over those of the shareholders. Indeed, whilst shareholders were interested in profits and high dividends, management was interested in growing the company, gaining a higher status, or receiving a higher salary. Berle and Means concluded that shareholders had exchanged control for liquidity (Weidebaum and Jensen 1991). Six years later, Chester Barnard wrote that firms must successfully manage economic and non-economic motives. Firms were required to obey the laws, pay taxes, pay creditors, pay reasonable dividends, give customers good service, pay managers well, and pay workers well. Thus the success of the firm—to make profits and pay dividends—depended on meeting all the other purposes. A number of Japanese thinkers have also been promoting this concept (Stretton 2000).[4]

8.1.1 Principal–Agency Theory and more

The findings from Berle and Means led to a debate on corporate governance. The Principal–Agency theory, as it became known, focussed on the inherent conflict of interest between the shareholders (dividend and profits) and management (remuneration, power, self-esteem). This theory sees shareholders as the owners and the principal of the company, whilst management are the agents who manage the company on behalf of shareholders. It led to discussions about information asymmetry and the costs of monitoring managers. It led to suggestions ranging from increasing controls exercised by the Board to devising schemes aligning the interests of management to those of the shareholders.

The solution for the latter was making available stock options or performance pay for managers (Bevir 2012).

By the 1970s, debates about corporate social responsibility re-emerged, noting that corporations had to consider the interests of key stakeholders (workers, communities, suppliers, and so on) and not just the interest of shareholders (Crane and Matten 2016). In the same period, Friedman strongly argued that management's only responsibility is to conduct business in accordance with the desires of the owners and in accordance with the law. The owners' desires were for management to increase profits (Friedman 1970). Friedman's viewpoint that the company's role was to maximise profits for shareholders coincided with the rise of neo-liberalism, and it became the mainstream view on the role of corporations (Zingales, Kasperkevic and Schechter 2020).

8.1.2 Scandals and Bankruptcies

Whilst the academic debates about corporate governance continued, a number of bankruptcies caused major concerns for legislators and financial markets. The first concern was raised in 1970 when Penn Central Transportation Company, the United States' biggest railway company, was declared bankrupt. A subsequent Senate report found mismanagement, high labour and supervision costs, high dividend payments since 1960, low investment expenditure, and a continually declining trade (Shabecoff 1973). In the 1990s, a period dubbed the 'roaring nineties' (Stiglitz 2004), a number of corporate scandals and bankruptcies came to prominence that led to serious questioning of corporate governance practices. The most high-profile cases[5] that led to national reviews of corporate governance included

- Bank of Credit and Commerce International in 1991 (United Kingdom). This bank was found to be involved in fraudulent activities, money laundering, bribery, arms trafficking, tax evasion, and illegal immigration. It collapsed with 20 billion USD in liability (Mufson and McGee 1991, Partridge 2020).
- Maxwell Fraud Scandal (United Kingdom). Robert Maxwell led a business empire based in London of some 400 companies, which was declared bankrupt in 1991. It was found that as chair, he had unfettered powers and could move money between accounts. It was found that he diverted 900 million pounds from public companies and the employees' pension fund into other accounts (AFR 1992).
- Enron, an energy commodity company based in Houston (United States) with a turnover of over 100 billion in 2000, went bankrupt in 2001. It was found that poor financial reporting and a lack of transparency hid the debt from shareholders. Auditors provided auditing and consulting services. Directors sold shares before the collapse. A key reason had been management's focus on increasing the share price because they owned stock and stock options (Bevir 2012).
- HIH Insurance was Australia's largest corporate collapse in 2001, with a debt of 5.3 billion AUD. Key findings from the Report of the Royal Commission on HIH revealed that the company had overpriced acquisitions, there was no consideration of the company's overall risks, management did not know how much money was actually in the business, and HIH did not have adequate provisions for insurance claims, which was its core business activity. The report also noted that the regulators failed to recognise the seriousness of the situation and failed to question the reliability of the information received from HIH (Bailey 2003).

- WorldCom, a long-distance carrier and largest mover of internet traffic, collapsed in 2002, with 32 billion USD in debt. The company used improper accounting practices, managed to get banks to issue securities when needed, and it provided managers with loans worth hundreds of millions of dollars. Some brokers assessed the stock as a buy just before it collapsed (Stiglitz 2004).

These events led to shareholder activism. It was led by the large pension funds, mutual funds, and hedge funds, which began to monitor and influence company boards and management. In the 1980s, some shareholders found more aggressive means of curbing the authority of corporate managers by initiating 'hostile takeovers'. In response to these events, businesses started to rethink their understanding of corporate governance (Friedman 2020). More importantly, governments began to launch corporate governance reviews to restore public confidence in the market, to improve the perception of a country's business practices, and to prevent (or at least limit) large bankruptcies and fraudulent activities.

8.1.3 Reviews

A number of governments conducted high-profile reviews that led to new legislation and regulations to reform corporate governance practices. Professional associations also developed good practice guides to help boards develop better governance practices. Key reviews and national laws included *The Cadbury Report* completed in 1992 (United Kingdom); the *Sarbanes–Oxley Act* of 2002 (United States); the HIH Insurance Royal Commission 2003 (Australia); and the *King Report* of South Africa (2009). Legislation was passed to deal specifically with consumers (*Dodd–Frank Act* of 2010). Industry codes were developed to complement corporation laws.[6] Approaches to corporate governance favoured either prescriptive regulations or industry-based self-regulations.

The legal requirements and industry-based codes of practice, whilst they differed, dealt with the powers, duties, and responsibilities of the board, management, and shareholders. Key features included clarifying and strengthening the role of the Board vis-à-vis management, strengthening the rights of investors vis-à-vis the board and management, and promoting ethical conduct. More specifically:

- The board was acknowledged as being ultimately responsible for corporate governance. Recommendations concluded that the board would be best served by having an independent Chair, separate from the Chief Executive Officer (CEO). It would be strengthened by recruiting independent directors and by establishing board sub-committees led by independent directors. These sub-committees included a remuneration committee, a governance committee (nominations sub-committee), and an audit and risk management committee. Boards would be expected to appoint and replace the CEO and senior managers; approve budgets and major capital expenditures; oversee accounting, reporting, and disclosure requirements; set the risk appetite and review risk management processes; approve the remuneration framework; and monitor governance practices (ASX 2019).
- The rights of shareholders were enhanced via a number of disclosure requirements. These would keep investors and the market regularly informed about the company's performance and administration. Key requirements included information on board and management qualifications, experience, and remuneration; disclosure of any information

that may influence the share price; regular information on financial results to be clearly presented; and information about their risk management and compliance procedures.

- There was a greater emphasis on ethical conduct. Codes of Conduct dealt with conflict of interest, fair dealing, and compliance. South Africa made it compulsory for all State-owned and listed companies to establish a Social and Ethics Committee and to report annually on laws, codes of practice, and social and economic development. In Germany, all Supervisory Boards and Management Boards of listed companies are required to make an annual declaration of compliance with the Corporate Governance Code (Du Plessis et al. 2015).
- Corporate governance codes or governance principles promoted good governance practices. These principles provided guidance on governance matters, including board composition and structure, the role of management, disclosure and reporting requirements, integrity in communication, respect for shareholders and stakeholders, managing risk, managing oversight, and so on. What was different about these new Codes is that, whilst voluntary, they demanded boards to comply with suggested good practice standards or explain why they did not comply. This provision informed investors about the board's intention on key areas of governance (Du Plessis et al. 2015).

It is clear from the key profile cases noted above and the various country-specific corporate governance reviews that good corporate governance requires more than just Board structures and greater competencies and transparency. The case studies noted how the law and regulatory bodies did not provide adequate oversight and were slow to intervene. It also noted how banks and other market players failed to understand the risks associated with those companies or question the way those companies operated. Du Plessis et al. have suggested the following criteria to establish good corporate governance standards. First, establishing effective board structures that recognise the supervisory role of the board (direct, govern, guide, monitor, oversee, supervise, and comply) and the managerial role of management (manage the day-to-day business of the corporation). Second, establish effective support mechanisms to assist the Board in fulfilling its functions properly. This would include Board committees (appointment, remuneration, audit, risk management, shareholders, and so on) and the company secretary. Third, establish effective statutory provisions in corporation law, banking law, capital markets, and auditing and accounting standards. Fourth, establish effective regulators in corporation law and capital markets. Fifth, establish effective codes of practice that apply the "comply or explain principle" (Du Plessis et al. 2015).

In addition, it would be beneficial to promote a vigilant and well-informed external environment comprising the media, universities, institutes of company directors, institutes of management, pension funds and fund managers, and a responsive public service. The external environment should have the ability to identify, discuss, and deal with any major risk that can have a detrimental effect on the economy and the share market.[7]

8.1.4 *Structures*

There are two dominant governance models that are used across the globe. The first is known as the Unitary Board, mostly adopted in the United Kingdom, the United States, and other English-speaking countries. The second model is the Dual Supervisory Board model, which is adopted in Germany and other European countries. Some countries adopt both models.

The Unitary Board model is a simple model. In this model, the shareholders elect the Board, which, in turn, appoints the company's CEO. The Board is ultimately accountable for the company's performance. To this end, the board is expected to develop the company's strategy (in cooperation with management), approve the budget and major capital works, ensure that effective governance processes are in place, including appropriate risk management and compliance policies and procedures, oversee remuneration policies, monitor the disclosure requirements, and have a regular reporting framework in place to monitor management's performance. The board is responsible for providing accurate annual reporting to shareholders. The board is usually led by an independent Chair. The board appoints independent directors and makes use of board sub-committees to fulfil its function of direction and control of the company on behalf of shareholders. It is good practice to have independent directors to chair board sub-committees. The board appoints internal and external auditors. It is expected that auditors are not engaged to provide consultancy services, as this constitutes a conflict of interest.

In a Unitary Board, the role of the CEO is to implement the company's strategy. To fulfil this function, the CEO appoints suitable staff to implement the strategic plan and is required to report regularly to the Board. When reporting to the board, the CEO, and senior management, must demonstrate how the company is achieving performance in alignment with the approved company strategy, in compliance with the law, and that it is operating within an acceptable level of risk. The Board is expected to oversee and support the CEO by ensuring that the CEO has adequate resources to implement the company strategy. Usually, the CEO makes decisions, and the board holds the CEO to account. The Board reserve the right to approve major decisions and major expenditures (Cadbury 1992, AICD 2010, Bevir 2012, ASX 2019).

The second corporate governance model is the two-tier Supervisory Board model. This model was introduced in Germany in 1861, after it had been introduced in the Netherlands. It is widely used in Europe and Japan. What follows is a description of the German model, as defined in the German Corporate Governance Code (the Code). This Model comprises a Supervisory Board and a Management Board. The Management Board is responsible for managing the enterprise; developing the business strategy, coordinating it with the Supervisory Board and ensuring its implementation; establishing appropriate risk and compliance management system; keeping the Supervisory Board informed; and considering women's representation and economic, social and sustainable goals when developing the business plan (Regierungskommission 2022).

The Supervisory Board appoints and supervises the Management Board. More specifically, the Supervisory Board may give advice to management and is expected to be involved in major decisions; comprises entirely non-executive directors; establishes various committees, including the audit committee to supervise the Management Board; appoints the external auditors; develops the executive remuneration policy and criteria; and it monitors and evaluates management's performance. The Supervisory Board, as well as management, are legally required to make a Declaration of Compliance with the Code (Regierungskommission 2022). It is important to note that the Supervisory Board cannot make decisions and cannot give formal orders to management. Even in a crisis, it is expected to monitor and advise the Management Board. The Supervisory Board, as it operates in Germany, is more removed from the process compared to a Board that operates in the United States (Deloitte 2021).

The other body that should also be mentioned is the general meeting of shareholders. This body elects shareholder representatives to the Supervisory Board. In companies with over 500 employees, up to 50 per cent of the Supervisory Board members are chosen by employees and their unions. The general meeting also approves the remuneration report and the resolution on the appropriation of profit, approves amendments to the Articles of Association, and deals with take-over offers (Regierungskommission 2022).

There are some variations to these two board structures. In the United States, the CEO can also be the chair of the board. In Denmark, the Unitary Board fully comprises non-executive board members, whereas in the United Kingdom, only the majority of members are required to be independent members. In Nordic countries, shareholders and the Annual General Meeting (AGM) seem to have more power than other models. For instance, the AGM appoints the external auditors who represent the interests of shareholders when reviewing the board and management practices; major shareholders are members of the nomination committee; and generally, 5–10 per cent of shareholders can request an extraordinary meeting or require a minimum dividend to be paid out. In addition, depending on the jurisdiction, 10–25 per cent of shareholders can request the public authority to appoint a special investigator whose findings are reported at the AGM (Lekvall et al. 2014).

8.1.5 *Defining Corporate Governance*

Corporate governance consists of many layers that include a board, management, shareholders, and a variety of stakeholders. There are policies, procedures, and processes that guide decision-making. There are Boards and corporate organisational structures with defined roles and responsibilities. There are laws, regulations, and oversight bodies. Companies need to perform in competition with other companies within the rules of a market economy. There are views on the overall purpose of a corporation: whether it is there to maximise profits or to operate in a way that considers the interests of all stakeholders.

There are many definitions of corporate governance, but two views stand out. One view focusses on corporate governance as a decision-making process, whilst the other focusses on a broader definition that includes stakeholders, responsible behaviour, and sustainable development. Here are two definitions that reflect these two approaches:

- Corporate governance describes "the framework of rules, relationships, systems and processes, within and by which authority is exercised and controlled within corporations. It encompasses the mechanisms by which companies, and those in control, are held to account" (ASX 2019).[8]

- [Corporate governance is] … the system of regulating and overseeing corporate conduct and of balancing the interests of all internal stakeholders and other parties (external shareholders, governments, and local communities) who can be affected by the corporate conduct, in order to ensure responsible behaviour by corporations and to create long-term, sustainable growth for the corporation.

  (Du Plessis et al. 2015)[9]

8.2 Cooperative Governance

The previous section discussed corporate governance from a conventional company perspective. This section analyses how cooperatives have engaged with the concept of cooperative governance over time. Three distinct historical phases define how the cooperative movement, nation States, and academia have engaged and debated cooperative governance. In the first phase, from the 1830s to 1945, cooperative governance focussed on defining the cooperative identity and promoting sustainable economic development. The second phase, from 1945 to 1990, discusses how cooperatives focussed on growing organically via mergers or acquisitions and how this strategy influenced cooperative identity and governance. The third phase, from 1990 until the present, is the corporatisation phase, with cooperatives attracting external capital and adopting dual structures to compete in the market. Cooperatives also experienced failures and scandals from 1945, and just like the private sector's experience, they led to cooperative governance reviews and subsequent recommendations.

8.2.1 Phase 1—Identity[10]

The first period, 1830–1945, consists of cooperative members finding a way to raise finance, promoting democratic management, preventing cooperative degeneration, preventing demutualisation, and promoting inter-generational wealth. To this end, Buchez promoted worker cooperatives that allowed open membership and democratic management based on the principle of one-person-one-vote, paid market wages, and held indivisible reserves. The Rochdale Model of 1844 added the principle of limited return on capital to 5 per cent, it required shares to be sold back to the cooperative and limited the number of shares held by each member to 100. Importantly, Rochdale also introduced cash trading only, the payment of quarterly dividends on purchases (patronage refund), and the devolution of 2 per cent to educational activities. Germany's people's banks and rural banks also promoted democratic management. However, the people's banks paid high dividends, but rural banks did not pay dividends and practised the concept of indivisibility of reserves and assets. The worker cooperative model in Italy after 1889 required workers to account for the majority of members, capital remuneration was fixed at 5 per cent, and the surplus had to be distributed according to work performed. The 1911 *Wisconsin Cooperative Law*, and later the Federal *Capper and Volstead Act* of 1922, required cooperatives to apply the principle of one-person-one-vote; limit capital remuneration to 8 per cent per annum, and require at least 50 per cent of cooperative transactions to be with members. The *Wisconsin Act* also required cooperatives to deposit 5 per cent of profits to an educational fund and to provide patronage rebates to members based on the surplus generated from transactions with members.

The governance structures at the cooperative and second-tier-level cooperatives included the GA, a Board of Directors, sub-committees, management, oversight, and reporting requirements. Rochdale governance included members electing the Board. The Board appointed and held store managers to account at its quarterly meetings. The Board appointed auditors and introduced a conflict resolution process. The German banks had already elected a Supervisory Board and a Management Board. The GA set a credit limit. The Management Board applied the GA's policies and directions. The Supervisory Board conducted quarterly performance and accounts reviews. The German rural banks and the Desjardins Bank expected managers and board members to work on a voluntary basis.

Cooperatives also extended democratic governance practices to second-tier cooperatives. The consumer cooperatives elected the 12-member board of the Cooperative Wholesale Society (CWS). The CWS Board appointed the general manager of operations and other financial administrators. It established four sub-committees (finance, drapery, grocery, productive operations) and required managers for each line of business to report to these sub-committees. The German Banking Federation provided annual auditing services to their members. The democratic model of the Swedish Central Consumer Cooperative Association (KF) was based on cooperative representatives elected from 18 electoral districts to the KF Congress.

In the United Kingdom, the governance debate raised the possibility of worker cooperatives having a tendency to degenerate. In response to many worker cooperative failures, Beatrice Webb's concluded that worker cooperatives failed because of inefficient management, an undisciplined workforce, and reluctance towards industrial change. Sydney and Beatrice Webb disapproved of worker cooperatives because they benefited only their members, exploited non-members, and cut wages to compete in the market. This explanation became known as the 'degeneration thesis' (Webb and Webb 1914, Thornley 1981, Webster 2012).

These early approaches to cooperative governance included policies on membership, profit distribution, limited capital remuneration, indivisibility of reserves, and a democratically elected Board. The 1937 International Cooperative Alliance (ICA) Cooperative Principles[11] reflected these cooperative policies and paved the way for establishing sustainable, democratically managed cooperatives whose focus was to serve current and future members. This emerging cooperative enterprise model was a different model from that adopted by capitalist firms. In capitalist firms, control was based on capital ownership, capital remuneration was unlimited, and profit distribution was designed to benefit current shareholders.

The governance structures indicate that some cooperatives were becoming professionally managed organisations (Boards, sub-committees, professional managers, appropriate oversight, and ownership of subsidiaries). Some other cooperatives relied on directors to work on a voluntary basis. The issue of degeneration was not a unique experience in one location; it would resurface again in the future. It is worth pointing out that in this period, cooperative growth was generally based on organic growth and the support from second-tier cooperatives that allowed individual cooperatives to achieve economies of scale. This was about to change with the rise of larger cooperatives and more centralised cooperative sectors.

8.2.2 Phase 2—Concentration[12]

From 1945 to 1990, cooperatives competed against large corporations in more competitive national, regional and world markets. In doing so, cooperatives grew across all sectors via organic growth, mergers, and acquisitions, and by attracting more internal and external capital. Fewer cooperatives dominated their respective cooperative sectors. Worker cooperatives in Italy and Spain employed thousands of employees.

To facilitate growth, cooperatives also found new ways to attract external capital. Some cooperatives chose to become joint stock companies so that they could attract external capital. Other cooperatives began to form separate holding companies through which they owned conventional subsidiaries. The German cooperative law removed any restriction on the amount of dividend or interest paid on share capital. Also, it allowed the cooperative to allocate a portion of the reserve funds to departing members (Münkner 2013).

This period also marked the failures or decline of many consumer cooperative movements. The cooperative sectors of the Netherlands, Belgium, France, Austria and Germany had either collapsed or reduced to holding a limited share of the retail market. Britain and Sweden, two of the leading consumer cooperative movements, experienced a decline in market share. Research conducted in France and Germany revealed inept or over-powerful management, low member participation, and non-payment of the dividend. There were also a number of incidents of fraud and corruption. In addition, State-led cooperative reviews concluded that cooperatives in India had been politicised, whilst, in Tanzania, cooperatives could not guarantee their democratic nature and contribution to the economy. Both countries suggested more government involvement in the governance of cooperatives.

The Laidlaw report, *Cooperatives in the Year 2000*, presented at the ICA conference of 1980 held in Moscow, described with clarity the governance issues faced by cooperatives. He found that the international cooperative movement faced a credibility crisis and a managerial crisis, and that cooperatives were behaving like capitalist businesses. More specifically, he stated that cooperatives operated industrial relations systems just like conventional businesses; in large cooperatives, member apathy and weak democratic management practices were a key concern; and that management began to exert more control in large cooperatives that operated with a complex business model (Laidlaw 1980). At the 1988 ICA congress held in Sweden, the ICA president, Lars Marcus, emphasised that Capitalism was influencing cooperatives and their subsidiaries. He was concerned with the decline of member participation and democratic practices, as well as the lack of co-operative international institutions and the weakness of cooperative national movements (MacPherson 2012).

The cooperative movement responded positively to Laidlaw's findings. In 1995, the ICA adopted the ICA *Statement on Co-operative Identity* and added principles four (autonomy and independence) and seven (concern for community). Cooperative movements also enhanced their democratic practices. For instance, the Japanese consumer cooperative members participated in district committees, in consumer panels, and in developing coop-label products (Kurimoto 2017, 2020). The larger worker cooperatives in Italy established branches in many locations and convened the workers' assembly many times during the year to discuss key issues (Holmstrom 1989). In Mondragon, cooperatives established the Social Council, a representative body of members and non-members to counterbalance the managerial focus of the Board and management. It provided input into matters relating to pay and conditions, health and safety, and work activities, and was consulted on all major issues (Morrison 1991).

During this period, cooperatives introduced new governance structures at the cooperative level and the cooperative network level. Individual cooperatives developed dual structures whereby a cooperative would own a holding company which owned subsidiaries. This added another layer of complexity to the traditional cooperative model. At the network level, Mondragon and the Lega Nazionale delle Cooperative e Mutue (LNCM)[13] established governance models that enabled them to make binding decisions on independent cooperatives. Mondragon's decision-making process included the Cooperative Bank's lending policies, the binding Contract of Association, and regular financial monitoring; inter-locking directorships; cooperative support structures; a common history; and a culture of solidarity. LNCM's Central Association was able to make binding decisions because cooperatives held a common vision on the economy and society; the large cooperatives and consortia were involved in LNCM's decision-making process; interlocking directorships throughout the organisation facilitated decision-making; the Socialist/Communist egalitarian values and traditions encouraged cooperation across all sectors; it provided effective support structures; and cooperatives operated within an accepted culture that promoted solidarity and equality.[14]

8.2.3 *Phase 3—Corporatisation*[15,16]

The third phase of cooperative governance commenced in the 1990s. From the 1990s until today, the need to compete in a global economy led many large cooperatives to embrace corporate legal structures so that they could attract capital, grow via acquisitions, and expand into international markets. As a result, the cooperative movement had to deal with isomorphism (cooperatives looking similar to private enterprises), degeneration, and demutualisation. Like the private sector, it had to deal with bankruptcies and scandals. Furthermore, just like the private sector, it promoted governance reviews and debates to identify issues and propose solutions.

In the 1990s, cooperatives developed into large, complex, international enterprises. Arla Dairy cooperative controlled 90 per cent of the Danish Dairy market. The manufacturing cooperatives from Italy and Mondragon controlled subsidiaries in many countries that included thousands of employees who were not members. Credit Agricole listed some of its shares on the stock market. Rabobank centralised all operations, and previously autonomous cooperative banks were converted into local branches. It is estimated that 60 per cent of the largest cooperatives were attracting external capital (Andrews 2015). Some cooperatives began to use the joint stock company structure to attract capital. Other cooperatives used the holding company structure. Others still listed tradeable bonds accessible to non-members.

The large size and complex nature of these cooperative's operations led to a series of governance issues. The major issue was that in large, complex organisations, management captured or dominated the decision-making process. Information and technical asymmetry meant that neither Board members, nor the GA, were able to question management proposals. Member apathy and the directors' level of competency meant members could not monitor or question management's proposals. Management's lack of cooperative background led to the prioritisation of economic growth rather than economic democracy. The neo-liberal political and ideological environment that favoured individualism and profit maximisation promoted the prioritisation of economic matters.

This state of affairs opened the possibility for a number of concerning scenarios. For instance:

- In scenario one, cooperatives could achieve growth but lose their identity because they behave like private enterprises. Key features in this scenario would be that most customers or employees may be non-members, the focus is on growth, on policies to increase salary differentials, and on policies to increase management's salaries to match market salaries.
- In scenario two, bad unchecked decisions from management could ultimately lead to failure and bankruptcy. Bad decisions led cooperatives to a weaker financial position and unable to provide competitive services. In these cases, members could leave the cooperative, which would lead to less member capital and a smaller market. Eventually, this process will lead to bankruptcy.
- In scenario three, cooperative growth could lead to cooperative degeneration. This may take place when management makes decisions without being challenged by the Board or the GA; the member participation rate is low; non-member trading exceeds member trading; and non-members exceed worker-members in a worker cooperative. It happens when cooperatives focus on profits.

- In scenario four, cooperatives could demutualise. In this scenario, management captures the decision-making process, a hostile neo-liberal environment encourages privatisation, government laws facilitate demutualisation, and consultants suggest converting to an investor-owned company. All these events may unfold whilst the cooperative is led by an ineffective Board and a passive membership that cannot prevent demutualisation (Battilani and Schroter 2012, Fulton and Girard 2015, Kasmir 2016, Ammirato 2018, Basterretxea, Cornforth and Heras-Saizarbitoria 2020).

In the 1990s, cooperatives also had their share of bankruptcies and scandals. The United Kingdom's Cooperative Bank failed after it accumulated debts of 1.5 billion pound sterling, and the Cooperative Group was in no financial position to save it. The Austrian Central Cooperative Bank was bailed out by the Austrian Government, which took a 43 per cent stake in the bank. Rabobank and Credit Agricole were fined by regulators for irregularities. Rabobank was involved in rate fixing and was fined by regulators in the United Kingdom, the United States, and the Netherlands. The Canadian Coop Atlantic collapsed in 2015. The Japanese Norin Chukin Bank lost money through investments in sub-prime mortgages (Birchall 2017). Large Italian construction cooperatives found it difficult to survive in the 1990s after the government cut public works spending. They filed for bankruptcy after losing all their inter-generational assets (Ammirato 2018). Mondragon's Fagor Electrodomésticos filed for bankruptcy in 2013 after accumulating unpayable debts following overseas expansion (Basterretxea, Cornforth and Heras-Saizarbitoria 2020).

The ICA conducted governance reviews to understand the organisational changes taking place. Sven Ake Book produced the *Cooperatives in a Changing World* Report tabled at the ICA Congress, held in October 1992 in Japan. The Report highlighted that democracy was problematic, that democratic participation should include employees, and that the tendency to make members' shares reflect the value of the cooperative deviated from cooperative principles. Book also suggested that the cooperative movement should study the advantages and disadvantages of cooperative transformation into joint-stock companies (Book 1992). ICA Europe released a report on corporate governance in 1995. It confirmed the previous findings from the *Laidlaw Report* of 1980 and the *Book Report* of 1992. It found corporate governance problems of mismanagement, financial scandals, poor management control, member apathy, and failure of democracy as directors and members were not able to exert their authority over management. The report, however, also noted that cooperatives were actively trying to encourage participation, including organising meetings near housing complexes, holding shop meetings, holding district meetings, organising study circles, organising debate evenings, holding consumer forums, or women's guilds, as well as cultural activities. The report found that members were informed via newsletters, annual reports, social reports, press releases, films, and television spots. The Report concluded that despite these activities, members still had a poor knowledge of cooperation and had not revitalised their interest in their cooperative societies (Volkers and Lees 1995).

Ivano Barberini, the ICA President, was very concerned that cooperatives were copying capitalist firms and losing their social function. He noted that cooperatives faced a crisis when they failed to manage change and, at the same time, copied the practices of capitalist enterprises. This led cooperatives to focus on profits and losing their social function. He suggested that Boards needed to be aware that their role is to preserve cooperative ideals and ensure cooperative practices align with cooperative values. To

Barberini, managers need to have technical knowledge as well as be able to understand and implement the cooperative mission. He is adamant that cooperatives should put in place control systems that limit the power of management, encourage participation by members, and measure the level of alignment between the cooperative mission and the cooperative practice (Barberini 2009).

A number of national cooperative associations concerned with the changes taking place conducted governance reviews. LCNM began discussing governance matters in the 1980s. It produced key governance guidelines in 2008 and participation guidelines in 2012. Guidelines focussed on cooperative autonomy, education and training, information, participation, cooperative groups, oversight practices, and internal governance. Key suggestions included separating the role of the Board (direction and control) with the role of management (operational responsibilities), electing independent directors, promoting a stakeholder model, limiting mandates for Board members, succession planning for Board members, and reducing the appointment of directors to other Boards (Legacoop 2008, Zarri and Badiali 2012, Ammirato 2018).[17] In 2003, Mondragon recognised a general decline in democratic control and the need to revitalise essential aspects of the Mondragon experience. It has focussed on participation, inter-cooperative cooperation, cooperative training and education, the role of cooperatives in promoting positive social change and expanding democratic management to cooperative subsidiaries (Bretos, Errasti and Marcuello 2019). The Cooperative Group in the United Kingdom commissioned Myners (2004) to conduct an independent governance review following the collapse of the Cooperative Bank. Myners found that there were inadequate collective capabilities and experience, there was a failure to understand the distinctive governance role of the Board (directors acted as delegates and not as independent representatives); the business strategy and the social agenda were disconnected; and it had an excessively complicated structure. Overall the governance arrangements were not fit for purpose. He suggested that individual members elect directors directly, appoint independent directors to the Board, establish a competency-based Board, and elect a 100-member Council as a consultative body and guardian of cooperative values. He also suggested establishing a nomination committee that included two members from the Council (Myners 2014). Coop Canada also commissioned a study on demutualisation in 2015. It found that key patterns leading to demutualisation included poor financial performance, poor capital planning and administration, member disengagement, and pressure from management and external advisors seeking significant financial benefits from demutualisation (Fulton and Girard 2015). Cooperatives UK commissioned Birchall to review the governance arrangements of the 60 large cooperatives. He found that large cooperatives were more complex and more difficult to govern. Their members were disengaged, their directors found it difficult to control management, and they did not focus on the needs of members. On the positive side, he found that cooperatives appointed independent directors and used nomination and governance committees, member councils, and expert advisory committees (Birchall 2017).

Academia began to take a greater interest in cooperative governance. In the late 1980s, cooperative studies by Whyte and Whyte (on Mondragon) and Zan and Holmstrom (on Imola cooperatives) considered the complexities of cooperative governance and approaches to self-management. They described the decision-making process and acknowledged that cooperatives faced governance difficulties but generally noted the cooperative's capacity to manage change and to find a balanced approach in dealing with economic and social issues (Zan 1987, Whyte and Whyte 1988, Holmstrom 1989).

More recent studies questioned whether the traditional cooperative governance model was appropriate for managing modern cooperatives. Spear noted members' apathy and the excessive power of management. The latter's power was most concerning since they could act without any external oversight, unlike managers of corporations who dealt with the external oversight function performed by the market. Spear suggested implementing countervailing measures on managerial powers such as competent Boards, professional management development, good practice guides, effective incentives (good pay), and better reporting (Spear 2004). Ricciardi found that whilst cooperatives encouraged participation, provided sufficient information, provided good working conditions, and developed formal induction programmes; power was concentrated in a few hands (the Chair of the Board and Board members also held executive positions), that members were passive, and that there were no succession plans (Ricciardi 2014). Cornforth explored in depth the relations between the Board and management and suggested appropriate practices for management and the CEOs to engage with and to support cooperative Boards (Cornforth 2015). A more recent study on the Fagor Electrodomésticos S. Coop collapse of 2013 found that the governance arrangements and the decision-making culture that prevailed between Fagor's GA, the Governing Council (The Board), and the Social Council were not suited to governing a multinational cooperative. They found there was a lack of competency, constant inaction, CEOs were readily removed after a period of bad results, and that the Social Council and the GA did not understand management's suggestions, or the decisions that were being taken. In addition, there was not a clear separation of duties between the three structures. The authors concluded that direct democracy exercised via the GA and the Social Council was inappropriate for governing a multi-national cooperative with 10,000 employees (Basterretxea, Cornforth and Heras-Saizarbitoria 2020).

The large cooperatives today, especially those operating in international markets with subsidiaries or their own branches, have adopted legal structures that resemble those of private enterprises. They have begun to separate the board from management, appoint independent directors, use Board sub-committees, formally adopt risk management practices, and operate at such speed that they often neglect the internal decision-making processes. In parallel to these evolutions, cooperatives have established member councils, Social Councils, internal committees with various responsibilities, and various information and educational activities to promote cooperative values. These changes will be discussed more in the next two sections on structures and risks.

8.2.4 *Summary*

The evolution of cooperative governance practices reflects the evolution of the cooperative enterprise and its endeavour to fulfil its economic and social goals. In doing so, cooperative governance is required to uphold cooperative principles whilst competing in the market. In their quest to compete in global markets, cooperatives have used some conventional approaches to raise finance and conventional legal structures to facilitate equity raising and cooperative growth. Various governance reviews conducted by the ICA, cooperative movements, and academics since the 1980s have identified the development of large cooperatives, management capture, member apathy, ineffective Boards, and influential external environments as reasons for the weakening of democratic values, of lower member participation, of forms of degeneration, and of demutualisation. These reviews have offered governance reforms that combine the governance structures adopted by conventional companies, augmented by cooperative-specific forms of democratic participation, democratic consultation, and democratic decision-making structures and processes. Governance structure reforms have included the separation of ownership and management, competency-based boards, the use of independent directors, the use of Board sub-committees, and better pay for managers and board members. Reforms designed to promote democratic participation included the formation of cooperative consultative councils supported by sub-committees, committees at the local level, Social Councils as was the case of Mondragon, Works Councils in Nordic countries, employee representatives (co-determination policies), decentralised cooperative branches, convening the GA multiple times to discuss key issues, and improved forms of communication and information. The next section will further explore the variety of approaches to cooperative governance.

8.3 Governance Structures

Cooperative use a variety of governance structures that suit the culture, size, and complexity of their operations. We could safely assume that direct democracy is most likely practised in small cooperatives, and that representative democracy is practised in larger cooperatives. We could also say that the trend is towards having governance structures that clearly separate ownership from management. This section describes six cooperative governance models. The first four governance models cover traditional cooperative governance arrangements for small and large cooperatives. The fifth model is the dual structure model, which allows individual cooperatives to own a holding company or conventional firms directly. The sixth model is that of the Mondragon Corporation because it is a governance model for a network of enterprises with a set of unique policies and procedures.

8.3.1 One-tier Model

The first governance model is a one-tier cooperative governance model. This model comprises the General Assembly (GA) as its only governing body. All members participate in the GA and make decisions based on direct democracy. It is suitable for small cooperatives, usually employing up to 20 members. Cooperatives that adopt this model make decisions collegially. The GA may appoint a cooperative representative and an auditor to audit its financial statements. In these cooperatives, every member is generally well-informed and is accustomed to participating in the decision-making process. All jurisdictions may adopt this model.

8.3.2 Tri-partite Model[18]

The second cooperative governance model is a mixture of direct and representative democracy. It is called the tri-partite model because powers are divided between the GA, the Board of Directors, and a Supervisory Committee. This model is suited for larger cooperatives. In this model, The GA appoints the Board of Directors, which also has executive management powers. The GA also appoints a Supervisory Committee that performs an oversight function over the operations of the Board on behalf of the GA. More specifically:

- The GA appoints both the Board of Directors and the Supervisory Committee. The GA approves the annual budget, policies and procedures. It decides how to distribute

profits, the annual dividend amount, and the annual patronage refund. It has the final say on membership matters. It appoints the external auditor directly or via the supervisory body; approves changes to the by-laws; and makes key decisions such as mergers, acquisitions, or international investments. In some cooperatives, the GA meets many times a year to discuss key issues and economic performance.
- The Board of Directors is elected by the GA. It also operates as a Management Board. As such, it may select a CEO among its board members, or it may select an executive committee which comprised Board members and professional managers. The CEO may also be the Chair of the Board. Usually, there is no separation of ownership and management in this model. Its role is to implement the strategic plan approved at the AGA. Some jurisdictions allow the board to include independent members, but others require only cooperative members. The board is required to report to the Annual GA and Supervisory Committee as requested.
- The Supervisory Committee is elected by the GA and reports to the GA. It can perform a minimum or a comprehensive set of functions. At a minimum, this body has financial oversight like an audit committee. A more comprehensive role would include oversight over the financial performance, the compliance programme, and membership-related matters; the appointment of the external auditor; dealing with complaints against management; and monitoring and reporting on compliance with cooperative principles. This body is not involved in the decision-making process. It reports directly to the GA (Bonfante 2011, Genco and Vella 2011, Fici 2013, Ammirato 2018).

There are variations to the above model. Uruguay and Argentina do not admit non-members as directors. The external auditors are appointed by the Supervisory Committee in Italy, the cooperative federation in Uruguay, and the GA in other countries. In countries that adopt co-determination policies and parts of Spain, the board will have to include employee representatives in cooperatives employing at least 30 employees.[19] Mondragon cooperatives use the Social Council to deal with industrial relations matters and be involved in the decision-making process. Works Councils representing employees are used in the Netherlands (Cracogna 2013, Fici 2013, Garcia 2013, Lavega 2013, Namorado 2013, Kutko 2021).

8.3.3 Two-Tier—Supervisory Board Model

The third cooperative governance model is the two-tier model, also known as the dualistic model and the German model. The key feature of this model is having a Supervisory Board that elects and controls the Management Board.[20] The Supervisory Board performs a more authoritative role than the Supervisory Committee of the tri-partite model. In Germany, the Annual GA elects a Supervisory Board and retains the authority to change the by-laws, to decide on annual returns and allocation of profits, and to decide on mergers and conversions. The role of the Supervisory Board is to appoint the Management Board and to perform an oversight function on behalf of the GA. Its directors cannot hold any management functions. Instead, it liaises with management and monitors their performance and compliance programme. It advises management if deemed appropriate but cannot make decisions. The Management Board may include members or professional managers; it may appoint management sub-committees; and is responsible for preparing the strategic plan, business plan, implementation plan, and risk and compliance programme (Münkner 2013, 2020).

In Germany, member control is mostly exercised via the Supervisory Board, whilst the GA is involved in major decisions and approves changes to the by-laws. Members with serious concerns about the cooperative management have the right to call a GA meeting if 10 per cent of members support such action. In addition, the German Cooperative Auditing Federation is legally required to audit large cooperatives every year and small cooperatives every two years. These audit reviews focus on auditing financial accounts and compliance with cooperative law (Münkner 2013).

There are variations to the German model. Rabobank, for instance, whilst it has centralised all operations and adopted this two-tier governance model, it has also maintained forms of member participation. Rabobank's 2.1 million members elect their representatives via 85 Local Member Councils. These Councils have the authority to monitor local bank branches and to elect their Chair to the General Member Council (GMC). The GMC has 85 members who elect the Supervisory Board, amend the by-laws, and approve major company decisions. The GMC acts as the custodian of Rabobank's values and identity. In doing so, it meets two times a year and has established five subcommittees[21] to help evaluate the governance and strategic principles. In accordance with Dutch law, Rabobank also has a Works Council representing employees, which is consulted on major decisions (Rabobank 2021a). In Rabobank's model, The AGM elects the Supervisory Board, which, in turn, elects the Management Board. The Supervisory Board has oversight over the performance, risk management, and compliance programme. It performs these duties by appointing the company auditors and by establishing a number of sub-committees, including the Risk Committee, Audit Committee, the Committee on Cooperative Affairs, the Remuneration Committee, the Human Resources Committee, and the Appointments Committee. The Management Board is led by the CEO and supported by professionals who effectively manage the company, including having full authority over Rabobank's subsidiaries and overseas offices (van der Sangen 2013, Rabobank 2021a, 2021b).

The major change from the one-tier and the tri-partite models to the two-tiered German Model is that there is a clear separation of roles between non-executives forming the Supervisory Board, and executives in the German Model that manage the Management Board. In the one-tier and tri-partite models, these roles co-existed. Secondly, there has been a transfer of power from the GA to the Supervisory Board, which has been given the responsibility to appoint the Management Board and supervise it via sub-committees and external auditors. The fourth model is the Unitary Board Model. This model transfers most powers to the Board of Directors, which has the authority to direct and control the enterprise and is responsible for its performance and conformance requirements.

8.3.4 *The Unitary Board Model*

The fourth cooperative governance model is called a Unitary Board because almost all powers are delegated to the Board of Directors. In this model, the Board provides direction and exercises control of the cooperative. It appoints the CEO. It provides direction by approving the strategic plan, business plans, and risk management plans. It keeps control by appointing an external auditor, by regularly monitoring the CEO and management's performance, and by regularly reviewing risk and compliance reports. The Board appoints sub-committees, such as an audit committee, risk committee, governance committee, and remuneration committee, to monitor cooperative activities. The CEO appoints a management team to implement the cooperative strategic plan. It is clear that the supervisory functions held by the GA and the Supervisory Committee, or by the Supervisory Council as per the previous model, are now held by the Board of Directors.

There are some governance variations to Unitary Boards. Arla members elect a Board of Representatives from four areas (Sweden, Denmark, Central Europe, and the United Kingdom). It has 175 members, including 12 employee representatives. The Board of Representatives and employees appoint a non-executive Board of Directors. The Board appoints the Executive Management responsible for implementing the cooperative's strategic plan and reporting to the Board (Arla Foods 2021). In the United Kingdom, the Cooperative Group members appoint a 100 Members' Council, which appoints four directors to the board, whilst the Board's Nomination Sub-committee proposes the remaining directors. The Board also includes the CEO and the Chief Financial Officer, whereas Arla appointed only non-executive directors. The 100 Members' Council sees its role as protecting the cooperative purpose, values and principles. A stakeholder working group arranges forums with directors, management, and council members to discuss key issues (Co-operative Group Limited 2022).

Fonterra's Board of Directors is elected by shareholders, of whom 60 per cent must be farmers. It has a plural voting system based on one vote per every 1,000 kilograms of milk solids sold to the cooperative. Fonterra has a traditional Unitary Board comprising 11 directors, of which seven are elected by shareholders, and four are competency-based Board nominees. Fonterra has introduced a 25 Member Shareholders' Advisory Council that is democratically elected by members. The Council reviews strategic plans, comments on quarterly reports, conducts training for directors, and it also appoints a Milk Commissioner in consultation with the Minister to deal with disputes arising between farmers and management (Fonterra 2022). In accordance with the cooperative law, directors have to make a declaration that Fonterra has been operating as a cooperative company. Thus alongside a traditional Unitary Board that transfers almost all powers to the Board of Directors, each cooperative has added an advisory body or representative body to engage with members and the Board.

8.3.5 Dual Structures Model

The fifth cooperative governance model is the Dual Structure Model. In this model, a cooperative enterprise competes in the market via owning or controlling subsidiaries that operate as conventional businesses. In this dual structure model, the cooperative is governed via any of the first four governance models described above, whilst the subsidiaries operate as conventional enterprises. These subsidiaries can be owned directly by the cooperative and governed by one of its managers or can be owned via a cooperative-owned (or majority-owned) holding company. The cooperative may also own many holding companies. The profits made from these subsidiaries form part of a cooperative's consolidated financial statement and are dispensed in accordance with cooperative law. In other words, rules regarding limited return on capital, deposits to indivisible reserves, payment of dividends according to transactions with the cooperative, and indivisibility of reserves and assets would apply [22]

8.3.6 Network Governance Model

The Sixth model is called a Network Governance Model. This model is used by the Mondragon Cooperative Corporation (MCC). The MCC has created a unique model in that it operates as a corporation whilst its members are autonomous cooperatives free to

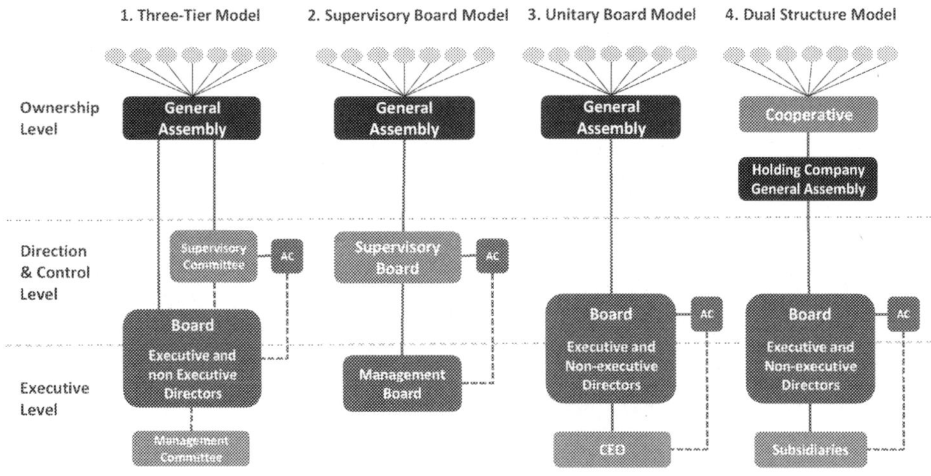

Figure 8.1 Cooperative Governance Structures

Source: Adapted from Huhtala and Jussila (2019).

join or exit MCC at any time. It is an integrated model that develops a common strategy and a common implementation plan that is then implemented by four divisions (industry, retail, finance, and knowledge), and over 95 cooperatives, which control 250 businesses. In 2020, the MCC employed almost 80,000 people, of whom over 14,000 work overseas. In 2020, MCC's total turnover amounted to 10.8 billion euros (Mondragon Corporation 2021).

The MCC's organisational structure comprises cooperatives, the Congress, a Standing Committee, and the General Council. The MCC Congress comprises 650 representatives elected by MCC cooperative members. It meets every four years, and its role is to approve the MCC strategy and MCC policies. The second body is the MCC Standing Committee (equivalent to a Board of Directors) which oversees strategy implementation. The members of the Standing Committee are elected by MCC's four divisions based on their share of membership. The third body, the General Council, is the executive management group responsible for implementing the strategy across the four industry divisions. It comprises a President and four vice presidents. Each vice president represents an MCC division. The first key feature to note is the level of interlocking directorships between cooperatives, their division, and MCC's key decision-making bodies. This ensures that decisions made have broad consensus, are understood, and have a good chance of being implemented.[23]

There are many policies and procedures that distinguish the MCC. These form a series of commitments by cooperatives and their members and agreed practices of inter-firm solidarity that improve competitiveness and manage change in a humane way. Key inter-firm solidarity mechanisms include:

- All cooperatives are members of the cooperative bank, which provides cooperatives with credit facilities as needed. In times of crisis, the bank can freeze payments or increase loans to facilitate change.[24]

- All cooperatives are members of Lagun-Aro, which provides employment insurance for Mondragon workers. It provides unemployment benefits, a pension on retirement, and support for members transferring to another cooperative.
- All cooperatives contribute to the Mondragon Inter-Cooperative Fund. Each year co-operatives contribute 10 per cent of profits to this fund, other than the Caja Laboral Bank, which contributes 20 per cent of its profits. This fund is managed by the Governing Council. It reviews each project before allocating funds for establishing new cooperatives, new developmental opportunities for existing cooperatives, and international investments.
- All cooperatives that make a profit, contribute 3 per cent to the Inter-Cooperative Compensation Fund managed centrally by the MCC. They also pool a portion of profits (15–45 per cent) at each divisional level. These funds are then redistributed across the cooperative members of each division according to their wage levels.
- Inter-firm employment support in times of crisis allows members from one cooperative to be transferred to another without losing their job.
- A support framework from cooperatives involved in the research and development and the University of Mondragon for the provision of training and research.
- All cooperatives support the Mondragon basic principles, which promote democracy, the sovereignty of labour over capital, education, wages solidarity, participation in management and open admission, inter-cooperation and social transformation (Bakaikoa, Errasti and Begiristain 2004, Bajo and Roelants 2011, Mondragon Corporation 2012, Barandiaran and Lezaun 2017, Mondragon Corporation 2021).

The MCC, through a democratic system of interlocking directorships, inter-firm solidarity mechanisms, and the management of the investment fund and the compensation fund, is able to provide strategic direction and an implementation process that enables it to operate as a quasi-corporation. The internationalisation strategy developed and implemented since the 1990s and how the Mondragon group managed the Global Financial Crisis (GFC) is evidence that this new governance model adds value to the Mondragon experience.

8.3.7 Summary

The cooperative governance structures have evolved in response to the need for cooperatives to compete in global markets, cooperative failures and malpractice, and the new corporate governance standards promoted via government law and industry codes. This has led cooperatives to develop more centralised decision-making structures. Power has shifted away from the GA and towards the Supervisory Boards, the Board of Directors, and management. The GA has delegated the supervisory powers to the Supervisory Board in the German model. It has also delegated the supervisory powers, as well as powers of direction and control, to the Unitary Board. Another trend is the strengthening of the competencies of the Supervisory Board and the Board of Directors vis-à-vis management. Supervisory Boards and Unitary Boards have achieved this by establishing sub-committees and appointing independent directors.

The governance models of one-tier, tri-partite governance models (and, to a lesser extent, the Supervisory Board model) have retained a greater level of direct decision-making powers. In these models, the GA retains powers over the cooperative by-laws, profit distribution, rebate remuneration, membership approval or dismissal, the direct appointment of the auditors or supervisory committees in some models, the appointment of member representative councils, and the right to decide on major matters such as acquisitions, mergers, or internationalisation of activities, and approval of the cooperative strategy.

The quest for being competitive whilst maintaining cooperative principles has also led to cooperatives operating within the Network Governance Model and the Dual Structure Model. The Network Governance Model is able to develop a united corporate strategy for the whole group allowing each cooperative to retain its tri-partite governance structures and autonomy. The Dual Structure Model allows cooperatives to retain their cooperative governance model and simultaneously own conventional companies either directly or via a holding company.

8.4 Issues and Risks

The discussion thus far has noted the evolution of corporate governance and cooperative governance and the six cooperative governance models. This section continues the discussion on governance by analysing nine key issues or risks[25] that, if not managed well, may prevent cooperatives from fulfilling their purpose and key objectives. The key issues that will be discussed include (i) balancing the needs of the enterprise and of the members; (ii) democratic deficit risks; (iii) the risk of cooperative degeneration by operating outside of cooperative principles; (iv) the risk of demutualisation when cooperatives decide to operate as capitalist enterprises; (v) the risks emanating from accessing external finance; (vi) the risk of operating within a hostile or indifferent external environment; vii) the risks emanating from cooperative diversity; (viii) the risks faced by the cooperatives operating alone; (ix) the risk of not reporting on cooperative principles and values.

8.4.1 Balancing Needs

Members form or join cooperatives because cooperatives can meet their particular need(s). These needs are unmet by the market or are needs that members consciously want to meet via a democratically managed cooperative. In order to meet their need, members must ensure that cooperatives are economically successful so they can provide them with a job, goods, or services that cannot be met on their own. In addition to meeting an essential need, cooperative members also receive a refund or bonus for being members of a cooperative. This distinctive feature of cooperative mutuality makes cooperatives different from private enterprises. To this end, cooperatives distribute members a dividend (consumer cooperatives), a patronage refund (agricultural cooperatives), or distribute a portion of the profits as bonus payments in a worker cooperative (Viviani 2013).

Balancing the distribution of profits in a way that meets the needs of the enterprise so it remains economically competitive and meets the needs of members is vital for the success of a cooperative. For instance, if 100 per cent of profits are distributed to members as refunds, there will be no funds for investment, which will jeopardise the cooperative's economic competitiveness. This will also lead to difficulty in attracting and retaining professional managers, marginalisation, or even bankruptcy. If 100 per cent is retained for investment, the needs of the enterprise and management will be met, and the long-term needs of current and future members will also be met. However, members' current expectations of receiving a refund for being an active member will not be met. This may lead to member apathy, non-participation at general meetings, less demand to become a member, less capital raising from new and existing members, limited generational change, and so on (Zanotti 2016). It may also lead to members considering themselves as employees and for Boards to operate as trustees just like the Boards of the Not-for-Profit sector (Birchall 2017).

A balanced approach would take care of current and future needs of members and potential members, and the current and future economic needs of the cooperative enterprise. This would require the cooperative law, or by-laws, and cooperatives' culture, to distribute profits appropriately. All the jurisdictions surveyed for this study provide cooperatives the opportunity to distribute profits to the indivisible reserve fund, and to members in the form of refunds and capital accounts remuneration. In some countries, the cooperative law prescribes the minimum and maximum amount that can distributed to indivisible reserves, to refunds, and for remuneration of capital accounts. In other jurisdictions the cooperative by-laws determine how to distribute profits.[26] Whatever approach is used, a balanced, approach to the distribution of profits must be found which will be able to meet the requirements of current and future members, and the economic needs of the cooperative enterprise. If a balanced approach is not found it will lead to the demise or the marginalisation of the cooperative.

8.4.2 *Democracy*

Cooperative members have chosen the principle of democratic decision-making to balance the needs of the enterprise and their immediate and long-term needs as members. It is accepted that small cooperatives (less than 20 members) adopt direct democracy via their GA to make decisions. It is also acknowledged that the larger cooperatives adopt representative democracy via a decision-making processes that includes the GA (with fewer powers than those held in small cooperatives), the Board, and management. Cooperative law allocates these bodies formal decision-making powers, with members always having the final say on key decisions via the GA. In spite of these legal requirements, a major risk for cooperatives is the likelihood that they can be effectively governed by management.

Cooperatives have experienced management accumulating more power from members and from the Board. This usually happens when members reduce their participation rate (apathy) in cooperative affairs whilst management has accumulated higher competencies compared to the Board, and the GA. The member participation rate may decline because members may not be aware of cooperative values; may not understand the operational complexity of large cooperatives; have made a low financial commitment (especially in consumer and credit cooperatives); feel that their participation will not make a difference; may be satisfied with the cooperative's performance and don't feel the need to participate; and because they may focus only on matters that impact job security, and pay and conditions. A low participation rate could be up to 1 per cent of total members in banks, up to 5–7 per cent in consumer cooperatives, and as low as 25 per cent in worker cooperatives. Management capture of the decision-making process is the result of management having higher qualifications, of information asymmetry, and because some cooperatives that operate in national and international markets may be led by non-professional Boards (Spear 2004, Birchall 2017).

Cooperatives manage the risk of management capture by having governance structures designed to simultaneously direct, appoint, and control management. These structures are fit for purpose when there is an alignment of intent between members, the Board, and management. Problems arise when management of large, complex cooperatives have more technical knowledge and expertise than cooperative members and the Board. In these cases, members and their Board do not have the knowledge and overall competencies to understand management's strategic suggestions. This state of affairs may result in management, with support of an acquiescent Board and a disengaged membership, to manage the cooperative as a trustee organisation (Birchall 2017). It may result in management, with support of consultants, and a weak Board, to propose demutualisation (Battilani and Schroter 2012). It may also result in poor decision-making leading to bankruptcy as the experience of Mondragon's Fagor has shown. In Fagor's case, cooperative members, via the GA, the Social Council, and their representatives on the Board, either accepted management's proposals without understanding their full consequences and risks, or delayed decisions that needed to be made, or disagreed with management's proposals to tackle financial and organisational problems that required imminent action (Basterretxea, Cornforth and Heras-Saizarbitoria 2020). Governance issues in Italy's construction companies resulted from having an entrenched management fully supported by members regardless of it not been able to manage change after the government reduced public works spending in the 1990s (Ammirato 2018).

The major risk for cooperatives is that if cooperative democracy is failing, it will result in an identity crisis, and ultimately it can lead to forms of degeneration, to demutualisation, and to bankruptcy. The cooperative movement has been aware of the 'democratic deficit' risk since at least Laidlaw's report in 1980 (Laidlaw 1980). In response, many cooperatives have taken practical steps to enhance democratic practices. These democratic practices have focussed on improving the level of awareness, of information, of the consultation process, of encouraging participation, and on developing better governance arrangements. Whilst not consistently applied throughout the sectors, many cooperatives provide induction programmes so members are aware of cooperative history and values. They also provide information on cooperative history and cooperative principles through their websites and annual reports. Information is supplied at the GA, at consultative committees, in newsletters, and at key events. Members are consulted through various consultative bodies such as the Social Council, members' councils, regional associations, mini-councils, specific committees, and during the budget planning process. Participation in decision-making is accessible via the powers retained in the GA. These powers include the powers to appoint and dismiss the Board, and the powers to make key decisions regarding membership, profit distribution, and mergers and acquisitions. Cooperatives have also developed governance structures that include independent directors with specialist skills, and board sub-committees that focus on key governance areas. As we have been observing throughout this study, cooperatives have simultaneously promoted professional boards and professional management with powers whilst maintaining or strengthening internal democracy to suit cooperative's governance arrangements. In all cases members always make key decisions via the powers reserved to the GA.

A key question that needs to be considered is whether democracy hinders cooperative growth. Is there a risk that direct democracy or forms of direct plus representative democracy prevents worker cooperatives from growing because the decision-making process is too slow? In France it was suggested that worker cooperatives should not employ more than 250 (FakhFakh, Perotin and Gago 2012). In Mondragon in the early 1980s, it was agreed that cooperatives should not grow beyond 500 members (Morrison 1991). Research in Italy in the 1980s indicated that even in cooperatives with less than 400 members, participation rates were low, except when discussing major issues. Holmstrom called it "Democracy by Exception" (Holmstrom 1989). A leader of a large manufacturing cooperative from Imola, which employed 84 workers in 1946, said that the decision-making process is slow; yet, the company today employs 4,000 employees of whom close to 400 are members (Hancock 2007, Sacmi 2021). Manutencoop, a large service cooperative from Bologna established in 1938, employed 11,000 employees whilst governed via a traditional tri-partite governance model. After 2003, it adopted a dual structure with the cooperative managing their business via a holding company, and subsequently increased its workforce to 20,000 employees by 2014 (Manutencoop 2014). It demutualised in 2022, citing that the cooperative form was a hindrance to growth? It now employs 28,000 employees (Bettazzi 2022). Further research along the lines conducted by Basterretxea et al. is required before this question can be answered fully (Basterretxea, Cornforth and Heras-Saizarbitoria 2020). One hypothesis could be that cooperatives have grown via making democratic decisions when members, the Board, and management are aligned, and members are informed to the point of being able to decide by balancing risks and rewards, and balancing the long-term and short-term needs of current and future members. Democratic decision-making becomes problematic when managers want to seize the opportunities offered by the market at a faster pace than allowed by members and their Board. But, is it really a problem if cooperatives that practice democratic decision-making take a little longer to grow compared to those that don't? If it is a problem, it is a problem for cooperative members or for management or for the cooperative enterprise?

The risk for cooperatives moving too fast without the legitimate consent of members leads to degeneration of the democratic process, management capture, and possibly demutualisation. Therefore, this risk could be managed by establishing a culture that promotes consensual growth within a cooperative, whereby

- Management promotes both economic efficiency and members' mutual goals (Barberini 2009).
- Management has the skills to explain how things should be done and how they could be improved; that change can take place in accordance with cooperative principles; the benefits and consequences of each proposal and decision to members; and encourage members to work together in alignment with cooperative principles, society's needs and stakeholders' needs (Viviani 2013).
- Management provides full support to the Board by helping structure the Board's work, provide timely information, raise awareness of key challenges and opportunities, assessing cooperative performance in compliance with cooperative principles and identity (Cornforth 2015).
- Cooperatives promote a culture of checks and balances, greater level of professionalism, and stakeholder engagements throughout the cooperative, and codes of practice that guide behaviours (Spear 2004).

Another key question is whether cooperative democracy should be just be left to members as a private affair or should it also be a matter of public concern, especially if cooperatives have a relatively strong presence in the economy? In the private sector, if large companies adopt unacceptable practices, the public, the media and eventually the government will intervene, possibly by establishing a Royal Commission. The public is also able to keep the government accountable. It keeps government accountable via parliamentary questions and parliamentary committees, via independent public bodies such as the Ombudsman and the Auditor-General, and public advocates of key areas (for instance healthcare) to whom citizens can appeal to review government administrative practices. Mondragon cooperatives used to rely on the Caja Laboral Bank to monitor whether cooperatives complied with the Contract of Association (Whyte and Whyte 1988, Bajo and Roelants 2011). In Italy, up to the 1980s, LNCM was able to intervene if members were not satisfied with the management of their cooperative. For instance, it was LNCM which suggested how best to allocate profits to benefit both the long-term interest of the cooperative enterprise (and management) and the short- and long-term interests of members (salaries, dividend and refunds) (Viviani 2022). Whilst the experience of LNCM and Mondragon may be unique cases that reflect the local culture at the time, cooperative movements should seriously consider establishing independent bodies that could perform a similar role. These independent bodies could monitor cooperative democratic practices and intervene whenever agreed democratic practices are not being met, or whenever a proportion of members are not satisfied with the decision-making processes. This approach may also be appropriate in cases when ordinary workers, considering their workload, and work practices, may not be able to keep management to account. This state of affairs is not dissimilar to that faced by shareholders who have not been able to hold Australian banks to account via their Boards, leading government to establish a Royal Commission (Bailey 2003, Hayne 2019). It is also not dissimilar to that state of affairs of electors who have not been able to hold governments to account via Parliament, so we have the Auditor-General's Office, the Ombudsman, Pubic Advocates, and anti-corruption bodies, to help electors hold governments to account.[27]

8.4.3 Degeneration

The debate on cooperative degeneration has mainly centred on worker cooperatives and it generally concludes that because cooperatives operate in a capitalist-led market economy (CME), they will eventually use capitalist organisational forms and behaviours in order to compete in CMEs. This is a major risk for cooperatives because if they mimic capitalist behaviours, a cooperative will be a cooperative only in name but not in practice. Cooperatives may violate the principle of open membership thus not allowing other workers from becoming members; or it may allow an elite or small group to effectively manage the cooperative; or it may compete in a CME and grow whilst neglecting to meet members' needs. This behaviour will harm the reputation of the cooperative movement.

The early criticisms from Democratic Socialists in the early twentieth century argued that workers cooperatives failed because of inefficient management, undisciplined workforce, and reluctance towards industrial change, and that because of these failures cooperatives would either fail or adopt conventional capitalist structures that would exploit other workers (Webb and Webb 1914). Marxists argued that a minority of cooperatives competing in a capitalist economy would not be able to transform society and would ultimately need to maximise profits (Jossa 2005). Others viewed cooperatives through the lenses of the 'Iron Law of Oligarchy', which determined that cooperatives would eventually be managed by an elite with superior knowledge and skills than the rest of the members.[28] The above views had a deterministic view of the degeneration process and had a view of democracy that fitted small organisations. They also had a view that all workers had to be members. They held the very high expectations that worker cooperatives on their own should transform the economic system. More recent studies have confirmed that cooperatives are also able to regenerate after periods of degeneration (Cornforth, Thomas et al. 1988, Storey, Basterretxea and Salaman 2014, Bretos, Errasti and Marcuello 2019).

Cornforth et al., identified three ways that cooperatives may degenerate and move away from their key cooperative principles. These are Constitutional Degeneration which occurs when cooperatives adopt capitalist forms when employees are excluded from the rights and benefits of cooperative membership; Organisational Degeneration (or democratic deficit) when decision-making is mainly captured by a management and technocrats and workers control is diminished; and Goal Degeneration refers to the focus on business goals over social goals (Cornforth, Thomas et al. 1988). The issue of democratic deficit was discussed in Part 8.4.2. In this section, we will discuss Constitutional Degeneration since this has been a major topic of debate since the 1990s as cooperatives developed dual governance structures.

Constitutional degeneration focusses on those practices when some members exclude others from becoming members. It assumes that the benefits derives from the proceeds of sales or services will benefit members only. This basically means that whilst some workers receive only a wage, worker-members will receive a bonus payment and other benefits on top of their wages. Underlying this critique, there is an assumption that every worker wants to become a member and that cooperatives should have everyone as a member. The ICA principles also promote an open membership. Having cooperatives operating with a workforce where everyone is a member is certainly the desirable objective. This objective, however, is quite difficult to achieve. First, becoming a member entails investing money into the cooperative (up to a year's salary in older cooperatives) and also being responsible for managing the cooperative by participating in making decisions. Not all employees may long for these responsibilities. Second, cooperatives may not be able to guarantee long-term full-time employment at all times, especially if they engage in winning fixed-term contracts from public or private operators. If public or private companies do not renew these contracts, cooperatives will jeopardise their economic stability if the whole workforce is retained without having a job. Third, cooperatives may operate in locations where there is little awareness of cooperative values and ideals, making it difficult to attract members. Fourth, cooperatives have acquired other businesses whose workforce have been accustomed to working as wage labourers and they are not familiar with cooperative practices. These are real practical issues that need to be considered, and perhaps a reason why cooperative laws do not force cooperatives to transact only with members. Indeed, most national cooperative laws either pose no limits on transacting with non-members, or impose a minimum requirement to trade with members ranging from 25 per cent to 75 per cent of total trade or transactions.[29]

The issue of excluding employees from membership has emerged during the neo-liberal globalisation era, since the 1990s. During this period, the larger worker cooperatives began to grow via mergers, and acquisition in order to compete against larger capitalist enterprises. This has led cooperatives to operate outside their local communities, to adopt conventional legal structures such as holding companies to attract finance, and to grow faster through managing separate companies (subsidiaries) at home and overseas. The growth through holding companies and conventional subsidiaries has allowed cooperatives to operate with dual structures: a cooperative operating within cooperative laws that at the same time owns conventional enterprises. In some cases, the employees of subsidiaries are more numerous than the cooperative members working at headquarters. This leads to a situation where the number of non-members far exceed the number of members. Some Mondragon and Italian cooperatives such as Ederlan and Camst have converted or incorporated domestic private companies into their cooperative, but generally overseas subsidiaries have remained as private companies (Ammirato 2018, Bretos,

Errasti and Marcuello 2019). Owning overseas companies poses a different set of problems for cooperatives. They pose obstacles such as different cooperative laws making it difficult to transform conventional companies into cooperatives; workers and unions may not support cooperatives; and, fear that a majority of overseas worker-members could make decisions at the expense of the local cooperative members (Errasti, Ignacio and Etxezarreta 2016).

The response to globalisation by growing through dual structures tells us, to a degree, that external environment does influence cooperative behaviours. Cooperatives, however, whilst influenced by the market have not fully turned into capitalist enterprises. Cooperative members may benefit from having subsidiaries, but the focus is not profit maximisation for distribution among members. Bretos notes that Mondragon cooperatives expanded because they wanted to save local jobs as competitors' costs were lower than those of Mondragon. In addition, In Mondragon, and in Italy, the cooperative by-laws and the cooperative law, limit the amount of profits that can be distributed to member accounts, and limit the level of remuneration on member loans. In Mondragon, a portion of profits is paid also to non-members who work is the Basque region and to the Mondragon Corporation's inter-cooperative funds. In Italy, all cooperatives pay 3 per cent of their profits into the cooperative development fund, whilst the large industrial cooperatives provide health benefits, free child care centre, free canteen services to all workers not just members. In addition, most profits are deposited into an indivisible reserve fund which cannot be distributed. It would appear that these cooperatives have adopted a dual structure, but they have not fully degenerated into capitalist enterprises.

The issue that members get better treatment than non-members, however, is real, and if unresolved it damages the reputation of cooperative enterprises. Cooperative members do have access to profit sharing, the right to manage the enterprise, and a greater level of job security. Fagor members for instance, found work in other Mondragon cooperatives, but workers in Fagor international subsidiaries lost their jobs (Barandiaran and Lezaun 2017, Bretos, Errasti and Marcuello 2019). This is a real issue that cooperatives need to correct. If it is not appropriate in the era of globalisation to ask cooperatives not to grow, it is equally not appropriate to operate dual structures when one set of workers exploits the other, whatever the ultimate aim may be. To this end, it is important for cooperatives to translate more rigorously cooperative practices to their subsidiaries in situations when they cannot be transformed into cooperatives. These may include the following:

- Introduce co-determination policies so workers can elect their representatives to the Board.[30]
- Automatic membership after a few years of good behaviour subject to workers wanting to invest in the cooperative, and wanting to participate in cooperative management.[31]
- Introduce profit-sharing arrangements for all workers. All workers contribute to making profits so all workers should have access to profit sharing.[32] Members can still be paid a bit more in lieu of their role in starting the cooperative, and because of the time taken to perform their duties as members.
- All workers to have access to child care, health care, catering benefits and so on.
- All workers to participate in educational and training programmes, as well as in the development of the strategic plan, in workers councils, or specific workers' commissions.[33]
- Workers from subsidiaries could become shareholders in the head cooperative also by becoming external investors with voting rights to elect their representatives. This is

allowed in many countries, including Italy and the Basque region. This would allow members of the head cooperative to retain control by holding the majority of votes, whilst all workers will participate in the governance arrangements and receive a dividend payment.[34]
- The cooperative law to regulate the relations between cooperatives with their subsidiaries at home or overseas to ensure compliance with cooperative principles and practices. The requirements could include a 'comply or explain' principle and the right of the Cooperative Ombudsman to review cooperative compliance with the legal requirements.
- The Board of a cooperative is to certify each year in the annual report that they are complying with their legal requirements in managing a subsidiary.[35]

An effective way to manage this risk is by having a practical, balanced approach whilst complying with cooperative principles. We have already discussed the positives in adopting a balanced approach between meeting the needs of the enterprise and the needs of members; and in making decisions by adopting forms of direct and representative democracy. On this occasion, in promoting open membership and egalitarian practices, cooperatives need to find ways to either transform conventional enterprises into cooperatives or introduce cooperative principles in their subsidiaries. This will enable cooperatives to grow, whilst promoting in their subsidiaries cooperative values in a practical, measurable, and substantial way.

8.4.4 Demutualisation

Demutualisation refers to the transformation of cooperative enterprises into capitalist enterprises. This practice became more pronounced during the neo-liberal era, especially from the 1990s until the 2008–2009 GFC. The demutualisation of mutual societies and cooperatives took place mainly in countries where neo-liberal values were more rooted, and in post-Socialist countries. In the United States, Australia, Britain, and Canada hundreds of mutual societies and cooperatives, mainly from the finance sector, demutualised (Battilani and Schroter 2012, Patmore, Balnave and Marjanovic 2021). Demutualisation poses a large reputational risk for the cooperative movement because it may signal a weakness of the model to compete in global markets, or signal that it is a transitory model. It may lead to disenchantment from those cooperative members who believed that cooperatives continued in perpetuity. It may also lead to outright disappointment considering that the wealth created is inter-generational and should not be dispensed in the interest of current members.

Cooperative studies have identified many reasons that have led to cooperatives and mutual associations to demutualise. First, cooperatives were forced to operate under a more deregulated environment which valued individualism and competition. This led some cooperatives to adopt governance structures, practices, and language of the private sector. Second, cooperatives were in financial difficulties and decided that the capitalist model could attract more capital. Third, managers with conventional training, with the support of hired consultants, promoted demutualisation as a way to attract capital and improve competitiveness. Fourth, ineffective cooperative Boards supported change, or were not able to challenge management and consultant's call to demutualise. Fifth, members were disengaged, not well-informed, or thought that the change would not make much difference since there was little difference between cooperatives and private firms. Finally, the cooperative law allowed cooperatives to demutualise (Chaddad and Cook 2004, Battilani and Schroter 2012, Fulton and Girard 2015, Patmore, Balnave and Marjanovic 2021).

In 2022, a large worker Italian worker cooperative, Manutencoop, demutualised whose circumstances were different to the ones described above. Manutencoop, commenced operating in 1938 in railway maintenance. It later diversified into cleaning, building maintenance, security work. The company grew and by 2003 it employed 11,000 employees. Competition from large companies and market demand for larger companies to provide more integrated services, led Manutencoop to establish a holding company, and to raise 23 million euros from the private investors and the cooperative sector. Through this capital raising, external investors held 28 per cent of the total stock (Levorato 2005). The holding company turned previous cooperative operational units, into separate conventional companies. In 2014, it employed almost 20,000 people. Manutencoop, achieved continuous growth, increasing revenue at the rate of 14 per cent per annum, and increasing employment at the rate of 11 per cent per annum from 1984 to 2018. By now it diversified into other areas like hospital services, elevator maintenance, and solar panel installation. In 2018, 1,000 people attended a public meeting where its members voted to leave Legacoop, and to join another cooperative association. In 2020 it also joined Confindustria, Italy's key industry association. In 2022, after long public debates noted in the major national and local media about the nature of the cooperative model, its members voted to demutualise. They voted in favour of demutualisation with clear knowledge that in accordance with the Italian cooperative law, members would have to forgo all the indivisible reserves accumulated since 1938. Following demutualisation, the reserves were deposited in General Fond, one of the three major cooperative development funds. The reason given for demutualisation was that the cooperative model did not allow the company to grow, and that it needed to demutualise to have better access to equity capital. In 2022, prior to demutualisation, Manutencoop employed 28,000 people, of which 18,000 are employed in Italy. Its annual revenue is close to one billion euros (Manutencoop 2014, Massaro 2018, Strocchia 2018, Bettazzi 2022). The significance of this demutualisation is that it occurred in a worker cooperative that was already growing using the traditional cooperative model, it just did not grow as fast as management wanted it to grow. It happened in a region renowned for its cooperative values. It happened after many years of public debate that included Legacoop's active participation. It happened regardless of the cooperative law making it difficult to demutualise. It does not appear that membership was passive since they participated in voting in favour of leaving Legacoop in 2018, and voted for demutualisation in 2022. This was not an uninformed or rushed decision.

There are many ways that cooperative members can prevent demutualisation from occurring. At the cooperative level, Boards should promote and maintain cooperative values; and management needs to consider the economic needs and the members' needs together with the need to apply the cooperative principles. At the cultural level, members should be encouraged to participate and become more aware of cooperative principles and values. They should appreciate the cooperative's unique features when compared with a capitalist enterprise. The law should prevent demutualisation. People have many choices when forming an enterprise—including forming a small business, a partnership, a not-for-profit, an investor-owned company, and so on—if they choose a cooperative, they do it for certain values, which should be maintained. It is morally wrong for the current generation of members to sell what was built by previous generations. It is also a betrayal of trust with the general public, the cooperative associations, and the original cooperative members that supported a cooperative in its initial stages. Demutualisation damages the reputation of the cooperative movement.

Cooperatives should find more effective ways to identify and manage early warning signs that may lead to demutualisation. Some warning sign include cooperatives not promoting cooperative history and identity; hiring external managers with no knowledge or regard for cooperative values; small groups forming a power base within the cooperative; discussions about personal gains; solving management and financial needs by adopting conventional methods; using corporate language that promotes profits without mentioning social goals; management hiring consultants to provide advice on demutualisation; boasting about going to market to raise funds; listing companies on the stock market; discouraging or making it difficult for employees or customers from becoming members; calling cooperative members customers or clients; cooperatives not complying with the law; cooperatives providing sub-standard goods and services; cooperatives sub-contracting a large amount of their work; managers proposing complex organisational models; large cooperatives operating on their own rather than supporting their second-tier cooperative associations and so on (Barberini 2009, Battilani and Schroter 2012, Fulton and Girard 2015, Ammirato 2018, Patmore, Balnave and Marjanovic 2021).

8.4.5 *Finance*

Accessing finance to start or grow a cooperative has always been more difficult for cooperatives than private enterprises, especially listed corporations. As discussed in Chapters 2–5, cooperatives traditionally have raised finance via members' capital, members' loans, retention of profits, and indivisibility of cooperative assets. This traditional approach to raising finance has been more suitable for cooperatives with large memberships, such as consumer cooperatives or cooperative banks, with social cooperatives that provide labour-intensive services and don't need much capital, and those profitable cooperatives that are leaders in niche markets. This approach has been less suitable for manufacturing cooperatives or cooperatives with a global dimension.

This traditional approach to raising finance has been augmented in two ways. The first approach has been to promote cooperative financial support structures. These may include credit guarantee companies, cooperative development banks, financial companies fully or partly owned by the cooperative movement that provide cooperative-specific loans or equity, and cooperative development funds. The second approach has been to go to the external market to raise capital. This second approach has resulted in cooperatives raising capital in a variety of ways, including issuing bonds (tradeable and non-tradeable), issuing equity with voting and non-voting rights, controlling holding companies that include external shareholders, and listing cooperative-owned or cooperative-controlled companies on the stock exchange.[36]

Raising funds externally to supplement the capital that can be raised from members and the enterprise is not a problem per se. It would not be a problem if the capital were raised under conditions that reflected cooperative values and principles. In other words, if the remuneration of external capital was limited, if external capital was invested as long-term patient capital, or if external capital also put cooperative members and the long-term preservation of the cooperative first. This approach to raising external capital would be acceptable and aligned with cooperative principles. However, once a cooperative issues bonds promising a set return or lists a company on the stock exchange that promises the regular payment of dividends, it has to meet those obligations. If cooperatives cannot meet those obligations due to a downturn of the economy, or because of poor financial results, they will encounter various risks that can damage the reputation, character, and the cooperative's future. A cooperative, for instance, may be forced to operate as a profit-maximising company to meet its obligation to shareholders or external investors. If the bond obligations cannot be met, it may be forced to sell cooperative assets or go into liquidation. Cooperatives may be forced to sell shares of listed companies if their core business is not doing well, thus losing control of a cooperative asset to private investors.

Cooperatives could explore further avenues to strengthen the traditional approaches to raising capital and the cooperative owned or cooperative-led financial support structures. One traditional approach that should be considered is that practised by the Japanese consumer movement whose members invest much more than a nominal sum in their cooperative (Kurimoto 2020). A second approach is to encourage the State to invest more in cooperative-led financial structures. The State's assets belong to all citizens and the co-operative sector should do more to get the State to understand and support cooperative specific financial policies. The State has performed this role in Italy, France, and Quebec but even in this countries its support has been limited when compared to the support the State provided the private sector during the GFC.[37] A third approach, is for the global co-operative movement to operate a number of cooperative development funds worldwide funded by the State and cooperatives. These funds would then promote new cooperatives or assist existing cooperatives to grow, to restructure, or to diversify their operations. A fourth approach is to promote cooperative development banks or cooperative-owned or civil society-owned financial institutions whose key purpose would be to promote cooperative and social enterprises. A fifth approach, which I have already mentioned on a few occasions, is to create a global cooperative-specific investment market where individuals, cooperatives, pension funds, and ethical funds could invest in cooperatives. These investments could be made knowing that cooperatives would operate under the ICA (or equivalent) cooperative principles framework. It would be expected that these investments would be regularly remunerated, at a non-speculative rate. If, the global cooperative investment market could operate under global cooperative-specific legislation providing cooperative-specific tax incentives (recognised worldwide), it could attract millions of socially minded individuals that want a non-speculative return on their investment whilst promoting the social economy.

8.4.6 *External Environment*

The external environment comprising the media, civil society organisations, government bodies, professional bodies, universities, fund managers, pension funds, and institutional investors, can have a negative or positive impact on cooperation. Cooperatives and co-operative associations need to engage with the external environment so that it becomes more aware of the cooperative purpose, cooperative principles, how they operate, and how they contribute to the economy and society. If the external environment dismisses cooperative enterprises or sees them as just another form of business, it will hold back cooperative development. One key risk is if the external environment continues to promote Investor-Owned Firms (IOFs) or private firms as the only legitimate form of enterprise. A second key risk is that if people are not aware of cooperatives because they have not heard about them in the media, or taught about them at school or university, then fewer people will form cooperatives. The third risk is public policy negligence.

If the bureaucracy is unaware of the actual economic size and potential contribution that cooperatives can make to society, they will not consider cooperatives when developing public policies. The fourth risk is that the external environment may portray cooperatives as being similar to IOFs, thus discouraging people from forming cooperatives.

Another major risk for cooperatives operating within a disinterested external environment is missing out on having a well-informed and vigilant external environment. The external environment already performs this positive function in relation to IOFs. To this end, specialist financial and business newspapers, business journals, business and governance schools, specialised television programmes, and unions keep businesses to account, whether it is in relation to governance practices, performance, compliance, the environment, industrial relations, and so on. Cooperatives do not operate in an environment that provides this level of scrutiny and oversight. Promoting an external environment that is able to scrutinise and question cooperatives that deviate from cooperative principles or that do not perform (economically and socially) as well as their peers would help identify and deal with key risks as they arise. The level of scrutiny would also encourage cooperative associations and State authorities to act where it is legally and desirable to do so. It would also provide cooperative members with relevant information that they can use to keep management and cooperative Boards to account.

One key area that clearly highlights the level of disinterest of the cooperative needs is the lack of an international cooperative-specific financial framework and cooperative-specific financial structures that can perform an equivalent role that stock exchanges perform on behalf of IOFs. Many of the large cooperatives access external finance by issuing corporate bonds, accepting equity from external shareholders, establishing holding companies, or being major shareholders of listed companies. Those that access investments via the stock market and financial markets need to operate within the same rules as IOFs. It would be desirable if an equivalent financial framework could be established which allows investors that do not support the profit maximisation concept to invest in enterprises that have social and general interest goals. This financial framework would possibly operate under cooperative-specific tax provisions and reporting requirements that would also highlight cooperative principles and values, and how the cooperative's value-added is distributed. It would allow a limited return on investment so that it would not have an adverse effect on cooperative principles and cooperative goals (Spear 2004, Viviani 2013, Zanotti 2016, Ammirato 2018).

8.4.7 Cooperative Diversity

The cooperative movement has always been a diverse cooperative movement. In each country, and at each historic moment, the cooperative sector has evolved in accordance with identifying and meeting people's needs, the prevailing ideas at the time, the opportunities and constraints imposed by the market, the capacity of the private sector to meet people's needs, the development of the Welfare State, and with the various public policies directed at mitigating market failures and overcoming economic crises.

Barberini noted that there have been four major views on cooperative's role in the economy and society. These include a holistic communitarian role where cooperatives provide everything needed by their communities (Israel); a marginal role within a capitalist economy (the United States and Canada); cooperatives as an integral part of a planned economy (Soviet Union, India, Tanzania); and cooperatives as a distinct third sector of the economy (Social Democratic view prevalent in Europe and Asia) (Barberini 2009).

In Chapter 6, where we considered the national cooperative legislative framework operating in 26 jurisdictions, we identified two major cooperative models and five types of cooperative enterprises. The two cooperative models include cooperatives as member-owned, capital-centred enterprises and cooperatives as members of a cooperative movement supporting community development. The five types of cooperative enterprises included traditional cooperative enterprises; member-owned capital-centred cooperative enterprises; cooperatives as active members of the cooperative movement; cooperatives as members of a community-focussed cooperative movement; and cooperative owned group of companies (dual structure model). These different cooperative models have significant differences: some allow the distribution of assets, whilst others do not (indivisibility of reserves); some limit the return on capital, whilst others do not; some have high salary differentials, whilst others do not; almost all promote the principle of one-person-one-vote, whilst some allow plural voting; some promote the cooperative enterprises only, whilst others are part of a cooperative movement that supports the community; some cooperatives engage with cooperatives from other sectors of the economy, whilst others do not; some see cooperatives as an alternative form of enterprise that operates in a CME, whilst others see them as a marginal component of the capitalist system; some grow organically, whilst others have adopted dual structures that own conventional companies; some adopt governance arrangements that provide members with a high level of decision-making powers via their GA, whilst others have devolved powers to the Board and management.

Investor-owned firms also have their differences. These may include different governance arrangements; dispersed versus concentrated ownership; different views on how to deal with the environment; traditional industrial relation arrangements versus the adoption of co-determination policies. However, the key focus of IOFs is clear. IOFs operate in the interest of shareholders (profit maximisation) and in compliance with the law, whilst all other costs (externality costs such as environmental, community, and job losses) are transferred to the State. The State is seen as an institution whose role is to maintain law and order, protect private property, regulate the market so corporations can invest and make profits, and intervene where the market fails to meet the needs of people, the community, and the economy (Mayer 2018).

The cooperative movement has not developed a holistic vision of its role in the economy and society and does not have an agreed position on the State.[38] The ICA provides a definition of the cooperative enterprise but not an overall vision of a cooperative economy, a cooperative-led market economy or the role of cooperatives in a pluralist CME. The ICA, and other national cooperative movements, have not developed a holistic vision of society that encompasses the role of individuals, the economy, and the State, to match the vision promoted by conventional enterprises. This is not surprising considering the differences in the various cooperative histories, cooperative laws, and types of cooperative enterprises. The cooperative sector, however, would benefit from developing its own unique vision of the role cooperatives can perform in a pluralist economy alongside the State and private enterprise. This will then enable it to propose cooperative-specific public policies and to organise cooperative support structures or financial frameworks that will help cooperatives access capital and to grow. A financial framework with unique cooperative characteristics, supported by fit-for-purpose legislation, to rival the stock market network available for IOFs worldwide is a must for the cooperative sector. Institutions and individuals that wish to develop a vision for the cooperative sector should consider the following

- Fauquet's argument and vision of cooperatives' contribution to a pluralist mixed economy as the third sector of the economy (Fauquet 1941) and Borzaga and Tortia's approach to cooperatives offering a coordinating market mechanism that is different to other mechanisms based on hierarchy (corporations) or authority (State) (Borzaga and Tortia 2017).
- The contribution that cooperatives have made in a market economy includes promoting market inclusion, engaging in market coordination mechanisms, promoting anti-monopoly behaviour, dealing with market and State failures; revitalising businesses that have failed; and promoting the general interest.[39]
- The successful second tier cooperative structures that operate in all cooperative sectors, cooperative development funds, and cooperative business development models based on inter-sectoral trade and collaboration.[40]
- Cooperative longevity record and the unique cooperative characteristics that have enabled cooperatives to navigate the difficulties that emerged after the GFC.
- The contribution that cooperatives make to expanding economic democracy and strengthening political democracy.
- The contribution that cooperatives can make in reducing income inequalities and wealth inequalities via building inter-generational assets (indivisibility of reserves concept) and practising egalitarian salary structures.[41]

8.4.8 Going Alone

A major risk for cooperatives and the cooperative movement occurs when cooperatives operate on their own without being integrated into the cooperative movement. This occurs when cooperatives are established independently from cooperative associations or do not participate in second-tier cooperative structures to access services or buy inputs to lower costs or to access the market via achieving economies of scale. It may also occur when cooperatives outgrow the services offered by their associations or second-tier structures and act with more autonomy neglecting the needs of the cooperative movement. Going alone may also refer to cooperative sectors, such as the cooperative banks, consumers, retailers, and so on, which, whilst cooperating within their sector, do not promote inter-sectoral cooperation with other cooperative sectors.

Cooperatives competing on their own weaken the cooperative sector in a number of ways. First, cooperative start-ups will have more difficulty competing without accessing the administrative and financial services and the trade links facilitated by cooperative associations or federations. Second, cooperatives that compete on their own are more likely to deviate from adhering to cooperative principles compared to cooperative that are members of cooperative associations that regularly promote and encourage compliance with cooperative principles. Third, cooperatives or cooperative sectors that do not promote inter-sectoral cooperation or inter-sectoral trade limit the economic and social potential of the whole movement. They limit the potential of the cooperative sector to achieve economies of scale, offer better services, and promote the cooperative sector nationwide. Fourth, a cooperative movement that is not united will have difficulty promoting a coherent vision, strategy, and structures to the State and society. This will limit their ability to influence public policy.

The research thus far has identified a number of cooperative development models (CDMs) that have succeeded in promoting, managing, and guiding the cooperative sector through change.[42] These CDMs include those developed in France, Japan, Italy, Korea,

Mondragon, Quebec. All these CDMs have in common a propensity to have broad goals that include support for their community, to develop forms of inter-sectoral cooperation, to develop cooperative support structures, and to have the capability and the capacity to manage change and to support cooperative members in times of economic crisis.[43] Cooperative sectors worldwide would benefit from promoting legislation, regulation, and practices that promote cooperative membership with an association; promote regular funding of cooperative associations; promote second-tier cooperative structures to provide administrative, legal, financial and other support; promote cooperative development funds; promote forms of inter-cooperative and inter-sectoral solidarity; and promote cooperative education and tertiary institutions.

8.4.9 Reporting

Annual reporting can be a valuable activity for cooperatives to demonstrate their uniqueness and value to their stakeholders. Annual reports allow cooperatives to demonstrate how they promote cooperative principles, how they are embedded with their local communities, and how they engage with the State and public institutions. Annual reporting could also demonstrate how cooperatives minimise or overcome externalities such as pollution, job losses, general waste, inequalities, exclusion, and so on. This activity could also demonstrate to all stakeholders, the external environment, and to governments the ways in which cooperatives differ from other forms of enterprises and how they uniquely contribute to the functioning of a pluralist market economy, how they solve people's problems, and how they engage constructively with the State. The key risk faced by cooperatives is their inability to differentiate themselves from IOFs. This risk emerges when cooperative annual reports use similar standards, formats, and language to IOF-produced annual reports. This approach to annual reporting damages the reputation of cooperatives, limits their potential to grow, and limits their capacity to influence public policy because they would not be able to demonstrate their unique contribution to the economy and society.

The cooperative movement has not produced and approved a cooperative reporting standard. In Chapter 6, we noted how some cooperative jurisdictions require national associations to audit cooperatives to ensure compliance with the cooperative law. However, there are no provisions for producing an annual report in a prescribed manner. The ICA has been promoting indicators for cooperative principles, but it has not produced a cooperative-specific format as yet. This author is not aware of any cooperative association prescribing an annual report format that would enable cooperatives to demonstrate their compliance with and promotion of cooperative principles. Thus, it is not surprising that the ICA-led research conducted on cooperative reporting among the top 300 cooperatives worldwide in 2016 found that only 21 of those cooperatives used an international reporting standard compared to 82 per cent of the world's top 250 conventional companies (ICA 2016). In 2021, Euricse found that 72 of the largest 300 cooperatives produced an annual report based on the Global Reporting Initiative standard or the United Nations Sustainable Development Goals[44] reporting guidelines (Euricse 2021). These and other reporting standards were designed for IOFs to promote transparency and good governance, and to demonstrate how to minimise negative externalities such as environmental risks and human rights violations. Companies applied these standards to appease their shareholders, future investors, consumers, local communities, and governments. This approach allows IOFs to continue to pursue profit maximisation policies whilst demonstrating that they are trying to limit the externality costs of their activities (Rixon and Beaubien 2015). It is important for cooperatives to develop their own annual reporting framework that reflects their purpose, their principles, and their practices.

There is evidence that cooperatives produce informative reports that, in addition to adopting an international standard, they also cover some of the cooperative principles (Viviani 2006, Brown and Novkovic 2015, Ammirato 2018, Co-operative Group 2021, Granarolo 2021, Vancity 2021). It is also reasonable to assume that compliance with cooperative law and adherence to cooperative principles helps cooperatives operate as socially responsible enterprises. To demonstrate their full potential, however, cooperatives need to comprehensively comply with cooperative principles, demonstrate how they solve people's needs, and contribute to solving society's current and future needs. In order to achieve this, cooperatives could develop their own unique reporting formats. For instance, cooperatives using conventional reporting formats mainly discuss financial, accounting and material risks that need to be mitigated. Risks that can negatively influence cooperative goals, such as democratic deficit, degeneration risk, demutualisation, and risk of isomorphism, are not mentioned.[45] The ICA, the national associations, and various academics have proposed a number of performance targets and formats that would demonstrate compliance with ICA principles (Legacoop 2002, Viviani 2006, Marino 2015, Nembhard and Kertilson 2015, ICA 2016, Theodos, Scally and Edmonds 2018, Novkovic 2021). In addition to compliance with cooperative principles, cooperatives could also report on how they contribute to reducing the costs of externalities as a result of their activities. To this end, they can also report on how they contribute to encouraging inclusion in the market; creating secure, full-time jobs; promoting a fair distribution of income and wealth; protecting the environment; practising fair trade engagement across the global economy; promoting respectful and productive relationship with all level of government; promoting resilient local communities; and supporting future generations. Cooperatives could adopt reporting the 'value added' created to clearly identify the value that is created on behalf of labour, capital, the State, the cooperative movement, and the community.[46]

Cooperatives that demonstrate that their enterprise model is aligned with cooperative principles, reduces externalities, and focusses on solving problems faced by current and future generations, will differentiate themselves from other types of enterprises and enhance their reputation. The next step in this process is for the ICA, in cooperation with national cooperative movements and Academia, to develop a formal cooperative reporting format suitable for each cooperative sector. These formats would then need to be approved and implemented by each cooperative federation. Further, it is desirable if cooperative reporting would become a legislative requirement of each country's cooperative law that would include formal independent auditing.

8.5 Defining Cooperative Governance

Cooperative governance is about providing direction and oversight so that the cooperative can meet its stated purpose in compliance with the law. As per corporate governance, cooperative governance consists of many layers. These include cooperative members, the GA, the Board, management, and a variety of stakeholders. It also includes policies, procedures, and democratic decision-making processes. It includes laws, regulations and public bodies that influence cooperative practices and behaviours. It also comprises the market economy, which influences the cooperative's strategy, structure, culture, and practice.

There are also cooperative principles, cooperative practices, and unique risks that need to be considered. Cooperative governance needs to align its arrangements with the seven cooperative principles to be considered a bona fide cooperative. Cooperative practices include promoting a democratic decision-making process; promoting inter-generational wealth via the indivisibility of cooperative assets; promoting fairer salary differentials; having support mechanisms to keep people employed or to provide cooperatives with credit during economic crisis; promoting the general interest by meeting the needs of the aged, people with disabilities, and long-term unemployed so that they are included in the market and in society. Cooperative practice also includes activities that have contributed to reducing exclusion, reducing or limiting income and wealth inequalities, and that promote fair trade, thus reducing uneven economic development. Cooperative governance also includes identifying and mitigating those unique cooperative risks that can negatively impact on the performance and reputation of cooperatives and the cooperative movement.

Before defining cooperative governance, we should note what cooperative governance is not. Cooperative governance does not focus on profit maximisation, and it does not operate with voting rights based on capital ownership.[47] It is also important to note that one single definition of cooperative governance would not be suited for all types of cooperatives. In Chapter 6, we identified two cooperative models and five types of cooperative enterprises. Each of these five types of cooperative enterprises has many principles in common (open membership, democratic management, limited return on capital, and so on). However, their overall governance approach may differ because their purpose and goals may differ. A cooperative that operates on its own for the benefit of only its members without any restriction on the distribution of profits and assets will have a different enterprise purpose to that of a cooperative that is part of a cooperative movement that supports their local community and that practices an inter-generational approach to the distribution of profits and the management of cooperative assets.

The ideal type definition of cooperative governance that has been developed here reflects the governance of those cooperatives that comply with the seven cooperative principles and are actively engaged in dealing with broader societal issues such as inequalities, exclusion, fair trade and fair economic development, and the environment. To this end, the ideal type of cooperative governance definition could be described as follows: *Cooperative governance comprises rules, policies, processes, democratic practices, and management oversight, through which cooperatives achieve their stated purpose and a level of competitiveness to the satisfaction of their members. Cooperatives achieve their purpose whilst being an active member of the cooperative movement; by safeguarding the interests of current and future generations; in full compliance with the law and cooperative principles; by actively supporting local communities to overcome their economic and social needs; and by operating anywhere in the world without harming people, society, and the environment.*

8.5.1 Good Practice

In order to practise good cooperative governance, cooperatives need to demonstrate a number of attributes. First, there shall be full alignment between members, the board, and management in promoting the cooperative's purpose in accordance with cooperative principles. Second, they shall operate as a democratic organisation via distributing powers between the GA, the board, and management, with the latter having clear but limited powers. Third, they shall be a part of and contribute to the development of the cooperative movement. This improves their competitiveness and strengthens the cooperative sector economically and politically. Fourth, they shall govern on behalf of current and future generations by ensuring that the cooperative assets are well-managed and transferred to future generations. Fifth, they shall support the community in which they operate by creating employment, engaging with local businesses, contributing to solving societal issues, engaging respectfully with local institutions, support social and cultural activities. Sixth, they shall manage all key cooperative-specific risks so that cooperatives do not degenerate, do not demutualise, and remain sustainable enterprises serving their members and their community in perpetuity. Seventh, they should demonstrate that the cooperative production of goods and services does not harm people directly or via their subsidiaries or suppliers. Eighth, they shall produce annual reports informing the public and stakeholders on its enterprise model, achievements, compliance with cooperative principles, contributions to alleviating inequalities, promoting inclusion, respecting the environment, and promoting fair trade.

8.5.2 Some Suggestions

Cooperative governance can be improved further by promoting cooperative governance reforms that improve cooperative accountability to their members, their stakeholders, and civil society. This study has identified eight reforms that would improve cooperative governance. First, cooperatives should focus on creating an external environment which comprised academia, the media, local authorities, the government, political parties, civil society associations, and so on, that understand the cooperative purpose and principles. This will enable these actors to praise cooperatives for their virtues and criticise them when they do not meet their stated purpose and principles. Second, cooperatives could develop a Code of Practice, backed by legislation, with which they must comply. The Code of Practice would require cooperatives to comply with cooperative principles; comply with disclosure requirements at least twice per year; produce an annual report that reports on compliance with cooperative principles; and apply the principle of 'comply or explain'.[48] Third, with approval from the GA, the cooperative board will declare annually that the cooperative has complied with the Cooperative Code of Practice. The board is required to explain the reasons why it did not comply with parts of the Code of Practice.[49] Fourth, in large cooperatives, provisions should be made to allow forms of direct democracy where members can vote on major issues. This is particularly useful for consumer cooperatives, cooperative banks, and cooperatives with subsidiaries.[50] Fifth, cooperatives should enhance the democratic practices of those cooperatives that own subsidiaries at home or overseas. The principles of co-determination, profit sharing, membership and ownership rights, and employee benefits should be promoted consistently and without prejudice throughout the cooperative.

The following reforms focus on oversight and accountability. The sixth reform requires cooperative's annual auditing should be conducted by an independent body. This means that neither externally engaged auditors nor audits conducted by the cooperative associations are regarded as independent because they constitute a conflict of interest. The best approach is for an independent body (it could be a public-cooperative statutory body) to conduct these audits. The independent body could be paid through an annual cooperative registration fee to the cooperative registrar, a government department, or a public-cooperative body.[51] The seventh reform should facilitate cooperative members' easy access to a Cooperative Ombudsman. The Ombudsman's role would be to review administrative malpractice, fraudulent cases, non-compliance with democratic practices, and so on. This would further enhance the democratic checks and balances and allow members to keep management and the Board to account. The eighth reform requires co-operatives to produce an annual report that, whilst it considers key international reporting standards, should primarily report on the operations of the cooperative enterprise model. This would include how the cooperative purpose and cooperative activities are aligned, how it complies with cooperative principles, how it distributes the value added, and how it contributes to solving society's major problems. The latter would consider the United Nations' 17 Sustainable Development Goals.

Applying this cooperative governance definition and implementing the suggested reforms will clearly differentiate cooperatives from conventional firms. It will provide co-operatives with the opportunity to be economic successful, engage positively with the external environment, be more transparent and open to scrutiny, and become an agent of change for the whole of society.

8.6 Summary

- Corporate governance or cooperative governance is a term that refers to how companies, cooperatives, and organisations make decisions and how they are held to account for their decisions, their performance, and their compliance with the law.
- The modern corporation began as a public institution and slowly developed into a private corporation with a separate legal entity. Corporate governance evolved in response to the separation of ownership from management and the risks that this posed for shareholders. The bankruptcies and scandals involving high-profile corporations led to government-led governance reviews, which made key recommendations to improve corporate governance. These recommendations included having a professional Board of Directors led by an independent chair; boards with independent directors; board sub-committees to improve its oversight capabilities; disclosure requirements to inform the market on materiality issues; industry codes of practices with the 'comply or explain' principle.
- There have been two major approaches to corporate governance. The first sees corporate governance as focussing on creating shareholder value whilst operating in compliance with the law. The second sees corporate governance as having to consider the interests of all stakeholders whilst pursuing long-term sustainable growth. Corporations have applied the Unitary Board structure or the Dual-Board structure to govern their businesses.
- Cooperatives' early approach to cooperative governance included policies on engagement with members, profit distribution, limited capital remuneration, and the creation of inter-generational assets via the indivisibility of reserves and assets. Cooperatives' promoted democratic structures with members electing a Board of Directors or equivalent. The 1937 cooperative principles reflected these cooperative policies and paved the way for establishing democratically managed cooperatives that focussed on meeting their members' needs.
- The larger cooperatives that operated in national and international markets began to attract external capital, own subsidiaries, use conventional legal structures similar to large corporations, and use holding companies which owned subsidiaries. ICA commissioned reports in 1980 and 1992, and academic research since the 1980s found

that some cooperatives were behaving like capitalist enterprises, members were not engaged, and management was accumulating more power. Cooperatives also incurred failures, loss of competitiveness, recorded instances of malpractice, and many demutualised. The cooperative movement responded by promoting ways to strengthen the oversight capabilities of the Board vis-à-vis management and to introduce forms of participation and representation within large cooperatives.

- Cooperatives have developed at least five governance structures to suit different types of cooperatives. Each structure divides decision-making powers between the GA, the Board of Directors, and management. Large cooperatives that use the Unitary-Board and Supervisory Board models have separated ownership from management and transferred more decision-making powers to the Board and management. They have also put in place consultative bodies and adopted co-determination structures. In all governance structures, the GA still retains powers over key decisions and reserves the right to re-arrange governance structures and the allocation of powers according to the wishes of its members.
- A key function of cooperative governance is to manage a variety of risks that may prevent cooperatives from achieving their goals and their full potential. Some risks can lead to their demise and weaken the whole cooperative movement. The key cooperative-specific risks that need to be managed include balancing the needs of the enterprise and those of members; democratic deficit risk; the risk of degeneration; the risk of demutualisation; the risk amenating from external finance; a hostile or disinterested external environment; cooperative diversity limiting the development of a comprehensive view of political economy and the role of cooperatives; cooperatives competing alone in the market; and annual reports that are not comprehensively aligned with cooperative principles and that mirror the reports produced by conventional companies. Key cooperative-specific risks, alongside conventional risk management practices, are a key component of cooperative governance.
- Cooperative governance is about providing direction and oversight so that the cooperatives can meet their stated purpose in compliance with the law. It consists of many layers that include cooperative members, the GA, the Board, management, and a variety of stakeholders; policies, procedures, and democratic decision-making processes; laws, regulations and public bodies that influence cooperative practices and behaviours; the seven cooperative principles; and practices designed to promote intergenerational wealth, fairer salary differentials, support mechanism for members during economic crisis; and cooperatives that promote the general interest of society by taking care of the most disadvantaged people, by promoting inclusion, by reducing income and wealth inequalities, and by promoting fair trade.
- Cooperative governance does not focus on profit maximisation, and it does not operate with voting rights based on capital ownership. A 'one size fits all' cooperative governance approach is not recommended because there are a number of different types of cooperative enterprise models, each reflecting their country's history, culture, cooperative law, and the cooperative's own history and aspirations.
- The ideal type of cooperative governance definition of those cooperatives that comply with all seven cooperative principles and that positively impact some of the major societal issues could be described as follows: cooperative governance comprises rules, policies, processes, democratic structures and practices, and management oversight, through which cooperatives achieve their stated purpose and an appropriate level of competitiveness to the satisfaction of their members. Cooperatives achieve their

purpose whilst being an active member of the cooperative movement; by safeguarding the interests of current and future generations; in full compliance with the law and cooperative principles; by actively supporting local communities to overcome their economic and social needs; and by operating anywhere in the world without harming people, society, and the environment.

- Good cooperative governance practices include: full alignment between members, the Board, and management in promoting the cooperative's purpose in alignment with cooperative principles; a democratically managed organisation that distributes powers between the GA, the Board, and management, with the latter having clear but limited powers; being an integrated member of the cooperative movement; governing on behalf of current and future generations by safeguarding and transferring cooperative assets to future generations; supporting the local community in solving needs and creating jobs; manage cooperative specific risks and avoid degeneration and demutualisation; ensure that all cooperative activity does not harm people, communities, institutions, and the environment; and the production of an annual report that informs the public and stakeholders on its enterprise model, its compliance with cooperative principles, its contributions to dealing with society's general interests.
- The cooperative governance model could be improved if it adopts some of the good practice standards adopted by corporations and governments, as well as responding to unique cooperative experiences. Key reforms or practices could include promoting a knowledgeable, critical, and constructive external environment that will keep the cooperative sector accountable; developing a Code of Practice with legal status with the 'comply or explain' provision; requiring cooperative Boards to issue an annual statement of compliance with the Code of Practice and the law; require annual auditing to be conducted by an independent body; allow cooperative members to have access to an Independent Cooperative Ombudsman to deal with administrative matters, malpractice, non-compliance with principles, and so on; the promotion of direct democracy via referendums in large cooperatives; development and application of policies and procedures for subsidiaries requiring all employees to be treated equally; the production of an annual reporting of how a cooperative is meeting its purpose, particularly how it is meeting its cooperative principles and contributing to solving key societal problems.

8.7 Questions

- Corporate Governance reviews since the 1990s have made recommendations to improve the operations of the Board and to provide more information to shareholders and the market. In your view, what are the key features of these reforms, and how have they made a difference to corporate governance? Are these reforms also relevant to cooperative governance?
- Corporate governance reforms have made improvements to corporate governance, but they have not stopped corporate governance failures and did not prevent the GFC. In light of the events leading to the GFC, comment on the relationship between corporations, regulators, and their broader external environment and whether there are lessons for the cooperative sector.
- Cooperatives have developed key features of their enterprise model that influence their governance principles, structures, and practices. What are the key features of a cooperative enterprise that the cooperative governance model needs to support and promote?

In what way do these features distinguish the cooperative governance model from the corporate governance model?

- Consider the five cooperative enterprise governance models noted in this study. According to you, which is the most appropriate governance model for a small and for a large cooperative? How would you allocate powers between the GA, the Board, and management? How would you encourage members to participate in the life of the cooperative and in the democratic decision-making process?
- Are cooperative dual structures necessary, or are they a form of degeneration? If you deem dual structures to be necessary, what should cooperatives do to make sure that subsidiaries at home or overseas operate in accordance with cooperative principles? In answering this question, consider the policies towards membership, profit sharing, participation in the decision-making process, forms of representation (such as co-determination or Social Council or workers' council), voting rights, enterprise welfare provisions, and other social benefits.
- It has been stated that the cooperative governance model may not be appropriate for a large multinational cooperative. Please read and comment on the findings noted in the article *Corporate Governance as a Key Aspect in the Failure of Cooperatives* (Basterraetxea Fagor 2020). Do you agree with the Authors' conclusion that cooperative governance failed Fagor Electrodomésticos? Can the cooperative enterprise model and cooperative practices be updated or modified to meet the requirements of modern multinational cooperatives?
- The Author has identified nine major risks that cooperatives should mitigate in order to compete in the market, to meet members' needs, and to uphold cooperative principles. Out of the nine risks mentioned, which is the most important, and what would you do to mitigate this risk? Are there other key risks that are not mentioned?
- Consider how large cooperatives are governed and identify the major risks to their democratic decision-making process. What would you do to ensure that cooperatives can grow, even internationally, whilst maintaining a healthy and participatory democratic process?
- Consider the discussion in Part 8.4.2 on democracy. It has been stated that an appropriate size for a worker cooperative is less than 500 employees. Do you agree with this suggestion?
- What are your views on having independent bodies such as independent auditors or an Independent Cooperative Ombudsman keeping cooperatives to account?
- Annual reports can demonstrate how cooperatives achieve their purpose in accordance with the law, with cooperative principles, and with community expectations. They can also demonstrate how they deal with the major questions of our time, such as income and wealth inequality, exclusion, environment, unfair trade, exploitation of labour, and so on. How would you structure a cooperative annual report so that it meets the above objectives?
- What are the key components of cooperative governance, and how would you define cooperative governance?
- What are the good cooperative governance features that would enable cooperatives to become successful, sustainable enterprises that operate in compliance with the law and with cooperative principles, as well as operate in alignment with community expectations?
- The Author has suggested a number of potential reforms to improve cooperative governance. Which reforms would you implement in your country, and how would they benefit the cooperative movement? You may prioritise the reforms and state the reasons why you have made this choice.

Notes

1 I will use the term corporate governance to refer to governance arrangements present in Investor-Owned-Firms or corporations.
2 A cooperative enterprise model refers to the way a cooperative is organised to produce and sell goods and services in the market in order to meet the needs of its members. Cooperatives meet the economic, social, cultural and aspirational needs of their members by competing in the market on their own, or as a member of a second-tier cooperative. Whilst the term enterprise model is synonymous with the term business model, this book will opt to use the term cooperative model interchangeably with the term cooperative enterprise model.
3 Corporations have existed since the Roman times and have evolved since then until the present form. Initially they performed a public function under the control of the State. Mayer identifies various formations of the corporations that have taken place over 2,000 years. Please refer to the book: Prosperity: Better Business Makes the Greater Good (Mayer 2018).
4 It is important to note that a number of Japanese thinkers (Fukuzawa Yukichi, Shibusawa Eiichi, Muto Sanji, Kawakami Hajime), from the early twentieth century also promoted concepts of the firm which included cooperation, social responsibility, and the material well-being of workers (Stretton 2000).
5 Bankruptcies and scandals as a result of fraudulent and mismanagement activities occurred all over the world. Other cases of note include: the Black Group from Canada, Euro–Asia Agricultural Holdings (Hong Kong); Parmalat (Italy); Vivendi (France); Ahold (Netherlands) (Stiglitz 2004).
6 Some of the corporate governance codes of practice include the Australia's Corporate Governance Principles and Recommendations; the UK Corporate Governance Code; Canada's Corporate Governance Guidelines; The German Corporate Governance Code; and the Organisation for Economic Co-operation and Development's G20/OECD Principles of Corporate Governance (Du Plessis, et al. 2015, OECD 2015, ASX 2019).
7 A vigilant external environment has been responsible in Australia of identifying and raising the profile of bad corporate behaviour that has led to the Australian Commonwealth Government to establish a Royal Commission to investigate the allegations made. The most recent case relates to The Royal Commission into Misconduct in the Banking, Superannuation and Financial Services Industry which was established on 14 December 2017 and completed in February 2019 (Hayne 2019).
8 Cadbury's definition of corporate governance is an even narrow definition to that provided by the ASX:

> Corporate governance is the system by which companies are directed and controlled. Boards of directors are responsible for the governance of their companies. The shareholders' role in governance is to appoint the directors and the auditors and to satisfy themselves that an appropriate governance structure is in place.
>
> (Cadbury 1992)

9 This definition is aligned with the key principles noted in the German Corporate Governance Code which explicitly requires boards to consider the interests of shareholders, the entire workforce, stakeholders, and ensure the continued existence of the enterprise and its sustainable value creation. The principles require compliance with the law and ethically sound and responsible behaviour (Regierungskommission 2022).
10 The information from this section is derived from Chapters 2 and 3.
11 The first four mandatory principles promoted by the ICA in 1937 included: open membership, democratic control, dividends to be paid on purchases, and limited interest to be paid on capital invested.
12 Please refer to Chapter 4 for further information on this section.
13 The LNCM changed its name to Legacoop post-1990. The name Legacoop will be used for events post-1990.
14 Please refer to the case studies on Mondragon and LNCM in Chapter 4.
15 I use the term corporatisation implying that cooperatives adopt the legal, organisational, governance structures, the language, and reporting formats that is similar to those of corporations.
16 Unless otherwise stated the information in this section is taken from Chapter 5.
17 Confcooperative and Federazione Trentina also developed membership charters for their members (Ammirato 2018).

18 The description of the tri-partite model is based on the Italian tri-partite governance model also described in Chapter 6, Part 6.3.3.
19 It is 30 employees in Finland; 50 employees in Spain.
20 I use the terms used by the German Corporate Governance Code: Supervisory Board and Management Board rather than the terms used in the Cooperative law: Supervisory Council and Management Committee. This allows us to make better comparisons with the corporate governance models and other cooperative governance models such as the tri-partite and the unitary model.
21 The five board sub-committees include: Urgency Affairs Committee, Coordination Committee, Confidential Matters Committee, Evaluation of Governance Committee, and the Cooperation Renewal Committee (Rabobank 2021a).
22 A number of large Italian cooperatives have adopted the dual structure model (Ammirato 2018).
23 A good diagram of the Mondragon Corporation Governance Structure is found in Babaikoa, Baleren; Errasti, Angel; and Begiristain, Agurtzane. 2004. "Governance of the Mondragon Corporacion Cooperativa." *Annals of Public and Cooperative Economics* 61–87 (Bakaikoa, Errasti and Begiristain 2004).
24 Prior to the establishment of the MCC, the Caja Laboral Popular Bank provided more services and actually coordinated Mondragon activities. Please refer to Chapter 4.
25 Risks are usually referred to events that if they occur are likely to prevent an organisation from achieving their objectives. There are various levels of risks and organisations apply mitigation strategies to reduce the risks to an acceptable level. Please refer to the ISO 3100:2018, Risk Management Guidelines.
26 Please refer to Chapter 6.
27 This reflects the Australian political context, but similar institutions are present in democracies around the world.
28 The term 'Iron Law of Oligarchy' was first used by Robert Michels in 1911 (Michels 2016).
29 The consumer sectors of Japan and Korea require consumer cooperatives to trade with members only (Jang 2013, Kurimoto 2013).
30 Co-determination policies are in place in Northern European countries and are already applied by cooperatives. The Danish Agricultural cooperative Arla is an example of this practice.
31 In Italy the law allows for a probationary member to become a full member after five 5 years provided the member has performed adequately and has paid up their minimum capital account requirement (Genco and Vella 2011).
32 This practice already is operational in France among CG-Scop cooperatives (Corcoran and Wilson 2010).
33 Bretos, Errasti, and Marcuello (2019) have noted that some of these practices were being trialed in Mondragon.
34 Chapter 6 discusses cooperative laws that allow external shareholders with minority voting rights.
35 The Fonterra Board is required to make a statement of compliance each year.
36 Please refer to Chapters 4 and 5.
37 Please refer to the case studies on France, LNCM, Quebec, and Trento in Chapters 4 and 5.
38 In fact, the Early Socialists such as Owen and others had developed an early critique of Capitalism and the role that cooperatives and their communities could play to overcome competition, private ownership, and the misery that this new economic and social system caused. Please refer to Chapter 2.
39 Please refer to Chapter 7, Part 7.1.
40 Please refer to Chapters 4 and 5.
41 Please refer to discussion in Chapter 9.
42 Cooperative development model refers to cooperative movements that are able to promote the whole cooperative sector. These are usually led by a cooperative association or federation providing political, strategic, cultural, and economic leadership to an inter-sectoral cooperative movement. Cooperative development models have the capability and capacity to promote new cooperatives, new cooperative sectors, support existing cooperatives, and manage economic or organisational crises that beset the cooperative movement.
43 Please refer to Chapters 4 and 5.

44 In 2015, the United Nations approved 17 Sustainable Development Goals with 169 associated targets which are integrated and indivisible. These goals cover a broad range of areas, including (1) no poverty; (2) zero hunger; (3) good health and well-being; (4) quality education; (5) gender equality; (6) clean water and sanitation; (7) affordable and clean energy; (8) decent work and economic growth; (9) industry innovation and infrastructure; (10) reduced inequalities; (11) sustainable cities and communities; (12) responsible consumption and production; (13) climate action; (14) life below water; (15) life on land; (16) peace, justice, and strong institutions; (17) partnerships for the goals (United Nations 2015).
45 Please refer to the following annual reports (Arla Foods 2021, Co-operative Group 2021, Granarolo 2021, Vancity 2021).
46 The "'value added approach' and it is very useful to compare the way cooperatives and private enterprises distribute the value created" (Cadiai 2016, Ammirato 2018, Sacmi 2021).
47 Although as noted in Chapter 6, few cooperatives allow voting based on share ownership.
48 The principle of 'comply or explain' is a standard practice for corporations around the world.
49 Fonterra is required to make such a statement. All German companies are required to make a statement of compliance with their code of practice.
50 This is a suggestion that Zingales, Kasperkevic, and Schekchter, made in relation to Investor-owned firms (Zingales, Kasperkevic and Schechter 2020).
51 This is Martin Wolf's suggestion. He made it in relation to IOFs. He suggested that the stock exchange should conduct audits for all listed companies by charging a fee. He claimed that the current system is corrupt because corporations pay their auditors therefore they are not independent (Wolf 2023).

References

AFR. 1992. "Maxwell the Master of Deceipt." *Australian Financial Review*, 18 June.

AICD. 2010. *Company Directors Course*. Sydney: Australian Institute of Company Directors.

Ammirato, Piero. 2018. *The Growth of Italian Cooperatives: Innovation, Resilience and Social Responsibility*. New York: Routledge.

Andrews, Michael. 2015. *Survey of Co-operative Capital*. ICA Think Piece on Cooperative Capital, Brussels: Filene Research Institute Publication.

Arla Foods. 2021. *Arla Foods Consolidated Annual Report 2021*. Annual Report, Copenhagen: Arla Foods.

ASX. 2019. *Corporate Governance Principles and Recommendations - 4th Edition*. Corporate Governance Guidelines, Sydney: ASX Corporate Governing Council.

Bailey, Brendan. 2003. *Report of the Royal Commission on the HIH*. Research Note, Canberra: Department of the Parliamentary Library.

Bajo, Claudia Sanchez, and Bruno Roelants. 2011. *Capital and the Debt Trap: Learning from Co-operatives in the Global Crisis*. London: Palgrave Macmillan.

Bakaikoa, Baleren, Anjel Errasti, and Agurtzane Begiristain. 2004. "Governance of the Mondragon Corporacion Cooperativa." *Annals of Public and Cooperative Economics* 61–87.

Bakan, Joel. 2004. *The Corporation*. London: Constable and Robinson.

Barandiaran, Xabier, and Javier Lezaun. 2017. "The Mondragon Experience." In *The Oxford Handbook of Mutual, Co-Operative, and Co-Owned Business*, by Jonathon Michie, Joseph R. Blasi and Carlo Borzaga, 17 Pages. Oxford: Oxford University Press.

Barberini, Ivano. 2009. *Come Vola il Calabrone*. Milano: Baldini Castoldi Dalai.

Basterretxea, Imanol, Chris Cornforth, and Iñaki Heras-Saizarbitoria. 2020. "Corporate Governance as a Key Aspect in the Failure of Worker Cooperatives." *Economic and Industrial Democracy* 1–26.

Battilani, Patrizia, and Harm G. Schroter. 2012. "Demutualization and Its Problems." In *The Co-operative Business Movement, 195 to the Present*, by Patrizia Battilani and Harm G. Schroter, Chapter 6. Cambridge: Cambridge University Press.

Bettazzi, Marco. 2022. "L'Ultimo Strappo di Levorato, L'ex Manutencoop non e` piu` Coop." *La Repubblica - Bologna*, 3 February: 1.

Bevir, Mark. 2012. *Governance: A Very Short Introduction.* Oxford: Oxford University Press.
Birchall, Johnston. 2017. *The Governance of Large Co-operative Businesses.* Governance Report for Co-operatives UK, Manchester: Co-operatives UK.
Bonfante, Guido. 2011. *Manuale di Diritto Cooperativo.* Bologna: Zanichelli.
Book, Sven Ake. 1992. *Cooperatives in a Changing World.* Report to the ICA Congress Tokyo, October, 1992, Geneva: International Cooperative Alliance.
Borzaga, Carlo, and Ermanno C. Tortia. 2017. "Co-operation as Co-ordination Mechanism: A New Approach to the Economics of Co-operative Enterprises." In *The Oxford Handbook of Mutual, Co-Operative, and Co-Owned Business*, by Jonathan Michie, Joseph R. Blasi and Carlo Borzaga, 55–75. Oxford: Oxford University Press.
Bretos, Ignazio, Anjel Errasti, and Carmen Marcuello. 2019. "Is There Life After Degeneration? The Organizational Life Cycle." *Annals of Public and Cooperative Economics* 435–457.
Brown, Leslie, and Sonja Novkovic. 2015. *Co-operatives for Sustainable Communities.* Altona: Friesens.
Cadbury, Adrian. 1992. *The Financial Aspects of Corporate Governance: "The Cadbury Report".* Government Review, London: The Committee on the Financial Aspects of Corporate Governance and Gee and Co Limited.
Cadiai. 2016. *Bilancio Sociale Consuntivo.* Annual Social Report, Bologna: Cadiai.
Chaddad, Fabio, and Michael Cook. 2004. "The Economics of Organizational Structure Changes: A US Perspective on Demutualization." *Annals of Public and Cooperative Economics* 575–594.
Co-operative Group. 2021. *Co-op Annual Report and Accounts.* Annual Report, Manchester: Co-operative Group Limited.
Co-operative Group Limited. 2022. *Co-op Annual Report and Accounts for 2021.* Annual Report, Manchester: Co-operative Group Limited.
Corcoran, Hazel, and David Wilson. 2010. *The Worker Co-operative Movements in Italy, Mondragon and France: Context, Success Factors and Lessons.* Calgary: Canadian Worker Cooperative Federation.
Cornforth, Chris. 2015. "The Eternal Triangle: The Crucial Role of the Chair and Chief Executive in Empowering the Board." In *Co-operative Governance Fit to Build Resilience in the Face of Complexity*, by International Cooperative Alliance, 95–103. Brussels: International Cooperative Alliance.
Cornforth, Chris, Alan Thomas, Jenny Lewis, and Roger Spear. 1988. *Developing Successful Worker Cooperatives.* London: Sage Publications.
Cracogna, Dante. 2013. "Argentina." In *International Handbook of Cooperative Law*, by Dante Cracogna, Antonio Fici and Hagen Henry, 189–206. Heidelberg: Springer.
Crane, Andrew, and Dick Matten. 2016. *Business Ethics.* Oxford: Oxford University Press.
Deloitte. 2021. *The German Supervisory Board: A Practical Introduction for US Public Company Directors.* Governance Guide for US Public Company Directors, Germany: Deloitte Global.
Du Plessis, Jean Jacques, Anil Hargovan, Mirko Bagaric, and Jason Harris. 2015. *Principles of Contemporary Corporate Governance.* Cambridge: Cambridge University Press.
Errasti, Anjel, Bretos Ignacio, and Enekoitz Etxezarreta. 2016. "What do Mondragon Coopitalist Multinationals Look Like? The Rise and Fall of Fagor Electrodomesticos S Coop and Its European Subsidiaries." *Annals of Public and Cooperative Economics* 433–456.
Euricse. 2021. *Exploring the Cooperative Economy Report 2020.* Cooperative Monitor Report, Trento: International Cooperative Alliance.
FakhFakh, Fathi, Virginie Perotin, and Monica Gago. 2012. "Productivity, Capital, and Labor in Labor-Managed and Conventional Firms: An Investigation of French Data." *ILR Review* 847–879.
Fauquet, Georges. 1941. "The Co-operative Sector." *Annals of Public and Cooperative Economy* 342–369.
Fici, Antonio. 2013. "Italy." In *International Handbook of Cooperative Law*, by David Cracogna, Antonio Fici and Hagen Henrÿ, 479–502. Heidelberg: Springer.

Fonterra. 2022. *Corporate Governance Statement and Statutory Information 2022*. Governance report, Auckland: Fonterra Cooperative Limited Group.

Friedman, Milton. 1970. "A Friedman Doctrine: The Social Responsibility of Business is to Increase its Profits." *New York Times*, 13 September.

Friedman, Walter. 2020. *American Business History: A Very Short Introduction*. Oxford: Oxford University Press.

Fulton, Murray, and Jean-Pierre Girard. 2015. *Demutualization of Co-operatives and Mutuals*. Cooperative Governance Report, Canada: Co-operatives and Mutuals Canada.

Garcia, Isabel Gemma Fajardo. 2013. "Spain." In *International Handbook of Cooperative Law*, by Dante Cracogna and Antonio, Henry, Hagen, Editors Fici, 701–718. Heidelberg: Springer.

Genco, Roberto, and Francesco Vella. 2011. *Il Diritto delle Societa' Cooperative*. Bologna: Il Mulino.

Granarolo. 2021. *Sustainability Report 2021*. Annual Sustainability Report, Bologna: Granarolo.

Hancock, Matt. 2007. *Compete to Cooperate: The Cooperative District of Imola*. Imola: Bacchilega Editore.

Hayne, Kenneth M. 2019. *Royal Commission into Misconduct in the Banking, Superannuation and Financial Services Industry*. Canberra: Commonwealth Government of Australia.

Holmstrom, Mark. 1989. *Industrial Democracy in Italy*. Avebury: Gower Publishing Company.

Huhtala, Kari, and Iiro Jussila. 2019. "Supervisory Board in the Governance of Cooperatives: Disclosing Power Elements in the Selection of Directors." *International Journal of Economics, and Management Engineering* 660–668.

ICA. 2016. *Sustainability Reporting for Co-operatives: A Guidebook*. Guidebook prepared by the Sustainability Solutions Group, Brussels: International Cooperative Alliance.

Jossa, Bruno. 2005. "Marxism and the Cooperative Movement." *Cambridge Journal of Economics* 3–29.

Kasmir, Sharryn. 2016. "The Mondragon Cooperatives and Global Capitalism: A Critical Analysis." *New Labour Forum* 52–59.

Kurimoto, Akira. 2017. "Building Consumer Democracy: The Trajectory of Consumer Cooperation in Japan." In *A Global History of Consumer Co-operation since 1850*, by Mary Hilson, Silke Neunsinger and Greg Patmore, 668–697. Leiden: Brill.

———. 2020. "Consumer Cooperatives' Model in Japan." In *Waking the Asian Pacific Co-operative Potential*, by Morris Altman, Anthony Jensen, Akira Kurimoto, Robby Tulus, Yashavantha Dongre and Seungkwon Jang, Chapter 21. London: Academic Press.

Kutko, Victoria. 2021. *National Report: Russia*. Legal Framework Analysis, Brussels: International Cooperative Alliance.

Laidlaw, AF. 1980. *Cooperatives in the Year 2000*. A Paper Prepared for the 27 Congress of the International Cooperative Alliance, Moscow: International Cooperative Alliance.

Lavega, Sergio Reyes. 2013. "Uruguay." In *International Handbook of Cooperative Law*, by Dante Cracogna, Antonio, Henry Hagen Fici and Editors, 779–802. Heidelberg: Springer.

Legacoop. 2002. *Una Forma Complessa di Normazione (tra il Micro e il Meso): il Bilancio Sociale*. Social Reporting Guidelines, Bologna: Legacoop Bologna, Stati Generali della Cooperazione di Lavoro: Soci, Democrazia.

———. 2008. *Linee Guida per la Governance Delle Cooperative Aderenti a Legacoop*. Governance Guidelines, Rome: Lega Nazionale delle Cooperative e Mutue.

Lekvall, Per, Ronald J Gilson, Jesper Lau Hansen, Carsten Lønfeldt, Manne Airaksinen, Tom Berglund, Tom von Weymarn, Gudmund Knudsen, Harald Norvik, and Rolf Skog, and Erik Sjöman. 2014. *The Nordic Corporate Governance Model*. Stockholm: Centre for Business and Policy Studies.

Levorato, Claudio. 2005. "Manutencoop Facility Management SPA Cresce e Apre le Porte a Partner Privati." In *Verso Una Nuova teoria Economica della Cooperazione*, by Enea Mazzoli and Stefano Zamagni, 90–95. Bologna: Il Mulino.

MacPherson, Ian. 2012. "What Is the Purpose of It All." In *The Cooperative Business Movement, 1950 to the Present*, by Harm G Schroter and Patrizia Battilani, Chapter 4. Cambridge: Cambridge University Press.

Manutencoop. 2014. *Bilancio Sociale 2014*. Annual Report, Bologna: Manutencoop Societa` Cooperativa.

Marino, Manuel. 2015. "The Cooperative Certification Process: Cooperation of the Americas." In *Co-operatives for Sustainable Communities*, by Leslie Brown et al, 310–321. Ottawa: Centre for the Study of Cooperatives and Co-operatives and Mutuals Canada.

Massaro, Fabrizio. 2018. "Legacoop Contro Manutencoop Dopo lo Stratto di Levorato dal Sistema." *Il Corriere della Sera*, 28 May.

Mayer, Colin. 2018. *Prosperity: Better Business Makes the Greater Good*. Oxford: Oxford University Press.

Michels, Robert. 2016. *Political Parties: A Sociological Study of the Oligarchial Tendencies of Modern Democracy*. Connecticut: Martino Fine Books.

Mondragon Corporation. 2012. *Corporate Management Model*. Corporate Model, Mondragon: Mondragon Corporation.

———. 2021. *Mondragon Corporation Media Kit*. Media Kit, Mondragon: Mondragon Corporation.

Morrison, Roy. 1991. *We Build the Road as we Travel*. Philadelphia: New Society Publishers.

Mufson, Steven, and Jim McGee. 1991. "BCCI Scandal: Behind the Bank of Crooks and Criminals." *The Washington Post*, 28 July.

Münkner, Hans. 2013. "Germany." In *International Handbook of Cooperative Law*, by Dante Cracogna, Antonio Fici, Hagen Henry and Editors, 413–429. Heidelberg: Springer.

———. 2020. *National Report Germany*. Legal Framework Analysis, Brussels: International Cooperative Alliance.

Myners, Paul. 2014. *The Cooperative Group: Report of the Independent Governance Review*. Governance Report, Manchester: The UK Cooperative group.

Namorado, Rui. 2013. "Portugal." In *International Handbook of Cooperative Law*, by Dante Cracogna, Antonio Fici and Hagen Henrÿ, 635–652. Heidelberg: Springer.

Nembhard, Jessica Gordon, and Lou Hammond Kertilson. 2015. "Identifying the Appropriate Indicators to Measure the Impact of Credit Unions and Other Cooperatives on their Communities." In *Co-operatives for Sustainable Communities*, by Leslie Brown et al., 180–204. Ottawa: Centre for the Study of Cooperatives and Co-operatives and Mutuals Canada.

Novkovic, Sonja. 2021. "Cooperative Identity as a Yardstick for Transformative Change." *Annals of Public and Cooperative Economics* 1–24.

OECD. 2015. *G20/OECD Principles of Corporate Governance*. Paris: OECD Publishings.

Partridge, Mathew. 2020. "Great Frauds in History:BCCI -Agha Hasan Abedi's Dodgy Bank." *MoneyWeek*, 28 January.

Patmore, Greg, Nikola Balnave, and Oliveira Marjanovic. 2021. "Resistance Is Not Futile: Cooperatives, Demutualization, Agriculture and Neoliberalism in Australia." *Cambridge University Press* 1–19.

Rabobank. 2021a. *Annual Report 2021*. Annual Report, Amsterdam: The Cooperative Rabobank.

———. 2021b. *Rabobank CLA 2021-2022*. Collective Labor Agreement, Amsterdam: Rabobank.

Regierungskommission. 2022. *German Corporate Governance Code*. Corporate Governance Code, Berlin: Regierungskommission.

Ricciardi, Mario. 2014. "I Risultati Della Ricerca su Partecipazione dei Soci e dei Lavoratori e Relazioni Industriali: I Primi Risultati." In *Rapporto Sulla Cooperazione in Emilia-Romagna: Una Prima Sintesi*, by Legacoop - Emilia-Romagna, 63–78. Bologna: Legacoop Emilia-Romagna.

Rixon, Daphme, and Louis Beaubien. 2015. " Integrated Reporting for Cooperatives: A Case Study of Vancity Credit Union." In *Cooperatives for Sustainable Communities*, by Leslie Brown et al., 337–352. Ottawa: Centre for the Study of Co-operatives and Co-operatives and Mutuals Canada.

Sacmi. 2021. *Annual Report.* Annual Report, Imola: Sacmi.
Shabecoff, Philip. 1973. "Collapse of Penn Central Reflects of Railroad." *The New York Times*, 11 February.
Spear, Roger. 2004. "Governance in Democratic Member-based Organisations." *Annals of Public and Cooperative Economics* 33–59.
Stiglitz, Joseph. 2004. *The Roaring Nineties.* New York: W W Norton and Company.
Storey, John, Imanol Basterretxea, and Graeme Salaman. 2014. "Managing and Resisting Degeneration in Employee-owned Businesses: A Comparative Study of Two Large Retailers in Spain and the UK." *Organization* 626–644.
Stretton, Hugh. 2000. *Economics: A New Introduction.* Sydney: University of New South Wales.
Strocchia, Giancarlo. 2018. *L'Assemblea del Cambiamento in Webambiente.* Accessed December 26, 2022. http://www.webambiente.it/28-l-assemblea-del-cambiamento.asp.
Theodos, Brett, Corianne Payton Scally, and Leiha Edmonds. 2018. *The ABC of Co-op Impact.* Guidelines, Washington: Urban Institute.
Thornley, Jenny. 1981. *Workers' Co-operatives: Jobs and Dreams.* London: Heinemann Educational Books.
United Nations. 2015. *Transforming Our World: The 2030 Agenda for Sustainable Development.* Resolution Adopted by the General Assembly on 25 September 2015, New York: United Nations.
van der Sangen, Ger J.H. 2013. "Netherlands." In *International Handbook of Cooperative Law*, by D. Cracogna et al. (editors), 541–561. Heidelberg: Springer-Verlag.
Vancity. 2021. *Change Makers - 2021 Annual Report.* Annual Report, Vancouver: Vancity.
Viviani, Mario. 2006. *Dire Dare Fare Avere: Percorsi e Pratiche della Responsabilita` Sociale.* Bologna: Il Mulino.
———. 2013. *Piccola Guida Alla Cooperazione.* Soveria Monnelli: Rubbettino.
———. 2022. *Piccola Guida Alla Cooperazione 2: Un'Immersione.* Forthcoming Publication.
Volkers, Reimer, and Moira Lees. 1995. *Corporate Governance and Management Control Systems in European Cooperatives.* Corporate Governance Report, Geneva: International Cooperative Alliance - Europe.
Webb, Sydney, and Beatrice Webb. 1914. "Special Supplement on the Co-operative Production and Profit Sharing." *The New Statesman*, 30 May: 1–34.
Webster, Anthony. 2012. "Building the Wholesale: The development of the English CWS and British Cooperative Business 1863-1890." *Business History* 883–904.
Weidebaum, Murray L., and Mark Jensen. 1991. "Introduction to the Transaction Edition." In *The Modern Corporation and Private Property*, by Adolf Berle and Gardner Means, 1–8. New York: Taylor and Francis Group.
Whyte, William Foote, and Kathleen King Whyte. 1988. *Making Mondragon.* New York: Ithaca Press.
Wolf, Martin. 2023. *The Crisis of Democratic Capitalism.* Great Britain: Penguin Books.
Zan, Stefano. 1987. *Organizzare L'Autogestione.* Conference Proceedings, Bologna: I Quaderni di Quarantacinque.
Zanotti, Antonio. 2016. *Cooperative e Imprese di Capitali: Quanto Sono Diverse e Quanto Sono Uguali: Una Analisi Comparata Dell'Analisi Cooperative.* Soveria Mannelli: Rubbettino Editore.
Zarri, Francesca, and Elisa Badiali. 2012. *Partecipazione in Cooperativa: Istruzioni per L'Uso.* Cooperative Democracy and Participation Guidelines, Bologna: Fondazione Barberini.
Zingales, Luigi, Jana Kasperkevic, and Asher Schechter. 2020. *Milton Friedman: 50 Years Later.* Chicago: Stigler Centre.

9 Cooperatives and Private Enterprises

This chapter compares private enterprises and cooperative enterprises. The key comparison is between cooperatives and the larger private enterprises, especially corporations. This chapter is divided into four parts. Part 9.1 considers some of the key features of both enterprises, including purpose, ownership, control, profit distribution, and industrial relations. Part 9.2 examines the behaviours of both firms by comparing their economic performance, entrepreneurship, and innovation. Part 9.3 examines the impact that cooperatives and corporations have on employment, equality, local economic development, and economic democracy. Part 9.4 considers whether corporations and cooperative enterprises are converging. Part 9.5 provides a summary. Part 9.6 suggests key questions for further consideration.

Key learnings from this chapter include the following:

- An appreciation of the core features of private enterprises and cooperative enterprises, their similarities, and their differences by analysing their purpose, ownership and control, profit distribution, and industrial relations.
- An ability to consider and assess the different approaches to entrepreneurship and innovation.
- An understanding cooperative's view of performance and how it differs to that of private enterprise.
- An appreciation of the contribution the cooperative sector makes to local economic development, equality, and economic democracy.
- The ability to consider whether cooperatives and private enterprises are converging or maintaining their core characteristics.

9.1 Features

9.1.1 Purpose

Firm behaviour is not static and is influenced by a mixture of individual morality, national custom and culture, market discipline, legal and regulatory provisions, community expectations, consumer behaviour, and enterprise business models (Stretton 2000, Amatori and Colli 2011, Bevir 2012). The behaviour of firms may differ between countries and may alter at different historical moments.

Companies began to appear in the sixteenth century and they were usually formed by a group of people to pursue a commercial interest. The participants would sign an agreement whereby the profits would be divided by the stock-in-trade. Two such companies

DOI: 10.4324/9781003269533-9

were The East India Company which was formed in 1600, and The Virginia Company of London which was formed a few years later in 1606 (Srinivasan 2017, Britannica 2021). They were both granted monopolies over a particular trade, and they reflected the business and political culture of the British Empire at the time (Howard 1989).

Economic theory assumes that the purpose of firms is to maximise profits. Milton Friedman has forcefully argued that the purpose of firms is to maximise profits on behalf of their shareholders. Friedman argued that the Board and management are only responsible to shareholders and that their role is to conduct business in accordance with shareholders' desires (maximise profits) whilst operating in accordance with the law and ethical customs. He did not believe that managers and the Board should engage in social responsibility using shareholders' money. Friedman promoted the firm as a profit-maximising firm and undermined any notion that the firm should act in a socially responsible way (Friedman 1970).

Another view considsers that the purpose of the firm is to look after all its stakeholders. Ideas about considering other stakeholders, in addition to shareholders, were implemented by paternalistic entrepreneurs like Titus Salt in the Village of Saltaire in West Yorkshire in 1853 (Amatori and Colli 2011). The concept was also promoted in Japan in the late nineteenth century (Stretton 2000), and by Goodyear and General Electrics in the United States (Bakan 2004). In 1932, Berle and Means noted that firms were led by a professional Board and professional management, and whilst managers had a fiduciary duty to manage the firm on behalf of shareholders, they focussed beyond short-term profit maximisation. They were also concerned with growth, market share, management status, respectability, reducing uncertainties through planning, and spreading risks through diversification (Galbraith and Salinger 1984, Stretton 2000). The stakeholder approach became more prominent after the Global Financial Crisis (GFC) under the catchphrases of 'inclusive Capitalism' or 'creating shared value' (Porter and Kramer 2011). These approaches promote a socially responsible form of Capitalism that considers the concerns of employees, communities or the environment whilst continuing to make profits. There are many examples of companies that are able to make profits whilst behaving socially responsibly (Henderson 2020). Donaldson, however, noted that the Boards and management's promotion of a diverse set of interests only shifted the focus to long-term profit maximisation rather than short-term profit maximisation (Donaldson 1984). Bakan informs us that the stakeholder or socially responsible approach is a way for multinational corporations to maximise profits whilst aligning their interests with society's interests. In other words: "doing well by doing good" (Bakan 2020).

The purpose of cooperatives is not profit maximisation. The International Cooperative Alliance (ICA) Cooperative Principles define cooperatives "as an autonomous association of persons united voluntarily to meet their common economic, social, and cultural needs and aspirations through a jointly owned and democratically controlled enterprise" (International Cooperative Alliance 2017). What stands out in this definition is that cooperatives are an association of people, not capital, and that they are established to meet not just the economic needs of members but also their social needs, their cultural needs, and their aspirations. The needs of members will differ according to people's economic needs, aspirations, culture, and history. The behaviour or characteristics of cooperatives will also differ and reflect the relations that cooperatives have with other cooperatives, with civil society, with the community, with political parties, with trade unions, and with the State (Book 1992, Ammirato 1996, Diamantopoulos 2011, Viviani 2013, Pestoff 2017).

The historical analysis conducted thus far has demonstrated that cooperatives have met their members' economic needs and non-economic aspirations. The early Socialist sponsored communities provided work as well as housing and educational facilities, hoping to improve working and living conditions and to help people achieve happiness. The Rochdale Society of Equitable Pioneers provided their members with safe food at low prices and provided housing and jobs for their members via other cooperatives. The Desjardins movement provided local businesses and the community access to credit but also supported the development of a financially independent province of French-speaking Quebec. The Danish agricultural cooperatives helped cooperatives compete in the market but also promoted a democratic society. The Italian Socialist leaning worker cooperatives promoted employment opportunities, better working conditions, as well as social justice and Socialist politics. The Mondragon cooperatives provide employment opportunities, but they are also committed to the social transformation of society, to social justice, to the sovereignty of labour over capital, and to Basque identity. The Korean consumer movement reconciled the needs of urban citizens and farmers by forming consumer cooperatives. The Japanese consumer movement has promoted a peaceful society, consumer protection policies, and health services since the 1950s. Most recently, social cooperatives (social enterprises) in many countries have been promoting the general interests of society through the provision of social services and essential community services.[1]

Cooperatives have managed to meet their members' needs through different types of cooperatives. The first types of cooperatives, such as marketing cooperatives, consortia, and social cooperatives, operate on a not-for-profit basis. These provide services to farmers or other cooperatives or provide social services to individuals and families by charging a service fee to cover administration and labour costs. The second and most popular type of cooperatives operate as profit-making enterprises. These cooperatives provide a service to their members; they pay a limited return on capital accounts and do not distribute cooperative assets. A third type of cooperative operates under jurisdictions that allow cooperatives to operate without imposing any limits on profit distribution and with access to the cooperative assets. These cooperatives could operate as profit-maximising enterprises if members choose to do so. Similarly, there are many cooperatives that own conventional enterprises or overseas subsidiaries that operate those subsidiaries as profit-maximising conventional enterprises. These include those worker cooperatives that own conventional enterprises; agricultural cooperatives that own plants overseas that purchase milk from non-members; banks that have subsidiaries overseas that engage with non-members; and cooperatives that fully or partly own listed companies.[2]

In summary, we can say that corporations use people and other factors of production for the purpose of achieving profit maximisation on behalf of their shareholders. This goal is also pursued in cases when corporations promote social responsibility. Cooperatives are enterprises that meet the economic and non-economic needs of their members. The economic need is sometimes met via a not-for-profit enterprise, but it is mostly met via a profit-making cooperative, and at times it is met via profit-maximising cooperatives.

9.1.2 *Ownership and Control*

In private companies and corporations, shareholders own the company. They hold shares that reflect the value of the company and which can be bought and sold in the open market. Ownership provides shareholders with various rights, which include the right to one-vote-per-share, elect the Board, receive an annual dividend as determined by the

Board, call an Annual General Meeting (AGM), be informed, sue managers for misconduct, and claim certain residual rights in case of liquidation. Corporations have their own legal identity and are independent from shareholders, employees, managers, and so on. They have perpetual succession and continue to operate under different management and under different shareholders. Corporations own and are responsible for managing and disposing of company assets (Crane and Matten 2016).

Cooperatives are democratically owned and managed enterprises. Each member contributes an initial amount to their capital account and is entitled to one vote regardless of the initial deposit.[3] In a cooperative, a member is also an employee or a user of the cooperative services. Membership provides members with many rights that include the right to approve the by-laws, approve new members, elect or be considered for election to the Board, propose and approve profit distribution, call a General Assembly (GA) meeting, approve key strategic decisions, and so on. Cooperatives do not adopt a uniform ownership model. In most cooperatives, membership entitles members to the right to manage the cooperative, but members do not own the cooperative assets. In some jurisdictions, cooperative members do own cooperative assets, and they can sell the cooperative and divide all remaining proceeds after debts and liabilities are paid. The prevailing practice, however, is for cooperatives to develop inter-generational assets that are passed-on to the next generation.[4]

Shareholders of corporations exercise control by electing a Board of Directors to act on their behalf. They do not exercise control directly. The Board has a fiduciary duty to protect the investment of shareholders and is required to operate on their behalf. The Board performs this role by providing overall direction and control of management and by setting performance goals in compliance with the law. It develops/approves the strategic plan, appoints the Chief Executive Officer (CEO), approves internal policies and procedures, and reviews management reports with the support of Board sub-committees and independent directors. The Board appoints internal and external auditors to review financial statements and other internal procedures (Bevir 2012). Companies generally adopt the Unitary Board Model, mostly used in English-speaking countries, and/or the Supervisory Board Model, also known as the German model.[5]

Cooperative members exercise control over their cooperative either directly or by electing a Board of Directors. In Chapters 6 and 8, we noted that cooperatives use a variety of governance models that distribute powers between the GA, the Board of Directors, and management. In the smaller cooperatives, members may exercise control directly via the GA, thereby exercising direct control through direct democracy. In larger cooperatives with a high membership, passive members may elect a Board to provide direction and control. These cooperatives also adopt the Unitary Board Model and the Supervisory Board Model used by private companies. Other cooperatives may use the tri-partite model. In this model, whilst members appoint a Board which appoints executive management, the GA retains key powers to appoint a supervisory committee, appoint the auditors, decide how profits should be distributed, and approve key decisions. The tri-partite governance model does not promote a clear division between ownership and management since members can be both managers and board members.[6]

9.1.3 *Profit Distribution*

In a corporation, the Board of Directors, in consultation with management, determines how profits are distributed. Shareholders can voice their disapproval at the AGM but do not decide the level of profit distribution. Shareholders have the right to remove the

Board, but most likely, disaffected shareholders will exit the company and invest in another company.

In a cooperative, it is the cooperative members that decide how profits should be distributed. This decision is made at the Annual General Assembly (AGA). In some jurisdictions, the cooperative law prescribes how profits should be distributed by setting minimum and maximum amounts for various categories such as dividend payments, cooperative reserves, education funds, and so on. Other jurisdictions allow cooperative members to decide profit distribution at their AGA or to codify profit distribution policies in the cooperative by-laws. In cooperatives with a large membership where decision-making powers have been devolved to the Board, the Board could decide how to distribute profits. In these cases, members could overturn the Board's decision at the AGA (if the by-laws permit), or change the Board, or cease to become a member.

In a corporation, profit distribution is a balancing act between retaining profits in the firm and returning profits to shareholders in the form of dividend payments. Re-investment in the firm allows the firm to achieve its strategic objectives, strengthen its competitiveness, and achieve long-term profit maximisation. Some companies do not pay a dividend to shareholders, preferring to keep all profits re-invested in the company in order to increase the net asset value of the firm and the share price. However, shareholders who rely on the dividend to sustain their livelihoods in retirement and pension funds pressure Boards to pay regular dividends. Oxfam reports that the percentage of profits returned to shareholders was 35 per cent in India, 70 per cent in Britain, and over 80 per cent in Australia and New Zealand (Oxfam 2017). It has been forecasted that in 2022 global dividends would reach 1.56 trillion USD (Henderson 2022).

Profit distribution practised by cooperatives is more complex. In addition to the limits imposed by cooperative law, cooperative profit distribution is influenced by the views and expectations of the members, the economic needs of the cooperative enterprise, and the ICA's seven cooperative principles. To this end, whilst not consistent across all jurisdictions, cooperatives may distribute profits as follows:

- Re-investing in the cooperative enterprise in order to remain competitive.
- Paying a patronage refund to members based on their transactions with the cooperative.
- Remunerating members' capital accounts and members' loans.
- Remunerating external investors' capital invested in the cooperative.
- Remunerating all employees, including non-members.[7]
- Contributing to cooperative federations or associations in return for services, promotional and educational activity, and political representation.
- Contributing to a cooperative development fund.
- Contributing to cooperative educational funds.[8]

Corporations have a more uniform and simpler approach to allocating profits. Whilst corporations can also distribute profits to employees as bonus payments or establish foundations for charitable works, it is clear that the Board allocates profits either to the firm or to shareholders. In a cooperative, whilst profit distribution is decided by members at the AGA, the level of distribution and the allocation may be either prescribed by law, or it may be left to cooperative members to decide. Cooperative profit distribution is more complex and inconsistent among jurisdictions when compared with the simpler profit allocation choice faced by corporations.

9.1.4 Industrial Relations

There is generally no difference in how employees are engaged and relate to management in a company and most cooperatives. The only cooperatives with distinct industrial relations practices are worker cooperatives where members are also employees.

Private enterprises and non-worker cooperatives employ employees as wage and salary earners under contractual arrangements in compliance with industrial relations laws. Generally, a cooperative or corporation pays employees a wage or salary in exchange for services or work provided. This agreement is enshrined in an employment contract. It is common for workers and employees to become union members and engage their union to negotiate enterprise-based agreements or industry-wide collective agreements to improve their working conditions and benefits.

In a number of European countries, namely Germany, Austria, Slovenia, Denmark, Sweden, and Norway, workers can elect their representatives to company Boards. This form of industrial democracy is referred to as 'co-determination'. Their level of representation on company Boards ranges from 33 per cent to 50 per cent of total Board members, but in Sweden, employees can elect two to three members depending on the size of the enterprise. Once elected, employee-elected board members have the same rights and duties as other Board members (Pendleton and Gospel 2013, Thomsen, Rese and Kronborg 2016, Thomsen 2016). These provisions apply to all companies, including cooperatives (Münkner 2020).

Worker cooperatives that employ only members, subject to local laws and customs,[9] would have different industrial relations because members would democratically decide their pay and working conditions, including bonus payments and capital remuneration. Where worker cooperatives also employ non-members, they would need to engage their employees via contractual arrangements that comply with that country's industrial relations framework and the enterprise or collective agreements signed with their union representatives. Finally, worker cooperatives that own subsidiaries, would engage their employees via contractual arrangements in accordance with local laws and local customs.

9.1.5 Summary

Overall, there are six features that distinguish cooperatives from corporations. First, the cooperative purpose is to serve the economic and non-material needs of members rather than the capital needs of shareholders. Second, in cooperatives, profit is a means to meet members' needs; it is not an end in itself. In a corporation, profit maximisation is the reason why they exist, and the production of goods and services are a means to this end. Third, cooperatives are democratic organisations based on the principle of one-person-one-vote rather than the principle of one-share-one-vote. Fourth, shareholders own the company's assets, whilst cooperative members have the right to manage the cooperative but, in most cases, do not own the cooperative assets. In corporations, shareholders have delegated powers to manage the corporations to the Board of Directors. In a cooperative, members are also users and workers, and are elected to the Board of Directors and other governance bodies. Fifth, in a cooperative, members decide the allocation of profit mostly within the prescribed legal limits across many categories. In a corporation, the Board decides whether profits should be retained or distributed to shareholders. Sixth, industrial relations practices are similar, except for those worker cooperatives where all workers are members.

9.2 Behaviours

Having discussed the key internal features of cooperatives and corporations, we now discuss how they behave externally when competing in the market. To make this comparison, the three broad categories of entrepreneurship, innovation, and performance are examined. Exploring these three categories should further our understanding of the differences and similarities between cooperatives and corporations.

9.2.1 *Entrepreneurship*

Entrepreneurship refers to the capacity of people, individually or collectively, to design, start, develop, and grow an enterprise to meet the needs of its owners, its shareholders, its members, or its community. Entrepreneurs are people who innovate, take risks, exploit opportunities, and make key decisions. They put ideas into practice and coordinate all the factors of production with the aim of producing goods or services that can be sold in the market (Amatori and Colli 2011).

The capitalist private sector distinguishes itself with the ease with which it can set up new businesses and the willingness, capacity, and speed with which it can grow a business. Capitalist enterprises can be formed by one person, who can then grow the business by hiring labour. The rights and responsibilities of capitalist owners and employees are well known; they are taught at schools and universities, discussed in the media, and enshrined in legislation. The core institutions of Capitalism are also well known. These include private property and ownership of the means of production; contract law governing business and labour relations; the market as a mechanism where businesses can engage labour, purchase production inputs, and sell products; and the right of the owners to keep profits (Azmanova 2020). The power or the ease with which this form of enterprise can expand has been displayed most recently following the development of market economies in countries previously part of the Soviet Union and in China.

The private sector and corporations in particular have the capacity and willingness to grow quickly into multinational enterprises. Capitalist enterprises have an innate propensity to grow, especially in capital-intensive industries. Their drive comes from their focus on maximising profits, from management's own goals to control more resources, and from business strategies and organisational structures designed to bring goods and services to market (Amatori and Colli 2011). Corporations have grown via organic growth, acquisitions, mergers, and by achieving economies of scale to cut costs. Growth allows corporations to control a market segment and have control over prices. Higher prices lead to higher profits (Hadas 2020).

Corporations dominate world markets. Their legal structure enables them to locate anywhere and to attract investment from world stock markets. Corporations have taken advantage of the expanding world trade, which increased from 57 billion USD in 1957 to 19.5 trillion USD by 2018 and have developed into transnational corporations (TNCs) with overseas subsidiaries. There were over 100,000 TNCs operating in 2018 (compared to 7,000 in 1970). In 2011, just over 1,300 TNCs controlled the majority of the world's blue-chip companies. The largest 200 TNCs account for over half of the world's industrial output, whilst the largest 2,000 TNCs produced profits of 3.2 trillion USD. TNCs account for 70 per cent of world trade (Steger 2020). In the United States, four US Airlines control 70 per cent of aviation and the five largest commercial banks hold 50 per cent of the nation's bank assets (Hadas 2020).

Corporations can grow to a formidable size. For instance, Apple was formed in 1976 and, by 2022, was the largest company in the world by market cap with a value of 2.65 trillion (IBIS 2022). In the United States alone, Apple employs 90,000 people directly and a further 2.4 million jobs indirectly via its 9,000 suppliers (Apple 2019). Walmart opened its initial store in 1962; yet by 2022, it became the world's largest employer with 2.43 million employees and the world's largest company via revenue with an annual revenue of 576 billion USD (IBIS 2022).

Corporations and businesses compete in a variety of business models. They could operate as a small business, as a business partnership, and as a single large company. They could form business groups, usually led by a holding company or parent company that fully owns or partly owns independent subsidiaries (Colpan and Hikino 2010). They could operate within Inter-firm networks, where firms work together to share information, complementary services, common values, and mutual benefits. Toyota's vertically integrated Keiretsu system, which relies on thousands of suppliers, is seen as an inter-firm network (Fruin 2007). They could operate within Industrial Districts, which allow small- and medium-sized private enterprises to achieve economies of scale and compete against larger companies. In this model, firms work together in the same location, have a shared business culture, and share professional services, research and development. The model is supported by government policies, business associations, local banks, and educational institutions (Zeitlin 2007, Becattini, Bellandi and De Propis 2009).

The initial drive towards cooperative entrepreneurship has been to meet the basic needs of their members. These needs may include wanting access to good quality products at reasonable prices, having a decent and secure job, accessing credit, selling primary produce, accessing social welfare services, accessing affordable housing, and buying out their enterprises in order to keep their jobs. In each case, members formed a specific type of cooperatives to provide these services, be it consumer cooperatives, credit cooperatives, agricultural cooperatives, worker cooperatives, social welfare cooperatives, or cooperatives formed from buying-out enterprises in crisis. The key point is that cooperatives are driven to solve a need, not to maximise profits.

Since the 1860s, cooperatives developed second-tier structures to allow cooperatives to achieve economies of scale whilst remaining small and anchored in local communities. Second-tier structures lowered the costs of inputs, facilitated access to public and private markets, and provided access to market information. Second-tier structures included wholesalers, marketing cooperatives, consortia to win public works, cooperative central banks acting as clearing houses, and Cooperative Associations or Federations providing administrative, legal, and accounting services to their members. This tradition has continued with cooperative movements making available development banks, credit guarantee companies, regional development offices, cooperative development funds, cooperative educational funds, and so on.

The third phase of cooperative entrepreneurship began in the 1970s but proceeded faster in the 1990s in response to globalisation, the formation of trading blocs, and neo-liberal policies. During this phase, cooperatives began to grow via mergers and concentration policies, acquisitions, joint ventures, establishing holding companies with subsidiaries and owning listed companies. The aim was to build larger cooperatives to compete against multi-national companies. However, there were also other drivers at play, such as professional managers wanting to grow cooperative enterprises; cooperatives wanting to exploit their capabilities in newly emerging markets; cooperatives required to locate closer to their supply chains; cooperatives having outgrown their local markets; but also the possibility to maximise profits by operating in global markets influenced their decisions.

Alongside the development of cooperatives, second-tier structures, and large cooperative enterprises, as noted in Chapters 4 and 5, the cooperative movement has also developed a variety of cooperative development models (CDMs). These CDMs developed more recently and can be found in France, Italy, Japan, Korea, Mondragon, and Quebec. Whilst all have developed their own unique features, they share common features such as having an association or federation, having inter-sectoral cooperation, the provision of support structures and services, the provision of financial support, the ability to promote new cooperatives, forms of reciprocal support and solidarity mechanisms, and the capacity to manage change and overcome economic crises.[10]

The ICA celebrates the creation of large cooperatives as a demonstration of cooperatives' capacity to grow and to compete in global markets. The ICA publishes the annual *World Cooperative Monitor Report* featuring the largest 300 cooperatives in the world, of which 81 per cent operate in the agricultural, retail and finance industry. Some of the largest cooperatives include Credit Agricole, with a turnover of 89 billion USD, employing 142,000 employees; Rabobank, with a turnover of 12.3 billion USD, employing close to 45,000 employees; Nippon Life insurance company has a turnover of 48 billion USD, with 95,000 employees; the REWE retail group, has a turnover of 77 billion USD and 256,000 employees; the Fonterra agricultural cooperative group, has a turnover of 13.2 billion USD, employing close to 20,000 employees; the Mondragon Corporation has a turnover of 13.11 USD, with 80,000 employees; Sistema Unimed, a confederation of health cooperatives, has a turnover of 14.8 billion USD, with 112,000 employees (Euricse 2022).

Cooperatives also hold prominent positions in key sectors of a country's economy. Consumer cooperatives hold more than 35 per cent of the domestic market in Denmark (International Cooperative Alliance 2016). Cooperative banks hold 40 per cent of the market in France and Holland. Mutual insurance companies hold 25 per cent of the world market. Agricultural cooperatives hold more than 70 per cent of the market in Japan (Zamagni 2012). Energy cooperatives provide electricity services to 42 million people in the United States (America's Electric Cooperatives 2016).

To sum up, we could say that the private sector's pursuit of profit and its universally accepted model facilitates the establishment of new businesses, access to equity, and quick growth worldwide. Members establish cooperatives to this day to service a need that the market and the State could not meet. Their focus is servicing their members within their local communities rather than maximising profits. From the 1970s, but especially after the 1990s, cooperatives began to grow in size, access finance, adopt new legal structures, develop more complex organisations, and even to expand globally. Cooperatives have grown but cannot match the dynamism of corporations. For instance, Walmart's turnover of 576 billion USD is five times the turnover of the entire European consumer sector, which is 103 billion euros. Walmart employs 2.3 million employees, whilst cooperatives employ 619,000 employees. Walmart commenced operating in 1962, whilst the Rochdale experiment started in 1844 (Cooperatives Europe 2016, IBIS 2022).

9.2.2 Innovation

Innovation and change are constant features of a capitalist-led market economy (CME). Innovation means the constant capacity and capability of enterprises to use the available knowledge and research to develop new products and services. This allows firms to differentiate from competitors and to gain a competitive advantage. This process leads to the development of new products, new markets, new forms of marketing and communication, new organisational models, new sources of finance, and new delivery modes. Innovation can lead to reduced costs, the production of higher quality products, and the realisation of higher profits (Lazonick 2008, Amatori and Colli 2011).

Innovation can be gradually implemented via minor changes that are regularly made to products, services, organisations, customer relations, and so on. However, innovation can also be disruptive and change the structure of markets or how people work. Schumpeter noted that businesses' drive for performance and maximising profits led Capitalism to constantly change and innovate modes of production, consumer goods, modes of transportation, and the industrial organisation to create new structures and destroy old ones. He called this a process of 'creative destruction' or the materialisation of new ideas on an economic level. This concept reflected the changes to the economic structure that had taken place as a result of innovations such as textile and metallurgy sectors, the railways, electricity, chemical and automobile industries, and today's Information, Communication and Technology industry (Schumpeter 1942, Amatori and Colli 2011).

Corporations, other conventional businesses, and cooperatives all implement gradual forms of innovations. It is inevitable if they wish to remain competitive. These may be innovations in strategies, organisational structures, processes, customer relations, human relations, financial management, and technology improvements. The fact that conventional and cooperative businesses existed for many decades, the cooperative wholesale society has existed since the 1860s, for instance, indicates that they have managed to innovate and change over time; otherwise, they would not exist today, let alone prosper. The key differences or uniqueness of corporations and cooperatives lay elsewhere.

The major innovation from corporations is the development of the corporation itself and the legal-financial framework within which it operates. For the first time, out of the industrial revolution, a type of company emerged that could attract capital from all over the world, grow quickly, and operate within an organisational structure that achieves economies of scale. Corporations operate with a governance structure that separates ownership from management, enabling them to make long-term decisions. They have demonstrated a capacity to bring goods to national and international markets very quickly. This type of organisation has achieved economies of scale, lowered costs, and it created economic growth and economic value for its shareholders at an unprecedented scale.

Another unique feature of corporations is the role performed by their own industrial research laboratories. These research laboratories enabled them to invent new ideas or to apply existing knowledge and technologies to develop new products which could be deployed in national and global markets (De Long 2022). Corporations bought to market those ideas and inventions that had a major impact on the economic structure, from the steam engine to the railroads, the telegraph, oil, steel, machines, automobiles, radio, television, computing, internet, and mobile technology (Srinivasan 2017). These were not invented nor developed solely by corporations. However, corporations were able to use existing knowledge, research funded by government, at times, government land, or tariffs to protect their products, in order to bring new products to market, which disrupted markets and local communities (Lazonick 2008). Apple is an example of a corporation using existing technology, mostly developed and disseminated by State agencies. It was able to recognise the potential of emerging technologies, apply complex engineering skills, and produce and market highly quality products for consumers (Mazzucato 2018).

Cooperative enterprises were developed in response to the industrial revolution, in response to the insecurities and poor working conditions generated by CMEs, and in response to the power of business. As a result, cooperatives promoted different types of innovations. In this case, too, the major innovation was the cooperative enterprise because it introduced economic democracy at the enterprise level. Cooperatives are a democratically owned enterprise whose purpose is to satisfy its members' needs. The cooperative enterprise introduced economic democracy in a market economy and an enterprise model designed to serve people and members and not to serve capital.

The second major innovation was the development of second-tier cooperatives. This cooperative innovation allowed their members some level of control over the market, providing them with a level of stability in their lives as opposed to the chaos and disorder created by the capitalist market economy. Cooperatives coordinated or distributed work among their members, ensuring that all farmer members received a fair price for their produce. Consumers could purchase goods at lower prices, whilst farmers and artisans could have access to loans so they could improve and grow their businesses. Cooperative's ability to help their members find stability from chaos and control from helplessness when dealing with corporations on their own was quite innovative and a humane way to manage market relations.

It is worth recalling that cooperatives have continuously innovated their legal, financial, and enterprise models. Key innovations include:

- The cooperative principles and their legal framework have evolved since 1844 to include the cooperative enterprise, the second tier structure, cooperative federations, cooperative groups, and cooperative corporations.[11]
- The cooperative mechanisms to access finance have continuously evolved. Key developments include cooperative members investing via their capital accounts and via providing loans, retention of profits in indivisible reserves, attracting finance from external shareholders, developing their own cooperative development funds, their own cooperative development banks, their own financial companies, and cooperative ethical banks.
- Cooperatives from all sectors have innovated their enterprises, including their strategies, structures, entrepreneurial and organisational cultures, governance, products, services, and the use of technology. Case studies from previous chapters have highlighted these changes in cooperatives from all sectors of the economy.[12]
- Research on innovation conducted in Canada covering 236 cooperatives from the Americas and Europe, and mostly from the banking sector, found that almost 70 per cent place innovation among their top three priorities. It found that over the next three to five years, cooperatives will prioritise the expansion of new services (91 per cent), the development of capacity in innovation (84 per cent), and technology platforms (83 per cent). It also found that cooperatives pursue innovation in order to take advantage of new opportunities (85 per cent), as well as to counter threats (81 per cent) (Brat, Buendía Martínez and Ouchene 2016).
- Manufacturing cooperatives from the Mondragon Corporation operate 15 research and development centres linked to the University of Mondragon, and it boasts 489 families of research patents (Mondragon Corporation 2019). Sacmi has established 100 active partnerships with universities and research centres, which have helped it file 4,960 patents by 2021 (Sacmi 2021, 2022).

The ever-changing nature of the CME forces all types of enterprises to innovate or face the consequences of becoming uncompetitive. Corporations and cooperatives have both been very innovative. This exercise is not meant to determine who is more innovative but to understand the different approaches to innovation. The corporation has shown a greater propensity to grow and to introduce 'creative destruction' type innovation which disrupts markets and society. Cooperatives have promoted economic democracy and have focussed on solving people's problems, thus creating order and stability in the lives of workers, consumers, farmers, artisans.

9.2.3 *Performance*

The discussion of performance within cooperative studies tested the neo-classical hypothesis that whilst corporations maximise profits (leading to high investment, high growth, and high employment), worker cooperatives maximise income per worker (leading to under-employment and under-investment). This hypothesis explained why private enterprises were more successful and why there were few worker cooperatives. It also predicted that maximising income per worker would eventually lead to their demise. Once cooperative studies disproved these theories, further research on firm longevity and dealing with the GFC highlighted other features worth exploring to further our understanding of cooperatives and conventional enterprises' performance.[13]

The maximisation of income per worker theory has been reviewed incessantly since 1992. Craig and Pencavel examined the plywood cooperatives in the United States from 1968 to 1986 (Craig and Pencavel 1992, 1993). Pencavel et al. and Jones compared worker cooperatives in Italy with conventional firms. Pencavel et al. in particular, examined the data of 2,000 cooperatives and 150,000 conventional firms (Pencavel, Pistaferri and Schivardi 2006, Jones 2007). Estrin and Jones, and FakhFakh et al. focussed on France. The latter compared 1,500 cooperatives and 12,000 conventional companies from 1987 to 2004 (Estrin and Jones 1992, FakhFakh, Perotin and Gago 2012). Burdi and Dean reviewed firms from Uruguay from 1996 to 2006 (Burdin and Andres 2012).[14]

These studies covered diverse industries, diverse timeframes, and at least four countries, yet they all refuted the hypothesis that workers focus on maximising income. Key findings can be summarised as follows:

- There was no evidence that workers focussed on maximising income.
- There was no evidence of under-investment.
- There was no evidence of under-employment.
- There was no significant productivity difference between the cooperatives and conventional firms.
- Cooperatives generally provided greater employment stability (although in France there was little difference between the two types of firms).
- Worker cooperatives tend to adjust pay scales rather than employment when needed. They focus on maintaining employment at the expense of reducing wages. This makes wages in worker cooperatives more volatile than in private firms, whilst employment in worker cooperatives is generally more stable compared to private sector firms.

These results should not come as a surprise. Since their inception, cooperatives have had multiple goals. As an association of people, members of worker cooperatives value job retention, being in control of their working lives, wanting better working conditions, wanting to promote an egalitarian society, and wanting to promote social justice. In addition, the cooperative laws operating in Italy and France, and Mondragon's internal mechanisms, ensured that a percentage of profits was deposited in cooperative reserves; and that bonus payments and capital remuneration were limited. The broader set of reasons and the requirements to compete in an ever-changing competitive market ensured that cooperatives re-invested most of their profits (Whyte and Whyte 1988, Morrison 1991, Ammirato 1996, Corcoran and Wilson 2010, FakhFakh, Perotin and Gago 2012).

During the GFC, the behaviour of worker cooperatives confirmed the previous findings, which noted that cooperatives place more emphasis on maintaining employment. Mondragon dealt with the crisis by cutting unnecessary costs, reducing their inventory, recovering late payments, and increasing cooperative payments to their pension system. Mondragon reduced salaries by 8 per cent, promoted mergers to save cooperatives, re-deployed workers within the cooperative group, and allowed early retirement. Despite these policies, the crisis reduced profits, and in two years 2008–2009, Mondragon cut its workforce from 92,000 to 85,000 (Bajo and Roelants 2011). Mondragon had used these same policies in previous downturns before the GFC of 2008. Supporting one another in solidarity had been embedded in Mondragon's cooperative culture that is applied when-ever there is a crisis (Whyte and Whyte 1988, Morrison 1991).

The Italian cooperative experience showed that from 2007 to 2013, a period of low or negative economic growth, cooperatives increased capitalisation and borrowings, increased investments, and increased value-added by 24 per cent, more than doubling that of the private sector. They also increased salaries more than the private sector. As a result, the cooperative sector created 80,000 more jobs, whilst the private sector lost 500,000 jobs. During the same time, however, the cooperative sector incurred lower profits (or losses) and a higher level of debt than the private sector. The private sector reduced costs and limited their level of debt, thus preserving the value of shares and enterprise competitiveness (Borzaga 2015). Like Mondragon, the Italian cooperatives reduced salaries when they had to but did not reduce jobs. They used the social security system, jointly paid for by workers and the cooperative, to temporarily lay off staff for short periods without losing their jobs. They used the cooperative development funds to help cooperatives resist the crisis, restructure their operations, or borrow to invest. They made use of their indivisible reserves and increased investments from members to survive the crisis and to make further investments. The cooperative sector lost jobs in the construction sector because there were fewer public works on offer, but created more jobs in the social services area. Large cooperative businesses were better able to withstand the crisis compared to smaller businesses that dominated the Italian economy (Ammirato 2018).

Interestingly, Caselli, Costa and Delbono, in comparing the performance of the cooperative sector with that of the private sector in Emilia Romagna, found that during 2010–2014, when the economy was stagnant, cooperatives performed better; but during 2014–2018, when the economy grew by more than 6 per cent, the private sector performed better. For the whole period of 2010–2018, however, cooperatives increased employment by 29 per cent and profits by 50 per cent, whilst the private sector increased employment by 19 per cent and profits 14-fold. This confirms the anti-cyclic role performed by cooperatives and the greater emphasis that cooperatives place on protecting employment. This also confirms the likelihood of the private sector to reduce costs and preserve capital in times of economic downturns (Caselli, Costa and Delbono 2021). This result is also consistent with the findings of FakhFakh et al. on French cooperatives.

They noted that the "differences between the two groups seem to vary across periods and stages in the business cycle, and are not homogenous across industries" (FakhFakh, Perotin and Gago 2012).

The competitiveness of cooperative enterprises is further demonstrated when comparing the survival rate of both enterprises. It is well-known that consumer cooperatives, cooperative banks, and agricultural cooperatives have been actively operating for more than 100 years. The English Cooperative Wholesale Society, for instance, was founded in 1863. In 2014, there were 134 agricultural cooperatives in the United States that had been operating for more than 100 years (Iliopoulos and Valentinov 2018). Longevity studies conducted in Canada, France, Italy, and Spain, all show that cooperatives survive longer than private enterprises. Key results include:

- A Quebec study on non-financial cooperatives from 1995 to 2000 found that 46 per cent of cooperatives had a ten-year survival rate, compared to 36 per cent for private enterprises (Government du Quebec 2003).
- Mondragon boasts a 90 per cent survival rate for new cooperatives compared to 20 per cent for conventional businesses (Corcoran and Wilson 2010).
- Five years after the GFC, 66 per cent of French cooperatives survived compared to 50 per cent of all French companies (Bajo and Roelants 2016).
- The Euricse-led study on Italian worker-buyouts (WBOs) since 1985 noted that the average lifespan of WBO-cooperatives was 11.9 years, compared to the average lifespan of newly formed manufacturing companies was two-to-five years (Vieta, Depetri and Carrano 2017).
- Unioncamere compared long-term survival rates of cooperatives and private enterprises in the region of Emilia Romagna and found that 20 per cent of cooperatives had been operating for more than 35 years, compared to only 4 per cent of private sector firms (Caselli 2014).

The reasons for cooperative longevity are a result of its cooperative model and the supportive, cooperative networks. Iliopoulos and Valentinov note that agricultural cooperatives have survived a long time because they have achieved economies of scale, have reduced transaction costs, have adapted to changing markets, and have a non-divided ownership structure (Iliopoulos and Valentinov 2018). The other examples from France, Italy, Mondragon and Quebec are all examples of cooperatives operating within a network of cooperatives. These are usually led by a Central Association and provide a variety of financial and non-financial support and assistance that enables cooperatives to grow, and to manage crises situations.[15]

9.3 Impact

It is quite difficult to compare the impact of cooperatives with the impact of conventional companies considering they have different objectives. For instance, what is more important: producing a world-class Apple watch or establishing a social welfare network for elderly people? Running an airline that flies people safely all over the world and promotes the tourism industry, or consumer cooperatives that promote genuine, organic, safe products for consumers? These are all legitimate products and services that showcase people's imagination, innovation, engineering, their technical skills, and concern for people. The impact of cooperatives and conventional enterprises will be explored by discussing four topics. The first topic is the impact on employment. The second topic is equality. Third, we discuss how they contribute to local economic development. Finally, we will discuss the relationship between economic democracy and political democracy.

9.3.1 *Employment Impact*

The impact on the world employment market is one simple measure to examine the impact of cooperatives and conventional enterprises. According to ICA's 2017 report, there were 2.94 million cooperatives employing 279.4 million people. These included worker cooperative members, staff employed by cooperatives, and producers (farmers) who relied on a cooperative for their livelihood. Considering that in the same year, the world's total workforce was 3.38 billion people, the world cooperative sector employed 8.25 per cent of the world's workforce (CICOPA 2017). Considering that public sector employment in Organisation for Economic Co-operation and Development (OECD) member countries is close to 18 per cent of the total workforce (OECD 2021), between 73 and 74 per cent of the labour force is employed in the private sector (this would include the Not-for-Profit sector).

9.3.2 *Equality*

The gap in income and wealth among people and countries is a major moral dilemma. Inequalities divide societies, limit opportunities for people on low income, and give people with money a greater level of political power and influence over society. The *World Inequality Report* of 2022 demonstrates the level of income and wealth gap within countries. Key data includes:

- The poorest 50 per cent of the world earn only 8 per cent of total income, whereas the wealthiest 10 per cent earn 52 per cent of the total income.[16]
- The income differentials between the average income earned by the top 10 per cent compared with the average income earned by the bottom 50 per cent, ranges from 6:1 in Sweden, 7:1 in France; 8:1 in Italy and Spain; 9:1 in the United Kingdom; 10:1 in Australia; 13:1 in Canada and Japan; 14:1 in China and South Korea; 17:1 in the United States; and 21:1 in India.
- The income differentials of the top 1 per cent of earners compared with the lowest 50 per cent, rise from at least 20:1 in France, to 70:1 in the United States, and to 80:1 in India.
- The poorest 50 per cent own only 2 per cent of total wealth, whereas the top 10 per cent own 72 per cent of the total wealth.[17]
- The top 1 per cent captured 38 per cent of global wealth growth since the mid-1990s (Chancel et al. 2022).

Inequalities are a result of many factors. These include the concentration of private property in few hands; the right of capital owners to keep profits; high level of salary differentials; lack of adequate progressive taxation policies to reduce inequalities; weak countervailing powers from unions; precarious employment and unemployment, especially long-term unemployment; level of education; inter-marriages between highly educated couples from top universities; and tax minimisation strategies from the wealthy. Inequalities are present within cities, within countries, and between countries (Atkinson 2015, Galbraith 2016, Milanovic 2017, Piketty 2017, 2022, Chancel et al. 2022).

Corporations, especially listed companies, are a major cause of inequalities in our society. They promote income and wealth inequalities. Income inequalities are promoted through policies of high salary differentials that can be as high as 312:1, according to the US-based Economic Policy Institute study conducted in 2018 (Steger 2020). Wealth inequalities are caused by paying dividends to shareholders of listed companies as well as increasing asset valuations or profit retention and asset growth in non-listed companies. Dividend payout can be as high as 80 per cent of profits, as is the case in Australia and New Zealand (Oxfam 2017), whilst the total global dividend payout 2022 was forecast to reach 1.56 trillion USD in 2022 (Henderson 2022).

The State has been active in developing public policies designed to redistribute wealth and reduce inequalities. It has been active since the nineteenth century when the first social insurance policies were implemented in Germany. Since then, it has implemented progressive taxation and welfare policies such as social housing, unemployment benefits, health cover, access to education, and so on. The State was most successful in reducing inequalities when corporate tax rates were high, at a time when working people and their union representatives could demand fairer wages and salaries from their employers. As noted in Chapter 5, the neo-liberal policies of the 1990s, which promoted lower taxes, along with the weakening power of the unions, led to higher income inequalities, as noted in the *World Economic Report*.[18]

Cooperatives generally have been known to reduce both income and wealth inequalities. They have reduced income inequalities by promoting lower salary differentials. Worker cooperatives generally have lower salary differentials than the private sector. In France, salary differentials do not exceed 3:1 (Juban et al. 2016). In Italy and Mondragon, maximum salary differentials used to be lower than 4.5:1 up to the 1980s (Whyte and Whyte 1988, Holmstrom 1989, Ammirato 1996), but have steadily increased on average up to 6.5:1, although in large manufacturing cooperatives salary differentials can be as high as 9–10:1 (Hancock 2007, Barandiaran and Lezaun 2017, Ammirato 2018). The banking law on ethical banks in Italy limits salary differentials in ethical banks to 5:1 (Banca Etica 2022).

Cooperatives promote wealth distribution by depositing a portion of profits in the cooperative reserves. In those jurisdictions where collective reserves are indivisible, these reserves become inter-generational assets passed on from generation to generation. These assets cannot be distributed to members during the life of the cooperative nor if the cooperative ceases to operate.[19] A number of jurisdictions set a prescriptive percentage of profits that are to be deposited into the reserve account. This ranges from 5 per cent in Argentina and South Africa to at least 30 per cent in Italy. The French cooperatives, however, deposited, on average, 45 per cent of profits. Mondragon cooperatives have deposited up to 70 per cent of profits into the indivisible reserves. Italian cooperatives have, at times, retained more than 80 per cent of profits (MacLeod 2009, Petrucci 2009, FakhFakh, Perotin and Gago 2012). Cooperative reserves form an important component of cooperative re-investment policies. In France, for instance, by 2006, capital reserves amounted to the equivalent of 36,000 USD per person (FakhFakh, Perotin and Gago 2012). In Italy, the top 250 cooperatives held 13.6 billion euros in their indivisible reserves accounts (Osservatorio Grandi Imprese 2016).

One way to assess how cooperatives distribute income and wealth is to analyse how a cooperative's 'value added' may be distributed. Value added constitutes revenue minus intermediary costs (goods and services purchased from other firms), leaving the 'value added' created (capital costs, labour costs, taxes, profits).[20] A study of 200 cooperatives in the city of Reggio-Emilia found that cooperatives' 'value added' was distributed as follows: labour (68.3 per cent); private capital (6.9 per cent); government taxes (4 per cent); and collective reserves (20.8 per cent) (Legacoop 2011).[21] The 6.9 per cent share paid to capital (which includes payments to cooperative banks, patronage refund for members, and members' loans) is much lower than the 30–35 per cent of 'value added' that corporations consistently paid to capital in the OECD countries (Piketty 2015).

As noted throughout this book, the cooperative movement is diverse, dynamic, and in flux. A matter of concern is that salary differentials are rising, especially in non-worker cooperatives. If we consider the larger cooperatives from other economic sectors, including cooperative-owned listed companies, it is evident that salary differentials are rising. For instance, the CEO of Vancity (Canada) earns just over 1 million CAD, and this equates to 26 times the median income of 39,500 CAD (Vancity 2021, Statistics Canada 2022). The CEO of Rabobank (Holland) earned 1.21 million euros, and this equates to 31 times the median income of 38,100 euros (Rabobank 2021, Statista 2021). The CEO of Arla (Denmark) earns 3.2 million euros, and this equates to 44 times the median income of 72,000 euros (or close to 45,000 DKK per month) (Arla Foods 2021, Statistics Denmark 2022). The CEO of the Cooperative Group Limited (UK), earns 1.46 million GBP per year, and this equates to 46 times the median income of 31,400 GBP (The Co-operative Group Limited 2021) (Office of National Statistics 2022). The CEO of Fonterra (New Zealand) earns 4.3 million NZD, and this equates to 62 times the median income of 62,000 NZD (Fonterra 2022, StatsNZ 2022). The General Manager of Unipol Insurance (Italy) earned 4 million euros in 2021, 137 times the total population average of 29,100 euros (Unipol Group 2021, Chancel et al. 2022).

The other concern is that some jurisdictions do not promote the concept of indivisible reserves or the concept of limited return on members' capital accounts. In these jurisdictions, members are allowed to distribute profits in accordance with their by-laws. It may be possible that, in addition to salary differentials, these cooperatives may distribute most profits as bonus payments for members, thus increasing salary differentials. Where jurisdictions assign members with shares that are linked to the value of cooperative assets, then it may also lead to wealth inequalities between members and non-members.

Cooperatives have the potential to reduce income and wealth inequalities and thus complement the State's income and wealth redistribution policies and create a more egalitarian society. Cooperatives have been known to reduce inequalities by practising lower salary differentials. They also limit wealth inequalities by placing a portion of profits in indivisible reserves, thus creating inter-generational wealth. Corporations and the private sector operate with high salary differentials and return profits to shareholders in the form of a dividend or increased asset value. In corporations, salary amounts or profit distribution are not limited. There are signs, however, that salary differentials in large cooperatives are increasing. In some jurisdictions, cooperatives do not have to establish an indivisible reserves account and members' shares are linked to the value of the cooperative enterprise and can be redeemed when they leave the cooperative at full value. These trends may limit the ability of cooperatives to reduce income and wealth inequalities. Further research, however, is required to assess the extent to which cooperatives effectively reduce income and wealth inequalities in order to obtain a more comprehensive understanding of cooperatives' behaviour and identify emerging trends.

9.3.3 Local Development

Local communities worldwide want to achieve full employment, promote social stability, provide appropriate educational and social services, and support inter-generational cohesion and engagement. Local communities have suffered as a result of de-industrialisation, the inability to provide adequate employment and services, and the negative spill-overs caused by emigration. In these situations, it is usually left to the State to intervene and deal with market failures. The nature of the cooperative enterprise and its cooperative principles, however, could offer practical short and long-term solutions to problems faced by local communities.

The neo-liberal CME place local communities at risk. Global firms sell their goods and services globally, and by reaching every market, they create more competition in local communities (Levitt 1983). Investor-owned capitalist firms' focus on maximising profits on behalf of shareholders leads firms to transfer production within a country or anywhere in the world, wherever regulatory, labour costs and taxes are cheaper. This leads to de-industrialisation and the closure of production facilities if deemed non-competitive.[22] Corporations' capacity to create new products, new services, and organisational innovations regularly creates those 'creative destruction' forces that disrupt sectors and communities at the same time. Management theories promoting outsourcing, privatisation, and contracting-out internally provided services create value for shareholders at the expense of closing parts of companies that often leads to the loss of jobs, lower-paid jobs, or insecure jobs.[23] All of these factors create a level of dissatisfaction and precariousness at all levels of society (Azmanova 2020).

There are many factors that place the cooperative sector in an ideal position to promote local economic development. First, the purpose of cooperatives is to solve a need of their members who are embedded in the community in which they live. This has led cooperatives to develop in ways that solve people's needs and not focus on profits. Second, cooperatives are owned and managed by members. As a result, cooperatives are embedded in local communities, and they cannot relocate to other locations. Third, cooperative laws or cooperative practice make sure that most investments are re-invested in the cooperative either via members' capital accounts or via placing profits in the indivisible reserves account. This ensures that the wealth created remains in the local economy and that cooperatives retain sufficient capital to exploit opportunities or manage economic crises. Fourth, cooperatives have demonstrated that they create inter-sectoral employment. Thus creating cooperatives in one sector may lead to solving problems in another. For instance, the Japanese consumer cooperatives providing health and well-being services are one of many examples. Fifth, cooperatives have formed cooperative associations and cooperative federations that perform acts of support and solidarity towards their members. This has led to the cooperative sector helping or bailing out other cooperatives that were experiencing difficulties, thus maintaining local employment. Sixth, Cooperative movements have supported the formation of cooperatives from capitalist enterprises in crisis, thus maintaining local employment and halting (or at least slowing down) the de-industrialisation process. Seventh, cooperatives have demonstrated, during the financial crisis, that they place people before profits. To this end, cooperative banks continued to provide loans whilst conventional banks did not; and worker cooperatives maintained full-employment or promoted work-sharing arrangements without resorting to dismissals. Eighth, cooperatives throughout the world are promoting community cooperatives which aim to promote cooperatives that provide services that serve the whole community, not just members. These may be essential services, sporting facilities, or a variety of services to revitalise small villages. Ninth, some cooperative sectors have established cooperative development funds or regional development offices to promote new cooperatives and to support existing cooperatives that are in the process of restructuring or managing change. Tenth, where cooperatives expand overseas, the various examples provided in this book from Mondragon, Sacmi, Arla, Fonterra, and Rabobank, indicate that overseas expansion is not done at the expense of their members or their local economies.

The argument just made does not suggest cooperatives are immune from the effects of a crisis. It also does not suggest that cooperatives can solve all the problems themselves. It is not meant to devalue the State's contribution in successfully managing crisis, nor neglect the contribution of the private sector. It does point out, however, that cooperatives offer a different model of local economic development that is more people and community focussed, rather than being focussed on profit maximisation. The cooperative model, via its principles, legislation, purpose and real-life practices, provides people and their communities with a greater chance to manage change in a more balanced way and the opportunity to create wealth and economic institutions that invest and operate locally in perpetuity. Communities can use cooperative networks to protect themselves and to grow whilst still being part of the global economy.

One question to consider is whether cooperatives support all the local economies with which they interact (trading or selling goods and services) or whether they only support the local economy in which they reside. This is an important question because if cooperatives support all the local economies in which they operate, then it may also lead to more even regional and national economic development. If they do not, local and regional inequalities may persist even if cooperative development expands. The Consumer cooperative movement's contribution to fair trade is well documented and positively contributes to promoting local communities' employment and wealth retention. In reflecting on this question, however, there are three examples that readers should consider as well. First, the Mondragon Bank operates throughout Spain; yet, 20 per cent of its profits are deposited only within the Mondragon Corporation (Bajo and Roelants 2011). Should the profits be shared with communities across Spain? Second, Unipol, the insurance company mostly owned by the cooperative sector, operates close to 30 per cent of sales offices in Southern Italy. However, its key investments in banking, agriculture, real estate, hotel management and other services are almost all located in Northern Italy (Unipol 2022). Should investments be spread throughout the country so that more even economic development is promoted across the country? Third, the retailer association, Conad, comprises six major consortia providing services to their retail members across Italy. They are all headquartered in Central and Northern Italy. One of their consortiums, based in Umbria, associates mostly members from Southern Italy (Conad 2021). Considering the majority of its members operate in Southern Italy, wouldn't it be fairer if the headquarter of this consortium were located in Southern Italy so that it would create local jobs and local capabilities and pay taxes to local authorities? It could be argued that decisions have been made on the basis of ownership rights or based on achieving economies of scale, based on a cost-and-benefit analysis, and simply following market opportunities. If these are the reasons, the decisions may follow a market logic, but they do not promote fair and even economic development across regions as would be expected from cooperatives adhering to the ICA principles. This is an area where more research needs to be conducted before conclusions can be reached.

9.3.4 Economic Democracy

Economic democracy is a term that refers to a market economy that predominantly comprises democratically owned and managed enterprises and State-owned enterprises and institutions. Economic democracy is a broader concept than industrial democracy and co-determination power-sharing arrangements (Schweickart 2011, Malleson 2013, Cumbers 2020). Economic democracy provides important economic, social, and political benefits. As noted earlier, democratically owned enterprises will be able to redistribute income and wealth more equitably among their members and non-members, thus overcoming a key market failure. Democratically owned enterprises are also a place where employees have a better chance of achieving their full potential and developing lifelong skills whilst practising collective decision-making. These firms enhance political democracy because they devolve economic and financial power among many producers, worker-members, consumer-members, and small business-owners. The dispersal of power contrasts with the high concentration of economic and political power held by corporations in CMEs.

Corporations and private enterprises do not practice economic democracy. Control is based on ownership. Ownership is based on how much capital is owned. The voting principle is based on one-share-one-vote, or one-share-multiple votes, in companies where dual shares are issued. A small percentage of firms allow employee-share-ownership arrangements, and power-sharing arrangements known as 'co-determination' are practised in a number of Northern European countries. Where co-determination arrangements are practised, the Chair can cast the deciding vote, and directors representing employees would be required to operate in the best interest of the company, as they do in every other company.

Henderson, Reich, and Stiglitz provide ample evidence of how corporations use their economic and financial power in ways that undermine political democracy. Corporations invest hundreds of millions of dollars in donations to election committees and billions of USD in lobbying to influence public spending and state laws. This power may translate into laws promoting deregulation, tax cuts, weak industrial and environmental laws, poor welfare measures, and inaction against permissive tax havens (Reich 2016, Stiglitz 2019). Most importantly, through their influence in the media and via think tanks, they are able to successfully block laws supported by 90 per cent of the population (Henderson 2020). Dahl succinctly explains the problem with a CME and its relations to political democracy. He notes that, "unequal ownership and control of the major economic enterprises, in turn, contributes massively to inequality in political resources … and thus to extensive violations of political equality among democratic citizens" (Dahl 1998).

The cooperative enterprise is a key contributor to economic and political democracy. Cooperatives are member-owned enterprises in which each member is entitled to one vote regardless of the amount held in their capital account. Cooperatives democratically make all key decisions on membership, investments, profit distribution, and strategic directions. This is achieved through forms of direct, representative, and participatory democracy. Cooperatives have been known to operate as schools of democracy. They provide members with the opportunity to understand how cooperatives make decisions, how they interact with the market, and are they are influenced by State legislation and public policies. Cooperatives train their members to accept different points of view and to make compromises when necessary. They also teach them to promote a culture of solidarity and to solve problems collectively. Overall they teach members how to manage a democratic enterprise and how to make collective decisions by following due process, respecting others' opinions, and being in compliance with the law.

Cooperatives also enhance political democracy. They primarily do this by distributing economic power and resources throughout the economy, preventing any concentration of power. They promote lower income differentials and create inter-generational wealth where cooperative reserves are indivisible. Cooperatives promote a more dispersed ownership model through cooperatives that provide services to small land-holding farmers, small retailers, and artisans. Cooperatives allow these cohorts to achieve economies of scale whilst remaining small. The second-tier cooperative model further supports the dispersion of ownership by allowing small- to medium-sized cooperatives from all sectors to achieve economies of scale. Through their capacity to promote a more just distribution of income and wealth, and their capacity to distribute economic power via first and second-tier cooperatives, cooperatives reduce those inequalities in political resources highlighted by Dahl.

In this section, too, it is important to note the diversity of cooperative experiences and their impact on economic democracy. Democracy is limited where cooperative employees are not members, especially in overseas-owned subsidiaries. Democracy is also limited in large cooperatives that operate with a passive membership and where more powers have been devolved to a better informed and more qualified management team that operates within centralised governance structures. Some large cooperatives are promoting high salary differentials that will lead to unequal distribution of resources among individuals. Some cooperatives allow shares to be linked to the value of assets and for members to access those assets when leaving the cooperative or upon its dissolution, just like the private sector. Thus, whilst the inherent characteristics of cooperatives provide a more fair and just way to distribute economic and political power compared to the inherent characteristics and practices of corporations, it is not inconceivable to imagine that management-led cooperatives, wider salary differentials, shares aligned with the value of the enterprise, may develop further. If this were to happen, it would limit the potential contribution that cooperatives could make to the advancement of economic democracy.

9.4 Convergence?

The research has noted that the unique features of both corporations and cooperatives remain, but some convergence is taking place with cooperatives emulating the behaviour of corporations.

Cooperatives are established to serve their members to meet their basic needs. They are democratically managed enterprises based on the principle of one-person-one-vote. They reduce income and wealth inequality by limiting salary differentials, distributing profits to members as patronage refunds, and depositing a portion of profits to the indivisible reserves. Cooperatives are more inclined to invest in local economies and promote local economic development. Cooperatives distribute decision-making powers within the enterprise and economic power throughout the economy and society by supporting farmers, retailers, artisans, and small- and medium-sized cooperatives via second-tier cooperatives so that they can achieve economies of scale. The distribution of power within the enterprise and within the economy promotes political democracy.

Corporations are profit-maximising enterprises. They will locate anywhere in the world in order to maximise profits for their shareholders. They pay salaries according to market rates leading to high salary differentials between executives and professionals, and working people. They distribute profits to shareholders in the form of dividends or retain profits to increase the value of shares. Their policies have led to increasing income and wealth inequalities throughout the world. Corporations will grow as much as they can within the limits imposed by law and use their resources to control markets and influence the political process to further enhance their economic and political power. Their policies and practices weaken political democracy.

Corporations and cooperatives have both been entrepreneurial in their own unique way. It is easier to form private enterprises because the capitalist business model is well-known and universally applied. Corporations have demonstrated that they can grow quickly into multinational enterprises. Corporations have fast access to credit and equity, can apply conventional contract-based industrial relations anywhere in the world, and are able to expand overseas through their universally accepted capitalist model. As a result, the private sector controls a greater market share and employs more people than cooperatives. It is more difficult to form cooperatives because the cooperative model is less known and more diverse. It requires more people to form a cooperative because the model places obligations to members who are also workers, producers or users of the cooperative. Their form of entrepreneurship, until the 1970s, generally evolved through the promotion of second-tier structures that helped small, locally based cooperatives achieve economies of scale. Since the 1970s, cooperatives have used legal structures, stock markets, strategies of mergers and acquisitions, and external finance to grow into large national and international enterprises.

Corporations and Cooperatives have both promoted innovations to suit their purpose and meet the expectations of their shareholders or their members. Corporations have created legal and organisational structures that enable them to attract capital, to grow, and to bring goods to the market rather quickly. Their innovation is of the 'creative destruction' type that disrupts markets and societies. Cooperatives have created the democratic enterprise to enable people to solve their economic and social needs democratically and with equal status. They have also created two-tier structures that enable farmers, small businesses, and small- and medium-sized cooperatives to achieve economies of scale. Cooperatives focus on solving people's needs to improve their well-being and to provide for a stable life. As a result, they have been less inclined to introduce 'creative destruction' type innovation.

Research findings have concluded that there is not much difference between the overall productivity performance of private enterprises and cooperative enterprises. Corporations have demonstrated a capacity to grow into multinational companies at a much faster rate than cooperatives. Cooperatives, however, have demonstrated a better survival rate than the survival rate of private enterprises. One major difference has been the tendency of cooperatives to act as anti-cyclic enterprises and to place more emphasis on maintaining employment. Corporations, instead, focus on maximising shareholder value and are more likely to respond to economic downturns with policies of disinvestment that lead to lower employment; and periods of economic growth with increased investment leading to higher employment.

A degree of convergence between cooperatives and the capitalist sector is taking place. This is evident among large cooperatives that are operating outside their local economies and those international cooperatives that own subsidiaries overseas. Areas where cooperative are converging with the private sector and corporations include conventional industrial relations where employees are simply wage or salary earners without representation; higher salary differentials have been slowly introduced in worker cooperatives, but especially in other cooperatives; the adoption of legal structures such as holding companies or joint ventures or corporate models that are similar to those of corporations; cooperative ownership of listed companies; more centralised governance arrangements where the Board and management make the key decisions on their behalf of passive members; and indifferent relations with other local economies and local communities. Cooperative law in some jurisdictions also allows cooperative by-laws to determine the unlimited distribution of profits, unlimited capital remuneration, and member access to cooperative assets, all of which pave the way for further convergence with capitalist enterprises.

It is interesting to note that Corporations are not converging towards the cooperative model. We have noted that corporations in some countries adopt co-determination policies. In the United States, employee ownership has been promoted. Concepts of 'inclusive Capitalism' and 'shared value', and 'sustainability' have also been promoted. However, it appears that these developments have been influenced by the trade unions, society, non-government organisations, government policies towards the environment, fund managers, and corporations' willingness to improve their image since the GFC. It appears that the cooperative model has not influenced corporations to the point of them considering altering their purpose, ownership model, democratic decision-making model, and views towards cooperation and the community.

Table 9.1 Cooperatives and Corporations: A Brief Comparison

	Corporation	*Cooperatives*
Purpose	Pursue a commercial interest for the purpose of maximising profits for shareholders.	Pursue an economic or social activity to meet the economic and non-economic needs of its members. Promote the general interests or community interests via social cooperative enterprises.
Ownership Control	Shareholders own corporations but do not manage corporations. They elect a Board of Directors to direct and control the company on their behalf via the principle of one-share-one-vote.	Cooperative members have the right to manage the cooperative but do not own the cooperative assets. In small cooperatives, members exercise control directly via the General Assembly. In larger cooperatives, members elect the Board of Directors through the principle of one-member-one-vote.
Profit Distribution	The Board of Directors decides on profit distribution policies: what percentage is to be retained and what percentage is distributed to shareholders.	Cooperative members decide on profit distribution policies. Profits are distributed either in accordance with cooperative law or cooperative by-laws. Cooperative laws or by-laws indicate what percentage is retained, and what percentage is distributed to members, to other activities, or to other stakeholders.

(*Continued*)

Table 9.1 (Continued)

	Corporation	*Cooperatives*
Industrial Relations	Companies employ employees via contractual arrangements in compliance with the law.	Cooperatives employ employees via contractual arrangements in compliance with the law. In worker cooperatives, members decide on working conditions and employment benefits in compliance with the law.
BEHAVIOURS		
Entrepreneurship	Private enterprises can easily form new businesses because the capitalist business model is well-known and easier to establish. Corporations have an innate capacity to grow quickly into multi-national companies in pursuit of profit maximisation.	The cooperative enterprise model is not well known and it is more difficult to establish. Cooperatives are established to meet members' needs. They have established second-tier cooperatives, inter-sectoral networks, and large cooperatives with subsidiaries in order to reduce costs, increase trade, and achieve economies of scale.
Innovation	The corporation itself is a key innovation because it enables the company to access capital, govern a large organisation, and bring goods to international markets. They have created value and wealth for shareholders at an unprecedented scale. The corporations, aided by their own research and development laboratories, have been responsible for developing "creative destruction type" innovations that have disrupted markets and communities.	The Cooperative model itself is a key innovation because it introduces democracy at the enterprise level, the goal of serving members and their communities and not profits, and second-tier structures that reduce costs and achieve economies of scale. Cooperatives have been more inclined to solve people's problems, thus creating order and stability in the lives of workers, farmers and consumers.
Performance	Productivity performance is similar to cooperative enterprises. More inclined to cut costs, to cut employment, and to preserve capital during times of economic crisis. Shorter survival rate compared to cooperative enterprises.	Productivity performance is similar to capitalist enterprises. More inclined to maintain employment through flexible work and pay arrangements during times of economic crisis. Better survival rate than capitalist enterprises.
IMPACT		
Employment	The private sector employs 73–74 per cent of total global employment (includes employment in the Not-for-Profit sector).	8.25 per cent of total global employment.

(Continued)

Table 9.1 (Continued)

	Corporation	*Cooperatives*
Equality	High salary differentials increase income inequalities. Profit distribution to shareholders and linking the value of shares to company assets increases wealth inequalities.	Worker cooperatives reduce income inequalities by promoting lower salary differentials and profit distribution policies. All cooperatives that practice the indivisibility of their reserves and assets reduce wealth inequalities. Large cooperatives have increased salary differentials. In worker cooperatives, non-members do not receive a share of profit distribution nor all benefits reserved for members. Where cooperative assets can be distributed, wealth inequalities will persist.
Local development	Private enterprises, especially investor-owned companies, can disinvest from a local community in search of higher profits creating insecurity, instability and a potential loss of local capabilities.	Cooperatives' purpose and ownership model makes them more embedded in their local economy creating more stable employment opportunities.
Economic Democracy	In corporations, shareholders who own capital control the business, based on the principle of one-share-one-vote. Corporations influence the political system to represent economic interests at the expense of the majority of the electorate.	Cooperatives are democratically managed enterprises that limit the concentration of power within the enterprise and disperse power in the economy, thus strengthening political democracy. There are instances where not all employees are members, where managers have more control compared to members, and tendencies for large cooperatives to influence second-tier cooperatives and cooperative federations. These trends lead to a concentration of decision making powers within cooperatives and within cooperative structures.

9.5 Summary

- The purpose of corporations (and businesses) is to maximise profits for their shareholders. In contrast, cooperatives are established primarily to meet a need or solve a problem for their members or the community.
- Shareholders own corporations but do not manage them. They elect a Board of Directors with functions to direct and control management on their behalf. Instead, cooperative members in most cooperatives have the right to manage a cooperative but do not own it. Cooperative members exercise control directly or via democratically electing a Board of Directors.
- Corporations distribute part of the profits to shareholders in the form of dividends, and part of the profits are retained to further economic development and shareholder value.

The Board of Directors of a corporation decides how profits are distributed. Cooperative profits are distributed to members (via limited remuneration of members' capital accounts and patronage refunds or bonus payments), to the indivisible reserves, the cooperative associations, the cooperative movement, and their community. In some jurisdictions, the law prescribes how profits are to be distributed; in others, it is left to the cooperative by-laws to determine how profits are distributed.

- Industrial relations are similar in both enterprises, other than in those worker cooperatives where all workers are members. Generally, all cooperatives enter into contractual arrangements with employees that provide a salary and other working conditions and rights in accordance with the law in return for working a set amount of hours. Employees do not participate in decision-making other than in countries that practice co-determination policies.
- Corporations' entrepreneurial culture is characterised by their ability to grow quickly into large national or multinational companies. Their desire to make profits, together with their high-quality management, easy access to capital, and accessible world capitalist markets create an enabling environment for corporations. Cooperatives have initially been locally based to serve their members and then developed second-tier structures to allow locally based cooperatives to achieve economies of scale. Cooperative inter-sectoral development models have developed in many parts of the world that are able to promote new cooperatives, manage crisis situations, and provide lifelong services and support to their cooperative members. Since the 1970s, cooperatives have developed strategies to grow their businesses beyond local and national markets.
- Cooperatives and corporations have been highly innovative. Their innovations have reflected their enterprise model's expectations. For corporations, the key innovation has been the development of the corporation itself which, as a result of all its attributes, is able to quickly deploy new products and services in world markets; and consistently promote 'creative destruction' type innovative products and services that disrupt markets. Cooperatives' key innovation has been to develop a democratically owned enterprise that meets the needs of its members and not the needs of investors. The other major innovations are the development of second-tier structures and inter-sectoral development models that help small- and medium-sized cooperatives to compete in the market whilst remaining small. In practice, it could be said that innovation from corporations produces chaos and uncertainty, whilst innovation from cooperatives produces stability, cohesion, and certainty for their members and the communities.
- Cooperatives have demonstrated that they promote economic growth, increase employment, and deploy long-term investment. Various studies have found that the productivity of cooperatives and the private sector is similar. Corporations have demonstrated a capacity to grow into multinational companies at a much faster rate than cooperatives, but cooperatives have a better survival rate than private enterprises. A key difference has been the cooperative's focus on maintaining employment in times of crisis, whereas the private sector is more inclined to cut costs. The cooperative's ownership model and networking arrangements (where they have been developed) have allowed cooperatives to establish supporting inter-cooperative solidarity-based arrangements that keep workers employed in times of crisis or restructuring.
- Worker Cooperatives promote a better distribution of income and wealth by maintaining lower salary differentials than the private sector, increasing members' income via limited remuneration of members' capital accounts, and depositing profits into the inter-generational reserve fund. Corporations adopt higher salary differentials,

distribute profits to shareholders, and retain profits in the enterprise, thus increasing the value of shares. Larger worker cooperatives have begun practising higher salary differentials, whilst large financial and agricultural cooperatives pay market-based salaries to their executives.

- Local communities are vulnerable to global markets. Corporations are renowned for relocating to places offering better opportunities to maximise profits. Cooperatives, instead, are embedded in local communities because this is where their member-owners live. Cooperatives retain their profits in the indivisible reserves and thus creating inter-generational wealth, and have provided social and essential services where the State and the market have failed. The task for international cooperatives is to find ways to translate this model into the overseas communities in which they operate and serve.
- Cooperatives operate under democratic structures that provide members with the opportunity to learn the art of democratic decision-making and promote a devolved economic model. Corporations, on the contrary, promote hierarchical decision-making models and concentration of economic power in multinational companies. Cooperative's model of economic democracy is further enhanced by their policies that lower salary differentials and wealth inequalities. The cooperative model devolves wealth and economic power across businesses and people. This strengthens political democracy and provides governments with a better opportunity to make decisions in the public interest.
- Cooperatives and private enterprises have maintained their unique character. Cooperatives have continued to meet their members' needs, adopt democratic management structures, limit capital remuneration, promote inter-generational wealth, and be embedded in local communities. Corporations have remained profit-maximising, hierarchical and non-democratic organisations whose purpose is to maximise shareholder value. They have shown a willingness to locate anywhere in the world in order to maximise profits.
- There is some evidence to suggest that cooperatives have been converging or emulating the corporation/capitalist model in a number of ways. Large cooperatives that operate overseas or own subsidiaries operate on a profit-maximising basis. Salary differentials in some cooperative sectors are almost similar to those practised in the private sector. Governance arrangements in cooperatives with a large passive membership delegate decision-making powers to a Board and professional management just like the large corporations. Cooperatives adopt the same legal structures as private businesses, including holding company-structure-owning subsidiaries that operate as conventional companies, joint ventures with the private sector, or cooperatives owning a listed company. Cooperative industrial relations, other than those practised by worker cooperatives where all workers are members, are similar to those employed by conventional companies where employees are employed via contractual arrangements. Cooperatives operating overseas do not offer overseas local communities the same benefits they offer their own local community.

9.6 Key Questions

- Consider and analyse the following core characteristics of cooperatives and corporations: purpose, ownership rights and control mechanisms, profit distribution, and industrial relations. What are the key differences between cooperatives and corporations? How significant are these differences?

- Most cooperatives adopt conventional industrial relations. What could be done to encourage employee participation in cooperative decision-making? Should profit-sharing arrangements in cooperatives be extended to employees, as is the case in France?
- Corporations distinguish themselves by being able to grow quickly into large TNCs. In your view, what are the key factors that prevent cooperatives from growing as quickly as corporations? How would you define the cooperative enterprise model, and what are its advantages and disadvantages? Should cooperatives attempt to grow as quickly as corporations?
- What are the major innovations that can be attributed to the cooperative movement? Consider the cooperative enterprise models, CDMs, how profits are distributed, how assets are managed, and so on. Which innovation would you regard as the most important and why?
- Cooperative productivity is comparable to the productivity of conventional enterprises. The survival rate of cooperatives is better than that of conventional enterprises. If this is the case, how can we explain that conventional businesses dominate markets and that the cooperative sector employs less than 10 per cent of the world's labour force?
- The larger cooperatives that have outgrown their local economy have adopted conventional business models: corporations, holding companies, subsidiaries, conventional industrial relations, higher salary differentials, profit maximisation, and so on. Does this mean that if cooperatives want to grow outside their local economies and become large cooperatives, they must imitate corporations? What are the factors that are leading large cooperatives and cooperative lawmakers to imitate practices previously associated with conventional firms? Can you identify large cooperatives that have not imitated conventional business models?
- Consider the purpose, ownership structure, and profit distribution policies of cooperatives. To what extent do cooperatives reduce income and wealth inequalities? Do all cooperatives reduce income and wealth inequalities?
- What are the key benefits that a cooperative-led economy brings to their local economy and their local community? What can be done to ensure that cooperatives extend their benefits to all the local economies and local communities in which they operate? Please comment on the examples provided in Part 9.3.3.
- To what extent do cooperatives contribute to economic and political democracy? In answering this question, compare and contrast the way cooperatives and corporations make decisions, how they engage with employees, how they distribute income and wealth, and how they engage with the State.
- If political democracy is based on one-person-one-vote, why do authors such as Bakan, Henderson, and Reich, are concerned about the excessive political influence of corporations? To what extent should the power of corporations concern the cooperative movement?

Notes

1 Please refer to Chapters 2–5.

2 Please refer to Chapter 5, which provides a number of cooperative examples that include Rabobank, Fonterra and Sacmi; and Chapter 6, which provides examples of five cooperative enterprise definitions.

3 The initial investment is called social capital in Europe, and members' shares in English-speaking countries. I use the term member capital accounts as is used in Mondragon and

Quebec, because social capital is not understood outside Europe, and the term 'shares' implies ownership of assets as in investor-owned firms, which is not the case in cooperatives.

4 It is important to note that whilst the cooperative law in some countries allows demutualisation and the distribution of assets, few cooperatives have demutualised. Those few cooperatives that demutualised operated in the finance and agricultural sector, and demutualised from the 1990s until the Global Financial Crisis. In addition, demutualisation mainly took place in English speaking countries where neo-liberal values were more rooted. Please refer to Chapter 5, Part 5.27; Chapter 6, Parts 6.3.4 and 6.3.8; and Chapter 8, Part 8.44.

5 Please refer to the Chapter 8.

6 Please refer to Chapters 6 and 8.

7 France seems to be the only jurisdiction from the 26 surveyed that requires a portion of profits to be distributed to all employees.

8 Please refer to Chapter 6 for an explanation of how profit is distributed among the various jurisdictions.

9 For instance, in Spain, cooperative members are treated as self-employed personnel. In Italy, collective agreements on pay and working conditions apply to members and non-members. Members, however, decide whether to provide extra benefits and remuneration policies for their capital accounts and the level of patronage dividend (Whyte and Whyte 1988, Ammirato 2018). Countries may pass legislations where minimum conditions apply to all types of enterprises, as is the case in Australia.

10 A cooperative enterprise model refers to the way a cooperative is organised to produce and sell goods and services in the market in order to meet the needs of its members. Cooperatives meet the economic, social, cultural and aspirational needs of their members by competing in the market on their own, or as a member of a second-tier cooperative. Whilst the term enterprise model is synonymous with the term business model, this book will opt to use the term cooperative model interchangeably with the term cooperative enterprise model.

11 Please refer to Chapter 6.

12 Please refer to Chapters 4 and 5.

13 Please refer to Chapter 7.

14 An overview on the various worker cooperative performance debates is provided by Perotin, and Dow (Perotin 2017, Dow 2018).

15 Please refer to Chapter 4 for information of the Mondragon and Legacoop cooperative development models, and Chapter 5 for information on the French and the Quebec cooperative development models.

16 Income refers to pay and earnings or compensation from work (wages and salaries) as well as income derived from dividends, interests, realised capital gains, rental income, and transfer payments from government such as unemployment insurance (Galbraith 2016).

17 Wealth is the value placed on a collection of possessions, or assets. It includes real estate and financial assets, such as money, and stocks and bonds at their market value (Galbraith 2016).

18 For discussions on inequality and also the role of the State please refer to these books (Atkinson 2015, Galbraith 2016, Reich 2016, Piketty 2017, 2022 and Gerstle 2022).

19 Chapter 6 provides more information about the various approaches used to allocate cooperative assets.

20 Value added refers to the difference between the firm's revenue minus the cost of intermediate consumption (the goods and services that the firm buys from other firms and consumes to produce its own goods and services). What is left is capital costs (dividends, interest on loans, taxes on profits, replacement of worn machineries and equipment (depreciation of capital or amortisation) and labour costs (wages, employer social contribution and employee paid social contribution) (Piketty 2015).

21 Sacmi, a very successful manufacturing cooperative, paid only 0.5 per cent of its value added to capital. The remaining value added amount was paid as follows: workers (63.7 per cent); cooperative reserves (28.9 percent); Taxes (5.7 percent); cooperative movement and the community (1.2 percent) (Sacmi 2021). Cadiai, a labour-intensive social cooperative, paid 96.4 per cent of its value added to workers and 2.4 per cent to cooperative reserves (Cadiai 2016).

22 Alan Greenspan notes how the United States lost 12 per cent of its manufacturing jobs (2.4 million) from 1979–1983 alone. He also notes that low-cost imports cost at least another 1.5 million jobs from 1990 to 2007 (Greenspan and Wooldridge 2019). There is currently a migration of firms from California to other parts of the United States, especially Texas. These may invest

in new facilities (Wells Fargo, Apple) or migrate their operations from California to Texas as Tesla, Hewlett Packard, Oracle have done (Lee and Vranich 2022).

23 Please refer to the books *Reinventing Government* to get an idea of how these ideas were promoted within the public sector and the book *Key Management Models* for an overview of management techniques adopted by the private sector over time (Osborne and Gaebler 1992, Van Assen, Van Der Berg and Pietersma 2009).

References

Amatori, Franco, and Andrea Colli. 2011. *Business History*. New York: Routledge.

America's Electric Cooperatives. 2016. *Powering America*. 22 December. Accessed June 14, 2017. http://www.electric.coop/our-mission/powering-america/.

Ammirato, Piero. 1996. *La Lega: The Making of a Successful Cooperative Network*. Aldershot: Dartmouth Publishing Company.

———. 2018. *The Growth of Italian Cooperatives: Innovation, Resilience and Social Responsibility*. New York: Routledge.

Apple. 2019. *Apple Newsroom*. 15 August. Accessed November 8, 2022. https://www.apple.com/newsroom/2019/08/apples-us-job-footprint-grows-to-two-point-four-million/.

Arla Foods. 2021. *Arla Foods Consolidated Annual Report 2021*. Annual Report, Copenhagen: Arla Foods.

Atkinson, Anthony B. 2015. *Inequality: What Can Be Done*. Cambridge: Massachusetts.

Azmanova, Albena. 2020. *Capitalism on Edge*. New York: Columbia University Press.

Bajo, Claudia Sanchez, and Bruno Roelants. 2011. *Capital and the Debt Trap: Learning from Cooperatives in the Global Crisis*. London: Palgrave Macmillan.

———. 2016. "Mainstreaming Co-operatives after the Global Financial Crisis." In *Mainstreaming Cooperatives after the Financial Crisis*, by Linda Shaw, Rachael Vorberg-Rugh Anthony Webster, 14–30. Manchester: Manchester University Press.

Bakan, Joel. 2004. *The Corporation*. London: Constable and Robinson.

———. 2020. *The New Corporation*. New York: Vintage Books.

Banca Etica. 2022. *Statuto di Banca Popolare Etica*. Company Statute, Padova: Banca Etica.

Barandiaran, Xabier, and Javier Lezaun. 2017. "The Mondragon Experience." In *The Oxford Handbook of Mutual, Co-Operative, and Co-Owned Business*, by Jonathon Michie, Joseph R. Blasi and Carlo Borzaga, 17 Pages. Oxford: Oxford University Press.

Becattini, Giacomo, Marco Bellandi, and lisa De Propis. 2009. *A Handbook of Industrial Districts*. Cheltenham: Edward Elgar Publishing.

Bevir, Mark. 2012. *Governance: A Very Short Introduction*. Oxford: Oxford University Press.

Book, Sven Ake. 1992. *Cooperatives in a Changing World*. Report to the ICA Congress Tokyo, October, 1992, Geneva: International Cooperative Alliance.

Borzaga, Carlo. 2015. "Introduzione e Sintesi." In *Economia Cooperativa: Rilevanza, Evoluzione e Nuove Frontiere della Cooperazione Italiana*, by Carlo Borzaga Editor, 5–35. Trento: Euricse.

Brat, Eric, Inmaculada Buendía Buendía Martínez, and Buendía Martínez Ouchene. 2016. *Innovation: Priorities and Practices in Cooperatives*. Montreal: Alphonse and Rorimene Desjardins International Institute for Cooperatives.

Britannica. 2021. *Virginia Company*. 5 April. Accessed June 1, 2023. https://www.britannica.com/topic/Virginia-Company.

Burdin, Gabriel, and Dean Andres. 2012. "Revisiting the Objectives of Worker-managed Firms: An Empirical Assessment." *Economic Systems* 158–171.

Cadiai. 2016. *Bilancio Sociale Consuntivo*. Annual Social Report, Bologna: Cadiai.

Caselli, Guido. 2014. *Osservatorio della Cooperazione in Emilia-Romagna: Partire dai Numeri*. Regional Cooperative Sector Review, Bologna: Unioncamere.

Caselli, Guido, Michele Costa, and Flavio Delbono. 2021. "What do Cooperative Firms Maximize, if at all? Evidence from Emilia-Romagna in the Pre-Covid Decade." *Annals of Public and Cooperative Economics* 1–27.

Chancel, Lucas, Thomas Piketty, Emmanuel Saez, and Gabriel Zucman. 2022. *World Economic Report 2022*. Paris: World Economic Lab.

CICOPA. 2017. *Cooperatives and Employment: Second Global Report*. Global Report on Cooperative Employment, Brussels: ICA.

Colpan, Asli M, and Takashi Hikino. 2010. "Foundations of Business Groups." In *The Oxford Handbook of Business Groups*, by Asli M Colpan, Takashi Hikino and James Lincoln, 15–66. Oxford: Oxford University Press.

Conad. 2021. *Annual Report 2021*. Annual Report, Bologna: Conad.

Cooperatives Europe. 2016. *Cooperatives Europe Key Figures 2015*. Cooperative Europe Statistics, Brussels: Cooperatives Europe.

Corcoran, Hazel, and David Wilson. 2010. *The Worker Co-operative Movements in Italy, Mondragon and France: Context, Success Factors and Lessons*. Calgary: Canadian Worker Cooperative Federation.

Craig, Ben, and John Pencavel. 1992. "The Behavior of Worker Cooperatives: The Plywood Companies." *The American Economic Review* 1083–1105.

———. 1993. "The Objectives of Worker Cooperatives." *Journal of Economic Literature* 288–308.

Crane, Andrew, and Dick Matten. 2016. *Business Ethics*. Oxford: Oxford University Press.

Cumbers, Andrew. 2020. *Economic Democracy*. Cambridge: Polity Press.

Dahl, Robert. 1998. *On Cooperation*. New Haven: Yale University Press.

De Long, Brad. 2022. *Slouching Towards Utopia: An Economic History of the Twentieth Century*. New York: Basic Books.

Diamantopoulos, Mitch. 2011. "Cooperative Development Gap in Québec and Saskatchewan 1980 to 2010: A Tale of Two Movements." *Canadian Journal of Nonprofit and Social Economy Research* 6–24.

Donaldson, Peter. 1984. *Economics of the Real World*. London: Penguin Books.

Dow, Gregory. 2018. "The Theory of the Labor-Managed Firm: Past, Present and Future." *Annals of Public and Cooperative Economics* 65–86.

Estrin, Saul, and Derek C. Jones. 1992. "The Viability of Employee-Owned Firms: Evidence from France." *Industrial and Labor Relations Review* 323–338.

Euricse. 2022. *World Cooperative Monitor* . Trento: Euricse and International Cooperative Alliance.

FakhFakh, Fathi, Virginie Perotin, and Monica Gago. 2012. "Productivity, Capital, and Labor in Labor-Managed and Conventional Firms: An Investigation of French Data." *ILR Review* 847–879.

Fonterra. 2022. *Corporate Governance Statement and Statutory Information 2022*. Governance Report, Auckland: Fonterra Cooperative Limited Group.

Friedman, Milton. 1970. "A Friedman Doctrine: The Social Responsibility of Business Is to Increase its Profits." *New York Times*, 13 September.

Fruin, Mark. 2007. "Business Groups and Inter-firm Networks." In *The Oxford Handbook of Business History*, by Geoffrey Jones and Jonathon Zeitlin, 244–267. Oxford: Oxford University Press.

Galbraith, James K. 2016. *Inequality: What Everyone Needs to Know*. New York: Oxford University Press.

Galbraith, J.K, and Nicome Salinger. 1984. *Almost Everyone's Guide to Economics*. Harmondsworth: Penguin.

Gerstle, Gary. 2022. *The Rise and Fall of the Neoliberal Order*. New York: Oxford University Press.

Government du Quebec. 2003. *Cooperative Development Policy*. Government Policy Document, Quebec: Government du Quebec.

Greenspan, Alan, and Adrian Wooldridge. 2019. *Capitalism in America*. New York: Penguin Books Ltd.

Hadas, Thier. 2020. *A People's Guide to Capitalism: An Introduction to Marxist Economics*. Chicago: Haymarket Books.

Hancock, Matt. 2007. *Compete to Cooperate: The Cooperative District of Imola*. Imola: Bacchilega Editore.

Henderson, Rebecca. 2020. *Reimagining Capitalism*. New York: Penguin Random House.

Henderson, Richard. 2022. "Global Dividend Payments Hit Record High." *Australian Financial Review*. 24 August. Accessed November 4, 2022. https://www.afr.com/markets/equity-markets/global-dividend-payments-hit-record-high-20220824-p5bc9h#:~:text=Dividends%20to%20edge%20higher&text=On%20a%20calendar%2Dyear%20basis,basis%2C%20accounting%20for%20currency%20fluctuations.

Holmstrom, Mark. 1989. *Industrial Democracy in Italy*. Avebury: Gower Publishing Company.

Howard, Colin. 1989. *Companies: What They Are and How They Work*. Oxford: Oxford University Press.

IBIS. 2022. *Global Biggest Industries by Employment*. November. Accessed November 11, 2022. https://www.ibisworld.com/global/industry-trends/biggest-industries-by-employment/.

Iliopoulos, Constantine, and Vladislav Valentinov. 2018. "Cooperative Longevity: Why Are So Many Cooperatives So Successful?" *Sustainability* 1–8.

International Cooperative Alliance. 2016. *Facts and Figures*. Accessed December 22, 2016. http://ica.coop/en/facts-and-figures.

———. 2017. *Guidance Notes to the Co-operative Principles*. Guidance Notes, Geneva: International Cooperative Alliance.

Jones, Derek. 2007. "The Productive Efficiency of Italian Producer Cooperatives: Evidence from Conventional and Cooperartive Firms." *Cooperative Firms in Global Markets: Incidence, Viability and Economic PerformanceAdvances in the Economic Analysis of Participatory and Labor-Managed Firms* 3–28.

Juban, Jean-Yves, Olivier Boissin, Hervé Charmettant, and Yvan Renou. 2016. "Pay Policy and Organizational Design of French Cooperatives (Des Scop)." *RIMHE - Management & Human Enterprise review* 64–83.

Lazonick, William. 2008. "Business History and Economic Development." In *The Oxford Handbook of Business History*, by Geoffrey G. Jones and Jonathon Zeitlin, 67–95. Oxford: Oxford University Press.

Lee, Ohanian, and Joseph Vranich. 2022. "California Business Exits Soared in 2021, and There Is No End in Sight." *Hoover Institute*. 25 October. Accessed November 26, 2022. https://www.hoover.org/research/california-business-exits-soared-2021-and-there-no-end-sight.

Legacoop. 2011. *Rapporto sulla Cooperazione Reggiana 2006-2010*. Congressional Report, Reggio Emilia: Legacoop Reggio Emilia.

Levitt, Theodore. 1983. "The Globalization of Markets." *Harvard Business Review* 92–101.

MacLeod, Greg. 2009. "The Mondragon Experiment." *Harvard International Review*, 4 April.

Malleson, Tom. 2013. "Economic Democracy: The Left's Big Idea for theTwenty-First Century?" *New Political Science* 84–108.

Mazzucato, Mariana. 2018. *The Entrepreneurial State: Debunking Public vs.Private Sector Myths*. London: Penguin Books.

Milanovic, Branko. 2017. *Capitalism, Alone*. Cambridge: The Belknap Press of Harvard University Press.

Mondragon Corporation. 2019. *Adding to Multiply*. Presentation, Mondragon: Mondragon Corporation.

Morrison, Roy. 1991. *We Build the Road as we Travel*. Philadelphia: New Society Publishers.

Münkner, Hans. 2020. *National Report Germany*. Legal Framework Analysis, Brussels: International Cooperative Alliance.

OECD. 2021. *Government at a Glance 2021*. Annual Government Statistics Report, Paris: OECD.

Office of National Statistics. 2022. *People Population and Community*. Accessed November 26, 2022. https://www.ons.gov.uk/peoplepopulationandcommunity/personalandhouseholdfinances/incomeandwealth/bulletins/householddisposableincomeandinequality/financialyearending2021.

Osborne, David, and Ted Gaebler. 1992. *Reinventing Government*. Reading: Addison-Wesley Publishing Company, Inc.

Osservatorio Grandi Imprese. 2016. *Le Grandi Cooperative Italiane.* Economic Statistics, Rome: Alleanza delle Cooperative Italiane.

Oxfam. 2017. *An economy for the 99%.* Oxford: Oxfam.

Pencavel, John, Luigi Pistaferri, and Fabiano Schivardi. 2006. "Wages, Employment, and Capital in Capitalist and Worker-Owned Firms." *Industrial and Labor Relations Review* 23–44.

Pendleton, Andrew, and Howard Gospel. 2013. "Corporate Governance and Labor." In *The Oxford Handbook of Corporate Governance*, by Mike Wright, Donald S Siegel, Kevin Keasey and Igor Filatochev, 634–657. Oxford: Oxford University Press.

Perotin, Virginie. 2017. "Worker Co-operatives: Good, Sustainable Jobs in the Community." In *The Oxford Handbook of Mutual, Co-operative and Co-Owned Businesses*, by Jonathon Michie and Carlo Borzaga Joseph Blasi, 131–144. Oxford: Oxford University Press.

Pestoff, Victor A. 2017. "The Social and Political Dimensions of Cooperative Enterprises." In *The Oxford Handbook of Mutual, Cooperative and Co-owned Business*, by Jonathon Michie, Joseph Blasi and Carlo Borzaga, 76–96. Oxford: Oxford University Press.

Petrucci, Paola. 2009. "La Distribuzione degli Avanzi di Gestione e la Practica del Ristorno nelle Imprese Cooperative." In *Colloquio Scientifico Annuale Sull'Impresa Sociale*, by Iris Network, 1–11. Trento: IRIS Network.

Piketty, Thomas. 2015. *Economics of Inequality.* Cambridge: Harvard University Press.

———. 2017. *Capital in the Twenty-First Century.* Boston: Harvard University Press.

———. 2022. *A Brief History of Equality.* Cambridge: Harvard University Press.

Porter, Michael E, and Mark R Kramer. 2011. "Creating Shared Value." *Harvard Business Review* 1–17.

Rabobank. 2021. *Annual Report 2021.* Annual Report, Amsterdam: The Cooperative Rabobank.

Reich, Robert. 2016. *Saving Capitalism.* London: Icon Books.

Sacmi. 2021. *Annual Report.* Annual Report, Imola: Sacmi.

———. 2022. "Sacmi Group, Revenues in 2021 Hit a Record of Over 1.53 Billion Euro." *Sacmi - Innovation and Sustainability.* 16 May. Accessed November 14, 2022. https://sacmi.com/en-US/corporate/news/14160/SACMI-GROUP,-revenues-in-2021-hit-a-record-of-over-1-53-billion-euro.

Schumpeter, Joseph A. 1942. *Capitalism, Socialism, Democracy.* Floyd: Sublime Books.

Schweickart, David. 2011. *After Capitalism.* Plymouth: Rowman&Littlefield Publishers.

Srinivasan, Bhu. 2017. *Americana: A 400 Year History of American Capitalism.* New York: Penguin Books.

Statista. 2021. *Average Annual Salary in the Netherlands in 2021 by Age.* Accessed November 26, 2022. https://www.statista.com/statistics/538406/average-annual-salary-in-the-netherlands-by-age.

Statistics Canada. 2022. *Income of Individuals by Age Group, Sex and Income Source.* 3 March. Accessed November 26, 2022. https://www150.statcan.gc.ca/t1/tbl1/en/tv.action?pid=1110023901.

Statistics Denmark. 2022. *Statistik.* Accessed November 25, 2022. https://www.dst.dk/en/Statistik/nyheder-analyser-publ/Publikationer/gennemsnitsdanskeren.

StatsNZ. 2022. *Labour Market Statistics (Income): June 2022 Quarter.* 17 August. Accessed November 26, 2022. https://www.stats.govt.nz/information-releases/labour-market-statistics-income-june-2022-quarter.

Steger, Manfred. 2020. *Globalization.* Oxford: Oxford University Press.

Stiglitz, Joseph E. 2019. *People, Power and Profits: Progressive Capitalism for an Age of Discontent.* New York: Penguin Random House.

Stretton, Hugh. 2000. *Economics: a New Introduction.* Sydney: University of New South Wales.

The Co-operative Group Limited. 2021. *Co-op Annual Reports and Accounts 2021.* Annual Report, Manchester, 2021: The Co-operative Group Limited.

Thomsen, Steen. 2016. "Nordic Corporate Governance Revisited." *Nordic Journal of Business* 1–12.

Thomsen, Steen, Caspar Rese, and Dorte Kronborg. 2016. "Employee Representation and Board Size in the Nordic Countries." *European Journal of Law and Economics* 471–490.

Unipol. 2022. *Company Profile*. Company profile, Bologna: Unipol.

Unipol Group. 2021. *Unipol Group Remuneration Policies*. Report on Remuneration Policies and Compensation, Bologna: Unipol Group.

Van Assen, Marcel, Gerben Van Der Berg, and Paul Pietersma. 2009. *Key Management Models*. Harlow: Prentice Hall.

Vancity. 2021. *Change Makers - 2021 Annual Report*. Annual Report, Vancouver: Vancity.

Vieta, Marcelo, Sara Depetri, and Antonella Carrano. 2017. *The Italian Road to Recuperating Enterprises in Crisis and the Legge Marcora Framework: Italy's Worker-Buyouts in Times of Crisis*. Trento: Euricse.

Viviani, Mario. 2013. *Piccola Guida Alla Cooperazione*. Soveria Monnelli: Rubbettino.

Whyte, William Foote, and Kathleen King Whyte. 1988. *Making Mondragon*. New York: Ithaca Press.

Zamagni, Vera. 2012. "A World of Variations: Sectors and Forms in the Comparative Business Movement." In *Cooperative Business Movement, 1950 to Present*, by Patrizia Battiulani and Harm Schroeder, Chapter 2. Cambridge: Cambridge University Press.

Zeitlin, Jonathon. 2007. "Industrial Districts and Regional Clusters." In *The Oxford Handbook of Business History*, by Geoffrey Jones and Jonathon Zeitlin, 219–243. Oxford: Oxford University Press.

10 Cooperatives and Globalisation

Cooperatives have consistently met their members' needs and have matched the private sector in economic performance and longevity. They have demonstrated a capacity to survive economic crises. Cooperatives have successfully intervened when there have been market, business, and state failures. They reduce income differentials and limit wealth inequalities, and their model is suited to address territorial inequalities. Cooperatives have grown since the 1750s and are estimated to employ close to 10 per cent of total global employment, but their share of the world's Gross Domestic Product is less than 5 per cent. Considering the benefits that cooperatives offer their members, the community, the market, and the State, it is important to propose strategies to grow cooperative sector so that it can become a significant player in the local and world economy. This is ever more pertinent considering that people's aspirations to have a full-time secure job, better working conditions, the ability to buy quality food at affordable prices, a home, access to education and health care, affordable aged care, and a retirement income, are still relevant today.

This question of how to grow the cooperative sector is also pertinent because, as Fauquet correctly noted in the 1930s, neither the State, the private sector, nor cooperatives, are able to solve all of society's problems on their own (Fauquet 1941). This has been true regarding capitalist-led market economies (CMEs) and state-led planned economies. CMEs have openly sought the support of the State to deal with periodic economic crises and inherent market failures. The State has become both the manager of the economy and the provider of welfare services in order to make CMEs more socially and morally acceptable.[1] State-led planned economies eventually sought support from the market and the private sector to diversify and revitalise their economies. This was achieved by attracting Foreign Direct Investment, accessing new technologies, and via nation-specific political and economic policies. This raises the question of what is an appropriate mix for the mixed economy. Is the best possible mix best determined by neo-liberal CMEs supported by welfare policies and programmes? Is it best determined by a planned economy supported by welfare policies and programmes? Or is it best determined by a pluralist market economy within which cooperatives perform a significant role alongside a socially responsible private sector and state enterprises governed by a State that supports all economic actors that operate in a pluralist economy? It is beyond the scope of this book to answer this question comprehensively. However, it will be argued that having a pluralist democratic state that supports a pluralist market economy where cooperatives hold a significant market share high enough to influence the market's operations significantly and significantly benefit society is the most preferred option.

DOI: 10.4324/9781003269533-10

This chapter discusses the contribution the cooperative sector could make in societies influenced by the global market and its global institutions. Part 10.1 discusses the impact of globalisation on the world today. It identifies its virtues and the negative impact that the neo-liberal, capitalist-led globalisation has on people, communities and countries. Part 10.2 will discuss cooperative longitudinal trends. This will examine the cooperative enterprise models,[2] cooperative development models (CDMs),[3] and cooperative law, finance, and governance. Part 10.3 discusses how cooperatives engage and improve the operations of the market, complement the role of the State, support local communities, and expand economic democracy. Part 10.4 will summarise why there are few cooperatives. Part 10.5 considers what policies and measures could be implemented to grow the cooperative sector significantly so that it can positively influence local and global markets and the societies in which they operate. Part 10.6 concludes the Chapter.

This chapter enables readers to:

- Consider the capabilities, the capacity to grow, the ability to innovate, and the limits of CMEs.
- Appreciate the cooperative enterprise models and CDMs trends since the 1750s.
- Examine the positive contribution that cooperatives make in the economy and society.
- Re-consider the reasons why there are few cooperatives.
- Critically consider what could be done—at the enterprise, movement, local, national, and international levels—to promote the cooperative sector.
- Consider whether the cooperative sector could be promoted in a similar way that the CME has been promoted since 1945.

10.1 A Capitalist-Led Market Economy

World trade today is conducted via a CME. This global market has been built by corporations, States, and global institutions. It speeded up its development after 1945, especially after the fall of the Soviet Union in 1989. Multinational companies dominate CMEs and the world economy. These corporations developed the public company, organisational innovations, financial markets, research laboratories, and a capacity to grow and to bring goods to market quickly. Corporations promoted universities worldwide that taught the Masters of Business Administration (MBA), facilitating the transfer of knowledge, ideas, and business practices worldwide. States protect private property and provide legal, regulatory, and economic environments for businesses to grow. They regulate labour and financial markets, provide essential infrastructure and educational services, and support research and development. They mediate the effects of market failures by managing the economy and providing welfare support to citizens left out of the market. Nation-states' quest for power and regular involvement in wars also helped corporations grow and develop new products. Nation-state-funded international institutions such as the International Monetary Fund (IMF), The World Bank, and the World Trade Organization (WTO) have promoted CMEs and world trade. Since the 1990s, these institutions have promoted neo-liberal policies across the world through international agreements and by forcing countries to deregulate and privatise their economy in return for receiving financial aid and infrastructure support (Chang 2014, Frieden 2020, Chomsky and Waterstone 2021).

The political-economic compromise that led to the development of CMEs, supported by state provisions of essential services and welfare measures, has increased productivity and generated more wealth. This political-economic system has supported a larger population worldwide, improved living standards, increased educational participation rates, improved health provisions, and enabled people to live longer. The neo-liberal approach to globalism, known as the 'Washington Consensus', has led to deregulation, privatisation, market-based foreign exchange rates, fewer trade barriers, and lower income and company tax. This approach to global markets has led to corporations gaining more market share and more economic power; nation-states having less control over the national economy; greater income and wealth inequalities among citizens and territories; and has led to insecurities and instability for citizens and their communities.[4] In addition, the current neo-liberal CMEs have not been able to prevent regular economic crises, global warming, and environment degradation; the mass migration of people leaving poor areas for richer countries; and corporations and a minority of the population having a disproportionate influence on the political system, thus undermining political democracy (Reich 2016, Steeger and Roy 2021).

There are a number of choices available. The first choice is to leave things as they are. This means accepting the inherent limits of CMEs and a society where the majority of people in wealthy countries are employed, most may be satisfied with their living standards, whilst a sizeable minority live in precarious and unsatisfactory living standards. The second choice is to revert to the Social Democratic policies of the 1930s and post-1945. This means accepting the inherent limits of CMEs as well as a State which mediates and corrects the inherent limits of CMEs. This would lead to a mixed economy, including state-owned enterprises, a progressive taxation system, a robust universal welfare system, and a regulated economy. This would allow states to provide universal educational, health, housing, and welfare services and to reduce income and wealth inequalities. The third choice is to promote a greater role for the cooperative economy because it would be able to solve some of the inherent problems associated with CMEs at the cooperative enterprise level and the cooperative movement level. This third option would imply having a mixed economy within which the cooperative sector would hold a significant share of the economy, with which it could influence the market, people's behaviours, and the State. A greater role for the cooperative economy could promote economic democracy within a pluralist market economy that could overcome the limitations inherent in CMEs. This third approach would establish a cooperative-led market economy that would complement the distributional policies as well as the welfare-related policies promoted via the Social Democratic State.

10.2 Cooperative Trends

This section considers the longitudinal trends of the cooperative enterprise model. It will synthesise the evidence provided in the previous chapters on the cooperative enterprise, CDMs, and cooperative law, finance, and governance.

10.2.1 Successful and Timeless

The first trend is that cooperatives have been consistently democratic and competitive and have demonstrated a universal appeal across all sectors of the economy. The cooperative enterprises have remained aligned with the cooperative principles of democratic management (one-person-one-vote), limited return on capital, patronage returns based on transactions, and mostly of holding collectively owned or community-owned assets.

Cooperative enterprises operate across the primary, secondary, and tertiary sectors of the economy. They have consistently met their members' need to have a secure job, access to unaltered food, access to markets and credit, access to child care and aged care, and so on. Cooperatives have proven that their performance, employment record, and longevity record matches that of the private sector. They have demonstrated their universal appeal by operating in every part of the globe.

10.2.2 Enterprise Models

The overall trend is for cooperatives to use the traditional first-tier enterprise model first, to then become members of a second-tier cooperative to improve their competitiveness, and then develop into large cooperative enterprises via organic growth and via mergers or acquisitions. Some internationally focussed large cooperatives have adopted dual structures.

The first tier is the original cooperative enterprise formed by workers, consumers, or producers. These are democratically managed and focus on meeting their members' needs. This first tier has been modified with the arrival of social cooperatives, which produce goods or services in the general interests of society. These first-tier structures have established second-tier cooperatives to achieve economies of scale whilst remaining small. These included consumer wholesale societies, agricultural purchasing or marketing cooperatives, consortia to access public works or to provide services to their members, and regional or central banking federations providing financial services to their members. Cooperatives then developed into large cooperative enterprises through organic growth, mergers, and acquisitions commencing in the 1980s. Some adopted dual structures that included holding companies owning and managing conventional companies. The holding companies could be fully owned or partly owned. Dual-structure cooperatives operate in all cooperative sectors.

10.2.3 Development Models

The appearance of CDMs that promote the whole cooperative sector is another major trend of the cooperative movement. These CDMs are usually led by a cooperative association or federation providing political, strategic, cultural, and economic leadership to an inter-sectoral cooperative movement. They have the capability and capacity to promote new cooperatives, new cooperative sectors, support existing cooperatives, and manage economic or organisational crises that beset the movement.

A number of CDMs were discussed in Chapters 4 and 5. These include the CDMs from Mondragon (Spain) and Legacoop (Italy)[5]; the CDMs from Japan, France; the CDM from the province of Quebec (Canada); and the CDMs centred in the cities of Trento (Italy) and Wonju (Korea). Although these CDMs have leadership, governance, organisational, size, and strategic differences, they display many common features. These features include a national or local lead association; a unique vision for society, or unique goals, that go beyond the needs of the cooperative enterprise; the provision of comprehensive administrative and financial support; the ability to promote new cooperatives; the ability to associate cooperatives from many economic sectors; the ability and the capacity to manage change and to overcome economic crises. All these CDMs display a level of engagement and cooperation with civil society. Most CDMs have developed a respectful relationship with the State.

The importance of CDMs is that they can promote cooperatives in perpetuity, accumulate knowledge, develop capabilities, and manage financial resources, all of which are passed on to the next generation of co-operators. These CDMs operate in many parts of the world with historical, language, and cultural differences, demonstrating that they can be established anywhere in the world.

10.2.4 Legislation

Cooperative law has been very flexible and comprises many elements. It reflects the needs of cooperative enterprises as they grow and compete in larger markets. It also reflects the type of cooperative activity, the national-specific cooperative needs, and enterprise culture. It reflects the International Cooperative Alliance's (ICA) Cooperative Principles. The key general trend is the constant incremental change of cooperative law. This approach allows the law to accommodate traditional and new cooperatives and allows diverse cooperative traditions to develop.

The first trend has been the progression from a member-focussed cooperative law to one that, since the 1990s, has also included social cooperative enterprises. These cooperatives promote society's general interests. Social cooperatives attempt to solve general problems such as aged care, long-term unemployment, and so on, and not just focus on meeting the needs of their members. The second major trend has been the progression from an enterprise-focussed cooperative law to cooperative law provisions promoting the cooperative movement and the community. To this end, cooperative law provisions include actively promoting cooperation among cooperatives; funding for educational activities managed by cooperative federations; development of cooperative development funds; and promoting inter-generational provisions such as preventing, or making difficult, the sale of cooperative assets that can be distributed to cooperative members.

These two major trends align with the ICA's sixth Principle, Cooperation Among Cooperatives, and the ICA's seventh Principle, Concern for Community. As noted in Chapter 6, jurisdictions whose cooperative law has shown a strong inclination to promote all or almost all of the seven cooperative principles include Argentina, France, Italy, Japan, Portugal, Quebec, Spain, and Uruguay.

10.2.5 Finance

The general trend relating to finance is the steady progression for cooperatives to access external capital to complement internal self-financing. The traditional means to access finance internally included members' capital accounts, members' loans, and retained profits. In addition to internal finance, traditional forms of finance, such as external loans from local banks, civil society-owned financial institutions, cooperative-owned financial companies, and cooperative development or solidarity funds, are also available. This type of funding is mostly suitable for small to medium cooperatives. However, it has also proven capable of meeting the financial needs of an international cooperative like Italy's Sacmi, Mondragon's manufacturing sector, and the expansion of the Japanese consumer movement.

Large cooperatives, especially those expanding overseas, have resorted to external equity capital. Some external equity capital (with or without voting rights) can also be provided by cooperative-owned or cooperative-friendly financial companies, whose capital may also include State equity funding. The mainstream capital market, however, is becoming a key source of external capital. Sources of external capital include cooperative tradeable and non-tradeable bonds; preference shares (non-voting shares); external capital accounts owned by non-members that may or may not provide voting rights; listing a limited amount of tradeable shares on the stock market; majority ownership of a listed company; and attracting external investment in a majority-owned cooperative holding company.

10.2.6 *Governance*

Cooperative governance has also introduced changes to how decisions are made to reflect the needs of larger cooperatives, local governance cultures, and public expectations following the governance scandals that impacted conventional and cooperative enterprises. Cooperative governance comprises a variety of governance models. However, the general trend for the larger cooperatives is to devolve powers from the General Assembly (GA) to the cooperative Board and management.

There are at least four core cooperative governance structures. The one-tier model practices direct democracy through the GA. In the tri-partite model, the GA retains key decision-making powers, including the powers to appoint the Board (which includes management) and the Supervisory Committee, which has powers to appoint the auditors. In the two-tier Supervisory Board model, the GA appoints the Supervisory Board, which, in turn, appoints the Management Board and the audit committee. Finally, the Unitary Board model is one where the GA appoints a Unitary Board, which appoints the CEO, the auditors, and the subcommittees. The Supervisory Board Model and the Unitary Board Model, just like conventional companies that use similar governance models, adopt the separation of ownership and management principle, the use of competency-based boards, the use of independent directors, and the use of board sub-committees to improve their effectiveness.

The GA has devolved powers to the Supervisory Board and Unitary Board, but especially in the one-tier, tri-partite (and to a lesser extent the Supervisory Board model) it still retains key powers such as changing the cooperative by-laws, making key decisions relating to investments (especially mergers and acquisitions), membership, profit distribution, rebate remuneration, and the direct appointment of auditors or supervisory committees. In addition, many cooperatives have elected member-based consultative bodies that engage with the Board and management. These have included the formation of cooperative consultative councils supported by sub-committees, committees at the local level, Social Councils as was the case of Mondragon, Works Councils in Nordic countries, employee representatives (co-determination policies), decentralised cooperative branches to encourage member participation, and improved forms of communication and information. Cooperatives can also convene the GA multiple times during the year to discuss key issues.

10.2.7 *Incremental Change*

The cooperative culture that is giving rise to these cooperative trends is one where continuity and constant change coexist. The cooperative culture displays an incremental approach to change within a diverse global cooperative movement. The original cooperative first-tier and second-tier enterprise models, the original cooperative growth strategies centred on a consumer cooperative or cooperative bank, the original cooperative focus on members, the focus on internal financing arrangements, the governance arrangements that favoured direct democracy and forms of representative democracy where ownership and management were not separated; have not been abolished, undermined, or rendered ineffectual. These traditional cooperative enterprise approaches continue to coexist with those new cooperative enterprise models. These new models include dual-structure co-operatives, cooperative networks, general interest cooperatives, cooperative movements with a community focus, cooperative development funds, provisions to access external capital, and the transfer of power from the GA to the Board and management.

10.3 Economy and Society

Cooperatives' 'reason to be' is to serve their members and their communities. The co-operative model is one organisation that people have used to protect themselves against the precariousness and insecurities created by economic liberalism and an economy that was based on self-interest (Polanyi 1957). Cooperatives have demonstrated that they are more than an economic entity that sells goods and services. They have always been an association of people that have used the cooperative model to solve problems that they and their communities encountered in a CME (Pestoff 2017).

10.3.1 Protection, Emancipation, and Inclusion

Consumers, farmers, artisans, small businesses, and working people turned to cooperatives to solve the many problems they encountered when dealing with the CME. Consumers formed consumer cooperatives to protect themselves from high prices, poor-quality products, and unsafe goods. In controlling prices, they also increased consumers' spending power. Cooperative rural banks provided farmers with loans and services so that farmers could survive, protect their lifestyle, safeguard their community, and eventually compete in the market. In Quebec, cooperative banks were also linked to safeguarding the community of the French-speaking population by promoting local economic development and preventing further emigration to the United States. Working people established worker cooperatives so that they could have secure jobs, better pay, and improved working conditions. Workers now owned their cooperative enterprise and made decisions affecting their lives. Social cooperatives served the general interests of society and provided work for long-term unemployed, people with disabilities, and the aged so that they could live a life with dignity.

As cooperatives grew, they began to perform a bigger role in the market and in society. This was made possible because they accumulated knowledge, capabilities, and resources; they developed second-tier support structures; they developed more ways to access credit; they achieved economies of scale and a stronger market position in key economic sectors, and a stronger presence in some local and regional economies. The roles they performed in the market and society included correcting the market, complementing the role of the State, and strengthening local economies. The total aggregate contribution to the economy and society has resulted in cooperatives and cooperative movements promoting economic democracy.

10.3.2 Correcting the Market

The term normally used when markets do not meet the needs of citizens or consumers is 'market failure'. This includes situations where a profit-maximising activity leads to costs that are paid for by society, a failure to create a competitive environment, a failure to provide consumers with adequate information on products and services, and so on. I use the term 'correcting the market' because cooperatives correct and improve the operations of the market. The current CMEs operate as they are meant to operate. Market failure implies that the CMEs could solve all society's problems such as employment, health, housing, provision of services and so on. This is not the role of the CME. CMEs are predominantly formed by corporations and businesses aiming to maximise profits on behalf of shareholders subject to complying with the law. Corporations will make decisions on behalf of shareholders and not in what is in the best interest of society. As a result, CMEs will continue to create regular economic crises, unemployment, and inequalities, grow until they become a monopoly or oligopoly, and will constantly threaten local communities by investing where it is most profitable. This is the inherent risk faced by societies that rely on CMEs.

Cooperatives correct the market by performing an anti-monopoly function. Cooperatives being member-based organisations can correct the market's tendency to have few companies control market segments and form monopolies. The Swedish consumer movement demonstrated how to develop anti-monopoly policies. It intervened in selected areas to the point of controlling at least 15 per cent of the market so that it could influence prices. Areas of intervention included margarine, rubber shoes, tires, fertilisers, building materials, and light bulbs. It was very successful as light bulb prices fell by 37 per cent; rubber shoe prices by more than 50 per cent; and margarine prices by nearly 60 per cent. It also led to higher levels of employment (Bonow 1938, Gillespie 1950, Hilson 2018).

Another limit of CMEs is their inability or unwillingness to provide essential services throughout the territory and to every citizen. The formation of electric cooperatives in the United States is a key example of cooperatives forming to provide a service that the private sector declined to provide because it was deemed unprofitable. In all, 800 cooperatives were established. They received state-loans and management support and built 350 miles of lines. By the 1940s, electric cooperatives provided 100 per cent electrification to a number of US states where electricity access was as low as 2 per cent of homes. These cooperatives have fully paid their loans and are still operating today (Taylor 2021). Cooperatives are also known to provide the only banking services in small towns,[6] and to provide essential proximity services to small and often isolated communities (Girard and Langlois 2009, Mori 2017).[7]

CMEs operations also lead to regular economic and financial crises. This is despite state regulations, oversight from public bodies, and improved governance arrangements. The Global Financial Crisis (GFC) of 2007–2009 provides a good example of how cooperatives mitigated the negative impact that the GFC had on workers, small businesses, consumers, and communities. During the GFC, whilst conventional banks were reducing their lending, cooperative banks continued to lend money to their members because their purpose is to serve their members and not to maximise profits for their shareholders. It was also not uncommon for cooperative banks to extend or reschedule payments (Birchall and Ketislon 2009, Birchall 2013, BCC 2016). When conventional companies resorted to laying off staff during the GFC, the Mondragon cooperative network reduced working hours or transferred workers to other cooperatives as much as possible. Italian cooperatives increased investment and increased employment. Research also indicated that where cooperatives had to reduce working hours to avoid job losses, the policy was implemented fairly between members and non-members. The Mondragon Corporation and the Legacoop Cooperative Development Fund also supported cooperative members in restructuring their operations in order to survive the crisis. Whilst cooperatives also have their limitations, they have demonstrated an inclination to save employment and to support other cooperative members in times of crisis (Bajo and Roelants 2011, Zevi, et al. 2011, Roelants, et al. 2012, Ammirato 2018).

It is also worth pointing out that based on our understanding of the non-speculative way that cooperative banks, insurance companies, credit unions (or mutual banks), and ethical banks like Banca Etica manage savings and allocate credit, a crisis like the GFC would have been avoided had cooperative banks been the dominant financial institution. The crisis was based on selling derivatives to retail and institutional investors based on real estate mortgages given to homeowners with no financial means to repay the loans. The lending practices of money lenders and the selling practices of institutional banks lacked due diligence. They displayed speculative behaviour designed to maximise profits at the expense of honest investors (Frieden 2020). The nature of cooperative banks, including their ownership structure, their policies to retain profits, their focus on providing their members with loans for their basic needs, and their close knowledge of their members, has so far prevented the kind of speculative behaviour that characterised investment banks that resulted in the GFC (Birchall 2013).

10.3.3 Complementing the State

In modern societies, citizens turn to the State via their representatives and associations to solve issues and problems encountered in the economic sphere and in society. These issues include matters related to industrial relations and employment opportunities, social security, local economic development, income and wealth inequalities, education, public health, housing, quality of life issues, concerns with law and order, aged care, family matters and so on. Everyone expects the State to intervene during an economic crisis. Most people expect the State to deal with income and wealth inequalities. The intervention of the State is expected to treat every citizen equally. To this end, State policies are either universally applied or are targeted in support of those whose life has been negatively impacted by the CMEs. Ideally, the State would want to achieve full employment, govern a law-abiding citizenry, promote high social mobility, establish a relatively equitable society, and achieve a good quality of life. Achieving these goals enhances the State's legitimacy and provides the State with adequate resources to govern society and to manage the economy.

Cooperatives can complement and support the State in fulfilling its public responsibilities. The focus of cooperatives on meeting their members' needs, their collective ownership model, their culture of re-investing profits, their adherence to the principle of limited return on capital invested, their practice of accumulating inter-generational assets makes them an enterprise whose purpose is clearly aligned with the public interest. For instance, housing cooperatives can provide housing facilities at fair rental. Consumer cooperatives can promote consumer protection practices, sell local produce, and provide food at fair market prices. Cooperative banks and credit unions make loans available to local businesses, families, and the social economy. This section will demonstrate how cooperatives can further complement the role of the State by providing welfare services and employment opportunities and distributing income and wealth more equitably.

Cooperatives have demonstrated they are very suitable for providing health and welfare services. Modern states, who are servicing high public debts, are struggling to meet the rising costs of welfare. Unmet needs and policies to outsource public services have provided cooperatives with an opportunity to complement the State in providing welfare and social services. The non-speculative nature of cooperatives, including the ability to operate on a cost-recovery basis in this area, makes them suitable for the provision of welfare services. For instance, in Japan, the Japanese consumer movement includes 104 cooperative societies with close to 3 million members, which own 75 hospitals, 333 primary health care centres, 75 dental facilities, and over 350 nursing care facilities. They provide employment to over 39,000 employees, including over 2,000 doctors and 235 dentists (HEW CO-OP 2020). In Brazil, 340 cooperatives associate 118,000 doctors and provide medical services to 19 million patients via 150 owned hospitals and 29,000 accredited hospitals. This model is practised throughout South America (Birchall 2011, Unimed 2023). Social cooperative enterprises also provide a variety of services in aged care, child care, disability care, and other social services. In Italy, it is estimated that they provide close to 50 per cent of all social services (Zamagni 2017).

Another area where cooperatives can complement the State is job creation. Cooperatives have displayed a genuine inclination to create employment for everyone. For instance, cooperatives have shown a firm commitment to creating employment for long-term unemployed people and people with disabilities. Cooperatives have been formed from private enterprises in crisis, thus maintaining employment in local areas. During the GFC, we noted how cooperative sectors either increased employment or ensured that staff remained employed through job-sharing policies or by transferring staff to other cooperatives, when possible, by using their financial reserves. France and Quebec have local cooperative development centres spread across their territory, helping people establish or support existing cooperatives. Italian and Mondragon cooperatives have established cooperative development funds, funded by cooperatives, to promote growth and new cooperatives, and to help cooperatives experiencing economic difficulties. The behaviours of these cooperatives complement the States' goals of promoting secure employment, social cohesion, and economic development.

They also promote a culture of solidarity and reciprocity rather than economic self-interest. They do not rely on the State to solve problems caused by the CMEs. Instead, cooperatives solve problems themselves or in partnership with the State. For instance, at times, the State has provided fiscal incentives, employment incentives, and contributed funds to job creation schemes. In return, cooperatives have used their support structures and their intellectual and financial resources to help any group of people wanting to form a cooperative; have ensured that profits are re-invested to create further employment opportunities; and have developed cooperative associations or federations that will provide financial and other services in perpetuity. The relationship between the State and cooperatives in job creation and job retention has the potential of a long-term, respectful partnership that could operate within clearly defined roles and responsibilities.[8]

Cooperatives can also complement the State's role in reducing income and wealth inequalities. The World Inequality Report of 2022 noted that the wealthiest 10 per cent earn 52 per cent of total incomes and own 72 per cent of total wealth (Chancel et al. 2022). This level of inequality has developed despite governments worldwide applying progressive taxation systems and redistributive social welfare policies. Inequalities prevent people from achieving their full potential, prevent families from living a life with dignity, lowers people's expectations of life, may cause social unrest and disharmony, and is immoral considering the abundant wealth generated by the CMEs. As the research has shown, the cooperative collective ownership structure and its policies of limiting the return on capital and limiting salary differentials reduce income and wealth inequalities. Cooperatives generally reduce income inequalities by limiting salary differentials. Whilst the larger cooperatives pay high salaries to CEOs, as we have noted, in worker cooperatives, salary differentials are usually below 6:1. Almost all cooperatives reduce wealth inequalities because the cooperative assets are collectively owned, and as such they are not distributed to members but passed on to the next generation. Cooperatives also adopt policies that limit the remuneration of member capital, further limiting wealth inequalities. Rarely have worker cooperatives, consumer cooperatives, cooperative banks, and social cooperatives demutualised, even though most jurisdictions permit members to do so.[9] The State could facilitate income and wealth distribution via cooperatives by continuing to provide tax concessions for profits retained in the indivisible reserves. The State could legally limit salary differentials, as is the case for ethical banks in Italy, where the maximum salary differential is legally set at 5:1.

10.3.4 Supporting Local Communities

Cooperatives are owned by local residents and are embedded in their local economy. This makes them the ideal enterprise to support local communities as they engage with the global market. Communities are constantly placed at risk as they interact with the global market. They can experience economic and population decline as a result of de-industrialisation when companies go bankrupt and are not replaced. Large retailers may sell non-locally made products because they can source them at a cheaper price from elsewhere. Large companies may establish disadvantageous relations with local farmers and local businesses in the pursuit of profits. Banks may close branches to cut costs and increase profits. Companies may prefer to invest overseas if deemed more profitable or closer to their supply chains. This results in communities having fewer job opportunities, experiencing population decline, and having difficulties attracting new businesses. Their predicament worsens when they do not have access to the financial and economic institutions needed to manage change in a global market.

The history of cooperatives informs us that cooperatives have always been formed to protect local communities as they engage with the CMEs. Cooperatives offer local communities the capabilities and resources to manage change and build stable and cohesive communities. Cooperatives are able to do this because they are embedded in local communities. They are embedded because local members own and manage cooperatives; because cooperatives engage with local businesses; because cooperatives serve their local members to meet their most pressing needs and aspirations; because profits remain locally invested; because cooperative assets are passed on to future generations; because cooperatives do not re-locate to other countries. The solidarity mechanisms of cooperatives, such as cooperative funds, support cooperatives throughout their lifecycles and the formation of new cooperatives to meet future community needs.

Cooperative movements can support local communities at various levels of engagement. This may include establishing new cooperatives; providing a comprehensive, multi-sector cooperative presence covering every sector of the economy; and providing a strong influential economic and social presence in a town, a region, or throughout a country. In very small communities, the proximity cooperatives or community cooperatives have allowed communities to access an essential service or a key recreational activity. In Japan and Korea, consumer cooperatives have established cooperatives that sell farm products directly to consumers bypassing intermediaries and the market. This allows consumers to buy fresh, organic products from local farmers, whilst local farmers have access to a secure, loyal local market. This creates social cohesion and a social bond between the urban and the rural population. The comprehensive, multi-sector CDMs of

Mondragon and those in Trento have become the key economic actors in their city-level communities. They provide financial, research, management, administrative and legal services. They promote new cooperatives. They are able to manage change and support their cooperative members during an economic crisis. CG-SCOP, Legacoop, and Quebec's CDMs provide the same level of support provided by Mondragon and Trento, but on a wider scale. The Quebec cooperative movement services cooperatives throughout the province of Quebec. Legacoop and CG-SCOP provide services throughout Italy and France. Japan's consumer movement, with close to 25 million members, provides retail, insurance, public health, and welfare services to Japan's urban population.

10.3.5 Economic Democracy

A cooperative economy ultimately promotes the principles of economic democracy. The CME promotes hierarchical relations where corporations and business owners decide where to invest, who to employ, who to dismiss, what to produce, what to buy, what to sell, how to distribute profits, and when to disinvest. In a cooperative, workers or consumers either own or have the right to manage their enterprise and they, directly or via their representatives, make key decisions.[10] This is really significant because this type of economic democracy, based on common ownership and the principles of one-person-one-vote, allows cooperative members to make decisions in the workplace that effect their working and quality of life, that effect the opportunities offered to the next generation, and that impact the well-being of their communities.

Economic democracy also enhances political democracy. First, cooperatives teach their members about the art of democratic decision-making and train them in the art of compromise. This allows cooperative members to accept majority-based decisions. Second, cooperatives reduce income inequalities and limit wealth inequalities, thus creating a more egalitarian society. A more even distribution of income and wealth will reduce the political influence of corporations, businesses, and wealthy individuals because they would no longer control the level of financial and intellectual resources that allows them to exert a disproportionate influence on the State. Third, cooperatives allow their members to be part of an association through which they can influence the State by proposing public policies that better reflect their needs and aspirations. This allows individuals to act with others and to feel part of the political system. Fourth, the experience of cooperative members in managing cooperative enterprises and engaging with their cooperative associations or federations enables them to develop a more holistic and realistic understanding of the interaction between political decisions, the economy, and society. This prevents co-operators from leaning towards having unrealistic solutions to economic problems, which can create distrust, political instability, and disharmony.[11]

10.4 Why Still So Few?

Despite cooperatives demonstrating their economic and non-economic value, there are still fewer cooperatives than conventional enterprises. There are also fewer people seeking cooperatives to solve the problems they encounter in society rather than the State. In Chapter 7, we discussed some of the key reasons why there are few cooperatives. One reason is a lack of awareness of what constitutes a cooperative and its potential. Another reason is that cooperatives may find it more difficult to grow than conventional enterprises because of their democratic structure, difficulties in raising or attracting capital, difficulties in attracting cooperative managers, and inconsistent cooperative laws. The cooperative movement has also found it difficult to promote an international common vision of a cooperative economy.

Most importantly, Chapter 7 also noted that the key reason that explains why there are few cooperatives has been the success of conventional enterprises and the ability of the State to solve economic and social problems. Conventional enterprises, especially corporations, have been very innovative, have developed legal and institutional structures that enable them to attract capital from all over the world, have developed organisational structures that enable them to bring goods and services to world markets, have the support of international organisations that promote CMEs and the interests of shareholders; operate under relatively homogenous tax, industrial relations practices, and property laws. This makes it easier for corporations to start, grow, invest overseas, and disinvest.

The modern State has evolved gradually over time, expanding its role into the economic and social sphere to overcome the limits of a CME and the minimalist Liberal States. It evolved from an institution that protected private property, maintained law and order at home, and managed foreign relations to one that managed the economy, provided education and health services, and social security and welfare provisions.[12] The State relies on tax revenue to fulfil its functions and responsibilities. To this end, the State has a strong interest in managing the economy so that it grows, creates jobs, and pays taxes. The combined efforts of the CME and the State have succeeded in providing most individuals with an opportunity to solve their problems, meet their needs, and pursue their goals in life.

The success of the State's involvement in the economy and society and the economic success of conventional enterprises have restricted the growth of cooperatives. Still, it has not prevented cooperatives from continuing to perform a valuable role in CMEs and in modern societies. As stated throughout this book, cooperatives have continued to exist because the State and the CMEs have never been able to address all needs, and they have never satisfied everyone's expectation of what a society should look like. To this end, considering the benefits that the cooperative sector can bring to market economies, the State, and society, it is pertinent to consider how to grow the cooperative sector so that it can significantly influence the operations of the global market economy and society.

10.5 A Way Forward

This book has identified the virtues and limits of the cooperative enterprise. It has identified good practices and forms of degeneration. In order to grow, the cooperative movement needs to overcome its limitations, learn from its own experiences, and learn from the experiences that have led CMEs to dominate global markets.

10.5.1 Awareness

One way to encourage cooperative growth is to promote cooperatives so that more people become aware of their existence and the benefits they bring. The cooperative sector needs to develop better ways to inform the public about the virtues and the benefits of cooperatives, what it takes to establish and grow one, how they operate, what are the risks and rewards, explain the importance of working with other cooperatives, and the value of being embedded in their community. Cooperatives must inform the public about their economic performances and longevity record. Associations and federations need to inform the public about the financial and management services they can offer and how they can support cooperatives throughout their lifecycles.

To my knowledge, the cooperative movement, including the ICA, organise conferences, seminars, celebrate International Cooperative Day, produce regular newsletters, publish books, and make available pamphlets on how to start cooperatives. All these activities are important and valuable, but it seems they mainly communicate with cooperative members or people who already support cooperatives. However, cooperative activities are rarely reported in the key news outlets—newspapers, television, radio, and so on. In countries like Italy, which boasts a high density of cooperatives, cooperatives are mentioned when they produce annual reports to highlight their economic performance but not to highlight how they distribute profits, how value added is distributed, or how they engage with the community. They also highlight negative cooperative experiences, and at times they publish an article on WBOs. Meanwhile, in Australia, which also has a high density of cooperative members, the mainstream media hardly mentions cooperatives, and there is rarely an article on cooperatives or mutual societies in the main media.

The cooperative movement needs to develop a strategy to create greater awareness. One way to achieve this is to introduce cooperative studies as part of the school curriculum. This would allow every school student to understand how cooperatives operate and be able to make a rational, educated choice when entering the workforce. The cooperative movement could engage with the mainstream media to ensure that it reports regularly and correctly about cooperative economic and non-economic achievements. It could also develop its own mainstream media outlet, which will inform the public about the cooperative sector alongside other relevant news of the day.

10.5.2 Education

The cooperative movement should strongly work towards teaching cooperative studies in every university, especially in the economics department. So, an equivalent cooperative economics and management course should also be taught wherever a mainstream classical economics course is taught. Cooperative studies should also be included in the study of history, politics, business administration, and community development. Cooperative studies should include a comprehensive list of subjects that could include cooperative history, cooperative principles, cooperative enterprise, cooperative management, cooperative finances, cooperative governance, cooperative strategy and marketing, cooperative human relations, cooperative legal structures and tax laws, comparative CDMs, cooperative entrepreneurship and innovation, the relationship of cooperatives with the State, the community, and so on. Cooperative studies should equip the student with a holistic understanding of the cooperative enterprise, the cooperative movement, and the political, economic, social, and cultural context within which they operate. This should enable students to lead and manage cooperatives and solve problems with a cooperative mind-set and cooperative-specific solutions. It should also enable students to develop cooperative-specific public policies with a capacity to articulate cooperative differences and uniqueness. Including cooperative studies in mainstream courses could also inform the general public about the cooperative movement.

As noted in Chapter 4, the cooperative movement has promoted educational centres worldwide. The International Labour Organization (ILO) noted that 86 countries had cooperative education centres by the end of the twentieth century (Shaffer 1999). Many universities across the world provide cooperative studies courses. Mondragon Corporation has established its own university. Whilst these activities are welcomed and contribute to further the knowledge about cooperative economic and management, their impact on the world of economics and management is dwarfed when compared with the impact and influence exercised by classical economics departments and the conventional business schools and legal schools. Whilst more cooperative studies centres have been established since Laidlaw noted that the cooperative movement had neglected cooperative education, cooperative education is still lacking compared to what is available to students of classical economics and conventional MBA courses (Laidlaw 1980). For instance, by 1980, 100,000 MBA degrees were awarded annually in the United States,[13] and by 1998, there were at least 1,600 MBA programmes worldwide, including in China (Amdam 2009). This kind of data on the cooperative movement is not available. It would be beneficial for the ICA to collect data on the cooperatives courses offered internationally, the types of courses and types of accredited degrees offered, the total number of students attending, and so on. It would also be beneficial to have an accredited cooperative studies system so students can choose a university that can meet their expectations. A review analysing whether cooperative studies meet student's demands and expectations would inform how to direct cooperative investments in the education sector. It would also be greatly beneficial if cooperatives would become as generous towards higher cooperative education as those philanthropists that established major universities in the United States[14] and those foundations that promoted MBA programmes across the globe (Amdam 2019).

10.5.3 Good Practices

One way the cooperative sector could promote a more competitive cooperative sector globally is to encourage cooperatives and cooperative movements to learn from one another. This would enable cooperatives and cooperative movements to implement 'good cooperative practices' that would improve their competitiveness and capacity to grow. This is something that conventional enterprises have always done well. The development of the public company, stock markets, the multi-divisional firm, scientific management, the just-in-time systems, world supply chains, holding companies, computerisation, marketing and human resources techniques, and so on, have quickly been implemented by conventional enterprises worldwide. The higher education system, the subsidiaries of multinational firms, quality performance standards, internationally based consultancy firms, and recruitment policies all contributed to this flow of information and ideas. Other factors that encourage conventional enterprises to learn from others and to initiate change include the pursuit of profit maximisation, responding to external pressure from shareholders, and responding to external pressure from their competitors. All these factors lead conventional businesses to continuously look for ways to improve their business models.

This book has identified good cooperative practices from many cooperative jurisdictions and cooperative movements. Chapter 4 highlighted good practice strategies, management, and democratic practices from the consumer sector. It also highlighted good practice examples of CDMs developed in Mondragon and in Emilia Romagna. Chapter 5 provided good practice examples of CDMs developed in France, Japan, Korea, Quebec, and Trento. It also suggested good practice approaches in establishing worker-buyouts. Chapter 6 informed on good practice in cooperative law. Chapter 8 noted good cooperative governance practices and risk management techniques specific to the cooperative sector. Chapter 9 noted how cooperatives are embedded in local economies. These good practice approaches are present in many countries. Every country could learn good practice approaches from another country regardless of their geographic location. Every cooperative movement could complement its experience with good practice standards applied by other cooperative movements. If cooperatives were to learn from other cooperatives, the world cooperative sector could achieve significant growth. Some key cooperative experiences and cooperative good practices that could help achieve cooperative economic growth in alignment with the ICA's seven cooperative principles include:

- Cooperative law requiring a minimum percentage of members, limited return on capital, the indivisibility of reserves, and promoting inter-cooperative support mechanisms.
- Cooperative regulations that allow external investors to invest in a cooperative whilst preserving the cooperative, democratic structure and the principle of limited return on capital.
- Mondragon's solidarity and network arrangements.
- Italy's inter-sectoral trade and cooperative support structures.
- Japan's consumer movement's development of hospitals, insurance, welfare services, and retail services.
- The cooperative development strategy of the Caja Laboral Popular and Banca Etica's social economy strategy.
- The regional cooperative development centres operating in France and in Quebec.
- The urban-rural collaboration promoted by consumer cooperatives in Japan and in Korea.
- State-cooperative financial companies or financial consortia partnership arrangements as practised in France, Quebec, and Italy.
- Cooperative development funds as developed in Mondragon, Uruguay, and Italy.
- The education funds promoted in Argentina, India, and Spain.
- The comprehensive role performed by the State in promoting agricultural and electric cooperatives in the United States comprising legislative, financial, managerial, and educational support.
- The Japanese consumer cooperative movements' successful strategy to ask consumers to invest more than a nominal sum to improve their self-financing capabilities.
- The successful anti-monopoly strategy of the Swedish consumer movement.
- The approaches to promote WBOs as practised in Argentina, France, and Italy.
- The democratic structure of Arla foods, the Danish agricultural cooperative.
- The Cooperative Group public governance review conducted in the United Kingdom in 2004.
- Developing annual reports that consider cooperative principles, cooperative-specific risks, cooperative value-added, and the United Nations Sustainable Development Goals.
- Creating a sound relationship between the cooperative movement and civil society, as is the case where the cooperative movement has developed successful, durable cooperative models.
- CDMs that have the financial and managerial resources to assist the formation of new cooperatives, to manage change, and to deal with an economic crisis.

These examples demonstrate the richness of cooperative ideas being practised across the world. It is important for these ideas and practices to become better-known and more widely practised. The cooperative movement has always promoted exchanges and information sharing at least since the ICA was formed in 1895. Information is shared at annual conferences, via the ICA website, via cooperative movement websites, at conferences and seminars, and at higher education courses. Cooperative movements do engage with other cooperative movements. Scholars and cooperative movements always mention Mondragon and Emilia Romagna. However, more research needs to be conducted in this area to understand the extent of the cross-pollination of good practices among cooperative movements, to explore what more could be done to get cooperatives to learn from each other.

10.5.4 Need a Vision

The cooperative movement needs to develop and promote a cooperative vision of politics, society and the economy, supported by an appropriate strategy and an implementation plan, which can create a better society. This requires the cooperative movement to articulate where the current political and economic system can be improved and develop an alternative path to solve the identified problems. In doing so, the cooperative movement could learn from the neo-liberal experience, especially how their supporters promoted the neo-liberal view of the world.[15] Neo-liberals identified in the size of the State, in a shrinking market, in high taxation, in high welfare costs, and in high public spending, the key problems States and the CME face. They then promoted the view that individualism, private enterprise, capitalist-led markets, and a minimalist liberal democratic state was the best hope to promote a free society that would benefit everyone. This, in turn, led to the election of Liberal-conservative governments whose public policies implemented the neo-liberal project: privatisation, deregulation, outsourcing of government services, public-private partnerships for delivering infrastructure, the marketisation of health and education, lower income taxed and lower corporate taxes, user-pay system, and balanced budgets. Internationally, neo-liberal policies became known as the 'Washington Consensus' and were systemically promoted by the IMF, the World Bank, the WTO, and the Organisation for Economic Cooperation and Development (OECD). This led to increased world trade and freer movement of capital and labour (Chang 2014, Steger 2020, Steeger and Roy 2021).

The cooperative movement has developed the seven ICA principles and supporting cooperative values but has not developed its own cohesive view of politics and society. A cohesive view of the economy and society will not be easy to achieve because of the different goals, culture, and history of the various cooperative sectors. There are also broad differences in how various cooperative movements see the role of cooperatives in the economy. For instance, there is a communitarian view where cooperatives provide everything a community needs; a liberal view where cooperatives perform a marginal role in market economies; another view which sees cooperatives as an integral part of a planned economy; and the Social Democratic view, which sees cooperatives as a distinct third sector of the economy. The Liberal view prevails in North America, whilst the Social Democratic view prevails in Europe (Barberini 2009).

The evidence gathered so far, however, indicates that the sum total of cooperative experiences could promote a unique view of the State and society and a constructive critique of the current CMEs. The current evidence would indicate that the cooperative sector would not be supportive of neo-liberal policies that allow financial speculation, create regular economic crises, promote income and wealth inequalities, allow large corporations to dominate the world economy, leave local economies consistently vulnerable to disinvestment from companies seeking profit maximisation elsewhere, and that create precarious living conditions for the majority of people.

The cooperative experience thus far would also indicate that the cooperative sector would support a pluralist market economy that would include all forms of enterprises. A cooperative-friendly state could promote a pluralist economy that could have the following features: a market economy limiting the power of large corporations whilst supporting small- and medium-sized businesses; a society that places limits on income differentials and wealth inequalities; a society where everyone has the right to have a home and to access education, public health cover, child care, aged care, and social security services; state policies promoting cooperative-specific funding, spending, and tax policies, that would benefit the whole cooperative sector; policies promoting full employment and life-long employment within the cooperative movement; and international trade relations promoting fair trading among all businesses and among developed and developing countries. These goals could be achieved through a working partnership between the State, cooperatives, and all socially responsible enterprises that operate in a market economy.

These broad goals could then lead to more cooperative-specific policies. Cooperative-specific policies could relate to cooperative law, finance, taxation, public spending, housing, public health, welfare services and so on. A broad vision would help the cooperative sector promote cooperative-specific public policies and develop appropriate strategies, organisational structures, supporting institutions, and a cooperative culture that could promote the cooperative movement worldwide.

In addition to policies creating more awareness, educational institutions, and promoting good practice among cooperatives, the cooperative movement could promote a global cooperative financial market and cooperative-specific global institutions that would mirror the roles that the IMF, the World Bank, and the WTO, and the OECD, performed for the CME.

10.5.5 Cooperative Financial Market

The financing of cooperatives has been challenging. It has been noted that cooperatives finance their operations in a variety of ways. First, they use internal mechanisms to access finance via members depositing money into their individual capital accounts, members' loans, and retained profits. Second, they can access loans from local banks. Third, the State has provided loans and co-invested in cooperative managed financial consortia or companies. Fourth, the cooperative sector has established their own financial institutions to fund cooperatives. These include cooperative banks, cooperative development banks, cooperative development funds, credit guarantee consortia, and cooperative-owned financial companies. Fifth, cooperatives have also accessed the external market through the issuance of bonds, through issuing preference (non-voting) shares, through the public listing of a portion of a cooperative's assets as tradeable shares. This study noted that mature CDMs may provide sufficient funds for small to medium cooperatives and that cooperatives with large memberships, consumer cooperatives, and cooperative banks, especially, can access large amounts of finance from their members. However, this study has also noted that the level of available finance may not satisfy the needs of cooperatives that operate in capital-intensive industries, that wish to grow quickly, or that are internationally focussed. In discussing cooperative risks, it was also noted how cooperatives that access external capital via bonds or via issuing of shares are under pressure to pay annual interests or dividends and to repay the bonds at maturity. These responsibilities towards external bond-holders or shareholders may lead to cooperatives having to focus on maximising profits, or selling assets, or declaring bankruptcy if unable to meet repayments.[16]

If the cooperative movement is to meet the needs of all cooperatives and if it is to effectively promote cooperative growth globally, it needs to attract capital or investment from a wider set of sources. The first source is for cooperative movements to learn from other cooperative movements. Cooperative movements would benefit if they applied those good cooperative practice examples implemented in other countries. They could also apply international regulations allowing cooperatives to attract external capital with or without voting rights. This would allow cooperatives to attract capital from cooperatives or cooperative-owned financial institutions. These reforms could lead to cooperative growth, inter-cooperative trade, and the quick transfer of knowledge and technology from mature and successful cooperatives to newly established cooperatives. This type of engagement could also take place between cooperatives from mature cooperative movements.

The second strategy is to attract capital from the State. The cooperative movement should convince the State that it is in its and society's interests to promote a pluralist market economy. To this end, the State should make sufficient funding available to support the cooperative sector becoming a significant component of a pluralist market economy. The State could provide funding via state-owned banks. It may establish banks that promote the whole cooperative sector; or establish banks that promote a specific cooperative sector; deposit funds in existing cooperative banks; cooperative development funds; or cooperative-owned financial institutions; or civil society-owned banks that promote cooperative development. These suggestions are based on past or existing State practices. What is suggested here, however, is that State funding should be part of a long-term state strategy to promote a more pluralist market economy that would complement the role of the State, and that would improve the operation of the market. State investment should be large enough to enable the cooperative sector to grow and to significantly influence the market and society.[17]

The third source from whom cooperatives can attract finance is those retail investors who would be inclined to support cooperatives, economic democracy, ethical investment, and whom generally would like to invest for the greater good.[18] Cooperatives could attract sympathetic global retail investors willing to accept cooperative-friendly remuneration policies. The remuneration should be limited to a couple of percentage points above the inflation rate. Investments could be in the form of bonds, loans, or preference shares that are not linked to cooperative assets. Investments can be made via accredited cooperative investment funds that promote cooperative principles and cooperative behaviours. A Global Cooperative Financial Framework (GCFF) would need to be established. This GCFF could include a cooperative-specific financial trading exchange enabling cooperative-specific funds to buy bonds or preference shares or make loans to cooperatives;[19] cooperative rating agencies providing retail investors information about cooperatives; accredited cooperative investment funds; remuneration rules in alignment with cooperative principles; harmonisation of cooperative laws; cooperative disclosure requirements; independent auditing of listed cooperatives; independent cooperative-specialist media coverage.

The GCFF should be supported by cooperative-specific tax incentives. The tax incentives should encourage investors to accept a limited return on capital, supported by adequate tax concessions when investing in cooperatives that re-invest profits in their indivisible reserve fund. This type of investment would benefit every stakeholder: cooperatives would access credit, retail investors would receive a return above the inflation rate whilst supporting the cooperative sector, the State would benefit from a more competitive cooperative sector and tax receipts, and future generations would access a mature and growing cooperative movement.

10.5.6 Cooperative Global Institutions

For the cooperative movement to grow to the point that it can complement the State and significantly influence the market and society, it must establish international organisations that can provide the cooperative movement with the same type of support that the IMF, World Bank, WTO, and the OECD have given CMEs since 1945. This would enable the cooperative movement to develop a holistic approach to promoting cooperative sectors and encouraging international inter-cooperative cooperation. The ICA has representative function status at the United Nations, and it helped establish the Committee for the Advancement of Cooperatives, which included the ILO and other United Nations agencies. At the turn of the twenty-first century, both the ILO and the United Nations endorsed the cooperative principles, the definition of a cooperative, and the cooperative sector. The cooperative movement, however, needs to do a lot more in order to be able to influence significantly the market and society.

A starting point is to consider emulating those four international organisations that have promoted CMEs and world trade. First, a Cooperative World Trade Organization (WTO equivalent) could also be promoted to reduce cooperative-specific trade barriers or limitations, harmonise cooperative legislation, promote inter-cooperative trade, and promote international cooperative joint-ventures. Second, a Cooperative Financial Support Fund (IMF equivalent) could be established to support the cooperative movement in times of crisis. Financial support may be given to federations or associations, cooperative development banks, or cooperative development funds.

Third, a Cooperative World Development Bank (World Bank equivalent) could fund cooperative-specific infrastructure projects to develop the cooperative movement by providing traditional loans, interest-free loans, and grants. Cooperative infrastructure includes all those structures that are necessary for the operation, the development, and the re-generation of the cooperative movement and the cooperative economy. Cooperative Infrastructure funding could be used to establish all those core features that helped establish those successful CDMs noted in Chapters 4 and 5. Key cooperative infrastructure projects could include cooperative federations or associations that provide legal, administrative, managerial, and financial services to their members; cooperative development banks that would fund cooperative development; cooperative development funds; the consumer cooperative sector so that it can attract many members and can help grow other cooperative sectors; the housing cooperative sector because they serve an important need and because they can help develop construction, manufacturing, and maintenance cooperatives; new greenfield cooperative sectors to allow local cooperative movements to be present in all sectors of the economy; cooperative universities or higher education cooperative institutes so that they can develop cooperative directors and managers, conduct research leading to public policy proposals; cooperative-specific 'enterprise quality standards' to improve cooperative competitiveness in compliance with cooperative principles and values; and independent cooperative auditing associations to assess cooperative compliance and performance.

Finally, a Cooperative Development Forum (OECD equivalent) could be established to promote the cooperative economy within a pluralist market economy. The Forum could discuss and promote cooperatives and the social economy; socially responsible enterprises; forms of collective ownership or community ownership models; widespread ownership within the community; policies to reduce income and wealth inequalities; stakeholder decision-making processes; the benefits of economic democracy; and fair trade between developed and developing cooperative economies, and between large and smaller cooperative enterprises.

The funding for these bodies could come from nation-states. The level of funding for these cooperative development bodies could be based on the size of the social economy or the contribution to national employment. It could be set at 5–10 per cent of the level of funding that nation-states allocate to these four existing CME-specific international bodies. The funding should be dispensed subject to local cooperative movements having clear development plans, showing a willingness to co-invest in projects, demonstrating good governance practices, demonstrating adherence to cooperative principles, and so on. Repayable low-interest or no-interest loans and long-term patient capital should be preferred to non-repayable grants. Funding should be made only where feasibility studies, and business plans indicate that projects have a high likelihood of success and demonstrate they have the full support of the local cooperative movement. The funds should be monitored to ensure proper implementation, continuous learning from experiences, and proper use of financial resources.

10.6 Concluding Comment

Cooperatives have been established since the end of the eighteenth century. The cooperative idea is present globally. Cooperative enterprises have grown into large enterprises, some operating globally. Cooperatives are present in almost all sectors of the economy. They are as productive as conventional firms, and their longevity record is deemed superior. They have developed a variety of second-tier support organisations and forms of inter-sectoral cooperation and solidarity mechanisms, enabling them to achieve economies of scale and compete in CMEs. They have become leaders or have a sizeable market share in agriculture, banking, insurance, retail, maintenance and transport services, and welfare services. They have become globally competitive in civil construction and manufacturing. They can correct the market economy and complement the role of the State. They have demonstrated that the cooperative idea is a global idea and the cooperative model is competitive and can withstand economic and political crises.

Cooperatives have been established to service people's needs and the needs of their communities. They have grown but have performed a marginal role in the economy and society. Cooperatives have never been seen as the prime movers of an entire economy. This privilege has always been offered to the State and private sector, especially corporations. This book has argued that the cooperative movement has grown but needs to do more to perform a significant role in the economy and society. This book has also argued that if the cooperative movement performs a significant role, a better economy and society will follow.

In order to perform a significant role, the cooperative movement needs to develop a clear vision of the economy and society it wants to create and how this will improve the current state of the economy and of society. The cooperative movement needs to create more cooperative awareness in society. It needs to make sure that cooperative studies are taught at schools, higher education institutes, and universities in every country; it needs to develop a global financial framework to fund cooperative development; and it needs to promote cooperative-unique global institutions to promote cooperatives globally, as their equivalent institutions have done for CMEs. This broad project could be achieved by having large cooperatives working together, by having cooperative associations engaging globally with each other, by having regional cooperative associations engaging with similar organisations, by having the ICA, academics, and intellectuals helping the cooperative movement develop a vision for society, and by having governments actively promoting a larger cooperative sector within a pluralist market economy.

The short- and medium-term goal is to promote a more pluralist market economy that operates within a society where people can make an informed choice of the type of enterprise they wish to work, shop, or use for their needs. This informed choice should be supported by laws, access to finance, and access to management expertise, so everyone can achieve their dream or actualise their choice. The ultimate aim is not to have more cooperatives as an end in themselves, but to create economies where income and wealth is shared fairly; societies that are more cohesive and able to meet their people's material and non-material needs; societies that offer a job, an education, health cover, and a peaceful and financially secure retirement for everyone; and a political system where everyone feels that their level of influence is based on their proposals and ideas and not the size of their wallet. This book has argued that a cooperative-led pluralist market economy would be better placed to achieve these goals than a CME.

Notes

1 Please refer to David Garland's excellent book on the Welfare State (Garland 2016).
2 A cooperative enterprise model refers to the way a cooperative is organised to produce and sell goods and services in the market in order to meet the needs of its members. Cooperatives meet the economic, social, cultural and aspirational needs of their members by competing in the market on their own, or as a member of a second-tier cooperative. Whilst the term enterprise model is synonymous with the term business model, this book will opt to use the term cooperative model interchangeably with the term cooperative enterprise model.
3 Cooperative development model refers to cooperative movements that are able to promote the whole cooperative sector. These are usually led by a cooperative association or federation providing political, strategic, cultural, and economic leadership to an inter-sectoral cooperative movement. Cooperative development models have the capability and capacity to promote new cooperatives, new cooperative sectors, support existing cooperatives, and manage economic or organisational crises that beset the cooperative movement.
4 Azmanova actually argues that 'Precarity Capitalism' is a new phase of Capitalism that impacts most people, not just those with insecure jobs or low income earners (Azmanova 2020).
5 In 1996, the Lega Nazionale delle Cooperative e Mutue changed its name to Legacoop.
6 In Italy cooperative banks are the only bank to operate a bank branch in more than 500 local towns (BCC 2016).
7 Proximity services may include services such as a supermarket, a service station, a café, the postal service, a pub, a sporting facility, a supermarket, tourism activity, and hospitality services (Girard and Langlois 2009, Mori 2017).
8 Please refer to Chapters 4 and 5 for information on Mondragon, Italy, France, and Quebec. Please also refer to Chapter 9 for information on economic performance, employment, and the GFC.
9 Whilst some demutualisation has taken place in the 1990s, it has affected only a small number of cooperatives (please refer to Chapter 5). For more information on cooperative law and demutualisation, please refer to Chapter 6.
10 Chapter 6 clarified that, in reality, cooperative members have the right to manage the cooperative enterprise but generally do not own the assets generated by the cooperative. These assets are passed on to future generations. Please refer to Chapter 6.

11 For a discussion on the relationship between economic power and political influence and how this negatively impacts political democracy, please refer to the works of Dahl, Reich, and Henderson (Dahl 1998, Reich 2016, Henderson 2020).
12 For information on how the modern state has evolved, please refer to the following books from Poggi, Garland, Sassoon, and Frieden (Poggi 1978, Garland 2016, Frieden 2020, Sassoon 2020).
13 The first business school was the Wharton School of Finance and Commerce, established in 1881 at the University of Pennsylvania. By 1914, 30 business schools were already educating 10,000 graduates each year (Amatori and Colli 2011).
14 Philanthropists also established or provided seed funding for prestigious universities such as the University of Chicago, John Hopkins University, and Stanford University (Srinivasan 2017).
15 The neo-liberal view has been promoted by intellectuals, conservative think tanks, mainstream media, business associations, members of parliaments, nation-states, and international organisations.
16 Cooperative finance is discussed throughout the book that is why there isn't a specific chapter dedicated to this important topic. Please refer to Parts 5.2.2, 7.2.5, and 8.4.5 for further information.
17 A recent report from Australia's Productivity Commission noted that Australia provided 13.8 billion AUD in industry assistance in 2021–2022. It also noted that the United States provided over 62 billion USD to the semi-conductor industry as well as tax concessions, and a further 500 billion USD via the *Inflation Reduction Act* to promote clean energy, whilst reducing inflation, the budget deficit, and prescription drug prices. The European Union also made available via the *EU Chips Act* of 2022, 43 billion industry assistance packages (Productivity Commission 2023).
18 In 2022, global assets held in Exchange Traded Funds that complied with the environmental, social, and governance screening criteria, amounted to 378 billion USD (Statista 2022).
19 The global cooperative financial trading exchanges could be established in the cooperative friendly cities of Bologna or Quebec City. Initially these exchanges could comprise the top 500 cooperatives.

References

Amatori, Franco, and Andrea Colli. 2011. *Business History: Complexities and Comparisons*. New York: Routledge.

Amdam, Rolv Petter. 2009. "Business Education." In *The Oxford Handbook of Business History*, by Geoffrey G. Jones and Jonathon Zetlin, 581–602. Oxford: Oxford University Press.

———. 2019. "The Internationalization of Executive Education." In *The Routledge Companion to the Makers of Global Business*, by Teresa da Silva Lopes, Christina Lubinski and Heidi JS Tworek, 125–137. London: Taylor Francis Group.

Ammirato, Piero. 2018. *The Growth of Italian Cooperatives: Innovation, Resilience and Social Responsibility*. New York: Routledge.

Azmanova, Albena. 2020. *Capitalism on Edge*. New York: Columbia University Press.

Bajo, Claudia Sanchez, and Bruno Roelants. 2011. *Capital and the Debt Trap: Learning from Co-operatives in the Global Crisis*. London: Palgrave Macmillan.

Barberini, Ivano. 2009. *How the Bumblebee Flies*. Milan: Baldini Castoldi Dalai Editore .

BCC. 2016. *L'Impronta del Credito Cooperativo sull'Italia*. Annual Report , Rome: BCC - Credito Cooperativo.

Birchall, Johnston. 2011. *People-Centred Businesses*. London: Palgrave MacMillan.

———. 2013. *Resilience in Downturn: The Power of Financial Cooperatives*. Financial Report, Geneva: International Labour Organization.

Birchall, Johnston, and Lou Hammond Ketislon. 2009. *Resilience of the Cooperative Business Model in Times of Crisis*. Geneva: Internatonal Labour Office.

Bonow, Mauritz. 1938. "The Consumer Movement in Sweden." *The Annals of the American Academy of Political and Social Science* 171–184.

Chancel, Lucas, Thomas Piketty, Emmanuel Saez, and Gabriel Zucman. 2022. *World Economic Report 2022*. Paris: World Economic Lab.

Chang, Ha-Joon. 2014. *Economics: The User's Guide*. London: Penguin Books.

Chomsky, Noam, and Mary Waterstone. 2021. *Consequences of Capitalism: Manufacturing Discontent and Resistance*. United Kingdom: Penguin Random House.

Dahl, Robert. 1998. *On Cooperation*. New Haven: Yale University Press.

Fauquet, Georges. 1941. "The Co-operative Sector." *Annals of Public and Cooperative Economy* 342–369.

Frieden, Jeffry A. 2020. *Global Capitalism*. New York: WW Norton and Company.

Garland, David. 2016. *The Welfare State*. Oxford: Oxford University Press.

Gillespie, James Edward. 1950. "Swedish Cooperatives." *Current History* 331–336.

Girard, Jean-Pierre, and Genevieve Langlois. 2009. "How Social Enterprises Can Combine Social and Economic Goals." In *The Changing Boundaries of Social Enterprises*, by OECD, Chapter 5. Paris: OECD.

Henderson, Rebecca. 2020. *Reimagining Capitalism*. New York: Penguin Random House.

Hilson, Mary. 2018. *The International Co-operative Alliance and the Consumer Co-operative Movement in Northern Europe, 1860-1939*. Manchester: Manchester University Press.

Laidlaw, AF. 1980. *Cooperatives in the Year 2000*. A Paper Prepared for the 27 Congress of the International Cooperative Alliance, Moscow: International Cooperative Alliance.

Mori, Pierangelo. 2017. "Community Co-operatives and Co-operatives Providing Public Services: Facts and Prospects." In *The Oxford Handbook of Mutual, Co-Operative, and Co-Owned Business*, by Joseph R. Blasi, and Carlo Borzaga Edited by Jonathan Michie, 13. Oxford: Oxford University Press.

Pestoff, Victor A. 2017. "The Social and Political Dimensions of Cooperative Enterprises." In *The Oxford Handbook of Mutual, Cooperative and Co-owned Business*, by Jonathon Michie, Joseph Blasi and Carlo Borzaga, 76–96. Oxford: Oxford University Press.

Poggi, Gianfranco. 1978. *The Developmental of the Modern State*. Stanford: Stanford University Press.

Polanyi, Karl. 1957. *the Great Transformation*. United States: Beacon Press Books.

Productivity Commission. 2023. *Trade and Assistance Review*. Canberra: Australian Government.

Reich, Robert. 2016. *Saving Capitalism*. London: Icon Books.

Roelants, Bruno, Diana Dovgan, Hyungsik Eum, Terrasi, and Elisa. 2012. *The Resilience of the Cooperative Model*. Economic Report, Brussels: Cecop.

Sassoon, Donald. 2020. *The Anxious Triumph: A Global History of Capitalism, 1860-1914*. London: Penguin Books.

Shaffer, J. 1999. *Historical Dictionary of the Cooperative Movement*. Lanham: Scarecrow Press.

Srinivasan, Bhu. 2017. *Americana: A 400 Year History of American Capitalism*. New York: Penguin Books.

Statista. 2022. *Global ESG ETF Assets from 2006 to February 2022*. 17 August. Accessed July 17, 2023. https://www.statista.com/statistics/1297487/assets-of-esg-etfs-worldwide/.

Steeger, Manfred, and Ravi Roy. 2021. *Neoliberalism*. Oxford: Oxford University Press.

Steger, Manfred. 2020. *Globalization*. Oxford: Oxford University Press.

Taylor, Keith. 2021. "An Analysis of the Entrepreneurial Institutional Ecosystems Supporting the Development of Hybrid Organizations: the Development of Cooperatives in the U.S." *Journal of Environmental Management* 1–8.

Unimed. 2023. *The Biggest Co-op System of Doctors in the World is Here*. Accessed July 5, 2023. https://www.unimed.coop.br/site/sistema-unimed.

Zamagni, Vera. 2017. "A Worldwide Historical Perspective On Co-operatives and Their Evolution." In *The Oxford Handbook of Mutual, Co-operatives and Co-owned Business*, by Jonathon Michie and Joseph, Borzaga, Carlo Blasi, 97–114. Oxford: Oxford University Press.

Zevi, Alberto, Antonio Zanotti, Francois Soulage, and Adrian Zelaia. 2011. *Beyond the Crisis: Cooperatives, Work and Finance*. Brussels: Cecop Publications.

Glossary

Capitalist-led Market Economy A Capitalist-led Market Economy refers to an economy that includes private, cooperatives, not-for-profit, and state-owned enterprises, that is led by global corporations that hold a dominant share of international trade and domestic markets.

cooperative enterprise model A cooperative enterprise model refers to the way a cooperative is organised to produce and sell goods and services in the market in order to meet the needs of its members. Cooperatives meet the economic, social, cultural, and aspirational needs of their members by competing in the market on their own, or as a member of a second-tier cooperative. Whilst the term enterprise model is synonymous with the term business model, this book will opt to use the term cooperative model interchangeably with the term cooperative enterprise model.

Cooperative Development Model Cooperative Development Model refers to cooperative movements that are able to promote the whole cooperative sector. These are usually led by a cooperative association or federation providing political, strategic, cultural, and economic leadership to an inter-sectoral cooperative movement. Cooperative development models have the capability and capacity to promote new cooperatives, new cooperative sectors, support existing cooperatives, and manage economic or organisational crises that beset the cooperative movement.

cooperative movement Cooperative movement refers to cooperatives from various economic sectors that are members of a national inter-sectoral association or federation through which they promote common ideas, beliefs, policies, and cooperative principles.

members' capital account Members' capital accounts include members' initial investment to join a cooperative as a member, further investments by members, bonus payments as practised in worker cooperatives, and dividend payments as per legal requirements or as per by-laws. This initial investment is called social capital in Europe, and members' shares in English-speaking countries. The book uses the term member capital account as is used in Mondragon and Quebec because the term social capital is not used outside Europe, and the term 'shares' implies ownership of assets as in investor-owned firms, which is not the case in cooperatives.

profits and surplus By 'profit' is meant revenue minus costs. At times, cooperatives also use the term surplus, which refers to revenue minus costs, taking into account only those transactions with their members. Throughout the book, the term profit will be used because it will be easier for the general public to understand and easier to compare with private enterprises.

Index

Note: Bold page numbers refer to tables.

Printed in the United States
by Baker & Taylor Publisher Services